Recreating the American Republic

*Rules of Apportionment, Constitutional Change, and
American Political Development, 1700–1870*

Rules of apportionment are vital elements of every social and political order. In marriages and families, in business partnerships and social organizations, and in every government and supranational relationship, rules of apportionment exist in various written and unwritten forms. In every form, the rule of apportionment affects not only how collective decisions are made and by whom, but also how and why a particular constitutional order develops over time. *Recreating the American Republic* provides a first and far-reaching analysis of when, how, and why these rules change and with what constitutional consequences.

This book reveals the special import of apportionment rules for pluralistic, democratic societies by engaging three critical eras and events of American political history: the colonial era and the American Revolution; the early national years and the 1787 Constitutional Convention; and the nineteenth century and the American Civil War. The author revisits and systematically compares each seemingly familiar era and event – revealing new insights about each and a new metanarrative of American political development from 1700 to 1870.

Charles A. Kromkowski is Lecturer in the Department of Politics at the University of Virginia.

Recreating the American Republic

*Rules of Apportionment, Constitutional Change,
and American Political Development, 1700–1870*

CHARLES A. KROMKOWSKI

University of Virginia

CAMBRIDGE
UNIVERSITY PRESS

CAMBRIDGE UNIVERSITY PRESS
Cambridge, New York, Melbourne, Madrid, Cape Town, Singapore, São Paulo

Cambridge University Press
The Edinburgh Building, Cambridge CB2 2RU, UK

Published in the United States of America by Cambridge University Press, New York

www.cambridge.org
Information on this title: www.cambridge.org/9780521808484

First published 2002
This digitally printed first paperback version 2005

A catalogue record for this publication is available from the British Library

Library of Congress Cataloguing in Publication data
Kromkowski, Charles A. (Charles Aloysius), 1963–
Recreating the American republic : rules of apportionment, constitutional change, and
American political development, 1700–1870 / Charles A. Kromkowski.
p.   cm.
Includes bibliographical references and index.
ISBN 0-521-80848-0
1. United States – Politics and government – To 1775.   2. United States – Politics
and government – 1775–1783.   3. United States – Politics and government –
1783–1865.   4. Constitutional history – United States.   I. Title.
JK31 .K76 2002
320.973′09′033–dc21
2002025929

ISBN-13 978-0-521-80848-4 hardback
ISBN-10 0-521-80848-0 hardback

ISBN-13 978-0-521-02272-9 paperback
ISBN-10 0-521-02272-X paperback

Contents

Tables and Figures

TABLES

FIGURES

Preface

The Paradox of Constitutional Consent

> *But of all the means we have mentioned for ensuring the stability of constitutions – but one which is nowadays generally neglected is the education of citizens in the spirit of their constitution.*[1]

Amidst the welter of discrete approaches and dispositions that happily constitute the social sciences, studies of past and present politics remain unified by a common interest in the conditions, causes, and consequences of collective authority. Across the disciplines of political science and history, many of these studies provide descriptions or measurements of various forms of collective authority. Other studies provide explanations of the causes or consequences of this authority; still others provide theories that account for its creation, transformation, or breakdown. This study speaks directly to these two disciplines and their common interest by describing, by explaining, and by proposing and testing a theory accounting for the development of the American political order between 1700 and 1870.

To engage these parallel but divided audiences in these purposes, this study's format not only enables a comparative historical analysis of the events and eras surrounding the American Revolution, the 1787 Constitutional Convention, and the American Civil War, it also facilitates the recognition and synthesis of the distinct scholarly contributions made by the disciplines of history and political science. This synthesis extends beyond a respectful acknowledgment of their unique disciplinary canons to include both the historian's aspirations to understand and to document

---

[1] Aristotle, *Politics*, Book V, ch. ix.

the particular and the contingent within an historical narrative and the political scientist's aspirations to analyze evidentiary domains without methodological bias in order to report general relationships and the logic of historical paths taken. In so doing, this study aspires to contribute to our historical understanding of the American constitutional experience, to methodological and theoretical debates concerning the analysis and dynamics of constitutional order and change, and to an emerging recognition and recovery of the benefits that follow from a union (or better yet, a fuller reconciliation) of the historical and political sciences.

The real possibility that this study's analytical format, synthetic purpose, or empirical and theoretical fields may initially appear unfamiliar to some individuals on either side of the disciplinary divide prompts the appeal for readers to suspend (at least temporarily) their respective disciplinary predispositions. Such a suspension, the following chapters demonstrate, must and will be justified by the double yield of a full and yet more rigorous historical account of American political development and of a rigorous and yet more realistic explanation and theory of constitutional order and change. For these readers and all others, *Recreating the American Republic* hopefully will be viewed as both a deep exploration of the substances and dynamics of constitutional order and a literary device for engaging and uniting disparate individuals and forms of scholarship divided by artificial boundaries that imperialistically and too often unproductively continue to divide the social sciences.

To engage these purposes and audiences, we can begin by pondering the nature of apportionment rules and the vexing constitutional action problem associated with their change. While this preparatory focus may not today be considered a common or neutral point of departure for the study of American politics and its development through time, the remainder of this Preface reveals how the logic and language of existing theoretical accounts fail to provide a ready-made means for engaging and understanding the problematics and possibilities of consensual constitutional order and the processes of apportionment rule change. With the nature of apportionment rules and their elemental relationship to order and change in full view, Chapter 1 identifies the three familiar American cases of apportionment rule change that this study subsequently examines. Whereas the analytical and literary tools of the historian's craft are recognized and employed in later chapters, Chapter 1 surveys the set of ideas and tools typically employed by political scientists to explain political change. This chapter, in addition, makes explicit the research design required to address the four questions that ground this study: namely, when, how, and why rules of apportionment change, and with what immediate and longer-term constitutional consequences. Definition of this study's theoretical problem, its set of cases, and its comparative research design likely will satisfy one discipline's initial methodological requirements, but it certainly will leave the other eager for the details and documentation of the three case studies completed in Chapters 2 through 9. Hopefully, these chapters will not disappoint students of either discipline, for they simultaneously tell the individual stories of three historically momentous apportionment rule changes and the general but equally intriguing story of American political development from the Revolution to Reconstruction.

What is a rule of apportionment and why do apportionment rule changes open windows onto the foundation, dynamics, and historical development of constitutional orders in general and of the American political order in particular? In brief, a rule of apportionment defines the intragovernmental distribution of collective decision-making authority. As such, every constitutional order (at whatever level of social aggregation) can be identified and assessed in terms of its rule of apportionment. Although these rules assume a variety of forms, one of the most familiar defines the basis for dividing political representation within a national legislative assembly. The original U.S. Constitution, for example, specified that representation in the U.S. House of Representatives shall be divided among the states according to the whole number of free persons and three-fifths of all other persons, excluding untaxed Indians. In the U.S. Senate, representation was to be divided equally among the states: two senators per state.

Most rules of apportionment, to be sure, reflect constitutional realities that extend significantly beyond their written constitutional forms. This lack of transparency between the nature of the object and its external appearance typically makes the systemic study of rules of apportionment intractable. Despite this, rules of apportionment remain highly significant. At lower levels of aggregation, rules of apportionment are embedded deep within individual decision-making behavior and within interpersonal relations such as marriages and business partnerships.[2] In

---

[2] The observation that apportionment rules are the psychological patterns that define human decision making prompts more reflection but it cannot detain or distract us here. At this level, apportionment rules are the deeply embedded and likely latent decisional rules that determine choices among rationally plausible alternatives. Dilemmas are paralyzing choice situations due to the lack of an operable decisional rule. For further illustration of the consequences of this observation, see Eric Voegelin's commentary on

marriages these rules typically are the unformalized or customary terms by which mutual decisions are made; in business partnerships the terms of these rules typically are defined within written, legally enforceable contracts.[3] At higher levels of aggregation (for example, inter- or supranational relations) rules of apportionment often can be conceived in terms of a panoply of material, territorial, and psychological factors that determine and affect the bargaining positions of two (or more) actors engaged in the expectation of some form of collective action.[4]

Although the full range of apportionment rules would be difficult to study comprehensively, these rules nevertheless are elemental parts of every constitutional order because they define the relationship between autonomous, uncoordinated interests. In so doing, apportionment rules establish a minimum level of decision-making coherence and coordination necessary for collective action. In constitutional orders where collective authority is not a momentary exchange, wholly dependent on force, monopolized by a single individual, or dispersed among self-representing individuals, the rule of apportionment has a special relationship to the stability of the order because it affects how socially organized interests and their agents will be embodied within the process of collective decision making. In this respect, modern forms of representative governance cannot fully be described or analyzed without recognition of a constitutional order's rule of apportionment. Indeed, the fact that some apportionment rules permit the *re-presentation* of a plurality of societal interests within the collective decision-making process (and, thus, reciprocal relations between governmental authority and society) offers a basis for distinguishing democratic forms of government from governmental forms characterized by either monocratic (or "unitary") apportionment rules or the general (and more simple) characteristic of existential representation.[5]

Aeschylus' *The Suppliants* in *New Science of Politics* (Chicago: University of Chicago Press, 1952), pp. 70–73. See also Alasdair MacIntyre, *Whose Justice? Which Rationality?* (Notre Dame, IN: University of Notre Dame Press, 1988).

[3] See Elizabeth S. Scott and Robert E. Scott, "Marriage as Relational Contract," 84 *Virginia Law Review 1225* (1998); Robert Scott, "Conflict and Cooperation in Long-Term Contracts," *California Law Review* (1987) 75: 2005–2054.

[4] See James D. Fearon, "Bargaining, Enforcement, and International Cooperation," *International Organization* (1998), 52(2): 269–305; James D. Fearon, "Bargaining Over Objects that Influence Future Bargaining Power," paper presented at the 1997 American Political Science Association Meeting, Washington, DC.

[5] See Eric Voegelin, *The New Science of Politics* (1952). Voegelin defines the historical existence of a society in terms of "existential" representation, or the presence of the capacity to act for a society as a whole. Aristotle's description of how Pisistratus came

Rules of apportionment are important for another elemental reason: Their stability has long-term informational consequences. Once established, that is, apportionment rules tend to remain in place. Although not immune to incremental adaptations, an established rule of apportionment – like all constitutional rules – is valued because it conveys information about the immediate position and longer-term prospects for various interests and individuals within a particular political order. In this respect, knowledge of the rule of apportionment provides a lens through which individuals and societal interests can assess their political capacities to secure the collective legitimization of their interests.

Finally, apportionment rules are important because the combination of their distributional and informational characteristics often prompts particularly contentious types of political conflict. Why, for example, should one set of interests be privileged over any other set of interests when the matter concerns a collectively binding decision? Moreover, if it is granted that a multiplicity of interests constitutes every society, then the rule of apportionment determines no less than who will govern and who will be the governed. This is an important distinction within every constitutional order, but its import is self-evident for all democratic forms of governance sustained by voluntaristic forms of consent.

Apportionment rule changes, thus, are important for several reasons. First, these rule changes offer nearly transparent opportunities for analyzing fundamental shifts in the distribution of collective decision-making

---

to rule Athens offers a classic example of existential representation under a "unitary" (and tyrannical) rule of apportionment. According to Aristotle, "When [Pisistratus] had finished the rest of his speech, he told the people what had been done with their arms, saying that they should not be startled or disheartened but should go and attend to their private affairs, and that he would take care of all public affairs" which he and his sons did for the next thirty-six years. (*The Athenian Constitution*, del. sp. trans. P. J. Rhodes, Harmondsworth, Middlesex; New York: Penguin Books, 1984), chapters 15.5, 15–19.

This study of "plural" apportionment rules and of governmental forms based on plural rules offers specialized insights concerning constitutional orders in which various individuals and interests are engaged in and consent to the creation and maintenance of a constitutional order. Whereas many have previously concerned themselves with the histories, the principles, and practical mechanics concerning the consensual maintenance of "plural" constitutional orders, few have fully engaged the additional difficulty of accounting for the consensual creation of this particular form of constitutional order. Modern theories of democracy, therefore, either note that the mechanics of founding moments are forever lost in the mists of time or they unwittingly mimic the Machiavellian logic that because "the many are incompetent to draw up a constitution" the founding of consensual democratic forms of governance necessarily requires nondemocratic and "reprehensible actions." See Machiavelli, *Discourses on the First Ten Books of Titus Livy*, W. Stark, ed. (London: Routledge and Kegan Paul, 1950), I, 9, 2–3.

authority. Second, wholesale apportionment rule changes are unexpected events because the decisions to abandon and to replace an existing apportionment rule will have adverse or uncertain effects upon presently empowered interests.[6] As a result, this type of rule change is not likely to occur without cost, resistance, and coercion.

In consensual constitutional orders – that is, where association with and recognition of collective authority is inherently noncoercive – the opportunity to choose among alternative rules of apportionment raises acute, if not paradoxical, order-making and order-sustaining problematics. For although rationally directed individuals would expect a new set of constitutional rules to provide a baseline of stability for all interests, it also would be evident that these new rules would have discrete (and potentially suboptimal or disastrous) distributional consequences. A paradox, thus, arises: Although a group of rational actors might desire to forsake the dark forests of anarchy, they still might not be able to negotiate their way back into either history or the constitutional gardens promised by a collective authority.

To understand this potential for failure more fully, consider the simplified representation of the paradox of constitutional consent in Figure 1. Assume that two individuals or socially organized interests (X and Y) face the decision whether to commit to the formation of a collective authority. Assume that the origin of the graph represents the expected utility of a preconstitutional status quo. When, therefore, both actors expect a proposed constitutional rule to return common or approximately equal benefits, their consent could reasonably be expected. The expected utility of this set of constitutional rules forms an axis of common informational gain represented by the southwest-northeast diagonal.

Consider the expected utilities of the additional bundles of proposed constitutional rules: A, B′, B″, C, and D. Each constitutional bundle is expected to return different relative gains to the two actors. Commitment to include these rules thus raises more complex, although not nec-

---

[6] One example will suffice. In 1844, John Quincy Adams, a member of the U.S. House of Representatives, attempted to introduce a resolution enacted by the Massachusetts legislature calling for amendment of the three-fifths clause of the Constitution's original rule of apportionment. So vigorous were the objections in Congress that both the House and Senate refused *to receive and print* the resolution. As Alabama Senator William King protested at the time: "Was there a man within the hearing of his voice that believed for one moment, that such an amendment could be made; and if it could be, by any possibility, that the federal Government would last twenty-four hours after it was made." *Congressional Globe*, 28th Congress, 1ˢᵗ sess. (January 23, 1844), p. 175.

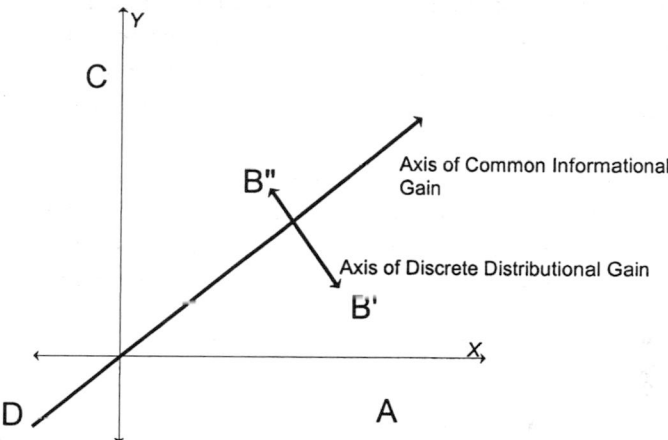

FIGURE 1. The Calculus of Constitutional Consent

essarily insurmountable, problematics. Actor X, for example, might exchange its consent for constitutional bundle "C" for actor Y's reciprocal consent for constitutional bundle "A." In so doing, the net expected value of the proposed constitutional order would be increased.[7]

When, however, actors X and Y care more about relative individual gains than net gains or when the values of different rules are not fungible, constitutional rule exchanges likely will not be completed or maintained. When, moreover, the rule choice is discrete (for example, between B' and B") and the expected utility difference is significant, consent also cannot be expected. For what would motivate either actor to forsake a relative distributional benefit? For one, the expected relative benefit may be so trivial that, at some point, a constitutional hold-up (and the resulting stream of "lost" gains) would not seem to be worthwhile. In rare circumstances, however, when the relative difference between two proposed constitutional rules is expected to distinguish the governing from the governed, consent would seem highly improbable and the imperative to sustain a constitutional hold-up would be almost indefinite. Choices among rules of apportionment are one of these circumstances.

Exposure of the inherent problematics associated with constitutional consent – especially the problem of discrete distributional differences –

---

[7] See Fritz W. Scharpf, "Coordination in Hierarchies and Networks," in *Games in Hierarchies and Networks*, Fritz W. Scharpf, ed. (Boulder, CO: Westview Press, 1993), pp. 125–165.

suggests a basis for the familiar opinion that the creation of consensual constitutional orders is either impossible or ironically dependent upon coercion. As David Hume, an eighteenth-century proponent of this idea, concluded: "Almost all the governments, which exist at present, or of which there remains any record in story, have been founded originally, either on usurpation or conquest, or both, without any pretence of a fair consent, or voluntary subjection of the people." The paradoxical problematics of constitutional consent, moreover, persist beyond the founding moments of a political order. Or as Hume additionally observed:

> The face of the earth is continually changing, by the encrease of small kingdoms into great empires, by the dissolution of great empires into smaller kingdoms, by the planting of colonies, by the migration of tribes. Is there any thing discoverable in all these events, but force and violence? Where is the mutual agreement or voluntary association so much talked of?[8]

What then are we to make of the familiar idea that many modern constitutional orders – including long-term exchange relationships at the supranational, international, and intranational levels – appear to have been established, altered, and maintained without naked usurpation, conquest, or domination? Are there credible accounts and a logical basis that explain both the consensual creation and maintenance of this type of collective authority? Three intellectual traditions offer a set of potentially useful answers that merit some consideration. In the first tradition the paradox is simply negated by explaining that the formation and maintenance of consensual unions occur by chance, by nature, or by convention. In addition to ignoring the core problem facing pluralistic constitutional orders, accounts built upon these tropological devices render human freedom and intentional political design secondary to arbitrary probability functions, preexisting communal dispositions, or unaccounted-for accidents of incremental drift. Moreover, the calculus of constitutional consent typically is portrayed against the backdrop of an apparently viable but unseen constitutional order. The utility of the logic and language of this intellectual tradition is limited by other considerations. Contemporary proponents of the "by chance" account, for example, overlook the inappropriateness of their reliance upon proba-

---

[8] David Hume, "Of the Original Contract," *David Hume, Political Essays*, Knud Haakonssen, ed. (Cambridge, UK: Cambridge University Press, 1994), pp. 189–190. For an interesting historical counterexample to Hume's generalization, see Joseph Felicijan, *The Genesis of Contractual Theory and the Installation of the Dukes of Carinthia* (Klagenfurt, Austria: Druzba sv. Mohroja v Celovcu, 1967).

bilistic models to simulate constitutional decision making.[9] Proponents of the "by convention" account, by contrast, implicitly assume or counsel obedience to, not consent for, collective authority. And proponents of the "by nature" account typically place severe restrictions on community scale – thereby revealing the inapplicability of this solution as well.

In the second intellectual tradition, consensual constitutional orders are explained in terms of a spontaneously generated motive to elect or to defer to the judgment of individual leaders who are deemed the best able to govern. This classic story portrays the presence of "valorous," "virtuous," or "visionary" leaders as a necessary condition for the creation and maintenance of a constitutional order. The unitary (and specifically "monarchical") rule of apportionment typically recommended in these accounts solves the paradox of constitutional consent in two ways. First, the extraordinary leader is authorized to select and to impose a particular solution among the various possibilities when founding a constitutional order. Second, different societal interests typically are barred from direct representation within the subsequent collective decision-making process.[10]

---

[9] The classic story of the so-called Theban Pair (Eteocles and Polynices) provides a cautionary reminder of the problematics of ascribing probability functions to individual or group-level calculi concerning constitutional choices and commitments. As recounted by Greek dramatists Aeschylus and Euripides and the Roman poet Statius, Eteocles and Polynices were the sons of Oedipus who, after their father's self-inflicted demise, agreed to rule Thebes on an annually rotating basis. After the first year, however, Eteocles refused to yield to Polynices. As a result, the Theban order faced civil war from within and foreign threats from without. In the midst of this constitutional crisis, the two brothers fought and killed each other. According to the story, their enmity was so enduring that their funeral flames refused to unite. (See Aeschylus, *Seven Against Thebes*; Euripides, *Phoenissae*; and Statius, *Thebaid*).

[10] This second account also includes heroic stories of deference to individual leaders who subsequently (and quite incredibly) established constitutional orders defined by "plural" apportionment rules. For example, the story of popular trust granted to Cleisthenes during his armed struggles against Isogoras in the wake of the collapse of the Pisistratid tyranny and Cleisthenes' subsequent division of the Athenians into thirty trittyes and one hundred demes is accounted as the birth of Athenian democracy. (See Aristotle's account in *The Athenian Constitution*, chapters 20–21).

Another form of this account of consensual collective authority, far too complex to be addressed in this study, enlightens part of the historical development of the Christian church. The origins of modern institutions of representation and democratic government (including "plural" apportionment rules and majority rule) are directly traceable to the theoretical concepts and practices that developed within this tradition. See Arthur P. Monahan, *Consent, Coercion and Limit: The Medieval Origins of Parliamentary Democracy* (Kingston, Ontario: McGill-Queen's University Press, 1987); Arthur P. Monahan, *From Personal Duties toward Personal Rights: Late Medieval and Early Modern Political Thought, 1300–1600* (Montreal: McGill-Queen's University Press, 1994).

The third intellectual tradition employs the language and logic of agreement and contract to explain the phenomena of political order. This tradition has ancient associations with the idea of covenant, yet its modern cast of storytellers warrants special attention for they aim to identify the individual motives and calculations that make consent and consensual orders possible. One of the most famous advocates within this tradition, Thomas Hobbes, proposed that individuals would freely consent to form a collective authority when they individually fear the violent consequences of an anarchic state of nature. Disappointingly, however, the particular political order created within the Hobbesian account is maintained perpetually by coercion, not by consent.

John Locke, writing after Hobbes and recovering and extending themes articulated during the English republican era, offered a different basis for his contractual account. Unlike Hobbes, Locke proposed that political order was maintained by specific limitations on the scope of collective authority, and by the direct consent of voters during elections and the tacit consent of nonvoters through their territorial residence. The Lockean account, however, explained that consent during the creation of a political order emerged spontaneously out of a shared set of societal interests – thereby solving the paradox of constitutional consent by denying the existence of important, discrete distributional differences.

Hume's subsequent critique of the Hobbesian and Lockean social contract accounts exposed the need for more rigorous and realistic accounts of the calculus of constitutional consent. In more recent years, most accounts within this intellectual tradition have tended to emphasize rigor over realism. Indeed, it has become widely accepted that a minimally rigorous explanation of macrolevel (or societal) phenomena like the creation, development, and breakdown of political orders must be built upon explicit microlevel (or actor-centered) assumptions concerning human motives and intentions. As political theorist Jack Knight argues, "[i]f social institutions are the product of human interaction, the substantive content of institutional rules" which frame and constitute social phenomena "should embody the goals and motivations underlying those interactions."[11] Moreover, as neocontractarian theorists James M. Buchanan and Gordon Tullock declared, the success of an account within this tradition can be evaluated in terms of how well it

---

[11] Jack Knight, *Institutions and Social Conflict* (Cambridge, UK: Cambridge University Press, 1992), p. 27.

answers the question: "Can the existing organization of the State be 'explained' as an outgrowth of a rational calculation made by individual human beings?"[12]

Beyond their microlevel orientations, neocontractarian theorists offer different solutions to the problems of constitutional consent. Two of the best-known solutions depend on the introduction of so-called "veil" devices. These devices, in brief, solve the problem of discrete distributional conflicts by altering the decision-making context in a way that detaches individuals from their interests in relative or discrete gains. Buchanan, Tullock, and Geoffrey Brennan, for example, place constitutional decision makers behind a "veil of uncertainty" that prevented them from anticipating the probable consequences of various constitutional rules.[13] Indeed, as Brennan and Buchanan contend, the "more general and more permanent" the rule, the less likely the capacity to forecast its consequences. As a result, "[t]he uncertainty introduced in any choice among rules or institutions serves the salutary function of making potential agreements more rather than less likely."[14] With similar consequences, John Rawls introduced a "veil of ignorance" that made it impossible for individual constitutional decision makers to anticipate how they would be affected by different rules. The resulting ignorance of consequences prompted these individuals to select rules impartially. Thus, as Viktor J. Vanberg and James M. Buchanan concluded, "[p]otential conflict in constitutional interests is not eliminated" behind the

---

[12] James M. Buchanan and Gordon Tullock, *The Calculus of Consent* (Ann Arbor, MI: University of Michigan Press 1962), p. 316.

[13] James M. Buchanan and Gordon Tullock, *The Calculus of Consent* (1962). Buchanan and Tullock, to be fair, do not attempt to engage the difficult questions concerning the consensual formation and consequences of apportionment rules. Consistent with their normative goals and their methodological individualism, they assume a "rule of unanimity or full consensus at the ultimate constitutional level of decision-making" (p. 6). They further contend that if the intragovernmental distinction between the majority and the minority is expected to vary stochastically, then consent for the establishment of the institution of majority rule would be rational because it would reduce the expected long-term costs of negotiating agreements. This assumption can be used to ground an account of the consensual establishment and maintenance of majority rule. However, prior to the selection of an apportionment rule the logic of stochastic variation loses much of its lustre because it requires the highly unusual generalization that individuals would not expect different consequences from different rules of apportionment. Rather, because rules of apportionment are almost never expected to have "stochastic" consequences, constitutional consent among discrete interests remains an elemental and prior-level problematic of constitutional order not addressed by Buchanan and Tullock.

[14] Geoffrey Brennan and James M. Buchanan, *The Reason for Rules* (Cambridge, UK: Cambridge University Press, 1985), pp. 29–31.

Rawlsian veil "but the veil of ignorance transforms potential interpersonal conflicts into intrapersonal ones."[15]

Rather than reconstructing the choice context to overlook or to exclude distributional conflicts altogether, other neocontractarian accounts more realistically permit a diversity of interests among the negotiating parties. One account, for example, explains that consent emerges when these parties agree "to split" their differences – thereby equalizing their absolute gains.[16] Another solution suggests a Hobbesian-like logic by maintaining that consent follows from the recognition that the gains from coordination exceed the minimalist gains or negative results of an anarchic (or noncooperative) status quo.[17] Moreover, once rational actors calculate negotiation costs and the "losses" from withholding consent, the benefits promised by the proposed collective authority do not necessarily have to be extensive.[18]

A third solution achieves consent by redefining the calculus of constitutional decision making to include evaluation of both immediate and long-term expected gains. By extending the "shadow of the future," the discounted value of future expected gains is added to immediate expected gains. Individuals, thus, are motivated to consent when the expected sum of immediate and longer-term gains exceeds the sum of possible short-term losses associated with consenting.[19]

A fourth solution achieves constitutional consensus by limiting the number of political actors during the constitution-making process. Larry L. Kiser and Elinor Ostrom, for example, contend that the formal determination of the size and responsibilities of a new "constitutional" order, the process of selecting its members and its operational procedures,

[15] See John Rawls, *A Theory of Justice* (Cambridge, MA: Belknap Press of Harvard University Press, 1971); Viktor Vanberg and James M. Buchanan, "Interests and Theories in Constitutional Choice," *Journal of Theoretical Politics* (1989), 1: 52–53.

[16] Fritz W. Scharpf, "Coordination in Hierarchies and Networks," in *Games in Hierarchies and Networks* (1993), p. 139. See also John R. Nash, "The Bargaining Problem," *Econometrica* (1950), 18: 155–162.

[17] James D. Buchanan, *The Limits of Liberty* (Chicago: University of Chicago Press, 1975). See also Adam Przeworski, *Democracy and the Market: Political and Economic Reforms in Eastern Europe and Latin America* (Cambridge, UK: Cambridge University Press, 1991), p. 85.

[18] See John G. Cross, *The Economics of Bargaining* (New York: Basic Books, 1969); and Fritz W. Scharpf, "Coordination in Hierarchies and Networks," in *Games in Hierarchies and Networks* (1993), pp. 125–165.

[19] See Robert A. Axelrod, *The Evolution of Cooperation* (New York: Basic Books, 1984); Michael Taylor, *The Possibility of Cooperation* (Cambridge, UK: Cambridge University Press, 1987). Cf. Adam Przeworski, *Democracy and the Market: Political and Economic Reforms in Eastern Europe and Latin America* (Cambridge, UK: Cambridge University Press, 1991), p. 19.

"must be made by individuals in the constitutional body functioning in a constitutional choice situation." These decisions are affected "by the composition of the community . . . , the rules governing the interaction that will establish the . . . [constitutional order], and the good that . . . [the constitutional order] represents." Moreover, according to Kiser and Ostrom, constitutional framers "may agree that all interested [parties] have one vote in the constitution of the association or that the larger [parties] have more votes in constituting the association than the smaller [parties]. The members may bar some [parties] from participating in the constitutional level of choice."[20]

Three final solutions have not been as fully developed as the others, although they share a similar Lockean logic. The fifth solution posits that the emergence of "focal points" permits unconnected individuals to perceive a single course of action around which their expectations converge.[21] The sixth and seventh solutions, more specifically, propose that consent follows when negotiating parties devise either "institutional arrangements that minimize the expected distributional effects" or "institutions that can easily be changed."[22] The former (or "minimization") solution implicitly proposes that consent becomes likely when negotiations are limited to constitutional rules that promise nearly similar expected benefits – in other words, when there is a liberal contraction of the set of constitutional possibilities to those nearest the axis of common interests identified in Figure 1.[23] The latter (or "metaconstitution") solution presumes that negotiating parties "are aware of the fallibility of their constitutional constructions" for future conditions and, therefore, are wary of long-term commitments to an inflexible constitutional design.[24]

[20] Larry L. Kiser and Elinor Ostrom, "The Three Worlds of Action: A Metatheoretical Synthesis of Institutional Approaches," in *Strategies of Political Inquiry*, Elinor Ostrom, ed., (Beverly Hills, CA: Sage Publications, 1982), pp. 212–213.

[21] Michael Hechter, "The Emergence of Cooperative Social Institutions," in Michael Hechter, Karl-Dieter Opp, and Reinhard Wippler, eds., *Social Institutions: Their Emergence, Maintenance and Effects* (Berlin: Walter de Gruyter, 1990), pp. 27, 13–33. See also Thomas C. Schelling, *The Strategy of Conflict* (Cambridge, MA: Harvard University Press, 1960).

[22] Knight, *Institutions and Social Conflict* (1992), p. 194.

[23] Elaboration of the liberal tradition since Locke is too extensive to summarize adequately here. For a sample of the varied applications of the "minimization" solution, see Louis Hartz, *The Liberal Tradition in America* (New York: Harcourt, Brace, 1955); Robert Nozick, *Anarchy, State and Utopia* (New York: Basic Books, 1974). Adam Przeworski implicitly contends that this "minimization" solution is most likely when the relative electoral strength of various societal interests is unknown [*Democracy and the Market* (1991), p. 87].

[24] Viktor J. Vanberg and James M. Buchanan, "Constitutional Choice, Rational Ignorance, and the Limits of Reason," in *The Constitution of Good Societies*, eds., Karol E. Soltan

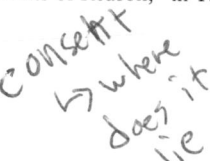
Consent → where does it lie

But why consent would follow from this seventh (or "metaconstitution") solution does not become clear until two further assumptions are more fully explicated. The first assumption is that the set of negotiating agents gains a degree of autonomy from the principal societal interests they represent. This autonomy, in turn, weakens the representation of discrete distributional differences during constitutional negotiations. The second assumption is that the relationship among the set of negotiating agents is grounded (at some level) in the reflexive norms (or general standards) of truthfulness, reciprocity, and trust. For without the advent of this common bond, the solution of institutional flexibility promises little more than future opportunities to become reengaged in discrete and likely disastrous distributional conflicts.[25]

Many of the logical and descriptive weaknesses of these solutions have been thoroughly debated, and they require no extended rehearsal here. The Buchanan and Tullock "veil of uncertainty" assumes that individuals possess the foresight to calculate the immediate and long-term benefits of a rule-based constitutional order but that these individuals are incapable of anticipating the likely distributional consequences of these rules. In a similar way, the Rawlsian "veil of ignorance" relies heavily on the unrealistic assumption that individuals behind the veil understand the general benefits of constitutional order but are ignorant that constitutional choices have discrete distributional consequences.[26] Both "veil" accounts, moreover, presume that individuals assent because of what is *not* known, when traditional philosophical discussions typically portray assent following the *acquisition*, not the absence, of knowledge.

The other neocontractarian solutions also fail to provide sufficiently realistic accounts of the process, outcomes, and consequences of consti-

and Stephen L. Elkin (University Park, PA: Pennsylvania State University Press, 1996), p. 53. Cf. Przeworski, *Democracy and the Market* (1991), p. 82.

[25] See Ian R. Macneil, "The Many Futures of Contracts," *Southern California Law Review* (1974), 47: 691–816; Ian R. Macneil, "Contracts: Adjustment of Long-term Economic Relations under Classical, Neoclassical, and Relational Contract Law," *Northwestern University Law Review* (1978), 72: 854–905; Ian R. Macneil, *The New Social Contract: An Inquiry into Modern Contractual Relations* (New Haven: Yale University Press, 1980); Elinor Ostrom, *Governing the Commons: The Evolution of Institutions for Collective Action* (Cambridge, UK: Cambridge University Press, 1990); Fritz W. Scharpf, "Coordination in Hierarchies and Networks," in *Games in Networks and Hierarchies*, ed., Fritz W. Scharpf (1993), pp. 125–165; Charles F. Sabel, "Constitutional Ordering in Historical Context," in *Games in Networks and Hierarchies*, ed., Fritz W. Scharpf (1993), pp. 65–123.

[26] Viktor Vanberg and James M. Buchanan, "Interests and Theories in Constitutional Choice," *Journal of Theoretical Politics* (1989), 1: 53.

tution making. The "splitting the difference" solution, for example, appears unrealistic when there are nontrivial differences in the bargaining positions of the actors engaged in negotiation. Under these circumstances, this solution yields clear advantages to comparatively "weaker" parties – thereby encouraging, not necessarily ending, constitutional hold-ups. Moreover, as Douglas D. Heckathorn and Steven M. Maser point out, comparatively "stronger" parties may refuse to consent to a proposed constitutional agreement because "it is politically irrational in the sense that it is judged to be inconsistent with the strength of the individual's strategic position."[27]

Other problems undermine the credibility of the "optimality" solution. The first problem is that constitutional decisions are almost never limited to a dichotomous choice between an anarchic status quo and a single constitutional order. Rather, prospective constitution makers typically are confronted with multiple alternatives that promise better conditions than the status quo. Thus, although the desire to leap from anarchy clearly exists, the particular leaping direction remains indeterminate.[28] The discrete interests problematic, moreover, reemerges once political actors are permitted to calculate the expected distributional consequences of particular rule proposals.[29]

The "iteration" solution is plagued by several apparent inconsistencies when applied to the constitutional choice process. This solution, in particular, requires ad hoc or reductive assumptions about how individuals discount future gains and calculate the risks of future commitments. As a result, individuals who value the future and who are risk-averse are likely to commit to long-term agreements. Yet, as Charles F. Sabel argues, "surely this is to say that cooperative parties cooperate, and it leaves open the question of whether cooperation is a likely outcome or not."[30] A second problem is that if the values of future gains are to be discounted, then why not also discount expected future losses attributable

[27] Douglas D. Heckathorn and Steven M. Maser, "Bargaining and Constitutional Contracts," *AJPS* (1987), 31: 156.

[28] The classic problem here is also known as the Buridanus ass paradox. A hungry jackass is confronted with two equidistant stacks of hay and dies of starvation because it cannot decide between the two appealing options.

[29] Douglas D. Heckathorn and Steven M. Maser, "Bargaining and Constitutional Contracts," *AJPS* (1987), 31: 156–157.

[30] Charles F. Sabel, "Constitutional Ordering in Historical Context," in *Games in Hierarchies and Networks* (1993), p. 83n. See also Michael Hechter, "On the Inadequacy of Game Theory for the Solution of Real-World Collective Action Problems," in Karen Schweers Cook and Margaret Levi, eds., *The Limits of Rationality* (Chicago: University of Chicago Press, 1990), pp. 240–249.

People know what
they don't want

to the adoption of a particular constitutional rule? For individuals may withhold their consent because they foresee that a small, seemingly trivial relative advantage projected over time would yield significant (and potentially threatening) differences among the contracting parties. At minimum, therefore, if the "shadow of the future" device is to be introduced then it must be utilized to calculate both the expected benefits and costs associated with constitutional consent.

The "focal point," "minimization," and "metaconstitution" solutions also are not beyond criticism. One obvious problem with the first two solutions is that it is not clear precisely how they "solve" the discrete distributional conflicts raised by different rules of apportionment. For "focal points" are temporary rhetorical devices and contraction beyond the inclusion of a constitutional rule of apportionment clearly does not seem possible. At minimum, therefore, the efficacy of these solutions requires deeper theoretical elaboration of the relationship between constitutional rules of apportionment and the larger framework of constitutional rules within which they ultimately are embedded.

The problems with the "metaconstitution" solution follow directly from the "agent autonomy" and "reflexive norms" assumptions relied on to explain this solution. More specifically, that is, how do agents become autonomous from the principal source of their authorization? And how do norms like reciprocity and trust emerge in the face of stubbornly discrete distributional differences? These elemental questions typically are not broached or given their required research focus, although an array of sources offers insights suggestive of various preliminary answers. Policy-oriented and journalistic accounts, for example, regularly expose how bribery or graft corrupts principal-agent relationships.[31] Scale changes – typically caused by demographic or electorate changes – are other significant conditions that promote the attenuation of representational relationships.[32] Other answers are suggested by behavioral science research that portrays human rationality as limited by computational capacities or affected by signaling or reference point changes.[33] Others have extended

---

[31] Kimberly Ann Elliott, ed., *Corruption and the Global Economy* (Washington, DC: Institute for International Economics, 1997); see also John T. Noonan, *Bribes* (New York: Macmillan, 1984); Jon Elster, *The Cement of Society* (Cambridge, UK: Cambridge University Press, 1989), pp. 263–272; Susan Rose-Ackerman, *Corruption: A Study in Political Economy* (New York: Academic Press, 1978).

[32] Charles A. Kromkowski and John A. Kromkowski, "Why 435?: A Question of Political Arithmetic," *Polity* (1991), 24: 129–145; ibid., "Beyond Administrative Apportionment: Discovering the Calculus of Representative Government" (1992), 25: 495–497.

[33] Amos Tversky and Daniel Kahneman, "Rational Choice and the Framing of Decisions," *Journal of Business* (1986), 59: 251–278; George A. Quattrone and Amos Tversky, "Contrasting Rational and Psychological Analyses of Political Choice," *APSR* (1988),

these insights by demonstrating that political preferences are multi-dimensional and that decision-making behavior is contextually sensitive.[34] As a result, the causes of "agent-autonomy" can be explained in terms of calculation errors, the framing of decision-making options, or real or anticipated changes in the context within which decision makers are embedded.

The spontaneous origins of inter-agent norms also are understudied. Traditional accounts, of course, simply assume that norms are static conditions that require no explanation – for example, the classic Hartzian synthesis of American political thought projects a liberal consensus across time and space.[35] Yet as decision theorist Christina Bicchieri recently argued, "Asking why social norms persist through time, or why we tend to conform to them, does not shed any light on the norm-formation process, since *how* norms emerge is a different story from why they tend to persist." Among others, Bicchieri proposes that norm-emergence can be explained as "the outcome of learning in a strategic interaction context" and that norms, therefore, are "a function of individual choices and, ultimately, of individual preferences and beliefs."[36] Bicchieri's account requires sequential actions among strategic actors. Notably, others contend that norm-formation and "learning" can emerge in response to long-term uncertainty about the efficacy of particular constitutional rules or in highly selective relationships through the process of bargaining and deliberation.[37]

CONCLUSION

How do these theoretical insights and their noted logical and descriptive shortcomings inform this study of apportionment rule change and the development of the American political order between 1700 and 1870?

82: 719–736; Lisa Anderson and Charles A. Holt, "Information Cascades in the Laboratory," *American Economic Review* (1997), 87(5): 847–862.

[34] Bryan D. Jones, *Reconceiving Decision-Making in Democratic Politics* (Chicago: University of Chicago Press, 1993).

[35] Hartz, *The Liberal Tradition in America* (1955).

[36] Christina Bicchieri, *Rationality and Cooperation* (Cambridge, UK: Cambridge University Press, 1993), pp. 228–230.

[37] See Viktor J. Vanberg and James M. Buchanan, "Constitutional Choice, Rational Ignorance, and the Limits of Reason," in *The Constitution of Good Societies*, eds., Karol E. Soltan and Stephen L. Elkin (1996), pp. 39–56; Charles Sabel, "Constitutional Ordering in Historical Context," in *Games in Hierarchies and Networks* (1993), pp. 65–123; Fritz W. Scharpf, "Coordination in Hierarchies and Networks," in *Games in Hierarchies and Networks* (1993), pp. 125–165; Jack Knight, *Institutions and Social Conflict* (1992).

For one, the paradox of constitutional consent identifies a set of problematics that calls into question the possibility and viability of consensual constitutional orders within modestly complex societies. To date, theoretical efforts (although fully endowed with the formalistic rigor of microlevel foundations) have failed to provide a satisfactory general solution for this most fundamental of modern political questions. As such, the causes of this failure offer useful negative examples for this study's narrowly circumscribed theoretical focus.

Clearly, one cause of the failure of prior theoretical efforts can be attributed to their disregard of the possibility that consensual constitutional orders are constructed and maintained over a multiplicity of potentially distinct interests. In this respect, the grand accounts of Hobbes and Locke are decidedly nonmodern because they do not fully accept the serious and perennial constitutional problematics of aggregation and consent in the midst of substantive and discrete distributional differences.

Contemporary efforts, to be sure, typically are keen on recognizing diversity within the human condition but they, thus far, have failed to address directly the fundamental question concerning the origins and constitutional consequences of rules of apportionment. In John Rawls's most recent account, for example, he disregards the elemental import of this question by simply "eliminating the bargaining advantages that inevitably arise within the background institutions of any societies from cumulative social, historical and natural tendencies."[38] Rawls often is singled out to bear the brunt of a seemingly permanent critique but on this particular limitation he stands in good company.[39]

---

[38] John Rawls, *Political Liberalism* (New York: Columbia University Press, 1993), p. 23. The lack of an "exit" or secession option from association with a single constitutional framework is another unrealistic and ad hoc limitation underlying the choice context within Rawls's account.

[39] In *Calculus of Consent* (1962), for example, Buchanan and Tullock concede that "the individual's evaluation of collective choice will be influenced drastically by the decision rule that he assumes to prevail" but they argue that this decision raises "a problem of infinite regression" (p. 6). In *A Theory of Justice* (1971), Rawls contends that without his "veil of ignorance," "the bargaining problem of the original position would be[come] hopelessly complicated" (p. 140). Larry L. Kiser and Elinor Ostrom acknowledge that apportionment rules have important consequences on subsequent alternatives and choices. They contend, however, that the complications that arise by examining the means by which constitutional rules are initially determined "add little to the explanatory and predictive powers" of their framework for institutional analysis [Larry L. Kiser and Elinor Ostrom, "The Three Worlds of Action: A Metatheoretical Synthesis of Institutional Approaches" (1982), p. 215]. Similarly, in *Governing the Commons* (1990) Elinor Ostrom engages the problematics of voluntary cooperation, but acknowledges

A final cause of theoretical failure (and a third negative example for this account) is a direct consequence of the widespread failure to construct rigorous *and* realistic accounts of the creation and maintenance of consensual constitutional orders. Whereas "rigor" customarily entails the specification of the individual motives underlying societal-level phenomena, "realism" minimally requires the explicit reconstruction of the "cumulative" background of human institutions and tendencies that make the constitution of consent both problematic in practice and paradoxical in theory. Self-styled constitutional apologists and normative theoreticians may privately relieve themselves of this additional requirement. So be it. Others, however, like political scientists Elinor Ostrom and Adam Przeworski, clearly demonstrate that rigor and realism are not mutually exclusive in their theoretically oriented accounts of consensually constructed and maintained institutions of collective authority.[40]

Informed by all of these examples, this study seeks to complement and extend the language and logic of existing theoretical accounts on the formation and maintenance of constitutional order in several ways. First, this study seeks to understand constitutional consent within a context defined by the possibilities and problematics raised by the presence of multiple and discrete interests. Second, this study directly confronts the acute difficulties and consequences associated with consensual apportionment rule creation. Third, this study moves beyond a purely abstract discussion of constitutional order to construct analytically rigorous *and* historically realistic accounts of several creations, transformations, and

that "[a]nalyses of deeper layers of rules are more difficult for scholars and participants to make" so that "[w]hen doing analysis at any one level, the analyst keeps the variables of a deeper level fixed for the purpose of analysis. Otherwise, the structure of the problem would unravel" (p. 54). Significantly, although without explanation, Ostrom includes a "rule" for aggregating individual-choice calculi in her general model: see figure 6.1, p. 193. See also Ostrom's suggestion that this rule is typically imposed or exists by convention (pp. 200–201). In arguably the most penetrating theoretical analysis to date, Adam Przeworski readily admits that constitutional agreement is problematic because "institutions have distributional consequences" that "affect the degree and manner in which particular interests and values can be advanced." Yet when the interests of negotiating agents are discrete, "balanced and known," Przeworski admits he is not sure how a constitutional choice among different constitutions will be completed [*Democracy and the Market* (1991), pp. 81, 83–84]. Finally, it can be added that the problematics raised by the choice of an apportionment rule are not typically addressed by state-centered theorists who view the process of state creation in terms of a zero-sum struggle to control the monopoly of organized violence. See Margaret Levi, *Of Rule and Revenue* (Berkeley: University of California Press, 1988), pp. 41–47.

40 Elinor Ostrom, *Governing the Commons: The Evolution of Institutions for Collective Action* (1990); Adam Przeworski, *Democracy and the Market: Political and Economic Reforms in Eastern Europe and Latin America* (1991).

breakdowns of the American political order. Fourth and finally, this study complements existing theoretical accounts by proposing that a general solution to the vexing problem raised by apportionment rule change, a diversity of interests, and the commitment to consensual constitutionalism likely will not emerge as a chance deduction of an as yet undiscovered general law. Rather, a fuller understanding of both the problem and the path to its solution will be secured more quickly and appropriately from the recovery and collection of the particular solutions devised, sustained, and renegotiated by specific individuals within specific historical contexts.

The political development of the United States between 1700 and 1870 offers a near ideal set of conditions to probe more deeply into the constitution of consent amidst the problematics of diversity. For not only is this extended period of constitutional stability generally unaffected by destabilizing influences from without and from below, this period is twice punctuated by the decidedly coercive actions that triggered and ended the American Revolutionary War and the American Civil War. In effect, therefore, this period offers a rare opportunity to assess not only the emergence and development of consensual order over an extended period of stability but its breakdown by both coercion from above and secession from below.

Other conditions also are nearly ideal. For example, for much of the period between 1776 and 1861 (that is, from the Second Continental Congress to the Secession crisis) the rule of apportionment corresponded closely with the terms defined within a written constitutional form. This time period, therefore, provides an unusually transparent opportunity to track the terms and processes defining the intragovernmental distribution of collective decision-making authority by focusing (at least, initially) on the written form and consequences of apportionment rules articulated in the Articles of Confederation and the U.S. Constitution. Finally, and most fortunately, because of the professional stewardship of numerous generations of dedicated archivists, librarians, publishers, scholars, and their benefactors, the depth and accessibility of the historical record over the selected period and series of political events are quite likely without parallel in the history of human civilization. The following analysis and synthesis of American political development and whatever fruits they may bear are therefore grounded in and emerge from fields that have been diligently prepared and cared for by others.

Recreating the American Republic

Questions:
①+② when+how cons.
changes in rule of app
occur

Introduction
③+④ why changes AND
consequences

rules of app.
cons. change
dev. of Am. pol. order 1700 - 1870

Four research questions frame this inquiry into the elemental import of rules of apportionment, the process of constitutional change, and the development of the American political order between 1700 and 1870. The first two questions ask when and how do constitutional changes in the rule of apportionment occur. The final two questions ask why these changes occur and what are their immediate and longer-term consequences.

In the Preface, rules of apportionment were defined not only in terms of the allocation of collective decision-making authority, but of their particular informational and distributional qualities as well. The general relationship between these rules and the process of constitutional change thus seems clear. Constitutional changes are a type of political change that alters or establishes seemingly permanent organizational structures, institutional procedures, or customary practices that determine the practical limits of collective authority. These changes are easily recognized when they are coterminous with explicit formal changes like constitutional amendments or written legal decrees, but they also occur with the establishment or transformation of unwritten, customary political practices.

easy to
determine
w/ amends
BUT can
be unwritten
too

Because every type of constitutional order requires some form of apportionment rule, constitutional changes in the rule of apportionment are further signified by two distinguishing events: the abandonment of an existing rule and the establishment of a new rule of apportionment. As a consequence, answers to the questions of *when* and *how* constitutional change occurs require detailed descriptive accounts of the contextual conditions which precede, and the sequences of decisions which effect, historical instances of this particular type of political change.

2 IMPT events:
abandonment &
establishment

The third research question framing this inquiry asks *why* constitutional changes in the rule of apportionment occur. Because apportionment rules, as defined in this study, establish relatively fixed and self-reproducing divisions of collective decision-making authority, constitutional changes in these rules cannot properly be characterized as spontaneous, unintended, or randomly occurring events. The causes of this type of change are extraordinary and likely (although not necessarily) to share similar characteristics. At a minimum, therefore, the search for an answer to the question why these changes occur requires a comparative analysis of the special conditions associated with these changes as well as the specification and clarification of the causal mechanisms which link these conditions to particular instances of this type of constitutional change.

Comparative causal explanations of this sort inexorably raise the classic analytical problem defined by the structure-agency antinomy. This core analytical problem of the social sciences concerns the causal primacy of structural (or macrolevel) conditions compared to actor-centered (or microlevel) conditions. More recently, the theoretical bar for causal explanations has been raised to engage a second analytical problem, the linkage between macro- and microlevel conditions. This second problem, in brief, transcends the first by exposing and requiring specification of the reflexive connection between macrostructural conditions and microlevel agency.[1]

Beyond this explicit acknowledgment of these core analytical problems, a fuller explanation of the three identified changes requires specification of a general theory which accounts for the abandonment and creation of rules of apportionment as well as for a fourth and final research question: What immediate and longer-term consequences have changes in the rule of apportionment had upon the American political order? To broach this question, it is necessary to gain an understanding of the relationship between an apportionment rule and the whole order of which it is but a part. This is no simple task. For not only is the complexity and beauty of the whole beyond the measures of the mind, the three apportionment rule changes examined in this inquiry are sequential changes extending over nearly two centuries.

---

[1] For informed theoretical discussions of these analytical problems, see Anthony Giddens, *Central Problems in Social Theory* (London: Macmillan, 1979); Anthony Giddens, *The Constitution of Society* (Berkeley: University of California Press, 1984); Jeffrey C. Alexander et al., eds., *The Micro-Macro Link* (Berkeley: University of California Press, 1987); Margaret S. Archer, *Realist Social Theory* (Cambridge, UK: Cambridge University Press, 1995).

Before attempting to clarify a general theoretical relationship between rules of apportionment and their respective constitutional orders, let us first consider the process by which this study's three cases of national apportionment rule change were identified and selected, the contributions, limitations, and range of existing explanations of political change by political scientists, and the research design that frames the subsequent analysis of each case. For only after these analytical preliminaries have properly been addressed can the more difficult task of theorization be engaged with the requisite seriousness.

CASE SELECTION

The process used to identify the set of constitutional changes in the national rule of apportionment began initially as an attempt to identify the conceptual and historical precedents of the U.S. Supreme Court's well-known "one person, one vote" apportionment rulings in the early 1960s. This attempt subsequently led to deeper historical inquiries into the institutional and conceptual development of representative government in the United States. One of the first memorable historical discoveries was a series of legal decisions in the 1920s and early 1930s. The first decision came in the aftermath of the 1920 Census. This Census revealed that for the first time in the nation's existence more Americans resided within urban areas than within rural areas. Rather than transfer representative power in the House (and, thus, also in the Electoral College) to states with the most rapidly increasing populations, Congress failed repeatedly throughout the decade to reapportion the House of Representatives in accord with the 1920 Census. Prior to this failure, Congress had succeeded every decade since the 1790 Census in enacting new legislation authorizing a reapportionment of representation within the U.S. House.[2]

In 1929, Congress made a second important decision. It determined that the then-existing interstate division of House representation (enacted in 1911) would not continue after completion of the next U.S.

---

[2] For more on Congress's unprecedented failure to complete a decennial reapportionment of the House of Representatives in the 1920s, see Louis C. Boochever, *A Study of the Factors Involved in the Passage of the 1929 Bill for Reapportionment of the House of Representatives* (M.A. thesis, Cornell University, 1942); Sister Mary Consolata Jennings, V.H.M., *History of Congressional Reapportionment* (M.A. thesis, St. Louis University, 1948); Orville J. Sweeting, "John Q. Tillson: Reapportionment Act of 1929," *Western Political Quarterly* (1956), 9: 434–453; Charles A. Eagles, *Democracy Delayed: the Urban-Rural Conflict in the 1920s* (Athens, GA: University of Georgia Press, 1990).

Census. In the 1929 Census Act, Congress authorized a new set of procedures for the completion of the 1930 Census, and it provided for an "automatic" House reapportionment process designed to take effect if Congress failed to enact separate legislation authorizing a new House apportionment.[3] Hailed by some as a pragmatic response to Congress's decade-long failure to reapportion the House, this "automatic" process of reapportionment continues today as the standard (and largely unrecognized) method for completing the decennial reapportionment of the U.S. House of Representatives. As a consequence of this "automatic" process, the House size has remained fixed at 435 members for almost ninety years.[4]

The third noteworthy decision came three years after enactment of the 1929 Census Act. In *Wood v. Broom* (1932), the Supreme Court reviewed a case involving a federal district court injunction against a state's congressional redistricting plan.[5] The lower court ruled that the state's plan violated federal standards that congressional "districts [be] composed of a contiguous and compact territory, and containing as nearly as practicable an equal number of inhabitants." These standards had been included in the last decennial apportionment act enacted by Congress in 1911, but not in the automatic apportionment section of the 1929 Census Act.[6] Writing the opinion of the Court in *Wood*, Chief Justice Charles Evans Hughes overturned the lower court injunction and definitively declared that "[i]t was manifestly the intention of the Congress not to re-enact" the 1911 districting standards.[7]

---

[3] Ch. 28, 46 Stat. 26 (June 18, 1929). The automatic apportionment section of the 1929 Census Act is known today as Title 2, Sec. 2(a) of the U.S. Code. After enactment of the 1929 Act, Congress enacted two minor procedural modifications. In 1940, after ratification of the Twentieth Amendment, which modified the congressional calendar, Congress altered the timing of the President's reapportionment report to Congress. (See 54 Stat. 162, April 25, 1940.) A year later, in 1941, Congress resolved a partisan controversy over the state assignment of the 435th House seat by adopting a single mathematical formula to reapportion the House. (See 55 Stat. L. 761, November 15, 1941.)

[4] The House size was increased temporarily to 437 on the admission of the new states of Alaska and Hawaii in the late 1950s. It automatically returned to 435 members after completion of the 1960 decennial reapportionment. For an assessment of the longer-term consequences of the 1929 Act, see Charles A. Kromkowski and John A. Kromkowski, "Why 435?: A Question of Political Arithmetic," *Polity* (1991), 24: 129–145; and "Beyond Administrative Apportionment: Discovering the Calculus of Representative Government," *Polity* (1992), 25: 495–497.

[5] *Wood v. Broom*, 287 U.S. 1 (1932).

[6] 37 Stat. L. 14 (August 8, 1911).

[7] 287 U.S. at 7 (1932). Notably, before the Supreme Court's decision in *Wood*, state supreme courts in Minnesota, Illinois, New York, and Virginia held that the 1929 Act

The effects of the now nearly eclipsed decisions of Congress in the 1920s and by the Supreme Court in 1932 were far from innocuous. Together, they signaled the national government's wholesale retreat from its traditional management of the decennial reapportionment process. State legislatures, as a consequence, were free to ignore the districting standards that Congress previously had included in prior decennial re-apportionment legislation.[8] Many state legislatures reacted by simply not redistricting, whereas others completed only nominal redistricting plans.[9] As a result, in many states congressional district populations grew increasingly disproportional over time. Indeed, district inequalities became so egregious in several states that individuals sought relief in federal and state courts. Although several state courts intervened to correct state legislative inequalities, it was not until the U.S. Supreme Court declared its "one person, one vote" rule in 1964 that a branch of the national government redressed – at least, in part – the longer-term consequences of the 1929 Census Act and the 1932 *Wood* decision.

What compelled Congress's failure to reapportion the House after the 1920 Census, or the omission of national districting standards in the 1929 Census Act, or Chief Justice Hughes's interpretation of this Act as nullifying the 1911 districting standards may forever remain matters for reasoned debate and speculation. These decisions, nonetheless, were an undeniable part of the political context within which the Supreme Court subsequently decided to establish a new apportionment rule in the 1960s.

Discovery of the relationship between and the similarities among the striking changes effected by Congress in the 1920s and by the Supreme Court in the early 1960s catalyzed additional questions and further

---

was enacted to prevent a recurrence of Congress's decennial reapportionment failure and not to void the 1911 districting principles. Two lower federal courts in Kentucky and Mississippi similarly held that the 1911 principles remained effective. For contemporaneous interpretations of Congress's intent, see Harold M. Bowman, "Congressional Redistricting and the Constitution," *Michigan Law Review* (1932), 31(2): 149–179; and the separate opinion of four Supreme Court justices in *Wood* 287 U.S. at 8–9.

[8] In 1842, for example, Congress began requiring single-member congressional districts that were territorially contiguous (5 Stat. L. 491, June 25, 1842). In 1872, Congress added the requirement that congressional districts within a state have "as nearly as practicable an equal number of inhabitants" (17 Stat. L. 28, February 2, 1872). In 1901, Congress additionally required territorially compact congressional districts (31 Stat. L. 733, January 16, 1901).

[9] These districting practices were already well established in several states by the time the Supreme Court decided *Wood* (1932). The Court's decision did not, therefore, trigger the conditions of malapportionment that ultimately were addressed by the Supreme Court in the 1960s. However, the *Wood* decision clearly bestowed a judicial blanket of legitimacy on these practices.

inquiry into the historical prevalence and causes of change in the rule of apportionment. Three additional constitutional changes were easily identified because the abandonment of the existing apportionment rule was coterminous with historic ruptures in the American political order and because the establishment of a new rule of apportionment was formalized within either a new national constitution or a national constitutional amendment. In chronological order, these three changes were initiated within the wake of the American Revolution, the 1787 Constitutional Convention, and the American Civil War. The first change was completed with ratification of the Articles of Confederation in 1781. The second change was effected by ratification of the U.S. Constitution in 1788. The third change was completed with ratification of the Thirteenth, Fourteenth, and Fifteenth Amendments to the U.S. Constitution between 1865 and 1870.

More specifically, the first constitutional change established an apportionment rule that divided political representation within the national Congress on an equal state basis. The second change, in brief, established a new apportionment rule that divided representation proportionally among the states in the U.S. House of Representatives and equally among the states in the U.S. Senate. Finally, the third change ended the applicability of the so-called "three-fifths" rule with ratification of the Thirteenth Amendment, and the Fourteenth Amendment established a new basis and set of procedures for apportioning representation in the U.S. House of Representatives. The latter amendment also required, although never effected, a reduction of representation if a state denied or abridged the adult male suffrage. The Fifteenth Amendment explicitly prohibited federal and state suffrage restrictions based on race, color, or previous condition of servitude.

Historical regression from the U.S. Supreme Court's apportionment decisions in the early 1960s thus revealed a set of five constitutional changes in the national rule of apportionment. Table 1.1 identifies the year and rule of apportionment abandoned for each change as well as the historic event and the immediate outcome commonly associated with the initiation of each change.[10]

---

[10] Beyond the five identified cases that fit within this study's definition of a constitutional change, additional cases might come to mind: for example, the familiar and antecedent constitutional changes in England in 1641 and 1688. Other cases plausibly suggested by the definition of apportionment rule change might include the 1967 federal law mandating single-member congressional districts and the 1982 Voting Rights Act amendment requiring the maximization of majority-minority legislative districts. Given the

TABLE 1.1. *Apportionment Rule Abandonment*

Change (Year)	Apportionment Rule Abandoned	Rule Form	Historical Event Associated with Rule Abandonment	Immediate Outcome
I (1776)	"British-colonial" rule[a]	Customary	Declaration of Independence	Civil war
II (1787)	Equal state rule	Written	1787 Philadelphia Convention	Political process
III (1860 1861)	Equal/ proportional rules	Written	Confederate secession	Civil War
IV (1921–1929)	Decennial reapportionment rule	Customary	Failure to reapportion House after 1920 Census	Political process
V (1962)	No national districting standards	Customary	*Baker v. Carr* (1962)	Political process

[a] See Chapter 2 for a description of the allocation of governmental authority within Great Britain and the American colonies prior to 1776.

Given this study's stated interest in making apportionment rule changes and their constitutional consequences as transparent as possible, the eras and events associated with the first three cases were selected for closer examination. Selection of these three cases is justified not only by the depth of the evidentiary materials and scholarly works on these cases, but also by the fact that over the first three eras collective decision-making authority (at the national level) was manifested almost exclusively by and exercised most clearly through Congress. These cases, therefore, present a rare opportunity within which the formal terms for apportioning representation within Congress closely approximates (with subsequently noted qualifications) the actual divisions of collective decision-making authority. As Table 1.2 illustrates, the three apportionment

relatively insignificant constitutional disruptions and consequences associated with these cases, their inclusion seems, at best, contestable. On the former cases, see J. G. A. Pocock, ed., *Three British Revolutions, 1641, 1688, 1776* (Princeton, NJ: Princeton University Press, 1980); on the contestability of the final suggested case, see *Shaw v. Reno*, 509 U.S. 630 (1993); and *Miller v. Johnson* 515 U.S. 916 (1995); *Shaw v. Hunt*, 116 S.Ct. 1894 (1996); *Bush v. Vera*, 517 U.S. 952 (1996).

TABLE 1.2. *Apportionment Rule Creation*

Change (Year)	Form	Distributional Terms	Procedural Terms
I (1781)	Articles of Confederation	(Congress) [*EQUAL STATE REPRESENTATION*]	
II (1788)	U.S. Constitution	(U.S. Senate) Equal state (U.S. House) [*PROPORTIONAL AMONG STATES, PARTIAL POPULATION FORMULA, MINIMUM HOUSE SIZE, MAXIMUM HOUSE SIZE*]	(U.S. House) [*DECENNIAL LEGISLATION*]
III (1865–1870)	Thirteenth, Fourteenth, Fifteenth Amendments	Equal state Proportional among states, [*FULL POPULATION FORMULA*] Minimum state representation, maximum House size [*REDUCTION FOR SUFFRAGE DENIAL*]	Decennial legislation

Note: Constitutional changes are bracketed and capitalized. Written constitutional changes are boldfaced and italicized. Customary constitutional changes are underlined.

8

rule changes under study have established new terms and/or procedures for the division of political representation within the U.S. Congress – and, in turn, the Electoral College. Several of these rule changes were formalized as a written constitutional mandate: they are represented as boldfaced changes. Other constitutional rules, by contrast, were established over time as customary practices: they are represented as underlined changes.

Commitment to the description and explanation of the three identified constitutional changes invited recognition and closer study of the insights, approaches, and limitations of a wide range of scholarship in the disciplines of history and the social sciences. Whereas the historical literature related to each change is surveyed in more detail in subsequent chapters, the following review of political science scholarship accounting for political change is required to plumb a central question of this study: Why do apportionment rules change? The following synopsis, however, is not exhaustive in a bibliographical sense nor does it exhaust all of the topical areas that parallel or intersect with this study. This synopsis, rather, is merely suggestive of how this study draws from and extends prior explanations of the causes of political change.

EXPLANATIONS OF POLITICAL CHANGE

Like the topic of collective authority for the disciplines of history and political science, the study of political change offers a focal point that transcends and binds many of the subfield boundaries that presently constitute the discipline of political science. Regardless of these boundaries, many of these studies can be distinguished by the ways in which they describe and explain the patterns and causes of political change. Typically, patterns of change are described either as incremental adaptations or as abrupt, discontinuous breaks from a prevailing (and often static) status quo.[11] Given the generally stable nature of individual

---

[11] For studies which rely on the metaphor of incrementalism, see Aaron Wildavsky, *The Politics of the Budgetary Process*, 3rd. ed. (1979); R. Kent Weaver, *Automatic Government: The Politics of Indexation* (Washington, DC: Brookings Institution, 1988); Douglass C. North, *Institutions, Institutional Change and Economic Performance* (Cambridge, UK: Cambridge University Press, 1990); and James A. Stimson, *Public Opinion in America: Moods, Cycles, and Swings* (Boulder, CO: Westview Press, 1991).

Political scientists have used several metaphors to describe more discontinuous forms of change in the political status quo. One of the more prevalent is the "punctuated equilibrium" or "critical juncture" description of change. A related approach that also incorporates part of the incrementalist metaphor is the "threshold" or "tipping point"

apportionment rules, apportionment rule changes most resemble a discontinuous form of political change.

Whereas the causes of incremental change often can be numerous or beyond measurable detection, the causes of discontinuous forms of political change typically have been explained in terms of a more limited and discoverable set of general causes. One of the most commonly identified of these general causes is agenda change, or changes in the issues or ideas discussed or held by political actors. Political scientist E. E. Schattschneider, for example, argued in his classic study *The Semisovereign People* that the agenda of politics defines the parameters within which political decision making occurs. He therefore advised against undue focus upon the "complexities of the governmental structure," and instead concluded that the decision maker who determines the political agenda or "what politics is about runs the country, because the definition of the alternatives is the choice of conflicts, and the choice of conflicts allocates power."[12] Recent studies of agenda change do not discount the effect of other factors upon agenda formation as much as Schattschneider apparently did, but they similarly contend that "agenda dynamics lead to lurches in public policymaking."[13]

metaphor. A deficiency shared by both is their tendency to conflate accidents with causation. See Stephen D. Krasner, "Sovereignty, An Institutional Perspective," *Comparative Political Studies* (1988) 21: 77–80; Seymour M. Lipset and Stein Rokkan, "Cleavage Structures, Party Systems, and Voter Alignments: An Introduction," Lipset and Rokkan, eds., *Party Systems and Voter Alignments* (New York: Free Press, 1967), pp. 47, 54; Collier and Collier, *Shaping the Political Arena* (Princeton, NJ: Princeton University Press, 1991), pp. 27–31; Gourevitch, *Politics in Hard Times* (Ithaca, NY: Cornell University Press, 1986), pp. 34, 27; March and Olsen, *Rediscovering Institutions* (New York: Free Press, 1989), p. 166; Douglass C. North, *Institutions, Institutional Change and Economic Performance* (Cambridge, UK: Cambridge University Press, 1990), pp. 73–117; Paul Pierson, "Increasing Returns, Path Dependence and the Study of Politics," *American Political Science Review* (2000) 94(2): 251–268; Paul Pierson, "Big, Slow-Moving, and . . . Invisible: Macro-Social Processes in the Study of Comparative Politics" (n.p., 2001) 42 pp.

[12] E. E. Schattschneider, *The Semisovereign People* (New York: Holt, Rinehart and Winston, 1960), pp. 112–139, 60, 66.

[13] Bryan D. Jones, *Reconceiving Decision-Making in Democratic Politics* (Chicago: University of Chicago Press, 1994), p. 25; and Frank R. Baumgartner and Bryan D. Jones, *Agendas and Instability in American Politics* (Chicago: University of Chicago Press, 1993).
    For a range of applications of this explanatory approach, see Charles E. Lindbloom, *The Intelligence of Democracy: Decision-Making through Mutual Adjustment* (New York: Free Press, 1965); William Connolly, *The Terms of Political Discourse* (Princeton, NJ: Princeton University Press, 1983); John W. Kingdom, *Agendas, Alternatives and Public Policies* (Boston: Little, Brown, 1984); Edward G. Carmines and James A. Stimson, *Issue Evolution: Race and the Transformation of American Politics* (Princeton, NJ: Princeton University Press, 1989); James Stimson, *Public Opinion in*

Another commonly identified cause of discontinuous political change is actor change, or the wholesale recomposition of the set of political actors. Students of the U.S. Congress, the Presidency and the U.S. Supreme Court regularly attribute dramatic policy shifts to personnel changes in these branches. Among others, Walter Dean Burnham identifies "critical" or "realigning" congressional elections to explain long-lasting changes in "the universe of policy."[14]

A third common cause identified to explain discontinuous political changes is institutional change, or changes that redefine the organizational structures, procedural rules, or customary practices that sustain patterned political behavior. Proponents of this type of causal explanation contend that political institutions affect the decisions of political actors by shaping their ideas, their preferences, and their abilities to coordinate with other actors. For example, students of international relations and comparative government often explain the formation of national interest, the dynamics of international cooperation, and cross-national policy differences by referring to the presence or absence of particular political institutions.[15] Others, especially students of the U.S. Congress,

---

America: Moods, Cycles and Swings (Boulder, CO: Westview Press, 1991); Margaret Weir, "Ideas and the Politics of Bounded Innovation," in Sven Steinmo et al., Structuring Politics (Cambridge, UK: Cambridge University Press, 1992), pp. 188–216; Judith Goldstein and Robert O. Keohane, eds., Ideas and Foreign Policy: Beliefs, Institutions, and Political Change (Ithaca, NY: Cornell University Press, 1993); Judith Goldstein, Ideas, Interests, and American Trade Policy (Ithaca, NY: Cornell University Press, 1993).

[14] Walter Dean Burnham, Critical Elections and the Mainsprings of American Politics (New York: Norton, 1970). See also V. O. Key, "A Theory of Critical Elections," Journal of Politics (1955), 17: 3–18; Stephen Skowronek, "Notes on the Presidency in the Political Order," Studies in American Political Development (1986), 1: 286–302; David W. Brady, Critical Elections and Congressional Policy Making (Stanford, CA: Stanford University Press, 1988); Mark Schneider, Paul Teske, and Michael Minstrom, Public Entrepreneurs: Agents for Change in American Government (Princeton, NJ: Princeton University Press, 1995).

[15] For examples of institutionalist studies in international relations, see Stephen D. Krasner, Defending the National Interest (Princeton, NJ: Princeton University Press, 1978); Arthur A. Stein, "Coordination and Collaboration: Regimes in an Anarchic World," 36: 299–324, International Organization (1982); Robert O. Keohane, "The Demand for International Regimes," 36: 325–355, International Organization (1982).

For comparative institutionalist studies, see Sven Steinmo, Taxation and Democracy (1993); R. Kent Weaver and Bert A. Rockman, eds., Do Institutions Matter?: Government Capabilities in the United States and Abroad (Washington, DC: The Brookings Institution, 1993); Sven Steinmo, Kathleen Thelan, and Frank Longstreth, eds., Structuring Politics (Cambridge, UK: Cambridge University Press, 1992); Ruth Berins Collier and David Collier, Shaping the Political Arena: Critical Junctures, the Labor Movement, and Regime Dynamics in Latin America (Princeton, NJ: Princeton University Press, 1991); George Tsbelis, Nested Games (Berkeley, CA: University of California Press,

have studied the causes and effects of various institutional configurations on legislative decision making and policy outcomes.[16]

Focus on the relationship between institutions and political behavior has been a traditional part of the political science discipline since its formal inception at the turn of the century. Recent applications of this institutional (or presently-named "new institutionalism") approach, however, also share an intellectual lineage with a family of theoretical and formalized expectations commonly known as the General Impossibility or Chaos Theorem. In its barest form, this theorem demonstrates the logical impossibility of consensus formation among a set of actors under highly constrained decision-making conditions.[17] Generalized to more complex sets of actors within less constrained (and, therefore, more realistic) conditions, collective decision making still appears to be a near impossibility. Moreover, although the spontaneous formation of a political consensus always remains possible, once established a political order is continuously threatened with a reversion to a primordial state of decisional chaos. As a consequence, Robert Goodin astutely observes, "the specter of a perpetual disequilibrium . . . seems to be a (indeed, perhaps the) central problem in political life."[18]

1990); Peter A. Hall, *Governing the Economy: The Politics of State Intervention in Britain and France* (New York: Oxford University Press, 1986); Peter Gourevitch, *Politics in Hard Times* (Ithaca, NY: Cornell University Press, 1986); Peter Katzenstein, ed., *Between Power and Plenty* (Madison: University of Wisconsin Press, 1978).

[16] See Steven S. Smith and Thomas F. Remmington, *The Politics of Institutional Choice: The Formation of the Russian State Duma* (Princeton, NJ: Princeton University Press, 2001); Eric Schickler, *Disjointed Pluralism: Institutional Innovation and the Development of the U.S. Congress* (Princeton, NJ: Princeton University Press, 2001). Sarah A. Binder, *Minority Rights, Majority Rule* (Cambridge, UK: Cambridge University Press, 1997). See also Roger H. Davidson and Walter Oleszek, "Adaptation and Consolidation: Structural Innovation in the U.S. House of Representatives," *LSQ* (1976), 1: 36–67; Kenneth Shepsle, "Institutional Arrangements and Equilibrium in Multidimensional Voting Models," *AJPS*, 23: 27–59 (1979); William Riker, "Implications from the Disequilibrium of Majority Rule for the Study of Institutions," *APSR* (1980), 74: 432–446; Kenneth A. Shepsle and Barry R. Weingast, "The Institutional Foundations of Committee Power," *APSR* (1987), 81: 85–104; and John Mark Hansen, *Gaining Access: Congress and the Farm Lobby* (Chicago: University of Chicago Press, 1990).

[17] For a more formalized explanation of the Chaos Theorem, see Richard D. McKelvey, "Intransitivities in Multi-Dimensional Voting Models and Some Implications for Agenda Control," *Journal of Economic Theory* (1976), 12: 472–482, 480; and William Riker, "Implications from the Disequilibrium of Majority Rule for the Study of Institutions," *APSR* (1980), 74: 1235–1247. For introductory explanations, see Michael Laver and Norman Schofield, *Multiparty Government* (Ann Arbor: University of Michigan Press, 1998), pp. 119–129; and Charles Stewart III, *Analyzing Congress* (New York: W. W. Norton, 2001), pp. 1–49.

[18] Robert E. Goodin, "Institutions and Their Design," in *The Theory of Institutional Design*, Goodin, ed. (Cambridge, UK: Cambridge University Press, 1996), p. 11.

In response to the theoretical expectations of the Chaos Theorem, the new institutionalism literature attempted to solve the obvious observational anomaly that Gordon Tullock succinctly captured with the question: "Why so much stability?"[19] The common response offered by neoinstitutionalist scholars, according to Kenneth A. Shepsle, was "that *institutions matter* because institutions prescribe how collective choices are to be made" and, thus, the theoretically expected decisional chaos is overcome within the observable world either "directly because political institutions restrict agendas, or indirectly because political institutions assign agenda power to those who would impose these kind of restrictions."[20] Political stability, in other words, is institution-dependent and the essential characteristics of a particular political order are related directly to the particular types of institutions adopted.

Change the institutions, according to the implicit logic of the new institutionalism literature, and the characteristics and possibilities of a particular political order also change. Discontinuous political change, therefore, results when one set of order-producing institutions is replaced by another set of institutions.[21] These moments of change – that is, between institutional abandonment and institutional reconstitution – are the points at which a political order (or elements of an order) appears to diverge onto a new path of political development. To use the Frostian metaphor familiar to neoinstitutionalists, institutional decisions make "all the difference" in the historical life of a political order.

Ironically, the general solution celebrated by the new institutionalism approach to the "Why stability?" anomaly has raised the specter of a second anomaly concerning the process and dynamics of political change. Most studies, that is, highlight the effects of institutions during stable, not transitional or unstable, periods. As a result, how and why specific institutions are adopted and change, and how stability is maintained during meta-institutional transitions are puzzling questions that remain largely unaddressed.[22]

---

[19] Gordon Tullock, "Why So Much Stability," *Public Choice* (1981), 37: 189–202.

[20] Kenneth A. Shepsle, "Political Institutions and the New Institutional Economics," *Journal of Institutional and Theoretical Economics* (1993), 149: 347–350.

[21] See James G. March and Johan P. Olsen, "The New Institutionalism: Organizational Factors in Political Life," *APSR* (1984), 78: 734–749; and North, *Institutions, Institutional Change and Economic Performance* (1990).

[22] See Norman Schofield, "Modeling Political Order in Representative Democracies," in *Political Order: Nomos XXXVIII*, Ian Shapiro and Russell Hardin, eds. (1996), p. 92; Karol Soltan, Eric M. Uslaner, and Virginia Haufler, eds., *New Institutionalism: Institutions and Social Order* (Ann Arbor: University of Michigan Press, 1998).

As presently conceptualized, the new institutionalism approach is ill equipped to illuminate the process or causal dynamics of institutional formation and change. For if political institutions are assigned the all-important function of stabilizing and sustaining political order over time, they cannot simultaneously be identified as the causes of discontinuous political change as well. This problem becomes more serious – at least, theoretically – when institutions are conceptualized as defining "the outermost frame for political conflict."[23] For such a conceptualization literally means that the interstitial moments between old and new institutions would expose a political order to the decisional chaos that characterizes the institutionless state. Moreover, when an elemental institution like an apportionment rule is called into question or abandoned the meta-institutional suspension of a political order over the theorized anarchical abyss requires nothing less than a leap of faith.

Although the three cases of apportionment rule abandonment examined in this study triggered institutional cascades in the existing framework of government (with two of these ending in civil war), transitions *between* old and new institutions only rarely threaten a political order with destabilization of this magnitude. The stability and permanence attributed to institutions therefore are, in part, exaggerated and, in part, an effect of a shortened historical perspective. Political institutions, after all, do not last forever. In fact, from a longer view, institutional changes are altogether common political phenomena. As a consequence, what appears at one time to be the cause of political stability appears from a longer historical perspective to be coterminous with a near-continuous stream of institutional changes.

NEW INSTITUTIONALISM AND RATIONALITY MODELS

To be fair, new institutionalism scholars may be blinkered but they are not blind to the necessity of explaining precisely how political change occurs. Several studies, for example, have explained discontinuous political change as triggered by environmental changes – for example, by economic shocks, tidal shifts in public opinion, or by domestic or international "crises."[24] According to these accounts, changes within

---

[23] Ellen M. Immergut, "The Rules of the Game: The Logic of Health Policymaking in France, Switzerland, and Sweden," in Sven Steinmo et al., eds., *Structuring Politics* (1992), p. 85.

[24] See Peter Gourevitch, *The Politics of Hard Times* (1986); and Theda Skocpol, *States and Social Revolution* (Cambridge, UK: Cambridge University Press, 1979).

environmental configurations disrupt the existing institution-structured equilibrium and, thereby, destabilize a political order. Political actors, in turn, respond in the aftermath of these exogenously triggered opportunities to establish new institutional arrangements that subsequently alter the immediate and long-term development of a political order. The causal sequence linked to this instrumental account of institutional change may very well be conducive for convincing allegorical descriptions of discontinuous political change. If, however, the standards for explanation require grounding in the historical evidence and in the sequence of decisions made by specific sets of political actors, then environmental triggers of political change seem epiphenomenal or, worse yet, ad hoc when not directly related to a particular type of political change.[25]

For these reasons, an explanation that identifies endogenous causes of political change seems both more realistic and more aesthetically satisfying. If, however, individual actors become the agents of institutional change, then the essential cause of political change is a behavioral, not a materially determined, phenomenon. As a consequence, construction of this type of explanation necessarily reflects the way in which individual decision-making behavior is defined.[26]

Since the 1950s, several models of decision-making behavior have dominated this definitional debate.[27] The "instrumental rationality" model is the well-known foundation of neoclassical microeconomic theory. This model assumes that individual decision makers have full information of their interests and of the means for achieving them. The model, in turn, assumes that individuals make optimal decisions that maximize individual benefits.[28] Under these conditions, institutional

---

[25] For an insightful critique of the structural approach, see Youssef Cohen, *Radicals, Reformers and Reactionaries* (Chicago: Chicago University Press, 1994). For an interesting exchange on the methodological problems and utility of the structural approach, see Elizabeth Nichols, "Skocpol On Revolution: Comparative Analysis vs. Historical Conjuncture," and Theda Skocpol, "Analyzing Causal Configurations in History: A Rejoinder to Nichols," *Comparative Social Research* (1986), 9: 163–194.

[26] See North, *Institutions, Institutional Change, and Economic Performance* (1990), p. 5.

[27] For a fuller review of the range of behavioral models, see James G. March, "Bounded Rationality, Ambiguity, and the Engineering of Choice," *The Bell Journal of Economics* (1978), 9: 587–608. See also Karen Schweers Cook and Margaret Levi, eds., *The Limits of Rationality* (Chicago: Chicago University Press, 1990); and North, *Institutions, Institutional Change and Economic Performance* (1990).

[28] The instrumental rational actor model has been criticized for its failures to describe or explain actual decision-making behavior. These failures can be traced to several elements of the model's design. First, the model describes decision-making behavior outside of an environmental context. Second, it collapses actor interests, decisions, and their consequent benefits into a single hypothetical moment of time, thus only immediate (not

change would be driven by an evolutionary process aimed continuously toward more "efficient" political outcomes.

The "bounded rationality" model offers another and more realistic definition of individual decision-making behavior and, therefore, a different starting point for explaining institutional change.[29] This model, in short, relaxes the full information and optimal outcome assumptions that define the instrumental rationality model. According to economist Herbert A. Simon, individuals make decisions in accord with their interests and they attempt to obtain outcomes that maximize individual benefits. The decision maker, however, is constrained by his or her capacities to gather and to process information. Rather than decisions that result in optimal outcomes, individuals under these conditions make decisions that merely satisfy their interests. Institutional change under the bounded rationality model, thus, can be explained in terms of interest-maximizing actors making decisions with limited information among a finite range of possibilities. Unlike the instrumental rationality model, decisions for new institutional arrangements under this second model may in fact lead to suboptimal outcomes.[30]

longer-term) benefits typically are considered. Another fundamental problem with this model is that the definition of "rational" action is imputed exogenously into the model. Thus, the definition of rational individual behavior is primarily an artifact of a study's research question and design. See Herbert A. Simon, "Human Nature in Politics: The Dialogue of Psychology with Political Science," *APSR* (1985), 79: 293–304.

   Others have maintained that instrumental rationality is a normative, not a descriptive, model of individual decision making. See, for example, Jon Elster, "When Rationality Fails," in *The Limits of Rationality* (1990), Karen Schweers Cook and Margaret Levi, eds., pp. 19–51.

[29] See Herbert A. Simon, *Models of Bounded Rationality*, 3 vols. (Cambridge, MA: MIT Press, 1982).

[30] "Rationality" in the bounded rationality model is defined endogenously by each individual decision maker "within the constraints imposed *both* by the external situation and by the capacities of the decision maker." Thus, as Herbert A. Simon repeatedly suggested, what is most important about explanations of political phenomena are the empirical assumptions about goals and, even more important, about the ways in which people characterize the choice situations that face them. These goals and characterizations do not rest on immutable first principles, but are functions of time and place that can only be ascertained by empirical inquiry. In this sense, political science is necessarily a historical science, in the same way and for the same reason that astronomy is. What will happen next is not independent of where the system is right now. And a description of where it is right now must include a description of the subjective view of the situation that informs the choices of the actors. Herbert A. Simon, "Human Nature in Politics: The Dialogue of Psychology with Political Science," *APSR* (1985), 79: 294, 301. See also Herbert A. Simon, "Rationality in Psychology and Economics," *Journal of Business* (1986), 59(4–2): S223.

A third behavioral model is the "institutional rationality" model. It includes the prior models' assumptions of interest maximization, limited information, and the possibility of suboptimal outcomes. This model adds the additional constraint that individuals are limited and motivated by the institutional contexts within which they decide. Institutional contexts, according to this model, are not neutral environments. In addition, that is, to facilitating cooperation among political actors by reducing the uncertainty of making and maintaining agreements, institutions establish distributional hierarchies that favor specific actors and types of decision-making behavior.[31]

Several institutional theorists have combined the core behavioral assumptions of this third model with the logic of a transaction cost approach to explain the decision-making dynamics that compel institutional change. They propose, in short, that institutions endure as long as the benefits individuals receive under these institutions exceed the expected benefits of alternative institutions minus the expected costs of institutional transformation. Once the sum of the latter two exceed the former, individuals become motivated to pursue institutional change. Moreover, economic historian Douglass C. North contends, when a political order is open to regular but incremental institutional changes, minor shifts in transaction costs prompt decisions for incremental institutional adjustments. These adjustments, in turn, produce incremental patterns of political change. When, however, a political order is closed off to incremental change over extended periods, then the accumulation of minor shifts in transactions costs prompts more dramatic (and potentially more destructive) attempts to effect institutional change.[32] Only after a long train of costs has amassed, North implies, are conditions ripe for discontinuous forms of change.

A fourth model of rationality – the one strived for in this study – recognizes the core assumptions of the other rationality models but abandons their common but latent predictive purpose. That is, rather than defining the constitutive components of rational behavior so that future behavior can be predicted with greater accuracy, this new "historical

---

[31] North, *Institutions, Institutional Change, and Economic Performance* (1990); and Margaret Levi, "A Logic of Institutional Change," in Karen Schweers Cook and Margaret Levi, eds. *The Limits of Rationality* (1990), pp. 402–418; and Jack Knight, *Institutions and Social Conflict* (Cambridge, UK: Cambridge University Press, 1992).

[32] North, *Institutions, Institutional Change and Economic Performance* (1990), pp. 83–91; and Stephen Krasner, "Approaches to the State: Alternative Conceptions and Historical Dynamics," *Comparative Politics* (1984), 16: 223–246.

rationality" model more modestly binds the description of rational behavior to particular times, places, and individuals so that past actions can be more fully and faithfully understood. This fourth model promises more realistic reconstructions of the decision-making behaviors that effect unique historical outcomes among numerous alternatives, but the model burdens its adherents with a self-consciousness – shared with historians – that any adequate explanation of a particular institutional change would require a full immersion in the empirical sources that reveal the cultural, group, and individual referents of rational behavior for a particular period and moment in time.[33]

In sum, this study draws upon and extends the insights of existing studies on discontinuous political change. Of these, this study is most indebted to those that focus on institutional change as the primary cause and consequence of political change. Similar to accounts of "critical junctures," "punctuated equilibrium," and "the open moments when system-creating choices are made," this study also focuses on the interstitial transitions between old and new institutions – and specifically between old and new rules of apportionment. In tune with the central insights of the new institutionalism literature, this study demonstrates that changes in rules of apportionment have significant short- and longer-term consequences upon the behavior of political actors and the mediation of state-society relations. Unlike existing accounts, however, this study explicitly acknowledges the necessity of an historical model of rational behavior as a means of confronting the nagging "Why stability?" and "Why change?" anomalies that presently plague the neo-institutionalist and rational choice literatures. In so doing, this study contributes to previous works by explaining institutional change and stability in terms of historically defined contextual conditions and the interplay between these dynamic conditions and the dynamics of historically defined actors engaged in the definition of a common constitutional order.

---

[33] See John A. Ferejohn, "Rationality and Interpretation: Parliamentary Elections in Early Stuart England," in Kristen R. Monroe, ed., *The Economic Approach to Politics* (New York: HarperCollins, 1991), pp. 279–305; Robert H. Bates, Rui J. P. De Figueiredo, and Barry R. Weingast, "The Politics of Interpretation: Rationality, Culture, and Transition," *Politics and Society* (1998) 26(4): 603–642; John H. Aldrich and Keneth A. Shepsle, "Explaining Institutional Change: Soaking, Poking, and Modeling in the U.S. Congress," in William T. Bianco, ed., *Congress on Display, Congress at Work* (Ann Arbor: University of Michigan Press, 2000), pp. 23–45.

RESEARCH DESIGN

Again, four research questions frame this inquiry: when and how rules of apportionment are created and abandoned, why these changes occur, and with what constitutional consequences. To formulate answers to these questions, the goals, assumptions, methods, and organization of this study need to be made explicit.

Description

The first goal of this study is to provide an accurate and comprehensive description of the first three constitutional changes in the national rule of apportionment identified in Tables 1.1 and 1.2. Such a description, it is assumed, requires a detailed account of the context, the actors, and the sequence of decisions associated with each change. To ground these descriptions, a census of the available historical evidence was completed for each change. Given the breadth and depth of original sources, secondary interpretative accounts were used initially to explore the historical periods prior to and inclusive of each change. These accounts also were relied upon to describe the contextual conditions that framed each change. These secondary accounts, however, failed to illuminate fully the contexts which, the actors who, and the sequence of decisions that defined each constitutional change. Indeed the more familiar each historical period and change became, the clearer the contributions and limitations of existing accounts became evident. Whenever possible, therefore, original source data were collected to validate prior accounts and to identify (independent of these accounts) the specific actors who participated in and the particular sequence of decisions that effected each change.[34]

The historical evidence collected for each change also was arranged into general categories reflective of macrolevel and microlevel conditions. Macrolevel conditions defined the societal and political contexts within

[34] Among the many political scientists who presently have taken the "historical turn," few explicitly recognize the methodological necessity of redoing prior interpretative works by reengaging primary source materials. See Andrew Moravcsik, "De Gaulle and European Integration: Historical Revision and Social Science Theory," Center for European Studies Working Paper (May 1998); and Ian Lustick, "History, Historiography and Political Science: Multiple Historical Records and the Problem of Selection Bias," *APSR* (1996), 90(3): 605–618. The full implications of this higher empirical bar for political scientists and their work are not immediately evident.

which each constitutional change occurred. In particular, the specific elements of the societal context focused upon were the long- and short-term patterns of change in economic and demographic conditions. The political context was defined in terms of institutional and ideological conditions. In particular, this study focused on long- and short-term patterns of change in governmental structure and capacities, and in the conceptualization of political representation.

Microlevel conditions, by contrast, were defined in terms of the individuals and the decisions that brought about each constitutional change. In particular, historical evidence was collected to identify the political actors who initiated and participated in the sequence of decisions associated with the three apportionment rule changes. This evidence also was used to reconstruct the range of possible outcomes as it was understood by these actors prior to each change. The remainder of the historical evidence collected was used to define the preferences of the primary sets of political actors who were participants in each change.

The description of the three sequential rule changes proceeded in chronological order. Description of each individual change also proceeded chronologically: the development of macrolevel contextual conditions was described first followed, at the microlevel, by a description of the sequences of decisions which effected the abandonment of the existing apportionment rule and the creation of a new rule.

Explanation

The second goal of this study is to explain why the three identified constitutional changes in the national rule of apportionment occurred. Several assumptions inform this second goal. First, this study assumes the necessity of recognizing and competing against the explanatory contributions and boundaries of alternative accounts. For the weight and magnitude of a new explanation become evident not only in terms of its logical rigor or the extent of the empirical field covered, but also in terms of its capacity to incorporate rival accounts into a more encompassing and coherent metanarrative.[35] Second, it is assumed that explanations entail propositions concerning causation, that causation is not directly

---

[35] See Alisdair MacIntyre, "Epistemological Crises, Dramatic Narrative and the Philosophy of Science," *The Monist* (1977), 60(4): 453–472; Richard W. Miller, *Fact and Method: Explanation, Confirmation and Reality in the Natural and the Social Sciences* (Princeton, NJ: Princeton University Press, 1987); Charles Taylor, *Philosophical Arguments* (Cambridge, MA: Harvard University Press, 1995).

observable, and, therefore, that a causal explanation of a set of historical events necessarily entails some form of conditional generalization.
Construction of a causal explanation, it is further assumed, requires
demonstration of a regular relationship between a set of initial conditions and a set of effects, as well as an intermediary causal mechanism
that illuminates the process by which a specific set of initial conditions
produced a specific set of effects. A causal explanation, as defined here,
can be expressed in the general form:

Initial Condition — (causal mechanism) → Effect

Two additional expectations also influenced the construction of a
causal explanation for the three identified changes. The first was that
apportionment rule changes were not expected because an apportionment rule empowers a set of actors whose intragovernmental authority
subsequently depends on this rule. The logic of this expectation can be
expressed in the general form:

Expected:
Apportionment Rule — (Decision Rule Empowerment) → No rule change
[Initial Condition — (causal mechanism) → Effect]

Contrary to this expectation, this study identified three historically significant apportionment rule changes.

Observed:　　　　Apportionment Rule$_{1...3}$ — (?) → Rule change$_{1...3}$

The second expectation follows from the specific constitutional action
problem identified in the Preface and from the general problematic
formalized by the Chaos Theorem. More specifically, it is assumed that
in the absence of an established rule of apportionment the formation of
a consensus for a new rule of apportionment is a highly improbable
event. The logic of this expectation can be expressed in the general form:

Expected:　　　　**No Rule — (Chaos Theorem) → No Rule**
[Initial Condition — (causal mechanism) → Effect]

Contrary to this expectation, this study identified three historically significant cases of apportionment rule creation.

$$\text{Rule}_{1...3} — (?) → \text{New Rule}_{1...3}$$

Given these unexpected observations and the general form for speci-
fying causation, explanation of apportionment rule changes requires
identification of a set of conditions correlated with the abandonment and

creation of these rules. This study recognizes and analyzes five general types of conditions for their potential causal effects. The first four conditions are macro- or structural-level conditions. The fifth condition is a microlevel (or actor-centered) condition. Whereas the four macrolevel conditions receive a full and fair exposure for each apportionment rule change, their relationship to these changes is not constant and, therefore, logically insufficient to explain the phenomenon of apportionment rule abandonment. This study's alternative causal explanation, while including a representation of these macrolevel conditions, rests upon a microlevel (or actor-centered) condition.[36] In brief, this study explains constitutional changes in rules of apportionment in relation to changes in the expectations of political actors. At the most general level, this study contends that divergent or unfulfilled expectations among the set of politically relevant actors concerning the efficacy of governmental institutions create conditions conducive to the abandonment of a rule of apportionment. Conversely, the convergence of expectations among these actors creates conditions conducive to the creation of new rules of apportionment.

Indicators of changes in political expectations concerning the efficacy of organizational structures, procedural rules, and behavioral norms are not easily standardized for they invariably are embedded within the historical particularities of the individuals and contexts that constitute political action within specific moments of time and space. Identification of these changes, thus, requires an intimate knowledge and comparison of the various streams of action and belief that define a political order over time.[37]

---

[36] Inclusion of this macrolevel representation within this study's microlevel explanation of apportionment rule change forms the basis for this study's macro-micro synthesis. Rather than an extended discussion of the problems and solutions associated with this synthesis here, see its specific applications in Chapters 3, 6, and 9. For informed alternatives to this study's application of the macro-micro synthesis, see Jack Knight, *Institutions and Social Conflict* (1992); and Stephen Skowronek, *The Politics Presidents Make* (Cambridge, MA: Harvard University Press, 1997).

[37] To summarize, analytical approaches that avoid microlevel or actor-centered analysis or expediently forsake grounding in historical evidence for deductive assumptions about so-called "rational" decision-making behavior are ill-suited for penetrating fully into the specific historical contingencies, processes, and causal mechanisms associated with the phenomenon of constitutional change. Studies or analytical approaches that explain political change only in terms of societal or state-centered conditions are inadequate for this study's special focus. These accounts, although often offering accurate descriptions of correlations between contextual conditions and a particular type of political change, are not falsifiable at a level of analysis where the types and sequence of individual actions are recognized as causally significant.

Although judgments about the relative compactness and diffusion of political expectations must be made with reference to specific indicators within the available historical evidence, several generalizations can be made about why expectations among political actors change. Expectations, for example, change when political actors perceive that the continuation of existing institutional arrangements poses a threat to their short- or long-term interests. Expectations also change when political actors develop new interests or preferences which they perceive existing institutions are incapable of satisfying. Finally, expectations change when political actors are presented with alternative institutional configurations of governmental authority that they perceive would yield greater benefits than existing institutions.[38]

If variations in expectations create conditions that are supportive of the abandonment and creation of rules of apportionment, why do specific instances of rule abandonment and creation occur when they do? Certainly, the transition from conditions pregnant with expectations for some form of institutional change to the specific moments in which definitive action occurs cannot be determined except in hindsight. To assume otherwise (that is, that specific causal mechanisms are predictable) would require a level of political prescience that has not yet been (or likely can be) achieved.[39]

---

[38] Institutions project relatively predictable distributional patterns into the future. If it is assumed, however, or demonstrated that individuals make decisions to abandon (or to defect from) existing institutional arrangements based on both short-term and long-term interests, then the problem of attaining and sustaining cooperation among political actors is more difficult than has been conceptualized within much of the political science literature. Robert Axelrod and Robert O. Keohane, for example, propose a widely accepted solution to the classic problem underlying the so-called Prisoners' Dilemma by contending that cooperation among self-interested actors becomes more likely if longer time horizons and a regularity of stakes become part of the decisional calculus of each individual. See Robert Axelrod and Robert O. Keohane, "Achieving Cooperation Under Anarchy: Strategies and Institutions," *World Politics* (1985), 28: 226–254; and Robert Axelrod, *The Evolution of Cooperation* (1984); cf. James D. Fearon, "Bargaining, Enforcement and International Cooperation," *International Organization* (1998), 52(2): 269–305.

[39] Thus, an underlying assumption of this inquiry is that the study of politics is an ineluctably backward-looking enterprise. Political science (in its qualitative, quantitative, idiographic, and theoretical variants) is, as Herbert A. Simon concluded, "necessarily a historical science" and, in particular, a form of comparative history. This label may be disappointing or discouraging because it suggests that political science not only requires *both* cross-sectional and longitudinal analysis, but that it fundamentally has a non-nomothetic purpose. See Herbert A. Simon, "Human Nature in Politics: The Dialogue of Psychology with Political Science," *APSR* (1985), 79: 301; Jack A. Goldstone, *Revolution and Rebellion in the Early Modern World* (Berkeley: University of California Press, 1991), p. 61.

This is not to say general observations cannot be made about the transitional periods between diverging expectations and the abandonment of the established rule of apportionment, or between converging expectations and the establishment of a new rule of apportionment. One general observation, for example, is that the entrepreneurial initiatives of specific individuals create the framework for and function as the catalyst of these institution-breaking and institution-making moments. These entrepreneurs include both the individuals who engage in the creative process of devising alternatives to the status quo, and the much smaller set of individuals who also possess the unique capacities to draw others to follow in the wake of their visions.

A second general observation is that although constitutional entrepreneurs play a large role in the initiation and completion of moments of institutional change, the alternative arrangements they propose rarely prompt spontaneous consent. Indeed, more often than not, the proposals of these entrepreneurs fail because they challenge other political actors whose interests are firmly allied with the existing set of institutional arrangements. Constitutional entrepreneurs, thus, succeed in initiating the critical moments during which political change occurs but they rarely succeed in fully establishing the particular changes that they initially envision.

A third general observation concerning these transitional periods is that their final outcomes are typically negotiated products. The distinct decisional sequences that end with the abandonment and creation of apportionment rules therefore constitute the paths by which specific historical outcomes emerge from a range of possible alternatives. To uncover these sequentially traveled paths, this study employs the

For a sample of the theoretical and methodological issues associated with the study of comparative political history, see Peter D. McClelland, *Causal Explanation and Model Building in History, Economics and the New Economic History* (Ithaca, NY: Cornell University Press, 1975); Raymond Grew, "The Case for Comparing Histories," *AHR* (1980), 85: 763–778; Theda Skocpol and Margaret Somers, "The Use of Comparative History in Macrosocial Inquiry," *Comparative Studies in Society and History* (1980), 22: 174–197; George Huber and Andrew H. Van de Ven, eds., *Longitudinal Field Research Methods* (Thousand Oaks, CA: Sage Publications, 1995); Clayton Roberts, *The Logic of Historical Explanation* (University Park, PA: Pennsylvania State University Press, 1996). For earlier discussions of these issues, see Jean Bodin, *Method for the Easy Comprehension of History*, Beatrice Reynolds, trans. (New York: Columbia University Press, 1946, [1566]); Marc Bloch, "Toward a Comparative History of European Societies" (1928), J. C. Riemersma, trans., in Frederic Lane, ed., *Enterprise and Secular Change* (Homewood, IL: R. D. Irwin, 1953), pp. 494–521; and Francois Simiand, "Causal Interpretation and Historical Research" (1903–1906), in Frederic Lane, ed., *Enterprise and Secular Change* (1953), pp. 469–488.

approaches common to the disciplines of political science and history. To trace the decisional sequences that effect apportionment rule abandonment, this study marries historically grounded descriptions of political expectations and of the range of outcome possibilities with a game-theoretic analysis of actors' preferences among these outcomes – see Chapters 3, 6, and the first half of Chapter 9.[40] To trace the more open-ended and often more complex processes effecting apportionment rule creation, this study provides detailed narratives of the decisions that yield new rules of apportionment – see Chapters 4, 7, and the latter half of Chapter 9.

[40] In addition to appropriating the structural forms and conceptual tools common to a game-theoretic approach, this study's historically grounded game-theoretic approach is guided by five explicit assumptions. These assumptions are: (1) that the set of political actors who become engaged in these critical moments of institutional abandonment can be categorized into a smaller number of unitary actors; (2) that the decisions of these actors are delimited by a historically determined and commonly recognized range of possible outcomes, including a status quo outcome that is not necessarily neutral or static; (3) that each actor, at a defined moment in time, has a potentially identifiable order of preferences among these outcomes; (4) that each actor, given the opportunity, would attempt to maximize his or her expected benefits among the possible outcomes; (5) and that, except for the preexisting and historically constituted status quo, new outcomes are negotiated between and jointly produced by the actors engaged in these critical decision-making moments. For general introductions to game theory and its applications in political science and economics, see Scott Gates and Brian D. Humes, *Games, Information, and Politics: Applying Game Theoretic Models to Political Science* (Ann Arbor: University of Michigan Press, 1997); David M. Kreps, *Game Theory and Economic Modelling* (Oxford: Clarendon Press, 1990).

For other applications and discussions of the budding merger between the historical and rational choice game-theoretic approaches, see Robert H. Bates et al., *Analytic Narratives* (Princeton, NJ: Princeton University Press, 1998) and authors' responses in *Social Science History*, Winter 2000, 24(4) and *American Political Science Review*, September 2000, Vol. 94. For earlier precedents, see Morris Fiorina, "Legislative Choice of Regulatory Forms: Legal Process of Administrative Process," *Public Choice* (1982), 39: 33–66; Adam Przeworski, "Marxism and Rational Choice," *Politics & Society* (1985), 14: 379–409; Robert Bates and Da-Hsiang Donald Lien, "A Note on Taxation, Development, and Representative Government," *Politics & Society* (1985), 14: 53–70; Margaret Levi, *Of Rule and Revenue* (Berkeley: University of California Press, 1988); Charles H. Stewart, *Budget Reform Politics: The Design of the Appropriations Process in the House of Representatives, 1865–1921* (1989); Dennis Chong, *Collective Action and the Civil Rights Movement* (1991); Youssef Cohen, *Radicals, Reformers and Reactionaries* (1994); Steven Brams, *A Theory of Moves* (1994); John Aldrich, "Rational Choice Theory and the Study of American Politics," in Lawrence C. Dodd and Calvin Jillson, eds., *The Dynamics of American Politics: Approaches and Interpretations* (1994), pp. 208–233; John H. Aldrich, *Why Parties: The Origin and Transformation of Party Politics in America* (1995); and Jon Elster, "Equal or Proportional? Arguing and Bargaining over the Senate at the Federal Convention," in Jack Knight and Itai Sened, eds., *Explaining Social Institutions* (1995); Anna L. Harvey, *Votes Without Leverage: Women in American Electoral Politics, 1920–1970* (1998).

Theorization

The final goal of this study is to assess the consequences of apportionment rule changes on the American political order. Empirical measurement of these consequences is certain to fail not merely because of the magnitude of the suggested project, but also because the elementary verities of the relationship between apportionment rules and the constitutional orders within which they are embedded seem poorly understood or misspecified. To clarify this relationship and, thus, to appraise the consequences of apportionment rule changes, this study proposes a theoretical framework that relates apportionment rules to the formation, transformation, and breakdown of constitutional orders.

To open a window onto this theoretical framework, let us conceive of the American political order and of all forms of constitutional order as complex and dynamic wholes that can be studied from three distinct analytical levels or reference points. Let us name these levels: the external constitution, the domestic constitution, and the intragovernmental constitution. Analysis of a constitutional order with respect to its *external constitution* would define the order by its relationships to other orders. A similar analysis with respect to the *domestic constitution*, by contrast, would define this constitutional order in terms of the relationships between the governing part of the order and the populace over which it governs. Finally, a constitutional analysis with reference to the *intragovernmental constitution* of an order would define the order in terms of the relationships among the set of actors who hold and exercise the authority and power to make collective decisions.[41] Measurement of the development of a particular constitutional order over time thus requires comparative generalizations about changes observed at one or more of these three constitutional levels.

Although changes in the domestic and external constitutions of an order no doubt are important (especially, under the special circumstances created by war, revolution, and the processes of globalization[42]), the theory offered here relates the development of a constitutional order –

---

[41] The set of "politically relevant" actors includes the principal interests organized within society and their agents within government.

[42] See Theda Skocpol, *States and Revolution* (1979); Richard F. Bensel, *Yankee Leviathan: The Origins of Central State Authority in America, 1859–1877* (1990); Stephen M. Walt, *Revolution and War* (1996); Vivien A. Schmidt, "The New World Order, Incorporated: The Rise of Business and the Decline of the Nation-State," *Daedalus* (1995); Phillip G. Cerny, "Globalization and the Residual State," *Designs for Democratic Stability* (1997), pp. 285–329.

+ows is where→ wher

and, in particular, of the American political order between 1700 and 1870 – to changes within the intragovernmental constitution. This theory, therefore, focuses upon the set of collectively relevant actors and relates their expectations concerning relative decision-making capacities and preferences for levels of governmental authority to the formation, transformation, and breakdown of constitutional order.[43]

The *formation* of a constitutional order, in brief, requires a general convergence of two types of expectations. First, each actor must have a positive, long-term expectation concerning its capacities to direct or to affect the allocation of governmental authority and its collective benefits. Initial expectations about these decision-making capacities are based, in large part, on the terms specified within the rule of apportionment. Second, the formation of a constitutional order also requires a convergence of expectations or preferences concerning the general type and extent of governmental authority. These expectations are based initially on the set of institutions and practices that specify the constitutional boundaries of legitimate governmental action.

Figure 1.1 offers a visualization of the posited relationships between principal political interests and their agents and between these agents, the set of constitutional rules and their attendant expectations for relative decision-making capacity, and levels of governmental authority. These expectations, to be explicit, are assumed to be positively related along an idealized equilibrium curve. Given, however, that expectations are subjective and, therefore, never uniform among any set of constitutional actors – even those who establish or maintain an order by force – the nexus of these expectations is not represented as a precise equilibrium point but as an idealized space containing various (and sometimes contradictory) expectations. National political orders, like other constitutional orders, cannot be manufactured simply by tinkering with various combinations of apportionment rules and constitution length, nor do they spring forth spontaneously or fully developed every time political expectations converge on the two identified dimensions. Rather, these orders are created only after a set of actors assumes this

---

[43] Expectations are cognitive phenomena and, therefore, are not fully measurable. Moreover, the intensity and density of these expectations vary among political actors and over time. As a consequence, measurement of changes in political expectations is extremely difficult – especially over extended time periods. Arguably, the clearest indicator of a minimal level of convergence is the voluntary participation of political actors within a common form of government. It follows, therefore, that the absence of this form of political association is an indicator of the divergence of political expectations.

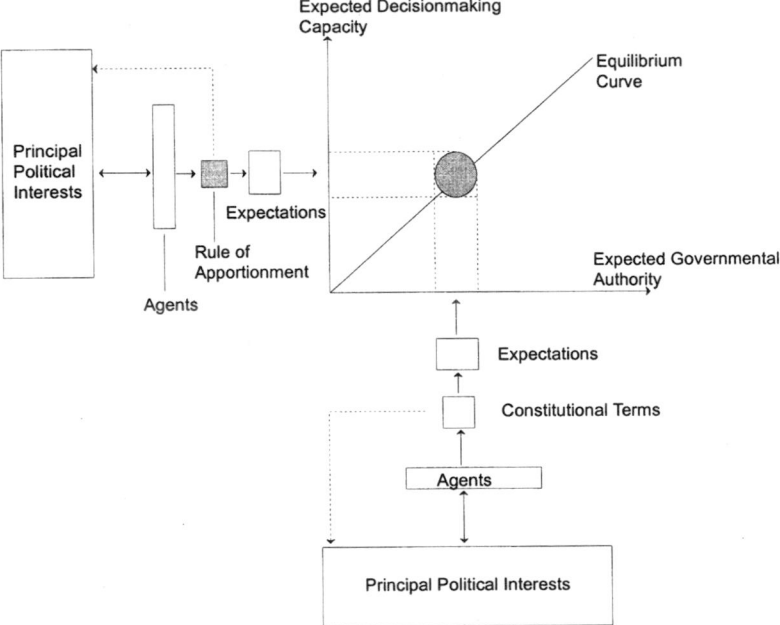

FIGURE I.I. Model of Constitutional Convergence

order-making authority and acts deliberately and successfully to effect this end. The formation of a constitutional order, in this respect, is a voluntary union among a set of constitutional actors who share similar expectations concerning the range of benefits made possible by participating within a common order and similar expectations concerning the range of individual capacities to renegotiate the terms of this constitutional union in the future.

The formation of a constitutional order is therefore like the completion of a long-term contract in that both agreements are grounded in a voluntaristic consensus that determines the parties to the exchange, the general form of the exchange, and the specific terms of the exchange.[44] What specifically is exchanged during the formation of an order is the autonomy of individual action for the benefits expected under a collective authority. The formation of an order, therefore, entails several agree-

---

[44] See Ian R. Macneil, *The New Social Contract: An Inquiry into Modern Contractual Relations* (1980).

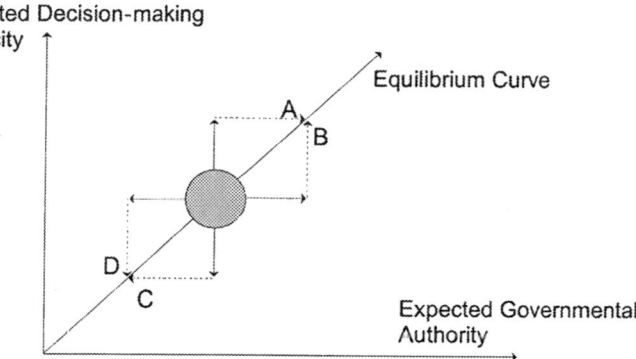

FIGURE 1.2. Model of Constitutional Development

ments. The first agreement defines the set of collectively relevant actors. The second agreement defines the general principles or framework of government. The third and final agreement specifies the institutions and practices that will shape and constrain the subsequent actions of a governing part of the constitutional order.[45]

If the convergence of expectations about decision-making capacities and governmental authority creates a general equilibrium space within which consensual collective action occurs, then the subsequent *transformation* of this space (and, thus, of a constitutional order over time) can be idealized in terms of four general dynamics. The first and second dynamics alter long-term decision-making capacities and, thus, the vertical dimensions of the equilibrium space. The first dynamic (denoted as "A" in Figure 1.2) is that the greater the expected increase in decision-making capacities, the greater the expected increase in levels of governmental authority. Conversely, the second dynamic (denoted "C") is that the greater the expected reduction in decision-making capacities, the greater the expected reduction in governmental authority. The third and fourth dynamics, by contrast, alter long-term levels of governmental authority and, thus, the horizontal dimension of the equilibrium space.

[45] For similar "layered" descriptions of the constitutional elements of political order, see James Buchanan and Gordon Tullock, *The Calculus of Consent* (1962), pp. 78–80, 119–120; Stephen D. Krasner, ed., "International Regimes" issue of *International Organization* (1982), 36(2); James D. March and Johan P. Olsen, *Rediscovering Institutions* (1984), p. 111; and Elinor Ostrom, *Governing the Commons: The Evolution of Institutions for Collective Action* (1990), pp. 50–52.

The third dynamic (denoted "B") is that the greater the expected increase in governmental authority, the greater the expected increase in decision-making capacity. Conversely, the fourth and final dynamic (denoted "D") is that the greater the expected reduction in governmental authority, the greater the expected reduction in decision-making capacity.

How large and small changes in expectations about decision-making capacities and levels of governmental authority ultimately transform constitutional orders at different levels of aggregation is too complex and understudied for this study to address in full. Suffice it to say here, the divergence or diffusion of expectations creates conditions that prompt attempts to redefine various elements of a constitutional order. When these attempts compel support from other constitutionally relevant actors, incremental and wholesale changes in existing political institutions are possible. In addition to the adjustment or replacement of existing institutions, a constitutional order can be redefined through the establishment of additional institutions or through alterations in the set of intragovernmental agents. When, however, attempted renegotiations of an order repeatedly fail or when a subset of actors begins to question the longer-term benefits of their association with other actors, then the consensus necessary to sustain a constitutional order weakens and, on occasion, breaks down.

The following four case summaries are illustrative of this theory of constitutional development. Less abstract than the foregoing explanation, these cases illuminate the explanatory power of the proposed theory across different levels of aggregation (national and subnational), different territorial units (England, France, United States, and Yugoslavia), and different temporal periods (1688–1715, 1789–1815, 1800–1850, 1960–1990). As a result, not only is the plausibility and applicability of this theory readily demonstrated, but the relationship between apportionment rule changes and their immediate and long-term consequences is specified for particular national political orders and, therefore, more easily perceived as an elemental part of every constitutional order.

The first case illustrates the path of constitutional development denoted as "A" in Figure 1.2. In particular, this case concerns the development of the English political order between 1690 and 1715.[46]

[46] See Aristide R. Zolberg, "Strategic Interactions and the Formation of Modern States: France and England," *International Social Science Journal* (1980), 32: 687–716; and Douglass C. North and Barry R. Weingast, "Constitutions and Commitment: The Evolution of Institutions Governing Public Choice in Seventeenth-Century England," *Journal of Economic History* (1989), 49: 803–832.

A. Expected Increase in Decision-making Capacity, Expected Increase in Governmental Authority

After the rout of James II in 1688 and the enthronement of the Dutch-born William of Orange in 1689, the intragovernmental division of authority within the English political order reflected a notable increase in the decision-making capacities of Parliament. As a result, the principal interests represented within Parliament gradually gained confidence about their long-term capacities to determine the policies of the national government.

This increase in Parliament's decision-making capacities was followed by a general expansion of the authority of the national government. A new and more equitable tax system, for example, was introduced in the 1690s that discarded the existing exemption-ridden system and, as a consequence, tripled the amount of tax revenue collected between 1689 and 1714. During this period, Parliament also chartered the Bank of England and made a significant institutional commitment to support a national system of public debt finance.

The effects of the constitutional change in the rule of apportionment following the Revolution of 1688 also can be measured beyond the noted expansion in Parliament's authority. For the new financial policies Parliament established catalyzed additional private sector innovations that, according to Douglass C. North, "were instrumental factors not only in England's subsequent rapid economic development, but in its political hegemony and ultimate dominance of the world."[47]

The second case illustrates the developmental path denoted as "B" in Figure 1.2. In particular, this case concerns the transformation of the first French republic into a constitutional dictatorship by the individual who ironically once proclaimed: "My only wish is that my time may mark the beginning of the era of representative government."[48]

B. Expected Increase in Governmental Authority, Expected Increase in Decision-making Capacity

The French political order broke down in 1789 after the Estates General failed to achieve a consensus about its rule of apportionment. Amidst

---

[47] North, *Institutions, Institutional Change and Economic Performance* (1990), pp. 138–139.

[48] This statement was made by none other than Bonaparte. As quoted in Irene Collins, *Napoleon and His Parliaments, 1800–1815* (London: Edward Arnold, 1979), p. 1.

See Irene Collins, *Napoleon and his Parliaments, 1800–1815* (1979); A. C. Thibaudeau, *Bonaparte and the Consulate*, trans. G. K. Fortescue (New York, The Macmillan Company [1827], 1908); and *Congressional Globe*, May 27, 1842, pp. 402, 403, 544.

the subsequent revolutionary fervor, reforms were debated continuously and several constitutions were proposed, but all efforts to establish a new political order failed to obtain the necessary political and social consensus required for political stability. In 1795, a new constitution established a bicameral legislature consisting of a Council of Five Hundred that was responsible for proposing and debating new legislation and a 250-member Council of Ancients which was charged with the authority to reject or to enact proposed legislation. The 1795 Constitution also provided for a national executive (the Directory) composed of five members who were appointed by the two legislative Councils.

In 1797 and 1798, national legislative elections were annulled by two coups d'etat. In 1799, General Napoleon Bonaparte led another coup d'etat which established yet another new constitution. Although Bonaparte (and his co-conspirators) were committed to establishing a national government dominated by a strong executive, they readily acknowledged that this required the support of a formalized legal system. The new constitution they proposed thus established a powerful executive Consulate (with Bonaparte as the First Consul) and a considerably weaker national legislature composed of several chambers. Notably, the size of these new legislative chambers was smaller than previous national legislatures and their policy-making authority was fragmented among four chambers. The net effect of this new constitutional design was to increase the decision-making capacity of the office of the First Consul and, therefore, of Bonaparte.[49]

Bonaparte's expectations for further increases in governmental authority (and, thus, for concomitant increases in his decision-making control over the national government) did not subside with the establishment of the 1799 Constitution. In 1802, for example, after a purge of his principal opponents in the Tribunate, Bonaparte used his influence over the Senate to impose additional constitutional reforms designed, in his words, "to reorganize the Constitution in such a way to give the Executive a free hand."[50] In addition to his lifetime appointment as First

---

[49] The constitution established a 300-member Legislative Body (*Corps Legislatif*) which was to vote on, but not debate, legislation enacted by a 100-member Tribunate (*Tribunat*). The Tribunate was authorized to debate legislation but was not permitted to vote. The new constitution further fragmented legislative authority by establishing a 40-member Council of State responsible for drafting legislation, and a 60-member Senate that was to act to conserve the constitution. The latter two chambers were appointed by the Consulate, and the Senate selected the membership of the Legislative Body and the Tribunate from national electoral lists.

[50] As quoted in A. C. Thibaudeau, *Bonaparte and the Consulate*, p. 46.

Consul, Bonaparte further consolidated his control of the national government by dividing the Tribunate into three sections and reducing its size from one hundred to fifty members.[51]

The consequences of Bonaparte's monopolization of the decision-making institutions of the national government extend well beyond the historical legacy of his personal career and demise. His dictatorial ascendancy and expansion of national political authority ended the upheavals that had raged since 1789 and established (for the first time) the institutional structures of a centralized French state.

The third case illustrates the developmental path denoted as "C" in Figure 1.2. This case, in particular, focuses on the path of development taken in the State of New York during the first half of the nineteenth century.[52]

C. Expected Decrease in Decision-making Capacity, Expected Decrease in Governmental Authority

Through much of the early national period of the United States – but extending far back into the colonial era – American state legislatures were active promoters of economic development. Prior to 1840, the legislature of the State of New York was one of the most active and successful promoters of economic growth. The legislature, for example, made significant commitments to infrastructure projects like roads and canals, and to other economic development aids like loans, subsidies, and corporate charters. Indeed, the state legislature's authority over and intervention into the state economy was constrained by few political or ideological boundaries.

In the 1820s and 1830s, voting participation rates and party politics increased dramatically not only in New York but across the American political landscape. At the same time, turnover rates among members of the state legislatures remained high and, as a result, the relationship between these legislatures and their constituent social interests remained highly fluid and reflexive. Concerned by the potential consequences of these newer interests within the political arena, long-established interests

---

[51] In 1802, Napoleon also exclaimed: "What is the *Tribunat*? – of what use is it? What the Government wants is a Tribune, a free rostrum. There is no need of a hundred men (the *Tribunat*) to talk over laws made by thirty (the Council of State). Then there are the three hundred, who must vote without debate (the *Corps Legislatif*). Three hundred men who never speak a word. What an absurdity!" As quoted in A. C. Thibaudeau, *Bonaparte and the Consulate*, p. 45.

[52] L. Ray Gunn, *The Decline of Authority: Public Economic Policy and Political Development in New York State, 1800–1860* (Ithaca, NY: Cornell University Press, 1988).

within the legislature engaged in a concerted campaign to curb the authority of the state legislature. The result of these efforts was no less than the deliberate withering of the legislature's policy-making authority, the legitimization of the judiciary as a restraint upon undesired legislative activity, and the privatization of the American economy.

The fourth and final case illustrates the path denoted as "D" in Figure 1.2. This case concerns the constitutional development of the Yugoslavian national government between 1960 and 1991.

D. Expected Decline in Governmental Authority, Expected Decline in Decision-making Capacity[53]

The death of long-time Yugoslavian ruler Josep Tito in 1980 escalated the process of political decentralization that had been an undercurrent of Yugoslavian politics since the 1960s. The Yugoslavian republics, for example, had assumed a substantial amount of the national government's political, economic, and administrative authority. In addition, this period was characterized by the devolution of the decision-making authority of the national Communist Party to republic-level organizations. As a result, the long-term expectation was that the republics were to become the centers of political and economic authority and this, in turn, prompted interested actors to make republic-level, not national-level, investments.[54]

Thus, as the efficacy of national governmental authority declined in real terms, expectations about the salience of a republic's decision-making capacities within the national government also declined. The latter development (that is, the decline of interest in the national government) continued until several republics voted for political secession in 1991. These decisions were not unimportant for they triggered a constitutional cascade that ended in civil war.

Cursory descriptions of these four cases cannot confirm the external validity of the proposed theory of political development. These descriptions, however, underscore the plausibility and potential range of this theory. More importantly, as Table 1.3 summarizes, the four cases vividly array the variety of immediate and long-term consequences that have resulted from changes in the rule of apportionment.

---

[53] Paula Franklin Lytle, "Electoral Transitions in Yugoslavia," in *Between States: Interim Governments and Democratic Transitions*, Yossi Shain and Juan J. Linz, eds. (Cambridge, UK: Cambridge University Press, 1995), pp. 237–254.
[54] Paula Franklin Lytle, "Electoral Transitions in Yugoslavia," p. 239.

TABLE 1.3. *Consequences of Apportionment Rule Changes*

Case	Time Period	Level	Immediate Outcome	Long-term Outcome
A	1690–1715	National	Increased legislative authority	Economic development
B	1790–1815	National	Executive dictatorship	Political centralization
C	1800–1840	Subnational	Reduced legislative authority	Privatized economy
D	1960–1991	National	Secession	Civil war

Further definition of the explanatory boundaries of this theory requires not only additional exploration and comparative analysis of additional types of cases, but also detailed, historically grounded examinations of the linkages between instances of apportionment rule change and their immediate and long-term consequences. Whereas it is certain that apportionment rules are not the primary cause of all political development, the three constitutional changes examined by this inquiry strongly suggest that their consequences upon the development of the American political order have been far more elemental than has presently been detected or imagined.

ORGANIZATION

To summarize, this study is an inquiry into the process, the causes, and the consequences of three constitutional changes in the rule of apportionment. Three sequential apportionment rule changes are examined individually and in chronological order. A "macro-micro" approach structures the account of each change. Macro-level conditions (defined as economic, demographic, institutional, and ideological conditions) are described in terms of their long- and short-term developmental patterns prior to each change. Microlevel conditions are described in terms of the expectations of the specific political actors who, in some direct way, participated in the abandonment of old or the creation of new rules of apportionment.

The first constitutional change is examined in Chapters 2, 3, and 4. Chapter 2 focuses, at the macrolevel, on British-colonial relations between approximately 1700 and 1774. Chapter 3 examines, at the microlevel, the escalation of British-colonial conflicts in the 1760s and 1770s. Game-theoretic models are used to order and to describe the sequence of British and American decisions between 1774 and 1776 and their culmination in civil war. Chapter 4 focuses on the process of constitutional reconstruction: Special attention is given to the deliberations of the Continental Congresses and to the formation of the Articles of Confederation.

The second constitutional change is examined in Chapters 5, 6, and 7. Chapter 5 focuses on the development of macrolevel conditions between 1776 and 1786. Chapter 6 focuses on microlevel conditions between 1786 and 1787 and describes the contributions of constitutional entrepreneurs to the process of constitutional change: James Madison is profiled as a prototypical agent of constitutional change. This chapter additionally describes how the failure to effect incremental institutional changes under the Articles of Confederation prompted interest in and a commitment to constitutional change among a handful of individuals, including Madison. This chapter also employs several game-theoretic models to explain the strategic calculations of the three largest states (Virginia, Massachusetts, and Pennsylvania) prior to their commitment to attend the 1787 Philadelphia Convention. Chapter 7 examines the Convention's deliberations and decisions for a new rule of apportionment.

Chapters 8 and 9 examine the third constitutional change. The former chapter describes macrolevel conditions between 1790 and 1860. The latter details the microlevel conditions that culminated in the 1860–1861 Secession crisis and, later, in the creation and ratification of the Thirteenth, Fourteenth, and Fifteenth Amendments. Chapter 10 concludes this study with an assessment of the specific answers this inquiry provides for the paradox of constitutional consent and the four stated research questions: When, how, and why do constitutional changes in the rule of apportionment occur? And what consequences have these changes had upon the American political order?

CONSTITUTIONAL CHANGE I: 1700–1781

2

Raising Leviathan: British-American Relations, 1700–1774

Chapters 2, 3, and 4 examine the context, the causes, and the immediate consequences of the first constitutional change in the rule of apportionment. This rule change begins with the constitutional breakdown of British-colonial relations in 1776 and ends with the formalization of a new American constitutional order in 1781. Whereas the former event signaled the abandonment of the unwritten but working rule of apportionment within the British Empire, the latter event established the written equal state rule of apportionment within the first American constitution, the Articles of Confederation.

Chapters 2 and 3 focus on how and why the imperial rule of apportionment was abandoned. In brief, Chapter 2 provides a macrolevel description of the broader context within which this event occurred. It specifically recounts the development of economic, demographic, institutional, and ideological conditions in Great Britain and the American colonies over the course of the eighteenth century. Assessment of these conditions over time is necessary given this study's interest in explaining the causes of apportionment rule change because it aids the identification and measurement of long-term patterns in these contextual conditions prior to (and, therefore, apparently independent of) a subsequent rule change. Chapter 3 follows with a microlevel account of the political actors most immediately responsible for the breakdown in the constitutional union between Great Britain and the American colonies between 1774 and 1776. Chapter 4 completes the story of the birth of the American constitutional order by focusing on the process by which the new equal state apportionment rule was established within the Articles of Confederation.

Chapter 2 consists of five parts. Part I recognizes the primary contributions and limitations of existing descriptions and explanations of the American Revolution. This interpretative survey serves two necessary purposes: First, it reveals the depth of the scholarly debt present works of American political history owe to those in the past; and second, this survey reveals why these prior works do not answer the elemental questions that compel this study of apportionment rules and constitutional change. The remainder of the chapter describes the development of four macrolevel conditions between 1700 to 1774. Part II describes the development of economic conditions in and between Great Britain and the American colonies. Part III describes the development of demographic conditions. Part IV completes a similar developmental account, but it focuses upon institutional developments within the different governmental levels of the British Empire. For the sake of analytical clarity, these governmental levels are referred to as the British, the colonial, and the imperial constitutions. Part V completes this assessment of contextual conditions prior to the American Revolution with a description of the development of British and American conceptualizations of political representation during the eighteenth century.

PART I: INTERPRETATIVE PERSPECTIVES

Historical accounts of the American Revolution typically describe its causes from one of three perspectives. Each perspective reveals essential elements of a complex process of constitutional change marked (at its midpoint) by the abandonment of the British-colonial order and (at its conclusion) by the establishment of a new and independent American constitutional order under the Articles of Confederation.

From the first perspective, the causes of the American Revolution are portrayed as essentially economic or social. Several historians, for example, identify colonial merchants, artisans, or western expansionists as the primary economic groups who drove the American colonies toward revolution.[1] Other historians suggest colonial opposition was

---

[1] See Arthur M. Schlesinger, *The Colonial Merchants and the American Revolution* (New York, Columbia University Press, 1918); Carl Bridenbaugh, *Cities in Revolt: Urban Life in America, 1743–1776* (New York: Capricorn Books, 1964); Gary B. Nash, *The Urban Crucible: Social Change, Political Consciousness, and the Origins of the American Revolution* (Cambridge, MA: Harvard University Press, 1979); Marc Egnal and Joseph Ernst, "An Economic Interpretation of the American Revolution," *William and Mary Quarterly* [hereafter *WMQ*] (1972), 29: 3–32; and Marc Egnal, *A Mighty*

triggered by Parliament's overbearing financial regulation of the colonies or by a credit crisis in the British home economy.[2] Still others identify the uncoupling of British and American commercial interests as an important precondition for the subsequent conflict.[3]

The second perspective offers a different view of the causes of the American Revolution. This perspective highlights ideological differences in American and British conceptualizations of governmental authority and political order. For historians within this interpretative school, particular sets of ideas "helped create a logical thrust toward revolution and independence."[4] For nineteenth-century historians, this thrust typically was portrayed as driven by an American desire for national independence. Contemporary historians, by contrast, highlight other sets of motivating ideas, for example, British fears that colonial anarchy or independence would lead to imperial ruin and foreign invasion; or colonial fears that British tyranny would lead to the social and moral corruption of the American colonies.[5]

A third interpretative perspective emphasizes institutional and political conflicts as the driving forces behind the American Revolution. Several historians focus on the eighteenth-century struggles for governing authority between the American colonial assemblies and the Crown's

   Empire: The Origins of the American Revolution (Ithaca, NY: Cornell University Press, 1988).

[2] John R. McCusker and Russell R. Menard, *The Economy of British America* (Chapel Hill: University of North Carolina Press, 1985); Edwin J. Perkins, *The Economy of Colonial America* (New York: Columbia University Press, 1988). See also Joseph Ernst, *Money and Politics in America, 1755–1775* (Chapel Hill: University of North Carolina Press, 1973); T. H. Breen, *Tobacco Culture: the Mentality of the Great Tidewater Planters on the Eve of Revolution* (Princeton, NJ: Princeton University Press, 1985); and Marc Egnal, "The Economic Development of the Thirteen Colonies, 1720–1775," *WMQ* (1975), 32: 191–222. See also J. Franklin Jameson, *The American Revolution Considered as a Social Movement* (Princeton, NJ: Princeton University Press, 1926).

[3] See Thomas C. Barrow, "Background to the Grenville Program, 1757–1763," *WMQ* (1965), 22: 93–104; and Michael Kammen, *Empire and Interest: The American Colonies and the Politics of Mercantilism* (Philadelphia: Lippincott, 1970).

[4] Pauline Maier, *From Resistance to Revolution* (New York: Knopf, 1972), p. xv.

[5] See Eric Robson, *The American Revolution* (New York: Da Capo Press, 1972); Louis Hartz, *The Liberal Tradition in America* (New York: Harcourt, Brace, 1955); Clinton Rossiter, *The Political Thought of the American Revolution* (New York: Harcourt, Brace & World, 1963); Trevor Colbourn, *The Lamp of Experience: Whig History and the Intellectual Origins of the American Revolution* (Chapel Hill: University of North Carolina, 1965); Bernard Bailyn, *The Ideological Origins of the American Revolution* (Cambridge, MA: Harvard University Press, 1967); Gordon S. Wood, *Creation of the American Republic* (Chapel Hill: University of North Carolina Press, 1969).

corps of colonial governors and administrators. Other historians focus on the tensions between these assemblies and Parliament over the definition of imperial authority. From either focus, the American Revolution is portrayed as the culmination of longer-term and seemingly irreconcilable conflicts between American colonial leaders intent on self-government and British officials dedicated to imperial governance by Parliament and the Crown.[6]

Each interpretative perspective reveals important elements of the economic, ideological, and institutional cleavages that no doubt contributed to the eventual breakdown of the British-colonial order in 1776. Alone, however, each perspective provides an incomplete account of the process by which American and British leaders ultimately committed themselves, their peoples, and their resources to the trials of civil war. The economic perspective, for example, clearly exaggerates the depth of the economic conflicts between Great Britain and the American colonies. Not only was the trans-Atlantic trade with Great Britain still profitable for the American colonies through the early 1770s, but comparatively little of the political debate during the late colonial period focused on colonial or British economic concerns. Moreover, the often-highlighted downturn in several colonial economies during the 1760s was not unusual for a postwar period nor were the commercial regulations or taxes imposed by Parliament during this period especially difficult burdens for the generally thriving colonial economies.[7] Most important, the American Revolution did not catalyze American attempts to establish a radically different kind of economic order. Thus, the allegedly critical economic causes of the conflict are not directly related to specific economic consequences.

---

[6] See George L. Beer, *British Colonial Policy, 1754–1765* (New York: P. Smith, 1933); Leonard W. Labaree, *Royal Government in America* (New Haven: Yale University Press, 1930); Lawrence H. Gipson, *The British Empire before the American Revolution*, 15 vols. (New York: Knopf, 1936–1970); Jack P. Greene, *The Quest for Power: The Lower House of Assembly in the Southern Royal Colonies, 1689–1776* (Chapel Hill: University of North Carolina Press, 1963); Jack P. Greene, "An Uneasy Connection: An Analysis of the Preconditions of the American Revolution," in *Essays on the American Revolution*, Stephen G. Kurtz and James H. Hutson, eds. (Chapel Hill: University of North Carolina Press, 1973), pp. 32–80; Jack P. Greene, *Peripheries and Center* (Athens, GA: University of Georgia Press, 1986); Richard R. Johnson, " 'Parliamentary Egotism': The Clash of Legislatures in the Making of the American Revolution," *JAH* (1987), 74: 338–362; and Theodore Draper, *A Struggle for Power: The American Revolution* (New York: Times Books, 1996).

[7] Egnal, *A Mighty Empire*, p. 149. See also Emory G. Evans, "Planter Indebtedness and the Coming of the Revolution in Virginia," *WMQ* (1962), 19: 511–533.

The ideological perspective, to its credit, provides more accurate descriptions of the British-colonial conflict because it focuses on the political ideas and arguments that dominated public discourse in the second half of the eighteenth century. Many of these descriptions, however, offer selective treatments of this discourse, and interpretative narratives constructed from this perspective typically are not connected to specific political actors or to the sequence of political decisions that preceded the American Revolution.

Accounts from the ideological perspective additionally suffer from a tendency to portray historical events in overly general and thematic terms. In nineteenth-century historiography, for example, the ideological core of the Revolution was commonly described in terms of an heroic and providential movement by American colonials to defend the principle of liberty for all of humankind.[8] In the 1950s, historians realigned the Revolution's ideological core around a so-called American consensus for a liberal, Lockean ideology in which government was portrayed as the guarantor of private rights.[9] In the 1960s and 1970s, the Revolution's core was repositioned yet again, this time around a more public-minded, republican ideology in which the purpose of government was identified as part of a much grander project to reform American society.[10] In recent years, more complex accounts have been formulated. Several argue for the restoration of a liberal ideological core without the 1950s consensus theme and for Locke as a dominant rather than the single ideological inspiration of the Revolution.[11] Others propose a liberal-republican synthesis between classical republican ideas and liberal, free-market ideas of "seventeenth-century English economic writers."[12] Still

---

[8] See George Bancroft, *History of the United States* (Boston: Little, Brown, 1864–1875), Vols. 4–7.

[9] Edmund S. Morgan and Helen Morgan, *The Stamp Act Crisis: Prologue to Revolution* (Chapel Hill: University of North Carolina Press, 1953); Rossiter, *Seedtime of the Republic* (1953); and Hartz, *The Liberal Tradition in America* (1955).

[10] Bailyn, *The Ideological Origins* (1967); Gordon S. Wood, "Rhetoric and Reality in the American Revolution," *WMQ* (1966), 23: 1–32; Edmund S. Morgan, "The Puritan Ethic and the Coming of the American Revolution," *WMQ* (1967), 24: 3–18; and Wood, *The Creation of the American Republic* (1969). Cf. Garry Wills, *Inventing America: Jefferson's Declaration of Independence* (Garden City, NY: Doubleday, 1978).

[11] Robert Webking, *The American Revolution and the Politics of Liberty* (Baton Rouge: Louisiana State University Press, 1988); and Scott D. Gerber, "Whatever Happened to the Declaration of Independence? A Commentary on the Republican Revisionism in the Political Thought of the American Revolution," *Polity* (1993), 26: 207–231.

[12] See Joyce Appleby, "The Social Origins of American Revolutionary Ideology," *Journal of American History* (1978), 64: 940, 957–958. See also Gary B. Nash, *The Urban Crucible* (1979); Robert E. Shalhope, "Republicanism and Early American Historiography,"

others suggestively point toward metanarratives composed of incommensurable and only partially reconcilable discourses.[13]

Although accounts from the ideological perspective reveal important elements of the British-colonial conflict prior to the Revolution, many of them share several methodological limitations. Many accounts, for example, use what allegedly are the American Revolution's *final* causes (or the consequences of the Revolution) to explain the Revolution's *efficient* or immediate causes (or why and how the Revolution came about). Thus, the historiography of the process by which the once viable British-colonial political order collapsed into civil war invariably becomes clouded by what are considered the more important, post-collapse consequences of the American Revolution. One account, for example, suggests that interpretative explanations of revolutionary ideology also must function as a source "for the aggressive individualism, the optimistic materialism, and the pragmatic interest-group politics" that subsequently dominated the early national period. In others, the interpretation of the Revolution is portrayed as determining "who we are as a nation – our origins, purposes, and ideals," or as "contain[ing] prescriptive implications for [contemporary] public policy" and "the essential source of historical legitimacy for any general political program."[14]

With such self-consciously important objectives in mind, leading accounts from the ideological perspective since the 1950s not surprisingly insist that the political ideas articulated by colonials in public debate prior to the Revolution were not merely rhetorical arguments intended to protest British policies or to sway colonial public opinion. Rather, according to one historian, these ideas explain "not merely positions taken but the reasons why positions were taken."[15] This literal fusion of word and motive was a literary technique used by a generation of historians intent on countering then-prevailing economic interpretations of the Revolution which dismissed colonial ideas as "propaganda" and identified only material motives for the Revolution. This fusion, nevertheless, is insupportable in light of historical evidence that clearly

WMQ (1982), 39: 334–356; and Steven M. Dworetz, *The Unvarnished Doctrine: Locke, Liberalism, and the American Revolution* (Durham, NC: Duke University Press, 1990).

[13] See Peter S. Onuf, "American Revolution and National Identity," Mellon Sawyer Seminar, Johns Hopkins University, April 1998.

[14] Appleby, "The Social Origins of American Revolutionary Ideology," *JAH* (1978), 64: 937; Scott D. Gerber, "Whatever Happened to the Declaration of Independence?," *Polity* (1993), 26: 231; and Dworetz, *The Unvarnished Doctrine* (1990), p. 4.

[15] See Bailyn, *The Ideological Origins of the American Revolution* (1967), pp. vi–x.

reveals a range of British and colonial ideas during the late colonial period.

In other accounts, the political ideas of the pre-Revolution period serve an even more expansive explanatory function: They are used to describe and to explain *social* motivations for supporting the American Revolution. One account, for example, goes so far as to assert that "the average man was content to echo the brave assertions of his delegate or minister," while another concludes that the American Revolution represented more than a political rebellion by colonials against Great Britain, it also was "a utopian effort to reform the character of American society."[16] Why and with what consequences these imaginative causal leaps from historical evidence of *political ideas* to *social motivations* for revolution are made are never adequately explored or acknowledged.

Others have identified additional methodological problems with accounts from the ideological perspective, especially with the civic republican interpretation of the American Revolution. Political scientist Robert Webking, for one, notes that leading accounts from this perspective fail "to treat the thought of the leaders of the Revolution as more important or more indicative of the thought of the period than that of more obscure people." Moreover, these accounts "quote phrases or sentences from one source and then move on to another without attempting to place the phrases in the larger context of the work from which they come."[17] Even more problematic, according to historian Marc Egnal, these accounts of the motivating ideas of the American Revolution typically "are linked to no specific groups in colonial society," and thus they "cannot explain the deep, sustained divisions within the ruling class of each colony."[18] Finally, historian Colin Gordon in a thoughtful essay notes that accounts made from this perspective are unrealistically static because "[t]he ideas themselves, their consistency, and their causal monopoly are essentially immutable. All that apparently changes is the Americans' capacity of desire to apply them." As a result,

---

[16] Rossiter, *The Political Thought of the American Revolution* (1963), pp. 5–6; and Wood, *The Creation of the American Revolution* (1969), p. 395.

[17] Webking, *The American Revolution and the Politics of Liberty* (1988), p. 13. See also Jack Greene, "Political Mimesis: A Consideration of the Historical and Cultural Roots of Legislative Behavior in the British Colonies in the Eighteenth Century," *AHR* (1969), 75: 340–341; Robert Shalhope, "Republicanism and Early American Historiography," *WMQ* (1982), 39: 334–356.

[18] Egnal, *A Mighty Empire* (1988), p. 4.

the American Revolution is portrayed as "a necessary and inevitable – and apparently passive – development."[19]

Arguably, the institutional perspective provides the most congruent and credible account of the American Revolution because it relates *political* causes (differences in American and British political interests and institutional structures) to *political* consequences (the British decision to use force to assert its authority over the colonies, and the American decision to resist). Admittedly, this perspective is not particularly insightful about the connection between these political causes and other nonpolitical conditions that preceded the American Revolution. Unlike the ideological perspective, moreover, the institutional perspective cannot explain fully the intensity of American and British commitments to their respective political positions – especially after 1774 when it became increasingly evident that a failure to negotiate a political compromise would precipitate a civil war. Thus, British and colonial interests and the sequence of political decisions that triggered the American Revolution remain obscured between the highlighted political and institutional conditions and the well-known consequence of civil war. As a result, the institutional perspective invariably telegraphs a British-colonial conflict that was seemingly inevitable and irreconcilable.

Given the complexity of an historical event like the American Revolution, this study's criticisms are not intended as a wholesale dismissal of interpretative accounts that begin and end within one of the three highlighted perspectives. At the same time, this study's account is not confined to a single perspective nor does it explore every cause or contextual condition related to the American Revolution. The eighteenth-century development of social and religious conditions in Great Britain and the American colonies, for example, are almost wholly neglected not because they were insignificant dimensions of the British-colonial relationship, but because they had little direct or systemically traceable influences on the subsequent collapse of the British-colonial consensus for a common political order.

This account, at bottom, explains the collapse in the British-colonial order by examining a series of political decisions made between 1774 and 1776. Before analyzing these decisions in Chapter 3, it is necessary to frame the general context within which these decisions were embedded. To accomplish this task, the remainder of this chapter describes

---

[19] Colin Gordon, "Crafting a Usable Past: Consensus, Ideology, and Historians of the American Revolution," *WMQ* (1989), 46: 683.

the development of economic, demographic, institutional, and ideological conditions between 1700 and 1774.

PART II: ECONOMIC CONDITIONS

Although changes in economic conditions in the 1760s and 1770s often
are highlighted as triggering the American Revolution, longer-term economic developments arguably were more important sources of tension
between Great Britain and the American colonies. One of the most significant of these trends was the eighteenth-century expansion of the colonial economy. According to most estimates, the colonial economy grew
twice as fast as the British economy after 1700, dramatically increasing
the economic importance of the American colonies.[20] As described by a
member of Parliament prior to the American Revolution, British trade
with the American colonies was "considerably more than a third of the
whole" in 1772, whereas it "was but one twelfth part" of this trade in
1704.[21] Even more representative of colonial economic growth was the
fact that by the 1770s the material standard of living for the average
white colonial family surpassed the British average and likely was the
highest in the world.[22]

Notably, this longer-term pattern of colonial economic growth
occurred without major structural change in either the colonial or British
economies. Throughout the eighteenth century, both economies were
dominated by their respective agricultural sectors. The British economy,
however, benefited greatly from an expansion in its manufacturing, commercial, and mining sectors, and the colonial economy benefited from a
small but growing seaboard commercial sector. At mid-century, however,
the colonial economy still employed as much as 90 percent of its work

---

[20] McCusker and Menard, *The Economy of British America* (1985), p. 55. For a
more detailed sector analysis, see Marc Egnal, *New World Economies: The Growth
of the Thirteen Colonies and Early Canada* (New York: Oxford University Press,
1998).

[21] Edmund Burke's remarks in House of Commons (March 22, 1775), *Proceedings and
Debates of the British Parliaments Respecting North America*, R. C. Simmons and
P. D. G. Thomas, eds. (Millwood, NY: Kraus International Publications, 1983), 5: 603.
Economic historian Edwin Perkins more precisely notes that the colonial gross
product was only 4 percent of the British economy in 1700, and by 1770 it had grown
to approximately one-third the size. Perkins, *The Economy of Colonial America* (1988),
p. 234.

[22] See Perkins, *The Economy of Colonial America* (1988), p. 212; McCusker and Menard,
The Economy of British America (1985), p. 55.

force in farming, and less than 8 percent of the colonial population lived in urbanized areas.[23]

The organizational structure of the American colonial economy in the eighteenth century was a legacy of seventeenth-century decisions that were designed to make the American colonies first self-sustaining and then producers of exportable agricultural products and raw materials. In the second half of the seventeenth century Parliament regularly en-acted legislation which promoted colonial agricultural production and restricted foreign competition from the trans-Atlantic trade between Great Britain and the American colonies. In addition, increased European demand for colonial products in the eighteenth century pro-vided a continuous market-based incentive to expand the export sector of the colonial economy. This expansion, in turn, enriched the American colonies and transformed them into new and increasingly attractive con-sumer markets for British and European manufactured products.[24]

Although the British and colonial economies benefited greatly from their commercial relationship and from Parliament's commercial regula-tions, British leaders grew increasingly concerned by French commercial and imperial interests in North America as well as by the potential devel-opment of rival American-based manufacturing interests. Indeed, by 1729 British essayist Joshua Gee was among several British voices that suggested that the latter development ultimately would allow the American colonies to "set up for themselves, and [to] cast off the English Government."[25]

Parliament responded in several ways to these perceived threats. In response to the French commercial threat, it enacted the so-called 1733 Sugar Act. The Act imposed heavy customs duties on American colonial imports of French sugar products and was intended to undermine the lucrative trade that had developed between New England colonies and the French-controlled West Indies. Parliament responded to the colonial

---

[23] See Perkins, *The Economy of Colonial America* (1988), p. 57; and Marc Egnal, "The Economic Development of the Thirteen Colonies, 1720–1775," *WMQ* (1975), 32: 200–201. The term "urban" refers to all towns with more than 2,500 residents. See McCusker and Menard, *The Economy of British America* (1985), p. 250.

[24] See Walton and Shepherd, *The Economic Rise of Early America* (1979), pp. 66–68; Beer, *British Colonial Policy* ([1907], 1933), p. 228.

[25] Joshua Gee, *The Trade and Navigation of Great-Britain Considered* (1729), as quoted in Bumsted, "'Things in the Womb of Time': Ideas of American Independence, 1633–1763," *WMQ* (1974), 31: 540. See also Jeremiah Dummer, *A Defense of the New-England Charters* (1721) in *Great Britain and the American Colonies, 1606–1763*, Jack Greene, ed. (Columbia, SC: University of South Carolina Press, 1970), p. 165.

manufacturing threat by imposing additional regulatory policies on the American colonies.[26] Among other policies, Parliament restricted certain types of colonial manufacturing, banned the exportation of several colonial-made products, imposed currency and financial regulations on the colonies, and offered bounties and subsidies to encourage colonial development of additional nonmanufacturing products like naval stores, indigo, and silk.[27] The Crown additionally instructed its colonial governors to enforce these restrictions and to monitor the progress of colonial economic development.[28]

Despite Parliament's persistent efforts to retain the rapidly expanding colonial economy within the trans-Atlantic commercial framework it had established in the second half of the seventeenth century, four developments during the eighteenth century altered the colonial economy and, more importantly, colonial and British understanding of the limits and dynamics of their economic relationship. One of these developments was the failure of the 1733 Sugar Act to restrict the West Indies-American colonies sugar trade. The Act failed because its duties were never adequately enforced by Great Britain. As a consequence, the Act – and thus Parliament's authority to regulate the colonial economy – was regularly disregarded in the American colonies.[29]

Increased colonial grain exports to southern Europe in the second half of the eighteenth century was a second development with important consequences. These exports not only benefited farmers and merchants in several colonies, they clearly demonstrated the economic benefits of increased colonial trade that were independent of British supervision. British political economist Josiah Tucker noted the third development in a treatise he published in Great Britain in 1753. According to Tucker, the colonies "not only [were] set[ting] up Manufactures of their own in Opposition to ours," with more expected in the future, "but they [were] purchas[ing] those Luxuries and Refinements of Living from *Foreigners*, which we could furnish them with." Tucker calculated that the colonies "are supplied with at least *one third* of these Articles from Foreign

[26] George L. Beer, *The Commercial Policy of England Toward the American Colonies* (New York, P. Smith, 1948), pp. 66–106. See also McCusker and Menard, *The Economy of British America* (1985), pp. 295–330.

[27] Oliver M. Dickerson, *American Colonial Government* (Cleveland: The Arthur H. Clark Co., 1912), pp. 299–314; Walton and Shepherd, *The Economic Rise of Early America* (1979), pp. 156–161.

[28] Beer, *Commercial Policy of England* (1948), p. 70; and Dickerson, *American Colonial Government* (1912), p. 300.

[29] Beer, *Commercial Policy of England* (1948), p. 122.

Nations, amongst whom the *French* come in for the *greatest* share." The fourth and final development was that resident colonial merchants gradually gained control over the distributional sectors of colonial commerce. After mid-century, economic historians McCusker and Menard note, "colonial merchants were not only fully in command of the coastwise commerce," they already "had begun to extend their operations into the transatlantic trades" that historically had been controlled by British-based operatives.[30]

PART III: DEMOGRAPHIC CONDITIONS

In addition to colonial economic growth, colonial population growth in the eighteenth century was a second longer-term trend that affected the relationship between the American colonies and Great Britain. Between 1700 and 1770, the American colonial population increased from approximately 265,000 to almost 2.3 million persons – a remarkably high growth rate, made extraordinary by the fact that many believed that the British population had been either stable or in decline during the same period.[31]

Demographic growth in the American colonies was a function not only of the fecundity of New World immigrants but also of colonial and English policies. Approximately 280,00 enslaved persons of African ancestry and 100,00 indentured servants and 50,000 convicts and prisoners from Europe were transported into the American colonies between 1700 and 1775. The colonies additionally promoted population growth by adopting immigrant-friendly policies like low taxes, religious tolerance, special surveying and plotting services, colonial naturalization, and, in several instances, by offering land and money bounties to new settlers. Policies enacted by Parliament also supported colonial growth. In the late seventeenth century, according to historian Emberson Proper, a policy promoting foreign immigration emerged as "Parliament voted considerable sums of money to assist Protestant refugees" from Europe "in making their way to the English colonies." In 1740, Parliament

---

[30] McCusker and Menard, *The Economy of British America* (1985), pp. 79–80; Josiah Tucker, "A Brief Essay on the Advantages and Disadvantages which respectively attend France and Great Britain with Regard to Trade with some Proposals for Removing the Principal Disadvantages of Great Britain" (London, 1753), in *Collected Works of Josiah Tucker* (London: Routledge/Thoemmes Press, 1993), I: 45–46.

[31] McCusker and Menard, *The Economy of British America* (1985), pp. 54, 211–235; D. V. Glass, *Numbering the People* (London: Gordon & Cremonesi, 1978), pp. 21–23.

offered another encouragement by enacting a general naturalization act for the British colonies.[32]

As early as the 1720s, a small number of British officials and essayists began to speculate on the potential longer-term consequences of colonial population growth.[33] Prior to this point, population growth generally had been welcomed as a positive indicator of British economic growth. More colonists, according to the traditional logic, predictably meant expanded colonial production, larger consumer markets for British manufactures, and increases in Great Britain's military strength in North America.[34] During the second third of the eighteenth century, however, the time-honored truth of this demographic formula was increasingly clouded by more anxious projections about the consequences of unfettered colonial growth.

In 1751, for example, one British writer voiced concerns about the "great Numbers" emigrating from Great Britain to the American colonies. This writer argued that "[t]his well deserves the Consideration of the Legislature, as by this Means we may become reduced to the same deplorable Condition as Sweden was by Charles XII who depopulated his Kingdom so much by War, that the Women were obliged to till the Ground."[35] Others projected that the continuous growth and westward dispersion of the colonial population would prompt increased interest in establishing colonial-based manufacturing. "[U]nless we can divert their Thoughts to some other *Projects*," one essayist predicted, the manufacturing established by colonials who settled in the western parts of the colonies "will extend itself downwards; and the Inhabitants on the Sea-Coast will be supplied by their Neighbours in the Up-Lands, upon cheaper and easier Terms than we can supply them."[36]

In addition to these economic consequences, others envisioned negative political consequences from sustained colonial population growth. Not only did a larger and more extended colonial population increase the

---

[32] Aaron S. Fogelman, "From Slaves, Convicts, and Servants to Free Passengers: The Transformation of Immigration in the Era of the American Revolution," *Journal of American History* (1998), 85(1): 43–76; Emberson E. Proper, "Colonial Immigration Laws," *Columbia Studies in History, Economics and Public Law* (1900), 12: 12–16.

[33] See, for example, Jeremiah Dummer, *A Defense of the New England Charters* (1721); and *Cato's Letters*, "Of Plantations and Colonies," Dec. 8, 1722 (London, 6th ed., 1755), 4: 3–12.

[34] See Charles Strangeland, "Pre-Malthusian Doctrines of Population: A Study in the History of Economic Theory," *Columbia Studies* (1904), 21: 5–356.

[35] "Extract of a private Letter from Beverly," in *Virginia Gazette*, February 13, 1752.

[36] Josiah Tucker, "An Essay on Trade" (1753), in *Collected Works* (1993), I: 95; I: 84, 90. See also Bumsted, "'Things in the Womb of Time'," *WMQ* (1974), 31: 541n.27; Greene, ed., *Great Britain and the American Colonies*, pp. 267–268; Robert V. Wells, *The Population of the British Colonies* (Princeton, NJ: Princeton University Press, 1975), pp. 29–30.

administrative costs associated with British supervision and participation in colonial governance, but expansion in the sizes of the American colonial assemblies in response to this growth produced an ever larger and increasingly independent pool of colonial political leaders. Once tensions between Great Britain and the American colonies escalated, British officials began to perceive colonial population growth more disconcertingly in terms of the colonies' capacity to resist British authority.[37]

Before 1760, economic and political concerns about colonial demographics remained on the periphery of the British ministry. After 1760, it was a different story as these concerns were absorbed increasingly into the mainstream of British political thought. In London, for example, essayist Oliver Goldsmith authored a widely circulated series of articles in which he argued in particularly forceful and memorable terms that "the colonies should always bear an exact proportion to the mother-country; when they grow populous, they grow powerful; and by becoming powerful, they become independent also; thus subordination is destroyed, and a country swallowed up in the extent of its own dominions."[38]

The immense territorial spoils of Great Britain's victory over France in the Seven Years War prompted more vigorous British attempts to control colonial population growth. "The first move in this direction," historian Emberson Proper noted, "was to disallow certain acts of the colonial assemblies for the encouragement of immigration." Royal governors also "were instructed from time to time to grant no lands to new settlers" and the Royal Proclamation Line decreed in 1763 effectively established a permanent western boundary on future colonial settlements. "These prohibitory instructions increased until 1773, when all naturalization was abruptly ended by an order in council, forbidding the colonial governors to assent to any bills of that nature; and about the same time they were instructed to issue no warrants to surveyors, not to pass any patents for lands, nor to grant any licenses to private persons to purchase lands from the Indians."[39]

---

[37] Robert V. Wells, "Population and the American Revolution," in *The American Revolution*, William Fowler and Wallace Coyle, eds. (Boston: Northeastern University Press, 1981), pp. 108–109. See also Jack P. Greene, "The Seven Years' War and the American Revolution: The Causal Relationship Reconsidered," in *The British Atlantic Empire before the American Revolution*, Peter Marshall and Glyn Williams, eds. (London: Cass, 1980), pp. 85–105.

[38] "Citizen of the World: Letter XVII," in *Public Ledger* (1760), as quoted in Alfred O. Aldridge, "Franklin as Demographer," *Journal of Economic History* (May 1949), 9: 40. For earlier but similar imagery, see Charles Davenant, "On the Plantation Trade" (1698) in *Great Britain and the American Colonies*, Greene, ed. (1970).

[39] Proper, "Colonial Immigration Laws," *Columbia Studies* (1900), 12: 75.

Whereas British opinion finally settled decidedly against unregulated colonial growth sometime in the early 1760s, colonial leaders consistently gained confidence from this growth throughout the eighteenth century. No colonial was more confident in or did more to promote the significance of colonial population growth during this period than Benjamin Franklin of Pennsylvania. In 1749, for example, Franklin was one of the first colonials to observe publicly that "People increase faster by Generations in these Colonies, where all can have full Employment, and there is Room and Business for Millions yet unborn."[40] In subsequent years, Franklin frequently returned to the issue of colonial demographics in both his public and private writings. Publicly, Franklin's widely published claim that colonial population doubled "once in 25 years" and therefore "in another century . . . the greatest Number of Englishmen will be on this Side of the Water" quickly became the authoritative forecast not only in the American colonies and in Great Britain but throughout much of Europe.[41]

Privately and anonymously, Franklin also expected that colonial growth ultimately would lead to the transfer of the seat of the British Empire from England to North America.[42] Until this projected shift in

[40] "Poor Richard Improved, 1750" (1/49), *PBF*, 3: 441. See also Ezra Stiles, *Discourse on the Christian Union* (1760), as quoted in James H. Cassedy, *Demography in Early America* (Cambridge, MA: Harvard University Press, 1969), pp. 176–177; Edward Wigglesworth, *Calculations on American Population, with A Table for Estimating the Annual Increase of Inhabitants in the British Colonies* (Boston, Jan. 25, 1775).

[41] Benjamin Franklin, "Observations Concerning the Increase of Mankind, People of Countries, Etc." (1755), *PBF*, 4: 233.

[42] British political economist Josiah Tucker observed that Franklin was continuously "haranguing after this" transfer of the imperial center to North America. Tucker referred to the idea as Franklin's "darling Scheme, even before he came to reside in *England* . . . as well as his favourite Topic ever afterwards." Josiah Tucker, "An Humble Address and Earnest Appeal" (1775), in *Collected Works of Josiah Tucker* (1993), 5: 40. See, for example, Franklin, "Right, Wronged, and Reasonable" (April 18, 1767), *PBF*, 14: 131; "The Colonist's Advocate: I" (January 4, 1770), *PBF*, 17: 7. Although the source of Franklin's "darling scheme" is impossible to identify, the idea of transferring imperial power from England to America did not originate with him. In 1728, colonial George Webb wrote the captivating couplet: "Rome shall lament her ancient fame declined, And Philadelphia be the Athens of mankind." Several years before traveling to the American colonies, Bishop Berkely penned these prophetic stanzas in "Verses on the Prospects of Planting Arts and Learning in America" (1726):

> Westward the course of empire takes its way;
> The first four acts already past,
> A fifth shall close the drama with the day;
> Time's noblest offspring is the last.

As quoted in Charles Sumner, *Prophetic Voices Concerning America* (Boston: Lee and Shepard, 1874), pp. 9, 24.

the balance of imperial power, Franklin more pragmatically suggested that colonial population growth should be reflected more favorably in Parliament's economic policies. As Franklin explained in a letter to Massachusetts governor William Shirley in 1754: "if, through increase of people [in the colonies], two smiths are wanted for one employed before, why may not the *new* smith be allowed to live and thrive in the *new Country*, as well as the *old* one in the *Old*? In fine, why should the countenance of a state be *partially* afforded to its people, unless it be most in favour of those, who have most merit?"[43]

PART IV: INSTITUTIONAL CONDITIONS –
BRITISH, IMPERIAL, AND COLONIAL CONSTITUTIONS

British-colonial relations in the eighteenth century also were shaped by the institutional development of three distinct but related constitutional frameworks. As historian Jack P. Greene observes, these frameworks were "the British constitution for the central state" of Great Britain, the imperial constitution "between the center and the peripheries" of the British Empire, and "the separate provincial constitutions for Ireland and for each of the colonies in America."[44] Although a complete characterization of each constitutional framework is unwarranted, a sketch of the most relevant elements of each will be a useful reference point for assessing the relationship between Great Britain and the American colonies prior to the latter's declaration of independence in 1776.

The British Constitution

The eighteenth-century British constitution was an unwritten governing framework defined by its legal institutions, its political customs and practices, and by the various conceptual explanations used to justify existing institutional arrangements and governing practices. Its three most important legal institutions were the Crown, the House of Lords, and the House of Commons. Each of these institutions – at least, as it customarily was conceptualized – represented a specific element or estate of the English social order. The Crown represented the royal or monarchical element; the House of Lords represented the noble or aristocratic element; and the House of Commons represented the popular or demo-

---

[43] Benjamin Franklin to William Shirley, December 22, 1754, *PBF*, 5: 451.
[44] Greene, *Peripheries and Center* (1986), p. 68.

cratic element. Although this "mixed" constitution traditionally was described as a means of balancing the interests of the three social estates, the tripartite form of government was intended initially and functioned up through much of the seventeenth century as a check on the de facto governing authority possessed by the Crown.

Civil war and regicide in the 1640s, and James II's abdication and Parliament's assertion of control over the monarchy in the 1680s were two constitutional crises that fundamentally weakened the governing authority of the Crown. Indeed, historian Betty Kemp notes, "by 1716 the King could not, without infringing statute law, legislate outside of parliament or set aside Acts of Parliament, and he could not, without parliamentary sanction, supplement his ordinary revenue by taxation or maintain a standing army." In addition, statutory law restricted the King's once discretionary power to summon and to dissolve Parliament, and the necessity of Parliament's annual sessions in the eighteenth century effectively made the Commons as much a part of the constitution as the King.[45] Not until the mid-eighteenth century, however, did Parliament, and especially the House of Commons, effectively assume a dominant decision-making position within the British constitution and even then, monarchical influence remained an important (and, to some, still threatening) part of the British government. This shift in governing authority from the king to the Commons had obvious constitutional consequences, especially during the later conflict with the American colonies. For once de facto governing power retreated from its traditional pivot around the Crown, the British constitution increasingly came to be understood in terms of the authority of Parliament.[46]

Political customs were a second traditional and significant source of governing authority within the British constitution. Unlike the more familiar and formalized devices of royal decree and legislative statute, political customs were the commonly accepted practices of government which, although unwritten, obtained an authoritative status from their continuous usage.[47]

Both the formal and customary sources of governing authority were connected and animated by a third characteristic component of the British constitution: the conceptual explanations adopted to justify and to inform the arrangement of governing institutions and customary

---

[45] Betty Kemp, *King and Commons* (London: Macmillan, 1957), p. 141.

[46] Greene, *Peripheries and Center* (1986), pp. 57–58. See also Kemp, *King and Commons* (1957).

[47] Greene, *Peripheries and Center* (1986), p. 38.

practices. Two of the most important and revered explanations were built upon the constitutional concepts of consent and representation. These concepts were used initially as devices to empower and to sustain the governing authority claimed by the monarchy. In the ancient English constitution, representatives of various parts of the realm were called before the king and asked to consent to his rule – and, more often than not, to his requests for tax revenues. Once these representatives organized themselves into a Parliament that claimed institutional independence from the king, the concept of consent served two additional purposes. First, it functioned as a conceptual restraint on the king's prerogative powers because certain practices of government – especially the collection of taxes – were deemed constitutional only when they were consented to by the people's representatives in the House of Commons. Second, the concept of consent was employed to justify the constitutional authority of customary political practices because the continuity of these practices implied both their utility and their acceptance by the people over time.[48]

Parliamentary representation also developed additional conceptual functions. In addition to supporting the legitimacy of Parliament's legislative authority – especially its taxation authority – representation gave the House of Commons a source of popular legitimacy independent of the Crown.[49] It was the representative quality of the Commons that made the mixed or balanced constitution possible. Representation, moreover, was conceptualized as empowering the Commons with the responsibility and the legitimacy to hear and to correct popular grievances against Crown officials.[50] Once Parliament's governing powers expanded in the beginning of the eighteenth century, the concepts of consent and representation developed yet another function: They help to explain the transformation from a governing order traditionally defined by monarchical rule and political custom into an order increasingly defined by legislative majorities and statutory law.

In addition to these concepts, conceptual theories were devised and used at various times in the eighteenth century to explain the powers and purposes of government within the British constitution. These concep-

---

[48] John Phillip Reid, *Constitutional History of the American Revolution: The Authority to Legislate* (Madison, WIS: University of Wisconsin Press, 1991), p. 100.

[49] See Reid, *The Concept of Representation in the Age of the American Revolution* (Chicago: University of Chicago Press, 1989), pp. 19, 25–28; and Morgan, *Inventing the People: The Rise of Popular Sovereignty in England and America* (New York: Norton, 1988), pp. 39–46, 209–211.

[50] Reid, *The Concept of Representation* (1989), pp. 28–29.

tual theories were important not only because they offered subsequent generations of political actors condensed explanations of past governing practices, they also informed and directed British and colonial expectations for future political developments.

Two of the most important of these conceptual theories in the eighteenth century originated after English constitutional crises in the seventeenth century. In the aftermath of the collapse of the British political order in the 1640s, Thomas Hobbes proposed a new contractual explanation of political authority in his *Leviathan* (1651).[51] Hobbes argued for the establishment of an absolute sovereign power whose authority was not dependent on the then prevailing concepts of divine or hereditary right. Instead, according to Hobbes, sovereignty was granted initially by a people, and once given it became intractable and indivisible as long as the sovereign maintained civil order and peace.

Almost forty years later, and after Parliament's resolution of a second constitutional crisis in 1689, John Locke proposed a different explanation of the basis of political authority in his *Two Treatises of Government* (1690).[52] Locke, like Hobbes, maintained that the people held the initial right to establish a sovereign governmental authority. Unlike Hobbes, however, Locke placed sovereign authority specifically within the *legislative* branch where it existed as a fiduciary power for the purpose of protecting a people's natural rights to life, liberty, and property. Constitutional change, it followed, was justified only when the sovereign legislature failed its primary responsibility of protecting these rights.

Unlike Hobbes, Locke additionally contended that sovereign authority was made legitimate not only at the founding moment of a political order, its legitimacy was sustained continuously thereafter through the explicit and tacit consent of the people. Explicit consent was given by those individuals permitted to vote for their representatives in Parliament and tacit consent was given indirectly but automatically by all others who, although not allowed to vote, "consented" by residing within civil society.

The conceptual explanations of governmental authority proposed by Locke and Hobbes were not immediately accepted as constitutional canon in seventeenth-century England, nor in the political discourse of

[51] Thomas Hobbes, *Leviathan*, Richard Tuck, ed. (1991).
[52] See John Locke, *Two Treatises of Government*, Peter Laslett, ed. (London: Cambridge University Press, 1967).

eighteenth-century Great Britain. Nevertheless, by the mid-eighteenth century and throughout the subsequent British-colonial conflict, remnants of Hobbes's conceptualization of absolute sovereignty and of Locke's conceptualization of legislative supremacy and popular consent were woven together and used repeatedly by British political actors to explain Parliament's authority to govern both Great Britain and the American colonies.

The Imperial Constitution

Whereas a general political consensus gradually developed for the practices and conceptualizations of the eighteenth-century British constitution, definitive practices and conceptualizations never were clearly defined for the imperial constitution. Despite the lack of consensus, Great Britain and the American colonies were in fact bound together into a greater political whole. What then were the ties that bound them together during the first half of the eighteenth century?

Political and market-based institutions of commercial exchange were no doubt the most significant ties between the British and colonial economies. These institutions functioned as conduits for the trans-Atlantic transfer not only of goods and services, but of information and technologies as well. Cultural linkages were other important bonds binding the eighteenth-century imperial constitution. For many American colonists, cultural associations were organized around shared religious faiths and missions. For others, they hinged more narrowly on a tradition of legal rights commonly believed to be shared by all British citizens.[53] For most, however, the most salient cultural linkage between the American colonies and Great Britain was their common linguistic and ethnic traditions. Notably, however, even these linkages varied by time and place as more than half of the colonial population by the mid-eighteenth century is estimated to have had ancestral origins from some place other than England.[54]

---

[53] Greene, *Peripheries and Center* (1986), pp. 22–24. For a thoughtful analysis of the imperial linkages created by voluntary organizations and interest groups, see Alison Olson, *Making the Empire Work: London and American Interest Groups, 1690–1790* (Cambridge, MA: Harvard University Press, 1992).

[54] See Thomas L. Purvis, "The European Ancestry of the United States Population, 1790," *WMQ* (1984), 41: 98; Aaron Fogelman, "Migrations to the Thirteen British North American Colonies, 1700–1775: New Estimates," *Journal of Interdisciplinary History* (1994), 22: 691–709; and McCusker and Menard, *The Economy of British America*, p. 54.

Other imperial linkages were embedded within legal institutions. In the eighteenth century, for example, Parliament enacted commercial regulations that further defined and strengthened the economic relationship between Great Britain and the American colonies. In 1740, Parliament also attempted to formalize one aspect of the cultural relationship between the colonies and Great Britain by establishing a uniform process for naturalizing foreigners with at least seven years residence in the American colonies.[55]

In addition to these bonds, connections between the American colonies and the Crown were supported by a variety of political institutions. Among others, these institutions included colonial charters, royal instructions to colonial governors, and the Crown's appointment and supervision of colonial administrators. At the end of the seventeenth century, the Crown established additional institutional linkages, creating the Board of Trade to oversee colonial affairs[56] and requiring regular reports on the colonies from both this Board and its colonial governors.[57]

The colonial agency provided a similar connecting function between the colonies and Great Britain. Typically appointed by a colonial assembly, an agent was sent to London to represent the colony's interests before Parliament, the Privy Council, and in British courts. When instructed by an assembly, an agent also submitted colonial petitions and addresses to the Crown or to Parliament. Beyond this representative function, agents regularly corresponded with the assemblies on the latest developments in Great Britain, and because they resided in London the agents simultaneously served as a convenient source of colonial information for British officials. Occasionally, in fact, agents were contacted by the Board of Trade or called before Parliament to answer questions on colonial affairs.[58]

Aside from these linkages, conceptual explanations of the imperial constitution were never well defined or universally accepted on either side of the Atlantic. According to one eighteenth-century conceptual tradition, the colonies still were considered the primary responsibilities of

---

[55] Greene, *Peripheries and Center* (1986), p. 61.

[56] See Dickerson, *American Colonial Government* (1912).

[57] Labaree, *Royal Government in America* (1930), pp. 29, 122.

[58] See Edwin P. Tanner, "Colonial Agencies in England During the Eighteenth Century," *PSQ* (1901), 16: 24–49; Michael G. Kammen, *A Rope of Sand: Colonial Agents, British Politics and the American Revolution* (Ithaca, NY: Cornell University Press, 1968); and Jack M. Sosin, *Agents and Merchants: British Colonial Policy and the Origins of the American Revolution, 1763–1775* (Lincoln, University of Nebraska Press, 1965), pp. 66–89.

the king. Some time in the eighteenth century, Parliament's more active intervention into colonial affairs gave rise to a second conceptual explanation of the imperial constitution. As described by a member of Parliament in 1766, this second explanation declared that the "universality of the legislative power is the vital principle of the whole Empire, and it has been confirmed at the [1689] Revolution that wherever the sovereignty of the Crown extends, the legislative power extends likewise."[59]

The Colonial Constitution

Like the British and imperial constitutions, the eighteenth-century colonial constitution also was defined by its legal institutions, its political customs, and its conceptual explanations. Although each colony had a unique tradition of governance, royal authority had organized each colonial government into one of three basic types. In the eighteenth century, royal colonies were the most common type of colonial government and those favored by the Crown because the king's agents retained – at least in theory – the most discretionary authority. Proprietary colonies, like Pennsylvania, Maryland, and Delaware, were a second type, one in which proprietors were charged with governing responsibilities. Charter colonies, like Rhode Island and Connecticut, were a third organizational type, and one in which the basic terms of the governmental order were specified within a colonial charter. Despite these differences, the institutional framework of almost every colonial government – a governor and a bicameral legislature – closely resembled the familiar tripartite institutional structure of the British constitution.

The colonial constitutions shared other characteristics. Their development in the seventeenth century was directed, in large part, by royal authority. The governor was the primary agent and representative of this authority and the institution through which the king formally exercised his prerogative power to govern the American colonies. With few exceptions, governors were appointed by or with the consent of the king, and they held the power to summon and to dissolve a colony's legislature, to veto legislation, to control appropriations and expenditures, and to appoint administrative officers.[60] In addition to a governor, colonial

---

[59] Speech of Charles Yorke, 3 Feb. 1766, *Proceedings and Debates*, Simmons and Thomas, eds. (1983), II: 137.

[60] Royal governors were controlled through royal commissions and instructions. The commission, read publicly at a governor's inauguration, outlined the king's delegation of powers to his governors. Royal instructions were private and contained the specific

governments typically included a council, which functioned as the upper house of a colony's legislature. Councils were small in size and in most colonies the colonial governor appointed its members. The council's primary functions were to advise the governor and to sit with him as a colony's highest court.[61]

Colonial assemblies, or the lower house of bicameral colonial legislatures, were established in every colony. In Maryland, the colony's original charter required that colonists consent to their proprietary government, and thus the first assembly was convened in the colony in 1637. A few years earlier, the first Massachusetts assembly was established, but only after residents of the plantation of Watertown refused to pay a small tax levied on them without their consent. Their protest, according to one account, was driven by the belief "that it was not safe to pay moneys after that sort, for fear of bringing themselves and [their] posterity into bondage." The colony's governor allegedly dismissed this protest but he nevertheless convened the colony's first assembly shortly thereafter.[62] Whatever the impetus, every colonial assembly initially was sanctioned in some way by royal authority. As a result, Crown officials consistently maintained that these assemblies had no legitimacy or purpose beyond the king's will. Assembly members, however, were popularly elected and, like Parliament, they were able to claim with a degree of credibility that their institutions, in fact, existed independently of the colonial governors and indirectly, therefore, of the Crown as well.

In addition to its organizational structure, the eighteenth-century colonial constitution was characterized by the gradual increase in the legislative activities and governing authority of the assemblies.[63] Several

---

objectives a governor was to pursue during his tenure. Dickerson, *American Colonial Government* (1912), p. 149; and Labaree, *Royal Government in America* (1930), pp. 98–99.

[61] Labaree, *Royal Government in America* (1930), pp. 134–135.

[62] As quoted in George H. Haynes, "Representation and Suffrage in Massachusetts, 1625–1691," *Johns Hopkins Studies* (1894), 12th ser., VIII–IX: 17–18.

  See also Morgan, *Inventing the People* (1988), pp. 38–46, 122–148. For additional discussion of the origins and development of the colonial assemblies and voting rights, see Andrew C. McLaughlin, *The Foundations of American Constitutionalism* (New York: New York University Press, 1932), pp. 31–61; Cortlandt F. Bishop, *History of Elections in the American Colonies* (New York: Columbia College, 1893); and J. R. Pole, *The Seventeenth Century: The Sources of Legislative Power* (Charlottesville: University of Virginia Press, 1969), pp. 32–69.

[63] Greene, *Peripheries and Center* (1986), pp. 45–46. See also Bailyn, *The Origins of American Politics* (1968), pp. 102–104; Jack P. Greene, "The Role of the Lower House of Assembly in Eighteenth-Century Politics," *JSH* (1961), 27: 454.

conditions facilitated this development. The mixed form of colonial government, for one, created an institutional tension between the king's colonial agents and colonial representatives that conditioned the assemblies to seek limitations on royal authority and greater clarification of their own institutional powers. Assembly leaders clearly recognized the similarities between their efforts and Parliament's prior successes in limiting monarchical power and many, in fact, self-consciously modeled their assemblies into mini-Parliaments.[64] As one Pennsylvanian assemblyman explained in 1728, "as the Methods of Proceedings in *Westminster-Hall* are made a Rule to us, in our *Courts of Justice*, so our *Assemblies* in like manner take their Rules from the *House of Commons* there." In short, this colonial claimed, the assemblies conducted themselves by "imitating the House of Commons in *England* as nigh as possible."[65] Crown officials added credibility to the mini-Parliament analogy in their instructions which denied the colonial assemblies "any power or privilege whatsoever which is not allowed by us to the House of Commons . . . in Great Britain."[66] Moreover, according to historian Jack Greene, colonial governors also accepted this analogy and, therefore, "could scarcely avoid interpreting any questioning of executive actions and any opposition to gubernatorial programs or imperial directives as . . . a challenge to the essential prerogatives of the Crown or proprietors."[67]

While structural dynamics supported the aggressive (often antagonistic) institutional dispositions of most colonial assemblies, other conditions in the early eighteenth century discouraged more strident royal supervision of colonial affairs. The unsettled domestic division of governing authority between Parliament and the Crown, the continual expenses or threats of war Great Britain faced with rival European powers, the success of the trans-Atlantic trade, and the initial military insignificance of the distant American colonies were all conditions which directed British attention away from the designs and actions of the colonial assemblies.

At the same time, the Crown's agents in the colonies were more often than not left with inadequate authority and resources to prevent the colo-

[64] Labaree, *Royal Government in America* (1930), pp. 214–217.
[65] *Remarks on the Proceedings of some Members of Assembly at Philadelphia: April 1728*, as quoted in Greene, *Peripheries and Center* (1986), p. 31.
[66] As quoted in Greene, *Quest for Power* (1963), p. 15.
[67] Greene, "Political Mimesis: A Consideration of the Historical and Cultural Roots of Legislative Behavior in the British Colonies in the Eighteenth Century," *AHR* (1969), 75: 350.

nial assemblies from encroaching on their governing powers. The Board of Trade, for example, was assigned only advisory and information-gathering duties, but never the authority to intervene directly or decisively in colonial affairs. Similarly, colonial governors – although armed with the power to veto colonial legislation – were denied the financial and administrative resources needed to fully subordinate the assemblies.[68] As a consequence, many governors and their councils were simply overwhelmed by the persistent demands of the assemblies, and many learned to avoid confrontations altogether by aligning themselves with a dominant colonial faction. Thus, as historian Jack Greene notes, "royal and proprietary governors in many colonies were fully integrated into the local political community and came to identify and to be identified as much with the interests of the colonies as with those of the metropolis."[69]

Colonial economic and social conditions were other catalysts of colonial political development. Individuals and groups representative of various economic interests, for example, began to use the colonial assemblies to establish common rules of economic exchange, to regulate the distribution of colonial lands, and to authorize private business ventures and public development projects. As a consequence, historian Bernard Bailyn writes, "the tradition of governmental intervention in the economy was well established, and the government's response to enterprising individuals and groups was positive."[70] The necessities and aspirations of the colonial experience also prompted a variety of social interests to seek legislative recognition or authorization.[71]

The political culture of the colonial assemblies was a final condition that encouraged their institutional development. This political culture was sustained, in part, by the emergence of dominant political families in many of the colonial assemblies. This occurred at different times in each colony. As early as 1716 the South Carolina assembly consisted

[68] Labaree, *Royal Government in America* (1930), pp. 102, 269; and Bailyn, *The Origins of American Politics* (1968), pp. 72–80.

[69] Greene, *Peripheries and Center* (1986), p. 47.

[70] Bailyn, *The Origins of American Politics*, p. 103, 103n.37. See also Michael C. Batinski, *The New Jersey Assembly, 1738–1775: The Making of a Legislative Community* (Lanham, MD: University Press of America, 1987), pp. 1–24; Thomas L. Purvis, *Proprietors, Patronage, and Paper Money: Legislative Politics in New Jersey, 1703–1776* (New Brunswick, NJ: Rutgers University Press, 1986); and Alan Tully, "Constituent-Representative Relationships in Early America: The Case of Pre-Revolutionary Pennsylvania," *Canadian Journal of History* (1976), 11: 139–154.

[71] Bailyn, *The Origins of American Politics* (1968), p. 104. For a more thorough analysis of governmental promotion and regulation of colonial economies, see McCusker and Menard, *The Economy of British America* (1985), pp. 331–348.

of members whose families had dominated the colony's politics for the past thirty years.[72] A steady decline in membership turnover in the assemblies during the eighteenth century was a second condition supportive of this political culture. Lower turnover, over time, generally meant that assembly memberships became more continuous, more politically skilled and increasingly more likely to associate their personal political interests with the longer-term, institutional development of their assembly.[73]

Supported by these conditions, colonial leaders adopted similar strategies to advance the institutional powers of their individual assemblies. Although their strategies were uncoordinated, assembly leaders commonly insisted on the authority to decide all matters related to public revenues. Because the assemblies also successfully resisted the Crown's efforts to secure permanent salaries for its colonial governors and administrators, the assemblies used their power of the purse to secure additional institutional powers. As one New Jersey assemblyman unashamedly described his assembly's strategy against their royal governors: "Let us keep the dogs poore, and we'll make them do what we please."[74] In Pennsylvania, at least, the assembly clearly fed their governors (and even their proprietors) a richer diet for, as Joseph Galloway explained, the "Practice of purchasing and paying for Laws . . . [was] interwoven with our *Proprietary* Constitution."[75]

---

[72] Pole, *The Seventeenth Century* (1969), p. 64. See also Jack P. Greene, "Foundations of Political Power in the Virginia House of Burgesses, 1700–1760," *WMQ* (1959), 16: 485–506; and George E. Frakes, *Laboratory for Liberty: The South Carolina Committee System, 1719–1776* (Lexington, KY: University Press of Kentucky, 1970). The prominence of these political families within several colonial assemblies was aided by the establishment of the legislative committee system. See J. R. Pole, "Historians and the Problem of Early American Democracy," *AHR* (1962), 68: 635.

[73] Jack P. Greene, "Legislative Turnover in British America, 1696 to 1775: A Quantitative Analysis," *WMQ* (1981), 38: 444–451. For a more detailed elaboration of this "political immobility" thesis, see James Kirby Martin, *Men in Rebellion, Higher Governmental Leaders and the Coming of the American Revolution* (New Brunswick, NJ: Rutgers University Press, 1973). For a discussion of the modern relationship between turnover rates and legislative institutionalization, see Nelson Polsby, "Institutionalization of the U.S. House," *APSR* (1968), 62: 144–168.

[74] As quoted in Marcus W. Jernegan, *The American Colonies* (New York, Longmans, Green and Co., 1941), p. 285.

Like Parliament, the assemblies also demanded and eventually won greater control over their internal institutional structure, including the authority to decide membership requirements, disputed elections, franchise qualifications, and indirectly, in most colonies, the size of their assemblies. Greene, *The Quest for Power* (1963), pp. 7–8; and Jernegan, *The American Colonies* (1941), pp. 285–288.

[75] As quoted in Alan Tully, *Forming American Politics* (1994), p. 281.

PART V: IDEOLOGICAL CONDITIONS

Ideological conditions, or the widely shared beliefs of political actors concerning the authority and responsibilities of government, are a final indicator of how the relationship between Great Britain and the American colonies developed prior to the American Revolution. Description of these conditions is problematic for several reasons. The beliefs of political actors, for one, are cognitive experiences bound to specific individuals at specific moments in time. As a consequence, examination of the development of these beliefs over several generations of British and colonial political actors is intelligible only if it is admitted that the resulting descriptive generalizations are analytical constructs.

The second problem associated with the description of ideological conditions is the incompleteness of the historical evidence of these conditions. Beliefs of political actors about the purposes or structure of government are only rarely recorded. As a consequence, the available historical evidence of these political beliefs or conceptualizations is unavoidably an unrepresentative sample of a much larger political discourse. Concentration upon the personal correspondence or writings of one or a few individuals only compounds this problem.

Despite these epistemological and evidential obstacles, the ideas that structure the behavior and self-understanding of political actors matter greatly. They matter because they define the boundaries of the political discourse, and in so doing define the range of expectations and possibilities of political actors at specific moments in time. The following description, therefore, is designed to capture the development of the range of beliefs about governmental authority, about representation, and about the relationship between the two as conceptualized by British and colonial political actors in the eighteenth century.

Conceptual Change and the British Constitution

Although the eighteenth-century development of colonial constitutions paralleled the seventeenth-century development of the British constitution, by the middle part of the eighteenth century the conceptual foundations of the constitutions had developed in notably different directions. Colonial leaders, for example, defended the rising powers of their assemblies with various conceptual explanations. Often these explanations affirmed the rights and institutions established in a colony's original charter; at other times, they relied on the familiar constitutional concepts of popular consent and mixed government, or on the long-accepted constitutional authority of legal precedent, perpetual usage, and established custom. Crown officials, by contrast, consistently resorted to an older, more traditional conceptual explanation of the colonial constitution that maintained that colonial governments were creations of the king and, thus, their constitutional development was not determined by local changes but was wholly dependent on royal authorization.[76]

Ironically, at the same time Crown officials were growing increasingly concerned by the expanding powers of the colonial assemblies, much of the king's governing powers already had been absorbed by Parliament and explained away – at least in Great Britain – by the concepts of parliamentary sovereignty and legislative supremacy. Not only, therefore, was there a fundamental disagreement about the basic character of the colonial constitutions, but fundamentally different conceptual foundations were relied on in the colonies and in Great Britain to explain and defend the legitimacy of the rule of law.

This conceptual divergence was nowhere more significant over time than in the constitutional functions of representation. Although differences in British and colonial conceptualizations of representation surfaced prominently in the 1760s during public debate over Parliament's authority to tax the colonies and the alleged "virtual" representation of the American colonies in Parliament, the substance of these differences was also reflective of the distinct ways in which institutions and practices of representation developed in Great Britain and the American colonies.

In the ancient English constitution, representation did not originate as a democratic institution. Instead, the king held the power to make grants of representation and he used these grants to legitimize his authority to govern. Initially, therefore, representation was considered more of an obligation than a right, and Parliament was less a policy-making institution than a judicial court and a means for executing the Crown's fiscal policies.[77] Moreover, as one student of Parliament summarized, up through the reign of Henry VIII (1509–1547) kings called "Parliaments when and how they pleased" and occasionally they "appointed by name who should be returned . . . [and] who should not, [even] though elected."[78] Later, according to historian Edmund S. Morgan, after

---

[76] Greene, *The Quest for Power* (1963), pp. 14–16; and Greene, "Political Mimesis," *AHR* (1969), 75: 337–360.

[77] George L. Haskins, *The Growth of English Representative Government* (Philadelphia, University of Pennsylvania Press, 1948), pp. 128–131.

[78] *Manuscripts of the Earl of Egmont, Diary*, "March 13, 1734" (1923), II: 57.

Parliament began to assert its institutional autonomy, grants of representation were made "not because the residents demanded it, but rather because powerfully connected country gentlemen persuaded the monarch to enfranchise boroughs where they could count on controlling elections."[79] In the seventeenth century, the House of Commons gained even greater control over its internal institutional structure, including institutions of representation. Indeed, between 1603 and 1660 the Commons added thirty new members by resolution, thus increasing its size without the king's assent. During this period, the king continued to grant representation to previously unrepresented boroughs, although only eleven members were added to the Commons this way.[80]

Dual authority over institutions of representation was not easily accepted by either the Commons or the king. The resulting tensions and conflicts prevented both institutions from developing and implementing reforms necessary to ensure that representation in the Commons reflected the dramatic economic and social changes of seventeenth-century England.[81] This failure to reform, according to historian Vernon F. Snow, gave rise to corrupt practices and ensured that "some areas, past their prime economically, still possessed political power in parliament, while other larger, more populated and prosperous areas lacked equivalent power in the lower house."[82]

During the 1640s, repeated attempts were made to effect a more equitable apportionment of representation in the Commons. In 1653 and 1654, representation in the Commons finally was reapportioned. Although not as radical as the reforms earlier advocated by the so-called Levellers, under the Cromwellian Protectorate plan many "rotten" or depopulated boroughs lost their representation in the Commons. The specific division of representation in the 1654 plan was notably more proportional than the older division had been, generally correlating with contemporaneous tax assessments although traditional electoral districting units of county, city, and borough still were recognized. Scotland and Ireland, moreover, were granted a small number of representatives in Parliament. This unprecedented inclusion of these non-English territories

---

[79] Morgan, *Inventing the People* (1988), p. 42.

[80] Kemp, *King and Commons* (1957), pp. 10–11.

[81] Shortly after his accession in 1604, James I vetoed a bill granting representation to the city and county of Durham. The king's refusal was answered by the Commons' decision to admit additional representatives without his assent. See Vernon F. Snow, "Parliamentary Reapportionment Proposals in the Puritan Revolution," *English Historical Review* (1959), 74: 435, 411n.2.

[82] Snow, "Parliamentary Reapportionment Proposals in the Puritan Revolution," *English Historical Review* (1959), 74: 434.

gave representation in the Commons a new and distinctly more imperial character. Finally, the Protectorate plan empowered the so-called Lord Protector in Council with the discretionary authority to effect additional reapportionments of Parliament.[83]

After Cromwell's death in 1658 these reforms were abandoned and the prereform apportionment system was reinstituted for subsequent Parliaments. As a consequence, the apportionment of representation within the Commons became decidedly less proportional and, thus, less reflective of English society. Rotten boroughs regained their political prominence within the Commons and encouraged other forms of electoral corruption. Scotland and Ireland also lost their rights to parliamentary representation, stalling the institutionalization of a more inclusive, imperial system of representation for the House of Commons. In addition, abandonment of the provision for an executive-initiated reapportionment left the prospects for periodic redivision of representation in the Commons in its previously undefined state, effectively ensuring that future reapportionments would not occur.

In the wake of the restoration of the English monarchy in 1660, the previously unreconciled conflicts between the king and the Commons over institutions of representation reemerged. In the 1660s and 1670s, for example, the king modified franchise qualifications in many boroughs in order to reassert his influence over their elections. In 1673, the Commons challenged these practices by refusing to seat two individuals elected from one of the boroughs recently chartered by the king. This refusal in effect denied the king's authority to include restrictive (and especially advantageous) electoral qualifications within the borough charters he granted. After several years without a resolution of this conflict, the Commons and the king settled on an informal but more definitive division of constitutional responsibilities. The Commons gained the authority to decide all election disputes without interference by the king, although its power to admit additional representatives was limited to statutory acts and then only to boroughs previously represented in the Commons. It also was decided that voter qualifications in all newly recognized boroughs were to be established by statute, thus undermining the king's capacity to shape the size and composition of a new borough's

---

[83] For more on the Leveller, Barebones, and Protectorate apportionment schemes see Snow, "Parliamentary Reapportionment Proposals in the Puritan Revolution," *English Historical Review* (1959), 74: 420–422; and Blair Worden, *The Rump Parliament, 1648–1653* (Cambridge, UK: Cambridge University Press, 1974), pp. 139–160.

electorate. The king, however, retained his ancient constitutional authority to grant new borough representation by royal charter and the power to alter franchise qualifications within existing boroughs.[84]

This informal division of authority over the design of institutions of representation had important consequences in the eighteenth century. Without the power to set franchise qualifications in new boroughs, the king did not make any additional grants of representation after the borough of Newark received its charter in 1673.[85] The Commons, similarly, made its final statutory restoration of borough representation the same year when it responded to petitioners from the city and county of Durham.[86] As a result, after the 1707 Act of Union extended a fixed number of representatives to Scotland no grants of representation were made by either the king or the Commons. The size of the House of Commons thus remained fixed at 558 members for the remainder of the eighteenth century. At the same time, representation in the Commons was never reapportioned and, thus, the institution's most elemental source of its authority to govern – its representativeness – was disconnected from the dynamic conditions of eighteenth-century Great Britain.[87] Ironically, the authority of the Commons grew without an adjustment in its internal division of representation and without a strengthening of its external connection to British society.

The informal decision to fix the number of seats in the Commons had important consequences. For once Parliament confirmed its constitutional prominence after 1689, interest in occupying these seats also increased. Electorally safe borough seats became highly prized by those seeking a voice in the Commons, and it was not long before these seats were sold or leased openly for whatever the political market would bear.[88]

Other forms of electoral corruption attained a new prominence within this more competitive electoral environment. Campaigns for seats in the Commons increasingly included open bribery of the electorate,

---

[84] Kemp, *King and Commons* (1957), pp. 10–13; Morgan, *Inventing the People* (1988), p. 42.

[85] The king was particularly successful, however, in restricting franchise qualifications in older boroughs. See Morgan, *Inventing the People* (1988), p. 106.

[86] Snow, "Parliamentary Reapportionment Proposals in the Puritan Revolution," *English Historical Review* (1959), 74: 411.

[87] Kemp, *King and Commons* (1957), pp. 13–14.

[88] Pole, *Political Representation in England and the Origins of the American Republic* (1966), pp. 386–387; and Edward Porritt, *The Unreformed House of Commons* (New York, A. M. Kelley, 1963 [1903]), I: 353–358.

candidate-sponsored entertainments, and candidate bidding wars for the right to pay borough or county expenses for market tolls, poor relief, public buildings, or the maintenance of roads, bridges, and harbors. The price of borough seats, the costs of campaigns, and the expectations of constituents rose so quickly and so overwhelmingly after 1689 that political leaders in many boroughs deliberately reduced the size of their electorates. Prompted by the House of Lords, whose members often bore the financial consequences of these new electoral dynamics, Parliament also enacted the 1716 Septennial Act extending the maximum number of years between parliamentary elections from three to seven.[89]

To discourage disputes over election results – especially, in boroughs where the electorate had recently been restricted – Parliament additionally enacted the 1729 Last Determinations Act, fixing the size of a borough's electorate at the level last decided by the House of Commons. Typically, several historians agree, the Commons settled these disputes in favor of the smallest possible electorate.[90] As a consequence, historian J. R. Pole concludes, the Commons not only "became decreasingly representative of what was in any case a very small electorate," its relationship to the "people of the kingdom" became, at most, "sketchy and fortuitous."[91]

Simultaneous with and accelerating these electoral changes was the Crown's realization that its governing powers within the eighteenth-century British constitution depended directly on its ability to affect the composition and disposition of the House of Commons.[92] To preserve this, the Crown relied on its influence over the electorate in approximately twenty-five Treasury, Admiralty, and Ordnance borough seats.[93] The finances of the Treasury and of sympathetic members of the House of Lords were used to buy or influence the election of additional members, and various forms of patronage and bribery were used to influ-

---

[89] Porritt, *The Unreformed House of Commons* ([1903], 1963), I: 152–163; and Morgan, *Inventing the People* (1988), pp. 158–159; 174–208. See also Kemp, *The King and Commons* (1957), p. 42; John Cannon, *Parliamentary Reform, 1640–1832* (Cambridge, UK: Cambridge University Press, 1973), p. 36.

[90] J. H. Plumb, *The Origins of Political Stability, England: 1675–1725* (Boston: Houghton Mifflin, 1967), pp. 94–95; Cannon, *Parliamentary Reform* (1973), pp. 34, 38.

[91] Pole, *Political Representation in England and the Origins of the American Republic* (1966), p. 386.

[92] Kemp, *King and Commons* (1957), pp. 88–90.

[93] A majority, or near majority, of the electorate in Treasury, Admiralty, and Ordnance boroughs were predisposed to elect members supportive of the king because they were limited, for the most part, to individuals who held Crown offices.

ence other members after their election to the Commons.[94] According to historian J. H. Plumb, the power over patronage, especially after the ascendancy of the Whig party in 1715, was what "cemented the political system, held it together, and made it almost an almost impregnable citadel, impervious to defeat, indifferent to social change."[95]

The consequences of these eighteenth-century changes in the electoral system were a notably more stable British political order. Not surprisingly, those who criticized these changes not only were few and safely assigned to the margins of public debate, but they demonstrated no interest in rekindling either the political heat or the democratic light that characterized the types of reforms instituted in the 1640s and 1650s.[96] For example, a group of reformers in 1765 endorsed a proposal for adding one hundred county members to the Commons. They did so, however, not to effect a more proportional distribution of seats but as a remedy for ministerial influence in borough elections. In any event, the reform failed, gaining little more than notice in Parliament or the nation.[97] Five years later, another group in London called on candidates to endorse a slightly more radical eleven-point reform program that called for a return to annual Parliaments, legislation banning place offices and bribery, and a "full and equal representation of the people in Parliament." Shortly after this program's announcement, however, a sympathetic observer disappointedly reported that the reforms "are either totally neglected in the country, or, if read, are laughed at, and by people who mean as well to the cause as any of us."[98]

Although British society remained deferential to its ancient monarchical and aristocratic political institutions, the new and more extensive cooperation between the Crown and Parliament that developed during the early decades of the eighteenth century was still a constitutional anomaly that required public justification. New conceptual explanations

---

[94] Reid, *The Concept of Representation* (1989), p. 110; Kemp, *King and Commons* (1957), pp. 91–93; and Porritt, *The Unreformed House of Commons* ([1903], 1963), I: 408–410; Kemp, *King and Commons* (1957), p. 87.

[95] Plumb, *The Origins of Political Stability* (1967), p. 189.

[96] See Caroline Robbins, *Eighteenth Century Commonwealthmen* (New York: Atheneum, 1968). See also Marie Peters, "The 'Monitor' on the Constitution, 1755–1765: New Light on the Ideological Origins of English Radicalism," *English Historical Review* (1971), 86: 706–727; J. C. D. Clark, *English Society, 1688–1832: Ideology, Social Structure and Political Practice during the Ancien Regime* (Cambridge, UK: Cambridge University Press, 1985), pp. 320–321.

[97] Clark, *English Society, 1688–1832* (1985), p. 321. See also Robbins, *The Eighteenth Century Commonwealthmen* (1968), p. 261.

[98] As quoted in Cannon, *Parliamentary Reform, 1640–1832* (1973), p. 65.

were thus employed to explain the deterioration of what had previously been a mainspring of the House of Commons: the customary claim that as representatives of the people the Commons must remain institutionally independent and uninfluenced by the Crown. By 1742, however, David Hume and other apologists for the close relationship between Westminster and White Hall explained with surprisingly little opposition that the influences "which arise from the offices and honours which are at the disposal of the Crown" restrained the Commons and thereby ensured "a proper counterbalance to the other parts of the constitution." "[W]e may," David Hume contended, "call it by the invidious appellations of *corruption* and *dependence*; but some degree and some kind of it are inseparable from the very nature of the constitution, and necessary to the preservation of our mixed government."[99] Indeed, others warned that without this corruption of the Commons "our Constitution would immediately degenerate into Democracy," or worse yet the "government would be tore to pieces by a factious parliament, or [the monarch] would be obliged to carry on without any parliament at all."[100]

Other conceptual changes in representation accompanied the ascendancy of the House of Commons. For example, once the locus of governing authority shifted decidedly from the king to the House of Commons, the traditional conceptualization of representation as a restraint against the arbitrary actions of the Crown was no longer needed and it fell quickly out of the constitutional mainstream. The remedial function of representation similarly was de-emphasized because the act of petitioning Parliament for relief implied what had been impossible in the ancient constitution: that the people's representatives in the Commons, and not the Crown, had abused its governing authority. Rather than apply this constitutional restraint to the eighteenth-century Commons and thus implicitly repudiate the constitutional orthodoxy of the 1689 settlement, eighteenth-century British constitutional thought proffered that popular grievances against government were to be remedied through the legislative process and not through the customary devices of "impeachment, attainder, or confrontation with the crown."[101]

The wholesale conceptual abandonment of the remedial and restraint functions of representation was a gradual and largely imperceptible

---

[99] As quoted in Kemp, *King and Commons* (1957), pp. 88, 144. See David Hume, "On the Independence of Parliament" (1742), in *David Hume's Political Essays*, Charles W. Hendel, ed. (New York: Liberal Arts Press, 1953), pp. 68–71.

[100] As quoted in Reid, *Concept of Representation* (1989), p. 114.

[101] Reid, *The Concept of Representation* (1989), p. 29.

process. To those who detected or promoted these conceptual changes, however, institutions of representation no doubt were understood as the means through which the real power in British government was to be gained, divided, wielded, and, most importantly, legitimized.

This starkly modern view of representation in the Commons was well known prior to the decapitation of the ancient constitutional order in 1649. Still, the full strength of the "Monster of a Democracy"[102] remained largely unarticulated throughout the seventeenth century – masked, in large part, by a succession of conceptual and institutional devices adopted to prevent England from degenerating into what the political generation of the 1640s witnessed as the anarchical conditions of civil war and the intractable tyranny of representative authority, or what Hobbes fictionalized so memorably for later generations as a grotesque "democratic" state of nature in which individuals warred persistently until death.

For the Puritans and the Long Parliament (1640–1653), the idea of a godly form of rule by the saintly was one of the conceptual devices used to explain and thus to stabilize the new political order in which only the "democratic" element of the old order remained.[103] When this proved ineffectual, Cromwell and the Protectorate Parliament (1653–1658) turned to less ethereal institutional devices to legitimize their infant republic. Among others, these devices included a written constitution, higher property requirements for the franchise, and a nearly omnipotent and wholly responsible Lord Protector. Once these devices apparently failed to stabilize the political order, a series of institutional restorations were made: the House of Lords in 1657, the prerevolutionary apportionment of the Commons in 1658, and the monarchy in 1660. To these familiar institutions of the old order, Charles II (1660–1685) subsequently added a resurrected conceptualization of the divine right of kings. He also engaged in a systematic campaign to restrict borough electorates. The net effect of these institutional and conceptual devices was the reestablishment of an ancient institutional equilibrium between the king and Parliament, and the restoration of the familiar conceptualization of the English government as a balanced or mixed constitution. These devices helped sustain the authority of government after 1660

---

[102] Anonymous, "Plaine English" (1643); as quoted in David Wootton, "From Rebellion to Revolution: the Crisis of the Winter of 1642/3 and the Origins of Civil War Radicalism," *English Historical Review* (1990), 105: 664.

[103] Judson, *The Crisis of the Constitution* (1949), pp. 274–348. See also Michael Walzer, *The Revolution of the Saints* (Cambridge, MA: Harvard University Press, 1965).

until, much to the dismay of the House of Commons, Charles II and the heirs to the Crown unilaterally disrupted the balance by revealing their Roman Catholic sensitivities.

In the aftermath of the Commons' escalation of the Exclusion Crisis in 1679, its role in forcing the abdication of James II in 1688, and its self-initiated reconstruction of the constitutional order in 1689, the naked display of the power of governmental institutions authorized through popular representation appeared even more impressive than it had been imagined since its last full exposure in the 1640s. Arguably, of all who thought seriously about representation in the seventeenth century it was Hobbes and Locke who were most acutely conscious of the potential of government authorized by representation. For not only do they both advocate institutional and conceptual devices related specifically to the authorization, division, and operation of the powers of their "representative" governments, they additionally prescribe fundamental purposes for their government as well. In short, whereas political order customarily was conceptualized as a stationary object requiring procedural devices to ensure its internal stability, the idealized governments of Hobbes and Locke attain their stability over time through their continual movement toward specific prescribed ends.

At first glance, the concept of representation in Hobbes's *Leviathan* is almost unrecognizable to the modern eye. His idealized government is established by a single and permanent contractual bond between a set of otherwise warring individuals and an omnipotent sovereign authority. Hobbes, moreover, does not provide for any additional institutions of popular consent or control subsequent to the initial establishment of the sovereign: there are no elections, no petitions to or instructions for governmental actors, nor are there any formal ways to redress individual grievances against particular actions of the sovereign government. Still, as political theorist Hanna Pitken correctly notes, "representation plays a central role in Hobbes' main political work," and the form of government described in the *Leviathan* is characterized repeatedly as representative.[104]

However, the fact that Hobbes charges his otherwise unaccountable sovereign with the overriding and affirmative mandate to procure "the safety of the people" offers the means for reconciling the conundrum of an all-sovereign but representative government.[105] For this mandate

---

[104] Hanna Pitken, *The Concept of Representation* (1967), pp. 14, 15–37.
[105] *Leviathan*, Ch. XXX, p. 231.

circumscribes a sphere of legitimacy – albeit an extremely large one – around one of the weakest representative governments ever conceived and, therefore, by implication on the actions of all governments based on representation as well. Hobbes's larger project and theoretical break-through is thus evident. He uses the concept of representation to solve the classical problem that political orders tend to degenerate into inher-ently instable forms of political order: monarchy into tyranny, aristoc-racy into oligarchy, and, especially for Hobbes, democracy into anarchy. The basis of this tendency, according to Hobbes, is the inexorable drive of human self-interest. Familial associations, fear of a common enemy, and even religious principles – as the English Civil War aptly demon-strated – are inadequate checks against this drive. And although these exogenous sources of authority may temporarily suppress the overzeal-ous and injurious pursuit of self-interest they also, according to Hobbes, legitimize equally as destructive attempts to fulfill self-interest through governmental institutions and the exercise of collective authority.[106]

The potential degeneration of a political order becomes especially acute in democratic orders once exogenous sources of governing author-ity are rejected. For what remains are individuals within society who invariably attempt to use the collective authority of government to secure personal gain. The result, not surprisingly, is that the authority of the political order typically is exhausted or frustrated: Democratic govern-ments thus lose much of their efficacy or legitimacy before devolving into anarchy or tyranny. Hobbes offers a two-part solution that, in essence, still serves as the conceptual blueprint of modern democracy. First, he makes representation the initial and singular basis of governmental authority, clearly rejecting other potential sources of political legitimacy. Government created by representation, in turn, is insulated from the din of individual demands that constitute large, pluralistic societies. Second, in return for the obedience of individuals within society to the collective authority of the government they established, Hobbes charges govern-ment with the responsibility of providing civil peace. Popular obedience, more specifically, requires that every individual outside of government forsake use of the collective authority of government to further his or her private interest. The latter responsibility imposed on government functions as a restraint on the self-interest of those who constitute the government. It is this unique combination of obedience and govern-mental purpose that generates a new kind of political order which

---

[106] *Leviathan*, Ch. XVII, pp. 117–121.

Hobbes calls "that great LEVIATHAN, or rather (to speak more reverently) of that Mortall God, to which we owe under the Immortall God, our peace and defence."[107]

Locke's *Second Treatise on Government* (1690) also addresses the unique authority of government derived from representation. Writing during a period of civil peace, and in support of the Commons' role in the Exclusion Crisis (1679–1681) and James II's abdication (1688), Locke portrays representation in a notably different light from Hobbes's minimalist rendition. In Locke's idealized government, representation is not only the initial source of political authority, it establishes a continuous relationship between government and society. Representation is reflected in the original social contract entered into by individuals who share common fundamental interests, and it is present between a people and their rulers (in a more limited sense) when government is first established. For Locke, representation exists as an evolving relationship between rulers and the ruled through the direct consent given by voters to those selected as representatives in government, and it is in the tacit consent continuously given for government through every individual's residence within civil society. By strengthening the relationship between those within government and those outside of government, Locke – like Hobbes – grounds the legitimacy of government on the authority of representation.

Locke additionally uses several conceptual devices to sustain and to limit the authority and legitimacy of government based on representation. The concept of legislative supremacy, for example, elevates lawmaking (or the traditional action of representative legislatures) above the arbitrary prerogative authority of nonrepresentative monarchs. At the same time, however, Locke also denies his idealized legislature the authority to use its supremacy in an arbitrary manner.[108]

Locke employs the concept of majority rule with similar countervailing effects. For example, after a majority of individuals within a society determine the form of government every individual within the society is bound to accept the decisions of the majority in government as authoritative.[109] Moreover, constitutional changes – even the right to rebel against a governmental order – also are dependent on a majoritarian

---

[107] *Leviathan*, Ch. XVII, p. 120.
[108] Locke, *Two Treatises of Government*, Laslett, ed., Book II, Ch. XI, Sec. 134–135, pp. 401–403.
[109] *Two Treatises*, Book II, Sec. 96, p. 375.

consensus within the government.[110] Thus, like Hobbes's Leviathan, Locke's idealized government (once established) is insulated from external demands or obligations, although it remains empowered through the concept of majority rule to make collective decisions binding on all. For Locke, the concept of majority rule also serves as a partial check against a government's abuse of its collective authority because its power to make binding decisions must be articulated at some point as a majoritarian consensus within government.

Locke uses another conceptual device, the social contract, to strengthen and limit the authority of representative government. Unlike that of Hobbes, Locke's initial contract is not between the people and government but among the individuals who first consent to form a society. Thus Locke's concept of a social contract binds individuals into a single community, which, in turn, makes possible the subsequent representative relationship between this community and the government it ultimately establishes. Locke, in addition, distinguishes the rights held by individuals within society as antecedent to the establishment and empowerment of government. As a consequence, although government receives authority because of its representative relationship to the people, it possesses no independent authority to define its own form or to alter the terms of the original social contract. Locke underscores the fundamental difference between government and society: The former is defined by the authority to make collectively binding decisions; the latter is defined by the types of relationships which exist between individual interests.

In addition to these conceptual devices, Locke adds a series of institutional devices to further stabilize his idealized government. Unlike Hobbes, Locke advocates a strict separation of legislative and executive powers to remove the possibility of one institution accumulating all the authority of government.[111] Locke, furthermore, recognizes the need for a "fair and equal Representative" according to "wealth and inhabitants" and he specifically empowers the executive, not the legislature, with the discretionary authority to effect this end "for the publick good."[112]

Like Hobbes, Locke circumscribes his representative government with an affirmative and enduring purpose. However, whereas Hobbes's Leviathan is circumscribed by the charge to preserve civil peace, Locke

---

[110] *Two Treatises*, Book II, Sec. 168, pp. 425–427.
[111] *Two Treatises*, Book II, Sec. 143, p. 410.
[112] *Two Treatises*, Book II, Sec. 157–158, pp. 418–420.

narrows the sphere of legitimate governmental action. In addition to civil peace, Locke's idealized government is also charged with the affirmative responsibility for protecting the terms of the original social compact: the individual rights to life, liberty, and property.[113] Locke ascribes a third but more general purpose which he applies to the supreme legislative power and, in the absence of legislative power, to the executive power as well: the responsibility to act in consonance with the public good.[114]

The relevance of the seventeenth-century conceptualizations of Hobbes and Locke to eighteenth-century British and colonial politics can easily be overlooked. After all, Hobbes's *Leviathan* (although widely studied after its publication in 1651) addressed a fundamental problem of political order that after 1660 was solved not through representation and popular contract but through the restoration of the ancient political institutions and conceptualizations of a mixed constitution. In a similar way, Locke's insights in his *Second Treatise* inspired few of his contemporaries.[115] In fact, in the wake of the 1689 settlement, those within government grew increasingly less likely to affirm or underscore the right of the people to overthrow their government. Neither, for that matter, did many initially trumpet Locke's conceptual arguments for legislative supremacy or private rights. The threat of an absolutist Crown was so remote after 1689 and the fear of a democratic influence within government so easily checked by a series of institutional devices that the deliberate establishment of a tradition of private rights beyond the purview of the Crown or of Parliamentary majorities seemed as unnecessary in the early eighteenth century as the presumption of legislative supremacy seemed an inviolable part of the constitutional settlement of 1689. Moreover, the political, administrative, and electoral solutions worked out between the Crown and Parliament during the early eighteenth century only compounded the discontinuities between the practices of British politics and the idealized governments proposed by Hobbes and Locke – for the former advocated either a monarch *or* an assembly, and the latter proposed a strict separation of legislative and executive powers.

Although not direct influences, the conceptualizations of Hobbes and Locke remain important because their timeless insights into government

---

[113] *Two Treatises*, Book II, Sec. 123–124, pp. 395–396.

[114] *Two Treatises*, Book II, Sec. 158–159, pp. 419–421.

[115] See John Dunn, "The Politics of Locke in England and America in the Eighteenth Century," in *John Locke: Problems and Perspectives*, John W. Yolton, ed. (London, Cambridge University Press, 1969), pp. 45–80.

based on representation provide deeper understanding of the paradox of an eighteenth-century House of Commons that grew more powerful as it became less representative of and less accountable to the British people. Elaboration of a final conceptual change in representation is necessary, however, before the relationship between these theoretical insights and the practices of the eighteenth-century British constitution can be seen. This conceptual change altered yet another customary function of representation. That is, in addition to its original restraint and remedial functions, representation also supported the Commons' claim to be independent from the Crown, an independence that – at least in the seventeenth century – had been understood by those in Parliament as necessary for maintenance of a balanced constitution. Representation in the Commons had thus been an integral part of the conceptual framework within which the authority of government and the legitimacy of the entire constitution were understood.

Prior to the eighteenth century, the basis of the Commons' claim to institutional independence and legitimacy rested on the direct relationship it had to the popular and local element of British society. In the ancient constitution, historian J. R. Pole explains, representatives of the "common people" called by the king "to sit in the lower House of Parliament" were considered "deputies of specific districts; not representatives of the general mass of common people."[116] Wages of members, for example, were paid by constituents during the initial centuries of the English constitution and, according to historian Edward Porritt, it was "customary for members, on returning from a Parliament, to address their electors when they presented their bills for wages and travelling-expenses."[117] Moreover, it was the directness of the Commons' relationship to localities – institutionalized in the customary practice of representatives binding their constituents to the decisions they consented to in Parliament, and in the assignment and the election of representatives from territorially defined electoral districts – which made the Commons' powers authoritative and its claims to institutional autonomy from the Crown credible.

In the early seventeenth century, this localist conceptualization of representation was transformed once the House of Commons began to

---

[116] Pole, *Political Representation in England* (1966), p. 399. See also Louise Brown, "Ideas of Representation from Elizabeth to Charles II," *Journal of Modern History* (1939), 11: 23–40.

[117] Porritt, *The Unreformed House of Commons* ([1903], 1963), I: 257; see also I: 261, 263–268.

describe itself not only as representative of localities and the popular part of English society, but more expansively as the representative of the entire realm as well. As early as the 1620s, Parliamentary leaders began describing the Commons as "the great eye of the kingdom," "the Counsel of the Land," and "the harte strings of the Commonwealth."[118] The new metaphorical self-descriptions did not, however, supplant the traditional local element of representation; instead, these descriptions originated as responses to divine-rights theorists who began to argue that the king alone – without the necessity of Commons consent – possessed the authority to determine and provide for the general welfare. In addition to the new claim to be coequal "national" representatives with the king, parliamentary leaders also responded to divine-rights advocates by cultivating greater popular support for their institutional powers, and by reconceptualizing the ancient constitutional concept of consent to include the idea that all parts of government (including the Crown) were restrained and, in fact legitimized, by an anterior, contractual relationship with the people.[119]

Development of this proto-democratic, proto-liberal vision of government – in many respects, the germ of the modern concepts of popular sovereignty and limited government – was undermined once the republican government of the Commonwealth period was abandoned and the previously discarded institutions of a mixed form of government were restored. Despite the failure of the English republican experience, both the "local" and "national" conceptualizations of representation endured and were sustained after 1689 by a resumption of the institutional tensions between Crown and Commons, and by Parliament's expanding interests in regulating imperial commerce.

Sometime in the eighteenth century, this dual concept of local *and* national representation in the Commons was replaced by a new orthodoxy.[120] As Edmund Burke explained to his electors in Bristol in 1774, Parliament was not "a congress of ambassadors from different and hostile interests; which interests each must maintain, as an agent and advocate, against other agents and advocates." Parliament, rather, "is a

---

[118] As quoted in Judson, *The Crisis of the Constitution* (1949), p. 304. See also Charles H. McIlwain, *Constitutionalism: Ancient and Modern* (Ithaca, NY: Cornell Univ. Press, 1947), pp. 114–115.

[119] Judson, *The Crisis of the Constitution* (1949), pp. 305–309. See also Derek Hirst, *The Representative of the People?: Voters and Voting in England under the Early Stuarts* (Cambridge, UK: Cambridge University Press, 1975).

[120] Pole, *Political Representation in England* (1966), pp. 441–442.

deliberative assembly of one nation, with one interest, that of the whole; where, not local purposes, not local prejudices ought to guide, but the general good, resulting from the general reason of the whole."[121]

Like all conceptual changes, when and how the shift to a "national-only" concept of representation occurred is difficult to identify with historical precision. Ingeniously, historian Betty Kemp discovered an indicator of this conceptual change in the annual editions of Edward Chamberlayne's *The Present State of England* and *The Present State of Great Britain* from 1669 to 1775. According to Kemp, these histories declare "that although every Member of the Commons' House be chosen to serve for one particular County, City, or Borough, yet he serves for the whole Kingdom, and his Voice is equal to any other, his Power absolute to consent or dissent without ever acquainting those that sent him, or demanding their Assent."[122]

In the editions before 1716, Chamberlayne's description of the duties of representatives also included that "they are to make it their special Care to promote the good of that County, City, or Borough, for which they serve, and from which heretofore they usually did receive Instructions and Directions concerning their Grievances, Wants, etc." In editions after 1716, Kemp astutely observed the omission of the special duty members originally were understood to owe their local constituencies.[123]

Notably, Chamberlayne's new description of representation first occurred the year after Parliament enacted the 1716 Septennial Act. The connection is not coincidental, for the 1716 Act overturned the practice of triennial elections, which had been considered a fundamental part of the constitutional settlement of 1689. Not only, therefore, were the electoral bonds between those outside of government and those within government weakened when triennial elections were abandoned, but the basic patterns of political order that defined the British constitution now appeared alterable through the statutory will of any given parliamentary majority. Even more significant, the Parliament that enacted the 1716 Act used it to extend its own institutional existence four additional years beyond what the electoral law and the last electorate explicitly authorized. Thus, as historian John Phillip Reid notes, the 1716 Act "taught a

---

[121] Edmund Burke, "Speech on Being Elected for Bristol in 1774" (November 3, 1774), *The Speeches of the Right Hon. Edmund Burke*, J. Burke, ed. (Dublin, 1854), p. 130. See also (William Pitt), *Parliamentary History*, Jan. 22, 1770, XVI: 753.

[122] As quoted in Kemp, *King and Commons* (1957), p. 43.

[123] Kemp, *King and Commons* (1957), p. 44.

lesson of parliamentary power and foreshadowed the shift of sovereignty from customary rights to legislative will and pleasure."[124]

Although the 1716 Septennial Act no doubt represents a major turning point in the eighteenth-century development of the British constitution, the new "national-only" concept of representation described in Chamberlayne's histories did not immediately displace the older, locally connected view of representation.[125] In 1745, for example, during a debate on repealing the 1716 Septennial Act and returning to the ancient custom of annual parliaments, Thomas Carew forcefully argued before the Commons that "it is necessary we should visit our constituents, at least, once a year, to know their sentiments, and to examine, upon the spot, the grievances they complain of." Instead, he charged,

We find by experience, that after gentlemen are once chosen for a long term of years, they fix their abode in this city, and seldom revisit their constituents, till it become necessary for them to go down to solicit their votes at a new election. Nay, since the establishment of Septennial Parliaments, we have often had gentlemen in this House, who never saw the borough that sent them hither, nor knew any thing of its constitution or interest, perhaps could not recollect its name, till they looked into the printed lists of parliament.[126]

No one in Parliament challenged the accuracy of Carew's account. What was contested instead was the normative claim that members of the Commons had an affirmative obligation to represent local interests. In response to Carew, for example, Sir William Yonge argued:

The word attorney has been artfully brought into the debate, as if the members of this House were nothing more than the attorneys of the particular county, city, or borough they respectively represent. But everyone knows that, by our constitution, after a gentleman is chosen, he is the representative, or if you please the attorney, of the people of England, and as such is at full freedom to act as he thinks best for the people of England in general. He may receive, he may aske, he may even follow the advice of his particular constituents; but he is not obliged, nor ought he to follow their advice, if he thinks it inconsistent with the general interests of his country.[127]

---

[124] Reid, *The Concept of Representation* (1989), p. 4.

[125] See Isaac Kramnick, "An Augustan debate: Notes on the History of the Idea of Representation," in *Representation*, J. Roland Pennock and John W. Chapman, eds. (New York, Atherton Press, 1968), pp. 83–91. For debate over representation in the 1730s, see also Isaac Kramnick, *Bolingbroke and his Circle* (Cambridge, MA: Harvard University Press, 1968); and *Manuscripts of the Earl of Egmont, Diary of Viscount Percival afterwards First Earl of Egmont* (London, H. M. Stationery, 1923), II: 56–58.

[126] *Parliamentary History*, January 23, 1745, XIII: 1058.

[127] *Parliamentary History*, January 23, 1745, XIII: 1078.

During subsequent decades, Yonge's view became constitutional orthodoxy and the local element of representation once thought so vital to the authority of the Commons and the balance of the constitution was dismissed as a nostalgic and misconceived longing for a lost (and, to many, long-forgotten) part of the ancient constitution. How the concept of representation changed so dramatically without destabilizing the British constitution is much too complicated to be explained here in full. The insights of Hobbes and Locke, however, offer glimpses into the dynamics driving this change. For in their idealized governments not only does the authority of government originate solely through the act of representation, but this authority is sustained and becomes, in large part, autonomous after an initial act of representation. Although they differ in the number and regularity of acts of representation necessary to make government authoritative – Hobbes proposes a one-time act; Locke acknowledges the need for periodic elections – the end result is the same: Those authorized as representatives become wholly independent from the original source of their authority. Thus, rather than a control over government, representation empowers government with collective decision-making authority and then detaches those empowered from exogenous sources of control.

The gradual detachment of the eighteenth-century House of Commons from its original association with localities and its realignment with an elusive but so-called "higher" national good discoverable only by its members parallel, in many respects, the conceptual perspectives offered by Hobbes and Locke. Beyond this conceptual similarity, the House of Commons periodically exercised the full extent of the authority latent within the act of representation. As early as 1701, for example, the Commons imprisoned several petitioners from the county of Kent who had asked that Parliament supply the king with the monies he had requested. Although the right of petition was still considered a customary right of individuals and groups, the Commons decided this particular petition was "scandalous, tending to destroy the constitution of parliaments, and to subvert the established government of these realms."[128]

Other demonstrations of the power of a government authorized through representation could be recounted.[129] Arguably, however, no

---

[128] As quoted in Morgan, *Inventing the People* (1988), p. 226.

[129] In 1733, for example, the Commons refused a petition from the colony of Rhode Island that protested the 1733 Sugar Act. The petition was rejected on the grounds that the right to petition against current taxation was denied in Great Britain and "as our

incident is more reflective of the completeness of the Commons' assumption of the authority to govern than its decision to deny John Wilkes his seat in the Commons in 1769. The voters of Middlesex elected Wilkes in three successive elections, yet after each election the Commons expelled him.[130] The decision for expulsion was not unanimous. Several members, in fact, protested that "the right of electors to be represented by men of their own choice" was "one of the most sacred parts of our constitution,"[131] and that "the right of judging upon the general propriety or unfitness of their representatives is entrusted with the electors," not with the Commons. "If it were otherwise," George Grenville complained in the Commons, "we should in fact elect ourselves, instead of being chosen by our respective constituents."[132]

Despite these protests and the nearly united voice of the Middlesex electorate, the Commons repeatedly expelled Wilkes. Several members defended the decision by arguing that any denial of the Commons' authority over its members would expose it more "to contempt, than to increase its dignity or importance." Others were more direct: They simply denied Middlesex voters "the right of doing wrong, of sending a member to parliament, who was certainly ineligible in the eye of reason." Voters, in short, were "bound not to return improper persons" to the Commons.[133]

Conceptual Dissension and the American Conceptualization of Representation

As the function of representation within the British constitution was changing dramatically in the eighteenth century, the practices and conceptualizations of representation in the American colonies continued to

---

colonies are all a part of the people of Great Britain, they are generally represented in this House as well as the rest of the people are; and in all the resolutions of this House, a due regard will certainly be had to the particular interest of every one of them, so far as it is consistent with the general interest of the whole." *Parliamentary History*, March 8, 1733, VIII: 1264. See also Morgan, *Inventing the People* (1988), pp. 226–227.

[130] John Wilkes was first elected in March 1768; on February 3, 1769, the Commons expelled him for a libelous publication. On February 16, 1769, the electors of Middlesex County chose him again for the next Parliament; the next day, however, the Commons declared this election void and Wilkes incapable of election. The same election-expulsion pattern was repeated in March 1769. In April 1769, after Wilkes was reelected again, his election was again voided and his opponent, Henry Luttrell, was seated by the Commons on April 15, 1769. See *Parliamentary History*, XVI: 546n.

[131] *Parliamentary History*, XVI: 589.

[132] *Parliamentary History*, February 3, 1769, XVI: 561; cf. 562–563, 574.

[133] *Parliamentary History*, XVI: 594.

be defined in the customary terms of executive restraint, remedial action, and legislative independence. The distinct evolutionary paths of British and colonial concepts of representation did not mean, however, that there were no shared experiences. For example, both the British House of Commons and the American colonial assemblies used their claim to be representative institutions to secure sole authority to determine their internal institutional rules and procedures.[134]

Electoral standards and campaign practices were additional areas in which Great Britain and the American colonies had some parallel experiences. Although most eighteenth-century colonial assemblies expected (or legally required) their members to be residents in the districts within which they were elected, district residency was not enforced in either the British House of Commons or in several colonial assemblies.[135] Like British electioneering, many colonial campaigns were marked by extravagant candidate donations and promises, spirited festivities, voter bribery and intimidation, and occasionally even election-day violence.[136] Moreover, as historian Chilton Williamson observes, "[t]he practice of creating freeholds at the time of a crucial election was fairly widespread in the American colonies" as it also had been in Great Britain.[137]

Despite these similarities, colonial practices and institutions of representation differed from those in Great Britain in several notable ways. The apportionment of representation in the colonial assemblies typically was not as disproportional as it was in the British House of Commons, although not one colonial assembly ever adopted a method for distributing representation proportionally. In several colonial assemblies,

[134] See Greene, *The Quest for Power* (1963), pp. 189–190; Tully, *Forming American Politics* (1994), pp. 402–403, 410.

[135] Hubert Phillips, *The Development of a Residential Qualification for Representatives in Colonial Legislatures*, Cincinnati, OH: Abingdon Press, 1921. Although not strictly required in the colonial assembly of New York, 91 percent of all eighteenth-century members resided in their electoral districts. See Patricia U. Bonomi, *A Factious People: Politics and Society in Colonial New York* (New York: Columbia University Press, 1971), pp. 258–259.

[136] See especially Sister Joan de Lourdes Leonard, C.S.J., "Elections in Colonial Pennsylvania," *WMQ* (1954), 11: 385–401. See also Morgan, *Inventing the People* (1988), pp. 184–185; see Tully, *Forming American Politics* (1994), pp. 343–345; Benjamin H. Newcomb, *Political Partisanship in the American Middle Colonies, 1700–1776* (Baton Rouge: Louisiana State University Press, 1995). Elections in other colonies, especially in New England, were more reserved and orderly events. See for example Tully, *Forming American Politics* (1994), p. 346.

[137] Chilton Williamson, *American Suffrage* (Princeton, NJ: Princeton University Press, 1960), pp. 50–51. See Albert E. McKinley, *The Suffrage Franchise in the Thirteen English Colonies in America* (Boston: Ginn & Co., 1905), pp. 38–39.

apportionment schemes were notoriously unequal. In 1770, for example, only 46 of 147 New Hampshire towns were permitted to vote for members of the colonial assembly, but more than one-third of the colony's taxes were assessed to communities without representation.[138] Unlike eighteenth-century Great Britain, colonial demographic patterns were less concentrated and, therefore, urbanizing areas in the American colonies were notably less underrepresented than their British cohorts. As a consequence, representation of depopulated towns or of "rotten" boroughs was almost nonexistent in the colonial assemblies.

Unlike the eighteenth-century House of Commons, most colonial assemblies successfully resisted executive-branch corruption of their members' independence. Several factors account for this difference. Many colonial assemblies made executive influence over colonial legislators more difficult by prohibiting their members from holding executive-sponsored offices. The Virginia House of Burgesses, in addition, required every member appointed sheriff by the colony's royal governor to resign his seat and stand for reelection.[139] As earlier noted, most colonial governors never had the personal, patronage, or financial resources necessary to influence the outcomes of colonial elections or the behavior of assembly members after their election.[140] Most significantly, unlike the diminu-

---

[138] Jeremy Belknap, *The History of New-Hampshire* (1791), II: 488–490; and Jere R. Daniell, *Experiment in Republicanism: New Hampshire Politics and the American Revolution, 1741–1794* (Cambridge, MA: Harvard University Press, 1970), p. 78. See also Robert J. Dinkin, *Voting in Provincial America: A Study of Elections in the Thirteen Colonies, 1689–1776* (Westport, CT: Greenwood Press, 1977), pp. 48–49.

[139] Greene, *A Quest for Power* (1963), p. 187; and Dinkin, *Voting in Provincial America* (1977), pp. 53–54.

[140] The financial expenditures of candidates were never a significant a factor in most American colonial elections. Although little data presently exist on the costs of colonial campaigns, several factors mitigated against the influence of a candidate's financial resources. For example, the common British practice of purchasing an electoral district was never established in the colonies. The colonial norm was that candidates reside within the districts they represented, and as the number of seats in the colonial assemblies increased throughout the eighteenth century, the demand for seats was aligned, to some degree, with their supply and accessibility. The fact that the American political elite was comparatively less wealthy than Great Britain's ruling class was another important factor. Whatever the weight of these factors, competitive colonial elections were generally characterized by voter mobilization efforts. British elections, by contrast, often were decided by a candidate's personal wealth or financial resources. As Benjamin Franklin observed during the 1768 elections for the British House of Commons, "this whole venal nation is now at market, will be sold for about two millions, and might be bought ... by the very Devil himself." As quoted in Kammen, *A Rope of Sand* (1968), p. 165. For a description of campaign costs in colonial Rhode Island, see David S. Lovejoy, *Rhode Island Politics and the American Revolution* (Providence, RI: Brown University Press, 1958), pp. 24–25.

tion of the Crown's authority in the wake of the 1689 settlement, royal authority in the American colonies remained a formidable – and often arbitrary and unchecked – element of the colonial constitutions. As a result, the institutional, conceptual, and behavioral practices that were cultivated by eighteenth-century British leaders to ensure cooperation between Parliament and the Crown were never established in the American colonies. As historian Jack Greene observes, "the specter of unlimited prerogative" that once dominated both English and colonial politics "continued to haunt colonial legislators" throughout the eighteenth century.[141]

Several unique practices of representation also developed in the American colonies. Unlike their ancient English predecessors, the earliest American colonial assemblies were born of colonial demands for representative assemblies and the right to vote for their representatives.[142] Unlike their eighteenth-century British contemporaries who stopped petitioning Parliament for representation after 1694, American colonials never stopped demanding more or a fairer apportionment of representation in their colonial assemblies.[143] In 1695, for example, colonials in South Carolina petitioned for the authority to control the apportionment of representation in their assembly. At a convention convened shortly thereafter by the colony's governor, the freemen of the colony agreed that there should be a total of thirty representatives for the colony's three counties and "as many more as the commons in the assembly shall from time to time think convenient."[144] In 1716 and over the objections of the colony's proprietors, the South Carolina assembly also changed the basis

---

[141] Greene, "Political Mimesis," *American Historical Review* (1969), 75: 351.

[142] The earliest indicator of this distinctly American political tradition of insisting on popular consent and the opportunity to participate in the political process is illustrated in the records of the Virginia Company prior to the first American colonial assembly election in 1619. Nine days before the election, the Company's records reveal, "Upon some dispute of the Polonians resident in Virginia, it was now agreed (notwithstanding any former order to the contrary) that they shalbe enfranchized, and made as free as any inhabitants there whatsoever." Susan M. Kingsbury, ed., *The Records of the Virginia Company of London*, July 21, 1619 (Washington, DC: Government Printing Office, 1906), I: 251–252.

See also McKinley, *The Suffrage Franchise in the Thirteen English Colonies in America* (1905); and Morgan, *Inventing the People* (1988), pp. 43–46; "Petition Demanding the Removal of the Sheriff, Sept. 12, 1727," in E. B. O'Callaghan, *The Documentary History of the State of New York* (1850), pp. 292–294; Breckinbridge Lodge, *Genesis of the Constitution of the United States* (New York, The Macmillan Company, 1926), pp. 14–18.

[143] Kemp, *King and Commons* (1957), p. 13n.1.

[144] As quoted in William Schaper, *Sectionalism and Representation in South Carolina* (New York: Da Capo Press, 1968 [1901]), p. 341.

of the assembly's apportionment system from equal *county* representation to a more proportional, *parish*-unit system of representation.[145]

There were other colonial innovations as well. Virginia, for example, permitted fractional voting whereby a group of joint-tenants (none of whom individually owned the required minimum acreage necessary to vote) was allowed to unite and cast a single bloc vote in assembly elections.[146] Pennsylvania did not permit its voters to vote for less than the number of offices listed on the ballot, voiding those ballots with less than the prerequisite number of votes.[147] Connecticut and Rhode Island (for a time) held assembly elections twice a year.[148]

Still other colonies enacted measures to mitigate various forms of electoral corruption. Several colonies conducted elections by secret ballot and not viva voce as was customary in Great Britain.[149] South Carolina required glass ballot boxes and, with Rhode Island, imposed heavy penalties for election fraud.[150] Georgia determined that half of all "fines and forfeitures" for electoral illegalities be "for the use of the poor" within a parish.[151]

Voting rights and electoral districts, moreover, often were defined in the American colonies to strengthen or dilute the political weight of specific religious or ethnic minorities. In the early eighteenth century, for example, Catholics and Jews were prohibited by colonial laws from voting in almost every colony. Members of various other religious groups were also singled out and denied access to the polls.[152] Ethnicity was

---

[145] Schaper, *Sectionalism and Representation in South Carolina* (1965), p. 343.

   Additional examples of colonial demands for control of institutions of representation are too numerous to report here. Among the more notable examples, Pennsylvania's "Paxton Boys" demanded a fairer assembly representation of the colony's western counties in 1763. See Pole, *Political Representation* (1966), pp. 254–255; Schaper, *Sectionalism and Representation in South Carolina* (1968), p. 347; Maier, *From Resistance to Revolution* (1972), pp. 17, 195–197.

[146] McKinley, *The Suffrage Franchise in the Thirteen English Colonies in America* (1905), p. 40.

[147] Tully, *Forming American Politics* (1994), p. 320.

[148] Lovejoy, *Rhode Island Politics and the American Revolution* (1958), p. 53.

[149] Williamson, *American Suffrage from Property to Democracy* (1960), pp. 40–41; and Schaper, *Sectionalism and Representation in South Carolina* (1968), p. 340.

[150] Schaper, *Sectionalism and Representation in South Carolina* (1968), p. 348; Samuel G. Arnold, *History of the State of Rhode Island, 1700–1790* (New York, D. Appleton, 1859), II: 117, 120.

[151] *Colonial Records of the State of Georgia* (Atlanta, GA: The Franklin Printing and Publishing Co., 1904-), 28: 266–272.

[152] How often this practice occurred cannot be determined because only anecdotal accounts remain and many of the events were irregular and isolated to particular localities. For

another condition that prompted political discrimination. Few individuals of non-English ancestry were elected to public office and several were excluded after their election because of this condition.[153] In 1716, South Carolina restricted the suffrage to "every white man, and no other" – an action likely prompted by previous elections in which free nonwhites had voted. Other Southern colonies had permitted this practice before they, too, enacted similar color-based restrictions.[154] In addition, colonial governors and administrators occasionally advocated assembly reapportionment in order to secure political and popular support.[155]

The apportionment of assembly representation was often motivated by similar exclusionary interests. In South Carolina, for example, the small French Huguenot community of a sparsely populated area was heavily overrepresented in the assembly prior to 1716, in part because they supported the colony's proprietors. After the 1716 change to a system of parish representation, county residents were notably underrepresented.[156] The Quakers who dominated eighteenth-century Pennsylvania politics drew new county boundaries and apportioned county representation to reduce the potential political strength of the colony's growing Dutch, German, and Scotch-Irish populations.[157]

A final unique characteristic of colonial representation was conceptual. Unlike eighteenth-century British constitutional thought, the idea of a proportional division of representation was a familiar part of the colonial constitutional discourse although no objective standard of

---

example, according to historian Robert J. Dinkin, "thirty-eight Quakers were excluded by the sheriff in the Westchester County, New York, election of 1733 as part of the attempt to defeat Lewis Morris." Dinkin, *Voting in Provincial America* (1977), p. 225n.88.

[153] Dinkin, *Voting in Provincial America* (1977), pp. 52–53.

[154] McKinley, *The Suffrage Franchise in the Thirteen English Colonies in America* (1905), pp. 137–146; and Dinkin, *Voting in Provincial America* (1977), pp. 31–32. South Carolina enacted its suffrage restriction in 1716. A year earlier, in 1715, North Carolina enacted the first American colonial voting restrictions based on color or ethnic characteristics, explicitly excluding the "Negro[,] Mulatto or Indians." In 1734–35 North Carolina repealed this legal restriction, although there is little evidence to indicate that free nonwhites resumed voting. McKinley, p. 92.

[155] See "Henry Ellis to Board of Trade, March 11, 1757," *Colonial Records of the State of Georgia*, Vol. 28.

[156] Schaper, *Sectionalism and Representation in South Carolina* (1968), pp. 340–341. For denial of representation for Craven County in 1696, see Pole, *The Seventeenth Century* (1969), pp. 65–66. See also James Glen to Board of Trade, October 10, 1748, *Great Britain and the American Colonies*, Greene, ed. (1970), p. 266.

[157] Tully, *Forming American Politics* (1994), pp. 189–190, 285–286; Pole, *Political Representation* (1966), pp. 109–124.

proportional representation was established and uniformly applied in any of the colonial assemblies. According to the so-called "Fundamental Orders of 1639," for example, representation in Connecticut's "General Courte" was to be divided in "reasonable proportion to the number of freemen that are in the said townes"; this rule was superseded, however, by a new royal charter in 1662 that provided that the number of representatives allowed each town or city was "not to exceed two."[158] In Pennsylvania, the original charter of William Penn (1682) similarly called for a reapportionment of representation on the basis of population growth. This provision was superseded by subsequent constitutional changes and the 1701 charter, which provided for a system of equal county representation and two representatives for the City of Philadelphia.[159] The colony of Virginia offers a final example. In 1662 and 1705, this colony enacted two electoral statutes that provided for additional assembly representation for counties that established towns or ports with a minimum number of inhabitants; yet, like the other proposals, these statutory entitlements to representation were not implemented and the 1705 act was repealed after five years in accord with the queen's instructions.[160]

In addition to population-based divisions, the colonial discourse on the institutional design of representational relationships included some discussion of proportional divisions of representation based on taxation.[161] This idea seems to have been especially attractive to individuals from the colony of Pennsylvania. In 1752, according to historian J. R.

[158] Melbert B. Cary, *The Connecticut Constitution* (1900), p. 16.

[159] Pole, *Political Representation in England* (1966), p. 262; and Bishop, *History of Elections in the American Colonies* (1893), pp. 29–31. The concept of proportional representation was also raised in a discussion of an intercolonial union plan proposed by Charles Davenant. See "An Essay upon the Government of the English Plantations on the Continent of America" (1701), in *History of the Celebration of the One Hundred Anniversary of the Promulgation of the Constitution of the United States*, Hampton L. Carson, ed. (Philadelphia: J. B. Lippincott Company, 1889), II: 456. For Davenant's plan, see "On the Plantation Trade" (1698), in Greene, ed., *Great Britain and the American Colonies* (1970), pp. 143–153.

[160] McKinley, *The Suffrage in the Thirteen English Colonies in America* (1905), pp. 26, 43.

There were similar, although slightly more successful, experiences in New Jersey and Georgia. See Stanley H. Friedelbaum, "Apportionment Legislation in New Jersey," *Proceedings of the New Jersey Historical Society* (October 1952), 70: 263–264, 274; Kenneth Coleman, *The American Revolution in Georgia, 1763–1789* (1958), p. 34; Bishop, *History of Elections in the American Colonies* (1893), p. 44.

[161] See, for example [Capt. Samuel Mulford], "A Memorial of Several Aggrievances and Oppressions of His Majesty's Subjects in the Colony of New-York" [1716–1717], in E. B. O'Callaghan, *The Documentary History of the State of New York* (Albany, NY: Weed, Parsons & Co., 1850), pp. 220–225.

Pole, residents of Philadelphia demanded a more equitable apportionment of assembly representation "on the ground that the City together with the old eastern counties, being much the richest, paid by far the heaviest weight of taxes, giving them a right to a proportionately greater weight of representation."[162]

Two years later, in his 1754 proposal for a new intercolonial government, Pennsylvanian Benjamin Franklin also linked the apportionment of representation with taxation. Franklin's "Albany Plan of Union" proposed a proportional division of representation according to the amount of annual taxes each colony paid to an intercolonial treasury. The Plan provided that "the number to be chosen by any one province" was not to be "more than seven nor less than two members." "After the first three years" of the new government "when the proportion of money arising out of each colony to the general treasury" was known, "the number of members to be chosen for each colony" was to be regulated "from time to time" in accord with this proportion. Until this time, Franklin's Plan provided for a temporary apportionment that carefully balanced representation along regional lines.[163]

Like population-based divisions of representation, tax-based apportionment proposals were unsuccessful. Although most of the latter proposals originated in Pennsylvania, the colony never reapportioned or redesigned its equal-county apportionment rule prior to the American Revolution. Moreover, the proportional division proposed in the Albany Plan (see Table 2.1) did not receive the endorsement of the Crown or of the colonial assemblies.[164]

Although no colony ever had a wholly proportional system of apportionment, eight colonial assemblies adopted rules of apportionment that included limited forms of proportional representation. Of these, most gave their largest towns more representation than the standard number assigned to a typical town. Several colonies also linked representation directly to population. In 1715, for example, a North Carolina law

---

[162] Pole, *Political Representation* (1966), pp. 263–264; C. H. Lincoln, "Representation in the Pennsylvania Assembly Prior to the Revolution," *Pennsylvania Magazine of History and Biography* (1899), 23: 33.

[163] *PBF*, 5: 405–407. See also Donald S. Lutz, "The Articles of Confederation as the Background to the Federal Republic," *Publius* (1990), 20: 60.

[164] For a summary of royal and colonial objections to the Albany Plan, see Harry M. Ward, *"Unite or Die": Intercolony Relations, 1690–1763* (Port Washington, NY: Kennikat Press, 1971), pp. 15–18. Rhode Island Governor Stephen Hopkins objected to the Plan on the grounds that the proposed system of proportional representation would leave the smaller states underrepresented.

TABLE 2.1. *Colonial Apportionment in Albany Plan "Grand Council"*

Colony	No. of Representatives	No. by Region (%)	
		New England:	16 (33%)
Massachusetts-Bay	7		
Connecticut	5		
New Hampshire	2		
Rhode Island	2		
		Middle:	17 (36%)
Pennsylvania	6		
New-York	4		
Maryland	4		
New-Jerseys	3		
		Southern:	15 (31%)
Virginia	7		
North-Carolina	4		
South-Carolina	4		
	48		

provided the right to elect one representative to every town with a population of at least sixty families, and several towns subsequently secured representation this way.[165] Ironically, given the nonproportional system of representation in the British House of Commons, the Board of Trade ended an eight-year controversy over the apportionment of assembly representation by recommending that the North Carolina governor "be instructed as the Province grows more people to erect such and so many Towns and Counties in the Southern District with the privilege of sending such a number of Representatives to the Assembly as that each different district or division [has] a reasonable and just proportion."[166]

This litany of eighteenth-century anecdotes about colonial institutions of representation should not be overvalued. None of the colonies ever established a formal process for regularly reapportioning their assemblies.[167] As a consequence, as colonial population grew and moved into

[165] McKinley, *The Suffrage Franchise in the Thirteen English Colonies in America* (1905), pp. 93, 114–115. See also Robert E. Brown, "Restriction of Representation in Colonial Massachusetts," *MVHR* (1953), 40: 463–476.

[166] "Representation of the Lords of Trade to the King," 14 March 1754, *Colonial Records of North Carolina*, 5: 92.

[167] Several New England colonial assemblies, it should be noted, regularly divided larger towns and granted each new town assembly representation. This practice was not formally required but it had the effect of reducing the problems of malapportionment

the western frontier and into larger towns, a colony's initial apportionment scheme typically became less proportional over time. Moreover,
even at mid-century, many colonials simply did not equate the apportionment of assembly representation with standards like population
or the amount of taxes paid. Petitions to the Pennsylvania Assembly,
for example, typically requested additional representatives or "an equal
Number" of representatives as enjoyed by the three original and consistently overrepresented eastern counties on the basis of "the acknowledged Principles of Justice and Equity." Rarely, however, did the
rationales that accompanied such requests advocate the adoption of a
uniform standard of proportional representation although such standards would promise many petitioners both immediate and longer-term
increases in political representation.[168]

Why there was little colonial support for a uniform standard of
proportional representation prior to the American Revolution is open to
conjecture. The fact that there were no British legal precedents supportive of such a standard likely explains a great deal. The lack of accurate
or publicly accessible population records was another important factor,
although records of taxes paid by each county or town were readily available in many colonies. More realistically, those who petitioned for assembly representation probably calculated that incremental changes were
far more likely to succeed than more radical and unpredictable constitutional changes in the existing rules of representation. A second and
equally plausible explanation is that eighteenth-century colonials simply
did not have a consistent or fully developed understanding of political
fairness grounded in the concept of proportionality.[169]

---

caused by rapid or irregular population growth. Patrick T. Conley, "Rhode Island
   Constitutional Development, 1636–1775: A Survey," *Rhode Island History* (1968), 27:
   93; and George H. Evans, "The Basis of Representation in New Hampshire," in *Manual
   of the State of New Hampshire* (1912), p. 260.
[168] See, for example, Lincoln, "Representation in the Pennsylvania Assembly Prior to the
   Revolution," *Pennsylvania Magazine of History and Biography* (1899), 23: 28n.1;
   Lawrence F. London, "The Representation Controversy in Colonial North Carolina,"
   North Carolina Historical Review (1934), 11: 260.
[169] For example, as historian Robert A. Becker observes in his study of the development
   of colonial taxation: "Few complained publicly about the regressive nature of the poll
   taxes or asked how such taxes could be squared with the ability-to-pay principle that
   in theory underlay New England's tax laws." Robert A. Becker, *Revolution, Reform,
   and the Politics of American Taxation* (Baton Rouge: Louisiana State University Press,
   1980), p. 40. See, however, protests against a disproportional tax assessment by the
   Rhode Island assembly: *Records of the Colony of Rhode Island*, Bartlett, ed., Nov.
   1756, V: 547–555.

American and British Concepts of Representation

Although eighteenth-century historical evidence of colonial institutions and conceptualizations of representation is fragmentary and anecdotal, the colonial concept of representation prior to the escalation of British-colonial tensions can be defined and measured (at least, at a general level) in terms of three characteristic conditions: (1) localism; (2) responsive elitism; and (3) dynamic institutionalism. The first term, localism, describes the close relationship that existed between colonial representatives and the specific localities they represented. Like members of the British House of Commons, most colonial representatives were elected from districts circumscribed by widely recognizable territorial boundaries. Unlike their British cohorts, however, eighteenth-century colonial representatives still perceived their legislative role and responsibilities as directed primarily by local needs and concerns. In New Hampshire, for example, assembly members were so closely attuned to local concerns that they "never find they have anything to do in the House [of Representatives] when there is nothing on the tapis in which the town or borough which chose them is not immediately concerned."[170] Even in two of the most oligarchical colonial assemblies (New York and Pennsylvania), historian Alan Tully observes, "[t]he most successful provincial politicians were well grounded in their local communities and felt many of the same concerns that touched their neighbors."[171]

Many factors supported differences in British and colonial conceptualizations of representation. Colonial and British social practices and norms no doubt yielded different sensitivities to and experiences with representative relationships.[172] One measurable difference was

[170] *New Hampshire Gazette*, November 3, 1758; as quoted in Jere R. Daniell, *Experiment in Republicanism* (Cambridge, MA: Harvard University Press, 1970), p. 22.

[171] Tully, *Forming American Politics* (1994), p. 354. Although localism predominated, in several colonies a dual concept of representation seems to have developed by the middle part of the eighteenth century. In addition to local interests, appeals were made with respect to colonywide interests. See, for example, the account of the Virginia assembly debate on "Whether a Representative was obliged to follow the directions of his Constituents against his own Reason and Conscience or to be Governed by his Conscience" in *Diary of Landon Carter*, Jack Greene, ed. (Richmond: Virginia Historical Society, 1965), II: 16–17.

[172] Historian John A. Schutz, for example, observed multiple centers of representation within revolutionary Massachusetts. In addition to the colonial assembly, the experiences of representation were woven into the organizational structures of and societal expectations for local councils, judges, militias, and various religious communities. See Schutz, "Representation, Taxation, and Tyranny in Revolutionary Massachusetts," *Pacific Historical Review* (1974) XLIII(2): 151–170.

the scale of representative-constituent relationships in the American colonies and Great Britain. As illustrated in Figure 2.1, the average number of persons per colonial assembly member after 1770 was approximately 2,800. In Great Britain, this ratio was one Member of Parliament for every 14,337 persons. By 1770, moreover, nine of the thirteen original American colonial assemblies had ratios of assembly members to adult white males that were less than 1:500.[173] Rhode Island's ratio was 1:167, prompting one observer to conclude that this colony's government was a "downright democracy" that was "entirely controlled by the populace."[174]

A second measurement of colonial representation will be described under the term "responsive elitism."[175] This term captures the fact that American colonial assemblies were considerably more open to expressions of popular consent and popular influence than was Parliament. The assemblies, to be sure, were never democratic in any modern sense because they typically were dominated by small groups of individuals who tended to be the most politically ambitious members of the highest social and economic classes within each colony. In the New York assembly, for example, more than 85 percent of its members were drawn from the colony's wealthiest class. Like British society, the colonial population generally seemed willing to defer to or be indifferent toward the elitist composition of their assemblies.[176]

In many colonies, political elites controlled the nomination and election of assembly candidates. As early as the 1720s, for example, groups like the "Boston Caucus" in Massachusetts exerted significant influence

[173] Greene, "Legislative Turnover in British America, 1696 to 1775," *WMQ* (1981), 38: 461.

[174] As quoted in Conley, *Democracy in Decline* (1977), p. 53.

[175] For analysis of the seventeenth-century origins of this "responsive elite" model, see John C. Rainbolt, "The Alteration in the Relationship between Leadership and Constituents in Virginia, 1660 to 1720," *WMQ* (1970), 27: 411–434; and David Jordan, *Foundations of Representative Government in Maryland, 1632–1715* (Cambridge, UK: Cambridge University Press, 1987).

[176] Dinkin, *Voting in Provincial America* (1977), p. 60. See also Jackson Turner Main, "Government by the People: The American Revolution and the Democratization of the Legislatures," *WMQ* (1966), 23(3): 391–407; Robert Zemsky, "Power, Influence, and Status: Leadership Patterns in the Massachusetts Assembly, 1740–1755," and Michael G. Kammen, "Quantification and the Study of Political Elites in Colonial America: A Comment," in *Representative Institutions in Theory and Practice* (Brussels: International Commission for the History of Representative and Parliamentary Institutions, 1970), pp. 155–178, 195–206; Thomas L. Purvis, "High-Born, Long-Recorded Families: Social Origins of New Jersey Assemblymen, 1703–1776, *WMQ* (1980) 37(4): 592–615.

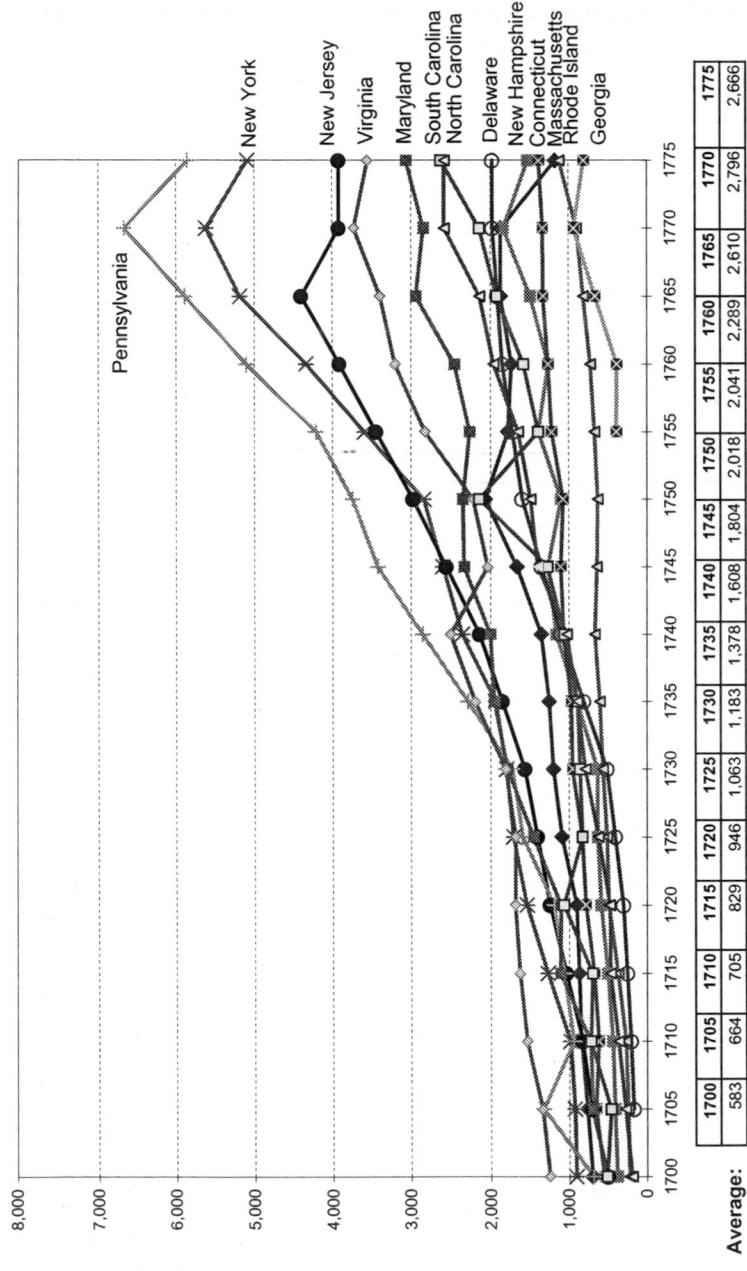

	1700	1705	1710	1715	1720	1725	1730	1735	1740	1745	1750	1755	1760	1765	1770	1775
Average:	583	664	705	829	946	1,063	1,183	1,378	1,608	1,804	2,018	2,041	2,289	2,610	2,796	2,666

FIGURE 2.1. Persons per Colonial Assembly Member: Colony Averages, 1700–1775

in colonial elections.[177] Political elites acted as gatekeepers in other colonial assemblies. In Pennsylvania, it was customary for unofficial election clubs or "a certain Company of leading Men to nominate Persons, and settle the Ticket, for Assemblymen" and other political offices "without ever permitting the affirmative or negative Voice of . . . a Mechanic to interfere."[178] Despite their elitism, colonial assembly members generally were more closely associated with and responsive to a wider range of interests outside of government than were their eighteenth-century cohorts in the British House of Commons.

Why colonial political elites grew more responsive as Parliament became increasingly less so can be explained, in part, by the fact that colonial cultural conditions and political norms were not deeply rooted in rigid social and economic distinctions. Colonials therefore were less deferential to political leaders than eighteenth-century British society was to their leaders. As one New York assemblyman bluntly acknowledged in 1734: positions in the colony's assembly were "but like a fine laced Livery coat of which the vain Lacquey may be stript at the pleasure of his proud Master [the electorate] & may be kikt out of Doors naked."[179] Landon Carter of Virginia was more succinct in his assessment of this phenomenon: Even if a gentleman "kiss[ed] the arses of the people and very servilely accommodated himself to others," he might "shamefully [be] turned out" at the next election.[180]

---

[177] G. B. Warden, "The Caucus and Democracy in Colonial Boston," *New England Quarterly* (1970), 43: 19–45; and Alan and Katherine Day, "Another Look at the Boston 'Caucus'," *Journal of American Studies* (1971), 5: 19–42.

[178] *Pennsylvania Gazette*, 27 Sept. 1770; as quoted in Leonard, "Elections in Colonial Pennsylvania, *WMQ* (1954), 11: 389. See also Gary Nash, "The Transformation of Urban Politics, 1700–1765," *JAH* (1973), 60: 605–632; Simeon E. Baldwin, "The Early History of the Ballot in Connecticut," *American History Association Papers* (1890), 4: 407–422.

In addition to "mechanics" and other tradesmen, German colonials in Pennsylvania apparently were the primary group disadvantaged by this process of nomination. Prior to 1764, few German colonials won election to the Pennsylvania assembly, although Germans constituted at least one-third of the colony's population. The pattern was repeated in other colonies. When a German-born candidate won election to New Jersey's assembly in 1740, the assembly expelled him because his naturalization was considered too recent. See Dinkin, *Voting in Provincial America* (1977), p. 52.

[179] As quoted in Bonomi, *A Factious People: Politics and Society in Colonial New York* (1971), p. 10n.

[180] *The Diary of Landon Carter*, April 1, 1776, Greene, ed., II: 1009. For several striking indicators of the limits of popular deference to political elites in Massachusetts, see Stephen E. Patterson, *Political Parties in Revolutionary Massachusetts* (Madison, WI: University of Wisconsin Press, 1973), pp. 28–29. See also James Iredell, "The Principles of an American Whig" (1775), *Life and Correspondence of James Iredell*, Griffith J. Mcree, ed. (New York: Appleton, 1857–1858), I: 247.

In addition to the possibility of electoral defeat, colonial leaders (including the many who never attempted to serve multiple terms) also recognized that American colonials were not bashful about participating in public demonstrations or, and not uncommonly, other more riotous forms of protest.[181] The emergence of active local colonial presses and pamphleteers, along with colonial expectations for governmental accountability, ensured that what legislators did during their terms would be made public. By mid-century roll-call votes were regularly published for public consumption in Maryland, New Jersey, and New York.[182]

Differences in voting rights and practices also distinguished British and colonial conceptualizations of representation. In Great Britain, the electorate consisted of approximately "a quarter or perhaps even a third of the adult males."[183] According to one estimate, however, "40 percent of the English boroughs had less than 100 voters . . . and only one-eighth had 1,000 or more."[184] The colonial electorate, by contrast, is estimated to have consisted of between 50 and 75 percent of the adult white, male population,[185] although historical evidence suggests the actual range was higher because most legal restrictions against voting – except those against free Negroes and Catholics – were not strictly enforced in the American colonies.[186] Because, moreover, colonial assemblies generally did not permit their governors to control voting qualifications as the Crown had for English boroughs, suffrage qualifications in each colony were often fixed by statute, and therefore more uniform and less arbitrarily restrictive than in Great Britain. As a consequence, the colonial electorate – at least, in eighteenth-century terms – was more fully repre-

---

[181] See, for example, Pauline Maier, "Population Uprisings and Civil Authority in Eighteenth-Century America, *WMQ* (1970), 27: 3–35; Edward Countryman, "The Problem of the Early American Crowd," *Journal of American Studies* (1973), 7: 77–90.

[182] John M. Murrin, "Political Development," in Jack P. Greene and J. R. Pole, eds., *Colonial British America* (Baltimore: Johns Hopkins University Press, 1984), pp. 408–456, 443.

[183] Morgan, *Inventing the People* (1988), p. 175.

[184] Williamson, *American Suffrage* (1960), p. 22.

[185] Williamson, *American Suffrage* (1960), pp. 12–16, 38. In a recent study of political development in the middle colonies Benjamin H. Newcomb suggests an "election day turnout of on average from 40 to 70 percent of the qualified voters." Newcomb, *Political Partisanship in the American Middle Colonies* (1995), p. 205.

[186] Dinkin, *Voting in Provincial America* (1977), pp. 46–47; Greene, *The Quest for Power* (1963), p. 186; Pole, "Suffrage and Representation in Massachusetts," *WMQ* (1957), 14: 560–592. In most colonies there were few efforts to reduce the electorate. See Williamson, *American Suffrage* (1960), p. 37; Pole, "Historians and the Problem of Early American Democracy," *AHR* (1962), 67: 339–351.

sentative of the colonial people than the British electorate ever was of the British people.[187]

In addition, the dynamics of colonial social and economic conditions in the eighteenth century made colonial voting qualifications increasingly less restrictive. Whereas the size of the British electorate remained relatively stable, a higher percentage of American colonials likely were allowed to vote during the second half of the eighteenth century than at the turn of the century. With a higher percentage of colonials typically participating in assembly elections than in parliamentary elections, the size of winning electoral coalitions in assembly elections increasingly began to extend beyond most candidates' personal constituencies.[188] The uncertainty of election thus bound assembly members to the colonial electorate in ways that clearly did not exist for many eighteenth-century members of Parliament. To further accentuate this electoral connection between assembly members and the colonial electorate, colonial elections typically occurred more often than parliamentary elections, especially after Parliament enacted the Septennial Act in 1716. Throughout the eighteenth century annual elections were customary in many colonies; in South Carolina and New Hampshire, assembly elections were triennial.[189]

American colonials – including nonvoters – also influenced representatives by exercising their customary right to petition those within government. Countless individuals sent private petitions to Parliament, but political petitions were legally prohibited in Great Britain for much of the eighteenth century.[190] More important, historian Edmund S. Morgan notes, British petitioners were considered "rivals of representatives" who "claim[ed] to speak the voice of the people but [who were] unrestricted by the qualifications placed on voting and uninhibited by the

---

[187] In Maryland, the original charter of Annapolis granted by the governor restricted the suffrage to the mayor, recorder, alderman, and common councilmen. The colonial assembly objected to this restriction and refused to admit the first two assemblymen elected from the city in 1708. The assembly subsequently extended the suffrage to all freeholders, to inhabitants worth 20 pounds, and to experienced tradesmen who resided within the city. McKinley, *The Suffrage Franchise in the Thirteen English Colonies in America* (1905), p. 73.

[188] See Newcomb, *Political Partisanship* (1995), pp. 99–100.

[189] Tully, *Forming American Politics* (1994), p. 88; Allan Nevins, *The American States During and After the Revolution, 1775–1789* (New York, The Macmillan Company, 1924), pp. 1–14; Greene, *Quest for Power* (1963), p. 199; and Evans, "The Basis of Representation in New Hampshire Previous to the Adoption of the Constitution of 1784," *Manual of the Constitution of the State of New Hampshire* (1912), p. 261.

[190] Peter Fraser, "Public Petitioning and Parliament before 1832," *History* (1961), 46: 201.

responsibilities of being part of the government."[191] Colonial assemblies, by contrast, "seem to have been less jealous than their British counterparts of the exclusive right to speak for the people" and "more willing to act on petitioners' requests in enacting legislation."[192] Historian Alan Tully additionally notes that although most petitions to the Pennsylvania assembly were from "people who had definite property rights to protect, social pretensions to uphold, or strong economic interests to further," there were also "proposals or requests from the lower levels of society." Whatever the social or geographic origin of a petitioner, "the petitioning procedure formed a broad, readily available method of political communications between rulers and ruled" that the colonial representatives responded to in a "relatively uniform" manner.[193]

Another form of popular influence on government was the practice of instructing legislative representatives. Although instructions to members of Parliament were not uncommon, they typically were engineered by national, not local, political leaders for purely rhetorical, not policy, ends.[194] By mid-century British instructions were rarely as direct or demanding as the instructions sent by American colonials to their assembly representatives.[195]

The third characteristic condition of colonial representation (identified as dynamic institutionism) was evident in the variability and mutability of colonial institutions, especially those related to the apportionment of assembly representation. As for the British House of Commons, the county and town were the units traditionally used to apportion representation in colonial assemblies. Apportionment rules, however, varied widely among the American colonies. In the New England colonies, towns usually received the right to send at least two

[191] Morgan, *Inventing the People* (1988), p. 226. Members of the House of Commons, according to Morgan, demonstrated their uneasiness with petitions "not only in such fits of hostility as their imprisonment of the Kentish petitioners but in the rule they apparently adopted around 1693 of refusing to hear any petitions having to do with current taxation."

[192] Morgan, *Inventing the People* (1988), p. 229. See also Purvis, *Proprietors, Patronage, and Paper Money: Legislative Politics in New Jersey, 1703–1776* (1986), pp. 182–185.

[193] Tully, "Constituent-Representative Relationships in Early America," *Canadian Journal of History* (1976), 11: 144, 145, 154. See also Raymond C. Bailey, *Popular Influence upon Public Policy: Petitioning in Eighteenth-Century Virginia* (Westport, CT: Greenwood Press, 1979).

[194] Reid, *Concept of Representation* (1989), p. 103.

[195] For a colonial example, see instructions of residents of Orange County, North Carolina, in McKinley, *The Suffrage Franchise in the Thirteen English Colonies* (1905), p. 113.

assembly representatives, with the larger towns often assigned additional representatives.[196] In the southern colonies, representation was customarily apportioned among counties, although grants of representation were made to individual towns as well. Within geographic regions, the rules of apportionment also varied. In southern colonies, for example, the Virginia House of Burgesses assigned two representatives to each county, and one burgess each to three towns and the College of William and Mary. In the Maryland General Assembly, by contrast, every county was assigned four delegates and several towns were assigned two assembly delegates each.[197]   *[handwritten: Inventd size 1700-1775]*

Colonial institutions of representation were dynamic in other ways. Whereas, for example, the size of the British House of Commons had been fixed since 1707 and never fully reapportioned (save the long-lost reapportionment of the Commonwealth period), many colonial assemblies doubled their size between 1700 and 1775 and several assemblies also managed to transfer the right of representation from older electoral districts to newer ones. The latter accomplishment was rare and not typically motivated by idealistic commitment to democracy or political equality. In 1716, for example, the South Carolina assembly reduced the number of representatives apportioned to Charles Town in order to undermine the influence of two unpopular governmental officials. The town of St. Mary's, Maryland, lost its assembly representation in 1708 as part of a plan to negate the influence of its Catholic residents.[198]

Legal and demographic conditions in the American colonies promoted this institutional dynamism. In all but the newest royal colony of Georgia, the rule for assigning assembly representation was defined in

---

[196] See 1719 Rhode Island charter; 1699 Massachusetts charter. In addition to town representation, according to historian Elmer C. Griffith, the Massachusetts legislature in 1765 incorporated a territorial area under the name of Paxton and granted it "liberty from time to time to join with the town of Leicester and the district of Spencer in the choice of a representative or representatives." Griffith, *The Rise and Development of the Gerrymander* (New York, Arno Press, 1924, [1907]), p. 24.

[197] See, for example, *The Laws of the Province of Maryland*, John D. Cushing, ed. (Wilmington, DE: Michael Glazier, Inc., 1978), p. 187; *The Earliest Printed Laws of Delaware, 1704–1741*, John D. Cushing, ed. (Wilmington, DE: Michael Glazier, Inc., 1978), pp. 4–5; Dickerson, *American Colonial Government* (1912), pp. 254–255.

[198] Pole, *The Seventeenth Century* (1969), p. 65. See also Schaper, *Sectionalism and Representation in South Carolina* (1968), pp. 345, 347; McKinley, *The Suffrage Franchise* (1905), p. 72; Friedelbaum, "Apportionment Legislation in New Jersey," *Proceedings of the New Jersey Historical Society* (1952), 70: 264, 272–274.

the colony's charter or by statute. Thus, as the colonial population grew and settled in newer areas, the apportionment rules fostered colonial expectations for representation, expectations fulfilled in almost every colony by increasing the size of the assembly's membership. As reflected in Figure 2.2, the average size of the thirteen colonial assemblies nearly doubled between 1700 and 1775 – with an average percentage decennial rate increase of fourteen percent. By 1775 the average American colonial assembly size was almost sixty-nine members.

The colonial practice of continuously extending assembly representation had several notable consequences. For one, it served as a mechanism for connecting newer western communities into colonial politics. Given legislative-executive antagonisms and the fact that the expansion of the assemblies was always incremental, additional representatives generally strengthened the assemblies. Although the continuous extension of representation reattuned the composition of the assemblies to the dynamic conditions of eighteenth-century colonial society, the popular legitimacy of these assemblies was continuously challenged by rapid colonial population growth and by the fact that new assembly representation was often not apportioned equitably between older, slow-growth areas and new, high-growth areas. The legitimacy of the colonial assemblies was not maintained by any measurable increase in colonial deference for their assembly representatives.[199] Instead, mid-eighteenth century colonial politics was characterized by increases in popular demands on government that were met by increases in the responsiveness of colonial political elites. Thus, where colonial assembly sizes increased, colonial assemblies gained greater popular legitimacy and became increasingly more likely to assert their political independence from the Crown's colonial agents. Where colonial assembly sizes remained small, colonial political elites maintained their popular legitimacy by becoming noticeably more responsive to popular demands.[200]

From the British perspective, increases in the size of the colonial assemblies had long been acknowledged as undermining the Crown's

---

[199] See, for example, Gary B. Nash, "The Transformation of Urban Politics, 1700–1765," *JAH* (1973), 60: 605–632.

[200] See Olson, "Eighteenth-Century Colonial Legislature and Their Constituents," *JAH* (1992), 79: 543–567. For more specific studies of colonies with small, stable assembly sizes, see Purvis, *Proprietors, Patronage, and Paper Money* (1986); Tully, "Constituent-Representative Relationship in Early America," *Canadian Journal of History* (1976), 11: 139–154; Bailey, *Popular Influence upon Public Policy* (1979).

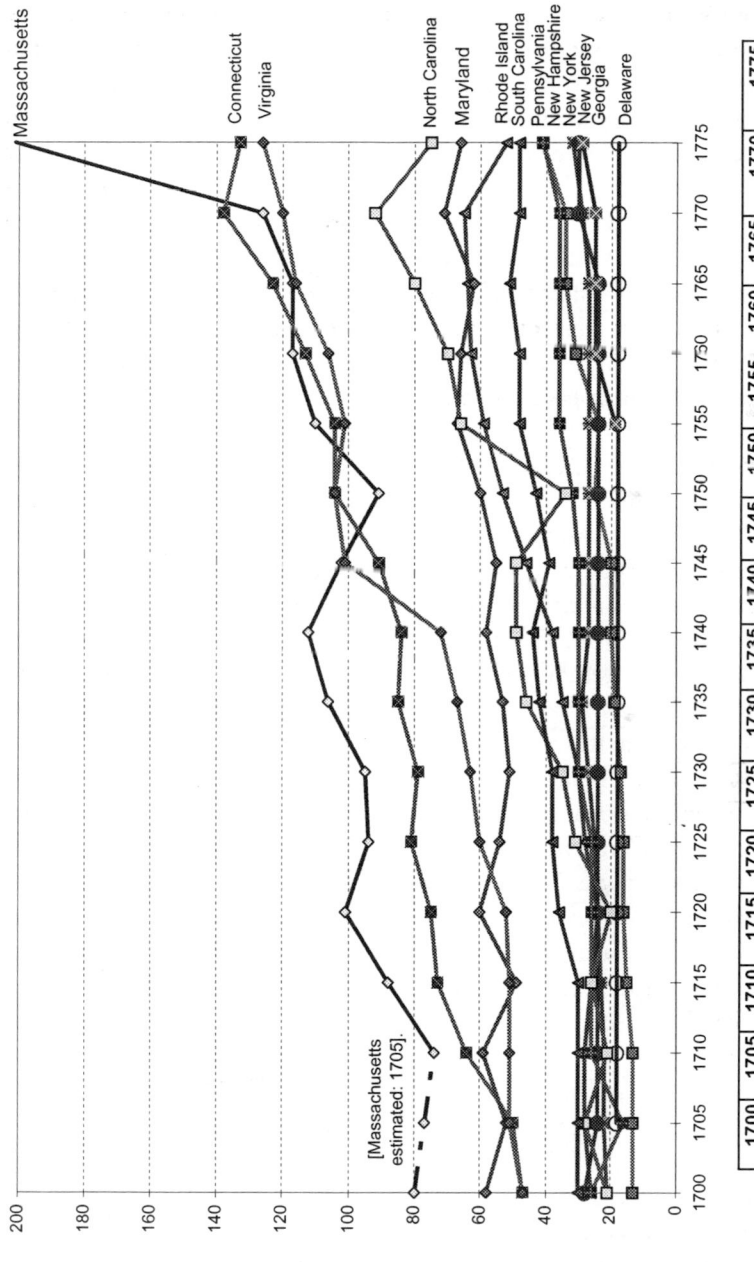

FIGURE 2.2. Colonial Assembly Sizes, 1700–1775

	1700	1705	1710	1715	1720	1725	1730	1735	1740	1745	1750	1755	1760	1765	1770	1775
Average:	36.1	34.1	35.8	37.4	39.7	41.3	42.3	46.2	48.0	50.2	51.3	54.1	57.2	59.8	64.0	68.6

[Massachusetts estimated: 1705].

Massachusetts
Connecticut
Virginia
North Carolina
Maryland
Rhode Island
South Carolina
Pennsylvania
New Hampshire
New York
New Jersey
Georgia
Delaware

authority in the colonies. Colonial legislators, like the seventeenth-century House of Commons, understood this effect. From as far back as the 1660s, for example, the Maryland assembly repeatedly attempted to secure the authority to increase the number of representatives apportioned to each of the colony's counties. The colony's proprietor consistently rejected these attempts, informing the assembly after one such attempt in 1682: "I cannot Deeme it Honourable Nor safe to Lodge it in the Freemen as you have desired, for it would be as reasonable for me to give away my Power of Calling and Dissolving of Assemblies, as to give that of Choosing the Number of Delegates."[201] In the eighteenth century, most colonial assemblies eventually secured statutory authority over the size and apportionment of their membership. The resulting increases in assembly size throughout the eighteenth century paralleled the institutional development of the colonial assemblies and the decline of British authority within the colonies. In an attempt to forestall this process by fixing the sizes of the assemblies, in 1768 the Crown instructed colonial governors to reject all changes in the membership of the colonial assemblies.[202]

To summarize, British and colonial conceptualizations of representation developed in notably different directions in the eighteenth century. Representative legislatures were dominated by political elites in both Great Britain and the American colonies, but British political actors increasingly conceptualized the duties of their representatives as focused wholly on the national interest, whereas the colonial conceptualization included a more traditional and more fragmented focus on local *and* colony-wide interests. The colonial conceptualization was further distinguished from its British counterpart by the tendency of the colonial assemblies in the second half of the eighteenth century to respond to the demands of a relatively wide cross section of the colonial population. Finally, whereas British institutions of representation were static throughout the eighteenth century, colonial institutions were dynamic.

---

[201] Quoted in Carl N. Everstine, *The General Assembly of Maryland, 1634–1776* (Charlottesville, VA: Michie Co., 1980), p. 140. See also Robert E. Brown, "Restriction of Representation in Colonial Massachusetts," *MVHR* (1953), 40: 467.

[202] According to historian Jack Greene, Henry Laurens of South Carolina considered the restriction "tyrannical" and declared it would "make the present Generation so watchful and attentive to their true Interests, as will defeat the Ends, which the Enemies of America have in View." Greene, *Quest for Power* (1963), p. 383.

CONCLUSION

The deep structure of the relationship between Great Britain and the American colonies was reshaped over the eighteenth century by the continuous development of various economic, demographic, institutional, and ideological conditions. The preceding reconstruction of these developmental trajectories advances this study's interests in several noteworthy ways. Foremost, this reconstruction provides a basis for assessing British and American political expectations that is independent of the subsequent constitutional crisis in their relationship. The benefits of this a priori description will be revealed more fully in Chapter 3's analysis of the American Revolution and in Chapter 10's comparative analysis of this study's three cases.

More immediately, the preceding reconstruction reveals few, if any, absolute changes in the relationship between Great Britain and the American colonies during the first three-quarters of the eighteenth century. Although British and American economies experienced dramatic expansion during this period, Great Britain in the 1770s retained its traditional economic dominance over the American colonies in terms of size and balance of trade. Great Britain's population also continued to exceed the total population of the American colonies, and the basic division and structure of political institutions remained relatively constant for the British, imperial, and colonial constitutions. Finally, although less clearly so than for the other conditions, British and American ideological conditions (especially the conceptualization of representation) continued to serve similar legitimating functions for Parliament and the colonial assemblies.

Although the preceding reconstruction reveals no absolute basis for identifying a cause of the subsequent constitutional crisis and apportionment rule change, it does reveal several relative changes in the relationship between Great Britain and the American colonies that likely aided the divergence of British and American political expectations by 1774. These changes have been described in detail within this chapter. In brief, the most significant relative changes were the faster rate of colonial economic growth, the remarkable growth rate and westward movement of the American colonial population, the parallel absorption of the Crown's governing authority by Parliament and the American colonial assemblies, and the increasingly divergent British and American colonial conceptualizations of representation. Alone, each one of these

rate of ec. growth
splitting of power
theories on rep.

developmental dynamics casts little light on British-colonial relations after 1774. Taken together, however, they suggest that the relationship was pregnant with political expectations for some form of constitutional transformation. What sort of transformation and who would act as its constitutional midwives are revealed in the story of the American Revolution told in Chapter 3.

3

Our Emperors Have No Clothes: The Macro-Micro Synthesis and the American Revolution

Like most relationships, the constitutional union between Great Britain and the American colonies was never a static relationship. Rather, as described in Chapter 2, over the course of the eighteenth century various economic, demographic, institutional, and ideological developments continuously redefined their relationship. Previous historical accounts typically agree that, despite these dynamic conditions, the constitutional union between Great Britain and the American colonies was generally stable and mutually beneficial as late as the early 1770s. Three questions therefore challenge every account of the American Revolution. First, why did British interests by 1774 commit to a reconfiguration of the terms of this union? Second, why were American interests generally unwilling to accept a reconfiguration? And third, why did this long-standing and valued relationship ultimately end in the civil war commonly known as the American Revolution?

The structural foundations of this constitutional union were not wholly immaterial to the sequence of decisions by which Great Britain and the American colonies committed themselves to civil war. For in addition to forming the context within which these historic decisions were made, this structure projected a future paradoxically constituted by relative American and absolute British gains. These crosscutting dynamics thus supported different (and often conflicting) perceptions of and expectations for the relationship between Great Britain and the American colonies. As a result, explanation of the subsequent constitutional crisis must extend beyond the structural context to the political actors and the decisional sequences that directly effected the final rupture of the British-colonial order.

An account of the microlevel (or actor-centered) conditions that produced this constitutional breakdown is the primary purpose of this chapter. Such an account cannot completely ignore the structural or macrolevel conditions described in Chapter 2. These conditions, however complex and contradictory when represented as a discrete totality, reflect the immediate context (or status quo) of British-colonial relations in the mid-1770s. For this reason, synthesis of these two types of conditions – the macro with the micro – is a secondary but necessary purpose that must be served by this chapter. To make the mechanics of this macro-micro merger as transparent as possible, Part I of this chapter identifies the general problems raised by the proposed synthesis and the particular methodological solutions employed to complete the chapter's dual purpose.

In Part II, the chapter approaches the American Revolution by first defining the five conceptualizations of the British-colonial constitutional order that framed the discourse and horizons of those who became engaged in this historic moment of constitutional failure. Reconstruction of the histories of these conceptualizations from the seventeenth century until the 1770s clearly illustrates that the relationship between Great Britain and the American colonies was never explicitly settled and that it was contested intermittently as far back as the Commonwealth era. In fact, until the mid-1770s, political opinions and preferences were neither fixed nor uniform on either side of the Atlantic.

Part III completes this new account of the American Revolution by embedding the five described constitutional conceptualizations within two game-theoretic models. The first model portrays British and American actors in terms of their decisions to adopt cooperative or non-cooperative strategies; the second model represents these actors' decisions as a choice among a set of possible outcomes. Whereas the first model represents the choices of Great Britain and the American colonies within the common game-theoretic format of a decision matrix, the second model represents their choices as a sequence of decisions made across five outcome axes. Both models serve the same purpose for they both cast attention upon the principal actors, interests, and decisions that ultimately ended the British-colonial union in 1776.

Some historians and political scientists may initially find these models and this new approach to the American Revolution unfamiliar or unrealistic, but the utility of these models (like the utility of a narrative trope or statistical technique) must be assessed in terms of whether their acknowledged distortions illuminate some portion of the historical evidence previously unrecognized or poorly clarified. In addition to answering the three identified questions that challenge every account of the American Revolution, these models also provide the media within which to complete the macro-micro synthesis. Within these models the macrolevel conditions described in detail in Chapter 2 are recognized as both the de facto structural dynamics that constituted the British-colonial relationship in the 1770s and one of the five constitutional conceptualizations that framed the set of negotiable possibilities between 1774 and 1776. The models thus facilitate a synthesis of macro- and microlevel conditions and they make clear why British-American negotiations concerning the terms of their relationship ultimately ended with the "sad alternative," as George Washington foresaw in 1775, of "a Brother's Sword . . . sheathed in a Brother's breast."[1]

PART I: THE MACRO-MICRO SYNTHESIS

The proposed synthesis of macro and microlevel conditions raises difficult and long-debated philosophical and methodological problems that warrant explicit attention by historians and political scientists interested in transcending their disciplinary divide.[2] This work cannot offer an extended discussion of the philosophical problems, although they open intriguing epistemological and ontological questions concerning the

---

[1] George Washington to George William Fairfax, May 31 1775, *Letters of Delegates to Congress, 1774–1789*, Paul H. Smith, ed. (Washington, DC: U.S. Government Printing Office, 1976), 1: 425.

[2] For theoretical discussions and applied solutions of these questions, see Margaret Archer, *Realist Social Theory: The Morphogenetic Approach* (Cambridge, UK: Cambridge University Press, 1995); David Dessler, "What's at Stake in the Agency-Structure Debate?," *International Organization* (1989), 43: 441–473; Alexander E. Wendt, "The Agent-Structure Problem in International Relations Theory," *International Organization* (1987), 41: 335–370; Jeffrey C. Alexander et al., eds., *The Micro-Macro Link* (Berkeley: University of California Press, 1987); Margaret Archer, "Structuration versus Morphogenesis," in *Macro-Sociological Theory: Perspectives on Sociological Theory, Vol. 1*, S. N. Eisenstadt and H. J. Helle, eds. (London: Sage, 1985), pp. 58–88; Anthony Giddens, *The Constitution of Society: Outline of a Theory of Structuration* (Berkeley: University of California Press, 1984); Herbert A. Simon, "Human Nature in Politics: The Dialogue of Psychology with Political Science," *APSR* (1985), 79: 293–304; Heinz Eulau, *Micro-Macro Political Analysis* (Chicago: Aldine Publishing Co., 1969); Stephen Skowronek, *The Politics Presidents Make* (Cambridge, MA: Harvard University Press, 1997); Walter Carlsnaes, "The Agency-Structure Problem in Foreign Policy Analysis," *International Studies Quarterly* (1992), 36: 245, 246; Jeffrey Berejikian, "Revolutionary Collective Action and the Agent-Structure Problem," *APSR* (1992), 86: 647–657; Thomas Gallant, "Agency, Structure, and Explanation in Social History: The Case of the Foundling Home on Kephallenia, Greece, during the 1830s," *Social Science History* (1991), 15: 479–508.

location and nature of causality. The ontological question inquires whether causal primacy ought to be assigned to free-willing human agents or to will-configuring environmental contexts. The epistemological question inquires whether the interests of individuals should be considered objective and socially determined or subjective and individually constructed. Historians and social scientists often share similar approaches to these questions, and it has become common within both disciplines to recognize that the (implicit or explicit) answers provided across this matrix of questions affect subsequent assumptions and decisions concerning the privileging of evidentiary domains and the employment of particular tropological devices and methodological techniques.[3]

In addition to these philosophical problems, the proposed macro-micro synthesis also raises immediate methodological problems. Five problems warrant explicit recognition. The first problem is the problem of *evidence inaccessibility*, or the difficulty of retrieving the types of evidence necessary to explain an historical event in terms of the decisions, perceptions, and preferences of individual actors. The second is the problem of *context dependency*, or the necessity of grounding an analysis of these decisions within a specific environmental context. The third is the problem of *evidence incomparability*, or the incommensurability of different types or categories of historical evidence. The fourth is the problem of *decisional interdependency*, or the difficulty of analyzing the decisions of multiple actors engaged in a jointly produced outcome. The fifth and final problem is the problem of *historical indeterminacy*, or the necessity of constructing an account of a well-known historical event in essentially nondeterministic terms.

The first problem, *evidence inaccessibility*, follows from the assumption that the immediate or efficient causes of the American Revolution can best be determined by examining the interests, calculations, and decisions of individual political actors during the period immediately prior to the constitutional collapse of the British-colonial union. However, even if the duration of these so-called "immediate" conditions is limited to the period between 1774 and 1776, the costs of retrieving and processing the evidence necessary for this type of actor-centered

---

[3] See Hugh Heclo, "Ideas, Interests, and Institutions," in Lawrence C. Dodd and Calvin Jillson, eds., *The Dynamics of American Politics* (Boulder, CO: Westview, 1994), pp. 366–392; Herbert M. Kritzer, "The Data Puzzle: The Nature of Interpretation in Quantitative Research," *American Journal of Political Science* (1996), 40(1): 1–32; Hayden White, *Tropics of Discourse: Essays in Cultural Criticism* (Baltimore: Johns Hopkins University Press, 1985).

analysis remain excessive. The number of individuals, the variety of institutional and decision-making contexts within which they acted, and the disparate and fragmentary condition of the historical record make this kind of analytical focus impractical if not wholly unmanageable.[4] Admission of this seemingly insurmountable difficulty, however, alters neither the location nor the importance of analyzing the immediate causes of the American Revolution. These causes, rather, remain fixed to the decisions of individual British and colonial political actors and their individual and collective capacities to draw others into their wake.

The second methodological problem, *context dependency*, arises from the expectation that the decisions of British and colonial political actors prior to the American Revolution relate, in some way, to the environmental conditions within which they were embedded. Constitutional changes, after all, occur within specific historical contexts and are only rarely unexpected or spontaneously generated events. Accounts of the causes of the American Revolution, it follows, necessarily must explain the collapse of the British-colonial order in 1776 with reference to the same set of environmental conditions that stabilized and sustained British-colonial relations during the first three quarters of the eighteenth century.

The third methodological problem, *evidence incomparability*, recognizes the difficulties associated with the simultaneous analysis of different types of historical evidence. Given that British-colonial relations were constituted, in large part, by the four types of conditions described in Chapter 2, explanation of the collapse of these relations must refer to these conditions in some way as well. Adherence to this commonsense standard is not easily or economically achieved and it presents an additional quandary regarding how the effects of different types of evidence – for example, evidence of *ideological* and *economic* conditions – are to be compared and ultimately integrated within a single explanation of the Revolution's immediate causes. Not surprisingly, the general failure to devise a method for analyzing different types of evidence yields historical reconstructions of the pre-Revolutionary period that either privilege one type of evidence over others or more glibly impute causality from a general and unspecified origin and location.

[4] For the best accounts of this period, see Bernard Donoughue, *British Politics and the American Revolution: The Path to War, 1773–1775* (London: Macmillan, 1964); David Ammerman, *In Common Cause: American Response to the Coercive Acts of 1774* (Charlottesville: University Press of Virginia, 1974), and Eric Robson, *The American Revolution In its Political and Military Aspects, 1763–1783* (New York: W. W. Norton, 1955).

The fourth methodological problem, *decisional interdependency*, demands the integration of both British *and* American decisions into a single explanation of the American Revolution. As with most civil wars, the immediate causes of this event cannot be attributed wholly to the decisions of a single set of political actors. After 1763, to be sure, British political actors repeatedly and aggressively attempted to redefine Great Britain's relationship with the American colonies. These attempts, however, necessitated neither a constitutional collapse nor a civil war. Rather, only after the American colonies decided collectively to resist these changes with force did civil war become both possible and probable. A fuller account of the American Revolution, therefore, must portray its immediate causes as a function of the political decisions made on *both* sides of the Atlantic Ocean.

The fifth and final methodological problem, *historical indeterminacy*, emerges from the assumption that political changes of the breadth and magnitude of the American Revolution are not produced by either random events or structurally required conditions. Causal but nondeterministic accounts of the American Revolution, it follows, must employ methodological approaches or narrative forms capable of accurately representing the uncertainty, contingency, and voluntarism of real-world decision-making moments.

This is not the place to review fully if or how well existing accounts of the American Revolution resolve each of these methodological problems. Historians – and notably not political scientists – have been the primary analysts of this constitutional crisis and they have adopted (or implicitly resorted to) several of the same types of methodological solutions. Economic interpretations of the American Revolution, for example, typically overcome the first problem of evidence inaccessibility by explaining the causes of the Revolution as a function of environmental or structural changes in British-colonial relations. Thus, the significance of individual interests and decisions, if acknowledged at all, is subordinated to explanations that emphasize the deterministic effects that economic or social class structures have on individual behavior.[5]

Historians of the American Revolution typically have solved the second problem of context dependency by highlighting similarities between immediate and longer-term environmental conditions. Ideological

---

[5] Like economic accounts, many accounts of the Revolution from the ideological perspective eschew explanations that assign causal significance to the intentions of individual actors. See Gordon S. Wood, "Rhetoric and Reality in the American Revolution," *WMQ* (1966), 23: 16, 22.

accounts of the Revolution, for example, often identify long-term currents of political thought that surfaced and intensified during the British-
colonial conflicts of the 1760s, before confronting individuals in the
mid-1770s as ideological tidal waves that moved, as one historian
claimed, "over the heads of the participants, taking them in directions
no one could have foreseen."[6]

Unfortunately, historians of the American Revolution have generally
not confronted or attempted to solve the final three methodological
problems. Thus, accounts of the American Revolution are typically given
from either a British *or* an American perspective, but not simultaneously
from both.[7] Few if any accounts have succeeded in comparing or
integrating different types of evidence within a single causal analysis of
this constitutional collapse. Hence, competing interpretations of the
American Revolution divide themselves almost effortlessly into categories defined by the most prominent type of empirical evidence on
which each focuses. Finally, although several accounts deny the
inevitability of the American Revolution, few adequately portray its historically unexpected civil war outcome.

This account resolves these methodological problematics by comple-
menting the macrolevel description of British-colonial relations arrayed
in Chapter 2 with a microlevel analysis of the American Revolution.
The analysis thus differs from existing accounts of the causes of the
American Revolution not merely because it approaches the event from
a different perspective but because it relies on a more comprehensive set
of solutions to the five identified methodological problems. The methodological solutions adopted to address the first three problems warrant

[6] Gordon S. Wood, "Rhetoric and Reality in the American Revolution," *WMQ* (1966),
23: 23. See also Jack P. Greene, *Quest for Power* (Chapel Hill: University of North
Carolina, 1963).
  Another ingenious way in which historians solve this second methodological problem
is to overlook longer-term conditions altogether and rely on what can be characterized
as middle-range conditions as proxies to explain the Revolution's immediate conditions.
Several accounts, for example, focus on British-colonial conflicts in the 1760s, triggered
by Parliament's attempt to tax the colonies, as a way of explaining (or, at least, strongly
suggesting a reason for) the subsequent constitutional crisis in the mid-1770s. See
Edmund S. Morgan and Helen M. Morgan, *The Stamp Act Crisis: Prologue to Revolu-
tion* (Chapel Hill: University of North Carolina Press, 1953); and Bernhard Knollenberg,
Origin of the American Revolution, 1759–1766 (New York: Free Press, 1960).
[7] See Marc Egnal, *A Mighty Empire: The Origins of the American Revolution* (Ithaca, NY:
Cornell University Press, 1988). A noteworthy exception is the multivolume work of
Lawrence H. Gipson, *The British Empire Before the American Revolution* (New York:
Knopf, 1936–1965), 12 vols.

Part II's reconstruction of the five constitutional conceptualizations that framed British-colonial negotiations after 1774. The game-theoretic solutions to the final two methodological problems aid and inform the analysis of British and colonial decisions completed in Part III.

The first methodological problem (evidence inaccessibility) is solved by defining the set of constitutional outcomes debated by British and colonial political actors. By 1774, this outcome set consisted of five distinct conceptualizations of their constitutional union. Thus, although evidence of the decisions, expectations, or preferences at the level of the individual actor remains questionable, the Revolution's immediate causes can be explained at a less immediate level by identifying the common set of conceptualizations within which British and colonial political leaders conceived, debated, and negotiated the future terms of their relationship. The reconstructed set of constitutional options completed in Part II thus becomes an alternative means of representing the historically un-recoverable set of individual preferences and decisions that produced the American Revolution.

In a similar way, solutions to the second and third methodological problems also display essentially ideational characteristics. The second problem (context dependency) is solved by sketching the development of these five constitutional conceptualizations from their approximate historical origins until tensions between British and colonial leaders escalated dramatically in 1774. The conceptual histories of each outcome provide the foundation for the game-theoretic analysis of British and colonial decisions constructed in Part III. The third methodological problem (evidence incomparability) is solved by reconceptualizing the structural conditions that framed and constituted British-colonial relations in terms of *British and colonial perceptions* of the benefits associated with these conditions. Thus, the different structural conditions measured in Chapter 2 are redefined into comparable sets of British and colonial speculations concerning how these conditions and their expected development might affect their relationship in the future.[8]

---

[8] Transformation of the four structural conditions arrayed in Chapter 2 into a single type of cognitive evaluation of the "status quo" solves the problem of evidence incomparability but raises an additional and admittedly difficult problem of differentiating historical evidence of the *intentions and perceptions* of political actors from evidence indicative only of their *rhetorical positions* in public or private debate. Neither political scientists nor historians have devised adequate solutions for this methodological quandary. Historian Bernard Bailyn adopts a literalist approach in his survey of the political literature of the late colonial period. He argues that the political pamphlets of this period "reveal not merely positions taken but the reasons why positions were taken; they reveal motive

The fourth and fifth methodological problems (decisional interdependency and historical indeterminacy) are solved by introducing two game-theoretic models to represent the interactions of British and colonial preferences and decisions prior to 1776. These models reflect both the sequential and the indeterminate nature of British and colonial decision making between 1774 and 1776. Like the other solutions, therefore, these models offer a new way of clarifying the causes and the dynamic conditions that compelled and ultimately completed the wholesale collapse of the British-colonial union and its working rule of apportionment.

PART II: DEFINING THE OUTCOME SET

In the 1760s and 1770s British and colonial leaders engaged in extended debates over the future of their relationship. In many respects, it was the resolution of this debate that preoccupied the calculations and decisions of British and colonial leaders throughout this period. As early as 1765, Massachusetts governor Francis Bernard noted (with an obvious British bias) "that all the Political Evils in America arise from the Want of ascertaining the Relations between Great Britain & the American Colonies."[9]

and understanding: the assumptions, beliefs, and ideas – the articulate world view – that lay behind the manifest events of the time." Bernard Bailyn, *The Ideological Origins of the American Revolution* (Cambridge, MA: Harvard University Press, 1967), p. vi.

This account finds a literalist approach too indiscriminate. At the same time, however, it is conceded that an analysis of the historical evidence indicative of "British" and "colonial" intentions and perceptions is mathematically intractable and therefore, at bottom, a matter for subjective interpretation. Acknowledgment that there is, as yet, no simple methodological solution to the problem of distinguishing the "intended and perceived" from the "rhetorical" is not an admission that every interpretation of a finite body of historical evidence ought to be considered of equal weight. Rather, given prior and prevailing scholarly conventions and standards, competing interpretations of the same historical event or period can continuously be assessed both in terms of their capacities to create a meaningful and full account of the historical record and of their capacities to recognize the contributions and limitations of rival interpretations. In the end, decisive distinctions between a small number of meta-interpretations may not always be possible, but at least trivial, incomplete, or biased interpretive representations can be identified as such. See Charles Taylor, *Philosophical Arguments* (Cambridge, MA: Harvard University Press, 1995); Richard W. Miller, *Fact and Method: Explanation, Confirmation and Reality in the Natural and the Social Sciences* (Princeton, NJ: Princeton University Press, 1987).

[9] *Barrington-Bernard Correspondence* [hereafter *BBC*], 23 Nov. 1765, E. C. Channing and A. C. Coolidge, eds. (Cambridge, MA: Harvard University, 1912), p. 96. See also Benjamin Franklin to Lord Kames, Feb. 25, 1767, *Papers of Benjamin Franklin* [hereafter *PBF*], Leonard W. Labaree, ed. (New Haven, CT: Yale University Press, 1959–), 14: 65.

Although the terms of British-colonial relations were discussed extensively during the two decades prior to 1776, only five conceptualizations of this relationship received serious attention. British-colonial relations were defined in terms of: (1) colonial subordination to Parliament; (2) colonial independence from Great Britain; (3) preservation of the status quo; (4) the admission of colonial representatives into Parliament; and (5) a dual sovereignty solution in which Parliament and the colonial assemblies would have independent governing authority but remain linked within an imperial union under a common Crown.[10] The histories of each conceptualization are sketched below.

Colonial Submission to Parliamentary Authority

The most prominently discussed conceptualization of British-colonial relations portrayed a future in which the American colonies acknowledged Parliament as their sovereign legislature. One of the earliest for-

---

[10] The historical evidence supporting the conclusion that British and colonial leaders gave serious consideration only to these five outcomes is bountiful. See, for example, John Adams, "Novanglus," No. VII (Boston, 1774); Thomas Jefferson, *A Summary View of the Rights of British-America* (Williamsburg, 1774); James Wilson, *Considerations on the Nature and Extent of the Legislative Authority of the British Parliament* (Philadelphia, 1774). See also Josiah Tucker, *Four Tracts: The True Interest of Great Britain Set Forth In Regard to the Colonies* (Gloucester, 1774), in *Collected Works of Josiah Tucker* (1993), II: 145–215; *An Humble and Earnest Appeal* (1775) in ibid., V: 4–5; James Otis, *The Rights of the British Colonies Asserted and Proved* (Boston, 1764); Thomas Pownall, *The Administration of the Colonies, wherein their Rights and Constitutions are Discussed and Stated*, 3rd. ed. (London, 1766); William Knox, *The Controversy Between Great Britain and her Colonies Reviewed* (London, 1769); Francis Maseres, *Considerations on the Expediency of Admitting Representatives from the American Colonies to the British House of Commons* (London, 1770); and Amor Patriae [Thomas Crowley], "A Plan of Union by Admitting Representatives from the American Colonies and from Ireland into the British Parliament" (n.p., 1770).

Other outcome possibilities were raised, but were either not widely discussed or were raised primarily on one side of the Atlantic. A small number of American colonials discussed the possibility of enacting an American Bill of Rights. See Samuel Cooper to Benjamin Franklin, March 15, 1773, *PBF*, 20: 114. See also Benjamin Franklin to Samuel Cooper, July 7, 1773, *PBF*, 20: 269; *Benjamin Franklin's Letters to the Press, 1758–1775*, Verner W. Crane, ed. (Chapel Hill: University of North Carolina Press, 1950), pp. 265–266. In Great Britain, especially after 1774, a variety of responses to the emerging constitutional crisis were discussed, although several cannot be associated with definitive constitutional outcomes. These responses included: British economic reprisals against the colonies, redrawing colony boundaries, restoring Canada to France, emancipation of the colonial slave population, and the encouragement of Indian attacks on western settlements. See Benjamin W. Labaree, "The Idea of American Independence: The British View, 1774–1776," *Massachusetts History Society Proceedings* (1970), 82: 15.

mulations of this idea was in the Commonwealth period when a then-kingless Parliament claimed to possess this authority over England's colonies in America. Although restoration of the monarchy in 1660 returned governing authority over the colonies to the Crown, in the second half of the seventeenth century Parliament began to regulate imperial commercial regulations, and thereby asserted indirect influence over the colonial economies.

In the eighteenth century, Parliament gradually extended its governing authority over the American colonies. It began regulating the colonial economy – including, among other things, the colonial money supply and the development of colonial manufacturing. This trend accelerated in the early 1760s when Parliament unilaterally asserted its authority to impose taxes on the colonies. In 1764, it imposed a series of customs duties on colonial imports and placed restrictions on colonial trade with the French West Indies. Although Parliament had previously imposed prohibitive taxes on selected colonial imports as a method of regulating imperial commerce, the 1764 Sugar Act was designed to generate revenue for the British Treasury.[11]

A year later, in 1765, Parliament imposed another tax on the colonies, the so-called Stamp Act, a direct tax on a variety of colonial goods including all materials printed within the colonies. With unexpectedly strong opposition in the colonies and by British commercial interests, Parliament quickly repealed this second tax. Unwilling to concede any limits on its legislative authority over the colonies, Parliament unequivocally proclaimed in the 1766 Declaratory Act that it "had, hath, and of rights ought to have, full power and authority to make laws and statutes of sufficient force and validity to bind the colonies and people of America . . . in all cases whatsoever."[12] Parliament, as one member explained prior to this declaration, "represents the whole British Empire, and [therefore] has authority to bind every part and every subject without the least distinction, whether such subjects have a right to vote or not, or whether the law binds places within the realm or without."[13]

In 1768, Parliament continued to claim full governing authority over the American colonies, imposing another set of customs duties on colonial imports. Parliament also decided that the revenues received from these duties would be used to pay the salaries of royal governors

[11] See Gipson, *The British Empire before the American Revolution* (1961), 10: 180–231.
[12] "The Declaratory Act, March 18, 1766," in *Prologue to Revolution*, Edmund Morgan, ed. (1959), p. 155.
[13] *Parliamentary History*, February 10, 1766, XVI: 173.

and judges in the colonies, thereby further extending its authority over colonial government. Colonial protests again were widespread and included an American boycott of British imports and violence in several colonial cities. Parliament again retreated from its tax policy, rescinding all duties except a small duty on imported tea.[14] These retreats sobered British expectations about the feasibility of enforcing the full extent of the authority Parliament claimed over the American colonies.[15] Nevertheless, members of Parliament and most of the British political elite continued to envision British-colonial relations in terms of the latter subordinated to the former.

American colonial leaders, by contrast, generally seemed united against any redefinition of the British-colonial relationship that established a form of Parliamentary authority over which there were no formal checks and in which they were not represented.[16] Throughout the 1760s, therefore, colonials not only resisted Parliamentary encroachments, they also began to question more openly the legitimacy of British influence in colonial affairs. As early as 1764, for example, Rhode Island governor Stephen Hopkins reportedly inquired: "What have the King and Parliament to do with making a law or laws to govern us by, any more than the Mohawks have?"[17] Over time, additional colonial leaders voiced their opposition to the idea of Parliamentary supremacy over the colonies. George Mason of Virginia, for example, declared in 1770: "We owe to our Mother-Country the Duty of Subjects but will not pay her the Submission of Slaves."[18] In late 1775 Thomas Jefferson not only echoed his fellow Virginian Mason, but claimed, "the sentiments of America" when he asserted "there is not in the British Empire a man who more cordially loves a union with Great Britain than I do, but by the God that made me, I will cease to exist, before I yield to a connec-

[14] Gipson, *The British Empire Before the American Revolution* (1965), Vol. 11.

[15] See *Parliamentary History*, XVI: 1021.

[16] For an indicator of colonial coolness toward the idea of unconditionally submitting to British authority, see Jonathan Mayhew, *Discourse Concerning Unlimited Submission and Non-Resistance to the Higher Powers* (1750); and Steven M. Dworetz, *The Unvarnished Doctrine* (Durham, NC: Duke University Press, 1990), pp. 148–172.

[17] As quoted in George L. Beer, *British Colonial Policy, 1754–1765* (New York: P. Smith, 1933), p. 310n.2. See also Charles Thomas to Benjamin Franklin, September 24, 1765, *PBF*, 12: 279–280.

[18] George Mason to George Brent, Dec. 6, 1770, *Papers of George Mason*, Robert A. Rutland, ed. (Chapel Hill: University of North Carolina Press, 1970), I: 129. See also Charles Thomson to Benjamin Franklin, November 26, 1769; James Iredell, "To the Inhabitants of Great Britain," September 1774, *Life and Correspondence of James Iredell*, Griffith J. McRee, ed. (New York: Appleton, 1857–1858), I: 205.

tion, on the terms as the British Parliament proposes."[19] Jefferson proclaimed that rather than submit to governance by the British Parliament, he "would level [his] hand to sink the whole island into the ocean."[20]

Colonial Independence

The second conceptualization of British-colonial relations was predicated on the American colonies becoming independent from Great Britain. The origin of this idea is impossible to identify, although it was discussed periodically throughout the eighteenth century. In the seventeenth century, also, the idea of a limited form of colonial autonomy was discussed.[21] As early as 1651, the Barbados Assembly claimed that Parliament had no authority to impose punitive trade regulations against the colonies when it defiantly inquired why they ought to suffer the will of a Parliament in which they had no representatives "to propound and consent to what might be needful to us, as also to oppose and dispute all what should tend to our disadvantage and harm."[22]

Although others no doubt debated the claims and limits of colonial autonomy during the early part of the eighteenth century, British officials were the first to become intrigued by the possibility of a more complete colonial separation. In 1711, for example, New York governor Robert Hunter reported that the level of governing authority claimed by the colony's assembly was then so extensive that if the colonial council acquiesced, the former would be "Independent of the great Counsil of the Realme."[23] British sightings of the spectre of colonial independence were not limited to the colony of New York. Another British observer reported in 1723 that he heard more treasonous discussions in Boston in one day "than in all my life before, such as his Ma[jes]ty has no business in this country, he is our nominal king, . . . the country is ours not

[19] As quoted in Samuel W. Patterson, *The Spirit of the American Revolution* (Boston: R. G. Badger, 1915), pp. 40–41.

[20] Thomas Jefferson to John Randolph, August 25, 1775, *The Portable Thomas Jefferson*, Merrill D. Peterson, ed. (New York: Viking Press, 1975), p. 354.

[21] See Theodore Draper, *A Struggle for Power: The American Revolution* (New York: Times Books, 1996), pp. 41–48.

[22] "Declaration of the Barbados Assembly, Feb. 18, 1651," in *Great Britain and the American Colonies*, Greene, ed. (1970), p. 48. See also James Harrington, *Oceana* (1656; *Cato's Letters*, "Of Plantations and Colonies," Dec. 8, 1722 (London, 6th ed., 1755), IV: 6–7; and Charles Davenant, *A New Discourse of Trade* (1698).

[23] Robert Hunter to Secretary Saint John, 1711; as quoted in Beer, *British Colonial Policy* (1933), p. 167.

his, ... [and] we have nothing to do with their country so they have nothing to doe with ours." Anxiety about the likelihood of colonial independence appears to have intensified during subsequent decades. One report found among British state papers for the period 1733–1748 remarked that "unless some Care be taken, the People born there, are too apt to imbibe Notions of Independency of their Mother Kingdom."[24]

Inferences from anecdotal evidence like this, however, should not be overdone. For despite the prescience of this early chorus of warnings, the idea of colonial independence was (at most) a faint siren amidst the din of mainstream British political discourses. Before 1750 the idea was either ignored altogether or discounted as highly improbable. In 1728, for example, a British essayist applauded "[t]he wisdom of the Crown of Britain" for "keeping its Colonies" separated from and jealous of each other's commercial interests "for while they continue so, it is morally impossible that any dangerous Union can be form'd among them."[25] In 1760, Andrew Burnaby concluded (after traveling through several American colonies) that "[a] voluntary association or coalition, at least a permanent one, is almost as difficult to be supposed: for fire and water are not more heterogeneous than the different colonies in North America."[26]

In the 1750s, several British leaders gradually became more receptive to suggestions that there was "a general disposition to independence" in the colonies that "prevailed throughout the whole."[27] Two developments prompted this change. The first was the British realization that although the colonies had become integral to British economic growth, colonial growth and development would likely make them less dependent on Great Britain and more successful in expanding their trade with other countries. The second development was a consequence of the Seven Year War (1754–1763) between Great Britain and France. In the aftermath of a French defeat, British leaders were left with the Pyrrhic spoils of an enormous national debt, a domestic population already heavily taxed, and prominent complaints that the wartime contributions of the

---

[24] As quoted in Beer, *British Colonial Policy* (1933), p. 168n.3; 166n.2.
[25] William Keith, "A Short Discourse on the Present State of the Colonies in America, with Respect to the Interest of Great Britain" (1728), in *Great Britain and the American Colonies*, Greene, ed. (1970), pp. 193–194.
[26] Andrew Burnaby, *Travels ... in North America in the Years 1759 and 1760* (New York: A. M. Kelley, 1970/[1798]), pp. 152–153.
[27] As quoted in Beer, *British Colonial Policy* (1933), p. 169. See also J. M. Bumsted, " 'Things in the Womb of Time': Ideas of American Independence, 1633 to 1763," *WMQ* (1974), 31: 544–557.

American colonies were inadequate and "wholly in conformity to their own selfish or rapacious views."[28]

Not only were the American colonies generally perceived in Great Britain as failing to shoulder their share of imperial burdens, but the once perceived benefits of securing France's territorial claims to the Mississippi Valley ironically left Great Britain with additional financial burdens at the same time they seemingly liberated the American colonies from their historic dependency upon British military protection. Freed from security concerns and presented with the opportunity for expansion into the new and largely uncultivated lands to the west, colonial economic development (several predicted) would continue unabated until it ultimately destroyed Great Britain's colonial markets.

From the British perspective, conditions in the early 1760s further ripened the possibility of American independence.[29] The colonies, as a consequence, were portrayed notably less often as disunited and jealous rivals, and increasingly "as now extremely populous, and extremely rich" who "are every day rising in Numbers, and in wealth, and must, in the nature of things, aspire at a total independence, unless we are beforehand with them, and wisely take the power out of their hands."[30]

The shift in British metaphors paralleled a shift in Great Britain's colonial policies. Royal supervision of the colonial assemblies became more stringent and restrictive throughout the 1760s. In 1763, the Crown additionally issued the Royal Proclamation Line, which banned colonial settlement and restricted colonial trade in the newly acquired western lands. After 1764, when Parliament imposed several new taxes on the colonies, resistance to these policies confirmed British anxieties about colonial interest in independence and heightened the imperative for more definitive demonstrations of British authority over the colonies. By the 1770s many British leaders were convinced that colonial independence was, perhaps, imminent and inevitably destructive to Great Britain's longer-term interests.[31]

---

[28] As quoted in Jack P. Greene, "The Seven Years' War and the American Revolution: The Causal Relationship Reconsidered," in Peter Marshall and Glyn Williams, eds., *The British Atlantic Empire before the American Revolution* (London: Cass, 1980), pp. 85–105, 88.

[29] See Thomas C. Barrow, "A Project for Imperial Reform: 'Hints Respecting the Settlement for our American Provinces,' 1763," *WMQ* (1967), 24: 108–126.

[30] As quoted in John C. Miller, *The Origins of the American Revolution* (Boston: Little, Brown and Co., 1943), p. 208.

[31] See Labaree, "The Idea of American Independence," *Massachusetts Historical Society Proceedings* (1970), 82: 3–20.

Ironically, the historical record prior to 1774 strongly suggests that American colonials rarely discussed the idea of colonial independence.[32] Virginian George Mason was not alone when he claimed in 1770 that "the wildest Chimera that ever disturbed a Madman's Brain has not less Foundation in Truth than this Opinion" because "there are not five Men of Sense in America who wou'd accept of Independence if it was offered." As late as October 1774, George Washington declared "that no such thing is desired by any thinking man in all North America; on the contrary, that it is the ardent wish of the warmest advocates for liberty, that peace & tranquility, upon constitutional grounds, may be restored, & the horrors of civil discord prevented."[33] Two years later, in 1776, this idea still had so few colonial advocates that John Adams of Massachusetts observed: "Independency is an Hobgoblin, of so frightfull Mein, that it would throw a delicate Person into Fits to look it in the Face."[34]

The Status Quo

The third conceptualization forecast a future in which British-colonial relations were shaped, in large part, by the long-term dynamics described in Chapter 1. Although it may be unorthodox to refer to the "status quo" as a nonneutral, dynamic condition this, in fact, is how British and colonial leaders projected the consequences of not settling the terms of their relationship. For most British leaders, continuation of the status quo became untenable because it ensured the eventual collapse of British authority within the American colonies. "[T]he colonies," Lord Chancellor Northington declared in 1766, "are become too big to be governed by the laws they at first set out with. They have therefore run

---

[32] See Bumsted, " 'Things in the Womb of Time'," *WMQ* (1974), 31: 533–564; and Appendix summary in Jared Sparks, ed., *The Writings of George Washington* (1838), II: pp. 496–502. For a range of colonial statements concerning independence in 1774 and 1775, see *LDC*, 1: 157, 166–167; 2: 21, 134–135, 219, 248–249, 193, 319–320). See also Thomas R. Adams, ed., *American Independence: The Growth of an Idea* (Providence, RI: Brown University Press, 1965).

[33] "George Mason to George Brent," Dec. 6, 1770, Robert A. Rutland, ed. (1970), *Papers of George Mason*, I: 129; George Washington to Robert Mackenzie, 9 October 1774, *LDC*, 1: 167. See also "Thomas Cushing to Benjamin Franklin," Dec. 10, 1773, *PBF*, 20: 497; Adams, *Diary*, 2: 121; Benjamin Franklin to William Franklin, *Franklin's Works*, I: 278; John Zubly to Lord Dartmouth, Sept. 3, 1775, *LDC*, 2: 21n.1; James Iredell, "[Causes of the American Revolution]" (June 1776), *Life and Correspondence*, I: 312.

[34] John Adams to Horatio Gates, March 23, 1776, *LDC*, 3: 431.

into confusion, and it will be the policy of this country to form a plan of laws for them."[35] Other British leaders, however, were more realistic: "It is impossible," one concluded, "that this petty island can continue in dependence that mighty continent, increasing daily in numbers and in strength," and therefore, "[t]o protract the time of separation to a distant day is all that can be hoped."[36]

Colonial leaders benefited from the dynamic developments associated with the status quo and therefore they consistently resisted every attempt to renegotiate the terms of their relationship with Great Britain. As Benjamin Franklin noted in 1773:

> our great Security lies, I think, in our growing Strength both in Wealth and Numbers, that creates an increasing Ability of Assisting this Nation in its Wars, which will make us more respectable, our Friendship more valued, and our Enmity feared; thence it will soon be thought proper to treat us, not with Justice only, but with Kindness; and thence we may expect in a few Years a total Change of Measures with regard to us; .... In confidence of this coming Change in our favour, I think our Prudence is mean while to be quiet, only holding up our Rights and Claims on all Occasions, In Resolutions, Memorials, and Remonstrances, but bearing patiently the little present Notice that is taken of them. They will all have their Weight in Time, and that Time is at no great Distance.[37]

Thomas Cushing was another colonial who was confident "that the [British] government at home are daily growing weaker, while we in America are continually growing stronger. Our natural increase in wealth and population," Cushing added, "will in a course of years effectually settle this dispute in our favor, whereas if we persist in openly and strenuously denying the right of Parliament to legislate for us in any case whatever. ... there will be great danger of bringing on a rupture fatal to both countries."[38]

Colonial Representation in Parliament

The fourth conceptualization of British-colonial relations envisioned a future in which the American colonies were granted representation in

[35] *Parliamentary History*, Feb. 10, 1766, XVI: 171.

[36] As quoted in Miller, *The Origins of the American Revolution* (1943), p. 210; cf. p. 209.

[37] Benjamin Franklin to Thomas Cushing, Jan. 5, 1773, *PBF*, 20: 10. See also Franklin to John Winthrop, July 25, 1773, *PBF*, 20: 330; William Hooper to James Iredell, April 26, 1774, *Life and Correspondence*, I: 197; and Silas Deane to Samuel Adams, Nov. 13, 1774, *LDC*, 1: 260–262. See also Charles Thompson to Benjamin Franklin, Nov. 20, 1769, *PBF*, 16: 239.

[38] Thomas Cushing to Arthur Lee, Sept. 1773, as quoted in Egnal, *A Mighty Empire* (1988), p. 14.

Parliament. The origin of this idea is not known, but as early as 1641 New England colonials were asked to send a delegation of representatives to Parliament. According to one contemporaneous account, the colonials declined this request after "consulting about it" because they believed "that if we should put ourselves under the protection of the parliament, we must then be subject to such laws as they should make," which although designed with good intentions "might prove very prejudicial to us."[39]

Although the historical record reveals little about the subsequent development of this idea in the eighteenth century, colonial representation in parliament was debated extensively in the 1760s after Parliament asserted its authority to tax the colonies. In response to the 1764 Sugar Act, James Otis of Massachusetts argued that "no parts of His Majesty's dominions can be taxed without their consent" and that "every part" of the British Empire "has a right to be represented in the supreme or some subordinate legislature." Notably, Otis proposed apportioning colonial representation in Parliament in "some proportion to their number and estates" and he argued that this extension of parliamentary representation to the colonies would provide an "effectual means of giving those of both countries a thorough knowledge of each others interests." This reform, moreover, "would firmly unite all parts of the British Empire in the greatest peace and prosperity, and render it invulnerable and perpetual."[40]

Other colonials repeated and extended Otis's proposal for colonial representation in Parliament. Richard Stockton of New Jersey recommended that each colony "send one or two of their most ingenious

---

[39] *Winthrop's Journal, "History of New England," 1630–1649*, James K. Hosmer, ed. (New York: Scribner's Sons, 1908), II: 24; as quoted in Miller, *Origins of the American Revolution* (1943), p. 227.

Near the end of the seventeenth century, the idea of colonial representation was raised again, this time, in the pamphlet of Barbadian planter Edward Littleton, *The Groans of the Plantations* (1689). In addition to noting a colonial desire for parliamentary representation, Littleton complained (as American colonials would eight decades later) that "our [English] Masters . . . think they have a great advantage over us" because "we have none to represent us in Parliament." Edward Littleton, "The Groans of the Plantations" (1689), in Greene, ed., *Great Britain and the American Colonies* (1970), p. 104.

In the first half of the eighteenth century, the idea of colonial representation in Parliament does not appear to have been discussed widely in Great Britain or in the American colonies. In 1754, the idea apparently was raised in a private exchange between Benjamin Franklin and Massachusetts governor William Shirley. See also Benjamin Franklin to William Shirley, December 22, 1754, *PBF*, 5: 449.

[40] James Otis, *The Rights of the Colonies Asserted and Proved* (Boston, 1764).

fellows" to the British House of Commons and "maintain them there till they can maintain themselves, or else we shall be fleeced to some purpose."[41] Like Otis, Joseph Galloway of Pennsylvania believed that colonial representatives would provide "a new door of Information" on colonial affairs for British legislators, and he predicted that colonials also "will conceive it their Duty to obey Institutions and Laws agreed on by their own representatives." This, in turn, "wou[l]d form the Strongest and most indissoluble Bond of Union, that can be invented, between the mother Country and her Foreign Dominions."[42]

Throughout the 1760s and early 1770s, colonial leaders continued both publicly and privately to debate the costs and benefits of gaining representation in Parliament.[43] Colonial enthusiasm for this idea seems to have declined steadily, however, after Parliament enacted the 1765 Stamp Act.[44] Colonials like Thomas Wharton of Pennsylvania noted that if the colonies were granted representatives in Parliament "their Number will be so small, as to be of little use, in the division of the House" of Commons. Wharton, moreover, questioned if "having a few Members to represent America, in Parliament, might not give the M[inist]ry, a better pretence of Laying heavier Burthens upon Us, without so much as letting the Colonies know, the Measure proposed; or offering a method which would be less injurious to them?"[45] Others were similarly fearful of parliamentary representation. Samuel Adams of Massachusetts, for example, definitively declared that "[t]here is nothing, therefore the colonies would more dread" than representation in Parliament.[46]

Still other colonials became wary of the idea of parliamentary representation not because of calculations about its potential consequences but because of their suspicions concerning British intentions. Support for this idea, reported the *Virginia Gazette*, was motivated by the British

---

[41] As quoted in Miller, *The Origins of the American Revolution*, p. 226.

[42] Joseph Galloway to Benjamin Franklin, Oct. 8–14?, 1765, *PBF*, 12: 304–305; Joseph Galloway to Benjamin Franklin, November 16–28?, 1765, *PBF*, 12: 376.

[43] See Franklin to Lord Kames, Feb. 25, 1767, *PBF*, 14: 65; William Hicks, *The Nature and Extent of Parliamentary Power Considered* (Philadelphia, 1768); *Virginia Gazette*, Feb. 9, 1769.

[44] The Stamp Act Congress and several colonial assemblies rejected the idea of colonial representation in Parliament in their protests against this Act. See "The Declarations of the Stamp Act Congress," Oct. 7–24, 1765; "The Massachusetts Resolves," Oct. 29, 1765, in Morgan and Morgan, eds., *The Stamp Act Crisis* (1953), pp. 56–67.

[45] Thomas Wharton to Benjamin Franklin, April 27, 1765, *PBF*, 12: 116–117.

[46] Samuel Adams to Dennys De Berdt, Jan. 30, 1768, *Writings of Samuel Adams*, Harry A. Cushing, ed. (1904), I: 178. See also account in *Pennsylvania Journal*, March 13, 1766; reprinted in Morgan and Morgan, eds., *The Stamp Act Crisis* (1953), pp. 88–92.

desire "to stop their [colonial] mouths" so "that they may no longer plead that as an excuse for their refusing to be taxed by the Mother Country."[47] The combination of colonial calculations and suspicions so badly eroded colonial support for the idea of representation in Parliament that Benjamin Franklin contended as early as 1767 that although "[t]he Time has been when the Colonies might have been pleas'd with it; they are now indifferent about it; and, if 'tis much longer delay'd, they too will refuse it."[48]

The idea of admitting colonial representatives into Parliament also was debated extensively in Great Britain. In 1764, the *London Chronicle* reported that this reform "was certainly on the carpet"[49] and Massachusetts governor Francis Bernard was convinced that parliamentary representation was "the Palladium of their [colonial] cause."[50] Initially, however, indirect forms of colonial representation dominated British discussions. According to one common argument, the colonists were like "nine tenths of the people of Britain" who were not permitted to vote but who were still *virtually* represented in Parliament. Thus, according to several British polemicists, it was of little consequence that the American colonies could not elect their own representatives because "every Member of Parliament sits in the House not as representative of his own constituents but as one of that august assembly by which all the commons of *Great Britain* are represented."[51]

The idea of "virtual" representation found little support on either side of the Atlantic. As a consequence, British leaders began to reformulate their views of representation and to consider the possible consequences of allowing more direct forms of colonial representation in Parliament. In late 1765, for example, Massachusetts governor Bernard privately sug-

---

[47] *Virginia Gazette*, Dec. 3, 1767.

[48] Franklin to Lord Kames, Feb. 25, 1767, *PBF*, 14: 65. See also "Draft" [Jan. 6, 1766], *PBF*, 13: 23; Franklin to William Shirley, Dec. 22, 1754, *PBF*, 5: 449–451.

[49] *London Chronicle*, Nov. 24, 1764, as quoted in Fred J. Hinkhouse, *The Preliminaries of the American Revolution as Seen in the English Press, 1763–1775* (New York: Columbia University Press, 1926), p. 122.

[50] As quoted in John Phillip Reid, *Constitutional History of the American Revolution: The Authority of Law* (Madison, WI: University of Wisconsin Press, 1993), p. 99.

[51] Thomas Whateley, *Regulations Lately Made Concerning the Colonies and the Taxes Imposed upon Them, Considered* (London, 1765), as quoted in Bailyn, *The Ideological Origins of the American Revolution* (1967), p. 166. See also Soame Jenyns, *The Objections to the Taxation of our American Colonies by the Legislature of Great Britain, Briefly Consider'd* (London, 1765), in Samuel Morison, ed., *Sources & Documents Illustrating the American Revolution* (New York: Oxford University Press, 1965), pp. 18–24.

gested that "30 [representatives] for the Continent & 15 for the Islands would be sufficient." "American Representation," Bernard subsequently explained, "will absolutely take away all Pretence of disputing the Ordinances of Parliament." For this reason, he privately suggested that if the American colonies "will not be obedient to Parliament without Representation, In Gods Name let them have them."[52]

In 1766, British pamphleteer Joshua Steele recommended for the "union and utility of the whole, a new sovereign council, consisting of deputies from each province of the Great Commonwealth."[53] Other proposals were formulated. Former Massachusetts governor Thomas Pownall proposed granting – or possibly forcing – the colonies to accept "a share in the legislature of Great Britain."[54] In 1770, former Quebec Attorney General Francis Maseres furthered this debate with his recommendation for admitting up to eighty new members from the North American and Caribbean colonies. This offer, Maseres and others believed, would resolve the ongoing dispute over British-colonial relations by forcing colonials to commit to the authority of parliamentary representation or to reveal their intention to become independent from Great Britain.[55]

---

[52] Governor Bernard to Lord Barrington, Nov. 23, 1765, *BBC* (1912), p. 98; Governor Bernard to Lord Barrington, Jan. 28, 1768, *BBC* (1912), pp. 137, 139.

[53] Joshua Steele, *An Account of a Late Conference on the Occurrences in America in a Letter to a Friend* (London, 1766), as quoted in Charles F. Mullett, "English Imperial Thinking, 1764–1783," *Political Science Quarterly* (1930), 45: 550.

[54] Thomas Pownall, *The Administration of the Colonies*, 4th. ed. (London, 1768), as quoted in Adams, *The Political Ideas of the American Republic* (1939), p. 31. For an insightful discussion of Pownall's ideas, see John Shy, "Thomas Pownall, Henry Ellis, and the Spectrum of Possibilities, 1763–1775," in *Anglo-American Political Relations, 1675–1775*, Alison G. Olson and Richard M. Brown, eds. (New Brunswick, NJ: Rutgers University Press, 1970), pp. 155–186.

[55] See Francis Maseres, *Considerations on the Expediency of Admitting Representatives from the American Colonies to the British House of Commons* (London, 1770); Miller, *The Origins of the American Revolution* (1943), p. 222.

See also "Scheme for the better uniting and cementing the mutual interest and peace of Great Britain and her Colonies by representation in Parliament of Great Britain and Dominions," n.d. (1764–1774, Chatham Papers); reprinted in *English Historical Review* (1907), 88: 757–758; Anonymous, *Reflexions on Representation in Parliament* (London, 1766); William Knox, *The Controversy Between Great Britain and Her Colonies Reviewed* (London, 1769); "Amor Patriae" [Thomas Crowley], *A Plan of Union by Admitting Representatives from the American Colonies and from Ireland into the British Parliament* (1770); Anonymous, *A Plan for Conciliating the Jarring Political Interests of Great Britain and her North American Colonies, and for Promoting a General Re-union throughout the Whole British Empire* (London, 1775); Samuel Clay Harvey, *Public Ledger* (London, Jan. 1775); and Adam Smith, *The Wealth of Nations* (London, 1776).

Despite these proposals, the idea of colonial representation in Parliament was widely denounced in the British press and in other published works. As Joshua Steele, an advocate of this solution, conceded in 1766 the idea "would go so much against the stomachs of some of our countrymen, that it could never be got down; nay would disgust them to that degree, that I think they would not suffer any plan to be brought before them that savoured of such a doctrine."[56] Critics complained that the apportionment standard ultimately settled on for colonial representation would establish a dangerous precedent for reforming representation in Great Britain. British political economist Josiah Tucker predicted "our own hair-brained Republicans, and our Mock-Patriots at Home will as certainly adopt" this basis "and echo back the same specious, tho' false Allegations, from one End of the Kingdom to the other."[57] At least one plan was published in London in 1775 that coupled a proposal for reconciling the British-colonial conflict with another for making representation "equal over all Great-Britain, in proportion to the number of Inhabitants."[58]

Notably, the idea of extending parliamentary representation to the colonies had few, if any, supporters in Parliament. It had become customary since the 1707 Act of Union to think of the House of Commons as having a fixed (and, thus, constitutional) size of 588 members.[59] Not surprisingly, as legal historian John Phillip Reid recounts, various objections were raised. The incorporation of colonial representatives into Parliament was opposed because it was feared they would become "a party, a faction, a flying squadron, always ready, and in most cases capable, (by uniting with opposition to administration, or with commercial factions,) to distress government, and the landed interest of the kingdom."[60] An increase in the size of the House of Commons was also

---

[56] Joshua Steele, *An Account of a Late Conference on the Occurrences in America* (1766), p. 23; as quoted in Miller, *The Origins of the American Revolution* (1943), p. 224.

[57] Josiah Tucker, *Four Tracts* (1774), *Complete Works* (1993), 2: 169.

[58] Anonymous, *A Plan for Conciliating the Jarring Political Interests of Great Britain and her North American Colonies, and for Promoting a General Re-union throughout the Whole British Empire* (London, 1775), as quoted in Reid, *The Concept of Representation* (1989), pp. 120–121.

[59] Secretary at War Lord Barrington informed Massachusetts governor Francis Bernard that "no influence could make ten Members of either House of Parliament agree to such a Remedy." Lord Barrington to Francis Bernard, 12 March 1768, as quoted in Reid, *Constitutional History of the American Revolution: The Authority of Law* (1993), p. 103.

[60] Thomas Pownall, *The Administration of the Colonies*, 5th ed., as quoted in Reid, *Constitutional History of the American Revolution* (1993), p. 104.

objected to because, according to one opponent, it would transform the institution into "such a numerous, tumultuous, unwieldy, and unmanageable body, as might give an opportunity to a powerful faction, to overset the throne; or, to a bold and able minister, to enslave the people."[61]

By mid-century, moreover, members of Parliament were neither accustomed nor inclined to associate the "representativeness" of the House of Commons with the legitimacy or effectiveness of the institution. Edmund Burke dismissed the idea of colonial representation as a "project of speculative improvement" because it added nothing "to the authority of [P]arliament" except "that we may afford a greater attention to the concerns of the Americans, and give them a better opportunity of stating their grievances, and of obtaining redress."[62] "It looks," Burke derisively remarked about one proposal, "as if the author had dropped down from the moon, without any knowledge of the general nature of this globe, of the general nature of its inhabitants, without the least acquaintance with the affairs of this country."[63]

Burke expected additional problems with the expenses and trans-Atlantic transportation of these new members as well as with the "infinite difficulty of settling that representation on a fair balance of wealth and numbers."[64] Isaac Barre deemed the idea "dangerous, absurd and impracticable" because the colonies "will grow more numerous than we are and then how inconvenient and dangerous would it be to have representatives of 7 millions there meet the representatives of 7 millions here."[65] Others complained that if the proportion of colonial representatives within the House of Commons was fixed permanently, then Parliament not only could expect continuous complaints about underrepresentation from the rapidly growing American colonies but, as a member noted in 1775, "what would be a reasonable proportion now" for colonial taxation purposes "will, in a few years, become, comparatively with their increased wealth, a miserable pittance."[66]

[61] Anonymous, *Constitutional Right*, as quoted in Reid, *Constitutional History of the American Revolution* (1993), p. 103.

[62] Edmund Burke, "Observations on a Late State of the Nation" [1769], *The Writings and Speeches of Edmund Burke*, Paul Langford, ed. (1981), 2: 178.

[63] Burke, "Observations on a Late State of the Nation" [1769], *Writings and Speeches* (1981), 2: 180.

[64] Burke, "Observations on a Late State of the Nation" [1769], *Writings and Speeches* (1981), 2: 178–179.

[65] Speech of Isaac Barre, 3 Feb. 1766, *Proceedings and Debates of the British Parliaments Respecting North America, 1754–1783*, R. C. Simmons and P. D. G. Thomas, eds. (1983), II: 144.

[66] 27 Feb. 1775, *Proceedings and Debates*, 5: 467.

Dual Sovereignty

The fifth and final conceptualization envisioned British-colonial relations in terms of a decentralized, confederal union. As with the other conceptualizations, the origin of the idea of dual sovereignty within British and colonial discourses is lost in the mists of time. As early as 1689, Edward Littleton of Barbados suggested this idea as an alternative to both colonial submission to Parliament and colonial independence. In his pamphlet Groans of the Plantations (1689), Littleton argued that "though we must part with our Country, yet we would not willingly part with our King: and therefore, if you please, let us be made over to Scotland. We are confident that Scotland would be well pleased to supply us with People, to have the sweet Trade in Exchange."[67]

The historical record suggests that the idea of dual sovereignty was not widely discussed during the first half of the eighteenth century. Benjamin Franklin's 1754 Albany Plan of Union was in this respect one of the first illustrations of how British-colonial relations could be reconstituted. Parliament's taxation of the colonies in the 1760s triggered additional colonial interest in the idea. In 1764, for example, Rhode Island governor Stephen Hopkins articulated the idea of dual sovereignty when he defined the British "imperial state" as composed "of many separate governments, each of which hath peculiar privileges . . . [and] no single part, though greater than another part, is by that superiority instituted to make laws for, or to tax such lesser part; but all laws, and all taxations, which bind the whole, must be made by the whole."[68] Five years later, in 1769, Benjamin Franklin suggested a similar form of imperial organization when he described the British, Irish, and colonial legislatures as the proper judges of their respective concerns and with the Crown "[t]heir only bond of union."[69]

Colonial advocacy of an imperial union bound under a common monarch intensified appreciably once tensions with Parliament escalated in 1774. James Wilson of Pennsylvania insisted that American colonials "are the subjects of the king of Great Britain" and "[t]hey owe him allegiance." According to Wilson, "the inhabitants of Great Britain and

---

[67] Edward Littleton, *The Groans of the Plantations* (1689), in Greene, ed., *Great Britain and the American Colonies* (1970), p. 112.

[68] As quoted in Beer, *British Colonial Policies* (1933), pp. 310–311. See also plan of William Smith reprinted in Robert M. Calhoon, "William Smith Jr's Alternative to the American Revolution," *WMQ* (1965), 22: 104–118.

[69] As quoted in Adams, *Political Ideas of the American Revolution* (1939), pp. 48–49.

those of America. . . . are under allegiance to the same prince; and this union of allegiance naturally produces a union of hearts." Moreover, this "connexion and harmony between great Britain and us, which it is her interest and ours mutually to cultivate, and on which her prosperity, as well as ours, so materially depends, will be better preserved by the operation of the legal prerogatives of the crown, than by the exertion of an unlimited authority by parliament."[70] Other colonials echoed these sentiments.[71] The colonial desire to deny Parliament's authority but to remain attached to the British Crown is captured in the lyrics of an anonymous Virginian poet who wrote in 1774:

> Our King we love, but [Lord Minister] North we hate,
> Nor will to him submissions own;
> If death's our doom, we'll brace our fate,
> But pay allegiance to the throne.[72]

British interest in or support for dual sovereignty was neither deep nor well defined. In the 1760s, several essayists in Great Britain advocated a form of colonial home rule that included Parliamentary supremacy on issues of direct imperial concern.[73] In 1774, John Cartwright advocated complete colonial independence from Parliament and the *voluntary* reunion of the colonies and Great Britain in a "brotherly and perpetual league" under a common king.[74] Several members of Parliament, like Edmund Burke, also became vocal advocates of a dual sovereignty solution as the British-colonial crisis escalated toward civil war. Most British leaders, nonetheless, were reluctant to support a solution that promised to circumscribe Parliament's legislative authority.

---

[70] James Wilson, *Considerations on the Nature and Extent of the Legislative Authority of the British Parliament* (1774), in *Works of James Wilson*, Robert G. McCloskey, ed. (Cambridge, MA: Harvard University Press, 1967), II: 744–745.

[71] See John Adams, *Novanglus* (Boston, 1774); Thomas Jefferson, *Summary View of the Rights of British America* (Williamsburg, 1774); and James Iredell, "To the Inhabitants of Great Britain" (n.p., 1774), *Life and Correspondence of James Iredell*, I: 205–220.

[72] Anonymous, "Virginia Banishing Tea" (1774), in Patterson, *The Spirit of the American Revolution* (1915), p. 55.

[73] See Charles F. Mullett, "English Imperial Thinking, 1764–1783," *PSQ* (1930), 45: 548–579; and Hinkhouse, *The Preliminaries of the American Revolution as Seen in the English Press* (1926), pp. 117–125.

[74] John Cartwright, *American Independence: The Interest and Glory of Great Britain* (London, 1774), as quoted in Adams, *Political Ideas of the American Revolution* (1939), p. 57. See also Labaree, "The Idea of American Independence," *Massachusetts History Society Proceedings* (1970), 82: 14; Granville Sharp, *A Declaration of the People's Natural Right to Share in the Legislature* (Philadelphia, 1774), in Adams, *Political Ideas of the American Revolution* (1939), p. 58.

Others, moreover, suspected that this solution was "a mere subterfuge" for colonial independence; as Samuel Johnson explained, "once they can obtain an exemption from the supremacy of Parliament, there is no power whatever to keep them in a state of submission to the crown." Still others predicted this solution would transform the empire into "at best but a Confederacy of petty states" or that it would destroy the "happy balance of the three estates which constitutes the great excellency of our justly-admired constitution."[75]

PART III: A GAME-THEORETIC ANALYSIS OF THE AMERICAN REVOLUTION

Given this set of five possible outcomes of British-colonial relations and assuming that the outcome preferences of individual British and colonial decision makers can be represented after 1774 as the collective preferences of two unitary actors, "Great Britain" and the "American colonies," consider the rankings of British and colonial preferences in Table 3.1.[76] Among the five possible outcomes, those most preferred by Great Britain and the American colonies are ranked first and assigned the highest numerical value of 5. Least preferred outcomes are ranked fifth and assigned the lowest value of 1.[77]

---

[75] See Hinkhouse, *The Preliminaries of the American Revolution as Seen in the English Press* (1926), p. 119; and Labaree, "The Idea of American Independence," *Massachusetts History Society Proceedings* (1970), 82: 14–15.

[76] These unitary actor categorizations represent the dominant political views in Great Britain and the American colonies. Among British and American political elites there were a variety of views about the future of British-colonial relations, especially prior to 1774. Generally speaking, however, by 1774 a "British" view and an "American" view had coalesced, and both were largely unaffected by dissenting voices in Great Britain or in the American colonies.

[77] The historical record is replete with evidence supportive of these preference rankings. After 1763, the most consistently advocated positions by most American colonial leaders were for the maintenance of the status quo and against colonial subordination to Parliament: hence, their placement as, respectively, the colonies' most and least preferred outcomes. In 1774 and 1775, colonial leaders repeatedly advocated the idea of dual sovereignty and an empire bound at the center under a single Crown: hence, the specification of the dual sovereignty outcome as the second most preferred colonial outcome. Colonial representation in Parliament was one of the first solutions advocated in the 1760s, yet colonial support for this idea dissipated after 1766. By 1775, Joseph Galloway's proposal of this idea as a means of averting a colonial decision for independence received almost no colonial support. For these reasons, this outcome was considered the fourth most preferred outcome. Finally, by the end of 1774 the colonial position on independence can generally be characterized as neutral, with little direct support for it but increasingly less overt resistance against it: hence, its assignment

TABLE 3.1. *British and Colonial Outcomes Preferences, 1774–1776*

Preference	American Colonies	Great Britain
Most	5. Colonial Status Quo	5. Colonial Subordination to Parliament
	4. Dual Sovereignty under Crown	4. Dual Sovereignty under Crown
	3. Colonial Independence	3. Colonial Representation in Parliament
	2. Colonial Representation in Parliament	2. Colonial Independence
Least	1. Colonial Subordination to Parliament	1. Colonial Status Quo

TABLE 3.2. *Decision Matrix of British-Colonial Relations, 1763–1776*

Great Britain:

American Colonies:	Compromise (C)	No Compromise (~C)
Compromise (C)	[Dual Sovereignty] [Colonial Representation in Parliament]	[Colonial Subordination to Parliament]
No Compromise (~C)	[Colonial Independence]	[Status Quo]

Beyond the obvious fact that British and colonial outcome preferences were not perfectly aligned prior to the American Revolution, what do these ordinal-level rankings reveal? Consider Table 3.2 where the British-colonial conflict is represented in a decision matrix in which two actors, "Great Britain" and the "American colonies," must select one of two strategies: "Compromise" (C) or "No Compromise" (~C). The outcome set again defines the range of possible outcomes, with the production

between the two positively perceived outcomes ("Status Quo" and "Dual Sovereignty") and the two negatively perceived outcomes ("Colonial Representation" and "Colonial Subordination to Parliament").

The historical record also supports British preference rankings. Unlike American Leaders whose preferences were evenly divided between "positive" and "negative" outcomes, British leaders generally considered the bottom four preferences in Table 3.1 "negative" outcomes. From the British perspective in 1774, "Colonial Subordination to Parliament" was the only "positive" outcome.

TABLE 3.3. *Preference Values among Outcomes*

Great Britain:

American Colonies:	Compromise (C)	No Compromise (~C)
Compromise (C)	(4, 4) [Dual Sovereignty] (2, 3) [Colonial Representation]	(1, 5) [Colonial Subordination to Parliament]
No Compromise (~C)	(3, 2) [Colonial Independence]	(5, 1) [Status Quo]

of any specific outcome dependent on both actors' decisions. If, for example, both actors decide to compromise, then two outcomes are possible: "Dual Sovereignty" or "Colonial Representation in Parliament." If, however, both actors decide not to compromise (as both British and colonial leaders essentially did after 1763), then the conflict remains unresolved, and the outcome (by default) is the "Status Quo."

In Table 3.3, the relative values of British and colonial outcome preferences are incorporated into the decision matrix as numerical pairs (x, y), where "x" represents the value of colonial preferences and "y" represents the value of British preferences. The outcome "Colonial Subordination," for example, receives the numerical pair: (1, 5), giving the "American Colonies" its least preferred outcome (x = 1) and "Great Britain" its most preferred outcome (y = 5).

Given this arrangement of strategies, outcomes, and preferences, and assuming that both actors pursue their highest possible preferences, what does this decision matrix reveal about the underlying dynamics of the British-colonial conflict after 1774? Neither actor, for one, has a dominant decision strategy because the value of x_C in every (x, y) pair for the "American Colonies" is not always greater than or equal to the value of x_{-C}, nor is y_C for "Great Britain" always greater than or equal to y_{-C}. In other words, neither actor is compelled to adopt a decision strategy without regard to the other actor's decision. If, for example, "Great Britain" unilaterally adopts a "No Compromise" strategy in order to obtain its most preferred outcome ("Colonial Subordination to Parliament"), the "American Colonies" would be compelled to adopt a "No Compromise" strategy in order to obtain its most preferred outcome. Ironically, the latter decision ensures "Great Britain" its least preferred outcome: the "Status Quo." Resolution of this conflict thus depends on cooperation between these two actors.

Although cooperation for both actors' second most preferred outcome ("Dual Sovereignty") is the outcome one might intuitively expect, such an agreement would have been unlikely given the logical relationships portrayed in this matrix. No agreement of any sort ought to have been expected. To illustrate this dynamic, eliminate the lower-value outcome ("Colonial Representation") from the upper left cell of the decision matrix in Table 3.3. Assume each actor selects a decision strategy in accord with its highest possible preference. Begin in any cell, allow consecutive decisions by each actor, and the resulting mix of strategies does not yield a single outcome but an endless, clockwise cyclic movement among the four remaining outcomes within the matrix. This failure to achieve a single outcome thus reveals that the underlying strategic logic of the British-colonial conflict was clearly more indeterminate than what some accounts of the American Revolution portray as an inevitable movement by American colonial leaders for Independence.

More than the strategic pursuit of interests prevented British and colonial leaders from resolving their conflict in the 1760s and early 1770s. Deep differences between British and colonial conceptualizations of representation meant that British and colonial leaders had radically different ideas and normative expectations about the boundaries of political legitimacy and the foundations of the authority to govern. In addition, the severe time lag for the trans-Atlantic transfer of information between Great Britain and the American colonies meant that decisions were made and received without complete information about the other's decisions. This lack of information was exaggerated by prevailing mental frameworks that consisted of seemingly indelible caricatures of the other actor's interests and intentions. Regardless of any contrary signals that might have been sent, most British leaders thought of the American colonies as a "thankless and ungrateful child" badly in need of discipline. "We have spoke the word, and must not falter," one Member of Parliament exclaimed in May 1774. "A radical correction of their constitution must take place. What have we to fear?"[78] Colonial leaders consistently viewed British decisions as evidence of a conspiracy to restrict American liberties and to establish a tyranny over the colonies.[79]

[78] House of Commons speech of John St. John, 2 May 1774, *Proceedings and Debates,* IV: 354–355.

[79] See Bailyn, *The Ideological Origins of the American Revolution* (1967), pp. 94–159; Gordon S. Wood, "Conspiracy and the Paranoid Style: Causality and Deceit in the

Institutional arrangements also affected British-colonial interactions. The underdevelopment of imperial institutions, especially the lack of a common British-colonial legislature, ensured that there were few formalized settings for discouraging negotiation brinkmanship or for brokering cooperative solutions. In addition, the absence of colonial representation in Parliament meant that the colonial assemblies remained the most prestigious governing institutions open to colonial political leaders. Not surprisingly, many assembly members became the most zealous opponents of Parliament's attempts to assert governing authority over the colonies. As British economist Adam Smith astutely but belatedly observed in 1776, "[a]lmost every individual of the governing party in America, fills, at present, in his fancy, a station superior, not only to what he had ever filled before, but to what he had ever expected to fill; and unless some new object of ambition is presented either to him or to his leaders, if he has the ordinary spirit of a man, he will die in defense of that station."[80]

Other impediments to a cooperative resolution of their conflict are masked by the ordinal-level numbers used to rank British and colonial outcome preferences. These numbers assign consecutive and equally distanced numerical values to preferences without consideration of the relative differences between these preferences. Thus, the difference between Great Britain's first and second preferences is assumed to be the same as that between its second and third preferences. By the 1770s, however, Parliament was accustomed to claiming and exercising unchallenged legislative authority and it was therefore extremely unlikely to return any of the governing authority it had acquired from the Crown since 1689.[81] As a consequence, the difference between Great Britain's most preferred outcome (Colonial Subordination = 5) and its second most preferred outcome (Dual Sovereignty = 4) was clearly greater than differences between the other possible outcomes. Just how much greater is not

---

Eighteenth Century," *WMQ* (1982), 39: 401–441; Thomas Jefferson to John Randolph, Aug. 25, 1775, *The Portable Thomas Jefferson*, p. 353.

  Other colonials, like James Iredell of North Carolina, made "a distinction between the Ministry, and even the Parliament, and the People of England. These last I do not consider as accessary in all the oppression we have sustained" for "the inadequacy of the Representation, and the Corruptions so universal leave little to the real voice of the People." James Iredell, "[Causes of the American Revolution]" (June 1776), *Papers of James Iredell*, I: 411.

[80] Adam Smith, *The Wealth of Nations* (1776), 1925 ed., II: 122.

[81] See Jack P. Greene, "The Plunge of Lemmings: A Consideration of Recent Writings on British Politics and the American Revolution," *South Atlantic Quarterly* (1968), LXVII: 141–175; and Greene, *Peripheries and Center* (1986), p. 143.

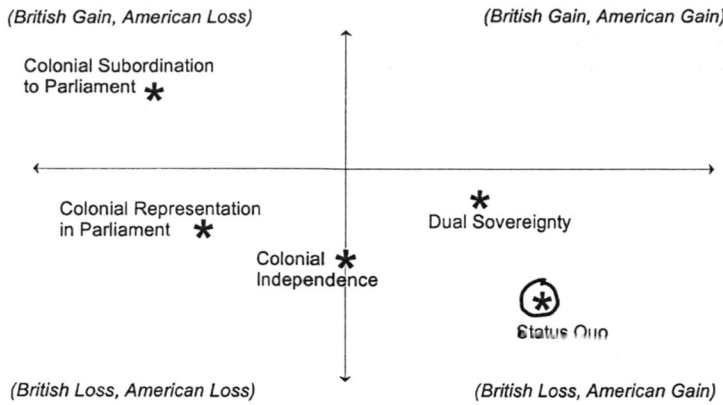

FIGURE 3.1. Expected Relative Outcome Values for Great Britain and the American Colonies

numerically translatable, but the greater the value of the British preference for the "Colonial Subordination" outcome the stronger the cyclical dynamic within the decision matrix because there would have been even less incentive for "Great Britain" to settle for an outcome that offered less than its first preference.

Figure 3.1 offers a more revealing perspective of the difficulties of achieving British-colonial cooperation without the assistance of a common institutional framework. The empty "British gain–American gain" quadrant clearly illustrates that none of the five outcomes was perceived as guaranteeing positive consequences for both actors.[82] Thus as long as both actors pursued courses they considered to be in their interests, no outcome could be expected to command their simultaneous support.

If spontaneous cooperative solutions were unlikely, then how can the indeterminacy of the British-colonial conflict (as observed in Table 3.3.) be reconciled with the historical fact that the American Revolution not only occurred but that this conflict ultimately ended outside the parameters of the original outcome set? Consider a second model of the British-colonial conflict in Figure 3.2. Rather than a decision matrix, the outcome set is represented now within a multidimensional space. As in the matrix model, assume that final resolution of this conflict will be for one of the five specified outcomes and, therefore, on only one of the five

[82] For a description of British and colonial views, see note 77.

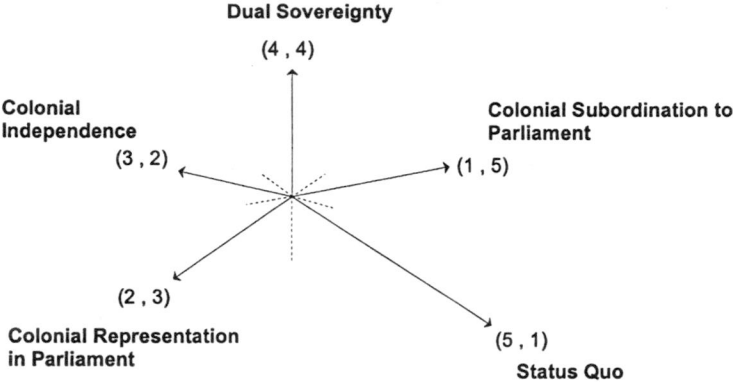

FIGURE 3.2. Model of Outcome Resolution space

axes defined within Figure 3.2. Let the original numerical values assigned to each outcome represent British and colonial preferences for resolution of the conflict on each axis.

The British-colonial conflict can be described more accurately as an historical event within this multidimensional model partly because the outcome set is portrayed directly in terms of individual outcomes and not as a consequence of the less realistic "compromise" or "no compromise" strategies that defined the range of actions within the decision matrix. In this alternative model, moreover, the original two actors ("Great Britain" and the "American Colonies") are removed completely from the structure of the model and are thus free to consider each proposal for resolving the conflict.

Several minor modifications further improve the descriptive utility of this second model. First, a temporal framework is added to mark time outward from the common center point of the five axes. To simplify the addition of this temporal framework, only two years, 1763 and 1774, are represented in Figure 3.3.

Inclusion of the element of time into this model does not affect the underlying indeterminacy of the British-colonial conflict. Rather, its only function is to illustrate that British and colonial efforts to resolve their conflict between 1763 and 1774 can be represented in terms both of its interaxial dynamics and as unique temporally ordered events. Every proposal for resolving the conflict between Great Britain and the American colonies, therefore, could be represented both as a point on an individ-

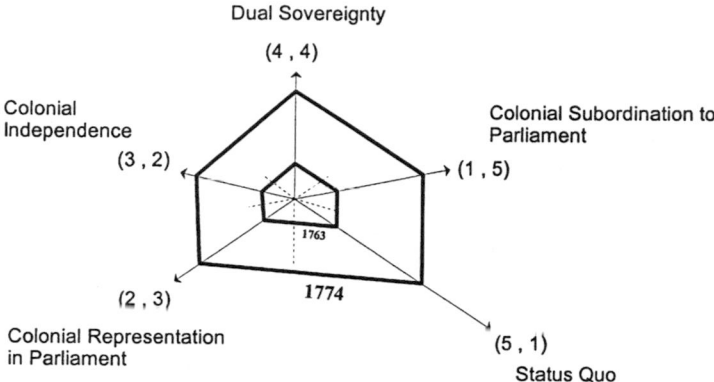

FIGURE 3.3. Outcome Resolution Space with Temporal Framework

ual axis and within a sequence of other points that moves outward from the model's center point.

A second and final modification reemphasizes that the "Status Quo" outcome was not only part of the conceptual framework within which the British-colonial conflict was debated, it also describes a set of real-world conditions as well. For the sake of clarity, only this latter real-world "status quo" is identified in Figure 3.4, where it is represented as an unbroken line that proceeds from a point in the past into the temporal framework clearly associated with this chapter's particular concern. Additional year markers are also included to distinguish this "real-world" outcome axis from the other purely "conceptual" outcomes. Reintegration of real-world conditions into the analysis of the immediate causes of the American Revolution underscores the point that regardless of the conceptual indeterminacy of the British-colonial conflict, British-colonial relations continued to be grounded on and continuously redefined by the dynamic set of economic, demographic, institutional, and ideological conditions described in Chapter 2.

Once modified to reflect both temporal and real-world conditions, this second model aids the resolution of the first model's representation of the indeterminacy of the British-colonial conflict with this conflict's ultimate civil war outcome. For what this modified model reveals is that the failure to resolve this conflict was not a neutral state, but rather it rewarded the American colonies with their most preferred outcome: the status quo. Leading colonials regularly predicted that if the colonies

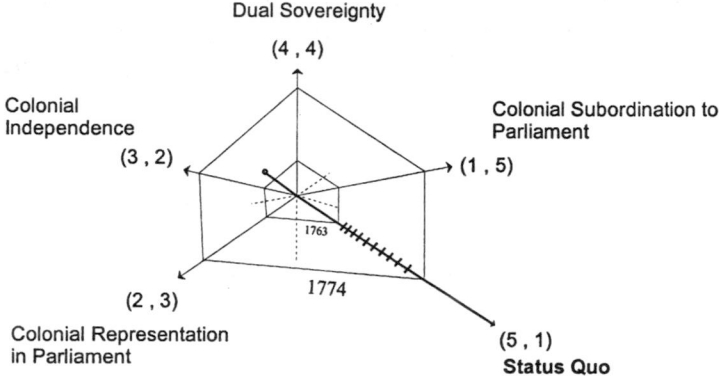

FIGURE 3.4. Outcome Resolution Space with Real-Time Status Quo

succeeded in simply blocking British interventions, their conflict with Great Britain ultimately would be resolved in their favor. Benjamin Franklin thus counseled against any rash actions by the American colonies, believing in 1773 "that by our growing Strength we advance fast to a situation in which our Claims must be allowed; [and] that by a premature Struggle we may be crippled and kept down another Age."[83] Moreover, when a military confrontation with Great Britain appeared increasingly likely in 1775, Edward Wigglesworth of Massachusetts lamented: "Happy had it been for America, if its present contest with the parent state had been postponed to the middle of the next century!"[84]

British leaders, by contrast, expected decidedly fewer benefits from "suffer[ing] Things to remain in statu quo." British essayist Josiah Tucker, for example, predicted that the American colonies would continue to secure additional governing authority and that "as they increase in Riches, Strength, and Numbers, and their civil and military Establishments" the financial costs of British participation in colonial governance also would continue to increase.[85] British realization that their position weakened the longer the terms of their relationship with the American colonies remained unresolved became the primary catalyst

[83] Franklin to John Winthrop, July 25, 1773, *PBF*, 20: 330. See also John Adams, *LDC* (October 1774), I: 157.

[84] Edward Wigglesworth, *Calculations on American Population, with A Table for Estimating the Annual Increase of Inhabitants in the British Colonies* (Boston, Jan. 25, 1775), p. 7.

[85] Tucker, *Four Tracts* [1774], in *Collected Works* (1993), 2: 160.

for their increasingly aggressive attempts to end this constitutional uncertainty. After more than a decade of failing to persuade the American colonies to acknowledge British supremacy, Parliament and George III used an act of colonial disobedience in Boston's harbor in December 1773 as an opportunity to impose a series of punitive measures known as the "Coercive" Acts.[86] These Acts, coupled with the British determination in late 1774 and early 1775 to use British troops to enforce them, represent a definitive decision to force the conflict from the real-world "status quo" to the "Colonial Subordination" outcome.[87]

As illustrated in Figure 3.5, Great Britain's decision had several dramatic consequences. From the British perspective cooperation was no longer understood as a necessary condition for ending the constitutional conflict. The parameters of the original outcome set were also altered. As the real-world "status quo" was irrevocably destroyed by Great Britain's resort to military force, its conceptual counterpart in the outcome set also was removed as a viable possibility. At the same time, George III made clear that he was "graciously disposed to join with Great-Britain against America in this Contest for Empire," thus eliminating the possibility of the "Dual Sovereignty" outcome as well.[88] From

[86] In 1773, Parliament granted the East India Company a monopoly on the American tea trade. Colonial opposition arose in several port cities, with the much celebrated Boston "Tea Party" occurring in December 1773. Parliament responded to the destruction of tea in Boston by enacting a series of policies known collectively as the "Coercive" or the "Intolerable" Acts which were intended to punish the colony of Massachusetts and to bolster Parliament's authority in the colonies. The Boston Port Act closed the port of Boston until the East India Company was reimbursed for its destroyed tea. The Massachusetts Government Act revoked the colony's charter and prohibited the convening of town meetings not approved by the royal governor. The Administration of Justice Act shifted the prosecution of certain cases from the American colonies to England. The Quartering Act empowered royal governors to quarter troops in private homes. Finally, the Quebec Act extended the boundaries of the Province of Quebec south to the Ohio River and west to the Mississippi River, and recognized a toleration for Catholicism in this region. See Gipson, *The British Empire before the American Revolution*, Vol. 12.

[87] For a more detailed account of British calculations and decisions, see Ammerman, *In the Common Cause* (1974), pp. 125–138. Arguably, British intentions are reflected in the preamble of a bill enacted by Parliament in 1774 which unequivocally stated that "the great increase of people in the said colonies has an immediate tendency to produce *independency*." Among other restrictions, this bill imposed a substantial tax (£50 per capita) on all colonial immigrants and, according to historian Emberson E. Proper, was designed to "practically shut off foreign immigration" and "the development of the colonies from an outside population." Emberson E. Proper, "Colonial Immigration Laws," *Columbia Studies* (1900), 12: 76.

[88] Josiah Tucker, *An Humble and Earnest Appeal* (1775), *Collected Works* (1993), 5: 41. See also George III to Lord North, Sept. 11, 1774, *The Correspondence of King George the Third*, John Fortescue, ed. (London: Cass, 1967), III: 131.

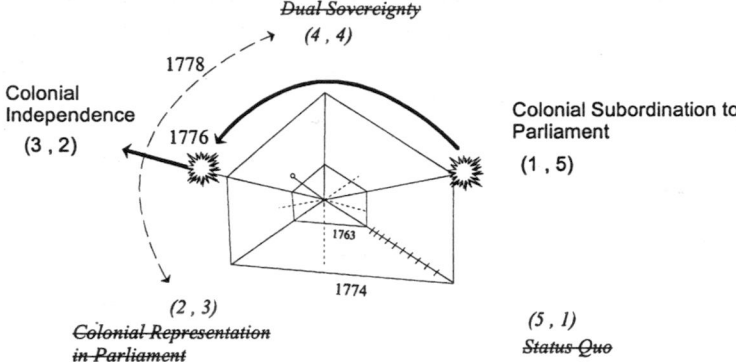

FIGURE 3.5. British and American Decisions, 1774–1778

the American colonial perspective, the outcome set was reduced to three possible outcomes: "Colonial Independence," "Colonial Representation in Parliament," and "Colonial Subordination to Parliament" – the third, fourth, and fifth most preferred outcomes by the American colonies. Faced with this more constrained set of choices and the British-induced "Colonial Subordination" outcome if no response was made, colonial leaders in the First and Second Continental Congresses decided to resist the British decision with force. In July 1776, colonial leaders made their historic decision for "Colonial Independence" – the highest remaining outcome preference of the American colonies.[89]

Ironically, after the unexpected American rout of British forces at Saratoga in late 1777 and France's formal alliance with the American independence movement in 1778, frantic efforts were made in Great Britain to reestablish their political union with the openly rebellious American colonies. House of Commons member David Hartley, for example, proposed "cement[ing] the two countries together by a mutual naturalization."[90] Others like William Pulteney attempted to reopen the original outcome set with proposals that called for the acceptance of the

[89] For a more theoretically oriented explanation of the consequences associated with the compression of a multidimensional issue space, see William Riker, "Heresthetic and Rhetoric in the Spatial Model," *Advances in the Spatial Theory of Voting*, James M. Enelow and Melvin J. Hinich, eds. (Cambridge, UK: Cambridge University Press, 1990), pp. 46–65.

[90] As quoted in Robson, *The American Revolution in its Political and Military Aspects* (1955), p. 81.

American colonies as equal members of the British Empire.[91] In addition, the Crown authorized peace commissioners to win the former American colonies back into the British Empire by offering the former colonies the original dual sovereignty solution and the opportunity to send a fixed "and very small" number of colonial representatives to Parliament.[92] These proposals were too late for serious consideration by American political leaders and those they represented. The visions and calculations of these individuals already extended past the known and seemingly meager possibilities of restoration toward the real and imagined benefits enchantingly promised by the creation of a new and now possible *American* constitutional order.

CONCLUSION

Accounts of the American Revolution invariably raise and are challenged by three questions: Why did Great Britain commit to a reconfiguration of the terms of their constitutional union with the American colonies? Why did the American colonies resist this reconfiguration? And why did these differences end in civil war in 1776? To answer these questions, this chapter extended Chapter 2's macrolevel analysis to include an examination at the microlevel of the expectations, preferences, and decisional sequences that ultimately produced the final constitutional rupture in 1776. The subsequent synthesis of these macro- and microlevel conditions into a new account of the American Revolution was facilitated by the historical reconstruction of the five constitutional conceptualizations that framed the debate between Great Britain and the American colonies. Given that both actors' preferences over this set of possible outcomes were determined, in large measure, by each constitutional outcome's expected rule of apportionment, two game theoretic models were introduced to illuminate why these different outcome preferences ultimately yielded an American declaration of independence and the subsequent civil war.

[91] William Pulteney, *Thoughts on the Present States of Affairs with America and the Means of Conciliation* [1778]; Adams, *Political Ideas of the American Revolution* (1939), p. 58.

[92] See "Royal Instructions to the Peace Commission of 1778, 12 April 1778," in *Sources & Documents*, Morison, ed. (1965), p. 200. See also "Carlisle Commission: Letter to Henry Laurens, President and Other Members of Congress, June 13, 1778; Congress' Rejection of the Carlisle Proposals, June 17, 1778," in *The American Revolution, 1763–1783*, Richard B. Morris, ed. (Columbia, SC: University of South Carolina Press, 1970), pp. 272–275.

Why, in sum, did British interests commit to and American interests resist a change in the fundamental terms of their long-standing constitutional union? The relationship between expectations about apportionment rules and their respective constitutional orders proposed in Chapter 1 offers a framework for answering these questions. The positions taken by Great Britain and the American colonies between 1774 and 1776 reflected their divergent expectations concerning both the division of decision-making capacities within the Empire and the level of imperial authority within the American colonies. In particular, whereas the historical record reveals that American leaders expressed little interest in constitutional change before 1774, British interests and their agents in Parliament grew increasingly dissatisfied with both their decision-making capacities and the level of governmental authority within the colonies. That British interests between 1774 and 1776 never appeared willing to entertain alternative constitutional outcomes – in particular, alternatives that did not acknowledge the absolute sovereignty of Parliament or a centralized form of imperial organization – sustains this work's theoretical expectation that the initial moments of the American Revolution were, in fact, a conflict induced by British leaders irrevocably dissatisfied with the then operative rule of apportionment over the American colonies.

But why the civil war outcome when so few on either side of the Atlantic foresaw, advocated, or prepared for this outcome before 1774? Clearly, few on either side of the Atlantic ignored or underestimated the high costs of suppression and rebellion. Yet as the second model revealed, the perceived costs of British acquiescence to a continuation of the status quo (especially, one defined by the long-term structural developments described in Chapter 2) and of American acquiescence to Parliament's new claim of sovereignty over the colonies compelled both sides to commit to resolving their differences through force and not the consent of the other.

The American Revolution, therefore, occurred because British and colonial political leaders failed to maintain a working consensus about the constitutional terms and limitations of their relationship. The breakdown of this consensus was no doubt made possible by various structural conditions, but it was given life and fueled by a divergence of expectations concerning the immediate and future terms of the governing relationship that would exist between Great Britain and the American colonies. Failure to negotiate a new and common understanding of these constitutional terms amidst these divergent expectations ultimately encouraged both parties to seek alternative means for resolving their constitutional differences. For American political leaders, the decision to abandon their long-standing relationship with Great Britain opened a rare opportunity for forming a new and independent constitutional order. Completion of this order was, however, by no means inevitable. The conventional wisdom at the time ominously predicted that without the protection of the British empire, the American colonies would never be able to establish or sustain a constitutional union and that "Anarchy and Confusion will every where prevail."[93] How the newly independent American colonies ultimately proved this wisdom wrong is the surprise that awaits the curious reader in Chapter 4.

[93] Josiah Tucker, "Four Tracts" [1774], in *Collected Works* (1993), 2: 138–139.

4

Union over Multiplicity: A Bond of Words, a Confederation in Speech, and the Constitutional Rule of Equal State Apportionment

The structural conditions described in Chapter 2 and the sequence of decisions analyzed in Chapter 3 constitute the remote and immediate causes of the collapse of the British-colonial order in 1776. This chapter completes this new story of the American Revolution with an account of the subsequent series of political debates, deliberations, and decisions that produced a constitutional consensus for a new national rule of apportionment and the first American constitution, the Articles of Confederation.

This chapter concentrates on the set of political actors who assumed the authority to define the governmental armature of the new American order, including its national rule of apportionment. The terms of this new rule were heavily contested. Many supported or contested other components of the proposed national order with reference to their expectations concerning the likely effect of different rules of apportionment. The latter phenomenon suggests a dynamic familiar to many constitutional transitions: constitution makers with positive expectations concerning the strength of their interests under a proposed rule of apportionment generally tend to support a more broadly empowered national government, whereas constitution makers with less positive expectations concerning the strength of their interests tend to support more limited forms of government. If, therefore, the set of constitution makers consists of individuals who do not share approximately similar interests and expectations, then the creation and maintenance of an order based on the consent of these individuals turns on the formulation of a rule of apportionment and a governmental structure capable of satisfying a multiplicity of interests and expectations. This, it is not difficult to imagine, is no simple task.

Construction of a full account of the creation of the first apportionment rule for the American political order is complicated by several additional obstacles. For one, the historical record of the individuals who debated, defined, and ratified this rule is incomplete.[1] Reconstruction of the sequence of decisions that yielded this rule and of the relationship between this sequence and the formalization of the new order therefore requires not only a descriptive account grounded in the available historical evidence but also an interpretative account that recognizes the central constitutional problem raised and solved during this original American founding experience: the problem of creating a national constitutional order – with a working rule of apportionment – based exclusively on the consent of the members of this common order.

Another obstacle to a full account arises once it is admitted that the makers of new constitutional orders of this magnitude generally engage in multiple (and often indistinguishable) discourses that address, at minimum, three distinct objectives.[2] One of these objectives is *external*

---

[1] The historical record of the debates of the Continental Congress between 1774 and 1777 is limited. Among the most complete subsets of this record, see John Adams, *Diary and Autobiography of John Adams* [hereafter *Diary*], Butterfield, ed. (Cambridge, MA: Harvard University Press, 1961), 4 Vols.; Thomas Jefferson, *The Papers of Thomas Jefferson* [hereafter *PTJ*], Boyd, ed. (Princeton, NJ: Princeton University Press, 1950), Vol. I; *Journals of the Continental Congress* [hereafter *JCC*], Ford, ed., Vols. I–XIII (Washington, U.S. Government Printing Office, 1904–1937); *Letters of Members of the Continental Congress* [hereafter *LMCC*], Burnett, ed., 8 vols. (Gloucester, MA: P. Smith, 1963); and *Letters of Delegates to Congress* [hereafter *LDC*], Smith, ed., 24 Vols. (Washington, DC: Library of Congress, 1976–1996). For the fullest interpretative accounts of this evidence, see Jack N. Rakove, *The Beginnings of National Politics: An Interpretive History of the Continental Congress* (New York: Knopf, 1979); H. James Henderson, *Party Politics in the Continental Congress* (New York: McGraw-Hill, 1974); Edmund C. Burnett, *The Continental Congress* (New York: The Macmillan Company, 1941); Merrill Jensen, *The Articles of Confederation* (Madison, WI: University of Wisconsin Press, 1940).

Somewhat surprisingly, the historical record of the ratification of the Articles of Confederation by the thirteen states remains highly fragmentary and, at times, the chronology of events based on the evidence is ambiguous and contradictory. See, for example, *LMCC*, 3: 323–324n.2. Among the fullest interpretative accounts of the available evidence, see Rakove, *The Beginnings of National Politics* (1979); Jensen, *The Articles of Confederation* (1940); George D. Harmon, "The Proposed Amendments to the Articles of Confederation, *South Atlantic Quarterly* (1925), 24: 298–315.

[2] For contemporaneous evidence that the American political leaders also recognized three distinct levels of discourse, see John Adams to Patrick Henry, June 3, 1776, *LDC*, 4: 122–123.

From a theoretical perspective, this account assumes that what is commonly referred to as a "two-level game" (consisting of "international" and "domestic" levels) can be described more accurately as a "three-level" game defined in terms of its "external-international," "domestic-operational," and "intragovernmental-elite" dynamics. See

legitimacy, or the recognition of an order's autonomy and domain by other similarly recognized orders. The discourse related to this objective was preceded by the debates, described in Chapter 3, between British and colonial leaders over the respective authority and domain of Parliament and the colonial assemblies. Once these debates ended in civil war, American political leaders became engaged in a new set of discourses with foreign governments concerning their recognition of the newly independent American nation.[3]

A second objective of constitution makers – and the primary focus of this chapter – is the *intragovernmental legitimacy* of a constitutional order, or the formalization of the rules and structures that shape the division of authority among those in a position to act collectively over an order. Determination of the most basic division of collective decision-making authority within a government – or a constitutional order's rule of apportionment – is an essential element of this second objective. The discourse related to this second dimension of constitutional order was defined not only by the political actors who became engaged in the creation of a new national government, but also by other sets of constitution makers who simultaneously attempted to secure the constitutional legitimacy of the new state governments in the wake of Independence.[4]

A third and final objective is the *operational legitimacy* of a constitutional order, or the administrative capacity and authority to govern others outside of the formal structures of government. The various concerns and actions prompted by this third objective are not addressed in

Robert D. Putnam, "Diplomacy and Domestic Politics: The Logic of Two-Level Games," *International Organization* (1988), 42: 427–460; and Aristide R. Zolberg, "Strategic Interactions and the Formation of Modern States: France and England," *International Social Science Journal* (1980), 32: 687–716.

[3] See Jonathan R. Dull, *A Diplomatic History of the American Revolution* (New Haven, CT: Yale University Press, 1985); and Samuel F. Bemis, *The Diplomacy of the American Revolution* (Bloomington, IN: Indiana University Press, 1957).

[4] See Rakove, *The Beginnings of National Politics* (1979). For additional accounts of the constitutionalization process at the national level, see Burnett, *The Continental Congress* (1941); E. James Ferguson, *The Power of the Purse: A History of American Public Finance, 1776–1790* (Chapel Hill: University of North Carolina Press, 1961); Henderson, *Party Politics in the Continental Congress* (1974).

For accounts of the constitutionalization of the new state governments, see Allan Nevins, *The American States During and After the Revolution, 1775–1789* (New York, The Macmillan Co., 1924); Stephen E. Patterson, *Political Parties in Revolutionary Massachusetts* (Madison, WI: University of Wisconsin Press, 1973); Willi P. Adams, *The First American Constitutions* (Chapel Hill: University of North Carolina Press, 1980); Robert A. Becker, *Revolution, Reform, and the Politics of Taxation, 1763–1783* (Baton Rouge: Louisiana State University Press, 1980).

this study. To do so would require the reconstruction of two fundamentally different and wide-ranging discourses. One discourse engaged the Continental Congress and the thirteen new state governments in a series of discussions and actions aimed at defining the terms of their relationship. The second discourse engaged both the national and state governments in separate discourses with the American people concerning the basis and purpose of the latter's collective authority and the extent to which these governments could make and implement decisions for the American people.

In addition to describing these external, intragovernmental, and operational objectives, historical accounts also highlight other aspects of the founding of the American political order. Several accounts emphasize the conflicts that dominated and delayed completion of the process.[5] Historian Merrill Jensen, for example, focused on the conflicts that arose among delegates to the Continental Congress, describing them as driven by various social and economic interests. Advocates of a weak national government and of a decentralized American union, according to Jensen, were radicals driven by expectations that their interests would be advanced within the new and hopefully more democratically structured state governments. By contrast, supporters of a strong national government and of a more centralized American union were conservatives motivated by their fears that democratic reform of state governments would undermine their short- and long-term economic and social interests. Ultimately, Jensen argues, the radicals won this grand constitutional struggle and, as a result, were able to define the structure of the national government formalized in the Articles of Confederation. Why or how the "loser" conservative group was convinced to consent to a form of government under which they expected their interests would not be secured is never adequately explained.

A second set of accounts of the creation of the American constitutional order has a different focus. These accounts generally overlook the problems of coordination and reconceptualization that arise during transitions between old and new constitutional configurations. Instead, they explain that the formation of an American constitutional consensus was compelled by common ideological motivations. Many of these accounts contend that liberal and republican principles of governance were the

---

[5] See Jensen, *The Articles of Confederation* (1940); Henderson, *Party Politics in the Continental Congress* (1974); Joseph L. Davis, *Sectionalism in American Politics, 1774–1787* (Madison, WI: University of Wisconsin Press, 1977).

shared constitutional idioms that unified American political actors prior to and after the dissolution of their political bonds with Great Britain.[6]

A third set of accounts describes both the conflicts which impeded the completion of this process and the specific motives contributing to the formation of a consensus among the delegates to the Continental Congress. In addition to a detailed description of the conflicts that divided the delegates, historian Edmund C. Burnett explained that a consensus for the Articles of Confederation ultimately was triggered by the delegates' sudden loss of confidence regarding their capacity to defeat Great Britain without foreign assistance.[7] Historian Jack N. Rakove provides a synthetic account of the constitutive elements of the American founding. Like Burnett, Rakove describes the delegates' conflicts and their common desire to secure international alliances. Rakove, however, additionally contends that the delegates were motivated to consent to a common constitutional plan because they were concerned that an increasingly inflationary American economy was jeopardizing the domestic legitimacy and operational capacities of the Continental Congress.

Like the accounts of Burnett and Rakove, this account describes both the conflictual and consensual elements of the original American constitutional founding moment. Unlike previous accounts, this chapter demonstrates that in addition to external and domestic concerns, the specific form of government crafted by the delegates between July 1776 and November 1777 provided a third (and necessary) motive supporting the formation of a constitutional consensus for the Articles of Confederation.

This new account of the creation of the American political order is presented in three parts. Part I focuses on the debates of the Continental Congress prior to Independence. These debates forecast the conflicts that would delay the formalization of the Articles of Confederation until 1781. They centered on three issues: the national rule of apportionment, the rule dividing the Union's expenses among the states, and the rules regulating state boundaries and the western territories. Part II recounts

---

[6] Robert W. Hoffert, *A Politics of Tensions: the Articles of Confederation and American Political Ideas* (Niwot, CO: University Press of Colorado, 1992); Gordon S. Wood, *Creation of the American Republic* (Chapel Hill: University of North Carolina Press, 1969); Louis Hartz, *The Liberal Tradition in America* (New York: Harcourt, Brace, 1955); Clinton Rossiter, *Seedtime of the Republic: The Origins of the American Tradition of Political Liberty* (New York: Harcourt, Brace 1953).

[7] Burnett, *The Continental Congress* (1941), p. 248.

Congress's deliberations on the initial drafts of the "Articles of Confederation." Part III illustrates how, amidst deep divisions over the provisions of the Articles, a consensus among delegates to the Continental Congress finally emerged for the rule of equal state apportionment and for the Articles of Confederation. Part IV completes this account with a brief summary of the final stage of the process of constitutional change: the unanimous ratification of the Articles of Confederation by the thirteen American states.

PART I: THE PROBLEMS OF UNION

The decision of American political leaders to dissolve their political bonds with Great Britain resolved one set of constitutional problems but created another concerning the terms of their common political future. The demands of a coordinated resistance against Great Britain and the ambitions of the individuals who became self-conscious of the moment and its constitutional possibilities were conditions that continuously supported the formation of an interstate Union among the thirteen former colonies. Nevertheless, the constitutionalization of this new American Union was never assured.

The unanimity rule which typically governed Congress's decision making and the diversity of state interests impeded the work of delegates to the Continental Congress. The former rule made Congress, in the words of one delegate, "a very unwieldy Body" because "no motion or resolution can be started or proposed but what must be subject to much canvassing before it will pass with the unanimous approbation of the Thirteen Colonies."[8] This difficulty was exacerbated by the fact that intercolonial acquaintance was extremely limited among the delegates. Religious, educational, and cultural differences were so apparent among the delegates that Massachusetts delegate John Adams observed the dissimilarities between "[t]he Characters of Gentlemen in the four New England Colonies" and the other delegates was "as much as several distinct Nations almost."[9] Adams privately believed the "other Colonies are too lazy and shiftless to do any thing untill you set them the example," and he attributed this regional difference to his belief that New Englanders were "purer English Blood less mixed with Scotch, Irish,

---

[8] Silas Deane to Mrs. Deane, June 3, 1775, *LMCC*, I: 111.

[9] John Adams to Joseph Hawley, Nov. 25, 1775, *LDC*, 2: 385–386. See also *Diary of Ezra Stiles*, 2: 237–238; and John Adams to William Tudor, Sept. 24, 1774, *Works of John Adams*, 9: 346.

Dutch, French, Swedish than any other colonials."[10] Different economic interests also separated the delegates. Those from northeastern states and coastal cities, for example, were bound by their interests in continental and international trade. Delegates from southern states and western areas, by contrast, shared longer-term interests in agricultural production and the untapped resources promised in the west.

Differences among the delegates also extended to their political discourse. Terms like the "common good," "public liberty," and "political virtue" were used often but their meanings and applications varied not only between delegates but across issues and time as well. In addition, delegates regularly claimed popular authorization for their positions at the same time as many delegates complained about the prevalence of the "Spirit of Levelling" and the dearth of disinterestedness on nearly every substantive proposal that came before Congress.

The allegedly common ideological idioms of liberalism and republicanism were also used in different and contradictory ways. Most delegates to the Continental Congress, for example, spoke freely for the liberal ideals of limited government, inalienable rights, and individual freedom. At the same time, however, they condoned state seizure of personal property, argued for the righteousness of human slavery, and tolerated the expediency of local justice. The promotion of republican ideals was riddled with similar contradictions. Before 1776 American political leaders rarely used the term "republican" in public or within the private deliberations of the Continental Congress. Indeed, Georgia delegate (and future loyalist) John Zubly declared (without a single recorded challenge from his fellow delegates) that "Republican Government is little better than Government of Devils."[11] Thus, as Continental Congress delegate Stephen Hopkins concluded, "Pleasing Theories [of politics] always gave Way to the Prejudices, Passions, and Interests of Mankind."[12]

The multiplicity of interests that filled the breach opened by the American decision to sever constitutional ties with Great Britain made the spontaneous creation of a new American order highly improbable. The forging of a new national union depended (at least initially) on the

---

[10] John Adams to John Lowell, June 12, 1776, *LDC*, 4: 197; and John Adams to Abigail Adams, as quoted in Davis, *Sectionalism in American Politics, 1774–1787* (1977), p. 10.

[11] Adams, *Diary*, 2: 204. See also W. Paul Adams, "Republicanism in Political Rhetoric Before 1776," *PSQ* (1970), 85: 397–421; and George M. Dutcher, "The Rise of Republican Government in the United States," *PSQ* (1940), 55: 199–216.

[12] Adams, *Diary*, 2: 248. See also Thomas Burke to Governor of North Carolina, Feb. 10 [16], 1777, *LMCC*, II: 257.

formation of a consensus among the delegates to the Continental Congress. At bottom, therefore, the initial cast of the American political order consisted of little more than a bond of words. The essential truth of this characterization of constitutional development was not unknown to the delegates. Massachusetts delegate John Adams, for one, optimistically observed as early as 1775: "It is certainly true that some of our Southern Brethren have not annexed the Same Ideas to the Words Liberty, Honour and Politeness that we have; but I have the Pleasure to observe every day that We learn to think and feel alike more and more."[13]

The formation of an American republic in speech began in earnest with the convening of the First Continental Congress in early September 1774.[14] In addition to confirming the American resolve to reject Parliament's authority to impose the so-called Coercive Acts, the debates and decisions of this Congress reveal that well before any formal commitment to American independence many of the delegates were looking beyond the present crisis to the formation of an intercolonial union.

The Architectonic Issue of Apportionment

Not surprisingly, given the elemental importance of the rule of apportionment, the first issue seriously debated among the delegates to the 1774 Congress was whether voting "should be by Colonies, or by the Poll, or by Interests." A single vote for each colony had been the rule adopted at previous colonial congresses like the 1765 Stamp Act Congress and the 1754 Albany Congress. Virginia delegate Patrick Henry declared, however, that "no former Congress could be a Precedent" for what "was the first general Congress which had ever happened." Henry instead defended a rule in which each colony's vote was proportionally weighted, arguing "it would be a great Injustice, if a little Colony should have the same Weight in the Councils of America, as a great one."[15]

New Hampshire delegate John Sullivan disagreed with Henry's suggestion, reminding Henry "that a little Colony had its All at Stake as well as a great one." With the different interests of the large and small

---

[13] John Adams to Samuel Osgood, Nov. 15, 1775, *LDC*, 2: 549. See also John Adams to Elbridge Gerry, June 18, 1775, LDC, 1: 504.

[14] See Burnett, *The Continental Congress* (1941), pp. 20–59; Andrew C. McLaughlin, *A Constitutional History of the United States* (1935), pp. 75–90; William Cocke, *The Constitutional History of the United States* (Philadelphia: J. B. Lippincott, 1858), pp. 28–34; Rakove, *The Beginnings of National Politics* (1979), pp. 42–62.

[15] Adams, *Diary*, 2: 123.

TABLE 4.1. *Estimated Population by Colony, 1774*

State	Population	Ratio (percent)
New Hampshire	150,000	5.0
Massachusetts	400,000	13.3
Rhode Island	59,678	2.0
Connecticut	192,000	6.3
New York	250,000	8.3
New Jersey	130,000	4.3
Pennsylvania/Delaware	350,000	11.6
Maryland	320,000	10.6
Virginia	640,000	21.2
North Carolina	300,000	9.9
South Carolina	225,000	7.5
Georgia	–	–
	3,016,678	100.0

Source: John Adams, Works of John Adams, Adams, ed. (1852), 7: 302. See also *The Literary Diary of Ezra Stiles*, November 23, 1774, I: 486–487.

colonies clearly distinguished on this issue, other delegates took sides in the debate. Massachusetts delegate John Adams argued: "If We vote by Colonies, this Method will be liable to great Inequality and Injustice, for 5 small Colonies, with 100,000 People in each may outvote 4 large ones, each of which has 500,000 Inhabitants. If We vote by Poll," however, "some Colonies have more than their Proportion of Members, and others have less." Adams concluded, "If we vote by Interests, it will be attended with insuperable Difficulties, to ascertain the true Importance of each Colony." For example, "Is the Weight of a colony to be ascertained by the Number of Inhabitants merely – or by the Amount of their Trade, the Quantity of their Exports and Imports, or by any compound Ratio of both." This question, Adams cautioned, "will lead us into such a Field of Controversy as will greatly perplex us. Besides I question whether it is possible to ascertain, at this Time, the Number of our People or Value of our Trade. It will not do in such a Case, to take each other's Words," perhaps in response to the inflated population estimates provided by several delegates (see Table 4.1). A proportional scale, he maintained, "ought to be ascertained by authentic Evidence, from Records."[16]

[16] Adams, *Diary*, 2: 123–124.

With no consensus after Henry's initial proposal, delegates returned to the voting rule debate several days later. Patrick Henry again advocated a proportional rule. This time, however, he more dramatically contended that "the present State of Things shew that Government is dissolved." "We are in a State of Nature," Henry claimed. "The Distinctions between Virginians, Pennsylvanians, New Yorkers and New Englanders, are no more." The voting rule, therefore, should be proportional because the people will complain if "10,000 Virginians have not outweighed 1000 others." The Virginia delegate further declared: "I hope future Ages will quote our Proceedings with Applause" because it "is one of the great Duties of the democratical Part of the Constitution to keep itself pure."[17]

Despite Henry's rhetorical flight, many of his fellow delegates remained unmoved. Thomas Lynch of South Carolina declared that although he thought the rule "ought to be a compound of Numbers and Property, that should determine the Weight of the Colonies," this issue "cannot be now settled." South Carolina delegate John Rutledge also opposed the adoption of a new rule. "Obedience to our Determinations," he warned, "will only follow the reasonableness, the apparent Utility, and Necessity of the Measures We adopt." "We have no coercive or legislative Authority," he reminded his fellow delegates, for "Our Constituents are bound only in Honour, to observe our Determinations."[18]

Other delegates offered additional reasons for their opposition to a proportional rule. Samuel Ward of Rhode Island noted that the rule advocated by Henry and others had not yet been tested in practice by any of the colonial assemblies. "There are," he directly reminded Henry, "a great Number of Counties in Virginia, very unequal in Point of Wealth and Numbers, yet each has a Right to send 2 Members." Other delegates, like Theodorick Bland of Virginia, argued that until it was possible "to ascertain the Importance of each colony, . . . [t]he Question" was not the justice of particular apportionment schemes but "whether the Rights and Liberties of America shall be contended for, or given up to [the] arbitrary Power" of Parliament. Despite the persistent pleas of proponents of a proportional rule, delegates to the First Continental Congress decided (at least, provisionally) that because "the proper materials for ascertaining the importance of each Colony" were not available "each Colony or Province shall have one Vote."[19]

[17] Adams, *Diary*, 2: 124–125. [18] Adams, *Diary*, 2: 125.
[19] Adams, *Diary*, 2: 125, 126; *JCC*, I: 25 (Sept. 6, 1774).

The Financial Costs and Constitutional Benefits of a
Coordinated Resistance

In May 1775, a second Continental Congress convened in Philadelphia. News of British militarism in Massachusetts prompted delegates to this congress to consider more definitive responses to the still unresolved conflict with Great Britain. With near unanimity, delegates consented to the establishment and support of a new Continental Army.

The ease by which a consensus for a coordinated resistance formed among the delegates to this second congress resulted from several conditions. In addition to their prior experiences at the 1774 Congress, delegates to the 1775 Congress were sobered by Great Britain's apparent commitment to force a resolution of the conflict and by the fragility of Congress's legitimacy to make decisions that would determine the future of millions of Americans.[20] Faced with threats of domination by Great Britain and of irrelevancy or revolt from Americans, congressional delegates recognized – at least for this moment – that building a consensus for an immediate display of collective action was more important than securing a relative advantage over other states.[21]

This effort to fashion a consensus for the common cause of resistance was made possible by specific acts of accommodation. Delegates from the larger states, for example, remained silent about the continued use of the equal colony voting rule adopted at the 1774 Congress. Decisions concerning the formation of the Continental Army were similarly intended to sustain intercolonial cooperation. For example, Congress's appointment of the Virginian George Washington to be commander general of the new Army was intended, in the words of one delegate, "to keep up the Union & more strongly Cement the Southern with the Northern Colonies."[22] Congress also increased the number of generals within the Continental Army to ensure a more inclusive representation of the colonies within the officer corps.[23] Such practices, no doubt, grew out of a common sense that a fair and full representation of all the states was required to sustain their common efforts against Great Britain.

---

[20] Fifty of the sixty-five delegates to the Second Continental Congress attended the 1774 Congress. Rakove, *The Beginnings of National Politics*, p. 71.

[21] Rakove, *The Beginnings of National Politics*, p. 76.

[22] Eliphalet Dyer to Jonathan Trumbull, Sr., June 16, 1775, *LDC*, 1: 496. See also John Adams to Mrs. Adams, 17 June 1775, *LMCC*, I: 130.

[23] Burnett, *The Continental Congress*, p. 78.

TABLE 4.2. *Congressional Division of Common Expenses, 1775*

State	Estimated Population	Ratio	Ratio Differential, 1775–1774 (percent)
New Hampshire	100,000	4.1%	−0.9
Massachusetts	350,000	14.5	1.2
Rhode Island	58,000	2.4	0.4
Connecticut	200,000	8.3	2.0
New York	200,000	8.3	0.0
New Jersey	130,000	5.4	1.1
Pennsylvania	300,000	12.4	0.8

Source: Silas Deane, *Diary*, June 13, 1775, *LDC*, 1: 482; and 1: 687; 689. See also *Diary of Ezra Stiles*, November 23, 1774, I: 486–488.

Shortly after Congress managed to coordinate a unified resistance against Great Britain, delegates to this Second Continental Congress again faced the problem of defining the relationship among the colonies when they discussed the costs of fielding the new Continental Army. Congress debated several methods of finance before finally agreeing to emit bills of credit totaling $3 million. Congress decided that each colony would be responsible for paying a proportional part of the resulting debt and all would be responsible for assuming the debt of any colony unable to repay its specified portion. Each colony's share of this common debt was to be "determined according to the number of Inhabitants, of all ages, including negroes and mulattoes." Because accurate population records did not exist, Congress adopted a revised estimate of each colony's population (see Table 4.2), and agreed their intercolonial ratios would be corrected on receipt of more accurate population records.[24] To ensure this revision, delegates "at the next Congress" were to "come provided with an exact account of the number of people of all ages and sexes, including slaves."[25]

In addition to meeting the immediate financial needs of the inter-colonial resistance effort, the debt repayment system adopted by Congress provided, according to one delegate, a "bond of union to the

[24] *JCC*, II: 103 (June 22, 1775); II: 207 (July 25, 1775); II: 221–222 (June 29, 1775). In December 1775, Congress again requested that each colony complete a census of its population. *JCC*, III: 458, Dec. 26, 1775. In February 1776, Congress established a committee to monitor this request. *JCC*, IV: 156, Feb. 17, 1776.

[25] Virginia delegates to the President of the Virginia Convention, July 11, 1775, *LDC*, I: 622–623.

Associated Colonies" because all the colonies "will be bound in interest to endeavour that ways and means be fallen upon for sinking" the debt. New England delegates – if John Adams was at all representative of the region – were especially pleased by the expected "Floods of Paper Money" that would result from this decision for they promised to "get the Continent nobly in our Debt."[26]

Territorial Lines as Constitutional Divisions

A third issue related to the formation of the American political order appears to have been discussed only briefly by the Continental Congress prior to independence. This issue concerned the definition and regulation of colonial boundaries. Delegates to the Continental Congress were aware as early as May 1775 that "the uncertainty of the Boundaries between Virginia & Penn[slyvani]a is the Cause of Great Uneasiness." Similar territorial disputes emerged between Pennsylvania and Connecticut, Maryland and Virginia, and several colonies and separatist groups. The Continental Congress consistently refused to intervene in these disputes, preferring to appeal for calm and a suspension of hostilities for the "preservation of everything that can make our common country dear to us."[27] By April 1776, however, there was a growing fear among several delegates that "the Continent would be torn in pieces by Intestine wars and Convulsions" without a resolution of these territorial disputes.[28]

In addition to intercolonial boundary disputes, the future of the so-called western lands – the vast region between existing colonial settlements and the Mississippi River – promised to emerge as yet another obstacle to the formation of a common American political order. Not only were there overlapping claims to these lands by several states, land speculators, and individual delegates to the Continental Congress, but the vast western territorial claims of eight states contrasted sharply with the limits of the five colonies that had fixed western boundaries.

---

[26] As quoted in Burnett, *The Continental Congress*, p. 81; John Adams to James Warren, July 23, 1775, *LDC*, I: 650.

[27] George Ross to the Lancaster County Committee of Correspondence, May 30, 1775, *LDC*, I: 421; Virginia and Pennsylvania delegates to the Inhabitants West of the Laurel Hill, July 25, 1775, *LDC*, I: 665–666; *JCC*, II: 76; and Adams, *Diary*, Oct. 25, 1775, 2: 218. See also Peter S. Onuf, *The Origins of the Federal Republic* (Philadelphia: University of Pennsylvania Press, 1983), pp. 8–10.

[28] Carter Braxton to Landon Carter, April 14, 1776, *LMCC*, I: 421.

Framing the Constitutional Debate

As delegates to the Continental Congress moved closer to a collective commitment for independence, it became increasingly apparent that debates over the rule of apportionment, the division of common expenses, and the regulation of territorial divisions could not (and would not) be resolved in isolation from one another. Rather, solutions to these issues (if there were to be any) would be made simultaneously within the context of a single constitutional framework. As a consequence, American political leaders were prompted to analyze a range of solutions to specific and general issues in terms of their possible combinations within a longer-term constitutional agreement.

Between 1775 and early 1776, at least three plans of union were proposed by members of Congress. Several delegates, including Connecticut delegate Silas Deane, privately discussed devising a formal plan of confederation in late 1774 and early January 1775.[29] Pennsylvania delegate Benjamin Franklin was the first to present Congress with a plan for framing a new national government. Franklin's plan, the "Articles of Confederation and Perpetual Union," included several notable provisions. Article VI of the plan's thirteen articles proposed dividing general expenses of this Union among each colony "in proportion to its Number of Male Polls between 16 and 60 Years of Age." Franklin's plan also required colonial delegates "to bring with them to every Congress, an authenticated Return of the number of Polls in the respective Provinces which is to be annually [or] triennially taken for the Purposes above mentioned." In Article VII, the Franklin plan proposed a proportional rule of apportionment that determined that the number of delegates for each colony "shall be regulated from time to time by the Number of such Polls return'd; so that one Delegate be allowed for every 5000 Polls."[30]

Other plans of union were devised by members of Connecticut's congressional delegation between 1775 and early 1776.[31] Silas Deane, according to most accounts, completed a draft of his plan in late summer of 1775.[32] The so-called Deane plan proposed a continental

---

[29] See Rakove, *The Beginnings of National Politics*, pp. 141–142.

[30] *JCC*, II: 195–199 (July 21, 1775).

[31] In addition to the Franklin and Connecticut plans, various terms of Union were proposed and discussed in American newspapers during the first half of 1776. See Leonard W. Levy, "Introduction: American Constitutional History," in *The Framing and Ratification of the Constitution*, Levy and Mahoney, eds. (New York: Macmillan, 1987), pp. 2–3.

[32] See Rakove, *The Beginnings of National Politics* (1979), pp. 137–138n.

"Confederation for the defence of their Liberties and immunities" and a proportional rule of apportionment that granted one delegate for every "Twenty five Thousand Souls" in each colony. "To preserve an equall Representation," Deane's plan proposed an annual census of "the Number of Souls, in each Colony." The rule for dividing common expenses was not specified, but the Deane plan proposed that a common Treasury of the United States would collect "all duties, custom, or excise laid on any Ware, Merchandize or Commerce."[33]

The Deane plan was modified in the winter of 1775 by other Connecticut delegates, with Roger Sherman the likely author of the revised plan that appeared in several American newspapers in March and April 1776.[34] This so-called Connecticut plan proposed a "General Congress" whose delegates were to be elected annually by the colonial assemblies. Like the two earlier plans, the Connecticut plan proposed a proportional rule of apportionment. The plan proposed that "[t]he number of delegates from each colony" was to "be in proportion to the number of inhabitants, of every age and quality; not exceeding one Delegate for every thirty thousand inhabitants." In addition, the plan proposed defraying the costs of the war and government proportionally among the colonies in accord with a census of all "inhabitants of every age and quality" which was to "be triennially taken and transmitted to the Congress."

Whereas each plan's rule of apportionment divided political representation in terms of population, the level of governing authority granted to Congress was a second general indicator of the type of political order proposed by each plan. Congress's authority under the Franklin plan extended "to the Determining of War and Peace, to sending and receiving ambassadors," the formation of alliances, "the Settling [of] all Disputes and Differences between Colony and Colony about Limits or any other cause," and "the Planting of new Colonies." Franklin's plan broadly empowered Congress to enact "general Ordinances" for "the General Welfare" including acts related to "Commerce; . . . Currency; the Establishment of Posts; and the Regulation of our common Forces." In addition, Congress was empowered to purchase land from native

---

[33] Silas Deane's Proposals to Congress [November 1775], *LDC*, 2: 418–419.
[34] The version of the Connecticut plan used here is taken from the *Boston Gazette and Country Journal*, April 22, 1776. The plan was first published in the *Pennsylvania Evening Post* on March 5, 1776, and subsequently in several other New England newspapers. See also Jensen, *Articles of Confederation* (1940), p. 124; and Rakove, *The Beginnings of National Politics* (1979), p. 426n.4.

American tribes "for the General Advantage and Benefit of the United Colonies" and to propose constitutional amendments subject to approval by a majority of the colonial assemblies.

Under the Deane plan, Congress's powers were similarly extensive. They included the authority to make war and peace, to approve all treaties, and to appoint state governors, lieutenant governors, and judges, to make final judgments in "All disputes between different Colonies," to appoint all Continental officers, to regulate a common currency, and to set and collect duties, custom, and excise taxes. Congress was further authorized to decide appeals by individuals who were elected, but later dismissed, by their state assemblies. Finally, the Deane plan broadly empowered Congress to decide all "other Concerns of a Lesser Nature."

The Connecticut plan, by contrast, provided a narrower range of powers to Congress. Congress's authority extended explicitly to the provision of the common defense and security, the formation of foreign alliances, a superintending authority over Indian affairs, post offices, intercolonial disputes, and the regulation of naval and land forces. The plan did not, however, include any provisions empowering Congress to make decisions on the issues of common expenses, state boundaries, the western lands, new states, or constitutional amendments.

A third indicator of the type of political order proposed by each constitutional plan was the range of restrictions each placed on the state governments. The Franklin plan only prohibited states from engaging in war "without the consent of Congress." The Deane plan subjected state governments to several limitations. State assemblies were prevented from holding sessions "longer than Three Years, or less than one, before a New Election shall take place." State governments were required to "transmit all Acts pass'd to the Next Congress to be by them approved or rejected." States were also denied "the power of laying any Duty, excise, or Custom" unless approved by Congress.[35] The Connecticut plan imposed only two restrictions on the states. They were prohibited from forming alliances or political connections "with the people of any other country or state, separate from the other United Colonies," and they were required to "always keep up a well-regulated and disciplined militia."

The Franklin plan and the two Connecticut plans are significant because their constitutional designs departed from traditional categories

[35] Silas Deane's Proposal to Congress [November 1775], *LDC*, 2: 418–419.

of government. They did not concentrate the authority of government within strong executive institutions and were thus not variations of a monarchical form of government. They did not conflate enduring social distinctions with political right and were thus not variations of an aristocratic form of government. All three plans, moreover, did not provide Congress with the seemingly boundless collective authority traditionally associated with a democratic form of government, but the authority of Congress was extensive. Yet in various ways, all three plans imposed specific restrictions on the exercise of this authority, acknowledging that the creation and maintenance of a new "American" government depended on the support of a diverse set of politically active centers – including the state governments, interstate coalitions of interests, and even the political actors most inclined to view any form of "national" political order with strong suspicion. The central problematic of formalizing a constitutional union among the American states was thus finding an acceptable combination of constitutional provisions capable of sustaining the rebellion against Great Britain and of strengthening the bonds of speech and trust required to generate effective compromises among different political interests.

The necessity of establishing a constitutional equilibrium among these interests was recognized implicitly in each of the plans proposed prior to independence. All three plans included auxiliary voting provisions mitigating the immediate consequences that a proportional rule of apportionment would have on the decision-making capacities of the smallest states. For example, Franklin's plan required delegates to vote individually, thus increasing the number of majority coalitions possible compared to a state delegation voting rule.[36] The Deane plan included other voting procedures that diminished the powers of the majority in Congress, requiring "a Majority of Numbers represented in Congress, independent of particular Colonies" to determine policies concerning "Supplies of Men, or Money . . . & other Concerns of a Lesser Nature." Decisions concerning war, peace, and the general privileges of the colonies would require "a Majority both of Colonies, and Numbers" of delegates in Congress. The Connecticut plan included the most stringent restraint on Congress's collective authority: For every vote in Congress, this plan required "the concurrence of a majority of the Colonies represented, and a majority of the Delegates present."[37]

---

[36] Rakove, *The Beginnings of National Politics* (1979), p. 144.
[37] Silas Deane's Proposals to Congress [November 1775], *LDC*, 2: 418–419; *Boston Gazette and Country Journal*, April 22, 1776.

Congress's authority was mitigated in several additional ways. The Franklin plan specifically linked the apportionment of representation and the division of common expenses to a periodic census, probably to remove the interstate transfer of representation from arbitrary manipulation by threatened majorities in Congress.[38] And Congress was prohibited from enacting constitutional amendments without the consent of a majority of the colonial assemblies.

The Deane plan limited Congress's authority to remove appointed Continental officers to cases involving "misbehavior in Office and for No other Cause." The Connecticut plan specified that Congress's authority to settle intercolonial disputes was not unbounded but was to be consistent with "the right of the parties by rules of law or equity." The Connecticut plan also did not permit Congress "to impose or levy taxes, or interfere with the internal policy of any of the Colonies," and it was prohibited from maintaining a standing army "in the time of peace."

Arguably, the most significant limitation on Congress's authority proposed by all three plans was the confederal structure of the proposed Union. Rather than a unitary form of national government, the Franklin plan explicitly recognized "That each Colony shall enjoy and retain as much as it may think fit of its own present Laws, Customs, Rights, Privileges, and peculiar Jurisdictions without its own Limits; and may amend its own Constitutions as shall seem best to its own Assembly or Convention." The Franklin plan also required its own submission to and approval by colonial assemblies or conventions. The Deane plan similarly recognized that "Each Colony shall in every respect, retain its present mode of internal police & legislation," and it specified that until directed by Congress, "[t]he Militia, of the several Colonies, shall remain under the direction of their respective Legislatures." Like the others, the Connecticut plan guaranteed that "Each colony shall retain and enjoy as much as it may think fit, of its own present laws, customs, privileges, and peculiar confirmations and have the sole direction and government of its own internal police."[39]

There are no records to suggest that Congress formally considered even one of these plans prior to independence.[40] The plans of Union proposed by Franklin, Deane, and the Connecticut delegation nevertheless remain important for two reasons. First, they provide reminders that new

---

[38] Rakove, *The Beginnings of National Politics* (1979), p. 143.

[39] *Boston Gazette and Country Journal*, April 22, 1776.

[40] Rakove, *The Beginnings of National Politics* (1979), pp. 136–137; Burnett, *The Continental Congress* (1941), p. 213.

political orders do not emerge *ex nihilo*. The creation of a new political order, rather, is informed by a preexisting framework of ideas and expectations concerning possible arrangements of institutions of governance. Second, these pre-Independence plans suggest that a general path to achieving a constitutional consensus among constitution makers with diverse interests required balance between the interests benefiting from the rule of apportionment and the provisions empowering the national government and the alternative interests benefiting from the inclusion of auxiliary voting procedures, explicit limitations on Congress's powers, and a federal national Union.

PART II: DELIBERATIONS TOWARD A
CONSTITUTIONAL CONSENSUS

Although a majority of the delegates to the Continental Congress were convinced by the end of 1775 of the necessity of American Independence, a consensus among the delegates concerning the specific organizational form of a new national government was not as well developed. Several conditions naturally supported the creation of such a consensus: the administrative demands of the American war effort, the uncertainty of Congress's popular legitimacy, the hearty vigor of nascent nationalism, and the protocol of international relations. Delegates, in addition, had similar experiences of colonial politics and they generally shared similar conceptualizations of the general type of national government they were committed to forming.

Despite these supportive conditions, the primary impediment to the formalization of the American political order was the commitment of the delegates to do so without recourse to force, deference to a single law-giver, or appeals of divine right. To what degree the delegates' requirement for the consensual establishment of this common political order was a principled commitment or merely one necessitated by the exigencies of the war and the lack of an established national political tradition is impossible to determine. What is significant is that a commitment of this sort impeded the constitutionalization process by requiring consent among the delegates within Congress and among the various sets of actors who constituted the new state governments. Overcoming the formidable obstacles to founding a consensual Union became the task to which congressional delegates turned in the wake of independence.

On the same day Congress appointed the much-heralded committee to draft the Declaration of Independence, 12 June 1776, it appointed another committee to prepare a plan of confederation to be submitted to, amended, and approved by Congress. Ratification of this plan required the unanimous consent of the thirteen state governments. One delegate from each colony was appointed to this committee, Pennsylvania delegate John Dickinson appointed its chair. A month later, the Dickinson committee completed a plan of union it presented to Congress as the "Articles of Confederation."[41]

Like the three plans of union crafted prior to independence, the Dickinson committee "Articles" can be understood as proposing a balance between the governing authority available to the majority within the national government and the protections afforded to the minority. The specific provisions related to the latter defined the rule of apportionment, the powers of Congress, and the restrictions on the state governments. The provisions of the "Articles" constituting the former protections included a set of auxiliary voting procedures, restrictions on Congress's powers, and a federally structured Union.

The Rule of Apportionment and the Powers of the National Government

More specifically, the Dickinson committee plan proposed a rule of apportionment that granted each state delegation a single vote within a unicameral Congress. According to accounts of the committee's deliberations, no rule was more contentiously debated than the rule of apportionment. After less than a week of deliberations one committee member (New Hampshire delegate Josiah Bartlett) privately reported that "[t]he affair of voting, whether by Colonies as at present or otherways is not decided and causes some warm disputes."[42]

As in the pre-Independence debates over Congress's voting rule, members of the Dickinson committee divided between those who supported an equal state apportionment rule and those who advocated a proportional rule. Supporters of the latter were again hindered by the lack of reliable measurements of state population or wealth from which objective interstate comparisons could be made. Advocates of a proportional rule also were disadvantaged by the fact that the Dickinson committee consisted of a single delegate from each state. If each committee member voted in accord with his state's interest, a majority of the states

---

[41] *JCC*, V: 433 (June 12, 1776); *JCC*, V: 546–554 (July 12, 1776).
[42] Josiah Bartlett to John Langdon, June 17, 1776, *LDC*, 4: 256.

TABLE 4.3. *State Representation under Equal State Rule and Proportional Rule of Apportionment, 1776*

State	Equal State Rule, %: One Vote Per State	Proportional Rule, %: Dickinson Committee	Proportional Rule, %: Stiles Estimates
New Hampshire	7.7	4.2	3.7
Massachusetts	7.7	14.5	16.6
Rhode Island	7.7	2.4	2.5
Connecticut	7.7	8.3	8.0
New York	7.7	8.3	6.4
New Jersey	7.7	5.4	5.4
Pennsylvania	7.7	12.5	12.4
Delaware	7.7	1.2	–
Maryland	7.7	10.5	10.4
Virginia	7.7	16.7	16.6
North Carolina	7.7	8.0	10.4
South Carolina	7.7	8.0	7.5
Georgia	7.7	–	–

would benefit from the shift to a proportional rule. As illustrated in Table 4.3, according to the one known set of interstate ratios discussed by the committee, the representation of as many as eight of the thirteen states – and thus a majority – would increase under a proportional rule of apportionment.

Why then was not a proportional rule of apportionment adopted by a majority of the Dickinson committee? For one, it was likely known that the ratios of New York and South Carolina were overestimated, therefore reducing the interest of at least two committee members. Moreover, if population estimates of colonial demographer and then Yale President Ezra Stiles are used as a less biased measurement of interstate ratios, then only six states – and a minority of committee members – would increase their representational strength in Congress under a proportional rule of apportionment.[43]

More than net expected benefits of a proportional rule troubled committee members from the small and medium states. Regardless of the size of an individual state's representational gains, the political arithmetic of a proportional rule of apportionment ensured that more than half the members in Congress would be controlled by the four largest states:

[43] See *The Literary Diary of Ezra Stiles*, I: 486–488.

TABLE 4.4. *Cleavage Strength under Equal and Proportional Apportionment Rules*

Cleavage Type	Equal Rule–Votes (%)	Proportional Rule (percent)
State Size		
Large	4 (30.8)	54.2
Medium	4 (30.8)	32.6
Small	5 (38.4)	13.2
Region		
Northeast	4 (30.8)	26.6
Mid-Atlantic	5 (38.4)	34.8
South	4 (30.8)	38.6
Section		
North	8 (61.5)	50.8
South	5 (38.5)	49.2

Virginia, Massachusetts, Pennsylvania, and Maryland.[44] Thus, despite the fact that several medium-size states would have gained representation under a proportional rule of apportionment, as illustrated in Table 4.4 the formation of a permanent majority coalition consisting of the four largest states (54.2%) would always be possible. By contrast, under an equal state rule of apportionment a permanent majority seemed probable only if the state delegates divided along a then highly improbable North-South sectional cleavage.

In addition to the equal state apportionment rule, the Dickinson committee "Articles" identified a range of powers for the national government and several restrictions on the authority of the state governments. Specifically, Congress was granted the authority to incur and repay expenses for the "common Defense" and the "general Welfare." The plan additionally empowered Congress to declare war and peace, and to establish the regulations and treaties for their execution and cessation. Congress's powers related to the regulation of the so-called western lands were also extensive. Article XIV empowered Congress to purchase lands held by native Americans. Article XVIII permitted Congress to settle disputes concerning state boundaries, to limit state territorial claims, and to dispose of "Lands for the general Benefit of all the United Colonies."

[44] Josiah Bartlett's Notes on the Plan of Confederation, *LDC*, 4: 200. See also Adams, *Diary*, 2: 248.

Article XVIII also empowered Congress to establish a judicial system for maritime cases, to receive foreign ambassadors, to enter into treaties and alliances, to form new states, to establish post offices, to appoint military officers, to fix the expenditures of the national government, to borrow money, to make requisitions on states, and to establish a uniform system of weights and measures. Notably, the residuum of powers not expressly granted to Congress or reserved to the states was not explicitly assigned to either Congress or the states under the Dickinson committee plan, thus leaving a constitutional aperture through which future Congresses might claim additional unspecified powers.

The Dickinson committee plan also proposed a Council of State to be constituted by one delegate from each state. The plan granted the Council an extensive list of powers and determined that seven of its "Members shall have Power to act." Congress was authorized to appoint delegates to the Council of State if a state failed to make an appointment.

The Dickinson Committee plan further empowered the national government by proposing numerous restraints on the state governments. States were prohibited from having foreign relations and from entering into interstate treaties without the consent of Congress. They were required to honor the "Rights, Liberties, Privileges, Immunities and Advantages" of individuals from other states, and no state could exclude nonresidents from enjoying the rights and privileges of its commercial and trading laws. The Dickinson committee plan also required that states abide by the decisions of Congress, including those dividing common expenses and the settlement of state boundaries.

Securing the Consent of Uncertain Majorities and Certain Minorities

Although the Dickinson committee "Articles" offered a broad range of explicit and implicit powers to majorities within the national government, the constitutional plan also included several restraints on these majorities. The "Articles" included several auxiliary voting procedures, a series of explicit limitations on Congress's powers, and an explicit confirmation of the governing authority of the state governments. In so doing, the plan resembled the pre-Independence Franklin, Deane, and Connecticut plans. In contrast to these earlier plans, however, the Dickinson committee "Articles" clearly proposed a more limited form of national government.

For example, the auxiliary voting procedures included within the Dickinson committee plan effectively raised the threshold of intra-governmental consensus required to employ the powers of Congress. Specifically, the plan required the consent of nine states in Congress to engage in war, to grant letters of marque and reprisal during peacetime, to consent to treaties and alliances, to coin and borrow money, to raise naval and land forces, or to admit new states. On all other questions (except adjournment), the Dickinson committee plan permitted the votes of seven state delegations to determine the will of Congress. This seven-vote rule also applied to decisions made by the Council of State.

The second type of restraint imposed restrictions on Congress's authority. Congress was required to divide the expenses of the Union in accord with total state population and to make requisitions on the states "in Proportion to the Number of white Inhabitants." The plan explicitly prohibited Congress from imposing "any Taxes or Duties, except in managing the Post-Office" and from interfering "in the internal Police of any Colony." In addition, Congress was required to publish a journal of its proceedings and to record the vote of each delegate. The Dickinson committee plan further required unanimous state consent for ratification and amendment of the "Articles of Confederation."

The third type of restraint proposed by the Dickinson committee plan consisted of provisions that explicitly recognized the governing authority of state governments. Like the Franklin and Connecticut plans, the Dickinson committee plan included a general approbation that "Each Colony shall retain and enjoy as much of its present Laws, Rights and Customs, as it may think fit, and reserves to itself the sole and exclusive Regulation and Government of its internal police, in all matters that shall interfere with the Articles of this Confederation." The plan explicitly recognized the authority of the states to impose taxes and duties, and states were guaranteed control over their militias and the types of taxes they could impose to pay their respective shares of the Union's common expenses.

Although the Dickinson committee plan proposed a more fully developed balance between the powers and limitations of the national government than pre-Independence plans, the "Articles" were not visibly embraced by any delegates within Congress. Delegates, rather, became engaged in a series of debates over how different rules of apportionment and different combinations of national and state powers might satisfy their immediate and longer-term interests.

The Apportionment Rule Debated

One of the first provisions of the Dickinson committee "Articles" debated within Congress was the rule of equal state apportionment. Delegates understood the significance of this rule to their efforts to finalize a plan of Union. Nevertheless, the various positions they advocated in debate typically reflected the distinct and parochial interests of their particular states. Maryland delegate Samuel Chase, for example, observed that this debate "was the most likely to divide us of any one proposed" for "the larger colonies had threatened they would not confederate at all if their weight in congress should not be equal to the numbers of people they added to the confederacy; while the smaller ones declared against an union if they did not retain an equal vote for the protection of their rights." Chase maintained, however, that Union was necessary because "should we sever from each other, either no foreign power will ally with us at all, or the different states will form different alliances, and thus increase the horrors of those scenes of civil war and bloodshed which in such a state of separation & independence would render us a miserable people." The Maryland delegate insisted that "mutual sacrifices should be made to effect a compromise on this difficult question." He therefore proposed "that the smaller states should be secured in all questions concerning life or liberty & the greater ones in all respecting property" and that "in votes relating to money, the votes of each colony should be proportioned to the number of it's [sic] inhabitants."[45]

Despite Chase's proposal, delegates from the largest states displayed no interest in compromise. Pennsylvania delegate Benjamin Franklin "thought that the votes should be so proportioned in all cases" and that it was "a very extraordinary language to be held by any state, that they would not confederate with us unless we would let them dispose of our money." Certainly, Franklin argued, "if we vote equally we ought to pay equally: but the smaller states will hardly purchase the privilege at this price." Franklin contended that "without bearing equal Burthen, a Confederation upon such iniquitous Principles will never last long." "I hear many ingenious Arguments to perswade Us that an unequal Representation is a very good Thing." If "We had been born and bred under an unequal Representation We might bear it," Franklin concluded, yet "to sett out with an unequal Representation is unreasonable."[46]

[45] Jefferson, "Notes of Proceedings in the Continental Congress," July 30–31, August 1, 1776, *PTJ* 1: 323–324.
[46] Jefferson, *PTJ*, 1: 324; Adams, *Diary*, 2: 245, 248.

John Adams of Massachusetts was another delegate who voiced support for "voting in proportion to numbers." He argued "we stand here as the representatives of the people." "[I]n some states the people are many, in others they are few; that therefore their vote here should be proportioned to the numbers from whom it comes." Adams asserted that "reason, justice, & equity never had weight enough on the face of the earth to govern the councils of men, . . . it is interest alone which does it, and it is interest alone which can be the mathematical representatives of the interests without doors." Thus, "the individuality of the colony is a mere sound," for does "the individuality of a colony increase it's [sic] wealth or numbers? if it does, pay equally." If, however, "it does not add weight in the scale of the confederacy, it cannot add to their rights, nor weight in argument." In short, Adams asserted, "the question is not what we are now, but what we ought to be when our bargain shall be made." Moreover, "the confederacy is to make us one individual only; it is to form us, like separate parcels of metal, into one common mass," in which "we shall no longer retain our separate individuality, but become a single individual as to all questions submitted to the Confederacy."[47]

Other delegates agreed with Adams. "Were it possible," Pennsylvania delegate Benjamin Rush argued, "to collect the whole body of the people together, they would determine the questions submitted to them by their majority." Why then "should not the same majority decide when voting here by their representatives?" Rush furthermore contended "voting by the number of free inhabitants will have one excellent effect, that of inducing the colonies to discourage slavery & to encourage the increase of their free inhabitants." Note that the free-person basis would have increased Pennsylvania's representation in Congress by reducing the Southern states' estimated population figures by almost one quarter.[48] Rush added:

I am not pleading the Cause of Pennsylvania. In half a century she may be and probably will be as near the smallest as she now is the greatest states. New Hampshire & Georgia will probably receive most benefit . . . from representation by numbers. No Sir – I am pleading the cause of the Continent – of mankind – of posterity.[49]

Most significantly, Rush made clear that the delegates' decision on the terms of the apportionment rule had significant consequences for the type

[47] Jefferson, *PTJ*, 1: 325.
[48] Jefferson, *PTJ*, 1: 326. See also the conceptualization of representation by Pennsylvania delegate Benjamin Rush: Adams, *Diary*, 2: 247; "Benjamin Rush's Notes for a Speech in Congress" [Aug. 1, 1776], *LDC*, 4: 600, 602.
[49] "Benjamin Rush's Notes for a Speech in Congress" [Aug. 1, 1776], *LDC*, 4: 601.

of authority that could be assigned to Congress. "If we vote by numbers," the Pennsylvania delegate declared, "we cannot deposit too much of our liberty & safety in the hands of the congress. . . . But if we vote by colonies I maintain that we cannot deposit too little in the hands of the congress." For the latter idea "is a most dangerous one" because it will "contract millions to a span" and "invest the Congress with the power of a Caligula." "The Scheme is big with ruin, not only to one but to all the colonies."[50]

The debate over the rule of apportionment continued several days without resolution. Delegates from the largest states continued to insist on a rule "in Proportion to Numbers." Small state delegates continued to demand an equal state rule. Delegates from medium-size states suggested several solutions to this impasse. Henry Middleton of South Carolina proposed "that the Vote should be according to what" each state pays to support the new national government. Roger Sherman of Connecticut acknowledged that the "Consent of every one is necessary." "The Vote," therefore, "should be taken two Ways. Call the Colonies and call the Individuals, and have a Majority of both."[51]

After nearly a month of debate, there was no consensus for replacing the Dickinson committee apportionment rule with a proportional rule. Delegates from the most populous states were greatly disappointed by their failure to amend the terms of the apportionment rule. John Adams complained: "Equality of Representation in the Legislature" (by which he meant proportional representation) "is the first Principle of Liberty, and the Moment the least departure from such Equality takes Place, that Moment an Inroad is made upon Liberty." By granting equal voting strength to both small and large states, "we are sowing the Seeds of Ignorance, Corruption, and Injustice, in the fairest Field of Liberty, that ever appeared upon earth, even in the first attempts to cultivate it."[52]

The Rule for Dividing Common Expenses Debated

The second major issue debated by the delegates centered on the Dickinson committee plan's rule for dividing the Union's common expenses. The committee's "Articles" provided for a division of these

---

[50] "Benjamin Rush's Notes for a Speech in Congress" [Aug. 1, 1776], *LDC*, 4: 600, 601, 600. See also views of James Wilson in Jefferson, *PTJ*, 1: 326–327.

[51] Adams, *Diary*, 2: 247.

[52] See August 20 draft of "Articles of Confederation," Aug. 20, 1776, *JCC*, V: 674–689, 681; John Adams to Joseph Hawley, Aug. 25, 1776, *LDC*, V: 61–62.

expenses among the states "in proportion to the Number of Inhabitants of every Age, Sex and Quality, except Indians not paying Taxes, in each Colony." To determine each state's population the Dickinson committee plan provided that a census "be triennially taken and transmitted to the Assembly of the United States."

Like the debate over the terms of the apportionment rule, the "Articles" common expenses rule prompted delegates to articulate positions that typically and often unambiguously coincided with their respective state interests. Delegates from states with sizeable numbers of enslaved persons objected to using the total "Number of Inhabitants" as the basis for dividing common expenses. Maryland delegate Samuel Chase, for one, attempted to reduce his state's share of national expenditures by "mov[ing] that the quotas should be fixed, not by the number of inhabitants of every condition, but by that of the white inhabitants" only. Although "taxation should be alwais [sic] in proportion to property," Chase reportedly argued, "it was a rule which could never be adopted in practice" for the "value of the property in every State could never be estimated justly & equally." Chase consequently accepted population as the basis of taxation but he redefined the term "inhabitants" used in the Dickinson committee plan to exclude enslaved persons. "[N]egroes are property," Chase suggested, "and as such cannot be distinguished from the lands or personalities held in those States where there are few slaves." "There is no more reason therefore for taxing the Southern states on the farmer's head & on his slave's head, than the Northern ones on their farmer's heads & the heads of their cattle." Chase concluded "that negroes in fact should not be considered as members of the state more than cattle & that they have no more interest in it."[53]

Chase's redefinition of the meaning of property and political wealth was unpersuasive. John Adams rejected Chase's interpretation and "observed that the numbers of people were taken by this article as an index of the wealth of the states, & not as subjects of taxation, that as to this matter it was of no consequence by what name you called your people, whether by that of freemen or of slaves. That in some countries the labouring poor were called freemen, in others they were called slaves; but that the difference as to the state was imaginary only." Adams protested "the condition of the laboring poor in most countries, that of the fishermen particularly of the Northern states, is as abject as that of slaves. It is," Adams argued, "the number of labourers which produce

[53] Jefferson, *PTJ*, 1: 320–321. See also Adams, *Diary*, 2: 245.

the surplus for taxation, and numbers therefore indiscriminately, are the fair index of wealth."[54]

Benjamin Harrison, a Virginia delegate known to some for "his rough dress and speech," exhibited little interest in resolving the interpretative differences between Chase and Adams. He suggested instead an arithmetical solution to the dispute: "that two slaves should be counted as one freeman" for the purpose of dividing common expenses among the states.[55] Given the so-called "three-fifths" compromise subsequently included in the U.S. Constitution, it is ironic that Harrison's proposal found no support among delegates to this Congress. James Wilson of Pennsylvania ignored Harrison's proposal and argued that if Chase's "white inhabitants" amendment were adopted "the Southern colonies would have all the benefit of slaves, whilst the Northern ones would bear the burthen." For, as "slaves increase the profit of a state, which the Southern states mean to take to themselves, . . . they also increase the burthen of defence, which of course fall[s] so much heavier on the Northern" states. Wilson counseled his fellow delegates, it "is our duty to lay every discouragement on the importation of slaves; but this amendment would give the *jus trium liberorum* to him who would import slaves." In addition, "experience has shown that those colonies have been alwais able to pay most which have the most inhabitants, whether they be black or white, and the practice of the Southern colonies has alwais been to make every farmer pay poll taxes upon all his labourers whether they be black or white."[56]

Threatened by Wilson's frank assessment of slave labor, Thomas Lynch of South Carolina intervened to stifle additional discussion on the subject. "If it is debated, whether their Slaves are their Property," threatened Lynch, "there is an End of the Confederation." "Our Slaves," he insisted, are "our Property. . . . [W]hy," therefore "should they be taxed more than the Land, Sheep, Cattle, Horses, &c.? . . . Freemen," Lynch pointed out, "cannot be got, to work in our Colonies." Moreover, "It is not in the Ability, or Inclination of freemen to do the Work that the

---

[54] Jefferson, *PTJ*, 1: 321.

   On July 29, 1776, John Adams informed his wife of "two knotty Problems in Politicks": "If a Confederation should take Place, one great Question is how We shall vote. . . . Another is, whether Congress shall have Authority to limit the Dimensions of each Colony, to prevent those which claim by Charter, or Proclamation, or Commission to the South Sea, from growing too great and powerful, so as to be dangerous to the rest." John Adams to Mrs. Adams, July 29, 1776, *LDC*, 4: 556.

[55] See Burnett, *The Continental Congress* (1941), pp. 29–30. Jefferson, *PTJ*, 1: 322.

[56] Jefferson, *PTJ*, 1: 322; Adams, *Diary*, 2: 245.

Negroes do. Carolina has taxed their Negroes. So," he added, "have other Colonies, their Lands." Benjamin Franklin, did not allow the last comment to stand unchallenged. "Slaves," argued Franklin, weaken rather "than strengthen the State, and there is therefore some difference between them and Sheep. Sheep will never make any Insurrections."[57]

Although the rule for dividing common expenses split Congress primarily along sectional lines, several delegates stressed other factors that should be taken into account when resolving this issue. John Rutledge of South Carolina stated he would "be happy to get rid of the idea of Slavery" for "Slaves do not signify Property." Yet if slaves were to be taxed, Rutledge suggested, Southern states would bear the costs of the Union and the "Eastern Colonies will become the Carriers for the Southern" and thereby "obtain Wealth for which they will not be taxed." New Jersey delegate John Witherspoon acknowledged the importance of balancing various regional and economic interests within the new Union. He therefore proposed, "that the value of lands & houses was the best estimate of the wealth of a nation, and that it was practicable to obtain such a valuation. This is the true barometer of wealth. The one now proposed is imperfect in itself, and unequal between the States."[58]

At the end of the debate, Congress rejected Chase's amendment to divide the common expenses of the Union according to the number of "white inhabitants" in each state. The vote split Congress along a sectional divide: Five southern states favored the amendment, Georgia's delegation was divided, and the seven northern states were opposed. As compiled August 20, 1776, the revised draft of the "Articles" determined that the common expenses of the Union would be divided according "to the Number of Inhabitants of every Age, Sex and Quality except Indians not paying Taxes, in each Colony." Congress further provided that "a true Account" of population, which also distinguishes "the white Inhabitants[,] shall be triennially taken."[59]

Rules for Regulating State Boundaries and the Western Lands Debated

A third issue debated by congressional delegates centered on the Dickinson Articles' rules for regulating state territorial divisions and land

---

[57] Jefferson, *PTJ*, 1: 322; Adams, *Diary*, 2: 247.
[58] Jefferson, *PTJ*, 1: 322.
[59] Jefferson, *PTJ*, 1: 323; *JCC*, V: 678 (Aug. 20, 1776).

claims. The plan gave Congress broad powers to fix state boundaries, to establish the boundaries of new states, and to dispose of all other "Lands for the general Benefit."[60]

Unlike the issues of representation and common expenses, delegates were divided not only by state interests but, in several instances, by personal interests as well. To complicate this issue, many states were already involved in intense interstate boundary disputes and several states faced intrastate secessionist movements. Private land development companies also became more aggressive after independence and often pursued their interests by lobbying for state governmental recognition and with unauthorized purchases from Native American tribes.[61]

On the issue of the western territories, the division within Congress was the most clearly defined. Delegates divided between those who claimed their states had "South Sea" charters which extended their western boundaries to the Mississippi River – the landed states – and those from states with fixed western boundaries – the landless states.[62] Eight states claimed some type of western territorial rights. Virginia's claims were enormous: The state claimed boundaries extending beyond her existing settlements to the Mississippi River and northward to the Canadian border. Five colonies had fixed western boundaries.[63]

Differences among the delegates on this issue were exacerbated by other calculations. The uncertainty of the terms of the rule of apportionment, for one, made it difficult for delegates to calculate (with any precision) the probable benefits of the Dickinson committee plan's broad delegation of authority to Congress. Although the eight landed states collectively constituted a majority under either an equal state or proportional rule of apportionment, the overlapping territorial claims of these states and the possible formation of alternative majorities made uncertain the future protection of a state's claims. Longer-term calculations about the future benefits of controlling the western lands also widened divisions among the delegates.

Not surprisingly, delegates from states with western claims immediately attempted to limit Congress's regulatory authority over the western lands. Virginia delegate Thomas Jefferson was one of the most vocal proponents of this change. He contended that the "Limits of the Southern

[60] *JCC*, V: 549 (July 12, 1776).
[61] Jensen, *Articles of Confederation* (1940), p. 120; and Merrill Jensen, *The New Nation* (New York: Knopf, 1950), pp. 8–9.
[62] Adams, *Diary*, 2: 244.
[63] McLaughlin, *A Constitutional History of the United States* (1935), p. 122.

Colonies are fixed" according to their old colonial charters. The power of purchasing additional "Lands, not within the Boundaries of any Colony shall be made by Congress." But, Jefferson inquired, "what Security have We that the Congress will not curtail the present settlements of the States?" He suggested it reasonable to believe "that the Colonies will limit themselves."[64]

Delegates from states with fixed western boundaries feared the consequences of allowing the landed states to monopolize the development of the west. Maryland delegate Samuel Chase attacked the integrity of South Sea charters. "No Colony," he declared, "has a Right to go to the South Sea" because "[i]t would not be safe to the rest. It would be destructive to her Sisters, and to herself." Pennsylvania delegate James Wilson also asserted that "Claims to the South Sea" were "extravagant" but he argued they "were made upon Mistakes" by persons "ignorant of the Geography." At the time, Wilson reminded his fellow delegates, it was "thought the S[outh] Sea within 100 Miles of the Atlantic Ocean. It was not conceived that they extended 3000 Miles." Wilson moreover admitted "Pensilvania [sic] had no Right to interfere in those claims." But, he threatened, she did have "a Right to say, that she will not confederate unless those Claims are cut off."[65]

Thomas Stone, another Maryland delegate, also attacked efforts to restrict Congress's power to regulate state claims in the west. "This Argument," he protested, "is taken up upon a very wrong Ground. It is considered as if We were voting away the Territory of particular Colonies, and gentlemen work themselves up into Warmth, upon that Supposition. . . . The small Colonies," however, "have a Right to Happiness and Security" as much as the larger ones. They "would have no Safety if the great Colonies were not limited" because these states would be able to profit enormously from the sale of their western territory. Instead, Stone proposed, "We shall grant Lands in small Quantities, without Rent, or Tribute, or purchase Money," for "all the Colonies have defended these Lands vs. the K[ingdom] of G[reat]. B[ritain]., and at the Expence of all."[66]

Roger Sherman of Connecticut contended "the Bounds [of the states] ought to be settled" for "A Majority of States have no Claim to the South Sea." He believed that areas already settled or that had become private property should not be separated from a state. Proponents of "South

[64] Adams, *Diary*, 2: 241.   [65] Adams, *Diary*, 2: 241–242.
[66] Adams, *Diary*, 2: 249; 2: 250n.1.

Sea" charters, like Virginia delegates Benjamin Harrison, insisted that Maryland and the other states with fixed western boundaries would benefit by not limiting "the Colony of Virginia." Rhode Island, Harrison argued, "has more Generosity, than to wish the [State of] Massachusetts pared away" and "Delaware does not wish to pare away Pensilvania." Connecticut delegate Samuel Huntington also defended the charter claims by arguing: "admit there is a danger, from Virginia, does it follow that Congress has a Right to limit her Bounds? The Consequence is not to enter into Confederation," and to remain "a Spectacle to all Europe." "But as to the Question of Right," Huntington added, "We all unite against mutilating Charters. I can[']t agree to the Principle of limiting a state's charter claims." For "A Man[']s Right does not cease to be a Right because it is large." Rather, "The Q[uestion] of Right must be determined by the Principles of the common Law."[67]

Despite the arguments and threats of the Maryland and Pennsylvania delegates, Congress amended the Dickinson Committee Articles. In the plan compiled August 20, Congress no longer possessed the authority to fix the western boundaries of the states[68] or to define the boundaries of new states.

PART III: THE IMPOSSIBILITY OF THE CONSENSUAL UNION

Although the second version of the Dickinson committee plan compiled on August 20, 1776, included several modifications of the original plan, prospects for a constitutional consensus remained dim throughout the subsequent year. The disagreements that arose during Congress's initial debates over the "Articles" had been so divisive New Jersey delegate Abraham Clark privately surmised that "Nothing but Present danger will ever make us all Agree," and North Carolina delegate Joseph Hewes concluded "it probable that we may Split on these great points, [and] if so our mighty Colossus falls to pieces."[69]

The delegates' initial failure to agree on a plan for a common form of government was the result of three specific conditions. The first

---

[67] Adams, *Diary*, 2: 249.

[68] *JCC*, V: 680, 682n.1 (August 20, 1776).

[69] Abraham Clark to James Caldwell, Aug. 1, 1776, *LMCC*, II: 33; Joseph Hewes to Samuel Johnston, July 28, 1776, *LMCC*, II: 28. See also William Williams to Joseph Trumbull, Aug. 7, 1776, *LMCC*, II: 41; Samuel Chase to Philip Schuyler, Aug. 9, 1776, *LMCC*, II: 44.

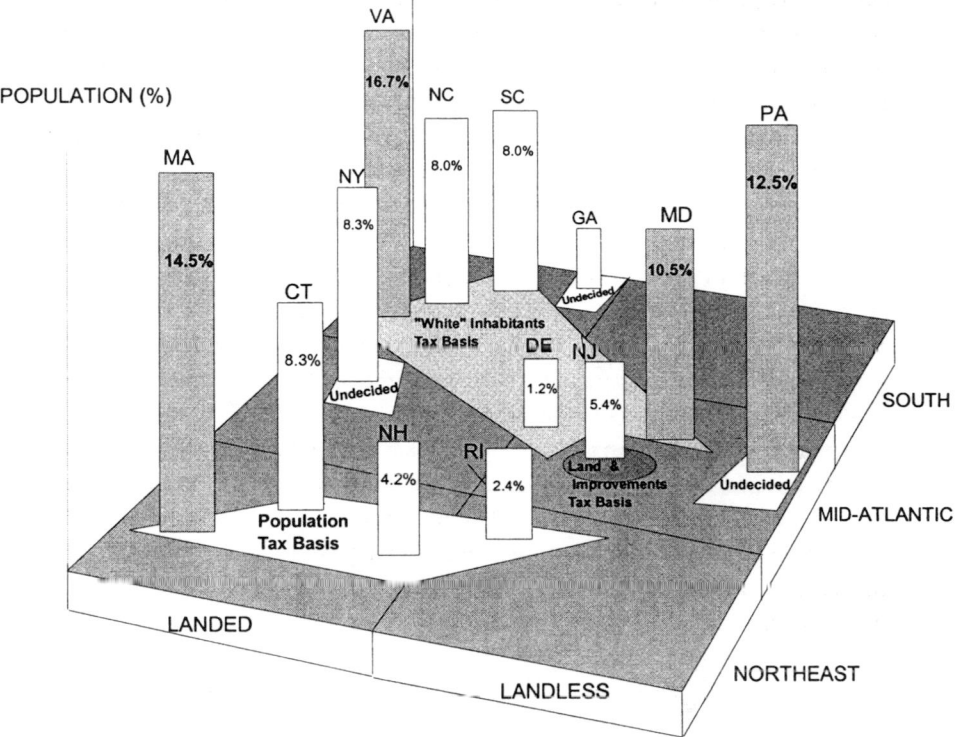

POPULATION (%)

FIGURE 4.1. Regional, Demographic, Tax Basis, and Land Policy Cleavages

condition was the diversity and intensity of interests that existed among the delegates. Differences of opinion and of state circumstances were real and made a spontaneous consensus on even single issues of constitutional design highly improbable. Moreover, as Figure 4.1 shows, across the most contested issues of the proposed constitutional plan – the apportionment of representation, the division of common expenses, and the authority over the western lands – state delegations divided into a series of nonconcurrent coalitions. If a consensus for a single constitutional plan was to emerge within Congress, then either the interests of the delegates would have to be made more uniform or the proposed political Union would have to be constructed over a multiplicity of interests.

The second condition that diminished the prospects of a constitutional consensus was the delegates' awareness of the immediate and profound consequences that followed from the formalization of the terms of the rule of apportionment. They understood the rule of apportionment defined the unit of voting within Congress and, thus, the type of governing coalition that would ultimately control the new national government. Given the convention of majority rule, the short-term conundrum of founding a political order on consent becomes apparent: Why would a set of constitution makers consent to a constitutional union and to the creation of a supreme, sovereign authority if their capacity to control this authority or to extract immediate or longer-term benefits from it was neither guaranteed nor highly probable?

This question paralyzed delegates to the Continental Congress for well over a year after the Dickinson committee submitted the initial draft of the "Articles of Confederation." It explains why delegates from the most populous states consistently attempted to amend the draft constitutional plan to include a proportional rule of apportionment. The largest and wealthiest states had the most to lose from entering a constitutional order in which representation within the new national government was divided equally among the states. The likely consequences of a proportional rule also explain why it was so consistently and "forc[e]ably opposed" by delegates who feared that under such a rule "the smaller Colonies will be in effect swallow'd up & annihilated."[70]

The third condition precluding the formation of a constitutional consensus was the delegates' awareness of the likely longer-term consequences of a new constitution. Constitutional rules, congressional delegates understood, establish patterns for distributing the benefits and costs of a political order. Every distributional difference associated with the terms of a new constitution – including relatively small differences – would have cumulative and forseeable effects that would lessen, not increase, the likelihood of achieving common consent. For even if a set of constitution makers was indifferent to a particular constitutional rule that guaranteed only a small benefit to another set of actors, iteration of this distributional asymmetry would appear as an enormous (and therefore unlikely) concession for the former group to make to the latter.

Evolution of Constitutional Consensus

The diversity of interests, the representational uncertainty associated with the equal state and proportional rules of apportionment, and the long-term distributional consequences of a written constitution were significant obstacles that hindered the formation of the first

---

[70] William Williams to Jonathan Trumbull, Sr., July 5, 1777, *LDC*, 7: 302.

American political order. Between August 1776 and November 1777, delegates repeatedly failed to achieve a consensus for a common plan of governance.

How then were the Articles of Confederation ultimately established? According to most interpretative accounts, dramatic environmental changes in the fall of 1777 functioned as the triggering mechanism for the formation of a constitutional consensus. One of these changes was the intensification of the British military threat to American independence. Despite the seemingly irreconcilable differences on issues of constitutional design, delegates within Congress responded to this new external threat by acknowledging the necessity of securing foreign alliances. The delegates became "exceedingly anxious to finish this business" of confederation, with many asserting "that the very Salvation of these States depend upon it" because "none of the European powers will publicly acknowledge them free and independent" without a plan of union.[71]

A second change that aided the formation of a constitutional consensus was the delegates' fears of an impending breakdown in Congress's operational legitimacy. In the fall of 1777, according to historian Jack N. Rakove, Congress faced "growing apprehension over the steady depreciation of continental currency." Congress responded by calling on the states to collect $5 million in new taxes, to end their paper currency emissions, and to impose specific price controls. Congressional delegates, according to this interpretation, were motivated to finalize a plan of confederation because their new demands on the state governments were, according to Rakove, "more controversial and potentially more explosive than" prior policies, and "because inflation was increasingly coming to be seen as the most dangerous source of popular 'disaffection'."[72]

The changes that occurred in the fall of 1777 offered congressional delegates strong incentives to complete a common plan of union. At best, however, these changes only intensified the delegates' shared interests in and commitment to achieving the constitutional objectives of international recognition and domestic efficacy. Neither the pressures of military defeat, the accepted norms of international protocol, nor the expected resistance of the state governments and the American people negated or dampened the underlying differences of interests among the

---

[71] Cornelius Harnett to the Governor of North Carolina, Oct. 10, 1777, *LMCC*, II: 514.

[72] Rakove, *The Beginnings of National Politics* (1979), p. 178. See also Charles Carroll to Benjamin Franklin, 12 Aug. 1777, *LMCC*, II: 450.

state delegations within Congress. The continuous presence of a multiplicity of interests – even after the completion of the final draft of the Articles of Confederation – was acknowledged in the circular letter Congress sent to the state legislatures requesting that they review the completed constitution in light of "the difficulty of combining in one general system the various sentiments and interests of a continent divided into so many sovereign and independent communities."[73]

Delegates were thus motivated to complete the American political order by both external and internal forces. The most salient external forces were the common fears of military defeat from without and popular revolt from below. The internal forces consisted of the multiple and invariably subjective motives that each state had to consent to a common form of government. How this complex set of internal motivations was coordinated (without recourse to force) into a constitutional consensus for the Articles of Confederation is, in fact, the definitive experience of the founding of the American political order.

To rediscover this process of coordination it is necessary to focus on the process by which the delegates ultimately resolved the contentious problem of the apportionment rule. As early as the spring of 1777, several delegates began to suggest alternative apportionment rules as a way of breaking the deadlock between advocates for an equal state rule and those for a proportional rule. North Carolina delegate Thomas Burke recommended transforming Congress into a bicameral legislature in which state representation would be proportional in one branch with each delegate controlling an individual vote, and a second branch in which the states would have equal representation and a single vote.[74] Thomas Jefferson and John Adams corresponded about another alternative rule that they believed would bring the "great and Small States ... as near together as possible." Their alternative apportionment rule provided "that any Proposition [in Congress] may be negatived, by the Representatives of a Majority of the People, or of a Majority of States."[75]

The type of solution offered by the dual rule of apportionment advocated by Burke and by Jefferson and Adams – namely, one ensuring two opportunities to participate in the formation of a majority coalition in Congress – was not fully appreciated by the Continental Congress.

---

[73] JCC, IX: 933 (Nov. 17, 1777). See also Cornelius Harnett to William Wilkinson, Nov. 30, 1777, LMCC, II: 578.

[74] JCC, VII: 328 (May 5, 1777). See also Rakove, *The Beginnings of National Politics* (1979), pp. 173–174.

[75] John Adams to Thomas Jefferson, May 26, 1777, LMCC, II: 374.

Delegates remained single-mindedly focused on securing the most favorable terms of apportionment for their individual states. Through the summer of 1777, delegates from several larger states remained steadfast in their support for a proportional rule, continuing their efforts to amend the draft Articles of Confederation.[76]

In early November 1777, Congress fixed the terms for the rule of apportionment in the Articles of Confederation on an equal state basis. In many respects, however, the equal state rule offered only a partial solution to the problem of founding a political order based on consent because it did not guarantee that even a single state would benefit by agreeing to the creation of a common sovereign authority. The equal state rule nevertheless minimized the possibility that the authority of the new national government would be monopolized by a majority coalition of states. Among the most prominently discussed coalition possibilities (see Table 4.5), a permanent majority coalition was probable under an equal state apportionment rule only if the state delegations divided on a landed-landless or North-South cleavage. However, formation of a majority coalition along either of these cleavages seemed highly unlikely to most, if not all, the delegates.

In addition to the equal state rule, several auxiliary voting procedures further reduced the likelihood that a state delegation would find itself permanently unable to participate in the formation of a majority coalition in Congress. The "Articles" required a nine-state majority in Congress to make decisions in several policy areas. The Articles also required the consent of nine states before another "colony" was admitted into the Union. The former rule institutionalized a continuous competition for broad-based majorities within Congress, whereas the latter rule made it extremely difficult for a temporary or simple majority to consolidate its power through the admission of new states.[77]

Settlement on a specific apportionment rule was a necessary condition for solving the problem of founding a political order based on

---

[76] See Samuel Adams to James Warren, June 30, 1777, *LMCC*, II: 391–392; *JCC*, IX: 779–780, 781 (Oct. 7, 1777).

[77] The problem of admitting new states was evident every time the "state" of Vermont appealed for formal recognition by Congress (and, thus, admission into the Union). New England state delegates supported the state's appeals, with the expectation that Vermont would strengthen their regional voting bloc in Congress, whereas southern state delegates typically rejected Vermont's appeals. Delegates from the State of New York sided with southern state delegates because their state held disputed land claims that coincided with the territorial boundaries of Vermont. See *LMCC*, II: 319, 321, 345, 388–389.

TABLE 4.5. *Cleavage Strength under Equal Apportionment Rules*

Coalition Type	Number of Votes (percent)
State Size	
Large	4 (30.8)
Medium	4 (30.8)
Small	5 (38.4)
Region	
Northeast	4 (30.8)
Mid-Atlantic	5 (38.4)
South	4 (30.8)
Tax Basis	
"White" Population	5 (38.4)
Total Population	4 (30.8)
Undecided	3 (23.1)
Land and Improvements	1 (7.7)
Land Status	
Landed	8 (61.5)
Landless	5 (38.5)
Section	
North	8 (61.5)
South	5 (38.5)

consent. A second condition was also necessary before the different interests of the thirteen states could be coordinated into a constitutional consensus. Ironically, the prolonged indeterminacy of the terms of the apportionment rule facilitated the development of this second condition. The year-long impasse over apportionment affected the delegates' willingness to make precommitments to other dimensions of the constitutional plan.

The delayed settlement affected deliberations on the types of powers that were to be entrusted to the new national government. As the experienced North Carolina delegate Thomas Burke reported in March 1777, Congress often divided between delegates "whose object on one side is to increase the power of Congress, & on the other to restrain it." Interestingly, Burke also noted that "[t]he same persons, who, on one day, endeavour to carry through some resolutions, whose tendency is to increase the power of Congress, are often on another day very strenuous advocates to restrain it."[78]

Burke's explanation of the cycling of opinions in Congress, although lengthy, deserves especially close attention because it transcends its immediate purpose and illuminates additional facets of the American founding experience. According to Burke, the erratic opinion reversals were an indication "that no one has entertained a concerted design to increase the power" of Congress.

[T]he attempts to do it proceed from ignorance of what such a being ought to be, & from the delusive intoxication which power naturally imposes on the human mind. This latter inevitably leads to an abuse & corruption of powers, & is in my humble opinion the proper object of political vigilance & jealousy. This is what will insensibly produce combinations of the States, & such combinations will be fatal to the liberties of many. It is of little moment to know what are now the subjects of political speculation. No State is in a condition to cherish projects of future ambition; but situation & comparative strength will always suggest such projects, & the powerful & conveniently situated will cherish them when they can. This will always be the case so long as man remains what his nature has determined him to be. Nor will human virtue be a sufficient security against it; on the contrary I am very suspicious that our greatest danger will arise from that source. This present is the period of public virtue & spirit: it is also the Era of inexperience. Simple nature walks almost without disguise. That profound dissimulation covered by an appearance of the most unreserved frankness, always inseparable from the accomplished political negotiator, is unknown amongst us, & must long be unknown, because it is to be acquired only by the most assiduous application, & long attentive exercise in the habit of it. Courts are the only schools where it can be learned, & we yet have them not, & probably shall not have them very soon.

Burke further remarked:

Every man's soul now stands forth; & in every one you read in very legible characters, that the State he represents is more wise, virtuous, or powerful than any other, & therefore ought to dictate to the rest. Where the more palpable advantage of power is wanting, each, in his own imagination supplies the superiority in wisdom or virtue; & this, I believe, in time will be realized. For conscious strength begets a security which relaxes the more painful efforts of wisdom & virtue; while conscious weakness spurs them to their highest mettle. But, strength, Sir, irresistible strength must in the end overcome all opposition. The more powerful States by combining, can doubtless subjugate the more feeble, & opposition will but rouse them to more effectual efforts.[79]

---

[78] Thomas Burke to Richard Caswell, March 11, 1777, *LDC*, 6:427.
[79] Thomas Burke to Richard Caswell, March 11, 1777, *LDC*, 6:428.

The classic constitution-making pathologies recounted by Burke were compounded by the delegates' determination to formalize the terms of their final consensus within a written constitution. This form of constitutional articulation required specification of a fixed set of governmental rules and an implicit precommitment that these rules would endure beyond the horizon of the moment. The former, in effect, guaranteed the constitutionalization of asymmetrical distributions of benefits among the states. The latter commitment extended the benefits (and costs) of these distributional asymmetries into the future.

Together, the structural rigidity and distributional biases inherent in the written constitutional form offered few incentives for more conciliatory relations to develop among the delegates. Indeed when two or more actors expect different benefits from different outcome possibilities, a unanimous decision for a single outcome cannot be expected because at least one actor would have to concede a relative advantage to another. Faced with this type of decision, David D. Heckathorn and Steven M. Maser argue, "Individuals may thus refuse to accept an offered outcome not because it violates individual rationality (i.e., because it would be worse than conflict), not because it violated joint rationality (i.e., because the offered outcome is inefficient), but because it is politically irrational in the sense that it is judged to be inconsistent with the strength of the individual's strategic position."[80]

Figure 4.2 illustrates this problem of constitutional design in an idealized form.[81] Assume actors X and Y are two sets of constitution makers with shared interests for the distinct sets of constitutional devices contained in sets A and B. Among the devices contained in set C, actor Y prefers the devices in subset C_1, whereas actor X prefers the devices in subset C_2. Subsets C_1 and C_2 are noncombinable and indivisible. Given these conditions, actors X and Y would be expected to consent to adopt constitution "A" consisting of the devices in set A, although both actors would prefer the more complex constitution "A + B" to constitution "A." Actors X and Y would be unable to agree, however, on the still more complex constitution containing the additional but incommensurable constitutional design devices from set C.

---

[80] Douglas D. Heckathorn and Steven M. Maser, "Bargaining and Constitutional Contracts," *AJPS* (1987), 31: 156.

[81] See Heckathorn and Maser, "Bargaining and Constitutional Contracts," *AJPS* (1987), 31: 154–156; and Fritz W. Scharpf, "Coordination in Hierarchies and Networks," in Fritz W. Scharpf, ed., *Games in Hierarchies and Networks* (Boulder, CO: Westview Press, 1993), pp. 127–140.

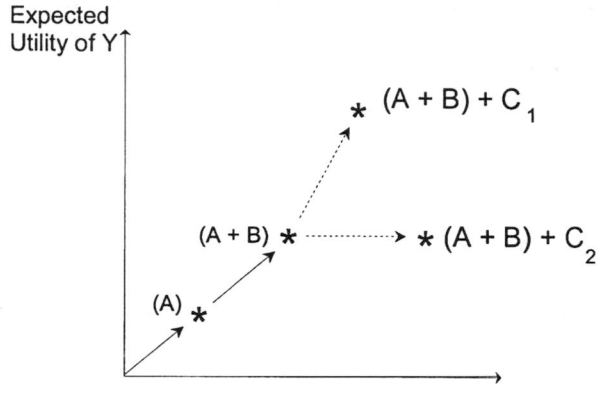

FIGURE 4.2. Constitutional Contracting over Common and Discrete Goods

Another and arguably more troublesome barrier to the formation of a constitutional consensus was the discontinuity between the delegates' apparent commitment to form a powerful common government and their capacities (as determined by the rule of apportionment) to extract benefits from such a government. Recall the remarks of North Carolina delegate Thomas Burke that all delegates appeared intent on increasing the powers of the national government but that they did so "from ignorance of what such a being ought to be, & from the delusive intoxication which power naturally imposes on the human mind." Burke also noted, "No State is in a condition to cherish projects of future ambition; but situation & comparative strength will always suggest such projects, & the powerful & conveniently situated will cherish them when they can."[82]

Figure 4.3 is an idealized model of the relationship between a constitution maker's expected capacity to extract governmental benefits (labeled decision-making capacity) and the expected level of governing authority available to the government. Other things being equal, there is a positive relationship between these two variables: low expected decision-making capacity correlates with low expected levels of governing authority, and higher levels of expected decision-making capacity correlate with higher expected levels of governing authority. In two classic forms, a single dictator or an oligarchical group with near-certain capacities to extract benefits from a new government are highly likely to

[82] Thomas Burke to Richard Caswell, March 11, 1777, *LDC*, 6: 427–428.

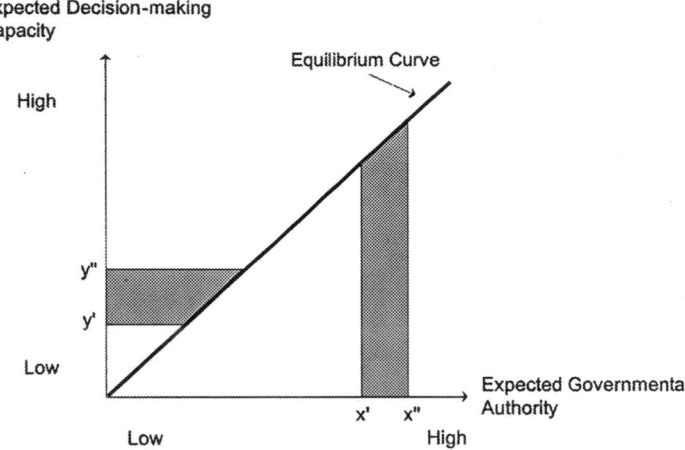

x'-x" = range of expected levels of governing authority
y'-y" = range of expected levels of decision-making capacity

FIGURE 4.3. Constitutional Consensus as Function of Expected Decision-making Capacity and Governing Authority

establish powerful (if not unlimited) forms of government. The delegates in Congress, by contrast, had limited representation under the equal state apportionment rule and the original Dickinson committee plan proposed a moderately high level of governing authority for the new national government. As a result, congressional deliberations designed to achieve common consent for a new political order were unsuccessful, in large part because there was a disequilibrium between the range of state decision-making capacities (y'-y") within the proposed national government and the range of national governing authority (x'-x") proposed in the initial drafts of the Articles of Confederation.

Although the historical conditions already described made unanimous consent for a plan of government improbable if not impossible,[83] delegates within Congress ultimately approved a final version of the Articles

---

[83] For theoretical and formalized explanations of this problem, see Kenneth Arrow, *Social Choice and Individual Values* (New York: Wiley, 1951), Charles R. Plott, "A Notion of Equilibrium and Its Possibility under Majority Rule," *American Economic Review* (1967), 57: 787–806; Richard D. McKelvey, "Intransitivities in Multidimensional Voting Models and Some Implications for Agenda Control," *Journal of Economic Theory* (1976), 12: 472–482; Norman J. Schofield, "Instability of Simple Dynamic Games," *Review of Economic Studies* (1978), 45: 575–594.

of Confederation in November 1777. This consensus was not achieved by nullifying the multiplicity of interests that existed among the delegates. Nor was it effected, historian Jack N. Rakove correctly contends, by a conceptual breakthrough that recast the terms of political discourse, nor by a single grand compromise in which disputed constitutional design issues were divided efficiently among contending state interests.[84] Rather, a constitutional consensus for the Articles of Confederation ultimately emerged only after an equilibrium was achieved among the delegates' expected decision-making capacities within the new national government and their expectations concerning the range of the national government's authority.

As suggested by Figure 4.3, development of a constitutional equilibrium required overcoming the discontinuity between the low levels of decision-making capacity (guaranteed to each state by the equal state apportionment rule) and the high levels of expected governmental authority proposed in the original drafts of the "Articles." In this respect, the decisions for an equal state apportionment rule and for supermajority voting procedures institutionalized high levels of competition for majority status within Congress. These decisions also fixed a y-axis floor on the equilibrium curve in Figure 4.3. Movement toward an equilibrium, as a consequence, necessitated further limitation of expected levels of national governmental authority – or, in other words, additional retraction along the x-axis.

South Carolina delegate Edward Rutledge was one of the first to identify this particular path to constitutional equilibrium. As early as June 1776, Rutledge assessed the security of his state's interests under the proposed national government and he privately concluded that "[u]nless it's greatly curtailed it never can pass, as it is to be submitted to Men in the respective Provinces who will not be led or rather driven into Measures which may lay the Foundations of their Ruin." Specifically, Rutledge cautioned that the destruction of "all Provincial Distinctions and making every thing of the most minute kind bend to what they call the good of the whole, is in other Terms to say that these Colonies must be subject to the Government of the Eastern Provinces." As protection against this possibility, the South Carolina delegate proposed granting "Congress with no more Power than is absolutely necessary" and thereby "to keep the Staff in our own Hands" for "if surrendered into the Hands of others a most pernicious use will be made of it."[85]

---

[84] Rakove, *The Beginnings of National Politics* (1979), p. 177.
[85] Edward Rutledge to John Jay, June 29, 1776, *LMCC*, I: 517–518.

Although many delegates no doubt shared concerns similar to those privately articulated by Rutledge, few in Congress initially understood how his solution could overcome their impasse concerning the formation of a new constitutional union. In early 1777, North Carolina delegate Thomas Burke refocused Congress's attention on the benefits of forming a more limited government. Specifically, Burke argued "that unlimited power can not be safely trusted to any man, or set of men, on earth." Like Rutledge, Burke also feared the consequences of ending up a staffless minority in Congress. For Burke, however, the "New England States" were not a long-term threat because "[t]heir situation & natural disadvantages will prevent their becoming formidable if uncombined with others." He speculated that "the most formidable combination would be Massachusetts, Pennsylvania & Virginia."[86] To protect against a coalition of these states, Burke "earnestly wish[ed] that the power of Congress was accurately defined, & that there were adequate checks provided to prevent any excess."[87]

Between August 1776 and November 1777, the revisions of the Articles of Confederation generally reflected the type of constitutional solution advocated by Rutledge and Burke. Most significantly, Congress's authority was redefined to extend only to those powers "expressly delegated" in the Articles of Confederation, thereby constitutionalizing a *formal* bulwark against future attempts to enact *informal* increases in the authority of Congress. The delegates agreed to limit Congress's treaty-making authority to protect "the legislative rights of any State, within its own limits."[88] Congress's authority to settle interstate disputes was also restricted in the final draft of the Articles of Confederation. These disputes, historian Jack N. Rakove notes, were to be mediated through a quasi-judicial process in which Congress was "the last resort on appeal."[89] Finally, the powers of the Council of State were more clearly defined to extend only to those agreed on by the "consent of nine

---

[86] Thomas Burke to Richard Caswell, March 11, 1777, *LDC*, 6: 428.

    Burke continued: "The first [Massachusetts] has power sufficient to overawe & consequently to direct the other three New England States. The second [Pennsylvania] could equally influence Jersey & Delaware. Virginia would be formidable to her Southern neighbors, & Maryland. New York could not resist a combination of Pennsylvania and Massachusetts; Maryland must fall a sacrifice to Pennsylvania & Virginia. Against this powerful confederacy, I fear, we should not be able to hold out long."

[87] Thomas Burke to Richard Caswell, March 11, 1777, *LDC*, 6: 428–429.

[88] *JCC*, IX: 845 (Oct. 28, 1777); IX: 841–843 (Oct. 27, 1777).

[89] Rakove, *The Beginnings of National Politics* (1979), p. 180.

states" and Congress was prohibited from delegating any authority to the Council that required "the voice of nine states."[90]

In addition to narrowing the range of powers available to future majorities in Congress, congressional delegates agreed on additional limitations to the powers of the state governments. As revised, the Articles of Confederation committed the states to the "Payment and Satisfaction" of the Union's debt. States also were required to give "full Faith and Credit" to the acts of other state governments and to extradite individuals accused of "treason, felony, or other high misdemeanor in any State." In addition, explicit restrictions were placed on the internal police powers of the states. The Articles specifically guaranteed citizens of each state "all privileges and immunities of free citizens in the several states," the freedom to travel between states, and "the privileges of trade and commerce" available within a state. Moreover, states were barred from imposing duties "on the property of the United States" or any of the other states.[91]

Finally, congressional delegates agreed to a more explicit recognition of the governing authority of the state governments. At Burke's prompting, in April 1777 Congress revised the draft Articles of Confederation to include the statement that: "Each state retains its sovereignty, freedom, and independence, and every power, jurisdiction, and right, which is not by this Confederation expressly delegated to the United States, in Congress assembled." Congress also agreed to recognize "the legislative rights of any State within its own limits" and to guarantee that "no State shall be deprived of territory for the benefit of the United States."[92]

The Calculus of Consent

This account acknowledges that the threat of military defeat, the demands of international protocol, and the concerns for the continued domestic legitimacy of Congress were powerful incentives compelling the thirteen American states to consent to a common form of government. It also contends that the development of another condition was neces-

---

[90] *JCC*, IX: 779–780 (Nov. 7, 1777).
[91] Rakove, *The Beginnings of National Politics* (1979), p. 181. See also final form of Articles of Confederations as printed in *JCC*, IX: 907–925 (Nov. 15, 1777).
[92] See *JCC*, IX: 907–925 (Nov. 15, 1777). See also Thomas Burke to Governor of North Carolina, April 29, 1777, *LMCC*, II: 345–346.

sary to achieve this end. This condition was the convergence between the states' expected capacities to extract benefits from the proposed government and their expectations concerning the level of collective authority available to the government. At bottom, the delegates' decisions to adopt the equal state rule of apportionment and an exceedingly limited form of national government were the decisive elements that permitted the formation of a constitutional consensus for the Articles of Confederation.

If a constitutional consensus (as defined in terms of the ideal equilibrium curve in Figure 4.3) is a necessary condition, what are the sufficient conditions for this particular form of collective political action?[93] This question cannot be breached fully here because a minimally adequate answer would seem to require a deeper cognitive-level inquiry into the decision-making calculations of *every* individual constitution maker who participated in constitutional deliberations. At this level of historical and analytical inquiry the calculus of consent likely would consist of a unique matrix of contextual contingencies and subjective behavioral tendencies to trust, to risk, to act under uncertainty, to be persuaded, to miscalculate, and to be magnanimous. At present, our theoretical capacities to model or explain the causes and consequences of subjective interactions like these remain nearly as underdeveloped as the body of empirical evidence required to ground an investigation of this sort is incomplete.

Although a full science of the causal mechanics of political foundings is not yet possible more plausible and informed stories of the American founding (and of the constitutive and degenerative dynamics of political

---

[93] In other words, the problematics of constitutional consent amidst diversity persist even when an "equilibrium" space is created because *identical* preferences or expected utilities are not held in common. As a consequence, although a constitutional agreement becomes more likely when the respective expected ranges of decision-making capacity and governing authority converge, the motives that prompt individual actors to make a final commitment for a specific constitutional agreement remain unspecified. This leap of consent can be explained in several ways: for example, with reference to the will and intellect of the individuals who become participants in these constitution-making moments. A momentary lapse or loosening of the representative relationship between individual agents (the set of constitution makers) and the diverse principal political interests they represent is another way to account for this special form of commitment. Political scientist and theorist Jon Elster provides a third account: that pre-existing or prior structures provide ready-made focal points around which constitutional assembly participants begin "the bootstrap-pulling enterprise of organizing political life." Jon Elster, "Constitutional Bootstrapping in Philadelphia and Paris," in *Constitutional, Identity, Difference, and Legitimacy: Theoretical Perspectives*, Michel Rosenfield, ed. (1994), p. 82.

These three explanations, however credible or promising, are admittedly ad hoc.

order) can be constructed. Thus far, most interpretative accounts suggest that delegates ultimately agreed to the Articles of Confederation because they feared the international, domestic, and personal consequences of not consenting. These accounts effectively retell the Hobbesian story of state creation: that constitution makers have individual and unshared interests but that a common and primordial fear ultimately motivates actors to consent to the creation of a nearly omnipotent form of government. Other interpretations of the American founding – primarily those told from the ideological perspective – retell what, in effect, is the Lockean story of state creation: that constitution makers are prompted to consent to the formation of a common government because they are embedded within a society of shared interests, ideas, and experiences.

This account, by contrast, suggests that a different state creation story more fully corresponds with the historical record of the decisions made by the constitution makers who engaged in the task of forming the first American political order. This alternative founding story contends that the state interests represented in Congress after 1776 were diverse, that these states and their delegates in Congress feared the consequences of consenting to a common Union as much as (if not more than) the consequences of not consenting, and that each state ultimately consented to a highly limited form of national government because it was perceived to be in each state's immediate and long-term interest to do so. Thus, in addition to the noted external conditions in the fall of 1777, the constitutional design of the political order proposed in the Articles of Confederation provided a motive for consent that appealed (in different ways) to each state. The original bond of the American Union was thus forged out of the perceived capacity of the Articles of Confederation to satisfy a multiplicity of state interests and expectations.

Table 4.6 offers a rough but functional measurement of the central claim of this new account of the American founding, illustrating how and to what degree each state stood to gain by consenting to the Articles of Confederation. Across the seven most prominently debated dimensions of the plan of government formalized in the Articles, state interests were valued on a "1, 0, –1" scale. As recorded in Table 4.6, total expected benefits for each state had net positive values.

The value of constitutional rules related to apportionment, common expenses, and the western lands varied among the states because these rules promised specific and asymmetrical benefits. The interests of the smallest states, for example, clearly benefited from the adoption of the equal state rule of apportionment over the alternative proportional rule.

TABLE 4.6. *The Calculus of Constitutional Consensus*

Constitutional Dimensions:

State	Rule of Apportionment	Powers of Congress on:		State Restrictions	Auxiliary Voting	Limited Government	Federalism	TOTAL
		Taxes	Western Lands					
MA	-1	-1	1	1	1	1	1	3
NH	1	-1	1	1	1	1	1	5
RI	1	-1	-1	1	1	1	1	3
CT	0	-1	1	1	1	1	1	4
NY	0	0	1	1	1	1	1	5
NJ	1	1	-1	1	1	1	1	5
PA	-1	0	-1	1	1	1	1	2
DE	1	1	-1	1	1	1	1	5
MD	-1	1	-1	1	1	1	1	3
VA	-1	1	1	1	1	1	1	5
NC	0	1	1	1	1	1	1	6

The five smallest states thus receive a score of "1" on this constitutional dimension. The interests of the four medium-sized states, however, were affected only marginally by the apportionment rule decision; they consequently received a "0" score. The interests of the four largest states were disadvantaged by the equal state rule, thus a "−1" score.

The value of the constitutional rules dividing common expenses and regulating the western lands were also assigned according to a "1, 0, −1" scale. New Jersey and five southern states supported the final constitutional rule, which divided common expenses according to state land value and improvements. These states received a score of "1."[94] Delegates from New England states opposed this rule: thus, a "−1" score. Three state delegations were undecided: thus, their "0" score.[95] The rules regulating the western lands provided a wider distribution of benefits: Eight states received a score of "1." Five states did not expect to benefit under these rules. They received a "−1" score.[96]

The four other constitutional dimensions included in Table 4.6 provided general benefits to each state. Thus, every state received a "1" for the restrictions placed on the state governments (State Restrictions), the auxiliary voting procedures placed on Congress (Auxiliary Voting), the restrictions placed on Congress's authority (Limited Government), and the Articles' explicit recognition of the authority and autonomy of the state governments (Federalism).

PART IV: RATIFICATION OF THE ARTICLES OF CONFEDERATION

Congress approved the final version of the Articles of Confederation on November 15, 1777, and submitted it to the state legislatures with the

---

[94] *JCC*, IX: 801 (Oct. 14, 1777).

[95] Nathaniel Folsom to Meshech Weare, Nov. 21, 1777, *LMCC*, II: 564.

[96] Additional attempts were made by delegates from states without western land claims to change the Articles' provisions on the western lands. On October 15, three amendments were proposed and debated. The first amendment proposed "that the limits of each respective territorial jurisdiction should be ascertained by the articles of confederation." The second amendment proposed that Congress shall have "the sole and exclusive right and power to ascertain and fix the western boundary of such states as claim to the South Sea, and to dispose of all land beyond the boundary so ascertained, for the benefit of the United States." The third amendment provided Congress with the power to establish "separate and independent states, from time to time, as the numbers and circumstances of the people thereof may require." Each amendment was defeated, leaving unresolved the question of how the western lands were ultimately to be incorporated into the Union. *JCC*, IX: 806–808 (Oct. 15, 1777).

recommendation that they review it by March 10, 1778.[97] Unanimous consent of the states was required for ratification of the Articles.

Several state legislatures were quick to ratify the Articles of Confederation. Other states had reservations.[98] Several New England state legislatures objected to the rule dividing the Union's expenses according to state land and building values. Connecticut proposed amending the Articles to divide these expenses according to population. Massachusetts proposed variation of the tax basis "until experience" reveals which "rule of apportionment will be most equal and consequently most just."[99] Several states objected to the Articles' provisions on the western lands. Maryland explained its initial rejection of the Articles on the fact that Congress was not empowered to limit the territorial claims of the so-called landed states. Maryland also petitioned Congress to recognize claims to part of the western lands, which were private property before the beginning of the War for Independence.[100]

Roughly half the states had authorized their delegates to sign the Articles by the March 1778 deadline set by Congress.[101] By the end of this year, eleven of the thirteen states had ratified the Articles of Confederation.[102] Several attempts were made to gain the consent of the final two states, Maryland and Delaware. In December 1778, Virginia threatened to confederate with as many states as were then willing.[103] In February 1779, delegates from Delaware were authorized by their state to sign the Articles.[104]

Maryland, however, withheld its consent for several more years, consistently insisting that without territorial cessions by the so-called "landed" states the interests of the "landless" states would not be adequately protected under the Articles. Maryland argued that it was disadvantaged because as a state without western land claims it was unable to grant land to troops in return for their service in the Continental Army or to sell land to support the state's treasury. Maryland also contended

[97] JCC, IX: 907–925 (Nov. 15, 1777); IX: 932–935.
[98] Virginia and New Hampshire adopted the Articles without qualification; Rhode Island's approval was conditioned on ratification by eight other states; and New York's required ratification by the other states. See JCC, XI: 663–665 (Feb. 18, 1777).
[99] JCC, XI: 638 (June 23, 1778).
[100] JCC, XI: 631 (June 22, 1778).
[101] JCC, XI: 662–671 (June 27, 1778).
[102] JCC, XI: 657–658 (June 26, 1778); XI: 677 (July 9, 1778); XII: 1162–1164 (Nov. 25, 1778).
[103] Jensen, *Articles of Confederation* (1940), p. 201.
[104] JCC, XIII: 186–188 (Feb. 16, 1779).

that these large western territories could never be easily governed by the states that claimed them.[105]

In March 1780, New York informed Congress of its willingness to cede part of its western claims to the United States in order "to accelerate the federal alliance."[106] In April, the Virginia delegation offered a similar territorial concession, declaring the state was open "to any just and reasonable propositions for removing the ostensible causes of delay to the complete ratification of the Confederation."[107] In December, the Virginia assembly reaffirmed the likelihood that "at a future Day one or more of the larger States already united may for their own Convenience and Accommodation effect a Division and claim a right of Representation in Congress for each State so divided."[108]

In October 1780, Congress made an effort to secure Maryland's consent. It enacted a resolution "On Public Lands and New States" which determined "that the unappropriated lands that may be ceded or relinquished to the United States, by any particular States . . . shall be disposed of for the common benefit of the United States, and be settled and formed into distinct republican States, which shall become members of the Federal Union, and shall have the same rights of sovereignty, freedom and independence, as the other States." This resolution also established that when nine or more states agreed, new states would be established that would "contain a suitable extent of territory" of not "less than one hundred nor more than one hundred fifty miles square."[109] On January 2, 1781, the Virginia assembly agreed to a conditional cession of her claims to territories northwest of the Ohio River and a month later Maryland became the final state to ratify the Articles, completing the process of constitutional reconstruction that began in earnest during the summer of 1776.[110]

CONCLUSION

The configuration of a framework of government within which the diverse interests of the former American colonies could be expressed as

---

[105] See *JCC*, XIV: 619–620 (May 21, 1779).

[106] Burnett, *The Continental Congress* (1941), p. 495; Morison, ed., *Sources & Documents*, p. xxx; Jensen, *Articles of Confederation* (1940), p. 226.

[107] Jensen, *The Articles of Confederation* (1940), p. 218.

[108] As quoted in Burnett, *The Continental Congress* (1941), p. 495.

[109] *JCC*, XVII: 808; "Resolution of Congress on Public Lands and New States," in Morison, ed., *Sources & Documents Illustrating the American Revolution*, p. 203.

[110] Jensen, *Articles of Confederation* (1940), pp. 229, 238.

a common warrant for a new American political order was neither inevitable nor simply a matter of committing prior colonial political experiences to paper. Rather, the architectonic work of formalizing a new governing partnership among these various interests required the formation of a consensus among the individuals who first engaged the serious business of founding a nation.

Formation of a constitutional consensus among these individuals (and, implicitly, among the politically relevant interests they represented) was no easy task as the debates and decisions of the First Continental Congress clearly forecast. The business of crafting the terms of the American political order took on a new earnestness in 1776 but not until 1781 did the interests and expectations of American political actors converge sufficiently to secure their unanimous consent for the national government defined in the Articles of Confederation.

The final rule of equal state apportionment incorporated into the Articles of Confederation was an elemental part of the successful statecraft that constituted the American founding. The immediate consequences of the debates and decisions that yielded this particular rule were visible not only as a formal constitutional articulation but in numerous beliefs and practices that determined how the united states subsequently prosecuted their efforts against Great Britain. As many have suggested before, the story of the American Revolution and of the early development of the new American political order is simply incomplete without acknowledgment of the formative effects of this particular rule. The longer-term consequences of the equal state apportionment rule were equally as significant for the American political order, but these effects are revealed and measured within the story of the second apportionment rule change unfolded in Chapters 5, 6, and 7.

CONSTITUTIONAL CHANGE II: 1781–1789

5

Contours of the Confederation:
Macrolevel Conditions, 1776–1786

new double app.

The equal state rule of apportionment adopted by the First Continental Congress in 1774 and formalized within the Articles of Confederation in 1781 endured until the Articles were set aside in 1787. The new constitutional order fashioned in that year promised to establish a more powerful national government and a new national rule of apportionment. This new rule divided national decision-making capacities among the states according to state population in the new U.S. House and equally among the states in the new U.S. Senate. The next three chapters retell the seemingly familiar story by which the Articles and their equal state rule were abandoned and replaced with the U.S. Constitution and its new "double" rule of apportionment.

Chapter 5 begins this new story of constitutional change and the framing of the Constitution by examining the same macrolevel conditions examined in Chapter 2, tracking their development from 1776 to the calling of the 1787 Constitutional Convention. As in Chapter 2, this chapter focuses on the economic, demographic, institutional, and ideological conditions that shaped the context within which the change occurred. Description of these conditions between 1776 and 1786 serves several purposes. First, it provides an opportunity for an assessment of potential causal relationships between these conditions and the subsequent change that is not predicated on the detailed account completed in Chapter 6. Second, it establishes external reference points for analyzing the decisions and outcome of the 1787 Convention. Third, description of the four conditions opens a window onto the developmental dynamics embedded within the status quo of late 1786 and early 1787, thereby infusing this outcome with an expected value relative to other possible constitutional outcomes.[1]

Chapter 5 is divided into five parts. Part I critiques existing explanations of the abandonment and replacement of the Articles of Confederation. Although much can be learned from these accounts, they typically do not provide complete or necessarily credible accounts of the constitutional change in the Articles' rule of apportionment. To begin the construction of a more credible account, Parts II through V reconstruct the contextual conditions within which this change occurred. Parts II and III focus on the development of economic and demographic conditions respectively. Part IV concentrates on the institutional development of Congress's structure and capacities after 1781. Finally, Part V measures the ways in which the concept and institutions of representation developed during the decade after 1776.

To forecast the remaining parts of this account, Chapter 6 complements this chapter's focus on macrolevel conditions with a microlevel (or actor-centered) analysis of the sequence of decisions leading up to the 1787 Constitutional Convention. Unlike Chapter 3, however, this chapter does not reconstruct the conceptual histories of each constitutional outcome envisioned during the mid-1780s. Chapter 6, rather, highlights another critical but often overlooked element of the process of constitutional change: the constitutional entrepreneurs who transform and direct divergent political expectations into attempts to effect wholesale change in a constitutional order. James Madison is profiled as one of the most important entrepreneurs behind this second constitutional change. Chapter 6 also focuses attention on the three most populous and politically powerful states (Virginia, Massachusetts, and Pennsylvania) prior to their commitments to attend the 1787 Convention. Although each of these states stood to gain from the adoption of a new population-based rule of apportionment, Massachusetts was notably apprehensive about attending this Convention with its likely attempt to abandon the Articles' equal state apportionment rule. The introduction of several game theoretic models helps to clarify the source of this apprehension and why Massachusetts ultimately committed delegates to the Convention. Chapter 7 completes the account of the second constitutional and apportionment rule change by closely examining the deliberations of the 1787 Constitutional Convention.

[1] See Fritz K. Ringer, "Causal Analysis in Historical Reasoning," *History and Theory* (1989), 28: 167–168.

The consequences of the Articles' rule of equal state apportionment on the subsequent development of the American political order thus become apparent. For the original and necessary coupling of this rule with a severely limited national government induced little interest in or attachment to the national government after the external threat of Great Britain was dramatically reduced by the treaty of 1783. As early as the mid-1780s few politically relevant interests or individuals attributed any significant immediate or long-term benefits to the national government established under the Articles. With few conceptual or customary attachments to existing constitutional arrangements, most political actors were not directly threatened by the movement to create a more powerful national government. It is not surprising, therefore, that as some began to argue openly for a division of the United States into two or more smaller unions, many others (including twelve of the thirteen state legislatures) supported the convention that assembled in Philadelphia in the spring of 1787. Why this expectation for a more fully empowered national government also precipitated a constitutional change in the national rule of apportionment is the unanswered puzzle that Chapters 5, 6 and 7 are designed to solve.

PART I: INTERPRETATIVE PERSPECTIVES

Prior accounts of the transition from the Articles of Confederation to the U.S. Constitution typically describe this constitutional transformation from one of three general perspectives. From the first perspective, attention is focused primarily on changes in underlying economic and social conditions. In *An Economic Interpretation of the Constitution of the United States*, for example, historian Charles Beard argued that the organizers of the 1787 Constitutional Convention were intent on establishing a stronger national government in order to protect their property and speculative interests.[2] *economic*

From a second perspective, the causes of this constitutional change are portrayed in terms of various types of ideological conditions. These accounts offer partial reconstructions of the era's political discourse in order to delineate the boundaries of political thought and the emotive

---

[2] Charles Beard, *An Economic Interpretation of the Constitution of the United States* (New York: The Macmillan Co., 1913); James Franklin Jamison, *The American Revolution as a Social Movement* (Princeton, NJ: Princeton University Press, 1926); Forrest McDonald, *E Pluribus Unum: The Formation of the American Republic, 1776–1790* (Boston: Houghton Mifflin, 1965).

ideological

forces that compelled political action. Among other accounts, Gordon
S. Wood's reconstruction of the discourse of American republicanism
grounds his contention that concerns for the preservation of public virtue
and political order compelled the calling of the 1787 Constitutional
Convention.[3] *institutional*

The third perspective offers a decidedly different view of the
Confederation period and of the making of the U.S. Constitution. This
perspective focuses attention on the efficacy of national political institutions. Several of these accounts concentrate on the national government's
limited capacity to collect tax revenues. Other accounts explain the
demise of the Articles with reference to the organizational capacities and
decision-making rules of Congress.[4] At bottom, accounts from this per-

---

[3] Gordon S. Wood, *The Creation of the American Republic, 1776–1787* (Chapel Hill:
University of North Carolina Press, 1969).

For other accounts made from the ideological perspective, see J. Allen Smith, *The
Spirit of American Government: A Study of the Constitution, Its Origin, Influence, and
Relation to Democracy* (New York: The Macmillan Co., 1907) and Merrill Jensen, *The
New Nation: A History of the United States During the Confederation, 1781–1789*
(New York: Knopf, 1950); Peter S. Onuf, "American Revolution and National Identity,"
Mellon Sawyer Seminar, Johns Hopkins University, 20 April 1998. These accounts
generally tend to emphasize the force of ideological commitments for political
centralization.

See also Louis Hartz, *The Liberal Tradition in America: An Interpretation of
American Political Thought Since the Revolution* (New York: Harcourt, Brace, 1955);
Joyce Appleby, *Liberalism and Republicanism in the Historical Imagination* (Cambridge,
MA: Harvard University Press, 1992). These accounts reconstruct different strands of the
political discourse of liberalism. For another variant of this interpretative perspective,
one that argues that the Articles of Confederation were abandoned because they offered
ineffectual protection of natural rights, see Scott D. Gerber, *To Secure These Rights* (New
York: New York University Press, 1995). For a counter interpretation, see Larry E. Tise,
The American Counterrevolution: A Retreat From Liberty, 1783–1800 (Mechanicsburg,
PA: Stackpole Books, 1998).

For a less thematic account made from the ideological perspective, one that searches
for the conceptual antecedents of specific ideas that came to the fore at the 1787
Constitutional Convention, see Edward S. Corwin, "The Progress of Constitutional
Theory between the Declaration of Independence and the Meeting of the Philadelphia
Convention," *AHR* (1925), 30: 511–536.

[4] See H. James Henderson, *Party Politics in the Continental Congress* (New York:
McGraw-Hill, 1974); Joseph L. Davis, *Sectionalism in American Politics, 1774–1787*
(Madison, WI: University of Wisconsin Press, 1977); E. James Ferguson, *The Power of
the Purse: A History of American Public Finance, 1776–1790* (Chapel Hill: University of
North Carolina Press, 1961); Dall Forsythe, *Taxation and Political Change in the Young
Nation, 1781–1833* (New York: Columbia University Press, 1977); Robert H. Brown,
Redeeming the Republic: Federalists, Taxation, and the Origins of the Constitution
(Baltimore: Johns Hopkins University Press, 1993); Rick K. Wilson and Calvin Jillson,
*Congressional Dynamics: Structure, Coordination, and Choice in the First American
Congress, 1774–1789* (Stanford, CA: Stanford University Press, 1994); Jack N. Rakove,

spective generally offer narrowly instrumental or functionalist explanations for the constitutional change in 1787.

Beyond these three general perspectives, the interpretative canon on
the formation of the U.S. Constitution can further be distinguished by
the use of one of two narrative frameworks. Accounts that use the
first framework, the so-called "Critical Period" narrative, portray the
national government and the young American nation as drifting inexorably into anarchy during the mid-1780s. Explanations for the cause
of this looming constitutional crisis vary. Economic historian Curtis P.
Nettls contends that the nation was threatened by economic chaos.
Historian Gordon S. Wood portrays the nation as threatened by the
corruptive forces of licentiousness. Political scientists Rick K. Wilson and
Calvin Jillson contend that a form of internal decision-making chaos had
paralyzed the Confederation Congress. Most recently, historian Jack N.
Rakove introduces a two-mechanism constitutional crisis initiated by
sectional divisions in Congress that exposed the possibility of disunion
and the realization that Shays's Rebellion "signaled a deeper crisis" concerning the capacity of existing state governments to withstand "popular
upheaval."[5]

Accounts made with the second narrative framework, by contrast, explain the abandonment and replacement of the Articles of Confederation
without an intervening or triggering "crisis." The process of constitutional
change is explained in terms of the deliberate actions taken by one of
several interest groups. In addition to Charles Beard's classic account
of the speculative interests who purportedly orchestrated the 1787
Constitutional Convention, the accounts of historians J. Allen Smith
and Merrill Jensen cast attention on a group of ideologues committed to
establishing a more centralized national government. Still other accounts
highlight other interest groups, for example, a Virginia-led faction of
southern states interested in western expansion, or a younger generation
of political actors committed to constitutional reform as a vehicle for the

---

Original Meanings: Politics and Ideas in the Making of the Constitution (New York:
Knopf, 1996).

[5] See Curtis P. Nettls, *The Emergence of a National Economy, 1775–1815* (New York:
Holt, Rinehart and Winston, 1962); Gordon S. Wood, *The Creation of the American
Republic* (Chapel Hill: University of North Carolina Press, 1969); Frederick W. Marks,
Independence on Trial: Foreign Affairs and the Making of the Constitution (Baton Rouge:
Louisiana State University Press, 1973); and Peter S. Onuf, *The Origins of the Federal
Republic: Jurisdictional Controversies in the United States, 1775–1787* (Philadelphia:
University of Pennsylvania Press, 1983); Wilson and Jillson, *Congressional Dynamics*
(1994); Rakove, *Original Meanings* (1996), pp. 33–34.

advancement of their nationalistic aspirations and personal political careers.[6]

The three identified perspectives and the two narrative frameworks illuminate essential elements of the conditions and actions that defined the abandonment of the Articles of Confederation. However, the accounts constructed from these perspectives and narrative frameworks have offered only partial views of this historic constitutional transition in American political development. The limitations of these accounts need no rehearsal here because they often reflect only the decision to combine a particular perspective with a particular narrative framework.[7] At a more general level, the interpretative canon of the Confederation period and of the making of the U.S. Constitution can be critiqued for both their incomplete recognition of alternative perspectives and frameworks and their failure to link this period's complex developmental patterns with the specific sequence of decisions that preceded and defined the 1787 Constitutional Convention.[8] Moreover and most significantly, existing interpretations rarely provide credible accounts of the process of constitutional change that ultimately yielded *both* an increase in national governing authority *and* a change in the national rule of apportionment. With this particular deficit in mind, let us turn immediately to the required assessment of the economic, demographic, institutional, and ideological conditions that existed from 1776 to 1786.

---

[6] See Robert A. Feer, "Shays's Rebellion and the Constitution: A Study in Causation," *New England Quarterly* (1969), 42: 388–410; Jensen, *The New Nation* (1950); Henderson, *Party Politics in the Continental Congress* (1974); Stanley Elkins and Eric McKitrick, "The Founding Fathers: Young Men of the Revolution," *PSQ* (1961), 76: 181–216; John P. Roche, "The Founding Fathers: A Reform Caucus in Action," *APSR* (1961), 55: 799–816; Cecilia M. Kenyon, "Men of Little Faith: The Anti-Federalists on the Nature of Representative Government," WMQ (1955), 12: 3–43.

[7] For perceptive reviews of this literature, see Peter S. Onuf, "Reflections on the Founding: Constitutional Historiography in Bicentennial Perspective," WMQ (1989), 46: 341–375; James H. Hutson, "The Creation of the Constitution: Scholarship at a Standstill," *Reviews in American History* (1984), 12(4): 463–477; Gordon S. Wood, ed., *The Confederation and the Constitution* (Boston: Little, Brown, 1973), pp. vii–xv, 181–189; Isaac Kramnick, "The 'Great National Discussion': The Discourse of Politics in 1787," WMQ (1988), 45: 3–32; Richard B. Morris, "The Confederation Period and the American Historian," WMQ (1956), 13: 139–156.

[8] The owl of Minerva flies only at dusk. The suggested synthesis can be completed only after several generations of archivists have labored (often without recognition) to make original sources accessible and after other scholars have analyzed and arranged these original sources into coherent and credible interpretative accounts. As French historian Marc Bloch noted, "The old maxim remains true that a day of synthesis requires years of analysis." Marc Bloch, "Toward a Comparative History of European Societies" ([1928], 1953), J. C. Riemersma, trans., in *Enterprise and Secular Change*, Frederic Lane, ed. (Homewood, IL: R. D. Irwin, 1953), pp. 519–520.

PART II: ECONOMIC CONDITIONS

Three obstacles impede any assessment of American economic conditions between 1776 and 1786. The first obstacle is the incomplete and un-compiled record of economic activity during this decade. The War for Independence no doubt interrupted or ended many imperial practices of record keeping in the American colonies. Initial American efforts at data collection were at best unconventional and erratic, and they focused almost exclusively on military and political matters. In addition, wartime economic activities (especially international commerce) were often redi-rected into new and more sparsely documented channels and the rapid destabilization of currency values in the late 1770s, economic historians John J. McCusker and Russell R. Menard note, "crippled the price system, with severe consequences for both the operation of the economy and the writing of economic history."[9]

The second obstacle is the conflicting interpretations of economic con-ditions during this decade. This study does not engage these debates but accepts the prevailing consensus that early American economic condi-tions varied over time and space. The war, for example, disrupted many sectors of the domestic economy but it negatively affected exports more than imports. It also destroyed trade linkages with several Native American communities and greatly diminished the southern labor force and New England's fishery and shipping materials sectors. For most Americans, none of these changes had much long-term significance. For these individuals, the end of the war in 1783 was a welcome opportunity to reattune themselves to the traditional rhythms of a noncommercial agrarian life. As much as 90 percent of the population became reengaged in modest forms of agricultural production directed primarily toward self-sufficiency or the demands of local economies. For many, the end of the war was defined by the unaccustomed uncertainties and disruptions of social displacement, financial risk, and, in some areas, true economic hardships; for others, especially the most entrepreneurial, these years opened new opportunities for short- and long-term growth.[10]

[9] John J. McCusker and Russell R. Menard, *The Economy of British America, 1607–1789* (Chapel Hill: University of North Carolina Press, 1985), p. 359. See also Gordon C. Bjork, "The Weaning of the American Economy: Independence, Market Changes, and Economic Development," *JEH* (1964), 24: 541–560.

[10] See Jensen, *The New Nation* (1950); Nettls, *Emergence of a National Economy* (1962); Gordon C. Bjork, *Stagnation and Growth in the American Economy, 1784–1792* (New York: Garland, 1985); McCusker and Menard, *The Economy of British America* (1985); Ronald Hoffman et al., eds., *The Economy of Early America: The Revolutionary Period, 1763–1790* (Charlottesville: University Press of Virginia, 1988); Richard Buel, Jr., *In*

A third and final obstacle emerges from the fact that without a single national currency and with few (if any) nationally organized economic interests, generalizations about a *national* economy invariably conceal significant differences among the thirteen states.[11] As a consequence, an accurate description of economic conditions prior to the 1787 Constitutional Convention must focus on subnational developments. Such a focus is problematic, however, because, as economic historian James F. Shepherd points out, "there were great variations in economic prospects among localities and regions of the country."[12] Given these obstacles and the present infeasibility of analyzing the range of local and state economic developments, this description focuses on regional patterns of economic development in the states of New England, the mid-Atlantic, the upper South, and the lower South.[13]

Of the four regions, the economies of the four New England states were the most dependent on Atlantic-based commerce. The region generally lacked staple agricultural exports and economic growth prior to

Irons: Britain's Naval Supremacy and the American Revolutionary Economy (New Haven: Yale University Press, 1998).

[11] As James Monroe contended in 1785, the American Union was "little more than an offensive and defensive" alliance because "the political oeconomy of each State is entirely within its own direction." James Monroe to Thomas Jefferson, June 16, 1785, *LMCC*, VIII: 143.

[12] James F. Shepherd, "British America and the Atlantic Economy," in *The Economy of Early America* (1988), p. 24.

[13] For similar justifications of this "regional" approach, see Gordon C. Bjork, "The Weaning of the American Economy," *JEH* (1964), 24: 541–542; McCusker and Menard, *The Economy of British America* (1985), pp. 31–32, 86–88.

Although a regional approach is adopted here, the four geographically defined regions faced common economic problems during the decade between Independence and the 1787 Convention. All four regions, for example, suffered the immense human costs of a civil war after 1776 and an economic depression during the immediate postwar years, the latter compounded by significant and long-term war debts. These debts required taxation which, when coupled with a negative balance of trade, placed significant constraints on the money supply and the possibilities for economic recovery. States and localities within the four regions also were affected by changes in international economic conditions. The war, in short, cast the long-term patterns of American economic growth described in Chapter 2 into disarray. American Independence ensured the loss of market security and its production incentives, which the colonies had enjoyed under the British mercantilist system. To secure new markets, Americans were forced to negotiate new commercial agreements with France, Spain, and the Netherlands. Near the end of the war, Great Britain imposed additional burdens on the nascent economy of the United States when it aggressively protected its international commercial interests by excluding U.S. ships from the British West Indies and from much of its domestic trade. See Shepherd, "British America and the Atlantic Economy," in *The Economy of Early America* (1988); and Buel, *In Irons: Britain's Naval Supremacy and the American Revolutionary Economy* (1998).

lost business b/c of lack of trade w/ England

Independence had been driven by codfish and whale oil exports, ship-building, and shipping services. The war decimated these growth sectors. New Hampshire's timber industry was especially hard hit by the loss of its best customer, the British navy. Merchant and trade groups in north-ern port cities were affected by British trade restrictions throughout the Confederation period. There is evidence, however, that by 1786 cod fish-eries were approaching prewar production levels and shipping-related services were resuscitated by the opening of new markets in the French West Indies and northern Europe.[14]

Mid-A

Unlike New England, the regional economy of the mid-Atlantic states between Connecticut and Pennsylvania contained more diversified forms of agricultural production. Prior to Independence, the region exported foodstuffs domestically as well as to the British West Indies and Southern Europe. During the War, the British blockaded the region's two major port cities, Philadelphia and New York, effectively shutting down the region's export sector. Independence, however, stimulated an expan-sion of the region's small processing and manufacturing sectors which, after the war, managed to compete directly with goods made in Great Britain. During the 1780s, Philadelphia and New York regained their populations and, like Boston for the New England states, developed into vibrant centers of regional commerce.[15]

Like the eight most northern states, the economies of the five south-ern states remained agricultural throughout the American Revolution. Given the lack of natural ports, its exhaustive agricultural practices, and its largely unsettled western frontier, the South remained predominantly rural throughout the Confederation period – although Baltimore and Charleston were rapidly developing into regional centers of commerce and two of the most populous cities in the nation. *upper - tobacco*

In the upper South states of Maryland, Virginia, and North Carolina, the postwar recovery was driven almost exclusively by high returns on tobacco exports which had returned to their prewar levels by 1786. *S.S.* During the 1780s, the region also began to diversify into wheat pro- *struggled* duction and various forms of agricultural processing. Like those of the other regions, the economies of the lower South states of South Carolina and Georgia were adversely affected by the war. Independence brought these states both British occupation and an end to Parliament's

[14] Bjork, *Stagnation and Growth in the American Economy, 1784–1792* (1985), pp. 31–38; Shepherd, "British America and the Atlantic Economy," in *The Economy of Early America* (1988), pp. 27–29.

[15] Bjork, *Stagnation and Growth in the American Economy* (1985), pp. 27–31.

traditional subsidization of their production of rice, indigo, and naval stores. And at the end of the war, Great Britain expropriated part of the region's enslaved labor force. With a labor shortage and without immediate access into new markets for their traditional staple exports, the export sector of the lower South decreased in per capita terms after Independence. After 1783, the purchase of additional slave labor and the expansion of tobacco production began to redefine the economic base of this region.[16]

2 generalizations

This survey, in sum, yields two generalizations concerning the development of economic conditions between 1776 and 1786. The first generalization is that the basic structure of the four regional economies remained centered around agricultural production. Relative differences among the regions existed during the Confederation period, determined for the most part, by geographically defined opportunities for economic specialization. Prior to 1783, the political significance of these exclusively regional interests was typically articulated within the state legislatures, not within Congress. After 1783, the salience of these divergent regional interests became more evident within Congress.[17]

The second generalization is that the end of the war presented each region with different opportunities for long-term economic growth. These opportunities, foreclosed by Great Britain prior to Independence, prompted different political expectations about economic development. New England statesmen, for example, envisioned their economic future in terms of an expansion of the region's commercial transport sector. Mid-Atlantic statesmen envisioned a future defined by their region's expansion into domestic markets in foodstuffs and manufactured goods. In southern states, the western frontier gave rise to regional political expectations that followed from visions of the near-boundless and yet untapped abundance in the west.

PART III: DEMOGRAPHIC CONDITIONS

ALSO prob's. w/ incomplete nature of population info

Assessment of the development of demographic conditions between 1776 and 1786 is hindered by the incompleteness of national population data prior to the first national census in 1790. Three general developments

---

16 Jensen, *The New Nation* (1950), p. 192; Bjork, *Stagnation and Growth in the American Economy* (1985), pp. 20–27, 157; Shepherd, "British America and the Atlantic Economy," in *The Economy of Early America* (1988), p. 32.

17 Jensen, *The New Nation* (1950), pp. 219–235.

3 developments ①

can nonetheless be noted. The first is that the American states lost population during the years immediately after 1776. The war undeniably disrupted conditions for natural family development and restrained the means and the motivation for both voluntary and involuntary forms of immigration. Tens of thousands of British loyalists returned to Great Britain or resettled in Canada or in the British-occupied areas of South Carolina and Georgia. Despite these losses, the American population is estimated to have grown by the remarkable rate of 82.9 percent between 1770 and 1790.[18]

② The second noteworthy development was the population growth of several American cities. Approximately three percent of the American population lived in "urban" areas between 1776 and 1786.[19] The population of several cities, including Philadelphia, New York, Charleston, and Baltimore, grew rapidly in the 1780s. The population of numerous towns, especially in New England and the mid-Atlantic states, also increased and urbanization (in its limited eighteenth-century form) was advocated directly or supported indirectly by every state legislature. Such advocacy typically envisioned only minor adjustments to the simple organizational forms of an agrarian economy and society. By the mid-1780s, however, several contemporaneous observers of the American political economy began to note that existing demographic, social, and international conditions were conducive to the establishment of more diversified forms of economic activity, including light manufacturing.[20] *IMPT*

③ The third notable demographic development was the southerly and westerly direction of interstate emigration. Again, the data are not available for a detailed measurement of the depth or extent of this trend. By 1790, slightly more than 200,000 Americans (of a national population of 3.9 million) lived west of the Allegheny Mountains. Southern leaders grew increasingly confident about the region's future significance within the Union. Emigration patterns appeared to lend credence to the expectation that the region's growth was, as George Washington put it, as inevitable as "the reflux of the tide when you had got it into your

[18] Jacob M. Price, "Reflections on the Economy of Revolutionary America," in *The Economy of Early America* (1988), p. 304.

[19] Everett S. Lee and Michael Lalli, "Population," in *The Growth of the Seaport Cities, 1790–1825*, David T. Gilchrist, ed. (Charlottesville: University Press of Virginia, 1967), p. 27; *A Century of Population Growth* (1909), p. 11; George Rogers Taylor, "Comment," in *The Growth of the Seaport Cities, 1790–1825* (1967), p. 39.

[20] See Drew R. McCoy, *The Elusive Republic: Political Economy in Jeffersonian America* (Chapel Hill: University of North Carolina Press, 1980), pp. 105–119.

rivers."[21] In 1783, a Baltimore newspaper editorialized that "it must be obvious to everyone that emigration from abroad prevails much more in the Southern States than those of the eastward, especially in the back settlements; no one therefore can falsely venture to predict, which part of the Continent will be consequential in a century."[22] New England statesmen concurred and they grew increasingly concerned that these demographic trends would intensify once the lands north of the Ohio River were opened for settlement by their most "industrious citizens."[23]

These political expectations, however, ran ahead of both the available data and actual conditions. For population growth during the 1780s was at near-unprecedented levels in every region. New England, for example, had a decennial increase of 30 percent, the mid-Atlantic region of 47 percent, and the south of 41 percent. Whereas much of the population growth within southern states was fed by interstate emigration, population growth in the other regions was aided after 1783 by increased immigration from European countries.[24] Table 5.1 reveals that according to the population estimates made by Congress prior to 1787, the five most southern states never comprised a majority of the national population.

PART IV: INSTITUTIONAL CONDITIONS

The institutional capacities and structures of the national government changed little between 1776 and 1786. If original intent is an appropri-

[21] Douglass C. North, *The Economic Growth of the United States, 1790–1860* (New York: Norton, 1966), p. 17; George Washington to William Grayson, April 25, 1785, George Bancroft, *History of the Formation of the Constitution* (New York: D. Appleton and Co., 1882), I: 432, 430–432.

[22] "A True American," *Maryland Journal*, July 29, 1783; as quoted in Davis, *Sectionalism in American Politics* (1977), p. 67.

Southern expectations were bolstered by the belief that once Spain opened the Mississippi River to American commerce, additional emigrants would be drawn from New England and the mid-Atlantic states. The Union, as a consequence, would admit new western states and this, in turn, would increase the South's voting strength in Congress. Otto to Vergennes, Sept. 10, 1786, in Bancroft, *History of the Formation of the Constitution* (1882), II: 389–393.

[23] Otto to Vergennes, Sept. 10, 1786, in Bancroft, *History of the Formation of the Constitution* (1882), II: 389–393.

[24] See Aaron S. Fogleman, "From Slaves, Convicts, and Servants to Free Passengers: The Transformation of Immigration in the Era of the American Revolution," *Journal of American History* (1998), 85(1): 43–76; J. Potter, "The Growth of Population in America, 1700–1860," in *Population in History*, D. V. Glass and D. E. C. Eversley, eds. (London: E. Arnold, 1965), pp. 638–640; Jensen, *The New Nation* (1950), pp. 122–124. Richard B. Morris, *Forging of the Union, 1781–1789* (New York: Harper & Row, 1987), pp. 12–20.

TABLE 5.1. *State Population, 1775–1790*

State	Congressional Estimates,				Actual Population,	
	1775, percent		1783, percent		1790, percent[b]	
New Hampshire	100,000	4.1	82,200[a]	3.5	142,000	
Massachusetts	350,000	14.5	350,000	15.0	474,000	
Rhode Island	58,000	2.4	50,400[a]	2.1	69,000	
Connecticut	200,000	8.3	206,000[a]	8.8	238,000	
		29.3		29.4		25.1
New York	200,000	8.3	200,000	8.6	340,000	
New Jersey	130,000	5.4	130,000	5.5	184,000	
Pennsylvania	300,000	12.4	320,000	13.7	434,000	
Delaware	30,000	1.2	35,000	1.5	59,000	
		27.3		29.3		27.7
Maryland	250,000	10.3	220,700[a]	9.4	320,000	
Virginia	400,000	16.5	400,000	17.1	692,000	
North Carolina	200,000	8.3	170,000	7.3	394,000	
South Carolina	200,000	8.3	150,000	6.4	249,000	
Georgia	–	–	25,000	1.1	83,000	
		43.4		41.3		47.2
TOTAL	2,418,000		2,339,300		3,678,000	

[a] Official state population record.

[b] 1790 population totals include 97,000 residents of Maine with Massachusetts; 110,00 residents of Kentucky and Tennessee are not assigned to the thirteen original states.

Source: JCC, XXIV: 231 (April 7, 1783).

[handwritten: 2 goals of creating Art. of Confed.]

ate baseline for assessing the development of a political order over time, the Articles of Confederation were a grand success of constitutional engineering because they achieved the two general goals that defined their creation: the prevention of a dominant majority within Congress and of the centralization of governing authority within the national government. The charge expressed by one newspaper essayist in August 1786 that Congress "may DECLARE every thing, but can DO nothing" was undeniably true, but this ineffectiveness was neither unintended nor unexpected given the institutional structures and processes formalized in the Articles of Confederation.[25]

[25] [A Bostonian], "A View of the Federal Government of America, Its Defects, and Proposed Remedy," *Boston Independent Chronicle*, Aug. 3, 1786; reprinted in *American Museum* (Philadelphia, April 1787), I(IV): 296.

The first general goal of the Articles, the prevention of a dominant majority within Congress, was achieved through several procedural devices designed to decrease the probability that a subset of the states would be able to control or to redefine the national government's decision-making processes. The Articles specifically required the votes of nine of thirteen state delegations within Congress for many decisions, including those related to foreign affairs, governmental spending, and the Continental Army. On all other decisions, the Articles required seven votes regardless of the number of state delegations present in Congress. Formation of decision-making majorities within Congress was rendered more difficult by the nullification of a state's vote if its delegation did not consist of at least two members or if its votes were divided. Moreover, constitutional amendments required the unanimous consent of the state legislatures – a threshold never met during the Articles' tenure.

The second general goal of the Articles, a national government of limited powers, was achieved through several explicit restrictions on Congress's authority. According to the Articles of Confederation, Congress possessed neither the authority to tax nor the coercive power to compel financial support from the state legislatures. Thus, even when Congress managed to enact new policies, it had no dependable or independent financial resources for their implementation.

The national government was not totally ineffective or completely devoid of creative acts of governance prior to 1787. The Continental Congress, it can be recalled, successfully declared independence from Great Britain, coordinated the subsequent war effort, gained international recognition, and secured the unanimous consent of the states for a written national constitution.

The accomplishments of the national government after ratification of the Articles in 1781 are comparatively less impressive, although accounts of Congress's death prior to the 1787 Convention are, no doubt, greatly exaggerated. Congress was never a paragon of state capacity or efficiency, but it seemed to muddle along quite nicely when the need arose. Lest we forget, between 1781 and 1783 the Revolutionary War and a favorable peace treaty were won from Great Britain. Throughout the 1780s, the Confederation Congress also collected nearly enough revenue to meet the national government's operating expenses. It did suspend debt payments to France after 1785; yet, as historian E. James Ferguson notes, by this date "France was insolvent and not a likely source of further loans." Moreover, Congress consistently managed to scrape up enough revenue to meet its debt obligations with Holland. Finally,

[handwritten: Congress did achieve some stuff BUT not much]

Congress enacted several major land policies in 1784 and 1785 designed to standardize the sale and political incorporation of the vast western territory ceded to the United States by Great Britain in 1783.[26]

Despite the consistency between the original intentions and the subsequent accomplishments of the national government, by 1786 almost no political leader publicly or privately expressed satisfaction with the form of national government defined under the Articles of Confederation. The *[handwritten: leaders not satisfied]* general cause of this widespread political dissatisfaction was a confluence of more specialized causes. The historical record is replete with examples of political actors who claimed that the national government *[handwritten: CLAIM]* under the Articles was too weak to defend the territorial, economic, and international integrity (in other words, the external constitution) of the United States. Other political actors claimed various social forces were threatening the national government's operational legitimacy (or the domestic constitution). Still others attributed the deterioration of the efficacy and cohesiveness of the national government to changes within the set of politically relevant actors (or the American political order's intragovernmental constitution).

This is not the place to catalogue or weigh all these more specialized claims. The final set of concerns for the intragovernmental constitution of the national government, however, offers an opportunity to revisit and to elaborate on the general equilibrium model proposed in Chapter 1 (see Figure 1.1). This model posited that the formation of a constitutional order requires a convergence of two types of political expectations: those concerning the content of collective governmental authority and those concerning the division of relative decision-making capacities among the set of politically relevant actors. The consequence of these moments of convergence is a negotiated settlement of the basic organizational forms and procedural patterns that will subsequently constitute the institutional framework of the order.

Whereas changes in both exogenous and endogenous conditions can prompt changes in political expectations, the basic structure of a political order's institutional framework generally remains fixed and impervious to spontaneous or unintended changes. The resulting dissonance between new political expectations and the existing institutional framework creates a tension between the former's motivation for and the

---

[26] Ferguson, *The Power of the Purse* (1961), pp. 235, 220–239. For a recent reevaluation of the national and state governments under the Articles of Confederation, see Keith L. Dougherty, *Collective Action under the Articles of Confederation* (Cambridge, UK: Cambridge University Press, 2001).

latter's latent resistance against intentional change of a political order's institutional framework.[27]

If the institutional framework of the national government underwent almost no changes prior to 1787, what were the new political expectations that fueled such widespread dissatisfaction with the Articles of Confederation? For one, political preferences for the extent and substance of national governmental authority clearly changed between 1777 (when the Articles were drafted) and the 1787 Constitutional Convention. Changes in economic conditions, especially in the eight most northern states where commercial activity was important, prompted expectations for a more active and interventionist role by the national government. Changes in Congress's revenue-generating capacities between 1777 and 1787 also inspired political expectations (especially concerning the repayment of debt obligations) that generally were at odds with the Articles' institutional structure. In particular, the wholesale collapse of the national currency system by 1780 and the subsequent failure of alternative forms of revenue generation left the national government fiscally strapped and dependent on the states.

The former set of exogenous changes exposed a primarily sectional-based divergence of political expectations between the eight northern states and the five southern states, whereas the latter set of endogenous changes produced a dissonance between the expectations of the most nationally minded American statesmen and the existing institutional

---

[27] Intentional institutional change can be conceived as occurring through either of displacement or of mitigation. Institutional change by displacement occurs when parts of the existing institutional framework are displaced by new institutional structures, or when this framework is retained but its original meaning or purposes are deliberately redefined. Intentional institutional changes through a process of mitigation establish new political institutions without displacing the existing institutional framework of a political order.

All forms of institutional change – those intended and discontinuous and those unintended and adaptive – are neither costless nor without longer-term consequences. See Douglass C. North, *Institutions, Institutional Change and Economic Performance* (Cambridge, UK: Cambridge University Press, 1990). In general, institutional change by replacement tends to be a high cost enterprise because it invokes distributional conflicts between those who benefit from existing institutions and those who expect to benefit from alternative institutions. In the end, the result of such change tends to be the continuation of a comparatively simple, but internally coherent and politically attuned institutional framework. Institutional change by mitigation, it follows, is a comparatively lower cost enterprise because rather than initiating distributional conflicts, such change differentiates opportunities for benefit by both new and old political expectations. Over time, the consequences of the latter gains-from-trade approach yield a more complex (and sometimes, internally contradictory) institutional framework.

framework of the Articles. Both forms of political dissatisfaction prompted a variety of state-supported and individual-based attempts to change the basic institutional structure of the national government. In 1780, Alexander Hamilton recommended a national constitutional convention to correct what he considered the most "fundamental defect" of the Articles of Confederation: the "want of power in Congress." Hamilton advocated several specific remedies but premised them all on the proposition that "the essential cement of union" required that Congress have full control over the military. Several years later, Hamilton participated in an unsuccessful plot to threaten intervention by the Continental Army to pressure Congress and the state legislatures into adopting a new national finance system.[28]

Others worked within more readily accepted boundaries to effect institutional changes in the national government. Congress, for example, deliberated over many constitutional amendments and several, in accord with the procedures of the Articles, were sent to the state legislatures for ratification. Shortly after the Articles were ratified, some congressional delegates (including a twenty-nine-year-old Virginia delegate James Madison) attempted unsuccessfully to use Congress's legislative authority to make five votes the minimum legislative majority rather than the seven state votes required by the Articles. A few months later, Madison promoted another form of institutional change when he led a three-member special committee that recommended Congress overcome its constitutional limitations by broadly interpreting the powers *implied* by the Articles of Confederation.[29] By 1787, however, both formal and informal methods of redefining national governmental authority had failed to reattune the institutional structure of the Articles of Confederation to the various political expectations existing among the thirteen American states.

Changes in relative decision-making capacities also prompted new political expectations that deviated from the distributional logic defined

---

[28] Hamilton to James Duane, Sept. 3, 1780, *Papers of Alexander Hamilton* (New York: Columbia University Press, 1961), II: 401–402. For Hamilton's subsequent views on the necessity of constitutional change, see "Hamilton to Robert Morris, April 30, 1781," *Papers of Hamilton*, II: 605. For various accounts of the Newburgh Affair, see Ferguson, *The Power of the Purse*, pp. 155–168; McDonald, *E Pluribus Unum* (1965), pp. 22–32; and Henderson, *Party Politics* (1974), pp. 328–335.

[29] See Thomas Rodney, *Diary*, March 5, 1781, LMCC, VI: 8–9; JCC, XIX: 236 (March 6, 1781); IX: 469–471 (March 12, 1781); 894–896 (Aug. 22, 1781). See also "Amendment to Give Congress Coercive Power of the States and Their Citizens, 16 March 1781," *Documentary History*, I: 141–143; and James Madison to Thomas Jefferson, April 16, 1781, *PJM*, 3: 71.

by the equal state apportionment rule formalized within the Articles of Confederation. Changes in exogenous and endogenous conditions were the source of these new political expectations. Among the former, the already noted demographic patterns and geographic conditions of the American South fueled new southern expectations about their region's future import fundamentally at odds with the Articles' equal state rule. As a consequence, by 1787 many southern statesmen were convinced that the replacement of the existing rule with a proportional state rule of apportionment would greatly increase their long-term decision-making capacities within Congress.

Changes in endogenous conditions also prompted consideration of a proportional-based alternative to the existing equal state apportionment rule. The Articles' equal state rule had been devised originally to make improbable the formation of a dominant coalition within Congress. By 1786, however, congressional delegates had divided into two distinct voting blocs, the eight most northern states comprising one voting bloc, the second bloc consisting of delegates from the five most southern states. Within the northern bloc, the three smaller New England states tended to follow the policies set by Massachusetts, effectively multiplying the weight of the latter's vote. By 1786, New York was another consistent member of this northern voting bloc, although it had tended earlier to align itself with several other mid-Atlantic states. According to James Monroe, Pennsylvania could "generally be calculated on in favor of all the measures of Massachusetts" although she independently had "some influence with Delaware & [New] Jersey." Maryland tended to divide its voting allegiance in Congress, occasionally extending the strength of the northern state bloc. Only in the latter half of 1786 did Maryland begin to vote consistently with Virginia and the other southern states.[30]

A final development between 1776 and 1786 prompting consideration of an alternative to the Articles' equal state rule of apportionment deserves noting. Recall that one of the conditions that influenced the First Continental Congress's historic decision to adopt the equal state apportionment rule in 1774 was the lack of "authentic Evidence" or a settled record for devising an interstate scale. In 1783, Congress sought state concurrence to make "the Number of inhabitants, under certain modifications, the measure of [financial] contribution for each state" rather than the Articles' unimplemented land basis. This request won little support

---

[30] Henderson, *Party Politics in the Continental Congress* (1974), pp. 357–358, 395, 390–391; Otto to Vergennes, January 10, 1786, Bancroft, *History of the Formation of the Constitution* (1882), I: 480; James Monroe to James Madison, May 31, 1786, *PJM*, 9: 70.

among the states.[31] Yet, by 1786 the want of a common political arithmetic had been surmounted as an unintended consequence of Congress's dependency on the states for its general operating revenues. The state requisition system used by Congress divided requested revenues proportionally among the states based on congressional estimates of state population. As Table 5.2 illustrates, the resulting interstate scale devised by Congress fluctuated slightly over time. Part of the variance was due to decisions to reduce the quota for individual states heavily burdened by the war. On several occasions, state delegates complained bitterly that Congress's requisition committee disregarded previous ratios or unfairly burdened a particular state or region.[32] In general, however, Congress's interstate division of the Union's financial burdens was accepted by members of Congress and the state legislatures. Over time, moreover, this practice established a semi-formalized means of defining interstate relationships in proportional terms based approximately on state population.

[margin handwritten notes: need to determine debt burden, need to define a ratio of population in two state relationships]

PART V: IDEOLOGICAL CONDITIONS –
THE CONCEPT OF REPRESENTATION

Measurement of the development of prevailing ideological conditions prior to the Constitutional Convention offers a final set of indicators of the American political landscape prior to 1787. Such a measurement is problematic not only because ideas and beliefs are irretrievable cognitive experiences of particular individuals at particular moments in time, but also because the historical record contains so many obscure and contradictory data that the scholarly trials necessary to collect and to master the set of relevant data between 1776 and 1786 would require a herculean effort.

Fortunately, the goal here is far less heroic: to describe only that portion of the American political discourse which concerns representation. A self-limited reconstruction of this sort cannot completely surmount the same types of selection bias problems that generally hamstring conceptual analyses constructed almost exclusively on pithy quotations. However, as the description and comparison of British and American

---

[31] John Adams, *Diary*, 2: 124; *JCC*, XXVI: 308 (April 27, 1783).
[32] See Edmund Randolph to the Governor of Virginia, Nov. 7, 1781, *LMCC*, VI: 260–261; *JCC*, XXIII: 564–571 (Sept. 10, 1782); James McHenry to John Hall, 28 Sept. 1785, *LMCC*, VIII: 223–224; Massachusetts Delegates to the Massachusetts Assembly, 27 Oct. 1785, *LMCC*, VIII: 242; Elbridge Gerry to A Committee of the Massachusetts Assembly, Sept. 21, 1780, *LMCC*, V: 382–386; *JCC*, XXII: 158–160, April 1, 1782; Edmund Randolph to James Madison, June 20, 1782, *PJM*, 4: 356; *PJM*, 3: 301, n.2; 328–329.

TABLE 5.2. State Ratios for Congressional Requisitions, 1775–1787 (percent)

State	1775	1777	1779a	1779b	1779c	1780	1781a	1781b	1782	1783	1784	1785	1786	1787
NH	4.1	4.0	3.3	3.3	2.7	3.2	3.1	4.7	4.0	3.5	4.5	3.5	3.5	3.5
MA	14.5	16.4	13.3	13.3	15.3	14.5	17.7	16.3	16.0	15.0	15.7	15.0	15.0	15.0
RI	2.4	2.0	2.0	1.7	1.3	2.5	1.9	2.7	2.4	2.1	2.6	2.1	2.1	2.2
CT	8.3	12.0	11.3	11.3	11.3	8.5	13.1	9.3	11.1	8.8	9.0	8.8	8.8	8.8
NY	8.3	4.0	5.3	5.3	5.0	8.5	2.9	4.7	4.5	8.5	4.5	8.5	8.5	8.5
NJ	5.4	5.4	5.3	5.3	6.0	5.1	6.9	6.1	5.5	5.6	5.8	5.6	5.6	5.5
PA	12.4	12.4	12.7	12.7	15.3	12.7	17.7	14.1	15.0	13.7	13.5	13.7	13.7	13.7
MD	10.3	10.4	9.4	9.4	10.6	9.3	12.1	11.7	11.0	9.4	11.2	9.4	9.4	9.4
DE	1.2	1.2	0.1	0.1	1.1	1.7	1.6	1.4	1.4	1.5	1.3	1.5	1.5	1.5
VA	16.5	16.0	16.0	16.0	16.7	17.0	19.2	16.3	14.5	17.1	15.7	17.1	17.1	17.1
NC	8.3	5.0	7.3	7.3	6.7	8.5	3.8	7.8	7.4	7.3	7.5	7.3	7.3	7.3
SC	8.3	10.0	12.0	12.3	8.0	8.5	–	4.7	6.0	6.4	8.3	6.4	6.4	6.4
GA	–	1.2	–	–	–	–	–	0.3	1.2	1.1	0.3	1.1	1.1	1.1
	100	100	100	100	100	100	100	100	100	100	100	100	100	100

Note: 1780, 1781, and 1786 ratios reflect only monetary sums, although Congress also requested additional material goods from the states.

Sources: JCC, II: 222 (July 29, 1775); IX: 955 (November 22, 1777); XIII: 28 (January 5, 1779); XIV: 626 (May 21, 1779); XV: 1150 (October 7, 1779); XVI: 45 (January 12, 1780); XIX: 299 (March 23, 1781); XXI: 1090 (November 2, 1781); XXIII: 564 (September 10, 1782); XXIII: 665–66 (October 18, 1782); XXIV: 259 (April 18, 1783); XXVI: 309 (April 27, 1784); XXIX: 745 (September 24, 1785); XXXI: 462 (August 2, 1786); XXXIII: 580 (September 29, 1787).

Jack P. Greene, "Legislative Turnover in British America, 1696 to 1775," WMQ (1981), 38(3): 442–463; Charles A. Kromkowski, *The Bond of Union: Rules of Apportionment, Constitutional Change and A General Theory of American Political Development, 1700–1870* (1998, Ph.D. diss., University of Virginia).

political institutions and practices prior to the American Revolution illustrated, it remains reasonable to expect that apportionment rule changes – including the one initiated by the 1787 Convention – would be preceded by historically observable traces of divergent ideas and beliefs concerning the authority of government and the purposes of political representation.

The historical record makes clear that the Declaration of Independence did not end the development of the American discourse on the concept of representation. As historian Gordon S. Wood observes, there was no "political conception" that was "more important to Americans in the entire Revolutionary era than representation."[33] After 1776 the pace and substance of the American discourse changed dramatically. American political leaders still discussed representation in terms of the familiar pre-revolutionary ideals of popular consent, shared interests and burdens, executive restraint, and local knowledge that had dominated the American exchange with Great Britain prior to 1776. Beyond the common lexicon of the pre-Independence era, however, two fundamentally different discourses on representation developed between 1776 and 1786.

The first discourse concerned the conceptualization of representation within the national government. As Chapter 3 noted, significant differences among the states were readily apparent throughout the process required to complete the Articles of Confederation. After 1781, however, a conceptual consensus emerged concerning various elements of national-level representation. Members of Congress, for example, were generally thought of as state delegates or ambassadors rather than as representatives of specific interests or popular constituencies. Delegates to Congress, moreover, were tightly tethered to the policy prescriptions articulated by their respective state legislatures.[34] And state legislatures rarely felt obligated to comply with the acts to which their congressional delegates consented. As one delegate conceded in 1786, the policy "Reccomendations" determined in Congress were often "as little regarded as the cries of an Oysterman."[35]

---

[33] Wood, *Creation of the American Republic* (1969), p. 164.

[34] In 1786, the Virginia legislature apparently replaced one of its delegates, Richard Henry Lee, because he *privately* suggested the state legislature reconsider its opposition to a commercial treaty with Spain. See James Madison to Henry Lee, Nov. 9, 1786, *PJM*, 9: 167; James Madison to Thomas Jefferson, Dec. 4, 1786, *PJM*, 9: 191. See also Rakove, *The Beginnings of National Politics* (1987), pp. 218–220.

[35] Allan Nevins, *The American States During and After the Revolution* (New York: The Macmillan Co., 1924) p. 623; Charles Pettit to Jeremiah Wadsworth, May 27, 1786, *LMCC*, VIII: 370.

The conceptual development of representation at the national level was constrained by acute concerns about the potential distributional consequences of seemingly minor changes in the institutional structure of the national government. Specialized forms of interest representation, for example, never enjoyed a favorable institutional environment within Congress because the body's committees were never empowered with autonomous policy-making authority.[36] Concerns about distributional advantage also prompted a regionally based deadlock over the admission of new states into the Union.[37] Southern states consistently managed to block every attempt to admit Vermont into the Union because they feared "the preponderancy it w[oul]d give to the Eastern scale" within Congress.[38] New England and the mid-Atlantic States were similarly fearful about admitting new western states, with several statesmen instead recommending, "that an entire separation must eventually ensue."[39]

A final indicator of the general convergence of expectations about national representation after 1781 is apparent in the attendance practices of state delegates to Congress. Rates of attendance generally declined after the end of the war as states lost interest in participating in a national government that was constitutionally enfeebled.[40] Congressional service became so unappealing that even the most active and nationalist-minded delegates voluntarily retired or dreaded their appointment to Congress. For several states the stakes of national governance fell too low to sustain even ceremonial forms of participation.

---

[36] See Jillson and Wilson, *Congressional Dynamics* (1994), pp. 91–131.

[37] See Rhode Island Delegates to the Governor of Rhode Island (William Greene), April 16, 1782, *LMCC*, VI: 329; Hugh Williamson to James Duane, June 8, 1784, *LMCC*, 8: 547; Francis Dana to the Massachusetts Assembly, July 22, 1784, *LMCC*, VII: 570–571; William Grayson to George Washington, April 15, 1785, *LMCC*, VIII: 97; William Grayson to George Washington, May 8, 1785, *LMCC*, VIII: 118.

[38] James Madison to Edmund Pendleton, Jan. 22, 1782, *LMCC*, VI: 296.
James Madison further claimed that "[t]he independence of Vermont and its admission into the Confederacy are patronized by the Eastern States . . . principally from the accession of weight they will derive from it in Congress." Moreover, once admitted, Vermont "will immediately connect her policy with that of the Eastern States; as far at least as the remains of former prejudices will permit." James Madison, Observations on Vermont and Territorial Claims (May 1, 1782), *LMCC*, VI: 340–341.

[39] Rufus King to Elbridge Gerry, June 4, 1786, *LMCC*, VIII: 380. See also Rufus King to Jonathan Jackson, Sept. 3, 1786, *LMCC*, VIII: 458.

[40] Jillson and Wilson, *Congressional Dynamics* (1994), pp. 116–117. See also George Washington to William Grayson, July 26, 1786, *Writings of George Washington*, Jared Sparks, ed. (Boston: American Stationers Co., 1837–), 9: 177; The Chairman of Congress (David Ramsey) to Certain States, Jan. 31, 1786, *LMCC*, VIII: 291; *LMCC*, VIII: 174–175, Aug. 3, 1785.

As political expectations concerning the processes and purposes of national-level representation tended to converge between 1776 and 1786, the post-Independence discourse on the meaning of state-level representation included a variety of conflicting and incongruous ideas and opinions. Much of this state-level conceptual variation was catalyzed by the task of fashioning new state constitutions, which necessarily required debates and decisions concerning each state's constitutional rule of apportionment.[41]

Although the historical record is more fragmentary and far less accessible at the state level than the records of the Continental and Confederation Congresses, examination of the conceptual development of representation at this lower level of aggregation offers another measure of this structural condition between 1776 and 1786. To add clarity and historical continuity to this state-level analysis, the concept of representation will be described with reference to the three characteristics employed in Chapter 2 to describe colonial conceptualizations of representation. These characteristics are localism, responsive elitism, and dynamic institutionalism.

Localism

The characteristic of localism reflects the general orientation and relationship between political representatives and those whom they represent. Like colonial assembly members, most state representatives had as their primary concerns the particular interests of their respective local communities. The parochial orientation of early American state politics was so prominent that it regularly prompted wholesale indifference toward the state legislatures. Numerous towns in the New England states, for example, ignored requests to attend constitutional conventions

---

[41] For a recent survey of state-level politics after 1776, see Marc W. Kruman, *Between Authority and Liberty: State Constitution Making in Revolutionary America* (Chapel Hill: University of North Carolina Press, 1997). For more specialized accounts, see Stephen E. Patterson, *Political Parties in Revolutionary Massachusetts* (Madison, WJ: University of Wisconsin Press, 1973); Richard Francis Upton, *Revolutionary New Hampshire: An Account of the Social and Political Forces Underlying the Transition from Royal Province to American Commonwealth* (Port Washington, NY: Kennikat Press, 1970 [1936]); Philip A. Crowl, *Maryland During and After the Revolution* (Baltimore: Johns Hopkins University Press, 1943); C. H. Ambler, *Sectionalism in Virginia from 1776 to 1861* (Chicago: University of Chicago Press, 1910); William A. Schaper, *Sectionalism and Representation in South Carolina* (New York: Da Capo Press, 1968).

and many more decided against sending representatives to their respective state legislatures. Occasionally, these localist tendencies were focused into concerted efforts to resist, or to secede from, state-level authority.

The political discourse during the decade after 1776 was stocked with continuous exhortations for consideration of a state's "general" interests above particular "local" interests. Yet only rarely did the former not coincide with an exhorter's particular interests. This common dimension of the discourse and practices of American representatives is captured by the classic statement by the residents of Essex County, Massachusetts, in 1778 that:

Representatives should have the same views and interests with the people at large. They should think, feel, and act like them, and in fine, should be an exact miniature of their constituents. They should be (if we may use the expression) the whole body politic, with all its property, rights, and privileges, reduced to a smaller scale, every part being diminished in just proportion.[42]

The localist orientation of state legislators was reinforced by a variety of devices formalized within the first state constitutions. Members of all but one lower state house, for example, were forced to stand for reelection at least once a year. In Rhode Island and Connecticut elections were

---

[42] [Theophilus Parsons], "The Essex Result" (1778), in *American Political Writing during the Founding Era, 1760–1805*, Hyneman and Lutz, eds. (Indianapolis, IN: Liberty Press, 1983), I: 497. The colonial heritage of this "localist" conceptualization of American representation is reflected in: James Otis, *Rights of the British Colonies Asserted and Proved* (1764); *Considerations on Behalf of the Colonies* (1765); James Wilson, *Considerations on the Nature and Extent of the Legislative Authority of the British Parliament* (1774); Alexander Hamilton, *The Farmer Refuted* (1775); and John Adams, *Thoughts on Government* (1776).

Whereas the localist orientation of the American conceptualization of representation was seemingly beyond reproach prior to 1776, the continuation of this characteristic within American state politics was attacked occasionally between 1776 and 1786. Arguably, the most widely accessible and most celebrated attack is James Madison's "Vices of the Political System of the United States" (*PJM*, 9: 348–357). Purportedly written prior to the 1787 Convention, "Vices" was not circulated publicly or privately. So the heavy emphasis given to it seems misplaced. More representative of these criticisms of American state politics are the attempts to reduce the size of the Connecticut lower legislative house in 1782 and 1786, or in the assessment of Rhode Islander Theodore Foster in 1777: "A form of Government so democratical as ours is liable to commit greater Error in the Administration of public Affairs than where the Government is Monarchical or Aristocratical." Foster, it must be noted, also conceded that over the long run popular forms of government are subject to less turmoil than elitist forms because popular participation in self-governance is more conducive to popular contentment. See Richard J. Purcell, *Connecticut in Transition: 1775–1818* (Middletown, CT: Wesleyan University Press 1963 [1918]), p. 124; Irwin H. Polishook, *Rhode Island and the Union* (Evanston, IL: Northwestern University Press, 1969), p. 28.

held twice every year. Figure 5.1 illustrates the immediacy of the Revolutionary era electoral connection in comparison to interelection frequencies during the colonial era. Nine state constitutions established explicit residency requirements for state legislators. And most states formally required that legislators reside within their particular electoral districts; in the other states, district residency remained an informal custom supported by a more general state residency requirement.[43] *[handwritten: IMPT of district residency]*

Another indicator of the localism of early American state politics is reflected in the various constitutional rules of apportionment adopted by the states. In almost every state, the constitution defined electoral districts that were coterminous with existing county or town boundaries.[44] The basis for allocating representation, moreover, was predominantly territorial and not proportional.[45] Among the upper state houses, nine

[43] Robert J. Dinkin, *Voting in Revolutionary America* (Westport, CT: Greenwood Press, 1982), p. 49.

[44] In New Hampshire, a form of pooled representation was permitted whereby towns with insufficient population would be grouped with other small towns in order to send a single representative. The upper legislative houses of Rhode Island and Connecticut were not elected by districts: they were elected statewide.

[45] Although this territorial idiom had pride of place in the early state constitutions, the American discourse on representation beyond these formal boundaries also included a good deal of discussion of alternative forms of representation. For example, by 1786 "The Free Republican" argued that state executives were the legitimate representatives "of the whole people, being chosen not by one town or country, but the people at large." In various American cities it also became commonplace to hear political exhortations that "respectable mechanics and carmen" were "entitled to the reins of government" and "that the man who can build a shoe, or a pair of breeches in the best manner, so as to sit right and tight about you; that the man who can build with taste and judgment, so as to answer all the purposes and intents of a house, is the most likely person to build laws that will answer all ends and purposes of legislation. Therefore, let us have mechanics – and mechanics only for our legislators." More formalized articulations of this interest-based conceptualization of representation are also apparent in the 1777 Georgia Constitution where "mechanics" were explicitly granted voting rights in lieu of the property requirements applicable to other segments of the population. Moreover, representation was granted to the port towns of Savannah and Sunbury to permit their residents "to represent their trade." *The [Boston] Independent Chronicle*, Jan. 5, 1786, XVIII: 897); Dinkin, *Voting in Revolutionary America*, (1982), p. 51; *The Revolutionary Records of the State of Georgia*, Allen D. Candler, ed. (Atlanta, GA: The Franklin-Turner Co., 1908), I: 285.

Compared to the colonial discourse, the post-1776 American discourse on representation included many more advocates of the ideal of proportionality as an elemental standard of representative governance. These advocates, as evidenced by state constitutional provisions, were still on the margins of the political mainstream. Nevertheless, they included, among others, Thomas Jefferson and James Madison in Virginia and many of the country towns in Rhode Island, and it is no exaggeration to claim that the disproportionality of the rule of apportionment was the primary reason why several proposed state constitutions were not ratified by voters in Massachusetts and New Hampshire.

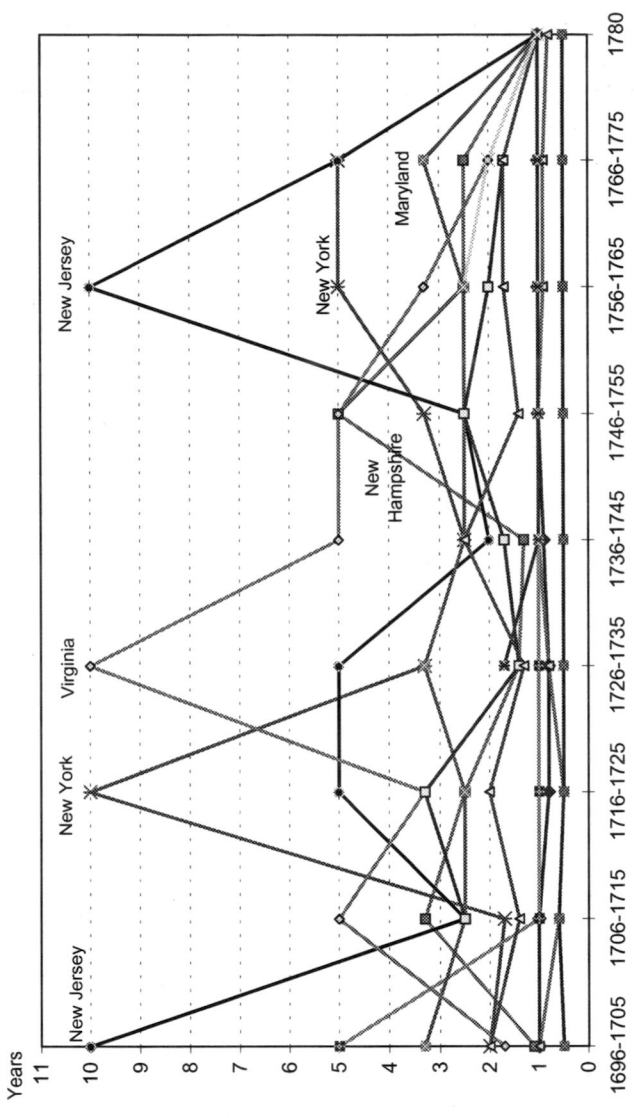

FIGURE 5.1. Colonial Assembly/State House Average Electoral Term Length, 1696–1780

	1700	1710	1720	1730	1740	1750	1760	1770	1780
Mean	2.8	2.0	2.9	2.5	1.8	2.2	2.6	2.1	0.9

TABLE 5.3. *Rules of Apportionment in American State Constitutions, 1787*

Apportionment Basis	Lower House	Upper House
Population	4	0
1. Taxpayers	MA, NH, PA	
2. Voters	NY	
Territory	8	9
1. Towns	RI, CT	
2. Counties	NJ, DE	NJ, DE, VA, NC, GA
3. Region		NY, MD
4. Mixed (1, 2, 3)	MD, VA, NC, GA	SC, PA
Other	1	4
1. "White population" and "taxable property"	SC	
2. Taxes paid		MA, NH
3. At-large		RI, CT

states apportioned representation on a strictly territorial basis, two on the basis of the amount of taxes paid, and members of two upper houses were elected statewide. Among the lower houses, five state constitutions established apportionment rules that defined a proportional basis for dividing political representation. (See Table 5.3.)

Other evidence could be presented sustaining the generalization that representation within the early state legislatures was oriented predominantly toward local interests and concerns.[46] Table 5.4 reflects an important dimension of this relationship by revealing that the immediacy of the representative relationship (as measured by the number of persons per representative) was approximately the same in 1786 as it had been in 1770.[47]

---

[46] In several states localities also continued the colonial practice of paying the salaries and expenses of their state legislative representatives. See Nevins, *The American States* (1924), pp. 181–182; J. R. Pole, *Political Representation in England and the Origins of the American Republic* (London: The Macmillan Co., 1966), pp. 285–286; Polishook, *Rhode Island and the Union* (1969), p. 34; Rosemarie Zagarri, *The Politics of Size: Representation in the United States, 1776–1850* (Ithaca, NY: Cornell University Press, 1987), p. 21.

[47] There is a crudeness to this measurement given that almost one-fifth of the American population was enslaved and well more than two-thirds were not permitted to vote due to their gender, age, wealth, or ancestry. If accurate and complete data on the voter population in each state were available this ratio would be significantly smaller and thus indicate a type of intimacy between voters and political representatives quite possibly unimaginable today.

TABLE 5.4. *Persons per Representative in State Lower House: State Means, 1770–1786*

	1770	1780	1786	Percent Change, 1770–1786
Northeast				
Average:	1,483	1,180	1,499	1.0
MA	1,868	1,227	1,894	
NH	1,835	1,187	1,612	
RI	895	945	983	
CT	1,332	1,360	1,506	
Mid-Atlantic				
Average:	4,543	3,324	4,583	0.9
NY	5,618	3,008	4,859	
NJ	3,914	3,580	4,627	
PA	6,668	4,546	6,033	
DE	1,972	2,161	2,814	
South:				
Average:	2,448	2,270	2,967	21.2
MD	2,849	3,230	4,207	
VA	3,725	3,736	4,673	
NC	2,143	2,548	2,461	
SC	2,588	891	1,186	
GA	935	945	1,376	
State Average:	2,796		2,941	

Sources: Regional and state mean measurements calculated from: Lower House Size/Total State Population. Data for 1770 and 1780, McCusker and Menard, *The Economy of British America* (1985), pp. 136, 172, 203 (Mid-Atlantic and South States); J. Potter, "The Growth of Population in America, 1700–1860," in *Population in History*, Glass and Eversley, eds. (1965), p. 638 (New England States). Population from the 1790 U.S. Census are used for the year 1786.

Responsive Elitism

The second characteristic employed in Chapter 2 to describe the colonial conceptualization of representation was responsive elitism, or the condition of an insulated and socially distinct political elite that was generally responsive to a variety of societal interests and demands. American politics after 1776 continued to possess similar elitist and responsive qualities. The elitist composition of state legislatures was aided by a continuation of colonial political customs against electioneering and office-seeking as well as by a variety of state constitutional provisions. Every state constitution, for example, required a minimum level of property or wealth for election to a state's lower legislative house. These requirements typically were increased for the state upper houses and for state governorships. In addition, three state constitutions explicitly required Protestants for state office-holding; two additional states defined this requirement more broadly as Christian.[48] Demographics and social norms often acted as equally effective barriers in other states.

The elitist composition of early American state legislatures was additionally supported by constitutional restrictions on voting. Women were not guaranteed the right to vote in any state, although they were not formally barred from voting by the New Jersey constitution. Several state constitutions also included property or wealth requirements, and two states had poll taxes. South Carolina and Georgia explicitly restricted voting to free "white" persons. For most adult males, however, the state property requirements proved less significant obstacles to voting.[49]

Although the first state constitutions restricted popular access into political decision-making circles, developments after 1776 were undermining part of the elitist character of colonial era political practices. Historian Robert J. Dinkin reports that although few persons of non-English ancestry were elected to American colonial assemblies, after 1776 an increased political presence of various ethnic groups became a new and generally accepted contour of the American political landscape. Whereas as many as 85 percent of colonial legislators were among the most materially wealthy within colonial society, their postwar cohorts had comparatively humbler and more diverse professional backgrounds.[50]

There were other changes that diminished the elitist character of American politics. The 1776 Pennsylvania constitution, among others,

[48] William C. Webster, "Comparative Study of the State Constitutions of the American Revolution," *Annals of the American Academy of Political Science* (1897), IX: 76–77.
      In addition, the elitist composition of Connecticut's upper legislative house, the Council, was secured through a double electoral system. See Richard Purcell, *Connecticut in Transition* (Washington, DC: American Historical Association, 1963), pp. 124–127.

[49] In New York, however, "[t]he right of suffrage was so restricted that as late as 1790 only 1303 of the 13,330 male residents of New York City possessed sufficient property to entitle them to vote for governor." De Alva Standwood Alexander, *A Political History of the State of New York* (New York: H. Holt, 1923), I: 15.

[50] See Gordon S. Wood, *The Radicalness of the American Revolution* (New York: Vintage Books, 1993), pp. 229ff; Dinkin, *Voting in Revolutionary America* (1982), p. 55; Jackson Turner Main, "Government by the People: The American Revolution and the Democratization of the Legislatures," *WMQ* (1966), 23: 405–406.

explicitly limited the maximum number of terms of her state and congressional legislators. This constitution also opened legislative sessions
to the public, required publication of legislative votes and proceedings,
and prohibited candidates and voters from giving or receiving gifts or
rewards of "meat, drink, monies or otherwise."[51] The 1776 Maryland
constitution permanently disqualified all involved with electoral bribery
from "any office of trust or profit in the state."[52]

Some states reformed their electoral processes: increasing the number
of polling places, standardizing election cycles and dates, replacing *viva
voce* voting with balloting voting procedures. The 1777 Georgia constitution provided for "free and open" elections by proscribing the appearance of military officers or soldiers, and by requiring the public
tabulation and declaration of vote tallies. Finally, the post-Independence
rejection of colonial forms of popular deference toward political elites
was ably demonstrated by the electoral rejection of the state constitutions proposed in Massachusetts in 1778 and in New Hampshire in
1778, 1781, and 1782.[53]

Dynamic Institutionalism

The third and final characteristic introduced in Chapter 2 to measure
American colonial conceptualizations of representation was referred to
as dynamic institutionalism. This characteristic provides a means of
describing two attributes conventionally associated with democratic
forms of government: the variability and mutability of institutions of
political representation. Like the two other characteristics identified, this
one can be employed to examine early state conceptualizations of representation, especially as they are reflected in decisions concerning state
legislative sizes, state rules of apportionment, and state election district
types.

Table 5.5 records the development of state legislative sizes after 1776.
Between 1776 and 1786, the average state house size varied from 115

---

[51] 1776 Pennsylvania constitution, Articles 8, 13, 14, 19, 32. William C. Webster,
"Comparative Study of the State Constitutions," *Annals* (1897), IX: 96–97.
    Seven states imposed term limitations on their governors. Dinkin, *Voting in
Revolutionary America* (1982) p. 49.
[52] 1776 Maryland constitution, Article 54. See also 1784 New Hampshire constitution.
[53] Dinkin, *Voting in Revolutionary America* (1982), pp. 91–106; 1777 Georgia constitution, Artciles X, XII, XIII; Donald S. Lutz, *Popular Consent and Popular Control* (Baton
Rouge: Louisiana State University Press, 1980), p. 83.

TABLE 5.5. *Average State Legislative Sizes, 1776–1786*

	1776	1777	1778	1779	1780	1781	1782	1783	1784	1785	1786
House	115.7	102.1	95.8	96.7	102.2	100.1	100.5	103.0	103.3	108.9	103.1
Senate	16.0	17.2	17.3	19.2	20.1	19.4	19.9	20.2	20.2	20.4	20.5

to 95 members – a notable increase when compared with the sizes of American colonial assemblies, which in 1770 averaged 68 members. Early American state senate sizes, by comparison, generally remained fixed between 1776 and 1786, but their average size increased slightly from 16 to 20 senators.

What do these institutional indicators reveal about the early conceptual development of representative government in the United States? First, the near doubling of the sizes of many American state legislatures after 1776 clearly opened new opportunities for political officeholding and representation that rarely, if ever, were available during the colonial era. Second, state decisions concerning their state legislature sizes varied widely among the states and within individual states throughout this period. In 1776, 1779, and 1784, for example, the Massachusetts House of Representatives had, respectively, 299, 174, and 231 members. The Virginia House of Delegates, by comparison, had 130, 146, and 160 members; and the Delaware lower house consistently had only 21 members. This variation provides partial evidence of the fluidity of early American conceptualizations of representation in addition to the political willingness – compelled by numerous factors – to experiment with the institutional structures of representative government.

As recorded in Tables 5.6 and 5.7, interstate and regional variations are manifest in the state rules of apportionment and state legislative districting types adopted during the early national years.

For all this early variation and experimentation with the form and practices of representative government, the conceptualizations of representation that emerged during the early national years remained rigid and restrictive in several ways. For example, election participation rates were about five percent of a state's total population – a surprisingly low rate of social participation for this so-called revolutionary period. By contrast, contemporary U.S. Presidential elections have voter participation rates between 37 and 41 percent of the U.S. population. With few exceptions, state elections were also characterized by low levels of electoral competition. Among the six New England and mid-Atlantic states

TABLE 5.6. *State Lower House Apportionment, 1787*

State and Year of Constitution	District Type(s)	Apportionment Unit	Basis for Allocation of Representation
MA-1780	MM, SM	town	Every incorporated town permitted 1 representative. New towns and additional representation allocated on proportional scale: 1 representative for 150 ratable polls; 2 representatives for 375 polls; and 1 representative for every 225 additional poll
NH-1784	MM, SM	town, pooled	1 representative for 150 ratable male polls; 2 representatives for 450 male polls; 1 additional representative for 300 male polls
RI-1663	MM	town	2 representatives per town, 6 representatives for Newport, 4 representatives each for 3 towns
CT-1662	MM	town	2 representatives per town
NY-1777	MM	county	number of qualified voters in county; between 10 and 2 representatives per county
NJ-1776	MM	county	3 representatives per county
PA-1776	MM, SM	county, city	taxable inhabitants
DE-1776	MM	county	7 representatives per county
MD-1776	MM	county, city	4 representatives per county; 2 representatives for Annapolis and for Baltimore (with population growth provision)
VA-1776	MM, SM	county, town	2 representatives per county; 2 towns each receive 1 representative yet any town with less than half of the smalllest county's population loses its representative
NC-1776	MM, SM	county, town	2 representatives per county; 6 towns with 1 representative each
SC-1778	MM	electoral district	initial basis unspecified, but districts received between 3 and 30 representatives; subsequent reapportionments with regard to number of white inhabitants and taxable property
GA-1777	MM, SM	county, town	10 representatives for 5 counties, 14 representatives for 1 county, 1 representative each for 2 counties; port towns of Sunbury and Savannah, 2 and 4 representatives

Note: MM = multimember electoral district; SM = single-member electoral district; pooled representative = smaller towns permitted to group themselves to send 1 representative.

TABLE 5.7. *State Upper House Apportionment, 1787*

State and Year of Constitution	District Type(s)	Apportionment Unit	Basis for Allocation of Representation
MA-1780	MM, SM	multicounty electoral district	taxes paid; size fixed at 40 members; maximum district representation is 6
NH-1784	MM, SM	multicounty electoral district	taxes paid by county electoral district
RI-1662	At large	state	10 representatives elected statewide
CT-1663	At large	state	12 representatives elected statewide
NY-1777	MM	section	9 representatives for southern section; 6 for middle; 6 for west; 3 for eastern
NJ-1776	SM	county	1 representative per county
PA-1776	SM	county, town	1 representative per county and city of Philadelphia
DE-1776	MM	county	3 representatives per county
MD-1776	At large[a]	section	9 western representatives, 6 eastern representatives
VA-1776	MM	multicounty electoral district	6 representatives per electoral district
NC-1776	SM	county	1 representative per county
SC-1778	MM, SM	electoral district	1 or 2 representatives per electoral district
GA-1777	MM	county	2 representatives per county

[a] Maryland upper house elected by lower house electoral college.

Note: MM = multi-member electoral district; SM = single-member electoral district.

with gubernatorial elections during the 1780s, the average percentage difference between the first- and second-place candidates was almost 30 percent. In the other states, governors were appointed by their respective state legislatures, and thus completely removed from electoral pressures and accountability.

In addition to electoral participation and competition rates, early conceptualizations of representative government differed from modern ones over the practice of reapportionment – the periodic, proportional transfer of legislative representation among political units. Slightly less than half the state constitutions included provisions for the reapportionment of state legislative representation. Four state constitutions (New York, New Jersey, Pennsylvania, South Carolina) provided for some type of reapportionment of lower state house representation. Two states (Massachusetts, New Hampshire) authorized but did not require reapportionment of upper house representation based on the amount of taxes paid by each county. Georgia's 1777 constitution established a similar proportional scale for future increases in the legislative representation of all subsequently created counties, providing for increases until these new counties achieved a number of representatives equal to those of the state's original counties. Despite their explicit constitutional authority to reapportion, the states failed to establish traditions of transferring the right of representation enjoyed by one locality or district to another (proportionally) more deserving locality or district. By 1786, only Pennsylvania in 1779 and 1786 succeeded in completing and publishing the necessary census of taxable inhabitants required to complete a proportional reapportionment of representation in its lower state house. This lone accomplishment is especially revealing because it suggests that, although the practice of regular elections provided opportunities to replace individual representatives, early American conceptualizations of representative government had still not formulated acceptable institutional mechanisms or working understandings of a means for completing peaceful, public, and limited transfers of governmental authority between different and geographically distinct interests.

CONCLUSION

Between 1776 and 1786, the structure of American politics was redefined by the development of various economic, demographic, institutional, and ideological conditions. Analysis of these conditions offers an opportunity to become reattuned to the general context within which the Articles of Confederation were abandoned by the 1787 Constitutional Convention and ultimately displaced by the second national constitution, the U.S. Constitution. Analysis of the development of these conditions prior to 1787 also provides a basis for discerning the development of American political expectations independent of the subsequent decisions to break and remake the constitutional framework of the American political order.

Two general developments and their immediate consequences deserve noting. The first development was the decline of political interest in the national government. The constitutional design of the Articles of Confederation offered a logic of limited decision-making capacities and governmental authority that made intense national political interest highly improbable. As evidenced by the decline in congressional delegate attendance rates and by the accompanying difficulties Congress had in securing the minimum number of delegates necessary for a quorum, the national government by 1786 "remained in a kind of political torpor."[54] One immediate consequence of this decline was a devolution of national power and its absorption by the state governments. The decline in the salience of the national government prompted one delegate to observe that "it seems as if many of the States had forgot the relation in which they stood to the Union as well as to foreign powers,"[55] and another to contend "that our federal Government is but a name, a meer shadow without any substance."[56] In light of subsequent constitutional changes, the lack of energy in, and the loosening of attachments to, the national government also reduced resistance to (and, thus, the costs of) abandoning the Articles of Confederation.

The second noteworthy development was the emergence of political expectations fundamentally dissonant with the governmental structures and rules established under the Articles. Out of this dissonance arose the possibility for constitutional change. Specifically what these new political expectations were, how they were directed into concerted efforts to displace the Articles of Confederation, and why they prompted a change in the national rule of apportionment are the subjects analyzed in Chapter 6.

[54] William Grayson to James Madison, March 22, 1786, *LMCC*, VIII: 332.
[55] William Grayson to Richard Henry Lee, [March] 22, 1786, *LMCC*, VIII: 333.
[56] Rhode Island Delegates to the Governor of Rhode Island (John Collins), Sept. 28, 1786, *LMCC*, VIII: 472. See also B. Lincoln to R. King, Feb. 11, 1786, *Life and Correspondence of Rufus King* (New York: G. P. Putnam's Sons, 1894–1900), I: 157; Charles Pinckney, Speech Before the New Jersey Assembly, [March 13, 1786], *LMCC*, VIII: 321–330.

6

Divide et Impera: Constitutional Heresthetics and the Abandonment of the Articles of Confederation

The contextual conditions described in Chapter 5 and the divergent political expectations they supported made constitutional change possible in the mid-1780s, but they neither required nor spontaneously prompted the abandonment and replacement of the Articles of Confederation. Constitutional change of this magnitude requires the timely intervention of individuals who possess the vision, commitment, and political skills to organize and to direct other dissatisfied individuals and groups toward the transformation of an existing order. The process of constitutional change must thus be understood as being entrepreneur-dependent.

However necessary constitutional entrepreneurs are for this account's explanation, they play an initial but clearly secondary role because they rarely dictate the final terms of the process of constitutional change. Not only are they constrained by their own capacities to envision both a new constitutional horizon and the immediate range of real possibilities, but, once initiated, transformative processes typically and often thankfully are propelled by and negotiated among a much larger and more diverse set of political actors. Regardless of the vision or charisma of any particular entrepreneur, his or her capacity to extend the political discourse of the day to include the possibility of constitutional change remains contingent on innumerable historical accidents of context and personality. As a consequence, constitutional change remains uncommon not only because of the high transformation costs but also because the convergence of the necessary macro- and microlevel conditions make real opportunities for wholesale transformation rare indeed.

Whereas Chapter 5 described the development of various macrolevel conditions between 1776 and 1786, this chapter focuses at the microlevel on the actors and sequence of decisions that made the 1787 Constitutional Convention possible. This possibility, this chapter argues, required not only a set of political interests and actors open to the abandonment of the Articles of Confederation, but a sequence of actions directed toward effecting this constitutional end. To unpack the initial problematics raised by the latter requirement, several game-theoretic models are introduced to illuminate the very real but largely ignored difficulties of securing state commitments to attend the 1787 Constitutional Convention. Chapter 7 completes this account by focusing on the sequence of decisions at the Convention that ultimately yielded a consensus for a new national rule of apportionment and a new constitutional framework, the U.S. Constitution.

In retelling the story of the road to the Philadelphia convention, this chapter consists of three parts which fill the gap between the macrolevel conditions described in Chapter 5 and the decisions by which the Articles of Confederation were effectively abandoned. Part I illustrates how processes of constitutional change can be initiated by profiling the political career of one of several constitutional entrepreneurs who played a significant role in catalyzing the 1787 Constitutional Convention: James Madison of Virginia, arguably an archetypical constitutional entrepreneur.

Part II extends the bridge this work seeks to build between macro- and microlevel conditions. Chapter 3 offered a set of conceptual genealogies as a way of spanning a similar divide for the first constitutional change. Part II offers a different type of linkage, defined by reconstructing the strategic interests and actions of Virginia directed toward securing state commitments to attend the 1787 convention. Finally, Part III completes the account by presenting several game-theoretic models to explain why Pennsylvania accepted but Massachusetts initially balked at the invitation to attend a convention widely expected to begin with a Virginia-led attempt to replace the Articles' rule of equal state apportionment with a new national rule of apportionment based on state population.

PART I: CONSTITUTIONAL ENTREPRENEURS

What is a constitutional entrepreneur? Constitutional entrepreneurs are individuals who perceive opportunities for altering the constitutional framework of a political order, who envision alternatives to the constitutional status quo, who bear the personal risk of promoting these alternatives, and who possess the interpersonal skills to persuade others to follow in the wake of their visions.[1]

Further definition of the specific significance of constitutional entrepreneurs can be made by recalling that this study assumes that constitutional changes in apportionment rules do not occur often or easily. How then can these discontinuous breaks with the political status quo be explained? Two explanatory traditions provide general, although ultimately unsatisfactory, accounts of discontinuous political change. According to one tradition, discontinuous changes are caused by individuals who possess extraordinary abilities to redefine the political landscape. Accounts that employ this charismatic political leader device, however, generally tend to overestimate the capacities of individuals to overcome complex environmental constraints and the costs of transforming institutionalized patterns of political behavior.

According to a second explanatory tradition, discontinuous political change is triggered by changes in exogenous, or nonpolitical, conditions. Individuals are portrayed as the immediate agents of political change but their emergence and their intentions are determined by environmental configurations. In addition to discounting the need to provide an alternative to a definition of political accountability grounded in human voluntarism and intentionality, this structural model of political change tends to underestimate the costs and skills needed to complete complex forms of collective action. Although environmental conditions provide the incentives and opportunities for political change, they do not spontaneously generate the vision, judgment, or interpersonal skills required. Such characteristics cannot simply be assumed to be randomly distributed or to be a matter of thoughtless serendipity. The development of these characteristics requires more specialized and longer-term investments of human energies and time than could possibly be attributed to general and more immediate changes in exogenous conditions.[2]

---

[1] For recent discussion of entrepreneurship, see Tony Fu-Lai Yu, "An Entrepreneurial Perspective of Institutional Change," *Constitutional Political Economy* (2001), 12: 217–236. Viktor J. Vanberg and James M. Buchanan, "Constitutional Choice, Rational Ignorance, and the Limits of Reason," in *The Constitution of Good Societies* (University Park, PA.: Pennsylvania State University Press, 1996), Karol E. Soltan and Stephen L. Elkin, eds., pp. 39–56; Mark Schneider and Paul Teske with Michael Mintrom, *Public Entrepreneurs: Agents for Change in American Government* (Princeton, NJ: Princeton University Press, 1995); and Margaret Levi, *Of Rule and Revenue* (Berkeley: University of California Press, 1988).

[2] For a perceptive critique of the logical flaws of structurally based causal explanations, see also Youssef Cohen, *Radicals, Reformers and Reactionaries* (Chicago: University of Chicago Press, 1994).

The role assigned to constitutional entrepreneurs by this study draws from both of these explanatory models of discontinuous political change. Rather than attempting further definition of this role in the abstract, attention is riveted onto a single individual who, by all accounts, was one of the most actively engaged in the promotion and organization of the 1787 Constitutional Convention.

Profile of An Entrepreneur: James Madison

Although several individuals made significant contributions to the process by which the Articles of Confederation were effectively abandoned, the actions of James Madison were central to the subsequent change in the national rule of apportionment. Prior to the convention, Madison declared that "[t]he first step to be taken is I think a change in the principle of representation."[3] Madison's interest in the process of constitutional change was apparent throughout his early public career. He read extensively during these years on "antient" and "modern foederal republics," the "laws of Nations," and the "natural & political [history] of the New World." With Philip Mazzei, he helped found the Constitutional Society of Virginia, one of the nation's first public interest groups committed to constitutional reform. The Society was chartered "to communicate by fit publications . . . facts and sentiments" on amending the Virginia constitution and on preserving "it from the innovations of ambition, and the designs of faction."[4]

Madison's theoretical and historical knowledge of the making and breaking of political orders was reinforced by his extensive political

---

[3] James Madison to Edmund Randolph, April 8, 1787, *PJM*, 9: 369. See also James Madison to Thomas Jefferson, March 19, 1787, *PJM*, 9: 318; James Madison to George Washington, April 16, 1787, *Writings of James Madison*, Gaillard Hunt, ed. (New York: G. P. Putnam's Sons, 1901), II: 345.

[4] James Madison to Thomas Jefferson, April 27, 1785, *PJM*, 8: 266; Rules of the Constitutional Society of Virginia, June 14, 1784, *PJM*, 8: 71–72.

With apparently little success, Mazzei attempted to establish similar groups in the other states. Without Mazzei's assistance, Benjamin Franklin established a similar organization in Philadelphia in 1787. The Society was chartered for "mutual improvement in the knowledge of government, and for the advancement of political science." In addition to Franklin, "The Society for Political Enquiries" included James Wilson, Gouverneur Morris, Robert Morris, Benjamin Rush, and Thomas Paine among others. "Rules and Regulations of the Society for Political Enquiries," 1787; as quoted in A. J. Beitzinger, *A History of American Political Thought* (New York: Dodd, Mead, 1972), p. 232; see also Charles P. Smith, *James Wilson* (Chapel Hill: University of North Carolina Press, 1956), p. 204.

experience. Madison was one of only seven persons who attended both the Annapolis convention in 1786 and the Philadelphia constitutional convention in 1787. In preparation for the former, he completed an extensive series of personal notes on the rise and demise of past confederacies. To prepare for the latter, he completed a private memorandum on the vices of the American political order that clarified his ideas on the necessity for wholesale replacement of the Articles of Confederation.[5]

Madison's experience with constitutional formation included the construction of several state constitutions. As a 25-year-old delegate to the Virginia constitutional convention in 1776, he witnessed the process and politics that preceded the framing and adoption of Virginia's first state constitution. A decade later, he advised leaders of the Kentucky statehood movement of his "Ideas towards a constitution of Government for the State in embryo." The formation of a political order, he explained, was a necessary experience of self-governance, but it was "both imprudent and indecent" for constitution makers "not to leave a door open for" subsequent constitutional revisions because a "handfull [sic] of early settl[l]ers ought not to preclude a populous Country from a choice of Government under which they & their Posterity are to live." Madison additionally recommended a rule of apportionment that assigned "the number of representatives of each county to its number of electors" and he suggested "the number of representatives allotted" among the counties could "be equalized from time to time" to account for population growth.[6]

Interestingly, as a delegate to Congress in the early 1780s, Madison consistently refused to entertain proposals for a national constitutional convention. In 1782, for example, he did not support a proposal by his congressional colleague Alexander Hamilton of New York. A year later, he opposed a convention proposal by the Massachusetts legislature, opting instead to support use of the constitutional amendment process defined in the Articles of Confederation.[7]

Ironically, after leaving Congress in the fall of 1783, Madison became the leading advocate for convening a constitutional convention to rewrite the Virginia state constitution. Prior even to his election to the General

[5] Ancient & Modern Confederacies, April–June 1786, *PJM*, 9: 4–24; Vices of the Political System of the United States, *PJM*, 9: 348–357.

[6] Marvin Meyers, *The Mind of the Founder* (Indianapolis, IN: Bobbs-Merrill, 1973), p. 5; James Madison to Caleb Wallace, August 23, 1785, *PJM*, 8: 350, 355–356, 354.

[7] *Papers of Alexander Hamilton* (July 20, 22, 1782), 3: 110–113, 117; *Magazine of American History* (1883), 10: 441n; *PJM*, 6: 425 (April 1, 1783).

Assembly, Madison went to great lengths to secure the support of Virginia's leading statesmen. On his return trip from Congress, he visited George Mason, the principal author of the 1776 Virginia constitution.[8] Several months later, he traveled to the home of another state leader, Patrick Henry, to discuss this reform and he also courted the support of Richard Henry Lee, an influential member of the Virginia House of Delegates.

Confident of this coalition of support, Madison pressed his case for constitutional reform on the floor of the House of Delegates. He denounced the 1776 state constitution, claiming that the "power of the people [was] no where pretended" in it. Madison pointed out that the constitution did not guarantee an "equality of Representation" among the counties and cities and he singled out the underrepresentation of the "district of [West] Augusta" which was still apportioned only two lower house delegates although since 1776 it had been subdivided into eight counties.[9]

Despite Madison's advance work and the strength of his arguments on the floor, he had clearly misgauged the level of support for constitutional reform within the General Assembly. After what must have been an embarrassing and unexpected rebuff from his colleagues, he quickly abandoned his efforts to win legislative endorsement for a state constitutional convention. Madison's failure was a pivotal moment in his political career for it gave him first-hand experience of the difficulties of building and sustaining interest in wholesale constitutional change within a legislative body directly affected by the proposed reforms. It also freed him to reconsider the possibilities and necessities of convening a national constitutional convention.[10]

Madison's interest in national constitutional reform emerged shortly after his state convention proposal failed. By December 1784, Madison privately professed that the question no longer was whether the Articles of Confederation needed radical reform but "in what mode & at what moment the experiment for supplying the defects ought to be made." With Madison's support, the Virginia legislature subsequently proposed convening a national convention in Annapolis to consider the establishment of national commercial regulations. Although initially disappointed that the Virginia legislature did not grant "a plenipotentiary commission

[8] James Madison to Thomas Jefferson, December 10, 1783, *PJM*, 7: 401.
[9] Notes for a Speech Favoring Revision of the Virginia Constitution of 1776, June 1784, *PJM*, 8: 77–79.
[10] See James Madison to Thomas Jefferson, July 3, 1784, *PJM*, 8: 93; "Notes for a Speech Favoring Revision of the Virginia Constitution of 1776," *PJM*, 8: 75–79.

to their deputies to the Convention," Madison calculated that the proposed Annapolis convention was "better than nothing" because it created a forum and an opportunity for the "recommendation of additional powers to Congress."[11]

Although the Annapolis convention was a colossal failure, Madison and Alexander Hamilton managed to convince the other delegates to call for a second convention to meet the following May in Philadelphia. Madison shepherded this invitation through the Virginia Assembly, was appointed a delegate to the Philadelphia convention, persuaded the retired but widely revered George Washington to attend, and had a heavy hand in crafting the so-called Virginia plan that provided the conceptual framework for much of the early deliberations of the 1787 Convention. Finally, as one of the primary authors of the *Federalist*, Madison was a participant in the post-Convention debates over the ratification of the U.S. Constitution.

PART II: STRATEGIC ACTORS FOR
CONSTITUTIONAL CHANGE

In addition to biographical assessment of the other individuals who contributed to the promotion and organization of the 1787 Constitutional Convention, the sequence of decisions that ultimately culminated in the abandonment of the Articles of Confederation can also be evaluated in terms of the interests and actions of each of the thirteen American states. More efficiently, although not as thoroughly, the sequence can be represented with reference to only those states that led attempts to convene a national constitutional convention.

Three attempts to convene a national constitutional convention were made after 1785. The first was issued by the Massachusetts state legis-

---

[11] James Madison to Richard Henry Lee, Dec. 25, 1784, *PJM*, 8: 201; Resolution Authorizing a Commission to Examine Trade Regulations, Jan. 21, 1786, *PJM*, 8: 471; James Madison to James Monroe, Jan. 22, 1786, *PJM*, 8: 482.

For additional exploration of Madison's public career and political thought, see Jack N. Rakove, *Original Meanings: Politics and Ideas in the Making of the Constitution* (New York: Knopf, 1996); Drew McCoy, "James Madison and Visions of American Nationality in the Confederation Period," in Richard Beeman, Stephen Botein, and Edward C. Carter II, *Beyond Confederation* (Chapel Hill: University of North Carolina Press, 1987), pp. 226–258; Charles F. Hobson, "The Negative on State Laws: James Madison, the Constitution, and the Crisis of Republican Government," *WMQ* (1979), 36(2): 215–235; Ralph Ketcham, *James Madison: A Biography* (New York: The Macmillaneo, 1971); Irving Brant, *James Madison: The Nationalist, 1780–1787* (Indianapolis, IN: Bobbs-Merrill, 1948), Vol. 2.

lature in June 1785, and was motivated by their interest in providing a general taxing power and commercial authority to the national government. The Massachusetts legislature was convinced that such reforms were possible only through extraconstitutional means.

The proposal failed after Massachusetts' congressional delegates unexpectedly refused to extend this invitation to the other states. The delegates explained their highly unusual action by arguing that the proposal would have prompted "an Exertion of the Friends of an Aristocracy" for a complete "Change of Government." Moreover, as the sponsor of the proposed convention, Massachusetts would be placed in the awkward position of having to accept "highly offensive" revisions to the fundamental principles on which the existing Union was founded. The Massachusetts delegates therefore recommended to their state legislature that "if a Convention of the States, is necessary on this occasion," it should be restricted to "the revision of such parts of the Confederation as are supposed defective" and strictly prohibit the adoption of "a plan of federal Government, essentially different from the republican Form now administered."[12]

What were these "highly offensive" revisions and who were the "Friends of an Aristocracy" that prompted such recalcitrance from the Massachusetts delegates? The historical record does not offer conclusive evidence for a definitive answer to either question. To date, legal historians William W. Crosskey and William Jeffrey have devised the most substantiated and credible explanation: that the anticipated revision was of the Articles' rule of equal state apportionment and that the "Friends of an Aristocracy" were the southern states.[13]

The subsequent actions of and proposals by Virginia (and the other southern states) sustain the contention that, by the mid-1780s, southern statesmen were interested primarily in increasing their relative decision-making capacities within the national government. In January 1786, for

[12] Massachusetts Delegates to the Governor of Massachusetts James Bowdoin, Sept. 3, 1785, *LMCC*, VIII: 206, 208; Nathan Dane to Rufus King, *Life and Correspondence of Rufus King*, Charles R. King, ed. (New York, G. P. Putnam's Sons, 1894), I: 67–70; Massachusetts Delegates to the Governor of Massachusetts, Nov. 2, 1785, *LMCC*, VIII: 245–246; Rufus King to Nathan Dane, Sept. 17, 1785, *LMCC*, VIII: 218; Samuel Adams to E. Gerry, Sept. 19, 1785, George Bancroft, *History of the Formation of the Constitution* (New York: D. Appleton and Company, 1882), I: 457.

[13] William W. Crosskey and William Jeffrey, *Politics and the Constitution in the History of the United States* (Chicago: University of Chicago Press, 1980), Vol. III. See also H. James Henderson, *Party Politics in the Continental Congress* (New York: McGraw-Hill, 1974).

example, the Virginia legislature reversed its previous indifference toward Kentucky statehood petitions and enacted legislation promoting the separation of the Kentucky District and its admission into the Union.[14] Later the same year, Virginia delegate James Monroe won congressional approval for a reduction in the number of new western states to be formed north of the Ohio River.[15] The proposed admission of Kentucky was intended to add another vote to the southern state bloc in Congress and the latter policy change orchestrated by Monroe was intended (over the short term) to strengthen the southern state bloc by accelerating the admission of yet another noncommercial state into the Union. The reduced number of western states also strengthened Virginia's congressional representation (over the long term) because, as Monroe suggested to Jefferson in 1785, it effectively prevented them from "outnumber[ing] us in congress."[16]

Table 6.1 offers a final form of corroboration of the southern states' interest in abandoning the Articles' equal state rule of apportionment. Recall that by 1785, the votes of the southern states had effectively been marginalized within Congress by the emergence of a voting bloc constituted of the eight most northern states. For the southern states (and especially for Virginia, the nation's largest state), a change from the existing equal state rule to a proportional state rule of apportionment promised

[14] James Madison led this effort in the Virginia General Assembly. Notably, Kentuckians had petitioned Congress and Virginia repeatedly for separation and statehood since 1780. When these petitions were ignored, they convened nine statehood conventions between December 1784 and September 1786. The final legislation enacted in January 1786 conditioned Kentucky's autonomy from Virginia on its admission as a new state. See *JCC*, XVII: 760, 763 (Aug. 23–24, 1780); XXII: 532 (Aug. 27, 1782). See also Caleb Wallace to James Madison, Oct. 8, 1785, *PJM*, 8: 378n.2; Act Concerning Statehood for the Kentucky District, December 22, 1785, *PJM*, 8: 452; Thomas Jefferson to William Carmichael, June 20, 1786, *Writings of Thomas Jefferson*, 4: 244.

[15] James Monroe chaired the congressional committee that proposed the reduction in the number of new western states. The 1784 Land Ordinance proposed forming nine states north of the Ohio River; the Monroe committee report recommended this territory be divided into at least two but not more than five states. *JCC*, XX: 252–255, (May 10, 1786). See also Monroe to Jefferson, July 16, 1786, *LMCC*, VIII: 404.

Once northern state delegates recognized a reduction of prospective number of northwestern states would automatically accelerate the admission of western states and thereby likely increase the number of states aligned with the southern states, they immediately had a "desire to rescind every thing they have heretofore done in it, particularly to increase the number of Inhabitants which sho[ul]d entitle such States to admission into the Confederacy and to make it depend on their having one 13th part of the free inhabitants of the U[nited] S[tates]." James Monroe to Thomas Jefferson, 16 July 1786, *LMCC*, VIII: 403–404.

[16] James Monroe to Thomas Jefferson, 16 July 1786, *LMCC*, VIII: 202–203.

TABLE 6.1. *Effects of Apportionment Rules on Southern State Representation in Congress*

Apportionment Rule:	Voting Ratio in Congress	Northern State Votes Required to Form Majority	% of Northern State Votes to Form Majority
Equal State Rule			
Southern Minority	$\dfrac{5}{8}$	$\dfrac{2}{8}$	25.0
Northern Majority			
Proportional State Rule[a]			
Southern Minority	$\dfrac{42}{58}$	$\dfrac{9}{58}$	15.5
Northern Majority			

[a] For illustrative purposes only, the size of Congress under a proportional state rule is set at 100 members. Note that legislative size increases would decrease the percentages in column three.

to provide a remedy for their seemingly permanent minority status within Congress. As Table 6.1 illustrates, under the existing rule of equal state apportionment the southern states had to secure at least two of the eight northern states to form a simple majority within Congress, or 25 percent of the northern state voting bloc. Under a proportional state rule, however, the costs of forming a similar southern-based majority would be reduced because only 15.5 percent of the northern state coalition would need to be realigned with the southern states. In addition, the probability of forming coalitions with northern state delegates would be increased for Virginia and the southern states if congressional delegates were permitted to vote individually rather than by state. However, this additional benefit was possible only under a proportional state apportionment rule.

Figure 6.1 plots the general expectations for constitutional reform that emerged in the wake of Massachusetts' 1785 convention proposal. The diagram clearly suggests a possible resolution of the differences between the southern states' expectations for increases in their relative decision-making capacities and the expectations of Massachusetts (and of the northern states) for increases in national governmental authority. The path to a new constitutional equilibrium becomes evident in coupling a change in the national apportionment rule with an expansion of the national government's authority.

A second proposal for a national constitutional convention – this one made by the Virginia legislature in 1786 – created an opportunity to

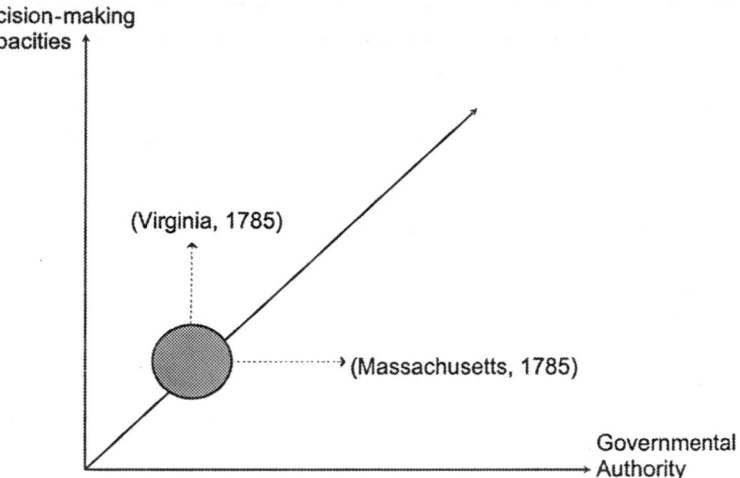

FIGURE 6.1. Divergent Political Expectations Concerning Constitutional Reform of Articles of Confederation, 1785

effect the suggested exchange. The Virginia legislature proposed that this national convention meet in Annapolis to deliberate over the national government's commercial authority. Given that this convention's stated purpose extended only to national commercial reforms, northern state interest in attending initially ran high. Every northern state except Connecticut appointed delegates.

Like Massachusetts' delegates the year before, Virginia's congressional delegates were less than sanguine about the wisdom of their state's proposal. William Grayson, for one, viewed the legislature's limitation of the convention's agenda to commercial reforms as ill-advised because "the Eastern people mean nothing more than to carry the commercial point" after which, he was certain, "they intend to stop." Future attempts to alter the Articles' rule of apportionment were thus still likely to fail. Grayson, therefore, suggested that "if all are brought forward at the same time one object will facilitate the passage of another and by a general compromise perhaps a good government may be procured."[17]

[17] William Grayson to James Madison, May 28, 1786, *LMCC*, VIII: 373–374. Compare also the change in views of James Madison: James Madison to James Monroe, Jan. 22, 1786, *PJM*, 8: 482; and James Madison to Thomas Jefferson, Aug. 12, 1786, *PJM*, 9: 96. According to Stephen Higginson of Massachusetts: "The ostensible object of [the] Convention is the regulation of Commerce; but when I consider the men who are deputed

As the Annapolis convention approached, however, the exchange recommended by Grayson for circumscribing a new constitutional ambit was complicated by the northern states' apparent willingness to consider abandoning the existing Union altogether.[18] Just how serious northern statesmen were about forming a separate Northern Union is immaterial because it compelled Virginian statesmen to refocus their efforts and strategies onto the maintenance of the Union. To prevent what was widely considered from the southern perspective to be the disastrous formation of an eight-state northern confederacy, Virginia attempted to construct stronger alliances with the middle states of Pennsylvania and New Jersey. As James Monroe advised Madison shortly before the Annapolis convention was scheduled to meet: "Upon [New] Jersey & Pen[nsylvani]a then it rests. To engage their leading men is now the object." Indeed, Monroe was convinced that the northern delegates were already "intriguing with the principal men in these States to effect that end in the last resort. They have even sought a dismemberm[en]t to the Potowmack & those of the party here have been sounding those in office thus far." To neutralize this northern initiative, "we must follow their mov[e]ments & counteract them every where, advise the leading men of their designs, the purposes they are meant to serve & e[c]t. and in even of the worst extremity prepare them for an union with the southern States." "I fear some of those in Penn[sylvani]a," Monroe continued, "will have a contrary affection – but it must be remov[e]d if possible. A knowledge that she was on our side wo[ul]d blow this whole intrigue in the air. To bring this ab[ou]t therefore is an important object to the Southern interest." However, "[i]f a dismemberm[en]t takes place" Pennsylvania "must not be added to the eastern scale. It were as well to

---

from New York, Pennsylvania, and Virginia, and the source whence the proposition was made, I am strongly inclined to think political Objects are intended to be combined with commercial, if they do not principally engross their Attention." As quoted in Crosskey and Jeffrey, *Politics and the Constitution*, (1980), p. 282.

[18] Massachusetts delegate Theodore Sedgwick, for example, argued it "well becomes the eastern and middle States, who are in interest one, seriously to consider what advantages result to them from their connection with the Southern States. They can give us nothing, as an equivalent for the protection which they derive from us. Should their conduct continue the same," he maintained, "[i]t becomes us seriously to contemplate a substitute; for if we do not controul events we shall be miserably controuled by them." Sedgwick proposed "contracting the limits of the confederacy to such as are natural and reasonable, and within those limits instead of a nominal to institute a real, and an efficient government." Theodore Sedgwick to Caleb Strong, Aug. 6, 1786, *LMCC*, VIII: 415–416.

use force to prevent it," Monroe declared, "as to defend ourselves afterwards."[19]

The commitments of Pennsylvania and New Jersey to attend the Annapolis convention offered some hope of foiling a northern secessionist movement. However, after the Maryland legislature refused to appoint delegates to a convention in its own state capitol, Edmund Randolph privately confessed to Madison: "what a dreadful chasm will the refusal of Maryland create? A chasm more injurious to us, than any other of the delegates." According to historian Joseph Davis, Maryland's refusal was significant because it "threatened to throw the weight of influence to the northern states and seemed to confirm a long-standing fear that the northern states would and could, with little difficulty, secure support in southern commercial centers like Baltimore and Charleston."[20]

PART III: A GAME-THEORETIC ANALYSIS OF STATE COMMITMENT TO THE 1787 CONSTITUTIONAL CONVENTION

Much to the surprise and disappointment of Madison and the Virginia legislature, only twelve delegates from five states attended the Annapolis convention.[21] The conspicuous absence of delegates from the New

---

[19] James Monroe to James Madison, Sept. 3, 1786, *PJM*, 9: 112–114.

    Monroe believed that the upcoming Annapolis convention was "a most important area in our aff[ai]rs" because the Eastern states "mean it as leading further than the object originally comprehended. If they do not obtain that things shall be arrang[e]d to suit them in every respect" they will work to break the Union. "Pen[nsylvani]a is their object," he again advised Madison. And "[u]pon succeeding or failing with her will they gain or lose confidence" (*PJM*, 9: 114).

    Slightly more than a week later, Monroe again wrote Madison: "It will depend much on the opinion of Jersey & Pena. as to the movements of Jay, and that of Jersey much on that of Mr. Clark now with you at Annapolis." As a consequence, "[i]t is well for the southern States to act with great circumspection & to be prepar[e]d for every possible event – to stand well with middle states especially." James Monroe to James Madison, Sept. 12, 1786, *PJM*, 9: 122–123. See also Otto to Vergennes, Sept. 10, 1786, Bancroft, *History of the Formation of the Constitution* (1882), II: 389–393).

    After the Annapolis Convention, Monroe again advised Madison: "I am inform'd [Jay] means to submit nothing further to the present Congress. Perhaps he waits the convention of the ensuing delegations, to sound them & to be govern'd by circumstances as they shall turn up. If Pen[sylvani]a & [New] jersey sho[ul]d move in the business this intrigue is at end." James Monroe to James Monroe, Oct. 7, 1786, *PJM*, 9: 142–143.

[20] Edmund Randolph to James Madison, June 12, 1786, *PJM*, 9: 75; Davis, *Sectionalism in American Politics* (1979), p. 142.

[21] George Washington to David Humphreys, Dec. 26, 1786, *Writings of George Washington*, Sparks, ed., IX: 223.

England states effectively tabled the convention's scheduled deliberations on national commercial reforms, and it foiled Madison's anticipated "intrigue" of piggybacking additional constitutional reforms onto the convention's agenda. Before adjourning, the Annapolis delegates decided to invite the state legislatures to send delegates to yet another national convention to be convened in Philadelphia the following May. The Annapolis invitation did not initially generate much enthusiasm. Congress simply ignored it until James Monroe insisted on referring the invitation to a congressional committee. Monroe's motion "was objected to by the Eastern states." After pressure from southern state delegates, Congress finally assigned the invitation to a committee where it remained unattended for the next four months.[22]

The response of most state legislatures was similarly ambivalent toward the proposed convention. Virginia, not surprisingly, was the exception. She was the first state to commit a slate of delegates and, in so doing, dramatically announced "that the crisis is arrived at which the good people of America are to decide the solemn question," whether to "reap the just fruits of   Independence," or give "way to unmanly jealousies and prejudices, or to partial and transitory interests."[23] The "crisis" that had arrived in Virginia by November 1786 was evidently a local sensation because the New England state legislatures remained uncommitted to the proposed Philadelphia convention. A full five months after the Annapolis convention adjourned only New Hampshire's lower house had responded positively to the invitation, although the full legislature delayed its official appointment of delegates until a month *after* the Philadelphia convention convened the following spring.[24]

The invitation to convene a national constitutional convention was greeted initially with caution or indifference in most states, but Massachusetts statesmen (and especially her congressional delegates) were actively hostile to the idea of a "general Revision of the confederation" and it became generally known that they "advised its non adoption in their Legislature." Massachusetts delegates Rufus King and Nathan Dane attempted to confine deliberations on constitutional

[22] James Monroe to James Monroe, Oct. 7, 1786, *PJM*, 9: 142–143; *JCC*, 31: 770n. (Oct. 11, 1786).

[23] The Virginia legislature authorized the election of convention delegates on November 23, 1786. See John P. Kaminski and Gaspare J. Saladino, "Introduction," *Documentary History of the Ratification of the Constitution*, 13: 35–36.

[24] Notes on Debates, February 21, 1787, *PJM*, 8: 291–292. Madison and others suspected these states "of leaning towards some antirepublican establishment . . . or of being less desirous or hopeful of preserving the Unity of the [American] Empire."

change to Congress because, as King alleged, the national legislature "can do all a convention can, and certainly with more safety to original principles."[25]

Despite Massachusetts' initial hostility and the apparent indifference of the other states toward the proposed constitutional convention, the subsequent sequence of decisions ultimately yielded commitments by twelve of thirteen states (including Massachusetts). Such a pronounced change in state preferences begs an explanation. Tracting out the decisional sequences within all thirteen states would, however, obscure the more interesting and telling sequence of decisions made by the three most populous states in the Union: Virginia, Massachusetts, and Pennsylvania. For of all the states, these three states stood to gain the most immediate benefit from the replacement of the Articles' rule of equal state apportionment with a new proportional-based rule.

Virginia, as expected, was the first state to commit to the Philadelphia convention. Thereafter the decisions of the two largest northern states, Massachusetts and Pennsylvania, would determine the fate of the proposed convention. To understand the sequence of decisions and the likely strategic calculations of these two states, several game-theoretic models will prove analytically useful. These models – like other more familiar analytical techniques – do not render previous historical narratives and their rich sets of details unnecessary or untrue; rather, these models illuminate and explain what previously has remained obscure.

To introduce the models, we follow the example in Chapter 3 and turn first to the definition of the outcome set.[26] The decisions and calculations of Massachusetts and Pennsylvania were delimited by the set of outcomes they perceived as viable possibilities for reconstituting the existing Union. Although additional constitutional outcomes had been discussed between 1776 and 1787, only three seem to have received serious attention.[27] The outcome set, therefore, included these three

---

[25] Rufus King to the Governor of Massachusetts (James Bowdoin), Sept. 17, 1786, *LMCC*, VIII: 469; Edward Carrington to James Madison, Dec. 18, 1786, *PJM*, 9: 218; Rufus King, Address to Massachusetts House of Representatives, Oct. 11, 1786, *LMCC*, VIII: 479; Rufus King to John Adams, Oct. 2, 1786, *LMCC*, VIII: 475; Nathan Dane, Address to Massachusetts House of Representatives, Nov. 9, 1786, *LMCC*, VIII: 504.

[26] For a more thorough discussion of the outcome set, see Chapter 3.

[27] Among other proposals, see Henry Drayton, "Commentary on the Articles of Confederation" (1778); Pelatiah Webster's Plan (1783); Rufus King and Jonathan Jackson, Sept. 23, 1786, *LMCC*, VIII: 459. See also Louise B. Dunbar, *A Study of "Monarchical" Tendencies in the United States from 1776 to 1801* (Urbana, IL: University of Illinois Press, 1922); *The Documentary History of the Ratification of the Constitution*, Kaminski and

possibilities: (1) maintaining the constitutional status quo defined by the Articles of Confederation; (2) reconstituting the Union by adopting a rule of proportional state representation; and (3) breaking the existing Union into two or three separate confederacies.

Framed by this set of possible outcomes and faced with Virginia's endorsement of the Philadelphia convention, the historical record strongly suggests that Massachusetts and Pennsylvania leaders seriously considered three responses to the Philadelphia convention invitation. These responses or strategies were: (1) abstaining from the convention; (2) attending (thus implicitly endorsing Virginia's expected attempt to enact a new rule of proportional state apportionment); or (3) dissolving the Union and forming separate confederacies.

Table 6.2 presents the likely outcomes of these options in terms of the representational strength or voting power of Massachusetts and Pennsylvania. If, for example, Pennsylvania and Massachusetts both decided to forgo the Philadelphia convention, the existing rule of equal state apportionment would likely remain unchanged. Given that the three smaller New England states consistently voted with Massachusetts,[28] Massachusetts would continue to control four of thirteen votes in Congress, or 30.8 percent of the body's voting power. Pennsylvania would continue to have one of thirteen votes in Congress, or a voting power of 7.7 percent. If both states decided to dissolve the Union and form a new northern confederation, Pennsylvania's new voting representation would be increased to one of eight states, or a voting power of 12.5 percent. Massachusetts' representation, however, would probably be reduced to a single vote among eight states because (without the opposition of the southern states) the three smaller New England states might not continue to align so consistently with Massachusetts. Finally, if both states decided to attend the proposed Philadelphia convention and accept the expected Virginia-led effort to establish a new rule of proportional state apportionment, the voting representation would be 29.4 percent for Massachusetts and 13.7 percent for Pennsylvania.

Several additional conclusions can be drawn if the probable effects of these decisions are given a numerical ranking, and if it is assumed

Saladino, eds. (1981), 13: 54–59, 168–178; Cathy D. Matson and Peter S. Onuf, *A Union of Interests: Political and Economic Thought in Revolutionary America* (Lawrence, KS: University Press of Kansas, 1990), pp. 82–100.

[28] Otto to Vergennes, Jan. 10, 1786, Bancroft, *History of the Formation of the Constitution*, I: 480; H. James Henderson, *Party Politics in the Continental Congress* (1974), pp. 355–358, 395.

TABLE 6.2. *Virginia's Gambit*

Pennsylvania selects:	Status Quo		Proportional Representation		Two Confederations	
Massachusetts selects:	Massachusetts	Pennsylvania	Massachusetts	Pennsylvania	Massachusetts	Pennsylvania
Status Quo	30.8% [Union]	7.7% [Union]	14.3% [7-state Northern Confederacy]	24.9% [6-state Southern Confederacy]	14.3% [7-state Northern Confederacy]	24.9% [6-state Southern Confederacy]
Proportional Representation	—	—	29.4% [Union]	13.7% [Union]	—	—
Two Confederations	14.3% [7-state Northern Confederacy]	24.9% [6-state Southern Confederacy]	14.3% [7-state Northern Confederacy]	24.9% [6-state Southern Confederacy]	12.5% [8-state Northern Confederacy]	12.5% [8-state Northern Confederacy]

Note: Proportional ratios among the states are based on Congress's 1785/1786 requisition apportionment ratios: See Table 5.2. The historical record offers little evidence that Massachusetts seriously considered a rule of proportional state apportionment prior to the decision to attend the 1787 Constitutional Convention. Given our interest in the realistic reconstruction of likely outcomes, Massachusetts' proportional representation outcome cells remain empty except for the outcome produced where both states select proportional representation. Additional definitions and assumptions related to the four bracketed ([]) outcomes are specified as follows:

1. *Union* constituted by the thirteen original states. Under an equal state apportionment rule, state representation is calculated as 1/13 (or 7.7%) for Pennsylvania and 4/13 (or 30.8%) for Massachusetts (and the other three New England States). Under a proportional state rule, state representation is calculated according to proportional ration, or 29.4% for Massachusetts (and the New England states), and 13.7% for Pennsylvania.

2. *8-state northern confederacy* constituted by eight most northern states, including Pennsylvania. An equal state apportionment rule is assumed, with each state receiving a representation equal to 1/8 (or 12.5%).

3. *7-state northern confederacy* constituted by seven most northern states, Pennsylvania not included. An equal state apportionment rule is assumed. Thus, the representation of Massachusetts is 1/7, or 14.3%.

4. *6-state southern confederacy* constituted by six most southern states, including Pennsylvania. A proportional state rule of apportionment is assumed. Thus, the representation of Pennsylvania is 24.9%.

TABLE 6.3. *State Representation under Alternative Apportionment Rules (Numerical Rank)*

OUTCOME SET	Massachusetts	Pennsylvania
Status Quo (Equal State Representation)	30.8% (4)	7.7% (1)
Proportional Representation	29.4% (3)	13.7% (3)
7-state Northern, 6-state Southern Confederacies	14.3% (2)	24.9% (4)
8-state Northern Confederacy	12.5% (1)	12.5% (2)

that each state prefers to maximize its representation. (See Table 6.3.)

As Table 6.4 illustrates, Pennsylvania's least preferred outcome (7.7 percent or "1") would be ensured under the existing rule of equal state apportionment, the constitutional outcome produced by both states opting for the "Status Quo." The State's leaders thus had a powerful incentive to support constitutional change in the apportionment rule because its relative voting power was expected to improve under any set of conditions that altered the status quo. In isolation from Massachusetts' decision, Pennsylvania's optimal strategy was to attend the Philadelphia convention because the expected change to a rule of proportional representation promised to yield the State its two highest levels of representation (24.9 or 13.7 percent) regardless of the decision of Massachusetts.

Massachusetts' "optimal" decision is more difficult to discern. The state's best voting representation (30.8 percent) is received under the "Status Quo-Status Quo" outcome. In isolation from Pennsylvania's decision, a decision by Massachusetts to forgo attending the convention might yield its third most preferred outcome (14.3 percent). Regardless of the decision of Pennsylvania, Massachusetts' representation decreases under all possible outcomes if it decides to dissolve the Union in order to form two confederacies. Interestingly, according to Madison's account, once the state delegates assembled in Philadelphia, "no suggestion was thrown out, in favor of a partition of the Empire into two or more Confederacies."[29]

---

[29] James Madison to Thomas Jefferson, Oct. 24, 1787, *PJM*, 10: 207.

TABLE 6.4. *Virginia's Gambit with Numerical-Rank Outcomes*

Pennsylvania selects:	Status Quo		Proportional Representation		Two Confederations	
Massachusetts selects:	Massachusetts	Pennsylvania	Massachusetts	Pennsylvania	Massachusetts	Pennsylvania
Status Quo	4 [Union]	1 [Union]	2 [7-state Northern Confederacy]	4 [6-state Southern Confederacy]	2 [7-state Northern Confederacy]	4 [6-state Southern Confederacy]
Proportional Representation	—	—	3 [Union]	3 [Union]	—	—
Two Confederations	2 [7-state Northern Confederacy]	4 [6-state Southern Confederacy]	2 [7-state Northern Confederacy]	4 [6-state Southern Confederacy]	1 [8-state Northern Confederacy]	2 [8-state Northern Confederacy]

Note: Outcome values: 4 + best; 1 + worst.

Why Massachusetts resisted attending the convention and the expected adoption of a rule of proportional state apportionment when, as Table 6.3 reveals, the representation of the four-state New England bloc would decrease only marginally from 30.8 to 29.4 percent, is not immediately evident. The resistance of Massachusetts to the proposal for a proportional rule seems even more anomalous because there is no evidence to suggest that the eight northern states would not continue to control approximately 60 percent of the votes in Congress.

By factoring in the expected costs of forming separate confederacies, and by accounting for the actual voting weight of each state among the eight northern states, the logic of Massachusetts' reluctance becomes less puzzling. Massachusetts and the three other New England states constituted four of the eight states within the majority coalition that had formed in Congress after 1785. In Table 6.5, this eight-state coalition is identified as: (Northern State Majority). The voting representation of Massachusetts with the three other New England states is more accurately represented as four of eight states or 50 percent, not 30.8 percent as recorded in Tables 6.2 and 6.3. Pennsylvania's weighted representation is more accurately represented as one vote within this eight-state northern majority, or 12.5 percent.

Table 6.5 illustrates the additional effect of breaking the Union into smaller confederacies by weighting the voting representation of Massachusetts and Pennsylvania in relation to the size of the resulting confederacies. The existing thirteen-state Union is assigned the maximum value of 1.00 under the assumption that the potential benefits of collective action were greatest within a Union including the most members. Smaller confederacies are assigned a relative value calculated by the number of states divided by the total number of states possible: for example, the six-state southern confederacy receives a value of 6/13, or .46. If, therefore, Pennsylvania elects to attend the Philadelphia convention and Massachusetts decides against attending, Pennsylvania's weighted voting representation in a six-state southern-dominated confederacy is not 24.9 percent as recorded in Table 6.3, but 24.9 percent multiplied by the relative value of this smaller confederacy (.46), hence 11.5 percent.

Despite Massachusetts' resistance to the convention invitation throughout the fall of 1786, two states followed Virginia's lead before year's end and appointed delegates to the Philadelphia convention. New Jersey selected delegates on November 24, and Pennsylvania appointed delegates on December 30. Virginia's grand constitutional strategy was strengthened immensely by the commitment of the two middle states,

TABLE 6.5. *Virginia's Weighted Gambit*

Massachusetts selects:	Pennsylvania selects:	Status Quo		Proportional Representation		Two Confederations	
		Massachusetts	Pennsylvania	Massachusetts	Pennsylvania	Massachusetts	Pennsylvania
Status Quo		50.0% (Northern State Majority) [Union-A]	12.5% (Northern State Majority) [Union-A]	7.7% [7-state Northern Confederacy]	11.5% [6-state Southern Confederacy]	7.7% [7-state Northern Confederacy]	11.5% [6-state Southern Confederacy]
Proportional Representation		—	—	29.4% [Union-B]	31.7% [Union-B]	—	—
Two Confederations		7.7% [7-state Northern Confederacy]	11.5% [6-state Southern Confederacy]	7.7% [7-state Northern Confederacy]	11.5% [6-state Southern Confederacy]	7.6% [8-state Northern Confederacy]	7.6% [8-state Northern Confederacy]

Note: Union-A: Union Value = 13/13, or 1.00. Assumes equal state representation. Massachusetts' voting weight is equivalent to 4/8 × 1.00, or 50.0%, and Pennsylvania's weight equals 1/8 × 1.00, or 12.5%.

Union-B: Union Value = 13/13, or 1.00. Assumes proportional representation; no consistent majority voting bloc because Pennsylvania can form majority with both northern and southern states; and New England states continue to vote as bloc (29.4%) in opposition to southern state voting bloc. Thus voting weights are relative to interstate proportional ratios multiplied by 1.00.

8-state northern Confederacy: Union Value = 8/13, or .62. Assumes equal representation; and equal weight for each state because no consistent majority voting bloc. Thus Massachusetts and Pennsylvania have voting weight equivalent to 1/8 × .62, or 7.6%.

7-state northern Confederacy: Union Value = 7/13, or .54. Assumes equal representation; and no consistent majority voting bloc. Thus Massachusetts has voting weight equivalent to 1/7 × .54, or 7.7%.

6-state southern Confederacy: Union Value = 6/13, or .46. Assumes proportional representation; and no consistent majority voting bloc. Thus Pennsylvania has voting weight equivalent to its population relative to the total southern union population, 24.9% × .46, or 11.5%.

especially Pennsylvania. The implications of the latter's decision were enormous for Massachusetts. On hearing of Pennsylvania's commitment, Rufus King immediately wrote Elbridge Gerry that it seemed both Virginia and Pennsylvania were committed to using the Philadelphia convention for a general revision of the Articles of Confederation. King advised caution especially if the state legislatures now decided to appoint delegates. "For God sakes," he exclaimed, "be careful who are the men; the times are becoming critical; a movement of this nature ought to be carefully observed by every member of the Community."[30]

Two days after Madison arrived in New York where Congress was then convened,[31] King had reversed his position and now advised Gerry: "Let the appointment be numerous, and if possible let the men have a good knowledge of the constitutions and various interests of the several states, and of the good and bad qualities of the confederation. Events are hurrying to a crisis; prudent and sagacious men should be ready to seize the most favourable circumstances to establish a more permanent and vigorous government."[32]

By mid February, five states south of New York had formally committed to attending the Philadelphia convention, and Maryland, according to Madison, had "entered into some vote which declare[d] as much."[33] South Carolina and Georgia were also expected to appoint delegates to attend, thus isolating the remaining bloc of northern states as the lone dissenters.[34] Interestingly, at this same time *The Independent Chronicle*, a

---

[30] *Documentary History of the Ratification of the Constitution*, 13: 26; Rufus King to Elbridge Gerry, Jan. 7, 1787, *LMCC*, VIII: 527.

Secretary of War Henry Knox of Massachusetts was one of the few New Englanders who initially supported the proposed Philadelphia convention. He recommended that the state appoint delegates to attend because, as he put it, "The Southern States are jealous enough already. If New England, and particularly Massachusetts, should decline sending delegates to the convention, it will operate in a duplicate ratio to injure us by annihilating the rising desire in the Southern States of effecting a better national system, and by adding to their jealousies of the designs of New England." Henry Knox to Stephen Higginson, Jan. 28, 1787, Francis S. Drake, ed. *Life and Correspondence of Henry Knox* (1873), pp. 93–94.

[31] Madison was reappointed to Virginia's delegation in Congress in December, and he arrived in New York by February 9, 1787. James Madison to James Monroe, Feb. 11, 1787, *PJM*, 9: 260.

[32] Rufus King to Elbridge Gerry, Feb. 11, 1787, *LMCC*, VIII: 539.

[33] James Madison to George Washington, Feb. 21, 1787, *PJM*, 9: 285–286. Maryland officially appointed delegates on April 23, 1787.

[34] James Madison to Edmund Pendleton, Feb. 24, 1787, *PJM*, 9: 294. See also Rufus King to Elbridge Gerry, Feb. 18, 1787, *LMCC*, VIII: 541; James Madison to Edmund Randolph, Feb. 25, 1787, *PJM*, 9: 299.

Boston newspaper, published an anonymous request for a five-state New England confederation that would "leave the rest of the Continent to pursue their own imbecile and disjointed plans."[35] Rufus King immediately recognized the political implications of the coalition that seemed to have formed between the mid-Atlantic and southern states, and he reported to Gerry that "Pennsylvania and [New] Jersey will be entirely under a *southern Influence*" and, therefore, there was "no mischief to public Credit, in the settlement of accounts, and in the just claim of the states, which may not be apprehended." Moreover, according to King, these new alignments made the decision to attend the convention "so problematical, that I confess I am at some loss. I am rather inclined to the measure from an idea of prudence, or for the purpose of watching, than from an expectation that much Good will flow from it."[36]

Pennsylvania's decision to attend the convention had neutralized Massachusetts' threat of dividing the existing Union into northern commercial and southern agricultural confederacies. Without Pennsylvania and commercially important Philadelphia, the viability of a New England confederacy did not seem particularly promising. Once Massachusetts delegates to Congress realized they had been outmaneuvered by Virginia and Pennsylvania, they moved to regain control over the process of constitutional change by not only proposing congressional endorsement of a convention "for the sole and express purpose of revising the Articles of Confederation," but also by requiring that "alterations and provisions" subsequently recommended be approved by "Congress and confirmed by the States."[37]

The Massachusetts legislature also resolved to send delegates to the proposed constitutional convention, although it instructed them "by no means to interfere with the fifth of the articles of the Confederation" – the article containing the rule of equal state apportionment.[38] To Madison,

---

Madison was confident "[t]he States South of Virg[in]ia still adhere as far as I can learn to the same ideas as have governed Virginia." New Jersey "instructed her Delegates ag[ain]st surrendering to Spain the navigation of the River even for a limited time. And Pen[nsylvani]a it is expected will do the same." James Madison to Thomas Jefferson, Feb. 15, 1787, *PJM*, 9: 268–269.

[35] *The Independent Chronicle and Universal Advertiser* (Boston, Feb. 15, 1787), XIX (955).

[36] Rufus King to Elbridge Gerry, Feb. 18, 1787, *LMCC*, VIII: 541.

[37] *JCC*, XXXII: 74 (Feb. 21, 1787).

[38] *Acts and Resolves of Massachusetts, 1786–87*, Feb. 21[22], 1787, in *The Documentary History of the Ratification of the Constitution* (1976), I: 205–206. Two weeks before Massachusetts imposed this restriction, the Delaware legislature imposed a similar but more explicit restriction against a change in "that Part of the Fifth Article" guaranteeing that "each State shall have one Vote" in Congress. See *The Documentary History of the Ratification of the Constitution* (1976), I: 203; Max Farrand, ed., *Records of*

this "fetter" against a change in the Articles' apportionment rule "denote[d] a very different spirit in that quarter from what some had been led to expect." The Massachusetts legislature subsequently rescinded this restriction after discovering, according to Madison's account, "the states own delegates, had voted in favor of an unlimited authority for the convention." Pennsylvania delegate William Irvine offered a different and slightly more realistic interpretation of this reversal. "It was," Irvine recounted, "with some difficulty [that] Congress carried the recommendation for a Convention. [T]he Eastern Delegates were all much against the measure. [I]ndeed I think they would never have come into, but they saw it would be carried without them," only "then they Joined." The result was that Congress's endorsement of the Philadelphia convention was "a piece of patch work" which, he confessed, "was thought better, than to keep up the smallest appearance of opposition to public view."[39]

Massachusetts' commitment to attend the Philadelphia convention proved a turning point for several other states as well. New York appointed delegates on March 6; Connecticut on May 2; and New Hampshire on June 27. Only Rhode Island, the final New England state, steadfastly refused to appoint any delegates.[40] With the commitment of all but one state for the Philadelphia convention, Madison left New York and Congress on May 5 and traveled to Philadelphia to prepare for the upcoming convention. Several weeks later, the Confederation Congress would lose its quorum and would not reconvene until early July when several delegates left the Philadelphia convention deadlocked over the rule of apportionment, traveled back to New York, and enacted a new western lands policy that settled the process for new state admissions and proscribed the establishment of slavery north of the Ohio River.

CONCLUSION

The road to Philadelphia was traveled by many interests. Nationalist-minded delegates journeyed to the 1787 Constitutional Convention

---

the Federal Convention of 1787 (New Haven, CT: Yale University Press, 1911), III: 574–575.

   The editors of the Madison Papers concluded that the "fetter" was a reference to the Articles' prohibition against serving more than "three years in any term of six years." See *PJM*, 9: 308n.3. Although plausible, this interpretation is at odds with the historical context and a preponderance of evidence to the contrary.

[39] James Madison to George Washington, Feb. 21, 1787, *PJM*, 8: 285; James Madison to Edmund Randolph, March 11, 1787, *PJM*, 9: 307; James Madison to George Washington, March 18, 1787, *PJM*, 9: 314–316; Farrand, *Records* (April 9, 1787), III: 584–485; William Irvine to James Wilson, March 6, 1787, *LMCC*, VIII: 551.
[40] Farrand, *Records*, III: 579–581; 585; 572–573.

hopeful of correcting the international reputation, the domestic irrelevancy and the "lethargic Imbecility" of the national government. Many delegates from New England and the mid-Atlantic traveled carrying their desires for a national government empowered with the authority to regulate domestic commerce and the leverage to open new foreign markets. Several delegates from southern states envisioned a reinvigorated national government that would spur on the development of the west. More financially minded delegates were motivated by their interests in the security of debt obligations and the value of public currencies. Other delegates expressed interest in controlling the "vices" of state governance and the need to reestablish a seemingly lost political world of disinterestedness and public virtue. Still others were no doubt motivated by more simple personal interests – not the least of which was the possibility of participating in the wholesale transformation of a political order.

Ahead of this caravan of interests were the delegates from Virginia. Like the other delegates, the Virginians had personal and political interests that prompted their enthusiastic endorsement of a national constitutional convention. Among the most important of these interests was a change in the national rule of apportionment. This change, James Madison suggested before the Convention, would be achieved without much difficulty for a "majority of the States conceive that they will be gainers by it." Madison reasoned: "To the Northern States it will be recommended by their present populousness; to the Southern by their expected advantage in this respect. The lesser States must in every event yield to the predominant will. But the consideration which particularly urges a change in the representation is that it will obviate the principal objections of the larger States" – both those in the present and those expected in the future – "to the necessary concessions of power."[41]

How this multiplicity of overlapping, conflicting, and contradictory interests and their attendant national, regional, state, group, individual, and historical purposes were ultimately coordinated into a consensus for a new constitutional framework and a new national rule of apportionment is a difficult question well worth pondering. For it strips the 1787 Convention of its familiar appearance, robs its historic product, the U.S. Constitution, of its schooled inevitability, and raises a bar that now must be confronted in Chapter 7.

---

[41] James Madison to Thomas Jefferson, March 19, 1787, *PJM*, 9: 318; James Madison to George Washington, April 16, 1787, *The Writings of James Madison*, II: 345.

7

The Veil of Representational Certainty: The 1787 Constitutional Convention and the Making of the U.S. Constitution

The economic, demographic, institutional, and ideological conditions described in Chapter 5 and the sequence of decisions analyzed in Chapter 6 constitute the remote and immediate causes of the abandonment of the Articles of Confederation. This chapter completes the story of this second constitutional and apportionment rule change by examining the deliberations and decisions of the 1787 Convention that produced a new national constitution and a new national rule of apportionment.

The new apportionment rule included within the U.S. Constitution established a dual form of state representation within the U.S. Congress: equal state representation in the U.S. Senate and a form of proportional state representation in the U.S. House of Representatives. In the former, each state was granted two senators regardless of its population and each senator voted individually. In the House, representation was divided among the states according to each state's respective "Numbers." These numbers were to be determined for each state by adding the whole number of free and indentured persons to three-fifths of the total number of enslaved persons. "Indians" who did not pay taxes were not to be included in a state's total. This constitutional rule required an initial enumeration of the American population within three years of the first Congress, and a new census every ten years. It also established that the number of representatives in the House of Representatives cannot exceed one representative for every 30,000 persons, and every state was guaranteed at least one member. Until completion of first national census, the House was to consist of 65 members distributed among the thirteen states as shown Table 7.1.

The process that produced this new "double" rule of apportionment dominated the deliberations of the 1787 Constitutional Convention from

TABLE 7.1. *Constitutional Apportionment of
the U.S. House of Representatives*

New Hampshire	3	Delaware	1
Massachusetts	8	Maryland	6
Rhode Island	1	Virginia	10
Connecticut	5	North Carolina	5
New York	6	South Carolina	5
New Jersey	4	Georgia	3
Pennsylvania	8		

its first full day of debate on May 30 to its final day September 17, 1787.[1]
As in previous continental congresses, discussion of the rule of apportionment both affected and was embedded within a much larger discourse concerning the external, the domestic, and the intragovernmental
constitutions of the American political order.

This chapter, although focused solely on the 1787 Convention, does
not provide a definitive account of its deliberations or the final word on
its decisions.[2] The historical record of this four-month long process is far
too fragmentary and the individual interests of the constitution makers
are far too complex to be reduced to simple or necessarily stable analytical constructs.[3] Unlike other accounts, however, this one reconstructs

---

[1] As Madison wrote to Martin Van Buren in 1828: "The *threatening contest*, in the Convention of 1787 did not, as you supposed, turn on the degree of power to be granted to
the Federal Govt: but on the rule by which the States should be represented and vote
in the Govt: the smaller States insisting on the rule of equality in all respects; the larger on
the rule of proportion to inhabitants: and the Compromise which ensued was that which
established an equality in the Senate, and an inequality in the House of Representatives.
The conflicts & compromises, turning on the grants of power, tho' very important in
some instances, were Knots of a less 'Gordian' character." *Records of the Constitutional
Convention* (New Haven, CT, Yale University Press, 1911), III: 477, May 13, 1828.

[2] Scholarship on the Constitutional Convention is too extensive to be fully recognized here.
See, for example, George Bancroft, *History of the Formation of the Constitution* (New
York: D. Appleton and Company, 1882); Charles Warren, *The Making of the Constitu-
tion* (Boston: Little, Brown, 1929); Clinton Rossiter, *1787: The Grand Convention* (New
York: The Macmillan Co., 1966); Forrest McDonald, *Novus Ordo Seclorum* (Lawrence,
KS: University Press of Kansas, 1985), pp. 225–260; Richard B. Morris, *Witness at the
Creation* (New York: Holt, Rinehart, and Winston 1985); and Jack N. Rakove, *Origi-
nal Meanings: Politics and Ideas in the Making of the Constitution* (New York: Knopf,
1996).

[3] Two obstacles impede every analysis of the formulation of the U.S. Constitution. The
first obstacle is the fragmentary quality of the historical record of the deliberations of
the 1787 Constitutional Convention. It was not open to the public and, therefore, there
are almost no independent accounts of its proceedings. The delegates generally refrained

the deliberations and decisions that yielded a new rule of apportionment and a second national constitution with a sensitivity to both the available historical evidence and the theoretical problematics associated with consensual constitutional change.

Like the formation of the Articles of Confederation, the process of redefining the American political order and of formulating the text of the U.S. Constitution pivoted on the definition of the apportionment rule. Unlike the earlier process, however, this second formative process was orchestrated largely by actors committed to or willing to accept an expansion of the authority of the national government. The primary concerns of these constitution makers were more focused on the determination of each state and interest's relative decision-making capacities within a new national government – and, thus, the terms of a new rule of apportionment.

The account of the establishment of the Articles of Confederation (in Chapter 4) subsumed the dynamics driving this process into a general claim concerning the formation of a political order based on the consent of its principal members: the claim that levels of governmental authority and decision-making capacity are positively and reflexively related and, therefore, that the founding of a new political order requires the convergence of political expectations on these two dimensions. This

from reporting on their deliberations in private correspondence. Reconstruction of the deliberations and decisions of the Convention must be based, therefore, on the Convention's journals and the notes taken by several delegates. None of this material was made public until decades after the Convention had concluded its business. The notes of James Madison provide the most extensive account, offering a virtual dialogue of several parts of the deliberations. These notes were made public posthumously in 1840. Although several historians have openly doubted the veracity of Madison's account, there is no conclusive basis for such doubt. But it must be noted that during the decades after the Convention, Madison edited and copied these notes. Compared to the limited quantity or questionable integrity of the published notes of other delegates, Madison's notes offer the most credible basis for reconstructing the Convention's deliberations. For more on these issues, see James H. Hutson, "Introduction," *Supplement to Max Farrand's The Records of the Federal Convention of 1787* (New Haven, CT: Yale University Press, 1987), pp. xv–xxvi; and Adrienne Koch, "Introduction," *Notes of Debates in the Federal Convention of 1787 Reported by James Madison* (Athens, OH: Ohio University Press, 1966), pp. vii–xxiii).

The second obstacle arises from the task of untangling the web of crosscutting cleavages that existed among and within the state delegations. Based on available records, it is clear that the voting behavior of several delegates and most state delegations was not consistent. Whether this inconsistency can be attributed to real changes in preferences, strategic voting, or to the evidential record is a matter for interpretative speculation. For more on shifts in state voting patterns at the Convention, see Calvin Jillson, *Constitution Making* (1987).

account of the redefinition of the American political order at the 1787 Constitutional Convention provides a corollary claim: when general preferences for the level of governmental authority are shared among constitution makers, the consensual formation of a political order requires that they possess a sense of security about the short- and long-term representation of their interests within the proposed order. Conversely, constitution makers who are uncertain or ignorant of their immediate and future representation (in other words, of their decision-making capacities) generally tend to refrain from making constitutional commitments. If, therefore, consent (and not coercion) is the basis for establishing a new framework of national-level governance, then a rule of apportionment must be crafted that offers a veil of representational certainty through which the constitution makers gain confidence concerning the relative strength of their positions in the immediate and long-term future.

The following account tracks the deliberations of the convention by focusing on the individual delegates, state delegations, and multistate coalitions that attempted to secure representation within the new and more powerful government widely expected to replace the Articles of Confederation. Part I centers on the deliberations of the first half of the Convention, which by early July were deadlocked over the rule of apportionment. Part II focuses on the resolution of this deadlock and the adoption of the double rule of apportionment ultimately incorporated into the U.S. Constitution.

PART I: A CONTEST FOR POWER, NOT FOR LIBERTY

Delegates appointed by their respective state legislatures began arriving in Philadelphia as early as the first week of May 1787, but most arrived several weeks later than expected. James Madison and the Virginia delegation made good use of the delay. They had arrived early; Madison on May 3, more than a week before the Convention was scheduled to convene and more than three weeks before its deliberations finally began. During this time, the Virginia delegation and several resident Pennsylvania delegates shared and refined their ideas and strategies on how to complete the wholesale changes in the national governmental framework they envisioned as necessary for reconstituting the Union.[4]

---

[4] This early collaboration between the Virginia and Pennsylvania delegations continued throughout the Convention as evidenced by their subsequent voting behavior. For a

As with previous continental congresses, the rule of apportionment was widely expected to be one of the first discussed by the delegates. Before the Convention officially convened members of the Pennsylvania delegation privately approached the Virginia delegation with a plan to insist on the adoption of new proportional voting procedures as soon as a quorum was achieved. The Virginia delegation rejected this stratagem, arguing that any change in the voting rules would lead the smaller, less wealthy states to abandon the Convention. This would disrupt the ratification process that Madison and others envisioned and jeopardize the entire project of reform. Better, the Virginians advised, to have the small states participate in the Convention's deliberations where they would be either convinced or cajoled to accept the much-desired change in the rule of apportionment.[5]

The Virginia Plan

The Convention's deliberations began in earnest on May 29 when Virginia delegate Edmund Randolph submitted fifteen provisions for consideration.[6] Among them, the so-called Virginia plan called for replacement of the Articles' rule of equal state apportionment with a proportional state rule. Representation in a new bicameral Congress, according to this plan, was to be divided in one house according "to the quotas of contribution, or to the number of free inhabitants, as the one or the other rule may seem best in different cases."[7] The Virginia plan additionally proposed popular election to this house. These representatives were then to elect the second house from a list of candidates nominated by the state legislatures. The net effect of this double-election process magnified the significance of the proposed proportional state rule for the first legislative house because the dominant interests represented there would likely be able to ensure the election of similarly interested persons to the second branch.

thorough, roll-call analysis of the voting coalitions within the Convention, see Jillson, *Constitution Making* (New York: Agathon Press, 1987); and S. Sidney Ulmer, "Sub-Group Formation in the Constitutional Convention," *Midwest Journal of Political Science* (1966), 10: 288–303.

[5] *Records*, I: 10 (May 28, 1787). Unless noted, all subsequent references to the *Records* are taken from James Madison's account.

[6] Charles Pinckney of South Carolina is also reported to have submitted a plan for confederation on the same day. See *Records*, Appendix D, III: 595–609.

[7] *Records*, I: 35 (May 30, 1787).

The Virginia plan proposed other novel institutions for reconstituting the national governmental framework. It called for a National Executive with "a general authority to execute the National laws" and "a council of revision" comprised of the Executive and the Judiciary that would have the authority to review national and state legislation before it became effective. Other provisions were less well defined. The tenth recommended only that the Convention provide for the "administration" of new states; and the thirteenth even more broadly called for a process for adopting additional amendments "whensoever it shall seem necessary." Congress was broadly empowered "to legislate in all cases to which the separate States are incompetent" and to veto state legislation that it deemed unconstitutional. Finally, as Madison had suggested before the Convention, the Virginia plan proposed a ratification process that required the assent of all changes by special assemblies "expressly chosen by the people."[8]

For two weeks the Convention debated the Virginia plan. Several provisions were readily accepted, whereas others were approved only after amendment.[9] Agreement on still other provisions, especially those related to the rule of apportionment, were more problematic because the delegates realized that this decision would affect their immediate and long-term decision-making capacities within the new and more powerful national government.

The Rule of Apportionment

Supporters of a proportional state rule of apportionment were well organized prior to the Convention and they easily dominated the first debate on the subject. Madison initiated the debate on May 30, proposing a change in the Virginia plan provision he had privately recommended months before and only days before had helped craft into its final form. He suggested that the words "*or to the number of free inhabitants*" might impede the Convention's progress, so he "moved that they might be struck out."[10]

---

[8] *Records*, I: 21–22 (May 29, 1787).

[9] On May 30, the Convention agreed that the first provision would call for the creation of a new national government consisting of legislative, executive, and judicial branches. The next day, it accepted without debate the plan's provisions for a bicameral Congress and for permitting legislation to originate in both houses. A week later, delegates provided for a single Executive and for life tenure for the national judiciary. *Records*, I: 35 (May 30, 1787); I: 48, 52 (May 31, 1787); I: 97 (June 4); I: 121 (June 5).

[10] *Records*, I: 35–36 (May 30, 1787).

Rufus King of Massachusetts, although a consistent advocate of the principle of proportional representation, disputed Madison's seemingly modest proposal. King remarked "that the quotas of contribution which alone remain as the measure of representation" would not be sufficient because the revenue collected by the national government from the states would continually vary. Another advocate of proportional representation, New York delegate Alexander Hamilton, apparently agreed with King and proposed that representation be apportioned only according "to the number of free inhabitants." With the basis for disagreement on the terms of apportionment exposed but confined to the options of taxation or population, Madison abandoned his amendment and recommended more broadly that representation be apportioned only according to "an equitable ratio."[11]

Delegates from several of the smaller states, not surprisingly, were troubled that the initial debate over the apportionment rule was limited only to proportional forms of representation because each proposal promised to transfer their existing decision-making weight within Congress to the more populous states. George Read of Delaware, one of the smallest states, declared his opposition to any change in the rule of apportionment that would leave his state without adequate representation. He also reminded the Convention that "the deputies from Delaware were restrained by their commission from assenting to any change of the rule of suffrage," and if a change occurred "it might become their duty to retire from the Convention."[12]

Gouverneur Morris of Pennsylvania, one of the organizers of the preconvention effort to change the Convention's voting rules, dismissed Read's threatened exit. Morris conceded that "the valuable assistance of [Delaware's] members could not be lost without real concern" but "the change proposed was however so fundamental an article in a national Govt. that it could not be dispensed with."[13]

James Madison appeared more tactful but no more convincing in his attempt to convince Read and the other small state delegates of the necessity of the apportionment rule change. He weakly reasoned that "as the acts of the Genl. Govt. would take effect without the intervention of the State legislatures, a vote from a small State wd. have the same efficacy & importance as ⟨a vote⟩ from a large one, and there was the same reason for ⟨different numbers⟩ of representatives from different States, as from

[11] *Records*, I: 35–36 (May 30, 1787).   [12] *Records*, I: 37 (May 30, 1787).
[13] *Records*, I: 37 (May 30, 1787).

Counties of different extents within particular States." Like most states at the time, however, Delaware had not yet adopted a rule of proportionality for representation within her state legislature. Perhaps recognizing his blunder, or perhaps conceding that his arguments had baffled more than they had persuaded their intended audience, Madison suggested that additional discussion of the proposed change in the rule of apportionment would best be continued at a later time.[14]

House Elections

With debate on the rule of apportionment temporarily tabled, deliberations on other provisions of the Virginia plan provided additional opportunities for indirectly continuing this pivotal debate. On May 31 and again on June 6, delegates debated the provision for popular election to the first branch of the new Congress. Connecticut delegate Roger Sherman opposed this provision because, he argued, it gave the people too much power. The people "are constantly liable to be misled," he contended, and therefore "should have as little to do with Government as possible." Elbridge Gerry of Massachusetts was similarly disdainful of popular involvement in government. "The evils we experience," he declared, "flow from the excess of democracy." The people "are the dupes of pretended patriots" and "they are daily misled into the most baneful measures and opinions by false reports circulated by designing men, and which no one on the spot can refute." Gerry further insisted that popular election would insure "the worst men get into the Legislature," while appointment of members of Congress by the state legislatures would allow "demogogues and corrupt members" to "creep in." He therefore recommended "that the people should appoint one branch of the Govt. in order to inspire them with the necessary confidence," and "the election of the other to be so modified as to secure more effectually a just preference of merit."[15]

George Mason of Virginia offered a different view. He "argued strongly for an election of the larger branch by the people." The House of Representatives, he envisioned, "was to be the grand depository of

---

[14] *Records*, I: 37 (May 30, 1787).

[15] *Records*, I: 48 (May 31, 1787); I: 132; Yates I: 140 (June 6, 1787); I: 132, King I: 142 (June 6, 1787). Gerry proposed popular nomination of double the number of candidates "in certain districts, out of whom the State Legislatures shd. make the appointment." I: 132.

the democratic principle of the Govt. . . . It ought to know & sympathize with every part of the community; and ought therefore to be taken not only from different parts of the whole republic, but also from different districts" within the states which often had "different interests and views." Mason "admitted that we had been too democratic but" he feared the Convention might "incautiously run into the opposite extreme." Instead, "We ought to attend to the rights of every class of people" and "to recommend such a system of policy as would provide no less carefully for the rights – and happiness of the lowest than of the highest order of Citizens."[16]

"Under the existing Confederacy," Mason continued, "Congs. represent the *States* not the *people* of the States: their acts operate on the *States* not on the individuals." This "will be changed in the new plan of Govt. The people will be represented; they ought therefore to choose the Representatives." Moreover, "[t]he requisites in actual representation are that the Rep[resentative]s should sympathize with their constituents, sh[oul]d think as they think, & feel as they feel; and for these purposes sh[oul]d even be residents among them." Mason admitted that much had been said against democratic elections, "but it was to be considered that no Govt. was free from imperfections & evils; and that improper elections in many instances, were inseparable from Republican Govts. But compare these" he advised, "with the advantage of this Form in favor of the rights of the people, in favor of human nature."[17]

James Wilson agreed. The Pennsylvania delegate proposed "drawing the most numerous branch of the Legislature immediately from the people" because "the federal pyramid" ought to have "as broad a basis as possible" and the authority of government ought "to flow immediately from the legitimate source of all authority" – the people. "No government," he warned, especially not a republican one, "could long subsist without the confidence of the people." The government, therefore, should have both the *"force"* and the *"sense* of the people at large." Indeed, it "ought to be the most exact transcript of the whole Society." Moreover, Wilson stressed, it was "wrong to increase the weight of the State Legislatures by making them the electors of the national Legislature" because it was "Officers of the States" who had opposed the national government in the past. The people, he claimed, cared only for

[16] *Records*, I: 48–49 (May 31, 1787).
[17] *Records*, I: 133–134 (June 6, 1787).

good government and would readily accept a stronger national government because it would be "more flattering to their pride."[18]

Madison concurred with Mason and Wilson. He "considered the popular election of one branch of the national Legislature as essential to every plan of free Government" and "that this mode under proper regulations had the additional advantage of securing better representatives, as well as of avoiding too great an agency of the State Governments in the General one."[19] If other methods of election were adopted "the people would be lost sight of altogether; and the necessary sympathy between them and their rulers and officers, too little felt." Madison admitted he "was an advocate for the policy of refining the popular appointments by successive filtrations," but election by the state legislatures pushed this policy too far.[20] Instead, he wanted "the expedient to be resorted to only in the appointment of the second branch of the Legislature, and in the Executive and judiciary." Madison concluded, "the great fabric to be raised" by a popularly elected House of Representatives "would be more stable and durable if it should rest on the solid foundation of the people themselves, than if it should stand merely on the pillars of the Legislatures."[21]

On May 31, the Convention approved the provision for popular election of the House; a week later, on June 6, the delegates reaffirmed this vote with an even larger consensus by rejecting a proposal to have state legislatures elect the House of Representatives.[22]

Senate Elections

The method of electing the second branch of Congress, the Senate, offered another opportunity for the delegates to debate issues related to

[18] *Records*, I: 49 (May 31, 1787); I: 132–133 (June 6, 1787); I: 49 (May 31, 1787); I: 133 (June 6, 1787).

[19] *Records*, I: 49–50 (May 31, 1787); I: 134 (June 6, 1787).

[20] Wilson, Mason (I: 134) and Madison (I: 144) recommended election of representatives from large districts. See contrary arguments by Charles Pinckney (I: 143) and Alexander Hamilton (I: 147).

On August 9, the Convention rejected a proposal to strip Congress of any authority to regulate congressional elections. *Records*, II: 240–241 (Aug. 9, 1787). The Convention subsequently agreed that "The Times, Places and Manner of holding elections for Senators and Representatives, shall be prescribed in each State by the Legislature thereof; but the Congress may at any time by Law make or alter such Regulations, except as to the Places of chusing Senators" (Art. I, Sec. 4 of the U.S. Constitution).

[21] Farrand, *Records*, I: 49–50 (May 31, 1787). On June 6, Madison continued his defense of a popularly elected House with arguments culled from his pre-Convention "Vices" memorandum. See *Records*, I; 134–136 (June 6, 1787).

[22] *Records*, I: 50 (May 31, 1787); I: 137–138 (June 6, 1787).

the proposed apportionment rule change. The Virginia plan called for the House to elect the Senate "out of persons nominated by the State Legislatures." The convention rejected this method of election on May 31 and unanimously adopted a proposal on June 7 that gave state legislatures the responsibility for electing the Senate.[23]

The rejection of the Virginia plan provision for senatorial elections confirmed that the Convention would not automatically accept all the constitutional changes envisioned by Madison and the Virginia delegation. It also opened the Convention's deliberations to the possibility of modifying the Virginia plan's proposal for a proportional state rule of apportionment. Opponents of the rule focused on the likely consequences of combining a rule of proportional state representation with state election of senators and the proposal for a small Senate.

Supporters of a proportional state rule of apportionment consistently advocated the necessity of establishing a small Senate.[24] Virginia delegate Edmund Randolph argued that the size of the Senate "ought to be much smaller than that of the first [branch]; so small as to be exempt from the passionate proceedings to which numerous assemblies are liable." James Madison agreed and added that the Senate was expected to proceed "with more coolness, with more system, & with more wisdom, than the popular branch. Enlarge their number and you communicate to them the vices which they are meant to correct." A large Senate, like the ancient Roman Tribunes, would lose "their influence and power, in proportion as their number was augmented. . . . The more the representatives of the people therefore were multiplied, the more they partook of the infirmities of their constituents, the more liable they became to be divided among themselves either from their own indiscretions or the artifices of the opposite factions, and of course the less capable of fulfilling their trust." The guiding principle, Madison recommended, was "[w]hen the weight of a set of men depends merely on their personal characters; the greater the number the greater the weight" but "[w]hen it depends on

[23] *Records*, I: 156 (June 7, 1787). See also Mason's explanation of this decision, *Records*, I: 155–156 (June 7, 1787).

[24] Opponents of proportional representation were more divided on the Senate's size. Roger Sherman of Connecticut proposed a small Senate, favoring "an election of one member by each of the State Legislatures." *Records*, I: 52; Pierce, I: 59 (May 31, 1787). John Dickinson of Delaware openly hoped "there would be 80 and twice 80 of them." *Records*, I: 150 (June 7, 1787). "[L]et their numbers be more than 200" in the Senate for "If their number should be small, the popular branch could not be [ba]lanced by them." Moreover, he thought, "[t]he legislature of a numerous people ought to be a numerous body." *Records*, I: 158, King; I: 150 (June 7, 1787).

TABLE 7.2. *Projected Apportionment of Senate Based on 1785 Requisition Quota*

States	1785 Quota (percent)	Number of Senators			
		(n = 30) Ratio/Number		(n = 90) Ratio/Number	
Virginia	17.1	5.13	5	15.39	16
Massachusetts	15.0	4.50	5	13.50	14
Pennsylvania	13.7	4.11	4	12.33	12
Maryland	9.4	2.82	3	8.46	8
Connecticut	8.8	2.64	3	7.92	8
New York	8.5	2.55	3	7.65	8
North Carolina	7.3	2.19	2	6.57	6
South Carolina	6.4	1.92	2	5.76	6
New Jersey	5.6	1.68	2	5.04	5
New Hampshire	3.5	1.05	1	3.15	3
Rhode Island	2.1	.63	–	1.89	2
Delaware	1.5	.45	–	1.35	1
Georgia	1.1	.33	–	.99	1
	100.0		30		90

Note: The method used by Convention delegates to assign representation for fractional remainders is not clear from the available evidence. According to Brearly's convention notes, Virginia would receive a "sixteenth" senator in a 90-member Senate. The state's fractional remainder was .39, but the fractional remainder for North Carolina was .57. From this, it can be inferred that average state population per senator was the criterion used to assign additional members beyond a state's whole number quota. Still, anomalies remain. Brearly's notes, for example, also note fractional remainders of "senators" for several states. See *Records*, Brearly, I: 574, (July 10, 1787).

the degree of political authority lodged in them the smaller the number the greater the weight."[25]

Opponents of a proportional state rule of apportionment pointed out, however, that either several of the smallest states would not be permitted to elect a single senator or that the Senate would have to be increased to between eighty and one hundred members.[26] As illustrated in Table 7.2, a thirty-member Senate would leave three states without any direct representation, and a ninety-member Senate would barely entitle the smallest state to elect a single senator.

[25] *Records*, I: 51 (May 31, 1787); I: 151–152 (June 7, 1787).
[26] *Records*, I: 51–52 (May 31, 1787); Pierce, I: 58–59 (May 31, 1787). See also *Records*, I: 150, 155 (June 7, 1787).

The Rule of Apportionment Revisited

Invigorated by the rejection of the Virginia plan provision for senatorial elections and by the exposure of the inconsistencies of Madison's all-too-bookish plan to couple proportional representation in the House with a small Senate, opponents of proportional state representation moved to resume the Convention's debate on the rule of apportionment. New Jersey delegate David Brearly, an opponent of a change in the Articles' apportionment rule, argued that the issue of representation "had been much agitated in Cong[res]s at the time of forming the Confederation and was then rightly settled by allowing to each sovereign State an equal vote." He contended that proportional representation of the states exuded an appearance of "fairness on the face of it; but on a deeper examination was unfair and unjust." If, for example, the 1785 tax ratio were used to apportion representation, the three largest states (Virginia, Pennsylvania, and Massachusetts) would have forty-two of the ninety members in the proposed Senate – or four votes short of a majority. The smaller states, as a consequence, would "be obliged to throw themselves constantly into the scale of some large one, in order to have any weight at all." Brearly additionally suggested that if the proponents of proportional representation were committed only to establishing a more effective national government, then let "a map of the U.S. be spread out, that all the existing boundaries be erased, and that a new partition of the whole be made into 13 equal parts."[27] Brearly's cartographic invitation was memorable but no doubt most delegates suspected there had to be a less outlandish means for balancing the various interests of the union. (See, for example, Table 7.3.)

Other small-state delegates added their voices to this debate. "The Convention," New Jersey delegate William Paterson reminded his fellow delegates, "was formed in pursuance of an Act of Cong[res]s" and "amendment of the confederacy was the object" of their state commissions. "We ought to keep" within the limits of the Convention's original purpose, the New Jersey delegate cautioned, "or we should be charged by our constituents with usurpation. . . . We have no power to go beyond the federal scheme, and if we had the people are not ripe for any other." In addition, he queried, what was "intended by a proportional representation? Is property to be considered as part of it? Is a man, for example, possessing of £4000 to have 40 votes to one possessing only

[27] *Records*, I: 176–177 (June 9, 1787).

TABLE 7.3. *Projected Proportional State Representation in 90-Member Senate, Calculated from 1785 Tax Ratio*

States	Representatives	Percentage
Most Populous States (3)	42	46.7
Virginia		
Massachusetts		
Pennsylvania		
Mid-size States (7)	36	40.0
Maryland		
Connecticut		
New York		
North Carolina		
South Carolina		
Least Populous States (5)	12	13.3
New Jersey		
New Hampshire		
Rhode Island		
Delaware		
Georgia	–	–
TOTAL	90	100.0

Note: For 1785 requisition ratio, see *JCC*, XXIX: 745. See also *Records*, Paterson, I: 190, (June 9, 1787); Brearly, I: 574 (June 10, 1787).

£100?" Paterson reminded the Convention that "[i]t was once proposed by [Joseph] Galloway & some others that America should be represented in the British Parl[iamen]t and then be bound by its laws. America could not have been entitled to more than 1/3 of the no. of Representatives which would fall to the share of G[reat] B[ritain]. Would American rights & interests have been safe under an authority thus constituted?" he asked. Paterson additionally declared that if several states wanted to unite "let them remember that they have no authority to compel the others to unite. N[ew] Jersey," he threatened, "will never confederate on the plan before the Committee" and "[h]e had rather submit to a monarch, to a despot, than to such a fate."[28]

Proponents of proportional state representation, like James Wilson, dismissed Paterson's arguments by boldly asserting that "a majority, nay

[28] *Records*, I: 177–178 (June 9, 1787); Yates, I: 183 (June 9, 1787); I: 179 (June 9, 1787).

even a minority, of the states have a right to confederate with each other, and the rest may do as they please." Because, Wilson added, "all authority was derived from the people, equal numbers of people ought to have an equal no. of representatives, and different numbers of people different numbers of representatives. . . . Are not the citizens of Pen[nsylvani]a equal to those of N[ew] Jersey? does it require 150 of the former to balance 50 of the latter? Representatives of different districts ought clearly to hold the same proportion to each other, as their respective constituents hold to each other. If the small States will not confederate on this plan," Wilson presumed that Pennsylvania and "some other States, would not confederate on any other."[29]

Over the objections of several smaller state delegates, the Convention again agreed that "the right of suffrage ought [to be] . . . according to some equitable ratio of representation." James Wilson then proposed that state representation in the House be "in proportion to the whole number of white & other free Citizens & inhabitants of every age sex & condition including those bound to servitude for a term of years and three fifths of all other persons not comprehended in the foregoing description, except Indians not paying taxes." With only New Jersey and Delaware opposed, the Convention adopted this proportional state rule of apportionment for the House of Representatives.[30]

After this vote Connecticut delegate Roger Sherman moved that the Convention turn to the rule of apportionment for the Senate. "Every thing," he declared, "depended on this" because "[t]he smaller States would never agree to the plan on any other principle" than equal representation in at least one branch. Sherman's proposal for equal state

---

[29] *Records*, Yates, I: 183 (June 9, 1787); I: 179–180 (June 9, 1787).

[30] *Records*, I: 200–201 (June 11, 1787).

The three-fifths ratio likely was familiar to all of the delegates. In 1783, on the advice of James Madison, Congress included this ratio in a constitutional amendment proposal that was designed to increase Congress's taxation powers. It was widely acknowledged that this 1783 ratio was a compromise between southern and northern state delegates. Madison boasted at the time that his compromise proposal "that Slaves should be rated as 5 to 3" free persons both proved "his professions of liberality" and would become the "material to future harmony and justice among the members of the confederacy." See *JCC* (March 28, 1783), XXIV: 215; *PJM* (March 28, 1783), 6: 407–408 (April 1, 1783), 6:425; James Madison to Edmund Randolph, April 8, 1783, *LMCC*, VII: 127.

At the 1787 Convention, Massachusetts delegate Elbridge Gerry was one of the first to protest the inclusion of the three-fifths ratio into the rule of representation. Gerry contended that if taxable wealth was the proper standard for granting representation, then why should "the blacks, who were property in the South, be in the rule of representation more than the cattle & horses of the North." *Records*, I: 201 (June 11, 1787).

TABLE 7.4. *Convention Votes for Equal and Proportional Representation in Senate – June 11*

For Equal Representation in Senate		For Proportional Representation in Senate	
Aye (5)	No (6)	Aye (6)	No (5)
Connecticut	Massachusetts	Massachusetts	Connecticut
New York	Pennsylvania	Pennsylvania	New York
New Jersey	Virginia	Virginia	New Jersey
Delaware	N. Carolina	N. Carolina	Delaware
Maryland	S. Carolina	S. Carolina	Maryland
	Georgia	Georgia	

representation in the Senate was rejected, however, by a coalition consisting of the three largest states and the three southernmost states. By a narrow six-to-five majority, the Convention agreed that "the right of suffrage in the 2d. branch ought to be according to the same rule as in the 1st branch."[31] After about two weeks of debate, proponents of proportional state representation had convinced a majority of the state delegations at the Convention to replace the Articles' rule of equal state apportionment with a new proportional state rule for both houses of a new national Congress. See Table 7.4.

Constitutional changes of this magnitude – especially within political orders formed and maintained with the consent of its members – are rarely implemented by simple majorities. True to form, delegates from several smaller states remained unwilling to accept the proposed change for both houses of the new Congress. During the following weeks, they organized and intensified their efforts to undermine the coalition of states that had supported the rule of proportional state representation for the Senate. The efforts of these delegates took a variety of rhetorical forms. They crafted and proposed an alternative constitutional plan which few, if any, of its proponents believed had a serious chance of adoption. William Paterson of New Jersey nevertheless presented the so-called New Jersey plan on June 15. This plan mirrored several provisions already agreed to by the Convention, thus creating an alternative set of provisions that could be negotiated away for a single compromise on the issue of state representation in the Senate.

---

[31] *Records*, I: 201–202 (June 11, 1787).

Supporters of a proportional rule like Wilson, Hamilton, and Madison used three days of debate to discredit the hastily constructed New Jersey plan, while others succinctly dismissed the plan by exposing the motives of its advocates. "Give N[ew] Jersey an equal vote," Charles Pinckney of South Carolina declared, "and she will dismiss her scruples, and concur in the Nat[iona]l system."[32]

Advocates of equal state representation in the Senate were undeterred by the wholesale rejection of the New Jersey plan. They refocused their protests against the proposed rule change by challenging the Convention's authority to propose constitutional changes. Although the Convention had already agreed in principle that sweeping constitutional changes were necessary, New York delegate John Lansing now contended that "the power of the Convention was restrained to amendments of a federal nature, and having for their basis the Confederacy in being." He also opposed the method of popular ratification earlier approved by the Convention not only because it could "be a source of great dissentions" but because "It could not be expected that those possessing Sovereignty could ever voluntarily part with it."[33]

Oliver Ellsworth of Connecticut and Luther Martin of Maryland, both opponents of the proportional state rule, agreed. Ellsworth contended that popular ratification would lead to "several succeeding Conventions within the States" which he deemed "better fitted to pull down than to build up Constitutions." Martin questioned the legitimacy of forcing constitutional change on unwilling states: "Is the old confederation dissolved, because some of the states wish a new confederation?"[34]

---

[32] *Records*, I: 255 (June 16, 1787). The provisions of the New Jersey plan were as unoriginal as they evidently were negotiable. The first provision repeated the Virginia plan's call for the Articles to be "revised, corrected & enlarged." The third provision included a recycled version of the 1783 requisition amendment that already failed to be ratified by the States despite Congress's repeated efforts to gain their unanimous consent. The New Jersey plan, moreover, failed to propose a new means for ratification, implicitly relying on the problematic requirement of the Articles that every state consent to constitutional amendments.

Other provisions of the New Jersey plan mirrored several already approved by the Convention. Where the new Committee of the Whole Plan called for a bicameral legislature with proportional representation, the New Jersey plan proposed a *unicameral* legislature with *equal* representation. Where the former called for a single Executive and judicial appointment by the Senate, the latter proposed a *plural* Executive and *executive* appointment of the national judiciary. The New Jersey plan, moreover, proposed empowering Congress with *specific* powers, whereas the Committee Report gave Congress broad power "to legislate in all cases to which the separate States are incompetent." *Records*, I: 242–244 (June 15, 1787).

[33] See *Records*, I: 214 (June 12, 1787); I: 336–337 (June 20, 1787).

[34] *Records*, I: 335 (June 20, 1787); Yates, I: 455 (June 28, 1787).

William Paterson continued this assault against proportional representation by doubting the level of popular support for a proportional rule of apportionment. The New Jersey delegate argued that the people desired a more powerful and efficient Congress, not more representation or democratic reform. "With proper powers," he contended, a Congress based on equal representation "will act with more energy & wisdom than the proposed Nat[iona]l Legislature" because it will be "fewer in number, and more secreted & refined by the mode of election." Paterson also raised financial concerns. "Allowing Georgia and Del[aware] two representatives each in the popular branch," he calculated, "the aggregate number of that branch will be 180. Add to it half as many for the other branch and you have 270 members. . . . In the present deranged State of our finances can so expensive a system be seriously thought of?"[35]

Connecticut delegate Roger Sherman complained that a bicameral and popularly elected Congress would "embarrass" the new government. "The People," he argued, "would not much interest themselves in the elections," and "a few designing men in the large districts would carry their points." The result would be that "the people would have no more confidence in their new representatives than in" the present Congress under the Articles. "If," however, "the difficulty on the subject of representation can not be otherwise got over," Sherman announced he could accept proportional representation provided "each State had an equal voice in" one of the branches. "This," according to the Connecticut delegate, "was necessary to secure the rights of the lesser States; otherwise three or four of the large States would rule the others as they please."[36]

This barrage against proportional representation prompted several delegates to defend the proposed apportionment rule change. Pennsylvania delegate James Wilson argued – with a surprising ignorance of the nonproportional apportionment schemes used in almost every state senate – that if equal representation was injected into any part of the constitutional plan it would be "a poison contaminating every branch of Govt." In Great Britain "this poison has had a full operation," and "the security of private rights" depends entirely on the courts because the judiciary "are neither appointed nor paid by a venal Parliament. . . . The political liberty of that Nation owing to the inequality of representation is at the mercy of its rulers" and the lesson to be learned is "that the

---

[35] *Records,* I: 251–252 (June 16, 1787).
[36] *Records,* I: 342–343 (June 20, 1787).

smallest bodies in G[reat] B[ritain] are notoriously the most corrupt" and least resistant to outside influences.[37]

Alexander Hamilton and James Madison also defended proportional representation. Hamilton argued that the principle of equal representation violated "the ideas of Justice, and every human feeling" and he declared that its proponents were engaged in "a contest for power, not for liberty."[38] Madison pointed out that a proportional rule was necessary if new states were ever to be admitted into the Union. Give these states representation according to their population and "all would be right and safe. Let them have an equal vote, and a more objectionable minority then ever might give law to the whole."[39] Girded, in part, by the arguments of Madison and Hamilton, a majority of the states reaffirmed their support for a rule of proportional state representatives in the House of Representatives on June 29.[40] Since the initial vote on this issue on June 11, Connecticut had withdrawn her support, thereby decreasing the number of states supporting the rule to six: the three largest states and the three southernmost states still comprising a winning majority coalition. After the June 29 vote, advocates of the equal state rule recognized that at least one of the six states in the majority would have to be convinced to change its vote in order for them to secure an equal state rule for the Senate.[41]

Although the idea of proportional representation may appear as the more easily defended position from a modern perspective, advocates of equal state representation offered arguments that resonated more strongly and clearly with the times. The small-state strategy of relentlessly attacking the idea of proportional representation raised questions among several proportional representation supporters. New York delegate Alexander Hamilton admitted that he had not been persuaded by Madison's arguments that proportional representation was necessary for "enlarging the sphere" of the Union. "The extent of the Country to be governed discouraged him" as did the expense of the new national

---

[37] *Records*, I: 253–254 (June 16, 1787).
[38] *Records*, I: 286 (June 18, 1787); I: 466 (June 29, 1787). Hamilton readily admitted that: "The State of Delaware having 40,000 souls will *lose power*, if she had 1/10 only of the votes allowed to Pa. having 400,000: but," he asked, "will the people of Del[aware]: *be less free*, if each citizen has an equal vote with each citizen of P[ennsylvani]a?"
[39] *Records*, I: 322 (June 19, 1787).
[40] *Records*, I: 468 (June 29, 1787).
[41] Maryland's vote was divided on proportional representation in the House. However, it consistently rejected proportional representation in the Senate. See *Records*, I: 202 (June 11); I: 510 (July 2).

government. The most serious problem, however, "was that of drawing representatives from the extremes to the center of the Community." "What inducements can be offered that will suffice?" Modest wages for representatives "would only be a bait to little demagogues." Hamilton thus concluded that the proposed plan was too "democratic" and would result in a "feeble and inefficient" government.[42]

Connecticut delegate Oliver Ellsworth, an equal state representation proponent, subsequently expanded on Hamilton's criticism to argue that the interests of the state legislatures needed to be protected. "Without their cooperation," he contended, "it would be impossible to support a Republican Govt. over so great an extent of Country. An army could scarcely render it practicable. The largest States are the Worst Governed." Virginia cannot "extend her Govt. to Kentucky," Massachusetts struggles to "keep the peace one hundred miles from her capitol," and Pennsylvania is not immune from similar problems. "If the principles & materials of our Govt. are not adequate to the extent of these single States; how can it be imagined that they can support a single Govt. throughout the U[nited] States."[43]

James Madison inadvertently bolstered the small state strategy to gain a compromise when he admitted during his attack on the New Jersey plan that the Convention's "great difficulty lies in the affair of Representation and if this could be adjusted, all others would be surmountable." Nathaniel Gorham of Massachusetts subsequently extended the logic of Madison's observation when announcing that he was now "inclined to a compromise as to the rule of proportion." Gorham also agreed "there was some weight in the objections of the small States," particularly the argument that Virginia's representatives would be inclined to vote as a bloc, and thus possess an "undue influence" in Congress.[44]

Madison further legitimized expectations for an eventual compromise when he informed the Convention he "was much disposed to concur in any expedient not inconsistent with fundamental principles, that could remove the difficulty concerning the rule of representation."[45] He suggested "Gradual partitions of the large, & junctions of the small ⟨States⟩." The Convention ignored Madison's compromise proposal, but on the following day Samuel Johnson of Connecticut proposed a more

---

[42] *Records*, I: 287–288; I: 310 (June 18, 1787).
[43] *Records*, I: 406–407 (June 25, 1787).
[44] *Records*, I: 321 (June 19, 1789); I: 404–405 (June 25, 1787).

realistic alternative: "that in *one* branch the *people*, ought to be represented; in the *other*, the *States*." Madison immediately rejected this compromise, arguing that the principle of equal representation "was confessedly unjust" and that "if admitted must infuse mortality into a Constitution which we wished to last forever."[46]

Despite Madison's dismissal, Connecticut delegate Oliver Ellsworth persisted with the small-state strategy to win a compromise. "We were partly national; partly federal," Ellsworth argued; "proportional representation in the first branch was conformable to the national principle & would secure the large States ag[ain]st the small. An equality of voices was conformable to the federal principle and was necessary to secure the Small States ag[ain]st the large. He trusted that on this middle ground a compromise would take place. He did not see that it could on any other. And if no compromise should take place, our meeting would not only be in vain but worse than in vain."[47] Ellsworth warned, "[i]f the Southern States contend for this plan of a popular, instead of State Representation we shall separate" and the Union "must be cut asunder at the Delaware" River.[48]

Although the arguments of the smaller state delegates had little effect on Madison, other delegates who previously supported proportional representation for the Senate hinted they were reassessing their positions. Abraham Baldwin of Georgia, "wished that the powers of the General Legislature had been defined" more clearly before a vote was taken on

---

[45] *Records*, I: 446–447 (June 28, 1787). Madison added, however, "he could neither be convinced that the rule contended for was just, not necessary for the safety of the small States agst. the large States." He asked: "Would 30 or 40 million of people submit their fortunes into the hands, of a few thousands?" "Why," moreover, "are Counties of the same States represented in proportion to their numbers? Is it because the representatives are chosen by the people themselves? So will be the representatives in the Nationl. Legislature. Is it because, the larger have more at stake than the smaller? The case will be the same with the larger & smaller States." *Records*, I: 447 (June 28, 1787). Again, however, Madison's rhetoric (or perhaps also his widely accepted erudition on American state constitutions and governments) seems to run ahead of reality because his association of the idea of proportionality with state apportionment rules does not correspond to the historical record of the early national era. See relevant data arrayed in Chapter 5.

[46] *Records*, I: 449 (June 28, 1787); I: 461–462, I: 464 (June 29, 1787).

[47] *Records*, I: 468–469 (June 29, 1787).

Ellsworth later observed "We are running from one extreme to another. We are razing the foundations of the building. When we need only repair the roof. No salutary measure has been lost for want of *a majority of the States*, to favor it." *Records*, I: 484 (June 30, 1787).

[48] *Record*, King, I: 478.

the rule of representation in the Senate. He still could not support the idea of equal representation, although he was uncomfortable with the provision for proportional representation "as it stood in the Report of the Committee of the [W]hole." William Davie of North Carolina was beginning to be convinced that proportional representation in the Senate was unrealistic. "There will according to this rule be ninety members in the outset, and the number will increase as new States are added" until it "may, in time, amount to two or three hundred. . . . It was impossible," he concluded, "that so numerous a body could possess the activity and other qualities required in it."[49]

Supporters of the proportional state rule sensed a softening of support and they adjusted their rhetoric accordingly. Madison tried to recast the Convention's debate in terms designed to maintain the support of the three southernmost states. He now argued that the states were divided not by their sizes as Ellsworth and others had insisted, "but by other circumstances; the most material of which resulted partly from climate, but principally from ⟨the effects of⟩ their having or not having slaves." Madison proposed "that instead of proportioning the votes of the States in both branches, to their respective numbers of inhabitants computing the slaves in the ratio of 5 to 3," representation of the states in one branch should be "according to the number of free inhabitants only; and in the other according to the whole no. counting the slaves as ⟨if⟩ free. By this arrangement," he submitted, "the Southern Scale would have the advantage in one House, and the Northern in the other."[50]

When Madison's proposal was not supported, two Pennsylvania delegates suggested other compromises designed to maintain support for proportional representation. To overcome the problem of a large Senate, James Wilson suggested modifying the ratio of representation to grant "one Senator in each [State] for every 100,000 souls" with every State having at least one Senator. Benjamin Franklin recommended an equal number of senators for each state, although on certain issues the votes of the states would be weighted in proportion to their contributions to the national Treasury.[51]

Opponents of proportional representation found these compromises unacceptable and they intensified their efforts to disengage one of the southern states from the coalition supporting proportional representation in the Senate. "Are not the large States evidently seeking to

[49] *Records*, I: 469 (June 29, 1787); I: 487 (June 30, 1787); Yates, I: 498.
[50] *Records*, I: 486–487 (June 30, 1787).
[51] *Records*, I: 488–489 (June 30, 1787).

aggrandize themselves at the expense of the small?" Gunning Bedford of Delaware asked, prodding the smallest states within the proportional rule coalition to reconsider their immediate interests and their alliance with the three largest states. Virginia, Massachusetts, and Pennsylvania, he continued, "think no doubt that they have right on their side, but interest had blinded their eyes. Look at Georgia," Bedford charged, "[t]hough a small State at present, she is actuated by the prospect of soon being a great one." South Carolina is similarly *"puffed up* with the possession of her wealth and negroes." She, too, "is actuated both by present & future prospects" and "hopes too to see the other States cut down to her own dimensions. N[orth] Carolina has the same motives of present & future interest," despite the fact that she has decidedly "different views" from the large states with whom she is aligned. "The Large States dare not dissolve the Confederation," Bedford added, "[i]f they do, the small ones will find some foreign ally, of more honor and good faith, who will take them by the hand, and do them justice."[52]

On Monday morning, July 2, the Convention reconsidered its June 11 vote in support of the rule of proportional state representation for the Senate. Although the Convention previously approved this rule, the vote this time was tied five to five, with the Georgia delegation unexpectedly divided.[53] The small-state strategy to gain a compromise on representation in the Senate finally broke Madison's carefully crafted coalition at its weakest point, the Georgia delegation. See Table 7.5.

When the July 2 vote was taken, Georgia had only two of its four delegates in attendance. On June 11, the delegation voted unanimously for proportional representation in the Senate. On July 2, however, one of Georgia's two remaining delegates, Abraham Baldwin, unexpectedly voted against the provision, thus dividing his state's vote. In his post-Convention report to Maryland's state legislature, Luther Martin suggested that Baldwin changed his vote because he thought a deadlocked Convention would allow him to go home.[54] Historians George Bancroft

---

[52] *Records*, I: 491 (June 30, 1787); Yates, I: 500 (June 30, 1787); I: 491 (June 30, 1787); Yates, I: 500 (June 30, 1787); I: 492 (June 30, 1787).

[53] Interestingly, if state votes at the Convention had been weighted proportionally (for example, according to the widely circulated 1785 requisition ratio), then the historic July 2 vote would not have ended in a deadlock. Rather, the Convention would have approved a rule for proportional state representation in the Senate by a 54 to 30 vote margin, with one state vote undecided.

[54] *Records*, III: 188.

Abraham Baldwin, the fourth and final Georgia delegate to arrive at the Convention, shifted his position on proportional representation sometime over the weekend

TABLE 7.5. *Convention Votes for Proportional Representation in the Senate – June 11, July 2*

(June 11)		(July 2)		
Aye (6)	No (5)	Aye (5)	No (5)	Divided (1)
Massachusetts	Connecticut	Massachusetts	Connecticut	Georgia
Pennsylvania	New York	Pennsylvania	New York	
Virginia	New Jersey	Virginia	New Jersey	
N. Carolina	Delaware	N. Carolina	Delaware	
S. Carolina	Maryland	S. Carolina	Maryland	
Georgia				

and Max Farrand offer less cynical explanations. Bancroft conjectured that Baldwin changed his vote because he feared "a disruption of the convention" and was convinced that a second convention was likely to fail. Farrand suggested Baldwin voted with the small state coalition because as a native of Connecticut he was naturally attracted to the compromise proposals consistently advocated by that state's delegates.[55] Baldwin perhaps more plausibly could have been convinced that proportional representation in both houses simply was not in his state's short-term interest. Georgia was the second smallest, if not the least populous, state in the Union. And, despite repeated assurances from the large-state delegates of its future weight in Congress, and although Georgia had one of the fastest-growing populations, a system of proportional representation virtually guaranteed that Georgia would have little decision-making weight well into the foreseeable future.[56] See Figure 7.1.

PART II: CONSTRUCTING A NEW CONSTITUTIONAL CONSENSUS

Faced with a deadlock on the pivotal issue of apportionment, most delegates were willing to consider some other method of resolving the seem-

---

before the July 2 vote. The other Georgia delegate, William Houston, voted for the provision of the Committee Report. The two other Georgia delegates who supported proportional representation were absent. William Few had already left the Convention (III: 587); and William Pierce was fighting a duel in New York. See Warren, *The Making of the Constitution*, (1937), pp. 261–262; John P. Roche, "The Founding Fathers: A Reform Caucus in Action," *APSR* (1961) 55: 809.

[55] Bancroft, *History of the Constitution*, II: 66; Farrand, *The Framing of the Constitution* (1913), p. 96. See also Warren, *The Making of the Constitution*, p. 262n.2.

[56] See description by Maryland delegate Luther Martin, *Records*, III: 187 and III: 154.

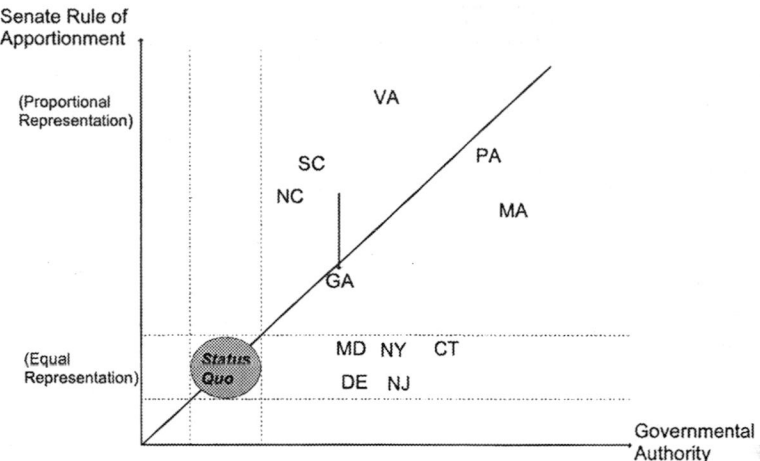

FIGURE 7.1. State Preferences for Rule of Apportionment in Senate and for Level of Governmental Authority, July 2

ingly indivisible matter. On July 2, the Convention authorized the creation of a special 11 member committee composed of a single delegate from each state. Abraham Baldwin, the Georgia delegate whose last-minute recalculation of his state's interests had deadlocked the Convention, was appointed Georgia's committee representative. Three days later, on July 5, the special 11-member committee reported the so-called Great Compromise plan for accommodating the representational needs of both the small and large states. It proposed a double rule of apportionment that granted each state "one member for every 40,000 inhabitants" in the House of Representatives and "an equal vote" for each state in the Senate.[57]

Although the Convention seemed closer to a compromise, disputes over representation continued to dominate its deliberations. The political arithmetic offered by the Great Compromise did become the starting point for more focused conflicts concerning the interstate distribution of representation in the new House of Representatives. Several delegates immediately objected to the special committee's proposal to use population as the standard for apportioning representation in the House. John Rutledge of South Carolina proposed basing apportionment instead on

[57] *Records*, Yates, I: 523 (July 3, 1787). See also comments by Mason, *Records*, I: 544 (July 6, 1787).

"Taxes paid in a given District" because "Property is the object of Society" and population is not "a proper Index of Wealth now" and "it will be much less so hereafter."[58]

Others delegates foresaw additional problems with the proposed "scale of apportionment." Gouverneur Morris, a Pennsylvania delegate, argued that a "range of New States" would "soon be formed in the west" and therefore "the rule of representation ought to be so fixed as to secure to the Atlantic States a prevalence in the National Councils. The new States," he said, "will know less of the public interest." Precautions, therefore, should "be made to prevent the maritime States from being hereafter outvoted by them." Morris concluded "this might be easily done by fixing the number of representatives which the Atlantic States should respectively have, and the number which each new State will have."[59]

Nathaniel Gorham predicted "great inconveniency from fixing directly the number of Representatives to be allowed to each State." The District of Kentucky, he pointed out, was on the verge of separating from Virginia, and Maine would soon hold a convention to discuss secession from Massachusetts. "In such events, the number of representatives ought certainly to be reduced." Gorham therefore recommended that the largest States be reduced "as much & as fast as possible."[60]

Rufus King pointed out two additional problems. He contended, "the Ratio of Representation proposed could not be safely fixed, since in a century & a half our computed increase of population would carry the number of representatives to an enormous excess." King also argued that the Land Ordinance of 1784 proposed ten new states in the Northwest Territory and established "that as soon as the number in any one State shall equal that of the smallest of the 13 original States, it may claim admission into the Union." If this plan were not amended, he argued, "10 new votes may be added, without a greater addition of inhabitants than are represented by the single vote of Pen[nsylvani]a."[61]

---

[58] *Records*, King, I: 536–537 (July 5, 1787).
[59] *Records*, I: 534 (July 5, 1787).
[60] *Records*, I: 540 (July 6, 1787).
[61] *Records*, I: 541 (July 6, 1787). Congress, meeting in New York at the time of the Constitutional Convention, enacted the Northwest Ordinance on July 13, 1787. This Act supplanted the 1784 Land Ordinance, reorganizing the territory north of the Ohio River into five states which, once acquiring a population equal to the smallest state would be admitted as states and as equals of the original states. For additional speculation on the connection between this Ordinance and the Constitutional Convention, see Louis W. Potts, "'A Lucky Moment': The Relationship of the Ordinance of 1787

TABLE 7.6. *Morris Committee House Apportionment (n = 56)*

New Hampshire	2		
Massachusetts	7	Maryland	4
Rhode Island	1	Virginia	9
Connecticut	4	N. Carolina	5
New York	5	S. Carolina	5
New Jersey	3	Georgia	2
Pennsylvania	8		
Delaware	1		
	[31]		[25]

The Convention responded to these objections by appointing a five-member committee to reexamine the apportionment ratio. This committee consisted entirely of delegates who had previously supported a proportional state rule of apportionment. Gouverneur Morris of Pennsylvania was appointed committee chair and James Wilson advised him and the others to "consider the propriety of adopting a scale" of apportionment that "would give an advantage to [the] small States without substantially departing from a rule of proportion."[62]

When the Morris committee reported back several days later, it proposed that the House of Representatives consist of 56 members. In keeping with Wilson's instructions, the committee awarded Virginia (the largest state) nine representatives and Delaware and Rhode Island (the smallest states) one representative each. The 9:1 interstate scale was a significant reduction from the 16:1 scale that traditionally defined the interstate range of Congress's requisition system. The Morris committee also recommended that Congress be given the authority "from time to time to augment [the] number of Representatives" and "to regulate the number of Representatives" of new states according not only to the "number of inhabitants" but "their wealth" as well.[63] See Table 7.6.

The Morris committee report did not end the conflict over the terms of interstate apportionment. Connecticut delegate Roger Sherman

and the Constitution of 1787," *Mid-America*, pp. 141–151; Staughton Lynd, "The Compromise of 1787," *PSQ* (1966), 81: 225–250; J. P. Dunn, *Indiana* (1905), pp. 210–218; and Frederick D. Stone, "The Ordinance of 1787," *Pennsylvania Magazine of History and Biography* (1889), XIII(3): 309–340.

[62] *Records*, I: 542 (July 6, 1787). The other members were Nathaniel Gorham (MA), Edmund Randolph (VA), John Rutledge (SC), and Rufus King (MA).

[63] *Records*, I: 559 (July 9, 1787).

immediately challenged the committee's arithmetic by demanding "to know on what principles or calculations the Report was founded" because "it did not appear to correspond with any rule of numbers, or of any question hitherto adopted by Congress." As Table 7.7 reveals, Sherman and the Connecticut delegation likely expected that the 40,000-person ratio would yield five representatives for their state. Connecticut, however, "lost" its fifth representative because several states were over-represented and the small House size prohibited other states from receiving their full "quota" of representatives. South Carolina, in particular, was overrepresented by two members – perhaps the result of John Rutledge's presence on the Morris committee or of Charles Pinckney's unexpected suggestion the day the committee was selected that "blacks ought to stand on an equality with whites."[64]

Members of the Morris committee admitted that the assignment of representatives among the states involved some guesswork. State population data, after all, were imprecise and often contradictory, and measurements of the relative wealth of the states was an anecdotal, not an empirical science. Nathaniel Gorham defended the committee's apportionment by explaining that the committee was guided by "[t]he number of blacks & whites with some regard to supposed wealth" of each state. He stated that fractional remainders – for example, New York's (.95) – "could not be observed" by the committee, but that Congress would be able "to make alteration from time to time as justice & propriety may require." Gouverneur Morris noted that his committee assigned additional representatives to rapidly growing states, although their present population did not warrant it. Morris also stated that the committee's decisions were designed to insure a small House initially and to permit the thirteen original states to "take care of their own interest, by dealing out the right of Representation in safe proportions to the Western States."[65]

The Morris committee's explanations were apparently unsatisfactory for a second committee was appointed to devise a more acceptable House apportionment plan. Chaired by another large-state delegate, Rufus King of Massachusetts, the composition of this second committee was more representative of the convention because each state selected one committee member.[66]

---

[64] *Records*, I: 559 (July 9, 1787); I: 542 (July 6, 1787).
[65] *Records*, I: 559–560 (July 9, 1787).
[66] The other members were Sherman (CT); Yates (NY); Brearly (NJ); Morris (PA); Read (DE); Carrol (MD); Madison (VA); Williamson (NC); Rutledge (SC); Houstoun (GA).

TABLE 7.7. Morris Committee Apportionment

State	Apportionment Population[a]	Apportionment Quota (1:40,000)	Whole Number Quota[b]	Number of Representatives (n = 56): Expected[b]	Actual	Difference: (Actual − Expected)/ (Actual − Whole no.)
NH	102,000	2.55	2	2	2	-/-
MA	360,000	9.00	9	8	7	-1/-2
RI	58,000	1.45	1	1	1	-/-
CT	202,000	5.05	5	4	4	-/-1
NY	238,000	5.95	5	5	5	-/-
NJ	138,000	3.45	3	3	3	-/-
PA	360,000	9.00	9	8	8	-/-1
DE	37,000	.93	1	1	1	-/-
MD	218,000	5.45	5	5	4	-1/-1
VA	420,000	10.50	10	10	9	-1/-1
NC	200,000	5.00	5	4	5	+1/-
SC	150,000	3.75	3	3	5	+2/+2
GA	90,000	2.25	2	2	2	-/-
		64.33	60	56	56	

[a] Population data taken from Charles Coatsworth Pinckney's speech in the South Carolina House of Representatives, January 1788, in Farrand, *Records*, III: 252.

[b] The "Expected" number represents the division of representatives when the total number of representatives is less than the whole number quota total. Under this condition, one or more states will not receive its respective whole number quota. Each state still receives at least one representative, but the size of each state's fractional remainder determines the order of the loss of representatives among the states. States with the smallest fractional remainders lose representatives before states with larger remainders.

TABLE 7.8. *King Committee Apportionment*
(Change from Morris Committee Report)

New Hampshire	3 (+1)		
Massachusetts	8 (+1)	Maryland	6 (+2)
Rhode Island	1	Virginia	10 (+1)
Connecticut	5 (+1)	North Carolina	5
New York	6 (+1)	South Carolina	5
New Jersey	4 (+1)	Georgia	3 (+1)
Pennsylvania	8		
Delaware	1		
	[36] (+5)		[29] (+4)
		TOTAL	65 (+9)

The next day, July 10, the King committee reported back to the Convention. It proposed expanding the House to sixty-five members and solved the unrepresented "quota" problem associated with a fifty-six-member House by judiciously allocating nine additional representatives among eight states. Maryland received two additional members; Connecticut, New York, New Jersey, New Hampshire, and Georgia each received one additional member. Massachusetts and Virginia also received one additional member, although the three largest states still did not receive the full "quota" of representatives demanded by the 40,000-person apportionment ratio. See Table 7.8.

Notably, under the King committee apportionment, eight states received five or more representatives. More than half of the states (and eight of the eleven states in attendance) maintained or improved their relative decision-making weight in the new House of Representatives compared to their existing representation in Congress under the Articles.[67] As Table 7.9 reveals, this high degree of representational parity between the Articles' rule of apportionment and the new proportional rule proposed for the House of Representatives was achieved by the voluntary underrepresentation of the three largest states. Arguably, Virginia, Massachusetts, and Pennsylvania delegates on the King Committee yielded a representative to the smaller states in the hope of securing their

[67] Under the Articles, every state had an equal representation in Congress, or 1/13 of the total representation. In a 65-member House in which representation is proportionally divided, a state would have to receive at least five representatives to maintain its existing decision-making capacity. Historian George Bancroft makes a similar observation in *History of the Formation of the Constitution of the United States* (1882), II: 73.

TABLE 7.9. Comparison of House Apportionment Plans

State	1785 Requisition Quota	1787 Ratio[a]	Apportionment Quota (1:40,000)	Morris Committee Apportionment (n = 56)			King Committee Apportionment (n = 65)		
				Expected	Actual	(Actual − Expected)	Expected	Actual	(Actual − Expected)
New Hampshire	3.5	3.96	2.55	2	2		3	3	
Massachusetts	15.0	13.99	9.00	8	7	−1	9	8	−1
Rhode Island	2.1	2.25	1.45	1	1		1	1	
Connecticut	8.8	7.85	5.05	4	4		5	5	
New York	8.5	9.25	5.95	5	5		6	6	
New Jersey	5.6	5.36	3.45	3	3		3	4	+1
Pennsylvania	13.7	13.99	9.00	8	8		9	8	−1
Delaware	1.5	1.44	.93	1	1		1	1	
Maryland	9.4	8.47	5.45	5	4	−1	6[b]	6	+1
Virginia	17.1	16.32	10.50	10	9	−1	11	10	−1
N. Carolina	7.3	7.77	5.00	4	5	+1	5	5	
S. Carolina	6.4	5.83	3.75	3	5	+2	4	5	+1
Georgia	1.1	3.50	2.25	2	2		2	3	+1
				56	56		65	65	

[a] Population data taken from Charles Coatsworth Pinckney's speech in the South Carolina House of Representatives, January 1788, in Farrand, Records, III: 252.

[b] Maryland, New Jersey, and Rhode Island, each with .45 fractional remainders, had legitimate claims to receive the 65th representative. Maryland was assigned the extra representative.

luther
reporting

support for the new constitution. No doubt, these delegates were confident that an accurate reallocation of representatives would occur shortly after the first census.[68] Later in the Convention, on August 20, the delegates agreed to shorten the time until the taking of the first census from six to three years from the first Congress. Not surprisingly the two states that were the most overrepresented by the King Committee apportionment – South Carolina and Georgia – opposed this resolution.[69]

Although the King committee apportionment was designed to settle the terms of the House apportionment, several delegates did not relent in their demands for additional representation. Despite the overrepresentation of several states (including South Carolina and Georgia), several southern state delegates were disappointed by the regional distribution of representation. South Carolina delegate Charles Pinckney claimed that if the proposed House apportionment was not altered and the national government was granted authority to regulate trade, then the southern states would be reduced to "nothing more than the over-

---

[68] One member of the King Committee, George Read of Delaware, recounted, after the 65-member apportionment had been agreed to, that within the Committee there was "a backwardness in some of the members of the large States, to take their full proportion of Representatives." Read recalled how Gouverneur Morris was unexpectedly satisfied with Pennsylvania's assignment of only eight representatives, and how unusual it was that Madison wanted additional representatives for North and South Carolina rather than for his own state of Virginia. He admitted that he "did not then see the motive" of these committee members, but that he later perceived "it was to avoid their due share of taxation."

James Madison and Gouverneur Morris denied the charge by Read pointing out that both Massachusetts and Virginia received an additional member from the King Committee and that the proposal to proportion direct taxes to representation was subsequently made by Morris. *Records*, I: 601 (July 13, 1787). Morris later proposed dropping the "direct taxes" clause, arguing he "meant it as a bridge to assist us over a certain gulph; having [now] passed the gulph the bridge may be removed." *Records*, II: 106 (July 24, 1787). And the additional representative assigned to Massachusetts and Virginia by the King Committee still did not grant these states their full proportional quota.

Additional support for the contention that representation was transferred from the large states to several smaller states is offered by several other delegates. Elbridge Gerry contended that "Massachusetts has not a due share of Representatives allotted to her." Maryland delegate Luther Martin explained that the House apportionment agreed to by the Convention was "not precisely agreeable to the rule of representation adopted by this system, and that the numbers in this section [Article I, Section 2] are artfully lessened for the larger States, while the smaller States have their full proportion, in order to prevent the undue influence which the larger States will have in the Government from being too apparent." See *Records*, II: 633 (Sept. 15, 1787). See also [House] Rep. No. 463, Report of the Minority, 22nd Congress, 1st Sess. (May 7, 1832), pp. 55–56).

[69] *Records*, II: 350 (Aug. 20, 1787).

seers for the Northern States." Southern interests had little reason to be comforted by their long-term prospects under the proposed apportionment rule because, as North Carolina delegate Hugh Williamson pointed out, the "North[er]n States are to have a majority in the first instance and the means of perpetuating it."[70]

Massachusetts delegate Rufus King denied the charge of a regional bias against southern interests and claimed, on the contrary, that the southern states received more representation than "entitled to them." The four northern states "having 800,000 souls, have 1/3 fewer representatives than the four Southern States, having not more than 700,000 souls rating the blacks, as 5 for 3." King allowed that "he had been ready to yield something in the proportion of representatives for the security of the Southern [states]. No principle," however, "would justify giving them a majority" nor could he "see how it could be done."[71]

Other delegates criticized other elements of the apportionment plan proposed by the King Committee. James Madison questioned the committee's decision to increase the House size to only sixty-five members and he "moved that the number allowed to each State be doubled." According to Madison, not only was "A *majority* of a *Quorum* of 65 members . . . too small a number to represent the whole inhabitants of the U[nited] States," but such a small number "would not possess enough of the confidence of the people, and w[oul]d be too sparsely taken from the people, to bring with them all the local information which would be frequently wanted. . . . The additional expence" of a larger House, Madison advised, "was too inconsiderable to be regarded in so important a case" and it "was overbalanced by its effect on the hopes of a greater number of popular Candidates."[72]

Other delegates offered additional reasons for expanding the number of representatives in the House. "The larger the number," Elbridge Gerry of Massachusetts argued, "the less the danger of their being corrupted. The people are accustomed to & fond of a numerous representation, and will consider their rights as better secured by it." Virginian George Mason agreed, arguing that even "[a]fter doubling the number, the laws might still be made by so few as almost to be objectionable on that account." Delaware delegate George Read supported the increase

[70] See *Records*, I: 567 (July 10, 1787); and II: 219 (Aug. 8, 1787). See also attempts by southern state delegates to decrease northern state representation: I: 566 (July 10, 1787); I: 601 (July 13, 1787).

[71] *Records*, I: 566 (July 10, 1787).

[72] *Records*, I: 568–569 (July 10, 1787).

because it gave more representation to the smallest states who, with only one member, might "have no representative present to give explanations or informations of its interests or wishes." Despite these arguments for more representation, the Convention rejected Madison's proposal and approved the apportionment and House size recommended by the King Committee.[73]

Completion of a consensus for the initial interstate distribution of political representation in the House did not end the delegates' disputes over the terms of the new rule of apportionment. Several delegates were concerned with the failure of the Morris and King committees to provide for a periodic reapportionment of the House. Virginia delegate Edmund Randolph worried that the initial northern majority in the House would never voluntarily relinquish its representational supremacy to the rapidly growing southern states. Mason also "considered a Revision from time to time according to some permanent & precise standard as essential to [the] fair representation required in the 1st branch."[74] "If equality between great & small States be inadmissable," Randolph stressed, "was it not equally inadmissable that a larger & more populous district of America should hereafter have less representation, than a smaller & less populous district?" If they could not secure "a fair representation of the people," then "the injustice of the Govt. will shake it to its foundations." Not only therefore should periodic reapportionment of the House be mandatory, Randolph added, Congress should direct the census because the "States will be too much interested to take an impartial one for themselves."[75]

Pennsylvania delegate Gouverneur Morris opposed such a mandate "as fettering the Legislature too much. . . . If we can't agree on a rule that will be just at this time," Morris argued, "how can we expect to find one that will be just in all time to come. Surely those who come

---

[73] *Records*, I: 569–570 (July 10, 1787).

Arguably, George Read was disappointed that as a member of the King Committee he failed to secure an additional representative for his state. Read also could have been upset by the assignment of three representatives to Georgia, in spite of the available estimates that consistently ranked Delaware's population equal to or higher than Georgia's. David Brearly of New Jersey recorded in his notes of the Convention that Delaware and Georgia had a population of 37,000 and 27,000 respectively. Records published on December 11, 1786, in the *Pennsylvania Packet* estimated the population of Delaware and Georgia at 50,000 and 56,000 respectively. *Records*, I: 573 (July 10, 1787); *Pennsylvania Packet*, Dec. 11, 1786, cited by Warren, *The Making of the Constitution*, p. 287n.

[74] *Records*, I: 578 (July 11, 1787).
[75] *Records*, I: 579–580 (July 11, 1787).

after us will judge better of things present, than we can of things future." In the end, the delegates again managed to resolve their differences, agreeing to require a decennial census but not to include an explicit mandate for a decennial reapportionment of the House of Representatives.[76]

[handwritten: decennial census But NOT decennial reapp.]

The Representation of Enslaved Persons

Several southern delegates were still not satisfied with their representation in the House and they anxiously campaigned for a change in the way enslaved persons were to be counted. On June 11, the Convention agreed without much debate that three-fifths of the number of enslaved persons would be included in each state's House apportionment population. When Georgia delegate Pierce Butler and South Carolina delegate Charles Pinckney "insisted that blacks be included in the rule of Representation, *equally* with the Whites," this projected change again threatened to deadlock the Convention.[77]

[handwritten: said they were contradictory]

Massachusetts delegate Nathaniel Gorham pointed out the hypocrisy of the Butler-Pinckney proposal, reminding the Convention that when the three-fifths ratio initially "was fixed by Cong[res]s as a rule of taxation" in 1783, southern delegates declared "that the blacks were still more inferior to freemen," although they now urge "they are equal." Pierce Butler ignored Gorham's history lesson and defended his proposal by contending "that the labour of a slave in S[outh] Carol[in]a was as productive & valuable as that of a freeman in Mass[achuset]ts" and therefore "an equal representation ought to be allowed for them in a Government which was instituted principally for the protection of property, and was itself to be supported by property."[78]

Although the Convention rejected the proposed adjustment in the apportionment ratio, delegates from several northern states remained

---

[76] *Records*, I: 570–571 (July 10, 1787); I: 583 (July 11, 1787); I: 588 (July 11, 1787).

The Convention initially agreed to a census every fifteen years, but on July 24, it agreed to a decennial census. *Records*, I: 596. On August 20, the Convention agreed, after several changes, that the first census would be taken within *three* years of the first Congress. *Records*, II: 350. The Convention also briefly agreed that after every census Congress "alter or augment the representation accordingly." By the end of the day, however, this mandate was rescinded. Thus, no explicit requirement for a decennial reapportionment was included in the text of Article I, Section 2, Paragraph 3 of the U.S. Constitution.

[77] *Records*, I: 580 (July 11, 1787).

[78] *Records*, I: 580–581 (July 11, 1787).

indignant and retaliated by agreeing to strike out the "three-fifths" ratio from the House apportionment rule. Gouverneur Morris justified his state's vote to rescind by arguing that "the people of Pen[nsylvani]a would revolt at the idea of being put on a footing with slaves." As he saw it, the ratio was either "doing injustice to the Southern States or to human nature, and he must therefore do it to the former. For he could never agree to give such encouragement to the slave trade as would be given by allowing them a representation for their negroes, and he did not believe those States would ever confederate on terms that would deprive them of that trade."[79]

Rufus King initially defended the inclusion of enslaved persons in the rule of representation by pointing out that "Eleven out of 13 of the States had agreed to consider Slaves in the apportionment of taxation; and taxation and Representation ought to go together."[80] After the defeat of the Butler-Pinckney proposal, however, King concurred with Morris that the inclusion of enslaved persons "along with Whites at all, would excite great discontents among the States," like his own, "having no slaves." King also "remarked that in the ⟨temporary⟩ allotment of Representatives made by the Committee, the Southern States had received more than the number of their white & three fifths of their black inhabitants entitled them to."[81]

Southern delegates were outraged by the withdrawal of northern support for the three-fifths ratio, and Butler and Pinckney again proposed counting enslaved and free persons equally. Other delegates, however, recognized the necessity of compromise. William Davie of North Carolina thought the three-fifths ratio was acceptable. And a more conciliatory Gouverneur Morris also acknowledged that "it is vain for the Eastern States to insist on what the South[er]n States will never agree to" as it is "for the latter to require what the other States can never admit." He therefore proposed adding to the apportionment rule "a

---

[79] *Records*, I: 581 (July 11, 1787); Bancroft, II: 81; I: 588 (July 11, 1787); I: 596 (July 12, 1787); I: 588 (July 11, 1787).

[80] *Records*, I: 561–562 (July 9, 1787). King's remarks were in response to the criticism of William Paterson. When the Morris Committee first proposed its apportionment, Paterson complained "Has a man in Virga. a number of votes in proportion to the number of his slaves? and if Negroes are not represented in the States to which they belong, why should they be represented in the Genl. Govt.?". . . . He was also agst. such an indirect encouragement of the slave trade; observing the Congs. in their act relating to the change of the 8 art: of Confedn. had been ashamed to use the term 'Slaves' & had substituted a description."

[81] *Records*, I: 586 (July 11, 1787).

proviso that taxation shall be in proportion to Representation" and hoped that any objections against his motion "would be removed by restraining the rule to *direct taxation*," thereby excluding "indirect taxes on *exports* & imports & on consumption."[82] Morris hoped the linkage would check southern demands for more representation in the House, while James Wilson acknowledged its rhetorical benefits for northern delegates who subsequently would have to explain the three-fifths ratio to their constituents. The Pennsylvania delegate "observed that less umbrage would perhaps be taken ag[ain]st an admission of the slaves into the Rule of representation, if it should be so expressed as to make them indirectly only an ingredient in the rule, by *saying* that they should enter into the rule of taxation: and as representation was to be according to taxation, the end would be equally attained."[83] As Morris later explained, the linkage was intended "to exclude the appearance of counting the Negroes in the Representation."[84]

The Convention unanimously agreed to Morris's "direct taxation" proviso.[85] Amendments to the apportionment provision along with the previously rejected three-fifths ratio were then bundled into a single

---

[82] *Records*, I: 592–593 (July 12, 1787).

There are other interpretations of this linkage between representation and direct taxation. Historian Charles Warren argued that "Morris and some other delegates from the North were actuated quite as much by their fears of conditions which might arise in the West, as by their anxiety over the South. They apprehended that the Western States, by increasing more rapidly in population than in wealth, might acquire a majority in Congress and tax unduly the property of the East." See Warren, *The Making of the Constitution* (1937), p. 290.

[83] *Records*, I: 595 (July 12, 1787). Emphasis added.

Before this vote, Elbridge Gerry stated that the principle of apportioning representation to direct taxation "could not be carried into execution as the States were not to be taxed as States." *Records*, I: 597 (July 12, 1787). Other delegates disagreed, but as historian Charles Warren argued there likely "was an implied understanding the power [of direct taxation], even though granted, would probably be seldom used." Warren, *The Making of the Constitution* (1937), p. 498.

[84] Madison conversely claimed Morris's intention had been "to lessen the eagerness on one side, & the opposition on the other, to the share of Representation claimed by the S.(Sothern) States on account of the Negroes. *Records*, II: 106n (July 24, 1787). On September 13, however, Morris explained that his linkage of taxation and representation was intended "to exclude the appearance of counting the Negroes in *the Representation* – The including of them may now be referred to the object of direct taxes, and incidentally only to that of Representation." *Records*, II: 607.

[85] *Records*, I: 592–595 (July 12, 1787). On July 24, Gouverneur Morris retracted his support for this proviso. He argued it had been intended only as "a bridge to assist us over a certain gulph" and that "having passed the gulph the bridge may be removed." For Morris, the principle of linking representation and taxation was too strict, and "liable to strong objections." Records, II: 106.

resolution. By this means, the Convention reaffirmed its support for counting three-fifths of each state's enslaved persons in the new rule of apportionment for the House of Representatives.[86]

Representation of New Western States

The July 12 vote for the amended version of the House apportionment rule did not satisfy the delegates' long-term expectations for representational security within the newly constituted national government. One of the more significant conflicts focused on the terms for allocating representation to new states subsequently admitted into the Union. Several delegates argued for a neutral application of the apportionment rule used for the thirteen original states, whereas others more anxiously sought to retain their existing decision-making capacity by limiting the representation of new states.

Gouverneur Morris advocated establishing constitutional restrictions on the representation of new western states. The Pennsylvania delegate warned against "the danger of throwing such a preponderancy into the Western Scale," predicting once "the Western people get the power into their hands they will ruin the Atlantic interests." These states "will not be able to contribute in proportion to their numbers," nor will they "be able to furnish men equally enlightened, to share in the administration of our common interests." Moreover, "they will inevitably bring on a war with Spain for the Mississippi."[87] Morris advocated giving Congress the discretion to apportion representation to new western states according not only to their population but their "wealth" as well.

Massachusetts delegate Elbridge Gerry was similarly consumed by the long-term representational consequences of admitting new western states

---

[86] *Records*, I: 597 (July 12, 1787). Connecticut, Pennsylvania, Maryland, Virginia, North Carolina, and Georgia voted in support; New Jersey and Delaware were opposed; Massachusetts and South Carolina were divided.

[87] *Records*, I: 571 (July 10, 1787); I: 583 (July 11, 1787); I: 583 (July 11, 1787); I: 604–605 (July 13, 1787).

Morris, an advocate of limiting western states representation, observed Madison's attempt to reunite the southern state coalition. "A distinction had been set up & urged, between the Nn. & Southn. States" he previously considered as "heretical" and "groundless." It now appeared "that the Southn. Gentlemen will not be satisfied unless they see the way open to their gaining a majority in the public Councils. The consequence of such a transfer of power from the maritime to the interior & landed interest will," the Pennsylvania delegate charged, "be such an oppression of commerce" that he would vote for the "vicious principle of equality in the 2d. branch in order to provide some defence for the N. States agst it." *Records*, I: 604 (July 13, 1787).

into the Union. He wanted to admit these states "on liberal terms," but could not accept "putting ourselves into their hands" and giving them the opportunity to "oppress commerce, and drain our wealth into the Western Country." Instead, "he thought it necessary to limit the number of new States to be admitted into the Union, in such a manner, that they should never be able to outnumber the Atlantic States." The problem for Gerry was that "[t]here was a rage for emigration from the Eastern States to the Western Country and he did not wish those remaining behind to be at the mercy of the Emigrants. Besides," he tellingly added, "foreigners are resorting to that Country, and it is uncertain what turn things may take there."[88]

Other delegates disagreed. "If the Western States are to be admitted into the Union as they arise, they must," George Mason insisted, "be treated as equals, and subjected to no degrading discriminations. They will have the same pride & other passions which we have and will either not unite with or will speedily revolt from the Union, if they are not in all respects placed on an equal footing with their brethren." Moreover, Mason added, the "number of inhabitants though not always a precise standard of wealth was sufficiently so for every substantial purpose."[89]

Pennsylvania delegate James Wilson also opposed the idea that the right of representation was conditioned on place of residence. "The majority of people wherever found ought in all questions govern the minority," he argued, and "If the interior Country should acquire this majority they will not only have the right, but will avail themselves of it whether we will or no[t]." Great Britain, Wilson continued, imposed disastrous policies on the American colonies because she jealously refused to recognize their right of representation. "The fatal maxims espoused by her were that the Colonies were growing too fast, and that their growth must be stinted in time." This produced "enmity on our part, then actual separation. Like consequences will result on the part of the interior settlements, if like jealousy & policy be pursued on ours." With respect to "[t]he cultivation & improvement of the human mind" and "to other *personal* rights, numbers were surely the natural & precise measure of Representation."[90]

"Besides," Connecticut delegate Roger Sherman eloquently explained, "We are providing for our posterity, for our children & our grand

[88] *Records*, II: 2–3 (July 14, 1787).
[89] *Records*, I: 578–579 (June 11, 1787).
[90] *Records*, I: 605–606 (July 13, 1787).

Children, who would be as likely to be citizens of new Western States, as of the old States. On this consideration alone, we ought to make no such discrimination." The Convention agreed with the principles espoused by Sherman and decided against granting Congress the discretionary power to apportion representation to the western states on a basis other than population.[91]

PART III: THE CALCULUS OF CONSENT

Finally, on July 16, the convention approved the amended provisions of the July 5 proposal for a double apportionment rule for the House and Senate.[92] Five state delegations voiced their approval, four were opposed, and one state delegation was divided. Again, the voting behavior of several states and individuals followed an unexpected path. Abraham Baldwin of Georgia, the delegate who made the subsequent deliberations and compromises possible by deadlocking the Convention on July 2, voted against the proposed rule of apportionment. Ironically, Baldwin's change of heart cast his state against the rule for equal state representation in the Senate. North Carolina voted for the compromise plan and the new double rule of apportionment – although, prior to July 5, it had been a consistent supporter of proportional representation for both the House and Senate. In another puzzling vote, the delegation from Massachusetts divided, thus nullifying the vote of another consistent supporter of the rule of proportional state apportionment.[93] See Table 7.10.

---

[91] *Records*, II: 3 (July 14, 1787); I: 606 (July 13, 1787). The Convention also rejected a proposal to prohibit the representation of the western states from ever exceeding that of the original states. *Records*, II: 3 (July 14, 1787). Later, the Convention finalized the provision for admitting new states into the Union. The Committee of Detail Plan (submitted August 8) required the consent of a state with jurisdiction and two-thirds of both branches of Congress before a new state could be admitted. It also added the requirements that new states "be admitted on the same terms with the original States" and that Congress could "make conditions with the new States concerning the public debt." The convention agreed to strike out these requirements. II: 454 (August 29). On August 30 it agreed that new states could not be admitted into the Union without the consent of any affected state and of Congress. II: 464–465 (August 30).

[92] *Records*, II: 15–16 (July 16, 1787). Notably, the amended plan voted on by the Convention contained no reference to the 40,000-person ratio originally proposed by the special 11-member Committee appointed July 2.

[93] The historical record does not offer sufficient evidence to make more than a conjecture explaining the unexpected votes of Massachusetts and North Carolina. Given Massachusetts' hesitancy to alter the equal state rule of apportionment prior to the Convention, the state's vote on July 16 might be explained as a form of strategic voting intended to gain additional representational security in the face of the expectation that

TABLE 7.10. *Convention Vote for Amended Plan of Special July 2 Committee (July 16)*

Aye (5)	No (4)	Divided (1)
Connecticut	Pennsylvania	Massachusetts
New Jersey	Virginia	
Delaware	S. Carolina	
Maryland	Georgia	
N. Carolina		

Although only a narrow majority approved of the new double rule of apportionment, the July 16 vote was subsequently accepted by the convention, altering the perspectives of individual delegates, state delegations, and multistate coalitions during subsequent deliberations concerning other elements of the new constitution.[94] This vote did not end all discussion of or attempts to alter or to mitigate the expected distributional consequences associated with the new double rule of apportionment. The various interests that had battled over this rule prior to the July 16 vote continued their contentious deliberations over the method for electing the President, the House size, and the population ratio for apportioning representation in the House of Representatives.[95]

the southern states would ultimately dominate the House of Representatives. To speculate beyond this is not presently possible. It must be noted, however, that the transformation in the view of these states occurred prior to the July 16 vote. On July 14, both North Carolina and Massachusetts voted against a proposal to establish proportional representation in a 36-member Senate. *Records*, II: 11. See also the suggestive vote on July 7 and exchange between Massachusetts delegate Elbridge Gerry and James Madison. *Records*, I: 549 (July 7, 1787).

[94] See Madison's brief note describing the meeting of large-state delegates the morning after the vote favoring the double rule of apportionment. *Records*, II: 19–20 (July 16, 1787).

[95] For an account of the Convention's deliberations on the method for selecting the President, see Shlomo Slonim, "The Electoral College at Philadelphia: The Evolution of an Ad Hoc Congress for the Selection of a President," *JAH* (1986), 73: 35–58. For additional discussion of an increase in the House size, see *Records*, II: 553–554 (Sept. 8, 1787); II: 563 (Sept. 10); II: 612 (Sept. 14, 1787); II: 623, 632, 633 (Sept. 15, 1787).

For additional discussion of the terms of the House apportionment, see *Records*, II: 221, 223 (Aug. 8, 1787). A final change in these terms merits recounting. On the final day of the Convention when only a ceremonial signing of the new U.S. Constitution was expected, a final revision of the rule of apportionment was proposed. Massachusetts delegate Nathaniel Gorham proposed reducing the House apportionment ratio from "forty" to "thirty" thousand "for the purpose of lessening objections to the Constitution." This change, he said, would not "establish that as an absolute rule, but only give Congress a greater latitude."

Despite this incomplete settlement, agreement on the double rule of apportionment for the House and Senate provided the delegates with a firmer basis for assessing their expected decision-making capacities within the new national government. Prior to the establishment of this foundation, the Convention's elaboration of and the delegates' commitment to a new framework of the national government were not feasible because most delegates were far too uncertain about their future positions to evoke much more than vague and tentative commitments to more effective forms of governance. Arguably James Madison spoke for his fellow delegates when he unequivocally declared that "it wd. be impossible to say what powers could be safely & properly vested in the Govt before it was known, in what manner the States were to be represented in it."[96]

The delegates' success in fashioning a consensus for the specific terms of the new U.S. Constitution and the subsequent ratification of this text by the states prompts revisitation of the general problematics associated with the definition of a rule for the intragovernmental apportionment of collective decision-making authority. These problematics turn on the vexatious question: If the establishment of collective authority requires the consent of the set of principal political interests and their political agents, how does this consent emerge when alternative rules of apportionment promise different immediate and long-term distributional consequences for these interests and actors? What motivated the delegates to consent to a particular rule of apportionment and the states to ratify this rule?

Recall the traditional accounts of consensual political foundings identified in the Preface and reviewed in Chapter 4. One of these accounts, the Hobbesian story of state creation, assumes that the set

---

Gorham's amendment would likely have been dismissed but for George Washington unexpectedly rising in support. Washington, silent during his four-month tenure as Convention president, declared that "[t]he smallness of the proportion of Representatives had been considered by many members of the Convention, an insufficient security for the rights & interests of the people," and he confessed "it had always appeared to himself among the exceptionable parts of the plan." Although "late as the present moment was for admitting amendments," Washington announced "he thought this of so much consequence that it would give much satisfaction to see it adopted." The Convention unanimously agreed with Washington and terms of the House apportionment rule were revised a final time by literally scratching off the word "forty" on the final hand-written version of the Constitution and replacing it with "thirty." *Records*, II: 644 (Sept. 17, 1787).

[96] *Records*, I: 551 (July 7, 1787). See also *Records*, II: 25 (July 17, 1787).

of constitution makers are defined by a multiplicity of interests but that a common and primordial fear of the consequences of not consenting ultimately motivates these individuals to consent to the establishment of a nearly omnipotent form of government. A second account, the Lockean story of state creation, proposes a different motivation for overcoming distributional conflicts, contending that the set of constitution makers is bound by their commitment to a shared set of interests, ideas, and expectations. As a consequence, the distributional differences that invariably arise from comparison of different rules of apportionment are superseded by the shared interest in attaining a higher set of interests.

Recall also the alternative account provided to describe the formation of the Articles of Confederation. This third story of political formation provided a more credible account by focusing on the consequences of a simultaneous reduction in the expected authority of the national government and in the collective decision-making capacities of each principal political interest and their intragovernmental agents. More specifically, commitment to a particular rule of apportionment and to a common political framework was prompted by two common expectations. The first was that no state or coalition of states would ever dominate the decision-making process within the Confederation Congress. The second was that subsequent majority coalitions within Congress would be temporary and generally enfeebled.

Unfortunately, this alternative story of the initial formation of the American political order does not account for significant elements of the proceedings of the 1787 Constitutional Convention. Delegates to the 1787 convention shared a general commitment to comparatively higher levels of collective authority in the national government. Moreover, the central proposal of the Virginia plan was a new rule of apportionment intentionally designed to increase, not equalize, the decision-making capacities of several states within the Union.

The Hobbesian account of state formation also does not seem to fit particularly well with the proceedings of the 1787 Convention. For all the talk of the Confederation tottering to its foundation prior to this convention, historian Jack N. Rakove reminds us "it would be incorrect to assert that the Convention assembled in an atmosphere of true crisis." Despite the concerns about foreign threats and domestic upheavals that dot the private correspondence of several individuals, most political actors in 1787 did not act as if the nation was ripe for anarchy or as if the American people had demanded a new constitutional framework of national government.[97]

At a general level, the Lockean story of state formation appears to provide a better fitting account of the making of the U.S. Constitution. Delegates to the Convention were undeniably bound by their common commitment to empower the existing national government, to establish republican institutions of governance, to diffuse decision-making authority within the national government, and to maintain both national- and state-level governments. The set of constitution makers who assembled in Philadelphia also shared common political experiences and expectations. In addition to sharing general youthfulness, forty-three of the fifty-five Convention delegates had some type of national political experience.[98] Almost all the delegates had recent political experience within their home states and many appeared committed to political careers. Many thus shared similar practical experience in addition to a general appreciation of the art and necessity of political compromise.

Unfortunately, the correspondence between the Lockean story of state formation and the specific proceedings of the 1787 Convention appears to lack contiguousness. This story cannot account for the prolonged conflicts that defined the Convention's deliberations over the rule of apportionment or for the deeply rooted sectional distrust that continued after the Convention. The essential Lockean assumption of shared interests and goals would seem to preclude the threats of disunion issued before and during the Convention, let alone the necessity of a constitutional convention altogether. The purported common orientation should have been equally evident within Congress under the Articles of Confederation. Moreover, the Lockean account's focus on the provision of greater general benefits does not suggest a motivation for a change in the rule of apportionment – especially, one that promises an inherently unequal distributional stream of benefits among the set of politically relevant actors who attended the 1787 Convention.

Given the diversity of interests within the Convention and among the states, how were the distributional conflicts over the proposed change in the Articles' rule of apportionment resolved and how was this resolution logically consistent with the establishment of a more powerful national

---

[97] Rakove, *The Beginnings of National Politics* (1979), pp. 396–399. See also John K. Alexander, *The Selling of the Constitutional Convention: A History of News Coverage* (Madison, WI: Madison House, 1990).

[98] See *Documentary History of the Ratification of the Constitution* (1981), 13: xlvi.

TABLE 7.11. *State Representation under Articles of Confederation and U.S. Constitution (Percent)*

	Articles of Confederation	U.S. Constitution: House	Senate	Combined	Date of Ratification
Smallest States					
Delaware	7.69	1.54	7.69	3.30	December 7, 1787
New Jersey	7.69	6.15	7.69	6.59	December 18, 1787
Georgia	7.69	4.62	7.69	5.49	December 31, 1787
New Hampshire	7.69	4.62	7.69	5.49	June 21, 1788
Rhode Island	7.69	1.54	7.69	3.30	May 29, 1790
Largest States					
Pennsylvania	7.69	12.31	7.69	10.99	December 12, 1787
Connecticut	7.69	7.69	7.69	7.69	January 9, 1788
Massachusetts	7.69	12.31	7.69	10.99	February 6, 1788
Maryland	7.69	9.23	7.69	8.79	April 26, 1788
South Carolina	7.69	7.69	7.69	7.69	May 23, 1788
Virginia	7.69	15.38	7.69	13.19	June 25, 1788
New York	7.69	9.23	7.69	8.79	July 26, 1788
North Carolina	7.69	7.69	7.69	7.69	November 21, 1789

government? As this chapter reveals, the delegates' disagreements over the new rule of apportionment were ultimately solved by adopting a new double rule, thereby splitting the seemingly discrete choice between equal state and proportional state rules of apportionment.

Why this "double rule" solution was deemed acceptable to the Convention delegates is related, in part, to the deliberative context of the Convention and, in part, to their common personal interests as participants in the potentially historic process of remaking the American political order. At a more general level, two additional interests supporting this new rule deserve noting for they apply to both the delegates that devised the new constitution and the principal political interests that subsequently ratified it.

The first interest was one that Madison ironically noted prior to the Convention: that most states would perceive they would be representational "gainers" under a new rule of apportionment. As Table 7.11 reveals, there was clearly an element of truth to Madison's astute observation. Under the new double rule of apportionment, every state benefited immediately from an aggregate increase in its representation within the national government – although not necessarily its relative

decision-making capacity. The smallest states maintained their existing
decision-making capacities in the Senate and gained additional representational opportunities in the House of Representatives. For the largest
states, the representational gain could often be measured in both absolute
and relative terms. Most southern states and their delegates remained
confident that over time their rapidly developing region would reap additional representation in the House and the Senate. As a consequence,
almost all delegates at the 1787 Convention (and ultimately all the states)
perceived their principal interests as better represented under the new
constitution than under the Articles of Confederation.

The second general interest prompting acceptance of the new double
rule of apportionment was the seemingly pervasive expectation that the
immediate and long-term distributional consequences suggested by this
rule were far less significant than the tacit recognition of the necessity of
maintaining a balance among the various political interests which constituted the Union. Commitment to the new rule of apportionment and
to the new form of national governance, therefore, turned not on a fixed
distributional calculus clearly articulated within the text of the new constitution. Rather, it was grounded more firmly in an open-ended willingness of American political leaders to commit themselves (and the
nation) to an ongoing process of deliberating toward general interests,
of negotiating among different interests, of validating stronger interests,
and accommodating weaker interests. From the various (and conflicting)
strengths and tensions of this commitment was forged the bond of a new
American Union.

CONCLUSION

Completion of a new constitutional framework for the American political order was neither inevitable nor simply a matter of aggregating
existing American political experiences. The architectonic work of formalizing a new process of governance and reformulating the existing
governing partnership among the states required the formation of a consensus, first among the individuals engaged in the serious business of the
1787 Constitutional Convention and second among the special state
conventions that were called on to ratify the U.S. Constitution.

Formation of a new constitutional consensus among these individuals (and the principal political interests they represented) was no easy
task as the intense deliberations of the 1787 Convention and of the subsequent state conventions clearly demonstrated. The new double rule of

apportionment incorporated into the U.S. Constitution was an elemental part of the statecraft that produced this new consensus and its most prominent immediate consequence: the wholesale but peaceful reconfiguration of the American political order. The relationship between the rule of apportionment crafted in 1787 and the subsequent development, breakdown, and reconstruction of the American political order is the story told in Chapters 8 and 9.

CONSTITUTIONAL CHANGE III: 1790–1870

8

The Relational Republic:
Macrolevel Conditions, 1790–1860

The double rule of apportionment fashioned at the 1787 Constitutional Convention served as the formal basis for the division of political representation within the U.S. Congress and the Electoral College for the next seventy-four years. The rule divided national representation among the states in three distinct ways: proportionally according to population in the U.S. House of Representatives, equally in the U.S. Senate, and the combined effect of these two methods in the Electoral College. The unique and combined distributional logics of these terms of apportionment sustained and oriented much of the constitutional development of the American political order until its collapse into civil war in 1861.

Given the deep sectional divisions that animated the 1787 Convention's debate over representation, the new rule of apportionment initially inspired different expectations and anxieties concerning each section's future political strength within the national government. Southern statesmen recognized that the new rule's demographic calculus likely guaranteed northern state majorities in the House and the Electoral College until at least the 1800 Census.[1] Many were convinced however that the new apportionment rule was particularly well designed for the South's rapidly growing population. The seemingly effortless development of the southwestern territory (and future states) of Kentucky and Tennessee's

[1] For more detailed accounts of these sectional expectations, see John R. Alden, *The First South* (Baton Rouge, LA: Louisiana State University Press, 1961); and Drew R. McCoy, "James Madison and the Visions of American Nationality in the Confederation Period: A Regional Perspective," in *Beyond Confederation: Origins of the Constitution and American National Identity*, Richard Beeman, Stephen Botein, and Edward C. Carter, eds. (Chapel Hill: University of North Carolina Press, 1987), pp. 226–258.

throughout the 1780s provided reassuring evidence of the section's future strength in the Senate as well.

Northern statesmen were decidedly less confident about the longer-term consequences of the new rule of apportionment. Emigration trends during the late eighteenth century promised to slow native-born growth rates in the northeast and, over time, to undermine the initial northern state majorities within both the House and the Electoral College. The comparatively slower settlement of the northern Ohio Valley during the 1780s and early 1790s coupled with initial expectations that this region would have distinct "western" (if not southward-leaning) interests also prompted doubts concerning the northeast's future strength within the Senate.[2]

Ironically, the nation's center of population continued to move westward during subsequent decades but never much further south than the latitude of Washington, D.C.[3] During the first half of the nineteenth century the distribution of political representation (and, thus, of national decision-making capacities) awarded neither the original northern nor the original southern states exclusive or effective control of the national government. Not surprisingly, the principal political interests within these sections and their agents within the national government made few commitments to expand national governmental authority or capacities between 1790 and 1860.[4] However, they expended considerable amounts

[2] The election of the Jeffersonian-Republicans in 1800 signaled the end of Federalist rule and the beginning, anxious New Englanders believed, of an irrevocable shift towards southern state control of the national government. Jefferson's election as President, not surprisingly, prompted both partisan attacks by the New England press and more serious complaints against the additional Electoral College votes the South received for its large enslaved population. Criticism of the Constitution's apportionment rule (and, in particular, its "three-fifths" formula) continued during subsequent years and several attempts were made to alter the Constitution's apportionment rule to include free persons only. See Herman V. Ames, *The Proposed Amendments to the Constitution of the United States* (Washington: Government Printing Office, 1897); Sereno Edward Dwight, *Slave Representation* (New Haven, CT, 1812).

[3] Margo Anderson, *The American Census: A Social History* (New Haven, CT: Yale University Press, 1988), p. 98.

[4] Between 1830 and 1860, the capacities of the national government increased in several ways. The number of federal employees increased significantly faster than population growth. Much of this increase was related to a scale change in the size of the national postal system. During this same period national governmental expenditures constituted about 2 percent of the total national income without any indication of inevitable increases in the future. (See William E. Geinapp, "Politics Seem to Enter into Everything": Political Culture in the North, 1840–1860," in *Essays on Antebellum Politics, 1840–1860,* Stephen E. Maizlish and John J. Kushma, eds. (College Station, TX: Texas A&M University Press, 1982), p. 43n.50; Paul B. Trescott, "The United State Government and

of time and resources toward strengthening their relative decision-making capacities within the national government. These efforts failed to achieve their desired end, not only because of the obvious diversity of interests among and within the states of both sections, but also because these coalition-building efforts were often directed toward the cross-purposes of forming and promoting transsectional political parties and of maintaining territorially cohesive sectional allegiances. Contrary to conventional wisdom, the fateful 1860 elections signaled the continuation of, not an end to, the general uncertainty concerning control of the national government because the Democrats – although internally fractured – retained the organizational and numerical capacity to control both the House and Senate while a relatively inexperienced Republican party and national political novice Abraham Lincoln won the Presidency.[5]

The American Civil War thus raises three questions. First, why did eleven southern states secede from the Union when the immediate consequences of losing the Presidency in 1860 seemed relatively insignificant and the longer-term consequences were, at best, highly ambiguous? Why, after a single electoral loss of a then clearly secondary branch of the national government, would any set of political actors be motivated to forsake the real and immediate benefits provided under the existing Union for the certain costs and projected (but still uncertain) benefits of forming a separate constitutional order? The second question mirrors the logic of the first: Why did the North resist secession in 1861 when the immediate benefits seemed, at best, marginal and the long-term costs of this decision were foreseeably high? The third and final question inquires why the sectional conflict in 1860–1861 ended in a civil war when prior sectional crises had been resolved peacefully.

To provide unequivocal answers to these classic questions (and, in turn, an account of the third constitutional change in the national rule

---

National Income, 1790–1860," *Trends in the American Economy in the Nineteenth Century* (Princeton, NJ: Princeton University Press, 1960), pp. 337–361).

[5] In the unusual 1860 elections, Lincoln received 39.7 percent of the popular vote and an Electoral College majority that did not include a single southern state. Without the subsequent series of state secessions the U.S. Senate and the House would not have been controlled by the Republican Party. Moreover, according to historian Michael F. Holt, Democrats "won almost 44 percent of the popular vote in the free states in 1860" and "few people in the 1850s and 1860s anticipated that the Republicans would remain the permanent successors to the Whigs as the major anti-Democratic party in American politics." See Roy F. Nichols, *Blueprints for Leviathan: American Style* (New York: Atheneum, 1963), p. 140; Michael F. Holt, *Political Parties and American Political Development from the Age of Jackson to the Age of Lincoln* (Baton Rouge, LA: Louisiana State University Press, 1992), pp. 325, 333–334.

of apportionment), Chapters 8 and 9 reconstruct respectively the contextual conditions and the sequence of political decisions associated with the dissolution of the American Union in 1861. The operational breakdown of the national rule of apportionment agreed to in 1787 begins with the voluntary secession of eleven southern states in 1860–1861 and ends with their coerced return to the Union in 1865 and the subsequent formalization of a new rule of apportionment in the Thirteenth, Fourteenth, and Fifteenth Amendments to the U.S. Constitution.

Chapter 8 provides a description of the general context preceding the South's abandonment of the original Constitution's rule of apportionment. This chapter brings into focus the development of various economic, demographic, institutional, and ideological conditions between 1790 and 1860. Description of these four conditions over time offers an opportunity to assess both relative and absolute changes in these structural conditions as well as changes in American political expectations prior to the sequence of decisions that initiated the American Civil War.[6]

Chapter 8 is divided into five parts. Part I briefly surveys the modern terrain of explanations for secession and the American Civil War. The remainder of the chapter turns to the task of reconstructing the general context within which this constitutional collapse occurred. Parts II and III focus on the development of economic and demographic conditions between 1790 and 1860. Part IV describes the long-term pattern of development in the institutional structures and capacities of the national government and offers numerous examples of how changes in the sectional distribution of political representation affected this development. Finally, Part V examines the ideological development of the concept of representation at the national and state levels between 1790 and 1860.

PART I: INTERPRETATIVE PERSPECTIVES

Like the American Revolution and the framing of the U.S. Constitution, the antebellum era and the American Civil War have been studied intensively and extensively by successive generations of political historians.[7]

---

[6] In accord with this study's general theory of political development, it can be recalled that changes in rules of apportionment become most probable when the set of relevant political actors have divergent or unfulfilled expectations concerning the level of governmental authority and/or their relative decision-making capacities.

[7] For reviews of this literature, see Edwin R. Rozwenc, ed., *The Causes of the American Civil War* (Lexington, MA: Heath, 1972); Eric Foner, "The Causes of the American Civil War: Recent Interpretations and New Directions," *Civil War History* (1974), 20: 197–214; David Potter, *The Impending Crisis, 1848–1861* (New York: Harper & Row,

Paradoxically, as the preconditions and the decisions preceding this constitutional breach have become broadly familiar, the causes of its breakdown have become more perplexing. The more that is known, the less satisfying the existing set of accounts has become.

Accounts of the causes of secession and the subsequent civil war are typically carried by two general logics.[8] The first general logic portrays the American Civil War as an inevitable and "irrepressible" culmination of deeply embedded economic, cultural, or ideological differences between the North and South. Sectional differences concerning the legality and morality of slavery are often highlighted in these accounts. Some, like historian John Ashworth, explain that "the origins of the American Civil War" can be traced to the differentiation of the northern and southern economies during the first quarter of the nineteenth century.[9] Accounts compelled by the second general logic typically deny the inevitability of the Civil War. These accounts generally downplay sectional differences or portray them as the source of common, if not entirely manageable, tensions within the American political order.[10] In these accounts, the subsequent constitutional collapse is attributed to the destabilizing combination of a small number of inflammatory extremists and the era's unfortunate dearth of statesmen.

Although contradictory in their methodological assumptions and explanatory conclusions, accounts made from both approaches clearly offer many important insights into the structural context and the personal forces present in late 1860 and early 1861. The fact remains that

---

1976), pp. 30–50; Charles Crowe, "Civil War: Meanings and Explanations," in Jack P. Greene, *Encyclopedia of American Political History* (New York: Scribner, 1984), pp. 251–272; *Political Parties and American Political Development* (1992), pp. 303–322; Hugh Tulloch, *The Debate on the American Civil War Era* (New York: Manchester University Press, 1999).

[8] The social science analogues of these two general logics are the "structural" explanation and the "punctuated equilibrium" explanation. The former attempts to correlate aggregate-level indicators of political behavior or environmental conditions with political decisions or outcomes. Political change is thus explained in terms of observed changes in aggregate-level phenomena. The punctuated equilibrium explanation presumes that political order is grounded on a generally stable and static set of relationships. Therefore, large-scale political changes are explained with reference to exogenous, destabilizing shocks or forces that destroy the set of working relationships of the existing order. In the aftermath of these tidal disruptions, there is a functional necessity to fashion a new set of political relationships and their attendant institutions.

[9] John Ashworth, *Slavery, Capitalism, and Politics in the Antebellum Republic* (Cambridge, UK: Cambridge University Press, 1995), p. 79.

[10] For a recent and more sophisticated version of this second general logic, see Brian H. Reid, *The Origins of the American Civil War* (London: Longman, 1996).

neither account provides a generally satisfying explanation for why a peacefully negotiated settlement of sectional differences failed in mid-1861. The basic explanation provided by the first set of accounts is unsatisfactory for two reasons. First, these accounts implicitly assume that environmental conditions broadly orchestrate the decisions of political actors. These accounts implicitly deny the voluntarism and accountability of political decision makers by assigning a rough functionalist form of causality to the structural conditions that existed in 1860. The second reason is empirical, and emphasizes that the specific causal leap taken from the structural context in 1860 to the particular sequences of political decisions is too retrospective because for all the obvious differences between the North and South there were as many and, in all likelihood, more similarities between the sections in 1860 than at any point since 1776.[11]

The second set of explanations is equally as unsatisfying although for entirely different reasons. These accounts typically ignore structural influences altogether and instead attribute the causes of the Civil War wholly to the era's political leaders whose political skills are dismissed as unusually inadequate. Secession and the American Civil War, in this view, seem to be the culmination of a process of political drift, without any notable compulsion or resistance from the existing context and without much thought or effort by the set of political actors prior to 1860. Not only is the idea of spontaneous political change of this magnitude difficult to imagine, there is little evidence these political actors were any less qualified than those who negotiated peaceful resolutions of prior sectional crises. Turnover rates for members of the U.S. House of Representatives remained consistently high throughout the antebellum era. And the question remains why the virulent rhetoric of secession became widely appealing in 1860 whereas it had customarily been ignored by most southern and northern statesmen during the preceding thirty years.

Given the benefits of a synthesis of structural conditions with critical decision sequences, a new account of the secession crisis seems in order.[12]

---

[11] See especially Joel H. Silbey, "The Civil War Synthesis in American Political History," *Civil War History* (1964), 10: 130–140; Edward Pessen, "How Different from Each Other Were the Antebellum North and South?," *AHR* (1980), 85: 1119–1149.

[12] Barry R. Weingast's account of the secession crisis is exceptional in one respect because it simultaneously explains why the stakes at the end of the 1850s were higher after the second party system collapse compared with prior sectional crises, and why secession and civil war remained highly contingent events. See Barry R. Weingast, "American Democratic Stability and the Civil War: Institutions, Commitment, and

To effect this end, this chapter follows the analytical format established in Chapters 2 and 5, turning first to examine and then to describe the content and development of economic, demographic, institutional, and ideological conditions between 1790 and 1860.

PART II: ECONOMIC CONDITIONS

In the early national period and for much of the nineteenth century, the U.S. economy was shaped by many of the agrarian institutions and practices that had structured the economies of the American colonies. All the original states shared this common economic ancestry. Shortly after Independence, small regional differences gradually emerged. In northern American states small home manufacturing sectors developed as did vibrant commercial sectors anchored around the coastal shipping business.[13] The climate and geography of the southern states, by contrast, encouraged a more single-minded focus on agricultural products, especially staple exports like tobacco, rice, and cotton.

In the aftermath of the War of 1812, a relatively small but significant process of economic conversion began in the northeastern and mid-Atlantic states that would have longer-term and fundamentally different economic and political consequences for the northern and southern

Political Behavior," *Analytic Narratives*, Bates, Greif, Levi, Rosenthal, and Weingast, eds. (Princeton, NJ: Princeton University Press, 1998).

Richard Bensel's account of secession in *Yankee Leviathan* (Cambridge, UK: Cambridge University Press, 1990) is exceptional in a second respect because it recognizes both fundamental structural differences between the sections and a calculus defined in terms of distinct sectional preferences for national governmental authority and an expected shift in sectional decision-making capacities. The latter calculus parallels the general theory of political development defined in this account, although this chapter and Chapter 9 offer alternative descriptions of the structural conditions as well as of sectional preferences and expectations. Our counterfactual speculations concerning the horizon of possibilities in late 1860 and early 1861 and the inferences we draw from them also differ. These differences may be artifacts of the methodological differences between our accounts, or they may well be effected by the different temporal frameworks within which our inquiries are embedded. Whereas Bensel's perspective on secession is essentially retrospective in that it is the pivotal event that precedes the Civil War, the subsequent failure of Reconstruction, and the creation of a national political economy, this account explains the secession crisis and the initiation of the Civil War from the perspective offered by the preceding eighty years of civil peace and contestation over the substance and meaning of the American Union.

[13] James A. Henretta, "The War for Independence and American Economic Development," in *The Economy of Early America*, Ronald Hoffman et al., eds. (Charlottesville: University of Virginia Press, 1988), pp. 45–87.

sections of the nation. Fueled initially by the depletion of New England's notoriously craggy soil and aided by the adaptation of European technologies, improvements in intrastate transportation, and an infusion of foreign capital, small but more specialized manufacturing industries developed within a corridor extending from Massachusetts to Maryland. Urbanization, modest at first, paralleled these advancements, transforming northeastern cities like Boston, Philadelphia, and New York into new domestic consumer markets and focal points of the nation's budding financial, manufacturing, and foreign trade businesses.[14]

As these nascent northeastern markets and industries developed in the 1820s and 1830s, the economies of the most southern states also enjoyed a notable expansion.[15] The South's expansion was driven primarily by increases in agricultural exports made possible by the nefarious institution of production: human slavery. As a consequence, the latter region never established the kind of control over its economy that followed the northeast's diversification into commerce and manufacturing. Ironically, the South's success with the production and exportation of cotton unwittingly aided the transformation of the northeast's economy. For increased cotton exports between 1810 and the 1830s meant more business for northern ports and, in time, more investment capital for extending and developing its markets and manufacturing industries.[16]

Other decisions widened the divergence between the paths taken by the economies of the original thirteen states. The south Atlantic states never managed to develop the demographic conditions or the cultural or business institutions needed to sustain more commercial and diversified economies.[17] The region generally tended to plow the bulk of its investment capital back into agricultural production rather than into the expansion of its commercial, manufacturing, or transportation sectors. By 1860, the South had only 9.5 percent of the national capital invested in manufacturing and only 8.4 percent of the total number of persons

[14] David Ward, *Cities and Immigrants* (1971), pp. 25–28; Robert R. Russel, *Critical Studies in Antebellum Sectionalism* (Westport, CT: Greenwood, 1972), p. 78; G. S. Callender, "The Early Transportation and Banking Enterprises of the States in Relation to the Growth of Corporations," *Quarterly Journal of Economics* (1903), 17: 139–146.

[15] Cotton production, for example, increased 400 percent between 1810 and 1830. *Encyclopedia of American History*, Robert Morris, ed. (New York: Harper & Brothers, 1961), p. 506.

[16] Douglass C. North, *The Economic Growth of the United States, 1790–1860* (New York: Norton, 1966), p. 68. See also G. S. Callender, "The Early Transportation and Banking Enterprises of the States" (1903), 17: 111–162.

[17] The south, for example, rarely marketed its exports or directly controlled the goods it imported. North, *The Economic Growth of the United States* (1966), p. 67.

employed in this sector.[18] Southern towns consequently rarely developed strong commercial or industrial sectors or, more important, the larger consumer markets needed to attract foreign investment or inclusion within the northeast's transportation systems.[19]

To compound the institutional deficiencies of the South's economy, the northeast's investment strategies in transportation improvements allowed it eventually to forge close economic bonds with the new northwestern states carved out of the territory north of the Ohio River. Networks of turnpikes and canals initially, and railroads increasingly after 1830, opened northwestern lands and integrated northeastern cities with the new communities established throughout the northern Ohio valley. In time, these transportation systems not only served as conduits for the northeast's manufactured goods, they also returned northwestern agricultural products to the growing urban markets in the northeast.[20] Thus, by the 1840s, the economic future of the region between Boston and Baltimore seemed inextricably bound to the new, emerging markets of the northwest.[21]

PART III: DEMOGRAPHIC CONDITIONS

Although too much can be made of the early economic indicators of the 1860–1861 secession crisis, the lines of division eventually chosen by northern and southern statesmen paralleled demographic and cultural differences inherited from the colonial and early national eras.[22] Sectional divisions were readily apparent during the American Revolution and the earliest moments of national politics under the U.S. Constitution. Indeed,

[18] Russel, *Critical Studies in Antebellum Sectionalism* (1972), p. 192.
[19] See George Rogers Taylor, *The Transportation Revolution, 1815–60* (White Plains, N.Y.: M. E. Sharpe, 1951), pp. 85–86; North, *The Economic Growth of the United States* (1966), p. 122. See also Harriet E. Amos, *Cotton City: Urban Development in Antebellum Mobile* (University, AL: University of Alabama Press, 1985); L. Ray Gunn, *The Decline of Public Authority* (Ithaca, NY: Cornell University, 1988).
[20] Yet as Barrington Moore astutely observed, "The West's trade with the South did not decline absolutely, but actually increased. It was the proportions that shifted and helped to draw the West closer to the North." Barrington Moore, *Social Origins of Dictatorship and Democracy* (Boston: Beacon Press, 1993), p. 128.
[21] Russel, *Critical Studies in Antebellum Sectionalism* (1971), p. 210; North, *The Economic Growth of the United States* (1966), p. 206. See also Thomas Cochran, *Frontiers of Change: Early Industrialism in America* (New York: Oxford University Press, 1981).
[22] See Joseph L. Davis, *Sectionalism in American Politics, 1774–1787* (Madison, WI: University of Wisconsin Press, 1977); Charles S. Sydnor, *The Development of Southern Sectionalism, 1819–1848* (Baton Rouge, LA: Louisiana State University Press, 1948); and Avery Craven, *The Growth of Southern Nationalism, 1848–1861* (Baton Rouge, LA: Louisiana State University Press, 1953).

there had always been divisions (handwritten)

Treasury Secretary Alexander Hamilton's ambitious economic initiatives divided the first Congress so clearly along geographical lines that James Madison – and later Thomas Jefferson – made the extraordinary effort to create and organize an opposition party and an opposition newspaper, the *National Gazette*.[23]

Hamilton's initiatives called for federal assumption of national and state debts, creation of a national bank, protective tariffs to promote American manufacturing, federal funding and coordination of internal transportation improvements, and a liberal immigration policy to restrain labor costs. At the time, it was commonly believed these programs would be especially beneficial to northern states.[24] Despite the oppositionist efforts of Madison and Jefferson, northern state majorities in early Congresses enacted most of the economic plan envisioned by Hamilton.

During subsequent decades, southern statesmen repeatedly managed to block or curtail implementation of national transportation policies.[25] Their national-level successes did not, however, prevent public and private interests in northern states from investing heavily in state-level transportation improvements. As a partial consequence of this new infrastructure, northern cities and markets experienced phenomenal growth rates after 1820.[26] According to the 1860 Census, only fifteen of the one

increase in transport in states (handwritten margin note)

N. pop growth rapidly (handwritten margin note)

[23] For discussion of early sectional divisions and party organization, see Joseph Charles, *The Origins of the American Party System* (Williamsburg, VA: Institute of Early American History and Culture, 1956), pp. 80–90; and Thomas P. Abernethy, *The South in the New Nation, 1789–1819* (Baton Rouge, LA: Louisiana State University Press, 1961), pp. 13–14, 225, 306–310.

[24] Northern commercial and manufacturing interests, for example, received favorable tariff protections, a shipping monopoly on coastal trade, harbor improvements, and, as economic historian Robert Russel notes, "[e]ven the commercial fishermen claimed and secured bounties for their catches." Russel, *Critical Studies in Antebellum Sectionalism* (1972), p. 78.

[25] The South's successes can be attributed, in large part, to President Jefferson's insistence on a constitutional amendment authorizing federal involvement in internal improvements, and to subsequent Executive vetoes by Presidents Madison and Monroe. See James S. Young, *The Washington Community* (New York: Columbia University Press, 1966), pp. 180, 187–189; G. S. Callender, "The Early Transportation and Banking Enterprises of the States in Relation to the Growth of Corporations," *Quarterly Journal of Economics* (1903), 17: 111–114; and Carter Goodrich, "National Planning of Internal Improvements," *PSQ* (1948), 63: 36–39; Paul Kantor with Stephen David, *The Dependent City* (Glenview, IL: Scott, Foresman, 1988), pp. 45–61; Stuart Bruchey, *The Roots of American Economic Growth, 1607–1861* (New York: Harper & Row, 1968), p. 127; Sydnor, *The Development of Southern Sectionalism* (1948), pp. 179–181.

[26] In the 1850s, for example, the population of New York City grew by 79 percent; Philadelphia grew by the even more remarkable decennial rate of 366 percent. The national decennial rate during this decade was 36 percent. See Dennis R. Judd, *The Politics of American Cities*, 3rd. ed. (San Francisco: HarperCollins Publishers, 1988), p. 15.

TABLE 8.1. *Population Growth and U.S. Cities,*
1790–1860

	1790	1830	1860
Northern Cities			
New York[a]	33,131	217,985	1,080,330
Philadelphia	42,520	161,410	565,529
Boston	18,038	61,392	177,840
Cincinnati	–	24,831	160,000
Chicago	–	–	109,000
Buffalo	–	8,653	81,129
Newark	–	10,953	71,941
Albany	3,498	24,238	62,367
Southern Cities			
Baltimore	13,503	80,625	212,418
New Orleans	–	46,310	168,675
St. Louis	–	5,852	160,000
Louisville	–	10,341	68,033

[a] New York total includes population of Brooklyn.
Source: Statistical View of the United States, DeBow, ed.
(1854), p. 192; *Statistics of the United States in 1860* (1866),
p. xviii.

hundred most populous U.S. cities were in southern states and as Table
8.1 illustrates, only Baltimore and two other marginally "southern" cities
(New Orleans and St. Louis) rivaled the largest northern cities in
population.[27]

In addition to the South's inability or unwillingness to sustain higher
urbanization rates, other decisions contributed to the section's comparatively slower population growth throughout the antebellum period.
Emigration patterns unexpectedly shifted from their southwesterly direction in the 1780s to a more westerly direction and the fertile lands north
of the Ohio River. Historian Andrew Cayton convincingly argues that
this shift was triggered, in part, by the Washington administration's decision to commit federal troops and resources to the Northwest Territory

[27] *Statistics of the United States in 1860* (Washington, DC: Government Printing Office,
1866), xviii–xvix; Bruchey, *The Roots of American Economic Growth* (1968), p. 86.
See also significant sectional and interregional differences in urbanization rates between
1790 and 1860 in North, *The Economic Growth of the United States* (1966), p. 258;
Historical Statistics of the United States, Colonial Times to 1957 (Washington, DC:
Government Printing Office, 1960), pp. 8, 14.

and not to the area south of the Ohio River.[28] Other decisions and conditions sustained and intensified this shift during the next several decades.[29] More important, this unanticipated demographic change meant that southern states began to lose population to the northwest. By 1860 there were three times as many natives of southern states residing in the North than northern-born natives in southern states.[30]

Dramatic increases in immigration in the 1830s and 1840s were other unanticipated changes that benefited the North more than the South. These welcome increases were a consequence of many unrelated developments in both Europe and the British Isles. In the early 1840s it was not uncommon to hear public arguments in favor of increased immigration. "We want population," George S. Camp extolled in 1841, because immigrants "compound our wealth in a geometrical ratio, by adding not only to its sum, but still more to its means. By every immigrant that comes to this country, every man already in it is made somewhat the richer; the circle of his customers is widened; the demand for his abilities, his goods, and his estate is increased, and with it their price."[31] The 1850 Census notably revealed that most of the foreign-born population resided in northern cities or states.[32] A decade later, as Figure 8.1 illustrates, the 1860 Census confirmed this settlement bias, recording 3.5 million persons of foreign ancestry residing in free northern states and territories and only half a million in southern states.[33]

---

[28] Andrew R. L. Cayton, "'Separate Interests' and the Nation State: The Washington Administration and the Origins of Regionalism in the Trans-Appalachian West," *JAH* (1992), 79: 1, 39–67.

[29] See, for example, Timothy G. Conley and David W. Galenson, "Nativity and Wealth in Mid-Nineteenth-Century Cities," *JEH* (1998), 58(2): 468–493.

[30] *Statistics of the United States in 1860* (1866): lxv. See also Charles Sumner, "The Barbarism of Slavery" (June 4, 1860), *Charles Sumner, His Complete Works* (1969), 6: 158; Russel, *Critical Studies*, pp. 187–188.

[31] George S. Camp, *Democracy* (1841), p. 240. For a contrary (and pro-southern) view of the costs associated with unrestricted immigration, see Samuel C. Busey, *Immigration: Its Evils and Consequences* (New York: Arno Press, 1969 [1856]).

[32] D. W. Meinig, *The Shaping of America: Continental America, 1800–1867* (New Haven, CT: Yale University Press, 1993), p. 410. By 1860, only three southern states (Missouri, Louisiana, and Maryland) had a foreign-born population of more than 10 percent. Half the southern states had foreign-born populations under 2 percent. Thirteen of sixteen northern and western states had foreign-born populations over 10 percent, and ten states were over 15 percent foreign-born. See *Southern Economic History*, Ballagh, ed. (1909), pp. 595–606; Emory Q. Hawk, *The Economic History of the South* (New York: Prentice-Hall, 1934), p. 224.

[33] See North, *The Economic Growth of the United States* (1966), p. 245; Russel, *Critical Studies* (1972), pp. 188–189.

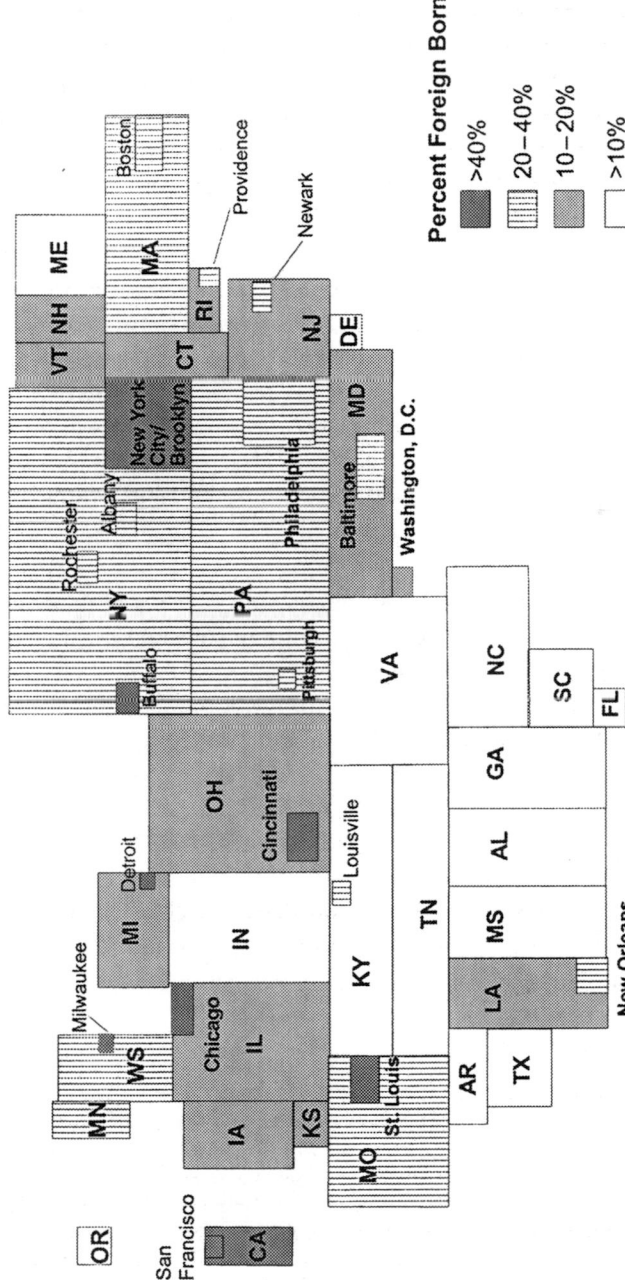

FIGURE 8.1. Foreign-Born Population, 1860. *Source: Population of the United States in 1860, U.S. Census* (1860). Cities identified have total population of more than 45,000

By the 1840 Census, southern statesmen recognized the longer-term political consequences of the North's commitment to economic development driven by technological improvements and a rapidly urbanizing, ethnically diverse population. Their responses reflected the diversity of ideas and interests that characterized the antebellum South. Popular opinion leaders like J. D. B. Debow, editor of *DeBow's Commercial Review*, and slavery apologist George Fitzhugh were long-time advocates of increased urbanization and commercialization. "The South," Fitzhugh urged, "must build up cities, towns, and villages, establish more schools and colleges, educate the poor, construct internal improvements, and carry on her own commerce." Others defended the virtues of a predominantly agrarian economy, and dismissed cities as "the seat[s] of free-soilism" which only would worsen "with every fresh arrival of European immigrants."[34] Still others like South Carolinian John C. Calhoun more romantically envisioned transportation improvements miraculously transforming the South from the "garden of the world" into "the centre of the commerce of the world."[35]

As sectional differences with the North widened, many in the South adopted the more simple solution of blaming northern prosperity on the latter's predominance in the national government. An editor of the *New Orleans Daily Crescent* repeated a common southern complaint that the Federal Government's "unjust, one-sided and partial policy of" encouraging "heavy annual immigration of foreigners" produced "enough foreigners to constitute a constituency for four or five additional representatives" for northern states. The editor additionally charged, "the whole policy of the Federal Government, from the beginning has been to build up and enrich the North at Southern expense." Tariff legislation "enabled the North to do nearly all the importing and exporting business of the country, with immense profit" and federal support of

---

[34] *Southern Economic History*, Ballagh, ed. (1909), p. 491; George Fitzhugh, *Cannibals All! or, Slaves without Masters* (Cambridge, MA: Harvard University Press, 1960 [1857]), p. 59, as quoted in David R. Goldfield, *Urban Growth in the Age of Sectionalism, 1847–1861* (Baton Rouge, LA: Louisiana State University Press, 1977), p. xxiii; *Southern Quarterly Review*, 26: 431, quoted in Herbert Wender, *Southern Commercial Conventions, 1837–1859* (Baltimore: The Johns Hopkins University Press, 1930), p. 47. See also John McCardell, *The Idea of a Southern Nation* (New York: Norton, 1979), pp. 103–104.

[35] John C. Calhoun, "Chair's Address, Southwestern Convention" (November 13, 1845) in *Report and Public Letters of John C. Calhoun*, Richard K. Cralle, ed. (New York: D. Appleton, 1855), 6: 274, 284.

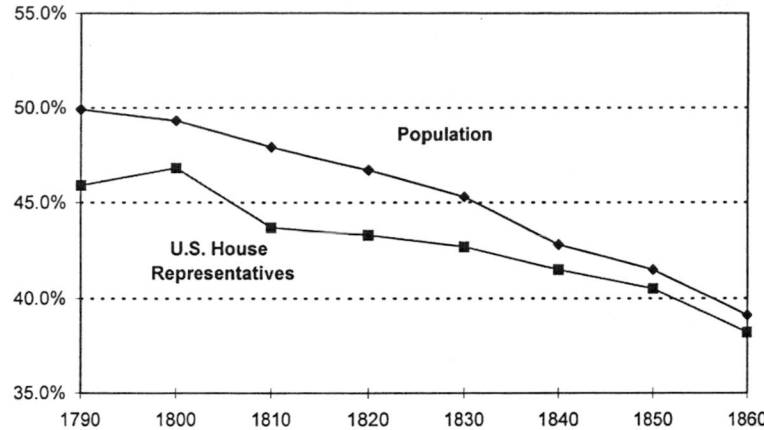

FIGURE 8.2. The South's Percentage of U.S. Population and the U.S. House of Representative, 1790–1860. Southern states include: Maryland, Delaware, Virginia, North Carolina, South Carolina, Georgia, Kentucky, Tennessee, Louisiana, Mississippi, Alabama, Missouri, Arkansas, Texas, Florida

fishing bounties, navigation laws, and large public land sales all "tend to aggrandize the Northern section of the Union."[36]

Although the effects of these national policies are not directly observable, by 1860 the South unquestionably had fallen behind the northern tier of states in wealth, investment, and production.[37] Nowhere were differences between the two sections more alarming and politically significant to the South as a distinct, definable section than in terms of population. As Figure 8.2 illustrates contrary to expectations in 1787, the South's population peaked at 49.9 percent of the national total in 1790 and steadily declined to 39.1 percent in 1860. And contrary to

[36] "Summer's Statistics," *New Orleans Daily Crescent* (June 15, 1860), in *Southern Editorials on Secession* (1964), pp. 126–127. See also *Southern Economic History*, James C. Ballagh, ed. (Richmond, VA: Southern Historical Publication Society, 1909), pp. 485, 664–666; and Busey, *Immigration: Its Evils and Consequences* (1969 [1856]), pp. 137, 149–150.

[37] See Charles Sumner's comparative analysis of regions in 1860: "The Barbarism of Slavery," in *Charles Sumner, His Complete Works* (New York: Negro Universities Press, 1969), 6: 144–161. For less polemical accounts, see North, *The Economic Growth of the United States* (1966); *Statistics of the United States in 1860* (1866), xviii–xix; Fred Bateman and Thomas Weiss, "Manufacturing in the Antebellum South," in *Research in Economic History* (1976), 1: 1–3; Taylor, *The Transportation Revolution, 1815–1860* (1951), pp. 84–86.

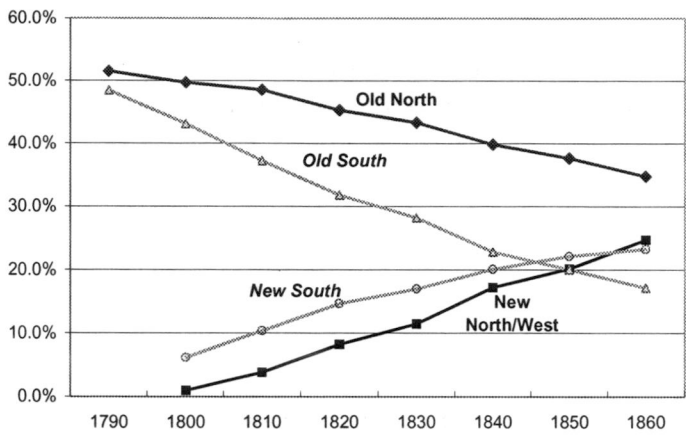

Key:
Old North: MA, NH, RI, CT, NY, NJ, PA, VT, ME
New North/West: OH, IN, IL, IO, WI, MN, OR, CA
Old South: MD, DE, VA, NC, SC, GA
New South/West: KT, TN, LA, MS, AL, MO, AR, TX, FL

FIGURE 8.3. Population Growth by Region, 1790–1860

initial complaints of New Englanders, the Constitution's three-fifths apportionment formula never gave the South a majority in the House of Representatives. The South's representation peaked at 46.8 percent in 1800 and declined to 38.2 percent in 1860.

Although the decennial trail of the South's representational decline is unmistakable, the section's overall economic conditions during the antebellum period were not in decline or on the verge of collapse in 1860. On the contrary, the economies of the southern states weathered the financial Panic of 1857 better than most and were growing modestly on the eve of secession, with cotton exports remaining immensely profitable and infrastructure and manufacturing investment on the rise.[38] Yet, as Figure 8.3 illustrates, by 1860 demographic trends of the older and newer regions of the South provided little basis for anticipating future relative gains against northern regions. On the contrary, the demographic reality recorded by the 1860 Census meant that as long as most southern statesmen remained wedded to the coalition strategy and ideology of sectional solidarity, the South would remain a national political minority well into the foreseeable future.

[38] North, *The Economic Growth of the United States* (1966), pp. 206–215.

[handwritten: looking for external forms]

PART IV: INSTITUTIONAL CONDITIONS

[handwritten: dominated natl politics]

Despite the erosion of the South's representation, southern statesmen dominated national politics throughout the antebellum period.[39] They accomplished this by relying on both their personal skills of political persuasion and a variety of institutional devices that effectively bolstered their decision-making capacities within the national government. Arguably the most important device was made possible by the emergence of national political parties defined by ideological rather than strictly geographical associations. James Madison, a member of the first U.S. House of Representatives, engineered this institutional solution with Thomas Jefferson and others shortly after northern congressmen aligned themselves into essentially the same voting bloc that had coalesced in the Continental Congress in 1785 and 1786.[40] Creation of the first national political party was thus essential to the political power of Madison, Virginia, and the southern states in general because it opened an alternative political dimension not immediately reflective of or affected by the distributional logic of the Constitution's rule of apportionment. In addition to increasing the number of coalition possibilities within Congress, the national parties institutionalized new behavioral norms that benefited the interests of southern statesmen conscious of their section's minority status. These party norms included the accommodation of member interests, resolution of controversies that avoided discrete geographical remedies, and the encouragement of a party identity that, on occasion, could be used to displace the more immediate, geographically discrete associations of economic interest and cultural identity.[41]

Other institutional devices also mitigated the South's relative decline in national representation. Southern members, for example, used party alliances with northern members to elect Speakers of the House sympathetic to southern interests. This strategy yielded more than ceremonial

[handwritten: Politicians sympathetic to S. interest]

[39] For illustrations of the dominance of southern statesmen, see *Congressional Globe*, 31st Cong., 1st sess., Appendix (July 8, 1850), p. 1178 (Rep. Truman Smith (CT-W)). See also Georgia Senator Alexander H. Stevens' 1861 survey in Jesse T. Carpenter, *The South as a Conscious Minority* (Gloucester, MA: P. Smith, 1930), pp. 180–181; and the fuller exposition in Leonard L. Richards, *The Slave Power: The Free North and Southern Domination, 1780–1860* (Baton Rouge, LA: Louisiana State University Press, 2000).

[40] See Charles, *The Origin of the American Party System* (1956), pp. 15–25. For a thorough account of the ideological rhetoric used to create the first Republican party, see Lance Banning, *The Jeffersonian Persuasion* (Ithaca, NY: Cornell University Press, 1978).

[41] See Carpenter, *The South as a Conscious Minority*, pp. 112–126.

benefits, for the Speaker during the nineteenth century controlled committee appointments and could provide southern members with critical opportunities to alter the pace and substance of the House's legislative agenda.[42] As the South's strength in the House became more tenuous with repeated decennial losses of representation, more ingenious and draconian devices were utilized. Most infamously, the House modified its debate rules in 1836 to include the so-called "gag rule" which systematically tabled abolitionist petitions. In the same year, Congress also refused to guarantee the delivery of abolitionist literature within South Carolina.[43]

As Southern representation declined in the House, southern statesmen turned increasingly to the Senate to protect their sectional interests. The Senate's function had shifted from what George Washington reportedly once described as "the senatorial saucer to cool" House legislation to what one U.S Senator in 1842 described as "the fountain, rather than the corrective of legislation."[44] The South's dependency on the Senate

[42] As northern members increased in number, contests for the House Speakership intensified. On several occasions, these contests were decided by plurality, not majority, voting. See Galloway, *History of the House of Representatives* (New York: Crowell, 1961), pp. 42–47; Allan Nevins, *The Emergence of Lincoln* (New York: Scribner, 1950), pp. 117–124; Shepsle, "Institutional Equilibrium, Equilibrium Institutions," p. 79n.28. For a vivid description of the 1859–1860 contest for the House speakership, see Bensel, *Yankee Leviathan* (1990), pp. 39–57.

[43] From 1790 to 1860, southern representatives also had substantially lower rates of turnover in the House than northeastern representatives. Southern representatives, as a consequence, typically had more political experience and were better positioned to benefit from seniority-based rules eventually adopted by the party caucuses. See Morris P. Fiorina, David W. Rohde, and Peter Wissel, "Historical Change in House Turnover," in *Congress in Change*, Norman J, Ornstein, ed. (New York: Praeger, 1975), pp. 34–35.

The contemporaneous account of Rep. John Quincy Adams provides additional evidence. After the Missouri Compromise, Adams noted significant differences in political skill between northern and southern members. In his diary, he wrote: "In the progress of this affair the distinctive character of the inhabitants of the several great divisions of the Union has been shown more in relief than perhaps in any national transaction since the establishment of the Constitution. It is perhaps accidental that the combination of talent and influence has been greatest on the slave side. The importance of the question has been much greater to them than to the other side. . . . They have threatened and entreated, bullied and wheedled, until their more simple adversaries have been half coaxed, half-frightened into surrender of their principles for a bauble of insignificant promises. . . . There must be at some time a conflict upon their very question between slave and free representation, but this is not the time, nor was this the proper occasion, for contesting it." John Quincy Adams, *Memoirs of John Quincy Adams*, Charles F. Adams, ed. (Philadelphia: J. B. Lippincott & Co., 1876), 5: 307–308.

[44] Galloway, *History of the House of Representatives* (1961), p. 224; and *Congressional Globe*, 27th Cong., 2nd. Sess. (May 27, 1842), p. 437: Senator Archer (VA-W).

affected its internal organization. After 1846, southern leaders used the extra-legislative device of the party caucus to dominate the committee appointment process. Historian Allan Nevins noted that "[o]f the twenty-two standing committees among which business was distributed" in 1858 "the chairmanships of sixteen went to slaveholding States, and of the six others to Northern Democrats politically sympathetic with the South. Not one really important Senate committee was allowed either a Northern chairman or a majority of Northern members."[45]

Not surprisingly, decisions to admit new states into the Union became intense political battlegrounds because they threatened to disrupt the representational equilibrium in the Senate on which the South's power depended. Tacit agreements and more explicit compromises like the 1820 Missouri Compromise were negotiated in Congress to pair the admission of free and slave states – ingeniously institutionalizing the practice and an expectation for a sectional balance in the Senate which contravened the distributional logic of the rule of apportionment for the House of Representatives and the Electoral College.[46] See Table 8.2.

The norm of paired state admissions worked for several decades until it became clear that territorial barriers against slavery in the Northwest Ordinance and the Missouri Compromise established definite and predictable limits on the South's representation within the Senate. Western and southern expansion of the Union became another salve for many southern statesmen who hoped additional territorial acquisitions could prevent the formation of northern state majorities in both houses of Congress.[47] Ironically, the South's success in admitting Texas as a slave state in 1845 initiated a war with Mexico that, in the end, resulted in the possession of an immense tract of southwestern territory (including California) and not one additional slave state. As Table 8.2 reveals, California's eventual admission into the Union in 1850 broke the representational equilibrium between the North and South, and for the first time in forty years a decade began without a sectional balance in the Senate.

---

[45] Nevins, *The Emergence of Lincoln* (1950), II: 119.

[46] In 1820, Congress resolved a sectional deadlock by enacting the so-called Missouri Compromise, which maintained a sectional representational equilibrium in the U.S. Senate by admitting Maine as a free state and Missouri as a slave state. As a condition of northern support, Congress banned slavery from the territory north of the line 36°, 30'.

[47] Carpenter, *The South as a Conscious Minority* (1963) [1930], pp. 179–180; and Potter, *Lincoln and his Party in the Secession Crisis* (New Haven, CT: Yale University Press, [1942]), pp. 219–222.

TABLE 8.2. *New State Admissions and Senate Representation, 1788–1861*

State (Year)	Northern/Nonslave	Southern/Slave[a]
(1788)	12 (+2)	10
NC, RI (1789, 1790)	14 (+2)	12
VT, KY (1791, 1792)	16 (+2)	14
TN (1796)	16	16
OH (1803)	18 (+2)	16
LA (1812)	18	18
IN, MS (1816, 1817)	20	20
IL, AL (1818, 1819)	22	22
MO, ME (1820, 1821)	24	24
AR, MI (1836, 1837)	26	26
FL, TX, IA[b] (1845, 1846)	28	30 (+2)
WI (1848)	30	30
CA (1850)	32 (+2)	30
MN (1858)	34 (+4)	30
OR (1859)	36 (+6)	30
KS (Jan. 1861)	38 (+8)	30

[a] Throughout the early national era, slavery was a legally sanctioned property right in every southern and several of the original northern states. In most of the latter states, a relatively small and diminishing number of individuals exercised this right. Of the approximately 40,000 northern-state slaves in 1790, three-quarters were held in New Jersey and New York [Levine, *Half Slave and Half Free*, (1992), p. 47].

[b] The admission of Florida and Iowa into the Union was paired. A boundary dispute between Iowa and a neighboring slave state, Missouri, delayed the territory's admission for over a year.

The widening of representational imbalances in Congress after 1850 prompted many southern leaders to support institutional remedies whose benefits were more conspicuously sectional. At the prompting of southern members of Congress and the Cabinet, for example, every Administration after 1848 offered to purchase Cuba from Spain in an undisguised effort to add another slave state to the Union.[48] When diplomatic

---

[48] As one newspaper derisively reported in 1860: "With the threats of secession ringing in his [President Buchanan's] ears, and an admission that he is powerless to prevent it, still upon his lips, he counsels still the purchase of Cuba. He would tax the people of these States hundreds of millions, to purchase Territory that may secede with the Gulf States before the ink used in drawing up the bill of sale is dry upon the paper. He knows . . . that a Southern Confederacy has long been a darling project of ambitious men in and out of South Carolina." "The President on the Crisis," *Iowa State Registrar*, Dec. 12, 1860, in *Northern Editorials on Secession*, pp. 154–155. See also "Third Joint Debate, Jonesboro, September 15, 1858," *The Lincoln-Douglas Debates*, Robert W. Johannsen, ed. (New York: Oxford University Press, 1965), p. 130; and "Fifth Joint Debate, Galesburg, October 7, 1858," pp. 234–235.

negotiations did not produce immediate results, military action was threatened and quasi-private efforts were encouraged to conquer Caribbean and Central American countries for their eventual admission into the Union.[49] When these ended in disaster or embarrassment, the search for other representational remedies continued unabated. Many southern leaders repeatedly accepted or cajoled sectionalist reactions and the perceived benefits of Democratic Party consolidation until the southern wing of the Whig Party withered and passed away.[50] With southern support, Illinois Senator and Democratic presidential aspirant Stephen Douglas pushed the ill-fated Kansas-Nebraska Act through Congress in 1854, thereby disrupting northern complacency toward southern sectionalism and the region's peculiar institution.[51] President James Buchanan also intervened on behalf of perceived southern interests, imploring Congress with rhetoric, patronage, and fraud to admit Kansas as a slave state under the illegitimately ratified Lecompton constitution. When these efforts failed to bolster southern interests in Congress, some southern statesmen embraced unprecedented judicial protection like that afforded by the U.S. Supreme Court in *Dred Scott v. Sandford* (1857).[52]

[49] For overview of southern expansionist schemes, see David M. Potter, *Lincoln and his Party* (1942), pp. 221–222; John Hope Franklin, *The Militant South* (Cambridge, MA: Harvard University Press, 1956), pp. 101ff.

[50] Michael F. Holt, *The Rise and Fall of the American Whig Party: Jacksonian Politics and the Onset of the Civil War* (Oxford: Oxford University Press, 1999).

[51] Don E. Fehrenbacher, *Sectional Crisis and Southern Constitutionalism* (Baton Rouge, LA: Louisiana State University Press, 1995); Barry Weingast, "Political Stability and Civil War: Institutions, Commitment, and American Democracy," in *Analytic Narratives*, Robert Bates, Avner Greif, Margaret Levi, Jean-Laurent Rosenthal, and Barry R. Weingast, eds. (Princeton, NJ: Princeton University Press, 1998), pp. 148–193.

[52] See Richards, *The Slave Power* (2000), pp. 52–106; *Dred Scott v. Sandford*, 19 Howard 393 (1857).

In *Dred Scott*, a highly fragmented Supreme Court denied African-Americans citizenship, voided the Missouri Compromise, and expanded Fifth Amendment protections of the property rights of slaveholders. The ill-fated attempt by the Court to remove the slavery question from the dictates of political negotiation seems highly improbable in hindsight. Not only was *Dred Scott* the first substantive federal policy overturned by the seventy-year old Supreme Court, but the logic of Chief Justice Taney's opinion concerning the rights of African-Americans contradicted long-settled jurisprudence and legal practices in northern and southern state courts. The modern conceptualization of an independent, rights-oriented federal judiciary has its historic roots in the Reconstruction era, not in the period prior to the Civil War. For an account of the rights protections afforded by antebellum state courts, see A. E. Nash Keir, "A More Equitable Past? Southern Supreme Courts and the Protection of the Antebellum Negro," *North Carolina Law Review* (1970), 48: 197–242; William Nelson, "Changing Conception of Judicial Review: The Evolution of Constitutional Theory in the States, 1790–1860," *University of Pennsylvania Law Review* (1972), 120: 1166. For other issues concerning the U.S. Supreme Court prior to the Civil War, see Jesse Carpenter, *The South as a Conscious Minority* ([1930], 1963), pp. 162–163.

TABLE 8.3. *Representation of the South in House of Representatives and Electoral College (1787–1861)*[a]

Year	House Size	No. of North Representatives	No. of South Representatives	South % in:	
				House of Representatives	Electoral College
1787	65	35	30	46.2	46.2
1792	105	57	48	45.7	45.9
1802	141	76	65	46.1	46.8
1811	181	103	78	43.1	43.7
1822	213	123	90	42.3	43.7
1832	240	141	99	41.3	42.7
1842	223	135	88	39.5	41.5
1852	234	144	90	38.5	40.5
1861	233	148	85	36.5	38.2

[a] House size, numbers of representatives, and Electoral College size do not reflect inter-decennial assignment of representatives to newly admitted states. Data for 1850 include 1852 supplemental apportionment act which added one member to House size. Data for 1861 include the admission of Kansas but not Congress's decision to add eight additional House seats in 1862. For the sake of consistent tabulation, Maryland, Delaware and Missouri are considered "southern" states. See 1 Stat. 253 (April 14, 1792); 2 Stat. 128 (Jan. 14, 1802); 2 Stat. 669 (Dec. 21, 1811); 3 Stat. 651 (Mar. 7, 1822); 4 Stat. 516 (May 22, 1832); 5 Stat. 491 (June 25, 1842); 9 Stat. L. 428 (May 23, 1850), 10 Stat. L. 25 (July 30, 1852), House Ex.Doc. No. 2, 37th Cong., 1st sess. (Aug. 2, 1852); Department of the Interior Report to H. of Rep., *Congressional Globe*, 37th Cong., 1st sess. (July 8, 1861), p. 26.

In the end, all these efforts did nothing to reestablish the desired sectional equilibrium in the Senate or to reverse the decline of the South's representation in the House of Representatives. As a consequence, those who sought to promote distinctly southern interests found themselves increasingly dependent on their influence over the Presidency. Yet as Table 8.3 reveals, the section's electoral influence over this institution of the national government diminished over time as well.

Long before these elemental indicators of national representation forecast the political decline of the South, southern leaders were resourceful in heightening their section's influence in presidential elections. From 1800 through 1824 these leaders used the practice of selecting presidential candidates by congressional party caucus to nominate three Virginians in six consecutive elections. As the South's representation in the House declined again after the 1822 reapportionment and with almost 89 percent of Congress affiliated with the Democratic-Republican Party

– including many northern members – nomination by congressional caucus and its per capita voting rule conveniently fell into disfavor among southern statesmen.[53] National nominating conventions permanently replaced the caucus by the 1832 elections, with the first convened in Baltimore in 1831. Southern members of the new Democratic Party quickly adapted this new institution to the advantage of their section by forcing the party to adopt a rule requiring that presidential nominees receive two-thirds of the convention delegates votes. The rule effectively guaranteed the section a veto power over the party's nominee throughout the antebellum period.[54]

In addition to these blatant attempts for sectional gain, other less obvious decisions and institutional reforms were instituted to bolster the representational strength of the South.[55] Congress's decision to decrease the House size after the 1840 Census is one example deserving closer attention. Although extant evidence may never allow a full portrait of this decision, the intense concerns for representation displayed by southern leaders throughout the antebellum period suggest a close connection to this pivotal yet understudied event in the institutional history of American representative government.[56]

After the 1840 Census, the House deliberated over its decennial reapportionment and agreed without much effort to increase the House size by 64 members to 306 members.[57] When the Senate took up the House

[53] South Carolinian John C. Calhoun credited himself and other party leaders for the demise of the caucus. Calhoun, *Works* (1856), 6: 249., as quoted in Charles W. McKenzie, *Party Government in the United States* (New York: Ronald Press, 1938), p. 292. See also *Diary of John Quincy Adams* (1951), p. 314.

[54] Southern delegates to the 1844 Democratic Convention used the super-majority requirement to deny the Party's nomination to Martin Van Buren of New York after he disclosed his opposition to the immediate annexation of Texas. At the convention, Van Buren delegates attempted but failed to repeal the two-thirds rule. Van Buren still received a majority on the first ballot. Southern delegates denied the New Yorker a two-thirds majority, however, and after eight more ballots James K. Polk of Tennessee received the Party's nomination. See Richard P. McCormick, *The Presidential Game* (New York: Oxford University Press, 1982), pp. 180–181.

[55] See Potter, *The South and the Concurrent Majority* (1972).

[56] For another account of this event, see Johanna Nichols Shields, "Whigs in the 'Bear Garden': Representation and the Apportionment Act of 1842," *Journal of the Early Republic* (1985), 5: 370–382.

[57] *Congressional Globe*, 27th Cong., 2nd sess. (April 26, 1842), p. 445. Unfortunately, analysis of this decision is not possible because the two votes taken on the 50,179 ratio were not roll-call votes. The vote totals recorded by tellers were 86–72 and 90–59. Of the 242 House members, 84 and 93 members, respectively, were either absent or not voting. A previous vote for a 60,500 ratio was agreed to 82–60, according to a teller count (April 21, 1842, p. 436).

bill, however, a chorus of southern Senators demanded an unprecedented reduction in the House size, with many advocating a House of only 200 members. Virginia Senator William Rives contended that James Madison "was in favor of a maximum of 200" members.[58] Others like Missouri Senator Benton corrected this revisionism by noting that George Washington and Alexander Hamilton favored a large House and that James "Madison looked forward to four hundred [representatives] although [the territory of] Louisiana was not then acquired."[59]

Others supporting the suggested decrease argued that the House had become "unwieldy." Several House members adamantly denied this characterization and were upset that the Senate and several public journals "could stigmatize it as a bear-garden, and contend that its number must be reduced."[60] At the time, the House possessed a long-running and relatively effective committee system that gave the institution and legislative process a suggestively modern organizational form. Moreover, the institution had repeatedly demonstrated its ability to adapt to new legislative conditions by imposing additional procedural restraints on its members.[61] More to the point, as one House critic of the Senate's decision put it:

> The nation's population increased by approximately 33 percent in the 1830s. The House-approved 64-member increase was a 26 percent increase – a rate of increase substantially higher than during prior decades.

[58] See *Congressional Globe*, 27th Cong., 2nd sess. (May 26, 1842), p. 539: "a proper number now would be 200" (James Buchanan, PA-D); p. 540: "the largest [ratio] number" (John Calhoun, SC-D); p. 540: "the best selection ... one hundred fifty members" (William Preston, SC-W); (May 27, 1842); p. 545: "reduced to that Standard which best qualified the House ... about 200 [members]," (Rives, VA-W).

Support for a reduction in the House size first surfaced during House deliberations on the apportionment ratio. On April 21, 1842, twenty apportionment ratios were proposed which would have reduced the House size. Eleven were offered by Whigs and nine by Democrats. Fifteen of the twenty proposals were offered by southern state members. *Congressional Globe*, 27th Congress, 2nd sess. (April 21, 1842), pp. 435–436.

[59] *Congressional Globe*, 27th Cong., 2nd. Sess. (May 27, 1842), p. 404.

[60] *Congressional Globe*, 27th Cong., 2nd. Sess. (June 13, 1842), p. 621; W. C. Johnson, (MD-W); p. 622, Samuel S. Bowne (NY-D).

[61] See Galloway, *The History of the House of Representatives* (1961), pp. 65–79; Thomas W. Skladony, "The House Goes to Work: Select and Standing Committees in the U.S. House of Representatives, 1789–1828," *Congress & the Presidency* (1985), 12(2): 165–187; Gerald Gamm and Kenneth Shepsle, "Emergence of Legislative Institutions: Standing Committees in the House and Senate, 1810–1825," *Legislative Studies Quarterly* (1989), XIV(1): 39–66; Joseph Cooper and Cheryl D. Young, "Bill Introduction in the Nineteenth Century: A Study of Institutional Change," *Legislative Studies Quarterly* (1989), 14: 74, 77; Sarah A. Binder, *Minority Rights, Majority Rule: Partisanship and the Development of Congress* (Cambridge, UK: Cambridge University Press, 1997).

Where was the evidence... [for] the assertion that the people were in favor of reducing the number of their agents here? Where was the popular meeting, the resolutions, or addresses, declaring that this body was too numerous? Where was the public press, the organ of any party, that had ever put forth such an opinion? So far as the public presses had spoken on the subject, they were in favor of a moderate increase of the number of Representatives, in proportion to the increase that has been made at every census.[62]

Other opponents of the Senate's amendment, like Massachusetts Representative John Quincy Adams, argued "[h]e could not conceive of any thing more perfectly [i]llogical than this effort on the part of the Senate to decimate the House of Representatives."[63] Others in the Senate "utterly denied the assumption that turbulence and incapacity of business characterized the present House." Even if partially true, Senator Allen of Ohio charged, "we must put up with these freaks of passion in the House and the people. We must take the great good, liberty with the little evil, instead of great evil with little good, which would be the converse of the state of things complained of." Besides "[t]hese temporary outbreaks of passion [in the House] are the guaranties of public liberty" and "keep the eyes of men fixed on their rights."[64]

The Senate eventually voted to reduce the House to 223 members, a 19-member reduction. The vote divided the Senate along geographical lines: 18 of the 25 votes for the reduction were southern state Senators; and 16 of 21 votes against were from northern Senators. Of the five

Notably, the House in 1841 adopted the hour debate rule, further streamlining its proceedings. See Thomas Hart Benton, *Thirty Years' View, or A History of the Working of the American Government for Thirty Years, from 1820 to 1850* (New York: D. Appleton, 1856) II: 247. Senator Thomas Hart Benton also noted the example of "Massachusetts, where five hundred members now sit in one House, and where seven hundred and fifty sat before the separation from Maine and where the order, the decorum the transaction, and the despatch of business are as eminent as the most fastidious could desire." *Congressional Globe* (May 27, 1842), pp. 403–404. See also *Congressional Globe*, 27th Cong., 2nd. Sess. (May 26, 1842), p. 540.

[62] *Congressional Globe*, 27th Cong., 2nd sess. (June 16, 1842), p. 643, Samuel Gordon (NY-D).
[63] *Congressional Record*, 27th Cong., 2nd sess. (June 13, 1842), p. 620.
[64] *Congressional Globe*, 27th Cong., 2nd. Sess. (May 27, 1842), p. 546.

Missouri Senator Benton also reminded the Senate of "the experience of France, in its transfer of government from a republican form to an imperial form. It was by Bonaparte's influence," he recounted, "first over the smaller body, the Council of Ancients, when he was First Consul, that he was enabled to make his rapid strides to imperial power." Moreover, Benton noted, "It was his policy to reduce the legislative bodies till he got each of them under 100; and then there was not a voice raised for public liberty" for "[a] body of 500 men was too strong for him, they whipped him with the intellectual power which they possessed." *Congressional Globe*, 27th Cong., 2nd. Sess. (May 27, 1842), p. 544.

southern Senators opposed to the reduction, four were from "border" states and the fifth Senator, William R. King of Alabama, voted against the bill because he wanted an even smaller House![65]

When the Senate's amended bill returned to the House, the House promptly rejected it.[66] Here, too, divisions of geography patterned voting. The House reconsidered the bill several days later, ultimately agreeing to the Senate amendment; on this vote, southern state members voted better than two to one in favor of the measure. Northern state members constituted approximately 83 percent of those voting against the reduction.[67]

Contemporaneous accounts reinforce these suggestive sectional-voting alignments. After the Senate approved the reduction, Missouri Senator Benton privately informed Martin Van Buren of New York that support for a smaller House and for the additional requirement of single-member districts was "from the South" and was "aimed against the populous States which are the nonslaveholding." Massachusetts Representative and former President John Quincy Adams was equally certain of the source of support. In his diary, he indicated, "[a]n out-of-door negotiation with Southern slave-holders and Northern Five-Points Democrats has accomplished this revolution in the voting of the House . . . It is an exact counterpart," he insisted, "of the restoration of the gag-rule, effected in the same manner and by the same tactics."[68]

Given the unexpected depth of support for a smaller House from southern members of Congress, what sectional benefits could have been expected from this unusual decision in 1842? In the House, a smaller membership was likely perceived as increasing the capacity of southern members to garner voting majorities by reducing the immediate costs and the longer-term consequences of building coalitions with northern members.[69] In terms of the South's interests in the Senate, a smaller

[65] *Congressional Globe*, 27th Cong., 2nd sess. (May 27, 1842), p. 546. In a series of roll-call votes on May 27, 1842, Senator King (AL-D) repeatedly voted for apportionment ratios between 77,000 and 72,354, or House sizes between 193 and 208 members. See *Congressional Globe*, 27th Cong., 2nd sess., p. 546.
   For further evidence that sectional (not merely party) divisions affected voting in the Senate, see vote to strike "50,179" (May 25, 1842) and vote to insist upon "70,680" (June 15, 1842).
[66] *Congressional Globe* (June 13, 1842), p. 623.
[67] *Congressional Globe*, 27th Congress, 2nd sess. (June 17, 1842), p. 649. The final vote was 113–103. Southern state members voted 59–28 for reduction.
[68] "Benton to Martin Van Buren, June 3, 1842," *Martin Van Buren Papers*, as quoted in Shields, "Whigs Reform the 'Bear Garden'," p. 317; and Adams, *Memoirs of John Quincy Adams* (June 16, 1842), 11: 179.
[69] For effects of larger House size on coalition formation in Congress before 1828, see also Young, *The Washington Community* (1966), pp. 198ff.

Also wouldn't be as strong as senate

House was also understood as weakening that institution's traditional claim to possess a popular authority superior to the Senate.[70] Arguably more significant than these legislative benefits, a smaller House also offered small but significant sectional rewards in the Electoral College.[71] As Figure 8.4 illustrates, as the House size increases, the South's percentage share of the Electoral College approaches its percentage share of the House of Representatives. Thus, a reduction of the House size to 200 members improves the South's Electoral College share by two votes compared to its share in a 306-member House – the number approved in the initial House bill.[72]

This institutional change benefits the South if measured over time – especially when viewed in terms of the following decade's reapportionment process. In 1850, not only was there again strong southern support

[70] See *Congressional Globe*, 27th, 2nd sess. (May 26, 1842), p. 538, William Preston (SC-W). According to Senator Preston: "A proper relation ought to subsist between the two legislative branches of this Government. The members of the other House had a direct interest in keeping up their numbers; but the Senate had a further interest in preserving the equilibrium, and in preserving its own powers undiminished by an apparently overwhelming majority. It was a difficult matter to stand up against the moral influences of large majorities. He (Mr. P.) did not desire to see the House of Representatives so exclusively popular as to overlay the Senate."

[71] For examples of electoral reform devised primarily for their sectional Electoral College consequences, see Noble E. Cunningham, "The Jeffersonian Republican Party," in *History of U.S. Political Parties*, Schlesinger, ed. (New York: Chelsea House Publishers, 1973), I: 239–272; and McCormick, *The Presidential Game* (1982).

An Electoral College reform before the 1800 election deserves particular noting. In preparation for that election, historian Noble E. Cunningham notes, Republicans searched for ways to overcome John Adams' three-vote Electoral College margin in 1796. They were especially "anxious to deny him votes in 1800 in states where under a district system he might carry one or two districts in an otherwise Republican state. Virginia was such a state, Adams having won one electoral vote there in 1796. Early in January, 1800, the Republican majority in the Virginia General Assembly pushed through legislation changing the method of choosing presidential electors from election by district to election on a general ticket throughout the state." Cunningham, pp. 250–251.

[72] Contemporaneous evidence reveals an appreciation of this effect on the Electoral College. See George Tucker, *Progress of the United States in Population and Wealth* (Boston: Little Brown, 1843), pp. 124–125. See also Calhoun's highly suggestive speech on an unrelated topic in February 1842: *Congressional Globe*, 27th Cong., 2nd sess., Appendix, pp. 164–168, (Feb. 28, 1842); and p. 538 (May 26, 1842), Senator William Preston (SC-W): "was in favor of the old notion, that the Representatives ought to be in the proportion of three to one." For similar evidence from a previous attempt to fix the House size at 200 in 1821, see remarks of Virginia Senator James Barbour: "As you multiply the number of the House of Representatives, you give to it more the form, and eventually more of the character of a National, in contradistinction to a Federal Government." *Annals of Congress*, 17th Cong., 1st sess. (Dec. 18, 1821), p. 31.

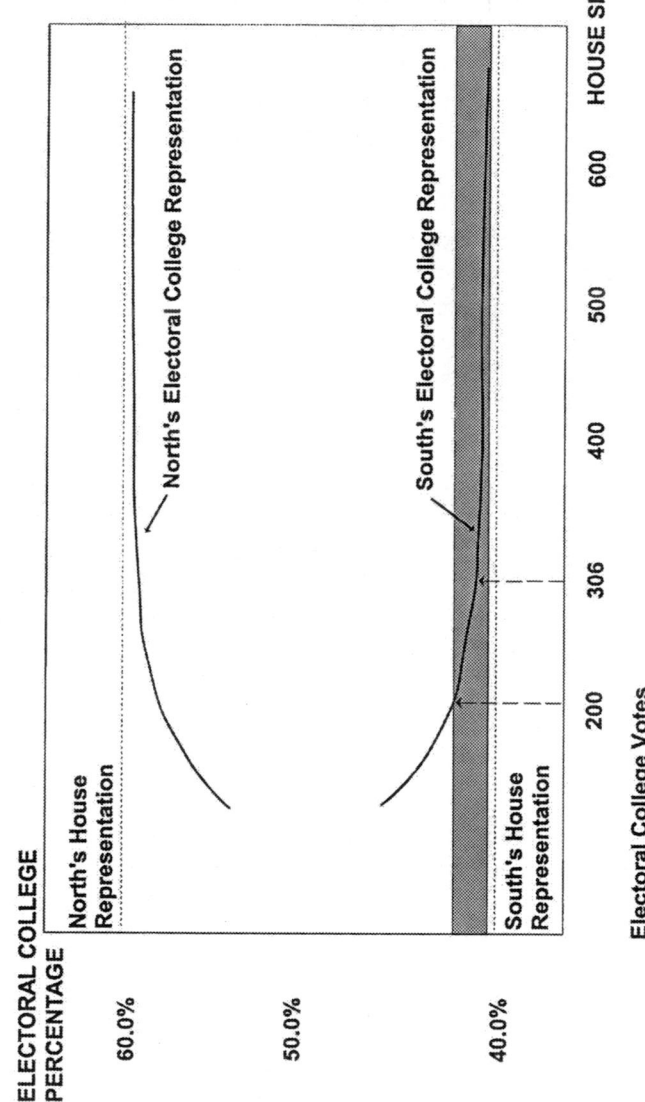

FIGURE 8.4. Sectional Effect of U.S. House Size on Electoral College Representation

338

for a further reduction in the House size, Southern members were a driving force behind using the bill authorizing the 1850 Census to establish an "automatic," nonlegislative House apportionment process. This clear violation of the congressional tradition of giving the House reapportionment legislation separate consideration *after completion of the decennial Census* and the hurried enactment of this unorthodox (if not procedurally unconstitutional) mechanism, were designed to have one obvious effect: the freezing of the House size.[73] Thus, over the long term, the 1842 reduction in the House size potentially increased the South's Electoral College representation by as many as eight votes compared to a House size that would have been allowed to increase to 600 members during subsequent decades.

In sum, the variety and sophistication of institutional structures devised and relied on by several generations of southern statesmen illustrate the centrality of their concerns for representation and their enduring desire to participate in governing the constitutional order established in 1787. As 1860 approached, however, these institutional strategies and structures increasingly failed to satisfy the political interests and aspirations of many southern statesmen. Once the bonds of political party fissured in the 1850s, many of these individuals were confronted by the reality that South Carolinian John C. Calhoun foresaw in his final Senate speech in 1850. According to Calhoun,

The census is to be taken this year, which must add greatly to the decided preponderance of the North in the House of Representatives and in the electoral college. The prospect is also, that a great increase will be added to its present preponderance in the Senate during the period of the decade, by the addition of new States. . . . There is not a single territory in progress in the southern section, and no certainty that any additional States will be added to it during the decade. . . . This great increase of Senators, added to the great increase of members of the House of Representatives and the electoral college on the part of the North, which must take place under the next decade, will effectually and irretrievably destroy the equilibrium that existed when the Government commenced.[74]

---

[73] See *Congressional Globe*, 31st Cong. (April 20, 1850), pp. 862–863; (May 6, 1850), p. 914; (May 7, 1850), pp. 923–930; (May 8, 1850), pp. 939–40.

[74] *Congressional Globe*, 31st Cong., 1st sess. (March 4, 1850), p. 451. Calhoun additionally cautioned the north that "[i]f you admit [California], under all the difficulties oppose her admission, you compel us to infer that you intend to exclude us from the whole of the acquired territories, with the intention of destroying irretrievably the equilibrium between the two sections. We would be blind not to perceive, in that case, that your real objects are power and aggrandizement, and infatuated not to act accordingly" (p. 455).

PART V: IDEOLOGICAL CONDITIONS – THE
CONCEPT OF REPRESENTATION

National and state-level discourses on the purposes, practices, and institutional forms of representative government between 1790 and 1860
offer additional opportunities to gauge American political expectations
prior to the 1860–1861 secession crisis. If southern and northern political leaders held fundamentally different views about the forms and functions of political representation, then the subsequent breakdown of the
American political order might be accounted for in terms of this underlying conceptual division. Over such an extended period, however,
generalizations concerning an ideological condition like the concept of
representation are problematic for several reasons. As noted in prior
chapters, conceptualizations are unobservable psychological phenomena.
Inferences concerning their development over time and place and among
different sets of individuals are riddled with selection bias problems and
highly tendentious assumptions regarding the consistency and universality of human cognition.

   Although a full assessment of the currents of political ideology during
the antebellum era exceeds the boundaries and goals of this study, a
partial measurement of the concept of representation can be completed
by focusing on national- and state-level organizational forms and practices between 1790 and 1860. This measurement is not easily completed.
The difficulties of compiling the record of American political development
(especially at the state and local levels) has proved so frustrating and time-
consuming that many elementary data (especially prior to 1900) remain
unavailable or only partially collected. Political historians and political
scientists have repeatedly noted this problem, the benefits to be gained
from coordinated efforts to preserve first-order research, and the necessity of multilevel data collection and theorization. Beyond the national
level, however, the empirical record today remains meager and fragmented, and therefore an obstacle to comparative historical analysis and
an embarrassment to most (if not all) generalizations concerning the
foundations and dynamics of American political development.

   Assessment of the development of the concept of representation prior
to 1860 is further complicated by the emergence and prominence of
transsectional political parties after the 1830s.[75] An attempt to track and

---

[75] For an exceptional comparative study of state political development, see McCormick,
The Second American Party System (1966).

disentangle the various national, state, and local discourses related to this significant political development is a necessary and highly complex research project but one, it seems, not particularly well suited to explain what, at bottom, was a geographically defined division of political expectations concerning the constitutional commitment established in 1787. To test for sectional differences concerning the conceptualization of representation, the following analysis focuses on the development of national- and state-level institutions of representation between 1790 and 1860.

With regard to the conceptualization of representation associated with the national government, the most significant development during this period was the already described redistribution of northern and southern state representation within Congress and the Electoral College. The emergence of national political parties at the turn of the century and their subsequent institutionalization in the 1830s opened a new dimension of coalition-building possibilities which allowed the southern states to mitigate the decennial decline in their national decision-making capacities.

Competitive political parties had other significant constitutional functions – not the least of which was the integration of national, state, and local political actors.[76] Too much can be made of the salience of political parties, however, if it is forgotten that real differences among the sections, the regions, and the states of the Union preceded and persisted after the construction of national political parties. Roll call analysis of congressional voting reveals that although party allegiance was important, members of Congress also remained loyal to (and were always circumspect about) their state, regional, and sectional interests.[77]

Other institutional developments prior to 1860 also affected the conceptualization of representation without regard to section or region. U.S. House district sizes, for example, increased continuously after 1790, but almost uniformly across the states. In 1790, the average House district size was slightly over 33,000 persons. By 1820, this average had increased to 40,000 and by 1850, the average House district contained almost 100,000 persons. These increases fundamentally altered the scale of the relationship between members of Congress and their constituents

[76] See Holt, *The Political Crisis in the 1850s* (1978), pp. 7–8.
[77] See Thomas B. Alexander, *Sectional Stress and Party Strength* (Nashville, TN: Vanderbilt University Press, 1967). For more on the salience of national party allegiances during the 1840s and 1850s, see Joel H. Silbey, *The Shrine of Party: Congressional Voting Behavior, 1841–1852* (Pittsburgh, PA: University of Pittsburgh Press, 1967); and Michael F. Holt, *The Political Crisis in the 1850s* (1978).

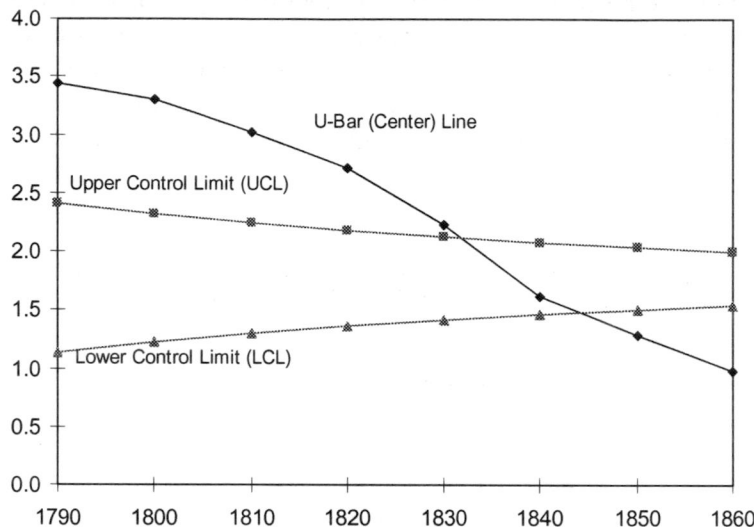

FIGURE 8.5. U.S. Representatives and U.S. Senators per 100,000 Persons, 1790–1860

Institutionalization/

→ led to IMPT of parties

and, along with other factors, encouraged the institutionalization of American political parties and of the U.S. House of Representatives. Figure 8.5 illustrates the general trend and timing of the scale changes in national representation. The causes of the rapid dissipation in the immediacy of the relationship between the American people and their representatives within the U.S. Congress after 1850 warrant special consideration.[78]

[78] In the 1920s, Dr. Walter Shewhart, who worked for Bell Telephone Laboratories, proposed and tested a theory for interpreting the causes of variation in manufacturing processes. W. Edward Deming subsequently applied Shewhart's theory of variation to numerous small- and large-scale processes, and he generalized its explanatory power to all causal systems. Demin's method for understanding his general theory of variation requires the creation of control charts that provide a means for distinguishing special variation from systemic variation. The type of chart is related to the type of data to be analyzed. For counts of items per unit of measure, for example, the u-chart is the most appropriate control chart for the assessment of variation. The u-chart is based on the Poisson mathematical model.

To assess variation in rates of "Representative per 100,000 persons," a u-chart has been created and is displayed in Figure 8.5. As with all control charts, the creation of this u-chart requires plotting individual "u" points and the determination of a central line as well as "upper" and "lower" control limits, UCL and LCL, respectively. In Figure 8.5, the data for each decade are represented as a "u" point that is calculated by dividing the number of occurrences (or U.S. Representatives) by the number of units observed

[handwritten: change to voting by popular vote]

Sectional differences are also not apparent in the general development of other institutions of representation adopted by the states. After 1832, for example, all but one state selected their presidential electors by popular vote.[79] The turnover rate for members of the U.S. House remained extraordinarily high by modern standards in both sections.[80]

[handwritten: turnover rate high]

(or total population in 100,000s). The center line, known as u-bar, represents the total number of occurrences (U.S. Representatives) in all subgroups (that is, for each decade) divided by "n," or the total number of units (population in 100,000s) in all subgroups. For the purpose of clarity, the center line which falls between the upper and lower control limits is not illustrated in Figure 8.5. UCL (the upper control limit) and LCL (the lower control limit) are calculated for each decade in order to account for different decennial population sizes. More specifically, the upper and lower control limits are calculated from the following equations:

Upper control limit (UCL):

$$\bar{u} + 3\sqrt{\frac{\bar{u}}{n}}$$

Lower control limit (LCL):

$$\bar{u} - 3\sqrt{\frac{\bar{u}}{n}}$$

See Gregory M. Bounds et al., *Beyond Total Quality Management: Toward the Emerging Paradigm* (New York: McGraw-Hill, 1994), pp. 357–371.

According to Deming, points that fall above UCL or below LCL can be considered so meaningfully different as to prompt the search for a special cause. The causes of variation associated with points that fall between UCL and LCL could very well be attributed to natural variation which affects all systems. In *The New Economics for Industry, Government, Education*, Deming also cautioned that "It is possible that a control chart may fail to indicate [the] existence of a special cause when one is actually present. It may send us scouting to find a special cause when there is none. It is wrong ([and a] misuse of the meaning of a control chart) to suppose that there is some ascertainable probability that either of these false signals will occur. We can only say that the risk to incur either false signal is very small." *The New Economics for Industry, Government, Education* (Cambridge, MA: Massachusetts Institute of Technology, 1993), p. 181.

[79] McCormick, *The Second American Party System* (1966), pp. 28–29.

[80] Between 1791 and 1831, the average percentage first-time members of the U.S. House was 42.5 percent. Between 1833 and 1859, this average increased to 50.6 percent. See Stuart A. Rice, *Quantitative Methods in Political Science* (New York, Knopf, 1928), p. 296; or Nelson W. Polsby, "The Institutionalization of the U.S. House of Representatives," *American Political Science Review* (1968), 62: 146. For a more precise measure of turnover that controls for the expansion of House size, see Morris Fiorina, David W. Rohde, and Peter Wissel, "Historical Change in House Turnover," in *Congress in Change* (1975), pp. 24–57. For House turnover averages between 1790 and 1798 by state, see Rudolph Bell, *Party and Faction in American Politics: The House of Representatives, 1789–1801* (Westport, CT: Greenwood Press, 1973), p. 8. For evidence that southern members generally served longer than northeastern members between 1789 and 1970, see Fiorina, Rohde, and Wissel, "Historical Change in House Turnover," in *Congress in Change* (1975), pp. 34–35.

TABLE 8.4. *U.S. House District Types, Number of States, 1790–1859*

Decade:	1790	1800	1810	1820	1830	1840	1850
District Type:							
Single-Member	7	8	7	13	14	25	28
At-Large	7 [1]	7 [1]	6 [1]	8 [4]	8 [2]	1 [1]	3 [2]
Mixed	1	2	5	3	3	0	0

Note: Number of states entitled to only one U.S. Representative are bracketed but included within the "At-Large" total. "Mixed" district type composed of single- and multimember districts.

TABLE 8.5. *State Failures to Complete Decennial Redistricting of U.S. House Districts, 1790–1859*

Decade:	1790	1800	1810	1820	1830	1840	1850
Section:							
Old North							Connecticut
New North/ West							
Old South		Maryland	Maryland	Maryland N. Carolina S. Carolina	N. Carolina S. Carolina		
New South/ West					Louisiana		Kentucky Texas

Table 8.4 illustrates that after 1820 almost two-thirds of the states established single-member districts for U.S. House elections. In 1842, Congress mandated this districting standard for every state entitled to two or more House members.[81] With few exceptions, U.S. Representatives were elected from single-member districts in the 1840s and 1850s.

Decennial redistricting of U.S. House representation became a well-established state practice during the first half of the nineteenth century. After excluding states with at-large congressional districts, there are only eleven cases prior to 1860 in which a state failed to enact a new decennial redistricting plan. Table 8.5 reveals that ten of these cases occurred in southern states, although after 1840 this sectional distinction disappears.[82]

---

[81] 5 Stat. L. 491 (June 25, 1842).

[82] For an impressive and comprehensive record of congressional redistricting by the states, see Kenneth C. Martis, *The Historical Atlas of United States Congressional Districts, 1789–1983* (New York: Free Press, 1982), Table 6.

Figure 8.6 offers a final subnational-level test for sectional differences by examining the development of intrastate variability in congressional district sizes for every state between 1790 and 1860. The states are grouped sectionally and the specific measure adopted for district variability is the decennial percentage standard deviation from each state's decennial mean district size.[83] Over these seven decades, district variability diminished from approximately 24 to 14 percent of the decennial district average. On average, intrastate congressional districts became more equal in population between the establishment of the U.S. Constitution and the South's decision to secede from the Union. Northern state congressional districts, as evidenced by Figure 8.6, approached the ideal of population equality more closely than southern state congressional districts. Sectional differences were typically small, however, and clearly did not forecast the South's dramatic exit from the Union.

Although this admittedly partial survey of institutions of national representation does not suggest a basis for the divergent political expectations prior to the 1860–1861 secession crisis, it does provide an empirical grounding for several generalizations concerning the conceptual development of national-level representation between 1790 and 1860. The most significant change was the precipitous decline in the South's representation in Congress and the Electoral College, a direct consequence of the rule of apportionment established by the U.S. Constitution. In 1860, this rule determined the relative decision-making capacities of the two sections and it provided sectionally minded political leaders with a fixed logic by which they could project their future decision-making capacities within the national government.

A second generalization runs counter to the first: Beyond the unequal sectional consequences of the original Constitution's House apportionment rule, there were few sectional differences in the institutional forms used to sustain national-level representation. Given the ultimate fate of the Union, it is ironic that the overall pattern of development prior to 1860 was toward greater, not lesser, institutional similarity among the states and sections.

[83] Percent standard deviation for each decade calculated by dividing the standard deviation of state congressional district populations by state mean district size. With one exception, population of congressional districts taken from Stanley B. Parson, William W. Beach, and Dan Hermann, *United States Congressional Districts, 1788–1841* (Westport, CT: Greenwood Press, 1978); Stanley B. Parsons, William W. Beach, and Michael J. Dubin, *United States Congressional Districts and Data, 1843–1883* (New York: Greenwood Press, 1986).

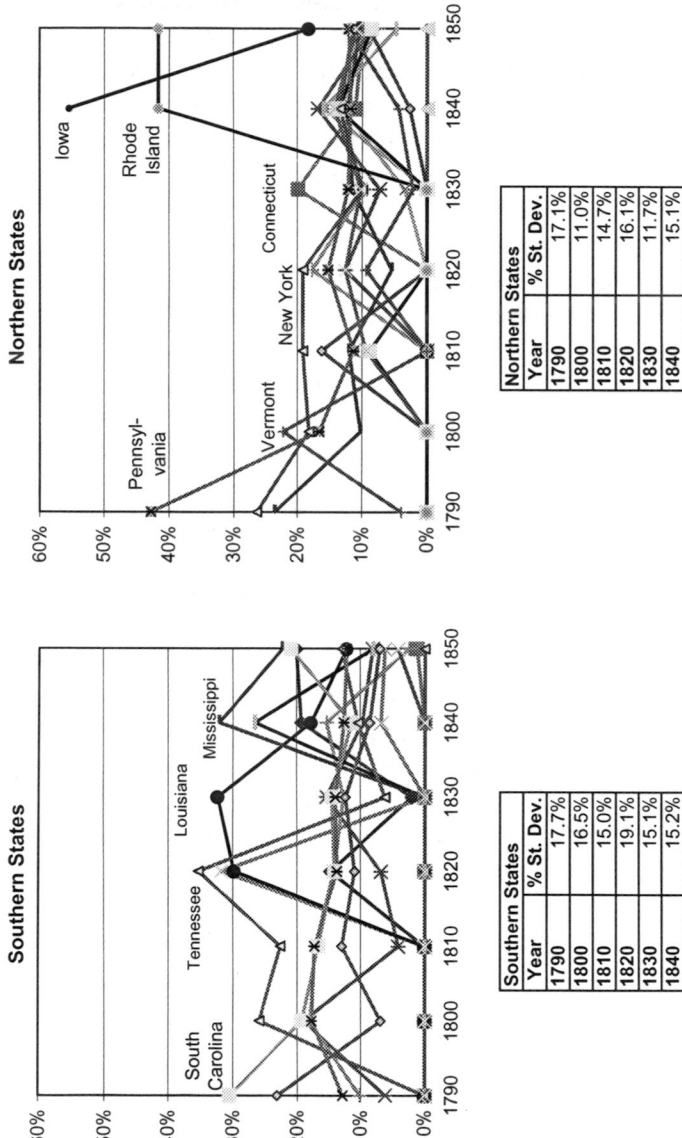

Southern States

Southern States	
Year	% St. Dev.
1790	17.7%
1800	16.5%
1810	15.0%
1820	19.1%
1830	15.1%
1840	15.2%
1850	14.3%

Northern States

Northern States	
Year	% St. Dev.
1790	17.1%
1800	11.0%
1810	14.7%
1820	16.1%
1830	11.7%
1840	15.1%
1850	11.4%

FIGURE 8.6. U.S. Congressional Districts in Northern and Southern States: Percent Standard Deviation from Ideal State District Size, 1790–1860

rep. definitely changed under new cons.

A third generalization is that national-level representation was seen in fundamentally different terms under the U.S. Constitution than under the Articles of Confederation. Rather than the comparatively simple ambassadorial forms of state representation commonly associated with the Articles, the concept of national-level representation after 1790 was differentiated by more complex and fluid combinations of local, state, sectional, nationalist, party, and interest-group orientations. These conceptual changes can be traced, in part, by closely examining the specific institutional forms that reflected and sustained each orientation.

The *localist* orientation of national-level representation was partly sustained through the practice of biennial U.S. House elections and by the standardization of contiguous, single-member House districts.[84] Whereas the former regularized a process for maintaining electoral accountability among House members, the latter anchored the representative-constituency relationship to territorially distinct, intrastate spaces. As a consequence, throughout the first half of the nineteenth century, conceptualizations of national representation were grounded in and, to a large extent, framed by the particular social and political conditions that were located within each House district.[85]

However, national politics was never simply the reflection or aggregated representation of local conditions. State, sectional, nationalist, party, and interest-group orientations also affected the conceptualization of national-level representation prior to the 1860–1861 secession crisis. These orientations reflected alternative sets of interests that transcended the particularities of individual localities and they were articulated within the national government through a variety of institutional devices and practices.

State orientations were always important conceptual guides for understanding the representative role and relationship within the national government. The original U.S. Constitution included numerous provisions

[84] The localist orientation of national-level representation was supported by the establishment of active local party organizations, the expansion and mobilization of local electorates, the coupling of local residency officeholding customs with high turnover rates for congressional representatives, the improvement of transportation and media linkages between members of Congress and their constituents, and by the persistence of the customary practice of petitioning. More thorough measurement and comparative analysis of these conditions and practices is necessary before a more complete assessment can be made.

[85] Edward Pessen, "How Different from Each Other Were the Antebellum North and South?" *American History Review* (1980), 85: 1119. For an important state exception to this generalization, see Kenneth S. Greenberg, "Representation and Isolation of South Carolina, 1776–1860," *Journal of American History* (1977), LXIV(3): 723–743.

that directly reinforced this orientation: for example, the apportionment of U.S. House representation *among the states*, and the direct election of the Senate by the state legislatures. Other practices, like senatorial recall and instructions, were less formalized but highly effective practices that sustained this orientation as well.[86] And the introduction of a state-based apportionment rule for the appointment of federal department clerks in 1853 is an indicator that this state orientation endured throughout the antebellum era.[87]

A nationally centered orientation of representation was another original and common conceptualization of national-level representation. This orientation directed a national representative to consider the *national* interest above less general interests. "The nation," one commentator argued in 1841, "are his constituents" and "[h]e is a representative, not of part, but of the whole. If the permanent interests of the nation at large clearly require the sacrifice of the particular interests of his state, he is ever conscientiously bound to vote for that sacrifice."[88] Prior to 1860, this nationalist orientation was sustained by a variety of proponents, practices, and national commitments, including western expansionism, national military engagements, the institutionalization of national political parties, the partial legitimization of the President as a direct representative of the American people, and the continuous promotion of nationalist ideologies and iconography.[89] Significantly this orientation toward higher-level interests did not mean the national representative had a "superior fitness for the station," "more wisdom," or "better understands the genius of our institutions, than his constituents." As a commentator in *United States Magazine and Democratic Review* concluded:

---

[86] See Robert Luce, *Legislative Principles* (Boston: Houghton Mifflin Co., 1930), pp. 460–491. See also William H. Riker, "The Senate and American Federalism," *American Political Science Review* (1955), 49: 459–460; C. Edward Skeen, "An Uncertain 'Right': State Legislatures and the Doctrine of Instruction," *Mid-America* (1991), 73(1): 29–47; "An Argument on the Right of the Constituent to Instruct his Representative in Congress," in *The American Review of History and Politics* (Philadelphia, July 1812), 4: 137–171.

[87] Leonard D. White, *The Jacksonians: A Study in Administrative History, 1829–1861* (New York: The Free Press, 1954), pp. 394–398.

[88] George S. Camp, *Democracy* (New York: Harper and Brothers, 1841), p. 209.

[89] See, for example, David Waldstreicher, *In the Midst of Perpetual Fetes: The Making of American Nationalism, 1776–1820* (Chapel Hill: University of North Carolina Press, 1997). For two interesting analyses of the origins and transformation of national Executive authority between 1790 and 1860, see Richard Ellis and Stephen Kirk, "Presidential Mandates in the Nineteenth Century: Conceptual Change and Institutional Development," *Studies in American Political Development* (1995), 9: 117–186; and White, *The Jacksonians* (1954), pp. 20–49.

Is not this idea frivolous? He may, indeed, be better qualified than any other *single* individual for the discharge of the high trusts committed to him; but that his wisdom excels the combined wisdom of his constituents, is paying but a poor compliment to the intelligence of this nation; and, were it true, would itself furnish evidence of the entire incompatibility of our form of government with such deplorable ignorance of the people.[90]

Sectional orientations were never directly sanctioned by the Constitution. They were nonetheless sustained by less formal but still highly effective means like sectionally defined business conventions, newspapers, journals, and universities as well as by the personal efforts of numerous sectionally minded ideologues like James C. Calhoun, James D. B. DeBow, and George Fitzhugh.[91] During the first half of the nineteenth century – and especially after the 1820 Missouri Compromise – the concept of sectional representation became a norm by which many national representatives assessed their role within and the operation of the national government. *Party centered*

A party-centered orientation of the concept of representation emerged initially and briefly near the turn of the eighteenth century and again, in a more permanent way, during the 1830s and 1840s. Like the concept of sectional representation, this conceptual orientation was promoted at first by a relatively small number of individuals but it, too, became increasingly significant for national representatives and the electorate without any direct constitutional warrant.[92] *Interest groups v. nat'l gov.*

The final view of national-level representation prior to 1860 was through the relationships formed between various interest groups and the national government. The increased prominence of this conceptual orientation over the course of the nineteenth century was no doubt promoted by several factors, including the institutionalization and expansion of the congressional committee system, the increased presence and

[90] "A Short Argument on the Doctrine of Instruction," *United States Magazine and Democratic Review* (Washington, DC: November 1841), 9: 436.

[91] See Sydnor, *The Development of Southern Sectionalism, 1819–1848* (1948); Craven, *The Growth of Southern Nationalism, 1848–1861* (1953).

[92] See Silbey, *The Shrine of Party* (1967); Ronald P. Formisano, "Deferential-Participant Politics: The Early Republic's Political Culture, 1789–1840," *American Political Science Review* (1974), 68: 473–487; Jean H. Baker, *Affairs of Party: The Political Culture of Northern Democrats in the Mid-Nineteenth Century* (New York: Fordham University Press, 1983). For two recent explanations of party emergence and development prior to the Civil War, see Martin Shefter, *Political Parties and the State* (Princeton, NJ: Princeton University Press, 1994), pp. 61–72; John H. Aldrich, *Why Parties: The Origin and Transformation of Party Politics in America* (Chicago: University of Chicago Press, 1995), pp. 65–156.

lobbying practices of various interest groups and their agents, and the organization and political mobilization of social groups with distinct political interests.[93] Clearly, more careful and systematic studies are required to cast new light on the displacement of the eighteenth-century delegate-trustee norm of the representative relationship with more direct (and not only financial) relationships between national representatives and particular political interests.[94]

Representation in the State Legislatures

Sectional differences in the conceptualization of representation, although not readily apparent when studied at the national level, can also be assessed in terms of the institutional development of American state governments.[95] The three general characteristics used to describe the conceptualization of representation between 1700 and 1770 (see Chapter 2) and between 1776 and 1786 (see Chapter 5) serve as reference points for the following examination of state-level conceptualizations of

[93] Too little, to date, has been written on the content of antebellum congressional petitions. An early example of interest group petitioning of Congress was the 1815 petition of a group of Kentuckians who requested that Congress reserve tracts of western federal lands for the settlement of emancipated slaves. See Joseph O. van Hook, *The Kentucky Story* (Chattanooga, TN: Harlow Publishing, 1970), p. 257.

[94] See Nichols, *The Disruption of American Democracy* (1948); Holman Hamilton, *Prologue to Conflict: The Crisis and Compromise of 1850* (Lexington, KY: University of Kentucky Press, 1964), pp. 118–132, 155–159; and Mark W. Summers, *The Plundering Generation: Corruption and the Crisis of the Union, 1849–1861* (New York: Oxford University Press, 1987). For an account of prominence of interest-group representation after the Civil War, see Susan M. Thompson, *"The Spider Web": Congress and Lobbying in the Age of Grant* (Ithaca, NY: Cornell University Press, 1985).

[95] For several general works on state political development across the nineteenth century, see Francis N. Thorpe, *A Constitutional History of the American People* (New York: Harper & Bros., 1898), 2 vols; Robert Luce, *Legislative Assemblies* (Boston: Houghton Mifflin Co., 1924); Sr. M. Barbara McCarthy, *The Widening Scope of American Constitutions* (1928, Ph.D. diss., Catholic University of America); McCormick, *The Second American Party System* (1966); George P. Parkinson, *Antebellum State Constitution-making: Retention, Circumvention, Revision* (1972, Ph.D. diss., University of Wisconsin). For accounts with a sectional or regional emphasis, see Fletcher M. Green, *Constitutional Development in the South Atlantic States, 1760–1860* (Chapel Hill: University of North Carolina Press, 1930); Ralph A. Wooster, *The People in Power: Courthouse and Statehouse in the Lower South, 1850–1860* (Knoxville, TN: University of Tennessee Press, 1969); Ralph A. Wooster, *Politicians, Planters and Plain Folk: Courthouse and Statehouse in the Upper South, 1850–1860* (Knoxville, TN: University of Tennessee Press, 1975); Don Fehrenbacher, *Sectional Crisis and Southern Constitutionalism* (Baton Rouge, LA: Louisiana State University Press, 1995). Numerous and more specialized accounts of the political development of individual states have also been completed.

representation between 1790 and 1860. These characteristics are localism, responsive elitism, and dynamic institutionalism.

Beyond Localism

Localism describes the relationship and orientation between political representatives and their respective local communities. Like the conceptual development of national representation between 1790 and 1860, conceptualizations of state-level representation also extended beyond their original localist moorings during this period. By 1860 state-level politics was affected by and commonly understood in terms of a diverse set of state-society linkages. Without question, however, the linkage between representatives and specific localities generally dominated the attention and policy making of state legislatures prior to 1860.[96]

The localism of state-level representation was grounded in and sustained by various institutional devices formalized within the state constitutions. Changes in these devices altered the framework and practices of state-level governance and, in turn, the conceptual norms that constituted the representative relationship. In 1790, for example, all but one state constitution required lower house elections at least once a year. By 1860, approximately one-third of the states were continuing to hold annual elections, with the remainder of the state constitutions mandating biennial lower house elections. A similar pattern of change increased state executive terms from an average of 1.7 years in 1790 to 2.5 years in 1860. Figure 8.7 clearly reveals a sectional distinction within this broader pattern of change: Southern state legislators generally became less electorally accountable than their northern cohorts.

Although American state legislatures, on average, became more detached from their electorates between 1790 and 1860, various changes in legislative districting strengthened the localist orientations of state legislators. By 1860, most state constitutions expressly prohibited the

[96] In Maryland, for example, historian Jean H. Baker observes "the state government served as a legislature not only for the state of Maryland, but for twenty-one counties and Baltimore city as well." For example, "of the 354 bills approved by the House in 1856, 34 (10%) affected the state as a whole, while 117 (33%) were of interest only to individuals, and another 203 (57%) concerned local communities and interest groups. In 1858 this same legislative pattern prevailed, as it would throughout the century, with 62 percent of the session's 432 acts involved with local issues, 29 percent with interests, and only 8 percent affecting the state as a whole." Baker, *Ambivalent Americans* (1977), pp. 92–93. See also Rodney O. Davis, " 'The People in Miniature': The Illinois General Assembly, 1818–1848," *Illinois Historical Journal* (1988), 81: 100; J. Mills Thornton, *Politics and Power in a Slave Society: Alabama, 1800–1860* (Baton Rouge, LA: Louisiana State University Press, 1978), p. 85.

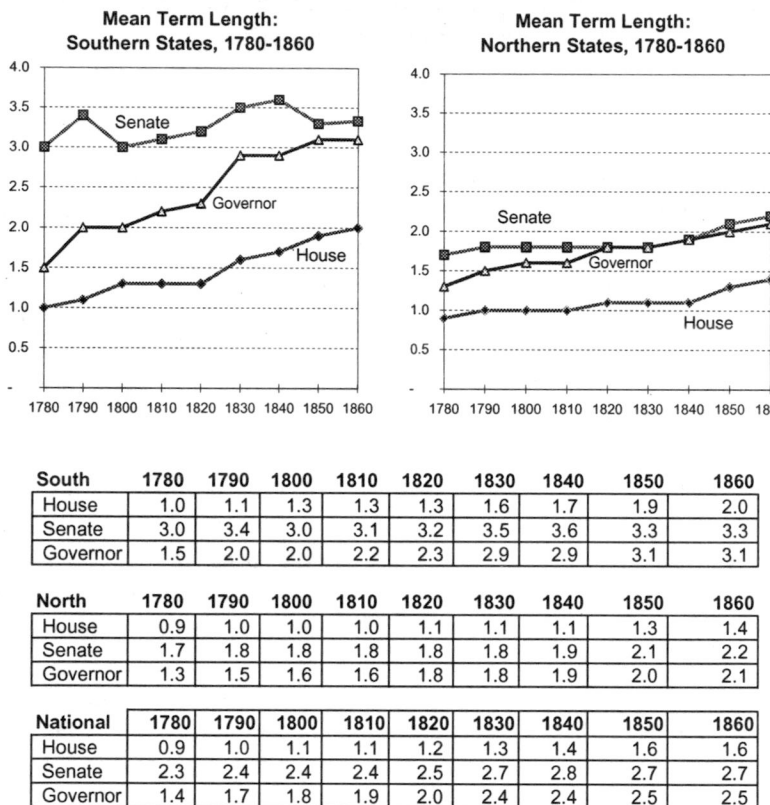

South	1780	1790	1800	1810	1820	1830	1840	1850	1860
House	1.0	1.1	1.3	1.3	1.3	1.6	1.7	1.9	2.0
Senate	3.0	3.4	3.0	3.1	3.2	3.5	3.6	3.3	3.3
Governor	1.5	2.0	2.0	2.2	2.3	2.9	2.9	3.1	3.1

North	1780	1790	1800	1810	1820	1830	1840	1850	1860
House	0.9	1.0	1.0	1.0	1.1	1.1	1.1	1.3	1.4
Senate	1.7	1.8	1.8	1.8	1.8	1.8	1.9	2.1	2.2
Governor	1.3	1.5	1.6	1.6	1.8	1.8	1.9	2.0	2.1

National	1780	1790	1800	1810	1820	1830	1840	1850	1860
House	0.9	1.0	1.1	1.1	1.2	1.3	1.4	1.6	1.6
Senate	2.3	2.4	2.4	2.4	2.5	2.7	2.8	2.7	2.7
Governor	1.4	1.7	1.8	1.9	2.0	2.4	2.4	2.5	2.5

FIGURE 8.7. State Term Lengths by Section, 1790–1860

division of counties and/or towns when forming state legislative districts. As a consequence, the shape of most state legislative districts assumed the familiar forms of local jurisdictional boundaries.[97] In addition to

[97] Not surprisingly, not every state legislative district formed a geometrically compact shape. See John S. Barry, *The History of Massachusetts* (Boston, The Author, 1857), pp. 369–370n.2; Elmer C. Griffith *The Rise and Development of the Gerrymander* (New York: Arno Press, 1974 [1907]), pp. 15–22, 115; Turner, *The Ninth State: New Hampshire's Formative Years* (Chapel Hill: University of North Carolina Press, 1983), p. 423n.16. The practice of forming irregularly shaped electoral districts also occurred occasionally for U.S. House districts. In particular, see the maps for these congressional districts: Pennsylvania 5th (1792); New York 7th (1792); New York 11th (1802); New York 17th (1812); New York 22nd (1822); Virginia 1st (1792–1822), in Martis, *The Historical Atlas of United States Congressional Districts* (1982). See also Micah Altman, "Traditional Districting Principles," *Social Science History* (1988).

[handwritten: rules and districting caused towns to stay together + united]

explicit proscriptions against division of these boundaries, numerous state constitutions required districts composed of contiguous or adjacent territory[98] and two state constitutions (Wisconsin and Kentucky) prescribed the most "compact" form possible for state legislative districts.[99]

Tables 8.6 and 8.7 display the development of state legislative districting systems between 1786 and 1860. The general trend over these years was away from multimember or at-large districts. In the state lower houses, the number of states with single-member legislative districts steadily increased after 1840, although two-thirds of the states in 1860 retained mixed districting systems. In the state senates, the preference for single-member senate districts clearly became more prominent over time.

Although most state legislators focused almost exclusively on local affairs during the first half of the nineteenth century, several developments undermining these localist orientations deserve noting. State governments increasingly assumed the responsibility for the salaries of state legislators, thereby severing the historic (and immediate financial) incentive that had been used to maintain a direct and intimate relationship between an individual representative and a particular locality. District residency requirements for state office holders also became notably less stringent after 1800, thus diminishing the necessity for candidates to have deep local attachments.[100] *[handwritten: less residency requirements]*

[handwritten margin: BUT state took over salaries AND]

Changes in state rules of apportionment between 1790 and 1860 also affected the localist orientations of state legislators. Tables 8.8 and 8.9 reveal a significant increase in the number of states with proportional rules for apportioning state legislative representation. As a consequence of this change, representation was no longer defined exclusively in terms of fixed spatial-corporate boundaries. Rather, the conceptual dimensions of state-level representation were deepened to include the relative weight of demographic conditions. Although these formal and

[handwritten: new rule → weighted for dem. purposes]

[98] 1817 Mississippi constitution, III, 13; 1821 Missouri constitution, III, 6; 1835 Tennessee, II, 6; 1837 Michigan constitution, IV, 3; 1846 Iowa constitution, III, 37; 1848 New York constitution, III, 5; 1848 Wisconsin constitution, IV, 4; 1850 Kentucky, II, 6; 1850 California constitution, IV, 30; 1851 Indiana constitution, IV, 6; 1851 Ohio constitution, XI, 5; 1857 amendment, Massachusetts constitution; 1859 Minnesota constitution, IV, 24.

[99] 1848 Wisconsin constitution, Art. IV, sec. 4; 1850 Kentucky constitution, Article II, sec. 5.

[100] Thorpe, *A Constitutional History of the American People* (1898), II: 413; Wooster, *The People in Power* (1969), p. 110.

TABLE 8.6. *State House Districts, 1786–1860 (percent)*

	Year (Number of states)								
	1786	1790	1800	1810	1820	1830	1840	1850	1860
	(n = 13)	(n = 15)	(n = 17)	(n = 18)	(n = 24)	(n = 24)	(n = 26)	(n = 31)	(n = 33)
District Type									
Single-Member	0.0	6.7	5.9	5.6	4.2	4.2	3.8	12.9	15.1
Multimember	53.8	33.3	23.5	22.2	16.6	16.6	3.8	6.4	6.1
Mixed	46.2	60.0	70.6	72.2	75.0	75.0	88.6	74.2	72.7
At-Large	0.0	0.0	0.0	0.0	0.0	0.0	0.0	0.0	0.0
Not Known	0.0	0.0	0.0	0.0	4.2	4.2	3.8	6.5	6.1
	100.0	100.0	100.0	100.0	100.0	100.0	100.0	100.0	100.0

Note: Mixed districting systems include any combination of single-member, multimember, at-large, pooled (or classed towns), fractional time, and floterial districts.

TABLE 8.7. *State Senate Districts, 1786–1860 (percent)*

	Year (Number of states)								
	1786	1790	1800	1810	1820	1830	1840	1850	1860
	(n = 13)	(n = 15)	(n = 17)	(n = 18)	(n = 24)	(n = 24)	(n = 26)	(n = 31)	(n = 33)
District Type									
Single-Member	23.1	33.4	35.3	38.9	45.8	50.0	53.9	51.6	54.5
Multimember	30.7	13.3	11.8	11.1	8.3	8.3	11.5	3.2	3.0
Mixed	23.1	20.0	29.4	22.2	29.2	25.0	23.1	35.5	27.3
At-Large	23.1	33.3	23.5	22.2	16.7	12.5	0.0	0.0	0.0
Not Known	0.0	0.0	0.0	5.6	0.0	4.2	11.5	9.7	15.2
	100.0	100.0	100.0	100.0	100.0	100.0	100.0	100.0	100.0

Note: Mixed districting systems include any combination of single-member, multimember, at-large, pooled (or classed towns), fractional time, and floterial districts.

TABLE 8.8. *State House Apportionment Units, 1786–1860 (percent)*

	1786	1790	1800	1810	1820	1830	1840	1850	1860
	(n = 13)	(n = 15)	(n = 17)	(n = 18)	(n = 24)	(n = 24)	(n = 26)	(n = 31)	(n = 33)
Fixed	62.5	66.7	53.0	44.4	33.3	33.3	15.4	12.9	12.1
(No. of states)	(8)	(10)	(9)	(8)	(8)	(8)	(4)	(4)	(4)
Proportional	37.5	33.3	47.0	55.6	66.7	66.7	84.6	87.1	87.9
(No. of states)	(5)	(5)	(8)	(10)	(16)	(16)	(22)	(27)	(29)
At-Large	0.0	0.0	0.0	0.0	0.0	0.0	0.0	0.0	0.0
(No. of states)	(0)	(0)	(0)	(0)	(0)	(0)	(0)	(0)	(0)
TOTAL	100.0	100.0	100.0	100.0	100.0	100.0	100.0	100.0	100.0

TABLE 8.9. *State Senate Apportionment Units, 1786–1860 (percent)*

	1786	1790	1800	1810	1820	1830	1840	1850	1860
	(n = 13)	(n = 15)	(n = 17)	(n = 18)	(n = 24)	(n = 24)	(n = 26)	(n = 31)	(n = 33)
Fixed	69.2	53.3	41.2	44.4	33.3	33.3	30.8	22.6	21.2
(No. of states)	(9)	(8)	(7)	(8)	(8)	(8)	(8)	(7)	(7)
Proportional	15.4	26.7	41.2	38.9	54.2	58.3	69.2	77.4	78.8
(No. of states)	(2)	(4)	(7)	(7)	(13)	(14)	(18)	(24)	(26)
At-Large	15.4	20.0	17.6	16.7	12.5	8.4	0.0	0.0	0.0
(No. of states)	(2)	(3)	(3)	(3)	(3)	(2)	(0)	(0)	(0)
TOTAL	100.0	100.0	100.0	100.0	100.0	100.0	100.0	100.0	100.0

conceptual changes redefined the coordinates of each state's political
culture, by 1860 this change was so widespread among the states that
there were few sectional distinctions of any significance.

Another notable (although often overlooked) development redefining
the localist orientations of state legislators was the growth in the population of state legislative districts. The following graphs display this
development in terms of the average number of persons per state
representative and state senator. Figures 8.8 and 8.9 reveal that the
average state district population generally increased between 1790 and
1860, with the most notable percentage increase occurring between 1820
and 1830.

Reaggregation of the displayed data along sectional and regional lines
exposes additional patterns of development.[101] Until 1830, southern state
house districts typically had slightly larger populations than northern
state house districts. After 1840, these sectional differences reversed and,
by 1860, northern state house districts, on average, were 16.5 percent
larger than southern state house districts. A similar, but accelerated,
growth pattern defines the differences between northern and southern
state senate districts. By 1860, northern state senate districts, on average,
were 22.9 percent larger than southern senate districts. A large part of
these sectional differences was due to district population increases in a
few northern states. At the same time, it must be noted that southern
state house district averages would be notably smaller if only the *free*
population were used to calculate the average number of persons per
district.

In addition to the transformation of the localist orientation of state-
level representation, the concept of representation became further
differentiated as additional conceptual forms of representation emerged
and grew in prominence. The conceptualization of state-society relations
in terms of *party representation* became common with the institutionalization of state political parties. The development of enduring party allegiances among state legislators and within the electorate occurred at
different times and rates across the states. In most states, this revolution
in the habits and manners of understanding the distribution and legitimacy of political authority did not begin to become significant until state

---

[101] Regional division of the states is as follows: (1) Old North, consisting of the eight
original states north of Maryland; (2) New North/West, consisting of the free states
west of Pennsylvania; (3) Old South, consisting of the five original states south of
Pennsylvania; (4) New South/West, consisting of the remaining slave states south of
the Ohio River.

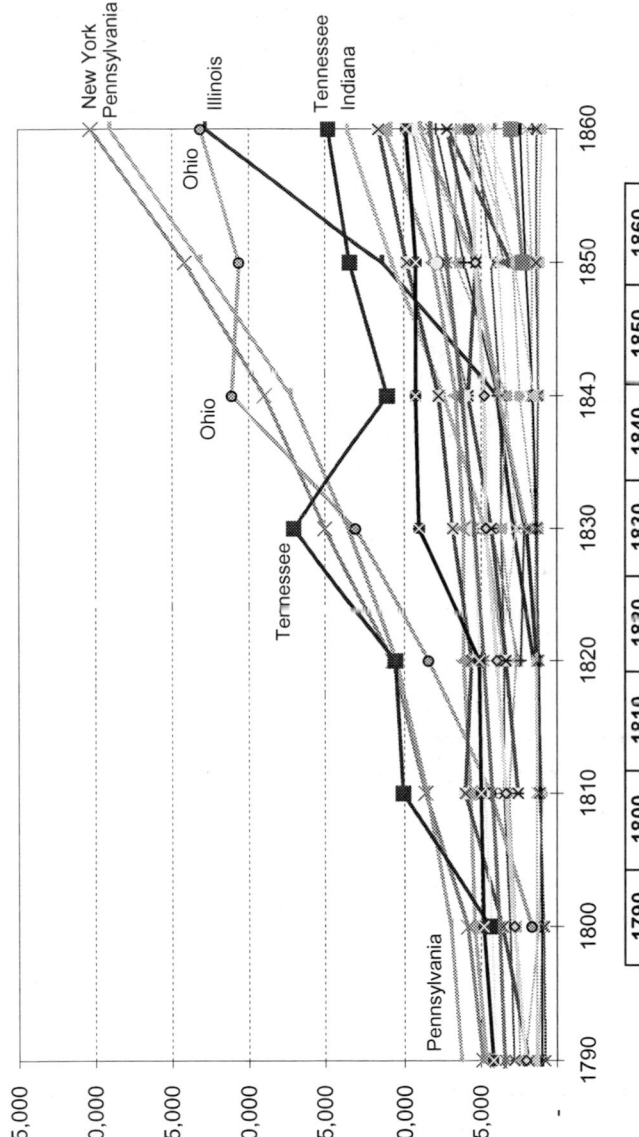

	1790	1800	1810	1820	1830	1840	1850	1860
Mean	2,858	3,210	4,137	4,231	5,561	6,309	7,187	9,108
Median	2,428	3,061	3,851	3,443	4,307	4,399	5,391	7,225
St Dev.	1,641	1,909	2,794	3,083	4,636	5,360	6,050	7,418
% Change (Mean)		12.3%	30.4%	-.1%	31.4%	13.5%	13.9%	26.7%

FIGURE 8.8. Persons per State House Representative: 1790–1860

357

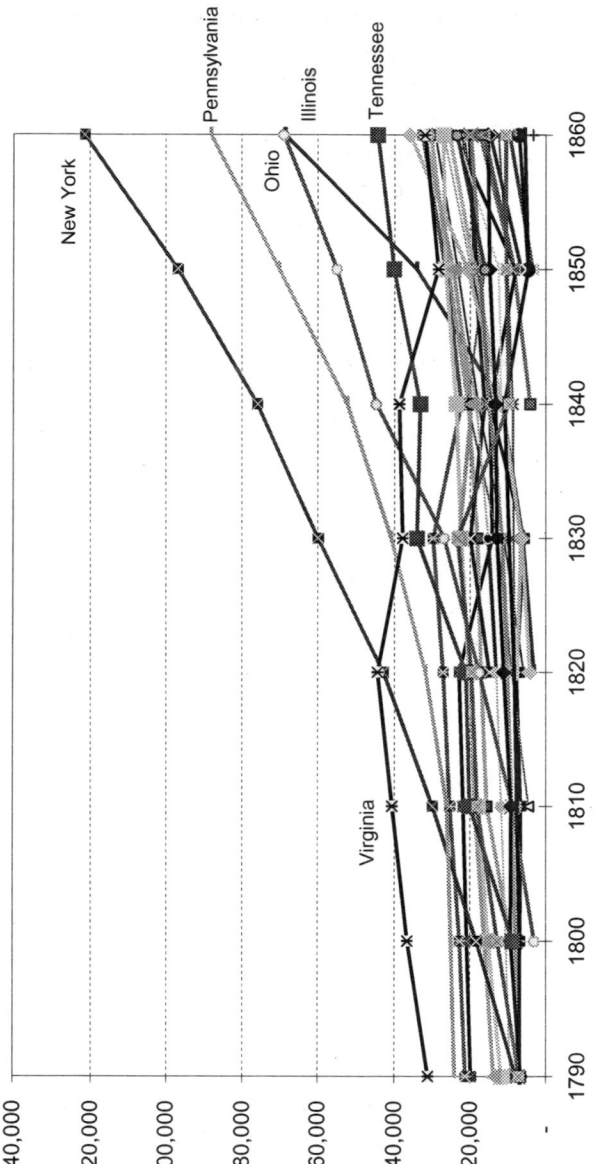

	1790	1800	1810	1820	1830	1840	1850	1860
Mean	12,554	14,003	16,687	16,548	19,508	21,380	22,998	29,359
Median	7,910	10,571	16,753	13,999	14,718	15,628	18,812	23,512
St. Dev.	7,846	8,585	9,597	11,145	13,356	15,879	19,890	24,774
% Change (Mean)		11.5%	19.2%	-0.8%	17.9%	9.6%	7.6%	27.7%

FIGURE 8.9. Persons per State Senator: 1790–1860

parties and their attendant electoral allegiances were integrated into the national party system during the 1830s.[102]

A second conceptual form of state-level representation to emerge in the nineteenth century, *executive representation*, signaled the recovery of a much older, pre-Revolutionary understanding of the representative-constituency relationship. This conceptual change extended the conceptual boundaries of representation beyond its original locus in the state legislature to include a state's governor as well. The conceptualization of executives as representatives was only partially established prior to 1860; most state governors remained, in practice, subordinated to their respective state legislatures and only rarely was it articulated that a state executive was an equal or better "representative" of the popular will than a state legislature.[103] Although governors were popularly elected in almost every state by 1860, many remained oriented toward and representative of local or party interests rather than more general statewide constituencies and their concerns.[104]

A third conceptual form that emerged and complemented the localist orientation of state-level representation was *interest-group representation*. This conceptual orientation followed the political mobilization of distinct social groups whose primary members or political interests transcended the boundaries of specific localities. This political and conceptual development during the nineteenth century has not been systematically or thoroughly analyzed at the state level.[105] What is known is that initially religious groups and, in time, social welfare organizations

---

[102] See McCormick, *The Second American Party System* (1966); Herbert Ershkowitz and William G. Shade, "Consensus or Conflict? Political Behavior in the State Legislatures during the Jacksonian Era," *Journal of American History* (1971), 58: 591–621; Ronald P. Formisano, "Deferential-Participant Politics," *American Political Science Review* (1974), 68: 480–481; Peter D. Levine, *The Behavior of State Legislative Parties in the Jacksonian Era: New Jersey, 1829–1844* (Rutherford, NJ: Fairleigh Dickinson University Press, 1977). For a contemporaneous description of this conceptual revolution, see Adams, *Diary of John Quincy Adams* (1951), pp. 511–513.

[103] A revisitation of the institutional and conceptual development of state executive authority prior to 1860 is needed. See Leslie Lipson, *The American Governor from Figurehead to Leader* (Chicago: University of Chicago Press 1939).

[104] For a list of the thirty-one states with elective governors prior to 1860, see McCarthy, *The Widening Scope of American Constitutions* (1928), p. 52n.1.

[105] Despite the exceptional work of a handful of scholars over several generations, many dimensions of state politics during the antebellum era remain as historian Ronald P. Formisano suggested "*terra incognita* to historians." Formisano concluded that "[b]etween the 1780s and 1830s, particularly, the historical landscape with respect to state legislative behavior is a great desert, and one to be approached with caution." Formisano, "Deferential-Participant Politics" (1974), 68: 480.

and nonlocalized economic interests interacted directly with state legislators and other governmental officials. The establishment of state legislative committee systems and the proliferation of professional lobbyists
facilitated these practical and conceptual changes in the representative
relationship. The former created policy-specific forums for defining the
legislature's agenda and new and more efficient access points for groups
to affect the state policy-making process. The latter development aided
the suspension of the more traditional representational linkages that
existed between state legislators and their local constituencies. The influence of lobbyists on the New Jersey legislature prompted one newspaper correspondent to observe in 1834 that the "people would be aston-
ished to hear how fully and familiarly these gentlemen offer the votes of
their representatives, to those who wish them. . . . I very much suspect
that they lay claim to quite as much influence as they possess: and if they
do not exaggerate, the other two houses are little more than merely
'mouthpieces' to express their decision."[106]

Additional conceptual forms of representation like *administrative representation* and *judicial representation*, although rudimentary compared
to their present-day forms, also became increasingly significant during
the second quarter of the nineteenth century. By 1860, slightly more than
half of the states were electing their state secretaries of state and their
state treasurers. Only two states held elections for these officials in 1840.
By 1860, roughly a third of the states were electing their state auditors
and attorneys general, and six states were electing their superintendents
of public instruction.[107] In Virginia and Louisiana, commissioners for the
Board of Public Works were elected from districts that were to be contiguous, compact, and, as nearly as may be, equal in population or
numbers of voters.[108]

The institutional forms for the concept of judicial representation were
slower developing. This, it seems, had less to do with a now widely

[106] As quoted in Levine, *The Behavior of State Legislative Parties* (1977), p. 57.
    State-level lobbying and interest-group activities prior to 1860 warrant greater
attention by historians and political scientists. See Douglas E. Bowers, "From Logrolling
to Corruption: The Development of Lobbying in Pennsylvania, 1815–1861," *Journal
of the Early Republic* (1983), 3: 439–474; Levine, *The Behavior of State Legislative
Parties* (1977), pp. 57–59, 185–206; Summers, *The Plundering Generation* (1987);
Rodney O. Davis, " 'The People in Miniature': The Illinois General Assembly,
1818–1848," *Illinois Historical Journal* (1988), 81: 103; and L. Ray Gunn, *The Decline
of Authority* (1988), pp. 155–156.
[107] See McCarthy, *The Widening Scope of American Constitutions* (1928), pp. 53–56.
[108] See 1850 Virginia constitution, V, 14; 1852 Louisiana constitution, VII, 130.

accepted distinction between law and politics and far more to do with the organizational immaturity of American state judicial systems. If the core elements of nineteenth-century representation required, at minimum, a direct connection between political actors and territorially bounded communities and a responsive orientation of these actors toward local or individual social demands, then state courts and especially lower-level state judges displayed the same quality of representativeness as their state legislative cohorts. The third common element of nineteenth-century representation, regular electoral authorization, was not associated initially with state judiciaries. Georgia and Indiana provided for the election of lower court judges as early as 1812 and 1816. It was not until 1832 that Mississippi became the first state to extend the possibilities of electoral legitimacy on its state supreme court. By 1860, twenty-one states (divided almost equally between North and South) had followed Mississippi and required election of their state supreme courts.

Electoral Elitism and a More Discriminating Responsiveness

The second characteristic used to describe colonial and early national conceptualizations of representation was responsive elitism, or the general condition by which a socially differentiated and electorally insulated political elite responded (without apparent discrimination) to the range of societal demands made on it. This condition described much but not all the political practices of the two earlier eras. Similarly uniform generalizations about the development of state-society relations between 1790 and 1860 are more difficult to make not only because of the extended length of time and the threefold increase in the number of states, but also because too little is known about the personal characteristics of state legislators, the range, intensity, and media of societal demands on state governments, and the content and consequences of state policy making.

Although additional monographic studies are necessary before a fuller synthesis of this dimension of state representation can be attempted, an impression of the relationship between state legislators and their constituents can be sketched from the measurements that are presently available. Legislative responsiveness can be measured in terms of the range of legislative accomplishments. State legislatures, especially during the first quarter of the nineteenth century, appear to have responded to a relatively wide range of societal demands. The legislative output of the

New Hampshire legislature between 1776 and 1818 suggests the breadth of this responsiveness. By 1818, according to one contemporaneous measurement, this legislature "had chartered 161 public libraries, 95 religious organizations, 22 academies, 27 musical societies, 10 banks, and 5 county agricultural associations." It had also provided "for 53 bridges, 52 toll turnpikes, 18 canals, 38 cotton and 'woolen' mills, 4 insurance companies, 8 fire engine companies, and 5 Masonic lodges."[109] Similarly diverse (and often more impressive) registries of legislative accomplishment have been (and no doubt could be) compiled for other state legislatures.[110]

Another indicator of legislative responsiveness is the volume of state legislation.[111] State legislative responsiveness increased significantly during the first half of the nineteenth century. The Illinois legislature enacted 136 statutes in 1830 and 273 statutes in 1841.[112] During the 1840s, the legislative output of the Pennsylvania legislature doubled to almost 500 acts annually.[113] Data on the legislative outputs of southern state legislatures generally remain uncompiled, but as historian Donald A. DeBats suggests "the legislatures of the South may have been relatively more important in the evolution of policy given the general absence of powerful governors who emerged more quickly in the North."[114]

Although state legislatures appear to have become more responsive if measured according to these indicators, the relationship between social demands and state policies between 1790 and 1860 never mapped a direct route from the former to the latter. One of the recurring social demands American state legislatures found particularly vexing concerned the distribution of political representation, especially requests

---

[109] Leon W. Anderson, *To this Day: the 300 of the New Hampshire Legislature* (1981), p. 119.

[110] See Louis Hartz, *Economic Policy and Democratic Thought: Pennsylvania, 1776–1860* (Chicago: Quadrangle Books, 1968), pp. 37–42; L. Ray Gunn, "The New York Legislature," *Social Science History* (1980), pp. 270–271; Rodney O. Davis, " 'The People in Miniature'," *Illinois Historical Journal* (1988), 81: 100; Donald A. DeBats, "An Uncertain Arena: The Georgia House of Representatives, 1808–1861," *Journal of Southern History* (1990), 56: 426–427. See also Kruman, *Parties and Politics in North Carolina* (Chapel Hill: University of North Carolina Press, 1983), pp. 55–85.

[111] There are other ways of measuring legislative output over time. State expenditures and state taxes collected are two of the more obvious. Ideally, what is required is the compilation and synthesis of the development of state financial and fiscal indicators.

[112] Davis, " 'The People in Miniature'," *Illinois Historical Journal* (1988), 81: 99.

[113] Bowers, "From Logrolling to Corruption," *Journal of the Early Republic* (1983), 3: 458.

[114] DeBats, "An Uncertain Arena," *Journal of Southern History* (1990), 56: 426.

[handwritten: However no state reapp.]

for constitutional revision of a state rule of apportionment. State legislatures regularly disregarded these demands. As a consequence, there
are numerous examples in which popular satisfaction with a particular
state government declined. In many states, this dissatisfaction catalyzed a range of extraconstitutional efforts to effect constitutional
change.[115]

Between 1790 and 1860, state legislative responsiveness also appears
to have become more restrictive in a second way. State legislatures during
the first quarter of the nineteenth century spent most of their time
responding to highly specialized demands like divorces or the settlement
of local disputes and land titles. During the second quarter of the century,
legislative responses increasingly began to provide much larger (although
still primarily specialized) types of political largesse like corporate charters, public works projects, or social welfare policies.[116] As a result of
this gradual shift in the scale of policy requests, individuals with small,
private, or purely localized interests increasingly found themselves
crowded out of state legislative agendas and were prompted to seek legal
remedies or resolutions in more accessible nonlegislative forums like state
courts and local governments.

[handwritten margin note: change in agenda forced to find legal remedies]

In several states, the responsiveness of the state governments was
restricted by adaptations and concerted efforts to distribute or dilute the
authority of the state legislatures. Explicit legislative restrictions were
incorporated into several state constitutions – a process that continued
throughout the nineteenth century.[117] The authority of state executives
also increased during the second quarter of the nineteenth century. Only
two of the original state constitutions granted governors the power to
veto state legislation. By 1860, twenty-four governors possessed this
authority and fourteen of these states required a two-thirds legislative
majority to override an executive veto.[118] In several states, governors
enjoyed part of the legislature's authority to appoint local officials.[119] By

---

[115] See Julian A. C. Chandler, *Representation in Virginia* (Baltimore, Johns Hopkins
University Press, 1896); Peter J. Coleman, *The Transformation of Rhode Island,
1790–1860* (Providence, RI: Brown University Press, 1969), pp. 218–294; Parkinson,
Antebellum State Constitution-Making (1972).

[116] For one measurement of the increase in the number of business charters granted by the
Pennsylvania legislature, see Hartz, *Economic Policy and Democratic Thought* (1948).

[117] See McCarthy, *The Widening Scope of American Constitutions* (1928).

[118] The ten other states allowed a simple legislative majority to override a veto. Notably,
of the fourteen states in 1860 that required a two-thirds legislative majority override,
four were southern states.

[119] See Levine, *The Behavior of State Legislative Parties* (1977), p. 57.

1860 most state judiciaries had secured the authority of judicial review, although the practice was limited.[120]

A final restriction on the responsiveness of the state legislatures prior to 1860 cannot be ignored, a restriction imposed by the rise of state interest groups and lobbyists. As this means of legislative influence became increasingly efficacious during the second quarter of the nineteenth century, legislative responsiveness increasingly reflected the demands, the competition, and the currency of the marketplace. By the 1850s, according to historian Douglas E. Bowers, these new political dynamics often were giving "large corporations and others with wealth a decidedly undemocratic advantage" within a state government.[121]

Like the uneven development of state legislative responsiveness between 1790 and 1860, the elitist qualities of American state legislators were transformed by similar crosscurrents, becoming less elitist in an eighteenth-century sense and more elitist in a new nineteenth-century sense. The origins of the decline, according to historian Gordon S. Wood, were partially latent within the set of possibilities opened by the American Revolution and subsequently although not perfectly encouraged

---

[120] The emergence and development of state-level judicial review across the nineteenth century is another topic of American political development requiring further comparative study. For a start, see Edward S. Corwin, "The Extension of Judicial Review in New York, 1783–1905," *Michigan Law Review* (1917), 15: 280–313; William T. Utter, "Judicial Review in Early Ohio," *Mississippi Valley Historical Review* (1927), 14: 3–24; Margaret V. Nelson, *A Study of Judicial Review in Virginia, 1789–1928* (1947); Oliver P. Field, "Unconstitutional Legislation in Indiana," *Indiana Law Journal* (1941), 17: 101–127; Oliver P. Field, "Unconstitutional Legislation in Minnesota," *American Political Science Review* (1941), 35: 898–915; Martin B. Hickman, "Judicial Review of Legislation in Utah," *Utah Law Review* (1954), 4: 50–64; William Nelson, "Changing Conception of Judicial Review: The Evolution of Constitutional Theory in the States, 1790–1860," *University of Pennsylvania Law Review* (1972), 120: 1166; Fehrenbacher, *Sectional Crisis and Southern Constitutionalism* (1995), pp. 96–102.

From another perspective, the gradual institutionalization of American state courts prior to 1860 suggests that the overall decline in state legislative responsiveness was offset, in part, by increases in judicially initiated and managed policy making. In addition to judicial affirmation of general rights like property, contractual obligations, and a minimalist variation of due process, state judicial policy making also extended occasionally toward more activist protection of so-called "minority" rights and, in rare circumstances, to the direct mediation of competing economic interests. In addition to the aforementioned article by Nelson, see A. E. Keir Nash, "A More Equitable Past? Southern Supreme Courts and the Protection of the Antebellum Negro," *North Carolina Law Review* (1970), 48: 197–242; Charles McCurdy, "Stephen J. Field and Public Land Law Development in California, 1850–1860: A Case Study of Judicial Resource Allocation in Nineteenth-Century America," *Law & Society Review* (1976), 10: 235–266.

[121] Bowers, "From Logrolling to Corruption" (1983), 3: 471.

by the idea of civic equality and the practices of geographic mobility, free markets, and the free exercise of religion.[122]

The decline in the older form of elitism was apparent in the types of modifications made to many of the state constitutions. Property qualifications and religious tests for state officeholding were deleted from most of the older state constitutions or never included in the newer state constitutions written prior to 1860. In 1790, slightly more than half the state constitutions required some type of property qualification for state officeholding. By 1860, twenty-six of the thirty-three state constitutions included no property qualification.[123] Religious tests – included in only a few state constitutions in 1790 – were also dropped in most states, although social customs and demographics often proved to have enduring exclusionary effects. Not until 1825 were Jews legally permitted to hold public office in Maryland.[124]

The electoral insulation enjoyed by eighteenth-century political elites also declined throughout the first half of the nineteenth century.[125] The rawness and unsettledness of frontier life that refracted through the politics of every western state offered little protection for elitist presumptions and little reason for popular deference toward elected officials. Winning elections in these newly settled states, as well as in the older states, had, it seemed, nothing discernible to do with the elevation of a "virtuous few" to govern the licentious rabble and a whole lot more to do with surviving long weeks of campaigning on horseback, pre-election duels, polling place roughhousing, and election day supplies of money, rum, and whiskey.

Candidates for state office often went to great lengths to portray themselves as similar to, and not better than, the general public. Several

---

[122] Wood, *The Radicalness of the American Revolution* (1991); Gordon S. Wood, "Ideology and the Origins of Liberal America," *WMQ* (1987), XLIV(3): 628–640.

[123] See McCarthy, *The Widening Scope of American Constitutions* (1928), p. 46n.3; Wooster, *Politicians, Planters, and Plain Folk* (1975), pp. 57–59.

[124] See *Constitutional Revision Study Documents of the Constitutional Convention Commission of Maryland* (Annapolis, 1968), p. 31. In North Carolina, a religious test requiring adherence to the Protestant faith for all public officeholding was included within the original state constitution and in an 1835 constitutional amendment. This restriction does not appear to have been enforced against either Catholics or Jews.

[125] In New Hampshire, for example, future President Franklin Pierce was known in the mid-1840s to have "scoured among [the] underground drunken holes and led men to the Ballot Box so drunk they couldn't stand without his aid." As quoted in William Geinapp, "'Politics Seem to Enter into Everything'" (1982), p. 47. See also Summers, *The Plundering Generation* (1987).

dressed themselves in homespun clothes when campaigning in order to appear as a candidate of the people. Others, as one North Carolina state house candidate reported on his 1846 campaign, became "busily engaged in proving to the people, the soundness of my political faith, and the purity of my personal character & playing the fool to a considerable extent, as you know, all candidates are obliged to do."[126] For many, regardless of state or section, this meant walking in parades, sleeping at strangers' homes, eating at public barbecues, drinking at local taverns, and the endless retelling of embellished stories about childhood hardships.[127]

The gradual lightening of constitutional restrictions on the suffrage was another factor that undermined the elitism of nineteenth-century state legislators.[128] By 1824, adult white males were generally eligible to vote in all but three states: Rhode Island, Virginia, and Louisiana. As recorded in Figure 8.10, the size of the electorate measured as a percentage of total population increased across time and every region.[129] This

---

[126] As quoted in Kruman, *Parties and Politics in North Carolina* (1983), p. 51.

[127] See Dinkin, *Campaigning in America* (1989), pp. 34–39.

[128] See Alexander Keyssar, *The Right to Vote* (New York: Basic Books, 2000); James Schouler, "Evolution of the American Voter," *AHR* (1897), II: 665–674. Another institutional change in the late eighteenth and early nineteenth centuries that aided the subsequent expansion in electoral participation was the localization of the voting process. The town remained the primary polling place for state election in New England states. But, as historian George D. Luetscher pointed out, "in all of the remaining States, there was a definite movement along the line of reducing the distance that an elector had to travel in order to exercise his political rights." In several states this was accomplished by making the township or hundred the voting district rather than the county; in other states, counties were divided into voting districts. George D. Luetscher, *Early Political Machinery in the United States* (New York: Da Capo Press, 1971 [1903 Ph.D. diss]), pp. 26, 27–30.

[129] Data on number of voters in gubernatorial elections are from Roy R. Glashan, *American Governors and Gubernatorial Elections, 1775–1978* (Westport, CT: Meckler Books, 1979). These data were combined with U.S. Census population data and straightline interdecennial annual extrapolations. Note that, contrary to prevailing opinions and a generation's worth of scholarly work, calculation of turnout based on *total* population is preferable for its analytical and normative qualities. The former quality ensures that we do not unwittingly accept biases imported from historical concepts of eligibility or the attendant folly that nineteenth-century turnout was "high" when in fact the vast majority of the population was never permitted to "turn out" on election day. The latter quality, I believe, places measurement of political participation on the natural and most acceptable basis within a modern democracy – that is, total population. Measurement of turnout based on total population has the additional benefit of revealing more fully the simultaneous growth and narrow breadth of electoral participation between 1790 and 1860. For a recent elaboration of the latter phenomenon, see Glenn C. Altschuler and Stuart M. Blumin, *Rude Republic: Americans and Their Politics in the Nineteenth Century* (Princeton, NJ: Princeton University Press,

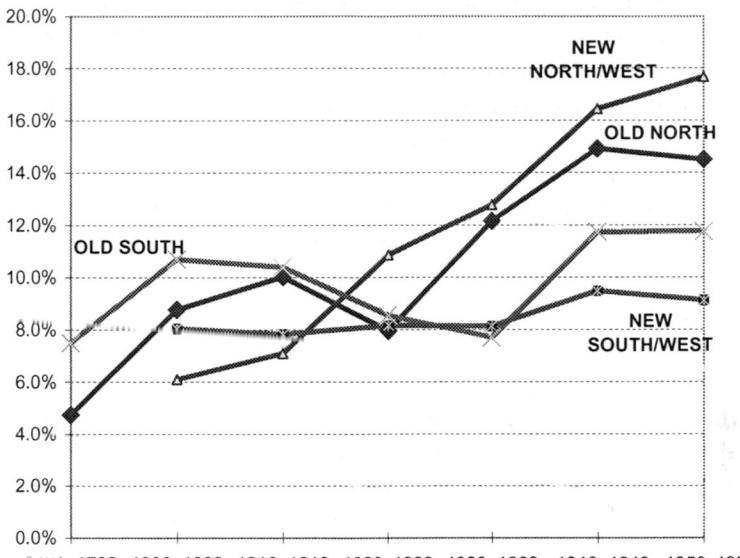

FIGURE 8.10. Electoral Participation Ratios, 1790–1859. (Electoral participation ratio represents percentage of voters per population in gubernatorial elections.)

expansion no doubt increased the complexity and uncertainty of electoral calculations far beyond the mathematical and political skills of most office seekers.[130] Unable to manage the enlarged and increasingly volatile electorate toward elitist electoral outcomes, American political parties (and their outwardly nonelitist orientations) had become an organizational prerequisite for electoral success in most states by the 1840s.

Additional changes in state electoral procedures further ensured that state legislators would remain bound to this new and seemingly unwieldy electorate. By 1860, most states had increased the number of polling places and many had limited their elections to a single (often constitutionally defined) day. As a consequence, the time commitment required of voters was reduced as was the pernicious and apparently prevalent electoral practice of multiple voting. Ballot voting also became the legal standard in most states, although a few continued to use the more socially

2000); Glenn C. Altschuler and Stewart M. Blumin, "Limits of Political Engagement in Antebellum America: A New Look at the Golden Age of Participatory Democracy," *JAH* (1997), pp. 855–885.
[130] See Formisano, "Deferential-Participant Politics" (1974) 68: 482; Silbey, *The American Political Nation* (1991), pp. 144–147.

restrictive (and thus more electorally predictable) *viva voce* method of electing state legislative representatives.[131] North Carolina replaced its paper ballot process with *viva voce* procedures in 1835 – a clear reminder that the process of electoral reform is not necessarily unidirectional.

The emergence, institutionalization, and competitiveness of state and national political parties further undermined the electoral insulation of state legislators. Competition among the parties prompted candidates to engage in new and more public forms of electioneering. Increased electoral competition, in turn, gave rise to more aggressive and public displays of political ambition by politically interested individuals who cast aside the eighteenth-century custom of appearing to wait for acclamation as the "best-suited" for public office.[132] Moreover, the hallowed rhetoric of disinterestedness, however unsubstantiated it may have been during the early national years, faded with little notice from the nineteenth-century American political lexicon. In an era when state governments seemed highly responsive, the last thing a candidate wanted to suggest was a disinterest in or lack of conviction toward his constituents' particular interests.

Another general condition that eroded popular deference toward state legislators was the public's increased exposure to state legislative proceedings. These proceedings generally were open to the public and, more important, they regularly were covered by a rapidly growing and highly competitive newsprint medium. The widespread use of the telegraph in the late 1840s and throughout the 1850s further accelerated the transfer of information from state capitals to local and regional newspapers. Because many newspapers were openly partisan, sensationalized reporting framed the public's perception of state politics and redefined the political rhetoric and cadences of state legislators.[133] American state

---

[131] See Albert O. Porter, *County Government in Virginia: A Legislative History, 1607–1904* (New York: Columbia University Press, 1947), pp. 171–174; Schouler, "Evolution of the American Voter," *AHR* (1897), II: 670–671.

[132] For different measures of the intensity of electoral and party competition from the 1830s through the 1850s, see Michael Holt, *The Rise and Fall of the American Whig Party: Jacksonian Politics and the Onset of the Civil War* (Oxford: Oxford University Press, 1999); Joel Silbey, *The American Political Nation, 1838–1893* (Stanford, CA: Stanford University Press, 1991). Abandonment of the norm against self-promotion did not occur at the same rate across the states. See Joan W. Coward, *Kentucky in the New Republic: The Process of Constitution Making* (Lexington: University Press of Kentucky, 1979), pp. 164–165; and Formisano, *The Transformation of Political Culture* (1984), pp. 130–135.

[133] See Andrew W. Robertson, *The Language of Democracy: Political Rhetoric in the United States and Britain, 1790–1900* (Ithaca, NY: Cornell University Press, 1995), pp. 36–53, 68–95.

legislatures, as a consequence, were rarely portrayed or conceived as inordinately cerebral, deliberative forums in which the brightest or the most virtuous legislators convened to divine public policies best aligned with the common good. Rather, the state legislature was understood more commonly as a highly contentious and artificial arena of political speech within which, as historian L. Ray Gunn observed, "individuals and narrow, often local, interests competed with one another for largess and favors."[134]

High rates of membership turnover in American state legislators only confirmed their nonelitist character during the second quarter of the nineteenth century. Compared to colonial and modern standards, these rates reached extraordinarily high levels in almost every state.[135] In Vermont, approximately two-thirds of the state legislature in the mid-1820s had prior legislative experience. By 1845, less than half of this state legislature had prior experience. In numerous other northern states, turnover rates generally increased during the second quarter of the nineteenth century.[136] Remarkably, almost ninety percent of the New York legislature in the mid-1840s were legislative novices, and between 1829 and 1844 no member of the New Jersey legislature had more than six years of legislative experience.[137]

Turnover rates also were high in southern state legislatures. In Georgia, membership turnover in the state house of representatives was almost 40 percent between 1809 and 1831; between 1832 and 1859, the turnover rate averaged nearly 55 percent. In North Carolina, the turnover rate was nearly 60 percent between 1836 and 1860. During the 1850s, moreover, approximately 60 percent served only one term in the Virginia and Mississippi state houses. In Florida and Texas, 80 percent or more of the state houses served only one term. And in Arkansas, only 6.1 percent of the 832 members of the state house between 1836 and 1861 served more than one term.[138]

Other elements of the social differentiation of American state legislators also lost their salience. Indeed, every state (at some level)

---

[134] Gunn, *The Decline of Authority* (1988), p. 254.

[135] Prior to 1818, Connecticut was an exception to this general trend. Richard J. Purcell, *Connecticut in Transition: 1775–1818* (Middletown, CT: Wesleyan University Press, 1963), pp. 134–135).

[136] See Bowers, "From Logrolling to Corruption," *Journal of the Early Republic* (1983), 3: 458n.51; Formisano, *The Transformation of Political Culture* (1984), p. 46; Davis, " 'The People in Miniature' " (1988), 81: 99; and Gunn, *The Decline of Authority* (1988), p. 191n.65.

[137] Gunn, "The New York Legislature," (1980), 4: 278–279; Levine, *The Behavior of State Legislative Parties* (1977), p. 76.

[138] Wooster, *The People in Power* (1969), pp. 42–43.

demonstrated a greater openness to the political participation of individuals and groups of different ethnic, religious, economic, and geographic backgrounds.[139] In no state was the breadth of this aperture comparable to modern standards and in several states it clearly contracted during the first half of the nineteenth century. In most northern states, cultural conditions were more diverse and, therefore, state legislators and state-level politics were affected in ways that generally were not possible in southern states. Yet, by no means was the nineteenth-century South culturally homogeneous. In both sections, cultural distinctions often were used in highly divisive ways to excite, to fragment, and to exclude large segments of the population from political participation.[140]

In at least one-third of the states, across both the North and South, free African-Americans were permitted to vote at some point between 1790 and 1860. Individuals of various religious and ethnic identities also participated voluntarily in nineteenth-century coalition politics – although not without resistance or costs.[141] Catholics and various non-English ethnic groups were significant forces within local- and state-level politics in addition to the northern coalition of interests that made the

---

[139] Although formal bars against female voting were standard across the states after 1807, the participation of American women in nonelectoral dimensions of the political process clearly increased under the second party system. See Gienapp, "Politics Seem to Enter into Everything" (1982), pp. 16–17; Elizabeth R. Varon, "Tippecanoe and the Ladies, Too: White Women and Party Politics in Antebellum Virginia," *JAH* (1995) 82: 494–521.

[140] See Lee Benson, *The Concept of Jacksonian Democracy* (1961).

[141] For evidence of the political skills and significance of various ethnic group organizations prior to 1860, see Busey, *Immigration* (1969 [1856]), pp. 13–46. Other evidence of the ethnic factor in antebellum politics is plentiful. In Tennessee, for example, "John Bell and Cave Johnson said that they were elected to Congress by the aid of colored men's votes, the latter boasting that he owed his election in 1828 to one hundred and forty-four free negroes who worked in his mills." Emil Olbrich, *The Development of Sentiment on Negro Suffrage to 1860* (Madison, WI: University of Wisconsin Press, 1912), p. 40.

For a general discussion of the deliberate creation and stimulation of negative reference group orientations in antebellum politics, see Benson, *The Concept of Jacksonian Democracy* (1961); Michael F. Holt, *Forging a Majority* (1969). See also *Niles Register*, December 13, 1834, p. 237, where it is reported that although only about 120 African-Americans voted in Boston elections, color distinctions were used as a wedge issue to divide the electorate. In other states and at other times, other groups were used in similar ways. In several northern states, Catholics (primarily of Irish and German ancestry) repeatedly were consigned to the margins of state and local politics. As one contemporaneous observer noted in 1842, Rhode Island's political elite "would rather have the negroes vote than the d–d Irish." (As quoted in Conley, *Democracy in Decline* [1977], p. 345). Not surprisingly, individuals associated with specific ethnic groups (rather than partisan allegiances) bore the brunt of election-day related violence.

Democratic party into a truly national party. This proto-pluralist commitment for drawing diverse social interests into the political process was manifested in other forms as well. Wisconsin and Indiana, for example, demonstrated an uncommon openness to the political integration of new immigrants. The former's 1846 constitution and the latter's 1850 constitution granted the right to vote to any foreign-born individual who expressed the *intent* to become naturalized. The state constitutions of Oregon, Minnesota, and Wisconsin were inclusive in other ways: The Oregon constitution, for example, expressly extended the right to vote to "Persons of Indian blood ... who have adopted the language, customs, and habits of civilization." In addition, in Maryland and Ohio (and likely other states) free African-Americans, mixed "race" persons, and resident aliens voted and held elected local offices despite explicit constitutional and statutory barriers.[142] "*political inclusiveness*"

Although the development of this norm of political inclusiveness was often motivated by electoral outcomes only, various ethnic groups also succeeded in electing members directly to their state legislators. In the Ohio and Pennsylvania legislatures, German Americans were politically relevant enough to warrant German publication of the state legal code and the House and Senate journals. Louisiana legislators were constitutionally permitted to speak in either French or English, and legislative officers were required to be bilingual. And Minnesota's first constitutional convention authorized the translation of the first state constitution into German, Swedish, and French.[143]

The noted demise of a socially differentiated, electorally insulated political elite within American state legislatures, however, ought not imply that nineteenth-century politics were any less elitist than during the eighteenth century. Elitism, like every suggestion of social differentiation, assumes numerous forms. For example, the available evidence strongly suggests that state legislators throughout the first half of the nineteenth century were professionally oriented, better educated, and possessed more personal wealth than their electors and constituents. As early as 1850, 17 percent of all legislators in the Vermont House of

HOWEVER still not less elite

b/c more educated, wealthier

---

[142] See Kenneth J. Winkle, "Ohio's Informal Polling Place: Nineteenth-Century Suffrage in Theory and Practice," in Brown and Cayton, eds., *The Pursuit of Public Power: Political Culture in Ohio, 1787–1861* (Kent, OH: Kent State University, 1994), pp. 180–182; Charles H. Wesley, "Negro Suffrage in the Period of Constitutionmaking, 1787–1865," *Journal of Nego History* (1947) 32(2): 143–168.

[143] William Anderson, *A History of the Constitution of Minnesota* (Minneapolis: University of Minnesota Press, 1921), p. 3106.

Representatives were attorneys.[144] Systematic comparisons of the personal characteristics of state legislators across the states and over time are not presently possible, especially for northern state legislators. Southern state legislators, according to the still unparalleled work of Ralph A. Wooster, became notably less like their constituents during the 1850s. Compared to their respective state populations, southern state legislators had notably more personal property wealth and were more likely to be slave-owning than most of their constituents. By 1860, slaveholders constituted a majority in every legislature in the lower South.[145]

New forms of political elitism also developed and became embedded as constitutional requirements. With the general expansion in the size of the electorate between 1800 and 1850, numerous states adopted new exclusionary restrictions on voting. Women remained the largest category of adult Americans formally barred from voting during the nineteenth century. In all but one state constitution, the suffrage was expressly reserved to adult males. The 1776 New Jersey constitution was the exception and women voted in state elections throughout the 1790s and very early 1800s. In 1807, however, the state enacted legislation barring women from voting, a restriction subsequently formalized within the state constitution.[146]

Additional restrictions on electoral access were adopted in other states. All adult male inhabitants in Vermont enjoyed voting privileges from 1793 until 1828 when a state law revoked this right for noncitizen residents.[147] In an 1810 constitutional amendment, South Carolina similarly retracted the right to vote from "paupers and non-commissioned

---

[144] Sidney G. Morse, "The Representation Issue in Vermont a Century Ago," *Vermont Quarterly* (1953), 21: 89.

[145] See Wooster, *The People in Power* (1969); Wooster, *Politicians, Planters and Plain Folk* (1975); Randolph B. Campbell and Richard G. Lowe, *Wealth and Power in Antebellum Texas* (College Station, TX: Texas A & M University Press, 1977); William G. Shade, *Democratizing the Old Dominion* (Charlottesville: University of Virginia Press, 1996).

[146] *History of the Woman Suffrage*, Stanton, Anthony, and Gage, eds. (New York: Fowler & Wells, 1881), I: 447–450; Olbrich, *The Development of Sentiment on Negro Suffrage* (1912), pp. 22–23. A noteworthy exception to this antebellum exclusion was Kentucky's 1838 grant of suffrage privileges to widows with school-age children. See Carrie C. Catt and Nettie R. Shuler, *Woman Suffrage and Politics* (New York: Charles Scribner's Sons, 1926), pp. 9, 13.

[147] Vermont constitution, 1828 Amendment, Art 1. The 1847 Illinois Constitutional Convention imposed a similar restriction: limiting voter eligibility under the 1818 constitution ("all white male inhabitants above the age of 21 years") to "all white male citizens." See Janet Cornelius, *Constitution Making in Illinois, 1818–1970* (Urbana, IL: University of Illinois Press, 1972), p. 37.

officers and private soldiers of the army of the United States."[148] In 1836, Pennsylvania legislators enacted a voter registration law motivated, in large part, by a desire to reduce the voter turnout in Philadelphia. Several other northern states enacted similarly biased registration laws; an 1840 New York restriction applied only to the city of New York.[149]

By 1860, additional restrictions had been imposed. Nearly every state had incorporated highly exclusionary racialist distinctions into their constitutional definition of the right to vote. In 1786, only two of the original thirteen states expressly defined voting qualifications in terms of racial or color characteristics. By 1860, as recorded in Table 8.10, only five states did not impose formal constitutional or statutory restrictions against free African-American males. A sixth state, New York, imposed a poll tax after 1811 and a special property restriction in 1821 which barred most of these individuals from voting. In 1849, a seventh state, Wisconsin, extended the right to vote in a statute which the state's voters approved; a state elections board, however, did not recognize the authority of the voters and the statutory grant did not become effective until after the Civil War.[150]

By 1860, several states had adopted new suffrage restrictions against other groups like the foreign-born and non-English speaking individuals. The 1842 Rhode Island constitution imposed an additional property requirement on its naturalized citizens, which, according to historian Patrick Conley, was "the most nativistic in the nation." The 1850 California constitution diluted the right to vote of "Indians or the descendants of Indians" into a privilege dependent on legislative approval. The 1858 Oregon constitution expressly prescribed that: "No Negro, Chinaman, or mulatto, shall have the right of suffrage." Several New England states established registration and educational tests to impede the voter turnout of foreign-born individuals. From 1855, Connecticut required electors to "be able to read any article of the Constitution, or any section of the Statutes of his State." Two years later, Massachusetts adopted a similar restriction that also exempted all prior voters in

---

[148] In 1830, Virginia added a similar set of restrictions: Article III, sec. 14.

[149] Chilton Williamson, *American Suffrage: From Property to Democracy, 1760–1860* (Princeton: Princeton University Press, 1960), pp. 275–276. See also Joseph P. Harris, *Registration of Voters in the United States* (Washington: Brookings Institution, 1929), pp. 67–73; Geinapp, "'Politics Seem to Enter into Everything'," (1982), p. 24.

[150] Sec. 2, ch. 137, Laws of Wisconsin (March 22, 1849). See Leslie H. Fischel, "Wisconsin and Negro Suffrage," *Wisconsin Magazine of History* (1963), XLVI: 180–196; *Gillespie v. Palmer et al.* (1866) 20 Wisc. 544.

TABLE 8.10. *Right to Vote for African-Americans, 1790–1860*

REGION	1790	1800	1810	1820	1830	1840	1850	1860
Old North	NJ	NJ (1807)						
	CT	CT	CT (1814)					
	NY	NY	NY[a]	NY[a]	NY[a]	NY[a]	NY[a]	NY[a]
	PA	PA	PA	PA	PA (1838)			
	RI	RI	RI	RI (1822)		RI (1842)	RI	RI
	ME	ME	ME	ME	ME	ME	ME	ME
	MA	MA	MA	MA	MA	MA	MA	MA
	NH	NH	NH	NH	NH	NH	NH	NH
	VT	VT	VT	VT	VT	VT	VT	VT
New North/West								
Old South	DE (1792)							
	MD[b]	MD (1802)[b]						
	NC	NC	NC	NC	NC (1836)			
New South/West	KY (1792–1799)							
	TN (1793)	TN	TN	TN	TN (1834)			

[a] New York adopted color-based registration and property-owning restrictions in 1811 and 1821, which severely limited voting by constitutionally eligible African-American males. See color-based residency and property restrictions included in 1846 state constitution (Art. II, Section 1).

[b] In a 1783 state law and in an 1802 constitutional amendment Maryland restricted voting to the eligible "white" population. Despite these restrictions, free African-American males voted in the state as late as 1810.

Sources: In addition to the individual state constitutions, see James T. Adams, "Disenfranchisement of Negroes in New England," *AHR* (1925), 30: 545–546; Charles H. Wesley, "Negro Suffrage in the Period of Constitutionmaking, 1787–1865," *Journal of Negro History* (1947), 32(2): 143–168; Joan W. Coward, *Kentucky in the New Republic: The Process of Constitution Making* (1979), p. 184 n. 23.

addition to individuals over sixty years. The Bay State also adopted voter registration requirements aimed at better managing the foreign-born (and primarily Catholic) vote.[151] In 1859, Massachusetts further required two additional years after naturalization before a foreign-born individual was permitted to vote.[152]

Beyond these formal restrictions, the political practices and expectations that emerged during the second quarter of the nineteenth century promoted new elitist characteristics among American state legislators. By 1860, the once-traditional delegate and trustee norms of political representation had become less salient after political parties came to dominate almost every element of the electoral process, including the drawing of electoral district boundaries, candidate recruitment and nomination, and the printing and "counting" of ballots.[153] As one observer concluded, independently minded legislators were highly improbable because "[t]he leaders of the party carry everything – none dare resist."[154]

The expansion of the American electorate in the 1830s had unexpected elitist consequences: In this new and more democratic electoral environment, candidates for state office were increasingly required to possess the physical presence and oratory skills necessary to win over mass audiences that, historian William E. Gienapp reminds us, were "willing – and able – to sit through speeches lasting three hours or more

---

[151] 1855 amendment to Connecticut constitution, Art. XI; 1857; Twentieth article of amendment to Massachusetts constitution.

[152] Formisano, *The Transformation of Political Culture* (1984), p. 333. Several state constitutions included additional restrictions which discriminated disproportionately against the foreign-born. By 1860, twenty-three of thirty-three state constitutions disenfranchised individuals classified as criminals, paupers, and the insane. More directly, the 1820 Maine constitution included a rule of apportionment that excluded "foreigners not naturalized and Indians not taxed." In 1822, the newly revised New York constitution redefined the basis of apportionment from qualified voters to "number of inhabitants, excluding aliens, paupers, and persons of color not taxed." In 1857, Massachusetts altered its apportionment rule from "inhabitants" to "legal voters" in order to dilute the representation of towns with significant numbers of foreign-born inhabitants.

In addition to formal restrictions, other common practices had a similarly dampening effect on political participation. In 1855, for example, members of the Know-Nothing Party deliberately singled out and seized ballot boxes from German-American wards in Cincinnati. See Stephen E. Maizlish, "The Meaning of Nativism and the Crisis of the Union," in *Essays on American Antebellum Politics, 1840–1860* (1982), pp. 190–192.

[153] Other common elements of the modern electoral process had less than auspicious beginnings. See, for example, Harris, *Election Administration in the United States* (1934), p. 17.

[154] J. Francis Fisher, *The Degradation of our Representative System* (Philadelphia: C. Sherman, 1863), pp. 8–9. See also Wooster, *The People in Power* (1975), p. 42.

without losing interest."[155] The combination of excited levels of partisan competition with relatively small increases in the sizes of most state legislatures, and high rates of population growth and increased interest among the electorate with generally activist but nonbureaucratized state governments, meant that the demand for state office generally outran the supply of electoral opportunities. As the size of the electorate and electoral competition increased, so did the dependency of candidates on nonpersonal financial resources for their campaigns. Political parties and their fund-raising devices – especially, the assessment of contributions from federal officeholders after 1829 – became an increasingly significant source of these resources.[156]

From Dynamic to Static Institutionalization

The third and final characteristic used to describe colonial and early national conceptualizations of representation was dynamic institutionalism, or the variation and mutability of the institutional structures and practices used to mediate the representational relationship between social interests and political agents. Between 1790 and 1860, state institutions of representation generally became less dynamic and more similar across the states. Between the adoption of the 1818 Illinois constitution and the state's 1848 constitution, there typically were four general elections per year and the method of election (either by ballot or viva voce) was altered four times. The 1848 constitution, however, established a single biennial date for state elections and the ballot method.[157]

In contrast to the colonial and early national eras, one of the most significant institutional developments between 1790 and 1860 was the near standardization of the practice of reapportioning state legislative representation. In the 1790s, one-fifth of the state constitutions mandated a regular reapportionment of representation within the state legislatures. By the 1820s, more than half the state constitutions included this mandate; and after 1840, more than 80 percent did so. Of these states, few failed to complete an expected reapportionment.[158] In other states, the legislature

---

[155] Geinapp, " 'Politics Seem to Enter into Everything' " (1982), p. 40.

[156] White, *The Jacksonians* (1954), pp. 332–343.

[157] Cornelius, *Constitution Making in Illinois* (1970), p. 37.

[158] In several states, additional strictures were devised to ensure that state legislators would remain bound to a constitutional promise for a regular reapportionment. The 1852 Louisiana constitution, for example, prohibited the state legislature from enacting "any law until an apportionment of Representation in both Houses of the General Assembly be made" (1852 Louisiana constitution, II, 16). In Alabama, an extra session

TABLE 8.11. *State Legislative Interreapportionment Intervals,*
1790–1860

	Number of States							
	1790	1800	1810	1820	1830	1840	1850	1860
No Reapportionment	9	8	8	7	7	3	2	2
1–5 years	2	3	3	8	7	8	3	3
6–10 years	3	5	6	8	9	12	25	25
11–20 years	0	1	1	0	0	1	0	1
Not Known	1	0	0	1	1	2	1	2

Note: If statutory interval not known, then constitutional interval used.

was granted a broad but unspecified authority to reapportion: Most of them also completed regular reapportionments. In the remaining states, there were no explicit or implicit expectations for legislative reapportionment. In these states, much more dramatic extraconstitutional pressures were typically required to establish a new distribution of legislative representation.[159] Although reapportionment became a constitutional norm during the first half of the nineteenth century, there were noteworthy differences in state reapportionment practices. Table 8.11 reveals that prior to 1840 interreapportionment intervals varied widely among the states. By 1860, however, most states had adopted reapportionment intervals of between six to ten years. (See Table 8.11.)

Interstate differences also existed with regard to state rules of apportionment. As previously noted, by 1860 most states had apportionment rules that divided legislative representation on a proportional basis. As Tables 8.12 and 8.13 reveal, the specific terms of apportionment varied

of the legislature was convened in 1821 to correct the body's failure to enact an expected reapportionment bill in 1820. Legislative resistance continued at this session as did public criticism of the legislature by Governor Thomas Bibb and several state newspapers. By December 1821, the legislature finally passed a new reapportionment act. Thomas M. Owen, *History of Alabama* (Chicago: The S. J. Clarke Co., 1921), II: 870.

[159] See Parkinson, *Antebellum State Constitution-Making* (1972).

Advocates of new apportionment rules used a variety of tactics to impress their interests on state legislatures. Of these, legislative petitions clearly were the most popular method. Legislative boycotts, threats of secession, and extra constitutional conventions were used in states where reform did not seem to be forthcoming. Finally, more violent interruptions of the authority of the political order are significant turning points in the political development of several American colonies and states. See, for example, Edgar A. Holt, "Party Politics in Ohio, 1840–1850," *Ohio Archaeological and Historical Publication* (1929), 38: 320, 319–353; Shade, *Democratizing the Old Dominion* (1996).

TABLE 8.12. *Apportionment Basis, State Houses of Representatives, 1790–1860*

	Number of States per Basis							
	1790	1800	1810	1820	1830	1840	1850	1860
FIXED (Total)	10	9	8	8	8	4	4	4
Territorial/Jurisdictional basis:								
County/district	4	3	2	2	2	1	1	1
Town	3	3	3	3	3	3	2	2
Mixed	3	3	3	3	3	1	1	1
PROPORTIONAL (Total)	5	8	10	16	16	22	27	29
Population basis:								
Total population	–	–	–	–	–	4	6	5
Ethnic basis:								
Population minus "foreign" classes	–	1	–	2	2	2	4	5
Population + 3/5 enslaved population	–	1	1	1	1	3	3	3
Free "white" population	–	–	–	3	3	4	6	7
"White" + "Indian" population	–	–	–	–	–	–	1	1
Gender/Age basis:								
Free white males	–	–	–	1	1	2	1	1
White males, 21 + years	–	1	1	2	2	2	1	1
Free males, 21 + years	1	–	–	–	–	–	–	–
Electorate-defined basis:								
Voters, qualified electors	1	2	3	2	2	2	2	3
Taxation-defined basis:								
Taxable inhabitants	1	2	2	2	2	1	1	1
Ratable polls	2	2	2	2	2	1	1	1
Mixed basis:								
"White" population + taxes paid	–	–	1	1	1	1	1	1

TABLE 8.13. *Apportionment Basis, State Senates, 1790–1860*

	Number of States per Basis							
	1790	1800	1810	1820	1830	1840	1850	1860
AT-LARGE (Total)	3	3	3	3	2	0	0	0
FIXED (Total)	8	7	8	8	8	8	7	7
Territorial/Jurisdictional basis:								
Section/region	1	1	1	1	2	1	1	1
County/district	7	7	7	7	6	5	4	4
Town	–	–	–	–	–	1	1	1
Mixed	–	–	–	–	–	1	1	1
PROPORTIONAL (Total)	4	7	7	13	14	18	24	26
Population basis:								
Total population	–	–	–	–	1	3	4	3
Ethnic basis:								
Population minus "foreign" classes	–	–	–	2	2	2	3	4
Population + 3/5 enslaved population	–	–	–	–	–	–	1	1
Free "white" population	–	–	–	2	3	4	5	6
"White" + "Indian" population	–	–	–	–	–	–	1	1
Gender/Age basis:								
Free white males	–	–	–	1	1	2	2	2
White males, 21 + years	–	1	1	2	2	2	2	2
Free males, 21 + years	–	1	1	1	1	1	–	–
Electorate-defined basis:								
Voters, qualified electors	–	1	1	–	–	1	3	4
Taxation-defined basis:								
Taxable inhabitants or freeholders	2	2	2	2	2	1	1	1
Free white taxables	–	–	–	1	–	–	–	–
Taxes paid basis:	2	2	2	2	2	2	2	2

considerably among the states between 1790 and 1860. After 1820, states increasingly defined apportionment in terms of ethnic or color distinctions. This peculiarly illiberal development reveals an early and enduring contradiction within nineteenth-century American liberalism.

State legislative size also varied among the states. In 1790, the total number of American state legislators was approximately 1,750. The average number of state representatives was 95 and the average number of state senators was 21. By 1860, the total number of state legislators exceeded 4,700, largely due to the admission of new states into the Union. The average state house size had increased to almost 115 representatives and the average senate size to more than 30. Between 1790 and 1860, the average number of state legislators increased by 26 members, or an average decennial rate of approximately 3.2 percent. Northern state legislative houses, on average, were notably larger than southern state houses between 1800 and 1840. By 1860, however, the size of northern and southern state houses were roughly similar. Southern state senates, on average, were consistently larger than northern state senates, although this difference had become notably smaller by 1860. State houses in the Old North and Old South regions were typically larger than in the new western states admitted to the Union. Interestingly, state senates in the new north/west region generally had more members than state senates in the old North region.

Two final observations offer additional insights into the institutional development of state-level representation between 1790 and 1860. The first is that although legislative reapportionment became a constitutional standard within most American states over the course of the nineteenth century, state institutions of representation ironically became less attuned to scale changes in state population. The resulting institutional dissonance between the organizational framework of state government and the dynamics of nineteenth-century demographic realities is reflected in the aggregate increases in the number of persons per state legislator illustrated in Figures 8.8 and 8.9. The attenuation of state-society relations (if measured by the total number of state legislators per population) became especially prominent and statistically meaningful during the latter decades of the antebellum era.

The thinning of the intimacy of the representational relationship between state legislators and their constituents was a direct consequence of the stabilization of the growth in the sizes of American state legislatures during the second quarter of the nineteenth century. By the 1840s the membership of approximately half of all state houses and senates had not increased in comparison to membership in the prior decade. Notably, state constitutional conventions typically provided both the forum and the format for reducing or capping the growth in the number of state legislators.[160]

A second observation concerning the nineteenth-century development of state institutions of representation exposes a final irony: As proportional rules of apportionment became the constitutional standard, a number of states established institutional devices or practices that withheld proportionate shares of representation from the most populous areas within their respective states. Four types of devices warrant special attention. The first device imposed an explicit cap on the maximum number of representatives permitted to any unit of apportionment. The 1819 Maine constitution, for example, provided that "no town shall ever be entitled to more than seven representatives." A second device restricted state house representation by imposing a cap on the size of the legislature and a minimum level of representation for every unit of apportionment. An 1835 amendment to the North Carolina constitution fixed the state house size at 120 and guaranteed that "each county shall have at least one member . . . although it may not contain the requisite ratio of population." In a slightly different way but with a similar effect, the 1851 Maryland constitution fixed the house size at eighty members, guaranteed Baltimore four more delegates than the next most populous county, and also provided two delegates each to twenty-one counties.[161] A third device with a similar bias against more populous areas was the sliding ratio scale. This scale established different and ascending levels of population for each additional state legislative representative.[162] A

---

[160] For a fuller account of these state-level developments, see Charles A. Kromkowski, *The Bond of Union: Constitutional Change, Rules of Apportionment and A General Theory of American Political Development* (1998 Ph.D. diss., University of Virginia).

[161] 1835 North Carolina constitutional amendment, I, 1, 2; 1851 Maryland constitution, III, 3.

See also 1808 South Carolina constitutional amendment; 1817 Mississippi constitution, III, 9; 1819 Alabama constitution, III, 9; 1821 Missouri constitution, III, 2; 1822 New York constitution, I, 2; 1835 Arkansas, IV, 34; 1836 Vermont constitutional amendment 4; 1837 Michigan, IV, 2, 4; 1838 Pennsylvania, I, 4; 1840 Massachusetts constitutional amendment (state senate); 1842 Rhode Island constitution, V, 1; 1844 New Jersey constitution, IV, iii, 1; 1845 Florida, IV, 18, IX, 1; 1845 Georgia statute: maximum size at one hundred thirty, each county at least one representative, no county more than one representative; 1846 New York constitution, III, 2, 5; 1849 Missouri constitution amendment, III, 1; 1852 Louisiana constitution, II, 8; 1857 Massachusetts constitutional amendment XXII.

[162] See 1837 Maryland constitutional amendment, sec. 10; 1849 Missouri amendment, sec. 1.

fourth device, resorted to infrequently prior to 1860, was to delay or ignore a constitutional mandate for a periodic reapportionment. In Louisiana the state legislature ignored an explicit constitutional directive when it failed to reapportion the state house of representatives between 1826 and 1841.[163] In the short run, the intentional bias of these devices was mitigated by prevailing levels of urbanization and by the fact that most states typically contained a single urbanizing city. In the long run, however, these devices were significant because they established precedents for more egregious distortions of the principle of proportionality that occurred in the late nineteenth and early twentieth centuries.

CONCLUSION

From the establishment of the U.S. Constitution to the initiation of the American Civil War, American political actors were embedded within and deeply affected by the development of various economic, demographic, institutional, and ideological conditions. Reconstruction of the developmental trajectories of these conditions between 1790 and 1860 serves two important purposes: First, it provides an opportunity for understanding the general context within which the subsequent constitutional collapse occurred; and second, it provides an independent and empirically grounded basis for assessing the immediate and long-term expectations of American political actors prior to the secession of the first southern state in December 1860.

These reconstructed trajectories additionally suggest a deep irony between the structural context in 1860 and the sequence of decisions by which northern and southern statesmen committed themselves and their states to the uncertainties and trials of civil war. In absolute terms, the states of the North and South were far more similar and interdependent in 1860 than they had been in 1787 or 1830. Both sections had productive and profitable economies and both remained predominantly rural and agricultural. In addition, by 1860 both sections shared the habits and the history of working for common national purposes and under a common set of national institutions. States within both sections had developed similar national- and state-level institutions of representative government. In the one area in which absolute sectional differences were undeniable, the legality of human slavery, states within both sections

---

[163] Emmett Asseff, *Legislative Apportionment in Louisiana* (Baton Rouge, LA: Bureau of Government Research-Louisiana State University, 1950), p. 14.

had similarly exclusionary legal and social orientations toward African-Americans.[164]

Although absolute differences diminished in many areas between 1790 and 1860, many American statesmen remained fixated on relative differences between the two sections. These differences were not trivial. Over the course of the nineteenth century many states in the North grew increasingly more commercial, more industrial, more technologically advanced, more urban, and more culturally diverse than the states in the South. Southern statesmen were decidedly more racist, more expansionist, more militaristic, and more sectionally cohesive than their cohorts in Congress and in northern state legislatures. No relative difference, however, seemed more important than the sectional division of decision-making capacities within the national government. On this difference, it often seemed, the American political universe revolved and gained much of its motion in the nineteenth century.

The complex set of relations that constituted the American republic founded in the American Revolution and peacefully reconstructed at the 1787 Constitutional Convention was continuously renegotiated between 1790 and 1860. By mid-1861, the calculus of consent that had sustained these relations for eighty-five years dissolved into the mists of time and the tragedy of civil war. How and why the constitutional bonds of the relational Republic were broken and later reforged are the serious and lingering questions that prompt the inquiry taken up and answered in Chapter 9.

---

[164] Leon F. Litwack, *North of Slavery: The Negro and in the Free States, 1790–1860* (Chicago: University of Chicago Press, 1961); Eugene H. Berwinger, "Negrophobia in Northern Proslavery and Antislavery Thought," *Phylon* (1972), 33: 266–275, republished in Paul Finkelman, ed., *Proslavery Thought, Ideology and Politics* (New York: Garland Publishing, Inc., 1989). For a broader and more detailed description of this inegalitarian ascriptive tradition in American history, see Rogers M. Smith, *Civic Ideals: Conflicting Visions of Citizenship in U.S. History* (New Haven, CT: Yale University Press, 1997).

9

Between Consent and Coercion: *Libido Dominandum* and the End of Representation

Chapter 9 completes the account of the third constitutional change in the national rule of apportionment. Whereas Chapter 8 described the development of various environmental (or macrolevel) conditions between 1790 and 1860, this chapter analyzes the microlevel (or actor-centered) conditions that effected the abandonment and replacement of the original Constitution's rule of apportionment. This chapter focuses on the sequence of decisions that preceded the wholesale breakdown in the political bonds between the northern and southern states. It also provides a brief account of the formalization of a new national rule of apportionment in the aftermath of the American Civil War.

The structural developments described in Chapter 8 offer no immediately obvious long- or short-term sectional differences that necessitated a constitutional crisis between northern and southern states in 1861. Since 1790, every state had reaped significant benefits under the constitutional Union established in 1787. In addition to sharing generally peaceful domestic and external constitutions, high rates of demographic growth, and sustained (although uneven) economic development, the principal interests within both sections had fashioned similar state governmental institutions and conceptualizations of representation, and they both had success in using the national government to promote or protect their particular interests.

During the first half of the nineteenth century, relative differences among the sections grew more prominent in several areas, although these differences were often mitigated by shared national experiences or by other more deeply embedded political commitments and capacities. By 1850, relative changes in the sectional distribution of national representation clearly prompted different sets of political expectations. Yet, this divergence of northern and southern expectations concerning each section's national decision-making capacities only created an opportunity for constitutional change in the rule of apportionment. It did not foreordain the initial secession of South Carolina and four other lower South states, the subsequent secession of the six upper South states after the provocation at Fort Sumter, or the commitments by the North and the South to engage in the American Civil War.

Several critical questions remain. Why did eleven southern states voluntarily abandon their long-standing commitment to the American Union? Why did the northern states and the national government resist secession? Finally, why did this attempt to redefine the constitutional relationship between northern and southern states culminate in civil war? As with the accounts constructed for the two prior changes, credible answers to these questions require recognition of both macro- and microlevel conditions and the employment of innovative methodological devices sensitive not only to contextual conditions and historical decision-making sequences but the set of possible constitutional outcomes as well.

For the first and second constitutional changes, the forms of several game-theoretic models were appropriated and modified in order to analyze the specific sequence of decisions by which the existing rule of apportionment was abandoned. Additional devices were also employed to aid the analysis.[1] The concept of a "dynamic status quo" was used to integrate macrolevel conditions with the sequence of decisions that

---

[1] The preceding account of the second constitutional change (especially Chapter 6) introduced another important analytical device: the "constitutional entrepreneur." As more fully explained in that chapter, the transition from structural conditions ripe for constitutional change to attempted constitutional changes are entrepreneur-dependent. The initiation of the process of constitutional change thus depends on the presence and engagement of particular types of individuals who possess the vision and skills to call into question elements of the existing constitutional framework.

Although not given special focus in this account, the transition from the set of structural conditions that existed in 1860 to the American Civil War by mid-1861 was heavily influenced by the entrepreneurial actions of various individuals in both the North and South. In particular, the actions of the so-called "Fire Eaters" from South Carolina and several other lower South states deserve special acknowledgment for their catalytic effects upon this transition process. For more on the interests and methods of these individuals, see Ulrich B. Phillips, *The Course of the South to Secession* (Gloucester, Mass., P. Smith, 1958), pp. 128–149; William Barney, *The Road to Secession* (New York, Praeger, 1972), pp. 85–122; Eric H. Walther, *The Fire-Eaters* (Baton Rouge, LA: Louisiana State University Press, 1992); and Brian H. Reid, *The Origins of the American Civil War* (London: Longman, 1996).

effected each change. Another device, the "outcome set," defined the set of decision-making alternatives and the relative ranking of these alternatives for each principal political actor. The "status quo" was included as an alternative within the outcome set, thereby establishing a means of evaluating the existing set of structural conditions for each principal decision maker. Game-theoretic models and these other analytical devices are again used to construct the following account of the third apportionment rule change and of the wholesale breakdown and reconstitution of the American political order between 1861 and 1870.

Part I of this chapter focuses on the unanswered questions of southern secession and northern resistance by describing the outcome set, or the common set of alternatives considered by northern and southern statesmen between late 1860 and mid-1861. In Part II, three game-theoretic models are employed to explain how and why the sequence of decisions between these statesmen culminated in the American Civil War. Part III concludes the account by sketching the process that formalized the terms for a new national rule of apportionment in the Thirteenth, Fourteenth, and Fifteenth Amendments to the U.S. Constitution.

PART I: THE OUTCOME SET

Although numerous proposals for restructuring the American political order were developed, debated, and occasionally enacted between 1790 and 1860, only six alternatives were given serious attention by northern and southern leaders after South Carolina formally seceded December 20, 1860.[2] This shared conceptual framework included proposals for: (1) constitutional reform of the existing Union; (2) enactment of legal reforms; (3) adoption of symbolic political reforms; (4) the peaceful division of the Union; (5) coercive resolution of the secession crisis; and (6) maintenance of the political status quo.

The meanings and likelihood assigned to each of these outcomes were neither fixed nor uniformly distributed among northern or southern statesmen. Historian Roy Nichols reminds us, "the confusing variety of plans and ideas whirling around in the minds of the many who attempted

---

[2] Following Herbert A. Simon, it is assumed that "to understand political choices, we need to understand where the frame of reference for the actor's thinking comes from – how it is evoked. An important component of the frame of reference is the set of alternatives that are given consideration in the choice process." Herbert A. Simon, "Human Nature in Politics: The Dialogue of Psychology with Political Science," *American Political Science Review* (1985), 79: 302.

new designs" is difficult to appreciate given the hindsight of their ultimate failure and displacement by the American Civil War. Moreover,
"[t]he most significant element in the confusion, and one sometimes
lost sight of, was the lack of anything like unity among the inhabitants
of the fifteen slave states and their leaders."[3] The initial declarations of
secession by the lower South states, for example, were compelled and
supported by a variety of interests and intentions among the statesmen
of the upper and lower South. For a small number of these individuals,
these formal declarations were intended to be the initial step toward
founding a new southern nation. For many others, however, the act of
secession was a means and not an end. As one "secessionist" advocate
argued in January 1861:

Secession is not intended to break up the present government, but to perpetuate
it . . . we go out for the purpose of getting further guarantees and security for
our rights . . . our plan is for the Southern States to withdraw from the Union
for the present, to allow amendments to the Constitution to be made, guaranteeing our just rights.[4]

Northern leaders also interpreted "secession" in a variety of ways.
Initially, most disregarded the initial declarations because the threat of
secession, although never before acted on, had become commonplace
during the past thirty years. As negotiations between the "secessionists"
and "Unionists" approached stalemate, northern state leaders increasingly perceived "secession" as a bargaining tool designed to increase the
South's political leverage within the national government. Numerous
individuals in the North therefore counseled strongly against any
capitulation to the demands of their southern cohorts.[5]

Before attempting to reconstruct the sequence of decisions that culminated in the American Civil War, three generalizations concerning the
orientations of American political leaders in early 1861 will prove useful.
The first generalization is that, although there clearly was a diversity of
opinions concerning the benefits and possibilities of renegotiating the

[3] Roy Nichols, *Blueprints for Leviathan: American Style* (New York: Atheneum, 1963),
pp. 141–142.
[4] As quoted in Jesse T. Carpenter, *The South as a Conscious Minority* (Gloucester, MA:
P. Smith, 1963 [1930]), p. 167. Additional contemporaneous observations could be
recited. See statement by former Tennessee Senator John Bell in December 1860 in
Nichols, *Blueprints for Leviathan* (1963), p. 145.
[5] See, for example, *New York Evening Post* editorials by William Cullen Bryant in *New
York Evening Post*, September 26, 1855, and October 1860 in *Power for Sanity: Selected
Editorials of William Cullen Bryant* (New York: Fordham University Press, 1994),
pp. 383–384, 380.

terms of the American political order, reactions to South Carolina's declaration of secession in December 1860 suggest that, at a more general level, there were also distinct "northern" and "southern" reactions. The latter sectional orientation can be further subdivided into distinct "Upper South" and "Lower South" reactions. These classifications are analytical constructs but they are not unimportant because they provide a historically grounded basis for modeling the diversity of opinions and interests concerning secession in terms of a smaller (and, therefore, more manageable) set of unitary actors.

The second generalization is that the differences between northern and southern orientations turned on their perceptions of the derivative benefits and costs of secession. Southern leaders (in both the Upper and Lower South) generally perceived secession as an opportunity to negotiate for more favorable terms than were provided under the existing constitutional order. Most northern leaders (especially Republican Party members) generally perceived secession in terms of relative and absolute losses. They were notably reluctant to engage in both formal and informal negotiations. President-elect Abraham Lincoln privately counseled his fellow Republicans: "Let there be no compromise on the question of extending slavery. If there be, all our labor is lost, and, ere long, must be done again. . . . Stand firm. The tug has to come, and better now than at any time hereafter."[6]

The final generalization is that during the initial months of 1861 neither the northern-state-dominated Union nor the secessionist states of the lower South possessed the capacity to establish the terms or boundaries of their political existence. There were some southern leaders who believed that when they unilaterally recalled their representatives from Washington, the national government would collapse. Still others confused the parchment framing of a southern Confederacy with the existence of a working and viable new constitutional order. There also were northern leaders who believed that by simply ignoring the secessionists the constitutional terms of the old Union would remain unimpeached and unaffected. More serious persons, never enchanted by these political fantasies, understood that the peaceful resolution of the secessionist crisis necessitated a bargaining process directed toward a commonly acceptable outcome. And the most sober of these individuals understood that beyond the consensual reconstruction of the American Union lay the

[6] Lincoln to Lyman Trumbull, December 10, 1860, as quoted in David M. Potter, *Lincoln and His Party in the Secession Crisis* (New Haven: Yale University Press, 1942), p. 157.

uncertainties of more coercive means of reconciling their differences. Negotiations between these consensual and coercive paths began in earnest only after the first secessionist declaration was issued in late December 1860. With these generalizations in mind, this chapter turns to the six outcomes that defined the set of real possibilities during the secession crisis.

Constitutional Reform

The first possible outcome called for the constitutional reform of the existing terms of the American political order. Numerous constitutional amendments were proposed publicly and privately by northern and southern political leaders.[7] Several of these amendments called for the constitutional affirmation of the individual right to enslave others as property. Others proposed modification to the existing rule of apportionment by guaranteeing sectional equality within the U.S. Supreme Court or by creating a new double national Executive consisting of a representative from each section.

Legal Reform

The second outcome called for the legal (or statutory) reform of the authority and capacities of the national government. These reforms included the addition of new slave states into the Union, active federal enforcement of the 1850 Fugitive Slave Act, federal recognition of the right of slave property in federal territories, and federal assistance against abolitionist agitation in the South.[8]

Symbolic Reform

The third possible outcome considered by northern and southern statesmen called for the establishment of symbolic political reforms. This outcome offered little to the secessionist states except a political opportunity to rejoin their fellow states within the existing Union. These reforms included a promise for a constitutional convention to address southern state concerns, repeated assurances that the federal government would not abolish slavery where it existed, and sectionally sensitive appointments to President Lincoln's Cabinet.

[7] See Carpenter, *The South as a Conscious Minority* (1963), p. 166.
[8] See Nichols, *Blueprints for Leviathan* (1963), p. 135.

Peaceful Separation

The fourth possible outcome of the secession crisis was the peaceful division of the United States.[9] Like the other outcomes, this was not a new idea in 1860: Separation from the Union had been proposed as far back as the 1787 Constitutional Convention – although, over the intervening years, the advocates and lines of division often had changed. By 1860, numerous individuals in the North openly advocated allowing the southern states to secede, but the most vocal advocates for separation and for the creation of a new southern confederacy were from the lower South states.[10]

Coerced Union/Separation

The fifth outcome possibility resolved the secession crisis through coercion. Few individuals, it seems certain, foresaw this outcome as leading to a protracted and massively destructive civil war. Southern proponents confidently suggested that only a small show of force by the secessionists would be necessary to repel the then minuscule Union army. In the North, few publicly pushed for the use of force against the secessionists. However, almost a full year before the secession crisis, the *New York Evening Post* had editorialized: "If the controversy ever comes to a division of the Union, the North will wait for no convention; the people of the free states will occupy first and negotiate afterwards with the advantage of possession on their side."[11]

Status Quo

The sixth and final outcome was maintenance of the political status quo. Like the other outcomes, this outcome had numerous interpretations. For many, the status quo was defined by its most immediate, short-term

---

[9] For detailed conceptual histories of the idea of Union prior to the Civil War, see Paul C. Nagel, *One Nation Indivisible: The Union in American Thought* (New York: Oxford University Press, 1964); John McCardell, *The Idea of a Southern Nation: Southern Nationalists and Southern Nationalism, 1830–1860* (New York: Norton, 1979); Clive S. Thomas, *American Union in Federalist Political Thought* (New York: Garland, 1991). For a briefer account of the idea of southern separatism, see Carpenter, *The South as a Conscious Minority* (1963), pp. 171–220.

[10] See Nichols, *Blueprints for Leviathan* (1963), p. 147.

[11] Bryant [editorial in *New York Evening Post*, January 20, 1860] in *Power for Sanity* (1994), p. 377.

characteristics. By the end of 1860, the political status quo had been disrupted in highly unusual ways. The election of Abraham Lincoln broke the Democrats' influence over the White House. Lincoln had won as had no prior presidential candidate, without a single southern state Electoral College vote. Despite this clear setback for the South, Lincoln received only 39.7 percent of the popular vote in a four-candidate race and as historian Michael F. Holt noted, "few people in the 1850s and 1860s anticipated that the Republicans would remain the permanent . . . anti-Democratic party in American politics."[12] The Democrats, not the Republicans, were positioned to control Congress in the immediate aftermath of the 1860 election and the Supreme Court was composed of the same individuals who had recently handed down the infamous *Dred Scott* decision. In the words of Stephen A. Douglas, the newly elected Republican President was effectively "tied hand and foot, powerless for good or evil."[13]

For many (and arguably most) of the individuals who became seriously engaged in the secession crisis in 1861, maintenance of the status quo had far more significant long-term consequences. For most southern statesmen, the long-term prospects associated with the status quo were especially worrisome. The abolitionist movement had been invigorated by the 1860 election and was no doubt encouraged to pursue its moral mission in future national and state elections. The South's traditional control of the Supreme Court was also threatened by the probable retirement of seven Justices on the Taney Court. At minimum, Lincoln's federal district court appointments promised a new kind of thinking about the normative dictates of the U.S. Constitution, the powers of the federal government, and the constitutional rights of slaveholders.[14]

More important, the anticipated decennial reapportionment of the U.S. House of Representatives in 1861 promised to transfer additional representation from southern to northern states.[15] In the Senate, the

---

[12] Michael F. Holt, *Political Parties and American Political Development* (Baton Rouge, LA: Louisiana State University Press, 1992), p. 333.

[13] See Roy F. Nichols and Eugene H. Berwanger, *The Stakes of Power* (New York: Hill and Wang, 1982), p. 92; Bruce Levine, *Half Slave and Half Free: The Roots of Civil War* (New York: Hill and Wang, 1992), p. 228.

[14] Dwight L. Dumond, *The Secessionist Movement, 1860–1861* (New York: The Macmillan Company, 1931), p. 18.

[15] The likely sectional consequences of the next House reapportionment was a subject of discussion in both the North and South. At the framing of the Confederate constitution, for example, most of the newspapers in Montgomery, Alabama, contained an

TABLE 9.1. *Distributional Frontiers of National Representation in 1860*

	House of Representatives[a]		Senate[b]		Electoral College[c]	
	1860	1863–1873	1860	1870	1860	1864
North	62.0%	63.5%	54.5%	58.3%	60.4%	61.8%
South	38.0%	36.5%	45.5%	41.7%	39.6%	38.2%

[a] Before the 1860 Census, northern states had 147 members in the House, southern states had 90 members. The House reapportionment was completed in July 1861: the North received 148 members, the South 85 members. Percentages do not include the 1862 Supplemental Apportionment Act (12 Stat. L. 353), which added 8 members to the House: 7 to northern states, and 1 to a southern border state.

[b] The distribution of representation in the Senate by 1870 requires more speculation than the apportionment of representatives in the House of Representatives. Calculation of the North's representation by 1870 is guided by the admission of three additional states before 1870 (Kansas, 1861; Nevada, 1864; Nebraska, 1867). Expectations for the admission of additional southern states were small in 1860, therefore the south's representation is assumed to remain stable.

[c] Calculations for the 1864 Electoral College representation account only for the admission of Kansas in January 1861 and the 1861 House reapportionment.

[handwritten marginal note: Kansas? / N. strong]

long-awaited admission of Kansas as a free state finally was completed in January 1861, further increasing the North's majority. These changes promised to reduce the South's Electoral College share before the next presidential election in 1864. Table 9.1 projects the South's relative strength as it likely appeared to those who surveyed the frontiers of national representation in 1860.

Although short-term changes in the distribution of national representation likely concerned only a small number of highly engaged individuals, the anticipation of longer-term changes prompted divergent

analysis of the sectional differences captured by the 1860 Census. In February 1861, the *Philadelphia Inquirer* editorialized that although the North and South were roughly equal in 1800, the southern states had fallen "eight votes behind the Free States in the Senate, and about sixty-two in the lower House, under the next apportionment, and consequently in a minority of seventy in the election of the President. This, so far as a political power in the Union depends upon mere representative force, puts them at our mercy, or our justice or magnanimity – a dependency that we would be as slow to accept as they are to rely upon. ... The North has been provoked and driven into sectionalism; the South is beaten, punished and humbled for its many transgressions." See Roy F. Nichols, *The Disruption of American Democracy* (New York: The Macmillan Co., 1948), pp. 460–461; Allan Nevins, *The Emergence of Lincoln* (New York: Scribner, 1950), II: 311; and "Adjustment, Compromise, Concession," *Philadelphia Inquirer*, February 23, 1861, in *Northern Editorials on Secession*, H. C. Perkins, ed. (New York: D. Appleton-Century, 1942), I: 284–285.

sectional expectations concerning future divisions of representation. Amidst numerous special causes, therefore, the distributional logic of the original Constitution's rule of apportionment was the common, general cause that made secession plausible to southern leaders and anathema among northern leaders. The fact that the original apportionment rule was elemental to the constitutional agreement in 1787, to the development of the American political order between 1790 and 1860, *and* to the wholesale constitutional collapse in 1861 exposes a latent contradiction embedded deep within the theory and practice of a republican constitution. Once the republican ideals of self-rule and majoritarianism became the traditional constitutional idioms by which the principal interests of the antebellum era and their political agents understood both their right to govern and the process of national governance, a breakdown in the constitutional consensus among these interests and agents became conceivable (if not, expected) when the latter process was anticipated as foreclosing the former right.[16]

---

[16] The public eruption of the contradiction between the constitutional traditions of majoritarianism and self-rule was, in 1860–1861, the surface phenomenon of a much deeper tension embedded within the original American synthesis of the discourse of republicanism with the American Revolution's nationalist (if not indeed imperialist) aspirations. For the former, despite the subsequent reworking in *The Federalist*, was and remained the genetic progeny of the Revolutionary era's oppositionalist discourse and the latter, despite unequivocal constitutional commitments to federalism, displayed inexorable tendencies toward expansion and consolidation. Whereas the latter aspirations for nation and empire building seemed relatively easy to satisfy through the trials and rewards of western expansion, the peculiar American form of republicanism continuously prompted the construction of political identities in relation to (or, more accurately, in opposition to) others. As long as this oppositional "other" was perceived to be external to the American constitutional order – for example, Great Britain, Spain, or the various indigenous nations – the expression of the idea of national consolidation within the familiar cadences of American republicanism did not seem particularly contradictory. However, when oppositional identities were imagined, constructed, and sustained almost exclusively from the substance of domestic antinomies – for example, North-South, Federalist-Republican, free-slave, native-immigrant, Protestant-Catholic – the ideas of nationalist consolidation and expansion were perceived by some to have especially disruptive, threatening, and likely exploitive consequences. The republican-nationalist synthesis nevertheless remained complete: for despite the persistent fears of victimization by a domineering metropolis, the desire for national expansion (albeit, in increasingly more selective forms) remained unsatiated. The integration of this oppositional form of republicanism into the political discourses of the southern states proved especially problematic. For the imagined racialist divisions that continuously and, in time, almost exclusively, were used to construct oppositional, hierarchical identities at the state level ultimately limited the possibilities and credibility of alternative identity formation at the national level. For deeper penetration of these core issues and of the republican-imperial synthesis, see Peter Onuf, "American Revolution and National Identity," Mellon Sawyer Seminar, Johns Hopkins University, 20 April 1998; and Peter Onuf,

By 1860, the self-styled intellectual leadership of the South had long been engaged in various (although often inconsistent) ways of recasting the republican tradition to avoid the adverse effects of this contradiction. Most prominently, the widely pronounced theory of "states rights" emphasized the primacy of the self-rule component within the republican tradition. Once an acceptable baseline of national representation was no longer anticipated by the South, renegotiation of the national rule of apportionment (broadly understood as the institutionalized division of collective decision-making authority) became a matter of both practical and theoretical imperative. For many, especially sectional ideologues like Calhoun, the need for and the theoretical justification of an alternative rule had been anticipated and conceived decades prior to 1860. For others, like the statesmen of the upper South, the projected benefits of a new apportionment rule were conceded but the risk and potential costs associated with this constitutional change tempered support for the act of secession until a negotiated resolution was foreclosed in the aftermath of Fort Sumter.

From its initial conceptualization, therefore, the common purpose and appeal of secession among upper and lower South statesmen did not arise from latent nationalist aspirations, but from the disappointment and anticipation of the past and future consequences of the apportionment rule adopted in 1787. As Virginian James Scott concluded in his 1860 treatise, *The Lost Principle*, so (no doubt) did many other southern statesmen: "The grand defect of the Constitution," according to Scott, "was to have rested the power upon a fluctuating basis like that of population. . . . The result of the arrangement," he added, "has been to swell the representative power of the commercial classes of the North, and to increase the preponderance over the South, by the wealth derived from the export and import trade of the South." In short, "the sages of Philadelphia had subjected the federal machine . . . to the control of that very despot, Numbers, against which the English constitution has so carefully guarded."[17] Scott concluded:

It is not going too far to say, that never was there a more splendid failure in government, never a more wretched conclusion of a grand and ostentatious

---

"Federalism, Republicanism, and the Origins of American Sectionalism," in *All Over the Map: Rethinking American Regions*, Edward L. Ayers et al., eds. (Baltimore: Johns Hopkins University Press, 1996), pp. 11–37.

[17] John Scott (pseud., "Barbarossa"), *The Lost Principle* (Richmond, VA: J. Woodhouse & Co., 1860), pp. 193, 217, 130. See also Edward A. Pollard, *The Lost Cause* (New York: E. B. Treat & Co, 1866), pp. 58–59.

experiment.... [I]t was the great delusion of the century that gave it birth – it has well nigh ruined the oldest and richest part of the Confederacy – it has pampered with ill-gotten riches the frozen hills and bleak valleys of New England – it has corrupted by the extravagant and lawless expenditures to which it has given birth, the morality of a portion, and will, unless amended or destroyed, gradually undermine that of the whole people – it has embittered into deadly hate the animosities between North and South . . . it has done all this, because of the vice which its makers introduced in the representation, which, like an error in the first concoction, must be followed by disease, convulsions and finally death itself.[18]

After 1820, northern leaders became increasingly optimistic about the long-term benefits they expected from the original Constitution's apportionment rule. As the national decision-making capacities of the northern states increased and began to coalesce as a viable coalition within Congress, so did the North's commitment to a more legalistic and more nationalistic conceptualization of the American Union.[19] Coupled with this conceptual change, northern statesmen had become increasingly indignant about the customary practice of capitulating to southern demands in the face of the North's clear numerical superiority over the South.[20] Northern antislavery advocates were not the only individuals who self-righteously envisioned a "northern tier of states, from one ocean to the other . . . pressing down thus more and more heavily on the confines of slavery . . . till finally it will be discovered that the laws of population are themselves abolitionists."[21] Northern statesmen not surprisingly regarded secessionist declarations as blatant denials of demographic realities and as brash attempts to renege on a constitutional agreement that had bound North and South alike for the past seventy years. As one northern newspaper editor argued in January 1861, the North's only "offence is that they are free. . . . Their crime is the census of 1860. Their increase in numbers, wealth, and power is a standing aggression" to the South.[22]

Given the incongruities between the raw northern-state dominance of the national government in 1860 and southern statesmen's persistent

---

[18] Scott, *The Lost Principle*, p. 217.

[19] See Kenneth M. Stampp, "The Concept of a Perpetual Union," *Journal of American History* (1975), LXV: 5–32. For a recent revisitation of the idea of union, see Rogan Kersch, *Dreams of a More Perfect Union* (Ithaca, NY: Cornell University Press, 2001).

[20] See Holt, *The Political Crisis of the 1850s* (1978).

[21] As quoted in Robert Wiebe, *The Opening of American Society* (New York: Knopf, 1984), p. 361. See also Hinton R. Helper, *The Impending Crisis of the South* (New-York: Burdick Brothers, 1857).

[22] "The Question of the Hour," *The Atlantic Monthly* (January 1861), 7: 117–120.

claims to retain their traditional right of self-rule, the majoritarian component of republican theory became the conceptual cudgel of choice for
many northern statesmen. In his First Inaugural Address, for example,
President Abraham Lincoln acknowledged that the core issue of the
secession crisis was: "[i]f by the mere force of numbers a majority should
deprive a minority of any clearly written constitutional right, it might
in a moral point of view justify revolution. But," he added, "such is not
our case." Without moral justification for revolution, the options for
resolving the crisis and for preserving the constitutional principle of
majority rule were clear to Lincoln:

> If the minority will not acquiesce, the majority must, or the Government must
> cease. There is no other alternative, for continuing the Government is acquies
> cence on one side or the other. If a minority in such case will secede rather than
> acquiesce, they make a precedent which in turn will divide and ruin them, for a
> minority of their own will secede from them whenever a majority refuses to be
> controlled by such minority.[23]

In addition to the clear divergence of sectional expectations concerning the long-term division of national decision-making capacities, expectations for national governmental authority also differed between the
two sections. Since 1787, the principal interests within both sections had
been successful in securing national-level commitments for many of their
particular interests. By 1860, both sections clearly expected the authority and capacities of the national government to expand. However, each
section wanted to extend national governmental authority toward
fundamentally different (although not mutually exclusive) purposes.

The principal interests within the northern tier of states generally
wanted their agents within the national government to secure new protective tariffs, more liberal federal land policies, and federal railroad subsidies. With a northern-state preponderance in Congress and the 1860
election of the pro-North and pro-growth Republican Abraham Lincoln,
fulfillment of these northern expectations was a conceivable, if not
probable, political possibility. The principal interests within the southern
tier of states were similarly activist: unlike their northern counterparts,
however, they wanted their national-level agents to secure credible
national commitment for territorial expansion into Central America and
the Caribbean, and for federal recognition and protection of slavery as

[23] Lincoln, "First Inaugural Address," in *A Compilation of the Messages and Papers
of the Presidents*, James D. Richardson, ed. (Washington, DC:, U.S. Congress, 1897),
6: 9.

a positive individual right.[24] Lincoln's election and the Republican Party's strength in Congress after the 1860 elections likely guaranteed that these southern expectations would remain unfulfilled for at least the immediate future.

The combination by late 1860 of southern expectations for smaller net benefits and higher negotiation costs within the existing Union suggests a plausible motive for the subsequent act of secession. Nevertheless, secession remains a puzzling overreaction to a single electoral loss. Not only was it conceivable that these unfulfilled expectations were only temporary short-term losses, it must also be conceded that the South (both as a section and as individual states) received a substantial and nearly certain stream of benefits under the existing Union. The suggested calculus of secession therefore would seem to entail forsaking a guaranteed and nontrivial stream of benefits under the status quo for an uncertain and costly attempt to secure an unpredictable stream of benefits under a hypothetical alternative constitutional order.

Southern secession thus awaits a more adequate answer. Consider the model of the expected utility streams of the South and North represented in Figure 9.1. For both sections, the *absolute* benefits accruing from their voluntary participation within the Union had increased over time according to most material measures and these streams were expected to continue their past paths into the future. The *relative* differences between the North and the South, however, were another matter: They had increased over time – especially when measured in terms of the apportionment of representation within Congress and the Electoral College – and these differences were expected to continue into the future as well. In the absence of any consideration of the risks and costs of change, therefore, a decision to secede from the Union becomes understandable when the aggregation of these relative differences was anticipated as ultimately destroying the decision-making parity that the section had originally secured.[25] Although the principal interests within the South had and likely would continue to benefit under the existing constitutional order,

---

[24] On the generally increasing nature of the demands of the South for national-level protection of their sectional interests, see William J. Cooper, *The South and the Politics of Slavery, 1828–1856* (Baton Rouge, LA: Louisiana State University Press, 1978).

[25] For a theoretical discussion of the conditions under which political actors focus on absolute and relative gains, see Robert Powell, "Absolute and Relative Gains in International Relations Theory," *American Political Science Review* (1991), 85: 1303–1320. For historical evidence of the motive of sectional parity, see Don E. Fehrenbacher, *Sectional Crisis and Southern Constitutionalism* (Baton Rouge, LA: Louisiana State University Press, 1995), pp. 1–76.

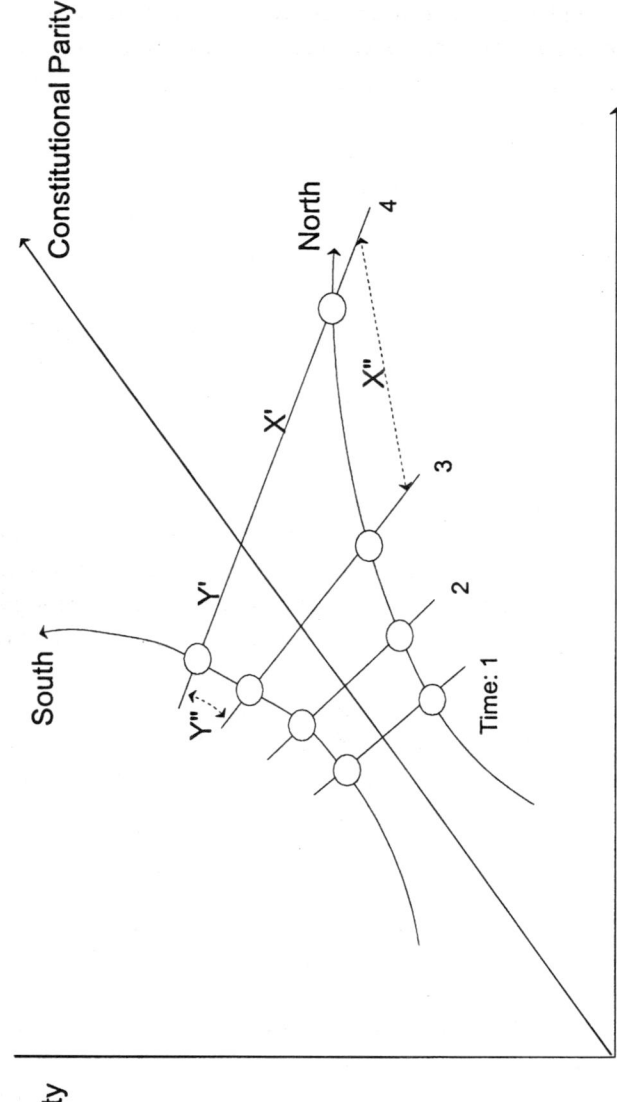

FIGURE 9.1. Absolute and Relative Utility Streams under Constitutional Contract

southern statesmen (especially those with heavy investments in or attachments to sectional political identities) were motivated to secede from the Union because they feared becoming politically irrelevant within the national government.

> *IMPT* [handwritten]

If the desire to rule was the general motive compelling secession, why did the North (despite its diverse interests) collectively resist the lower South's decision to secede and why were northern statesmen in this crisis seemingly unwilling to negotiate a peaceful resolution? Again, Figure 9.1 suggests a general logic for understanding the North's motives. Prior to the 1860 crisis, the North's willingness to negotiate with the South effectively allowed the former section to enjoy an uninterrupted stream of absolute and collectively produced benefits under the existing constitutional order. The secession of the states of the lower South was resisted by the North because it effectively diminished the North's expected stream of future constitutional benefits. But why not purchase the South's return with concessions? Figure 9.1 offers an answer in terms of the relative differences between the sections (expressed as the increase in the distance X' over time compared to Y' over time). Each time the North granted concessions under the shadow of southern demands or threats, the North conceded an increasingly greater potential gain. As a result, maintenance of the original constitutional parity between the sections became too costly for the North. And as the North grew conscious of its numerical supremacy, it no longer perceived an immediate basis for or longer-term benefit from acknowledging the South as an equal at the negotiation table.

> *Why N. unwilling to negotiate peace?,* [handwritten]

> *N gave S concessions ↓ became too costly* [handwritten]

PART II: A GAME-THEORETIC ANALYSIS
OF THE SECESSION CRISIS

Given that the configuration of political expectations by the end of 1860 made some form of constitutional change possible, what were the immediate conditions that transformed the long-term relationship between the northern and southern states into the American Civil War? Three game-theoretic models will aid this account's explanation of this final puzzle. Unlike many normal form game-theoretic models, each of these models contains a temporal dimension.

The first model, the decision tree in Figure 9.2, represents the process that ultimately yielded the Civil War as a sequence of decisions between two principal actors: the "North" and the "South." Both actors are motivated to act in response to their relative representational positions:

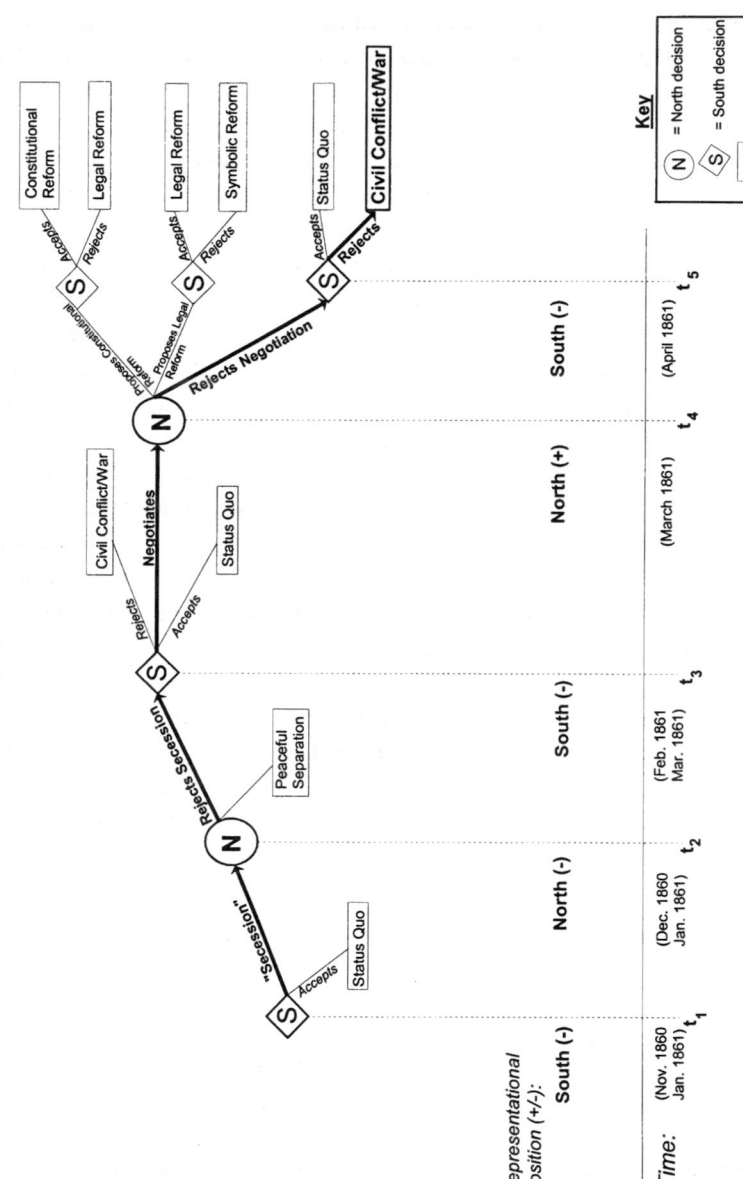

FIGURE 9.2. Decision-tree Model of Secession Crisis

a positive representational position prompts a response for the status quo; a negative representational position prompts a response for alternatives to the status quo.[26] On the far left of this model, the South is depicted in a negative representational position after the 1860 election. At t_1 (or between November 1860 and January 1861), the South rejects the status quo by declaring its intention to secede from the Union – note emboldened path. Between December 20, 1860, and February, 1, 1861, seven lower South states formally declared their intention to secede. The remaining upper South states did not issue similar declarations, although none formally renounced the possibility of secession. As signified after t_1, the South's decision to disrupt the status quo threatened to diminish the relative value of the North's representational superiority under the existing rule of apportionment. At t_2, the North responded by refusing to recognize the legitimacy of unilateral declarations for secession.

The North's de facto invalidation of the original secessionist declarations returned the South to its initial negative position – that is, under the Constitution's rule of apportionment – and forced the upper South states to reconsider the goals and likely consequences of secession. For these undecided states, three options emerged: (1) acceptance of the political status quo; (2) negotiation of a settlement to the crisis; or (3) rejection of the status quo and its likely effect of inducing some kind of civil conflict with the North, possibly even a civil war.[27] Faced with these options, the states of the upper South repeatedly refused to join the lower South in secession. They did not, however, disavow the secessionist states or their alleged right to secede. At t_3 (between February and March 1861), the South continued to support secession but implicitly signaled its willingness to negotiate an end to the crisis. Because it is plausible to assume that the North would have controlled the negotiation process, the North is represented as having a positive representational position at t_4 (or March 1861).

Why, then, civil war? The division of the states of the South into two distinct subgroups was a critical factor because it undermined the

---

[26] This account of events after the 1860 election parallels the historical accounts of Daniel W. Crofts, *Reluctant Confederates: Upper South Unionists in the Secession Crisis* (Chapel Hill: University of North Carolina Press, 1989); David M. Potter, *The Impending Crisis, 1848–1861* (New York: Harper & Row, 1976), pp. 485–554; William Barney, *The Road to Secession* (New York, Praeger, 1972), 161–209; and Potter, *Lincoln and His Party* (1942), pp. 156–375.

[27] Most historians agree that the introduction of force to the secession crisis was not understood at the time as necessarily inducing a protracted civil war. See Potter, *The Impending Crisis* (1976), pp. 223–224; and Barney, *The Road to Secession* (1972), p. 197.

[handwritten margin note: couldn't bargain for change]

[handwritten margin note: Also-N mulling]

section's capacity to bargain for constitutional changes (especially, changes in the rule of apportionment). Not surprisingly, few northern leaders were motivated to engage the South in negotiating an end to the secession crisis.[28] By April 1861, or at t_5 on the decision tree, southern leaders therefore faced the options of either accepting what they considered "the hated badge of a [minority] section" or testing the North's willingness to resolve this standoff with coercion.[29] Ultimately, the South elected to endure the latter trial with history.

As portrayed in this first model, the South's final decision was not only rational and irrepressible but the North's response and the subsequent initiation of the American Civil War seem inevitable. If, however, such gross violations of the civil peace require a more precise assignment of political accountability, this model clearly offers only a partial solution to the still puzzling civil war outcome. A second model supplements this account by providing a fuller elaboration of the indeterminacy and tragedy of the final decisions made by the North and South. To construct this model, consider the ordinal-level ranking of each section's preferences among six possible outcomes for resolving the secession crisis.[30] (See Table 9.2.)

---

[28] Before adjourning, the 36th Congress proposed a constitutional amendment prohibiting interference with slavery in the states where it then existed. Lincoln endorsed this amendment during his First Inaugural Address. The amendment was only a *symbolic* reform because it promised only to constitutionalize the political status quo in which the South was and could expect to remain a national representational minority.

　　Privately, President-elect Lincoln reluctantly endorsed one additional reform by which the territory of New Mexico would be admitted as a slave state. Again, the effect was primarily symbolic because the territory's population was minuscule. Moreover, few expected New Mexico to remain a slave state. Thus, the political or economic benefits of this concession were foreseeably small.

　　From the South's perspective, an example of an appealing legal reform with representational consequences was the westward extension of the 36°, 30' line. With this reform, the South would not receive immediate representational parity with the North, but it opened the possibility for admission or acquisition of additional states south of the line. Early in the crisis, according to historian William Barney, "Southern leaders indicated that this blank check for future expansion of slavery was the one plan that might possibly forestall secession." Barney, *The Road to Secession*, p. 192.

　　Examples of constitutional reforms discussed during the crisis include a "double" or "rotating" Executive, a concurrent sectional veto, and a broad reinterpretation of the constitutional right to own and acquire enslaved persons.

[29] Scott, *The Lost Principle* (1860), p. 127.

[30] This model, like each of the preceding models, is a means of representing the totality and complexity of a train of political decisions and their ultimate consequences in an historically accurate and logically consistent manner. These particular ordinal rankings were the result of the following method. First, the set of historically viable outcomes was identified. These possible outcomes were those perceived by the relevant political

TABLE 9.2. *North and South Outcome Preferences*

	Actor	
	North	South
Preference:		
Most	6. Status Quo	6. Constitutional Reform
	5. Symbolic Reform	5. Legal Reform
	4. Legal Reform	4. Peaceful Separation
	3. Civil Conflict/Civil War	3. Civil Conflict/Civil War
	2. Constitutional Reform	2. Symbolic Reform
Least	1. Peaceful Separation	1. Status Quo

[handwritten annotation: N–4 (+) – wanted cons. negot. 5 symbolic 4 legal]

For the North, four of the six outcomes had positive net values. Of these, the North's most preferred outcome was the constitutional status quo because the terms of the original Constitution promised both immediate and future benefits for the section. Its second and third outcome preferences were to end the secession crisis with either a symbolic or legal reform, for these solutions offered incentives for the South to abandon secession without necessarily or fundamentally altering the North's relative representational advantage. The remaining two outcomes had negative net values for the North. Of these, the North's least preferred outcome was the peaceful separation of the South because it not only undermined the North's constitutional authority to govern the nation, it squandered the section's superior capacities to coerce the South to capitulate.

actors engaged in the secession crisis between December 1860 and April 1861. Second, for each set of actors these outcomes were divided into categories reflective of their net values as they were contemporaneously perceived: the general values of "positive," "neutral/indeterminate," and "negative" are sufficient for locating each outcome along a positive-to-negative scale. Third, within each of these value categories, an ordinal ranking of the outcomes was completed. In many cases, this method of ranking will require interpretive judgments based on the available historical evidence and the relevant secondary literature – for example, the ordinal elevation of the North's preference for the "Status Quo" over the "Symbolic Reform" outcome is supported by both evidentiary and interpretive warrants. In other cases, these warrants will not be sufficient to produce a definitive ordinal ranking between two outcomes. Under these conditions, logical relational inferences can be drawn to support a ranking – for example, it can be inferred from the expected costs of even a limited military engagement with the North that the South preferred a "Peaceful Separation" outcome to the "Civil Conflict/Civil War" outcome, although there is ample support that both outcomes were generally perceived as having net positive values. Finally, to ensure the utility of this methodology, the ordinal rankings of outcome preferences were completed prior to their application within the subsequent game-theoretic matrices.

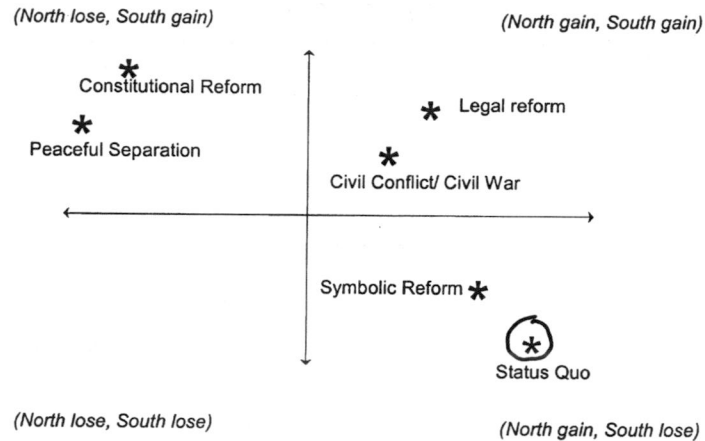

FIGURE 9.3. Expected Relative Outcome Values for North and South

(handwritten marginalia: "S / b_ans reform / Gllegal / Least → Status quo")

(handwritten above paragraph: "lohty of outcome preferences")

The order of the South's outcome preferences was conspicuously different. The South's most preferred outcome was to remain within the Union and to end the secession crisis with a constitutional reform that offered more permanent representational guarantees for the section's principal interests. A legal reform with representational benefits was the South's second best outcome because – as northern leaders feared – it also invited attempts to gain additional representational concessions in the future.[31] The status quo was the least preferred outcome because it promised a long-term decline in the South's national representation.

Figure 9.3 plots these sectional outcome preferences and thereby offers a partial glimpse of the difficulties and possibilities of achieving a consensus between the North and the South. Whereas the outcomes located in the northwest and southeast quadrants suggest outcomes that were not likely bases for a negotiated settlement, the two outcomes in the northeast quadrant (that is, "North gain, South gain") were perceived by both actors as mutually beneficial. It must be noted, however, that the North's most preferred outcome was the "Status Quo" which appeared obtainable either through the consent or coercion of the South, or upon the collapse of the secessionist movement.

---

[31] See, for example, "Abraham Lincoln to Rep. James T. Hale" (January 11, 1861), John G. Nicolay and John Hay, eds., *Works of Abraham Lincoln* (New York: F. D. Tandy, 1905), 6: 93; as quoted in Potter, *Lincoln and His Party* (1942), pp. 160, n.11; 218–224.

TABLE 9.3. *Secession Decision Matrix*

SOUTH: NORTH:	No Action	"Secession" to gain:		
		Legal Reform	Constitutional Reform	Separation
Reject	6, 1 [Status Quo]	6, 1 [Status Quo]	6, 1 [Status Quo]	3, 3 [Civil Conflict/War]
Negotiate	6, 1 [Status Quo]	5, 2 [Symbolic Reform]	4, 5 [Legal Reform]	2, 6 [Constitutional Reform]
Affirm	6, 1 [Status Quo]	4, 5 [Legal Reform]	2, 6 [Constitutional Reform]	1, 4 [Peaceful Separation]

Note: {X, Y} = {North, South}; 6 = Most Preferred Outcome; 1 = Least Preferred Outcome.

In addition to the configuration of outcome preferences, the decision matrix model presented in Table 9.3 presents the range of decision-making strategies available to each section during this crisis. The South's options were limited to "No Action" (column 1) or "Secession" (columns 2, 3, 4). Because the South was not capable of unilaterally effecting a final outcome to the crisis except by initiating some form of civil conflict, the option of "Secession" is depicted as a means to a range of intended outcomes.[32] Secession is portrayed as a means for attaining one of three intended outcomes: legal reform, constitutional reform, or separation. The range of the North's responses are defined as: "Reject," "Negotiate," or "Affirm" (rows 1, 2, 3).

Table 9.3 also identifies the most likely outcomes derived from the intersection of southern and northern choices. When an outcome is not immediately suggested and the historical record provides inconclusive guidance, the outcome selected reflects the North's superior negotiation and enforcement powers. If, for example, the South is perceived as using the threat of "Secession" to achieve only a legal reform (column 2) and the North "rejects" this outcome (row 1), then the probable outcome is the "Status Quo" because the South has neither the will nor the means to effect

[32] There is strong historical support for this treatment. See, for example, the statement of Alexander H. Stephens in Potter, *Lincoln and his Party* (1942), p. 230.

TABLE 9.4. *The Paradox of Civil War*

	SOUTH	
NORTH	"Secession" to gain: Constitutional Reform	"Secession" to gain: Separation
Reject	4, 1 [Status Quo]	2, 2 [Civil Conflict/War]
Negotiate	3, 3 [Legal Reform]	1, 4 [Constitutional Reform]

Notes: {X, Y} = {North, South}; 4 = Most Preferred Outcome; 1 = Least Preferred Outcome.

another outcome. If the South is perceived as committed to using "Secession" to achieve separation (column 4) and the North decides to "negotiate" (row 2) to preserve the Union, then the final outcome will likely fall short of the South's intended goal because of the North's superior resources to secure negotiations with a majority of the southern states.

By narrowing the options of the North and the South to those most reflective of the final stages of the secession crisis, the decision matrix can be streamlined and made even more historically realistic. The South's decision to take "No Action" (column 1) and the North's decision to "Affirm" (row 3) can be eliminated. Because the North's superior negotiation and enforcement powers effectively deny the South representational benefits if it is perceived as using "secession" only as a threat for "legal reform," this option (column 2) can also be eliminated.

As Table 9.4 illustrates, the South's final options were restricted to "Constitutional Reform" or "Separation," and the North's options were "Reject" or "Negotiate." After an ordinal re-ordering of the preferences of the North and South, the tragedy of the Civil War becomes readily apparent. The logical resolution of the crisis given this set of options and outcome preferences is civil conflict/civil war (row 1, column 2) because the North's highest outcome preferences (its "dominant strategy") are obtainable only if it continues to "reject" (row 1), and the South's highest preferences are obtainable only as long as it is perceived as committed to "separation" (column 2). The tragedy of the civil war outcome is that the North and South could both have attained more preferred outcomes if they had only agreed to compromise to effect a legal reform of the political status quo (row 2, column 1).

Political crises are not so easily or so favorably resolved as hindsight and the logic of a rational choice analysis might imply. Among other impediments, political actors regularly underestimate the intentions or resolve of those with whom they are negotiating. Decision makers can also become confused by their options or miscalculate the costs of coalition building, and all are invariably embedded within the horizons of their imaginations. Despite these impediments to achieving a consensus for optimal outcomes, deliberative politics generally tends to slow down the decision-making process to ensure that most political conflicts are not resolved with outcomes perceived as generally inferior. The process of deliberation accomplishes this by encouraging repeated consideration of the full set of outcome possibilities, including maintenance of the status quo. Over time, those outcomes mutually less preferred by the negotiating parties are eliminated and the remaining outcome possibilities continue to cycle in debate until a consensus is reached for implementing or combining the best of the remaining solutions. If this is the norm of deliberative politics, why were the North and the South not able to agree to some type of legal reform in order to avoid the mutually less preferred outcome of civil war?

Several impediments clearly made resolution of the 1860–1861 secession crisis more difficult than prior sectional crises. In prior crises, the options and outcomes were repeatedly debated and considered within Congress and in the state legislatures. Therefore, the withdrawal of many southern state members from Congress (and from the political community within the District of Columbia) restricted the effectiveness of the institutional procedures and social norms that arguably were best suited for resolving this particular political conflict. Even without the full benefit of Congress and of Washington's salon coterie, proposals and negotiations to end the crisis continued through other public and private channels.[33] Fragmentation of the deliberative process would not necessarily hasten decisions for civil war, especially when the benefits of avoiding civil war were unimpeachable to all but a handful on both sides. The paradox of the Civil War consequently remains: If both sections perceived they would receive better outcomes through compromise, how was it that the secession crisis ended in civil war when prior sectional crises did not?

A final model of the secession crisis addresses this vexing question by framing the sectional conflict in terms of its three most salient

---

[33] See Potter, *The Impending Crisis* (1976), pp. 551–565.

dimensions. On the first and most familiar dimension, the North and the
South are divided according to their numerical representation under the
original Constitution's rule of apportionment. Faced with a seemingly
permanent minority status on this dimension, southern leaders used their
threats and declarations of secession to open a second dimension within
which they could engage the North more equally. On this second
dimension, northern and southern statesmen divided more evenly
according to their commitments to the constitutional ideals of "Union"
or "Separation." The states of the lower South clearly declared their
preference for Separation, whereas the North declared its preference for
Union. The states of the upper South were undecided, declaring for neither
Union nor Separation. As a consequence of this indecision, there was no
immediate consensus for resolving the crisis on this second dimension.

As support for the ideal of Separation weakened the longer the upper
South states vacillated, the most zealous advocates of secession increasingly appealed to a third and more highly divisive dimension. On this
third dimension, the North and South divided according to their distinct
historical and ideological experiences. For northern leaders, the experiences of sectional identity were diffuse, or (where especially intense) isolated around subsectional moral, economic, or social commitments and
practices. For southern leaders, however, the invocation of this dimension was a highly charged and effective emotional appeal for southern
unity based on a common set of cultural experiences and a widespread
fear of northern domination.

Given these three dimensions or discourses of the secession crisis,
consider the sectional alignments illustrated in Figure 9.4. For each
dimension, the immediate preferences of the North, upper South, and
lower South are arrayed on a horizontal axis. The temporal diffusion of
the preferences of each section are represented vertically within a
two-dimensional area bounded by the expected range of intrasectional
preferences. In terms of the previously described decision tree model,
immediate preferences of each section correlate approximately to the
first three time periods in Figure 9.2 – or between December 1860 and
March 1861). Immediate preferences are assumed to be highly compact.
Posterior preferences reflect the expected diffusion and differentiation of
intrasectional opinion after the secession crisis deadlocked in March
1861. As far as reasonable speculation from the available historical
evidence allows, the breadth and direction of this differentiation are
illustrated as extending into the future (that is, from t_1 to t_n). It follows,
therefore, that – barring any intervening action – movement beyond the

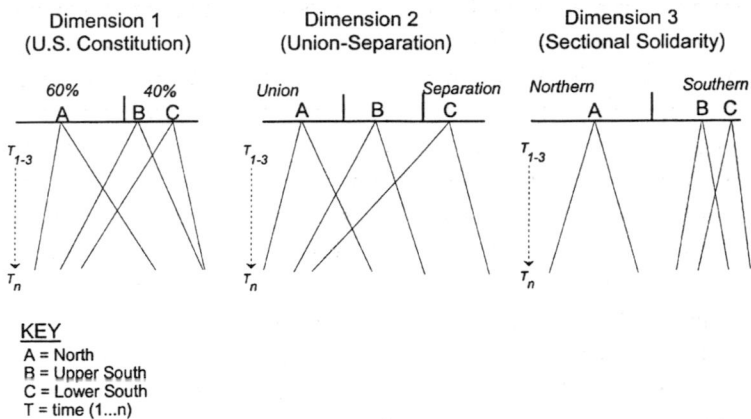

KEY
A = North
B = Upper South
C = Lower South
T = time (1...n)

FIGURE 9.4. The Diffusion of Interests over Dimensions and Time

sectional stalemate on Dimension^2 was probable only where there was a consensus for action – that is, where the preference ranges of at least two of the three sections intersected.

As illustrated on the horizontal axis of Dimension^1, the North (denoted as "A") is a representational majority; the upper South and lower South (respectively denoted as "B" and "C") are a minority. Given the customary practice of majority rule, the South's capacity to protect its interests during intersectional conflicts of interests consequently depends on either the North's magnanimity or the South's success in preventing northern statesmen from enacting their immediate sectional preferences. For decades, the South had been aided by the mitigating effects provided by the constitutional traditions of federalism, separation of powers, rights, and constitutional revision as well as by the mediation provided by credible trans-sectional political parties.[34]

On Dimension^2 (the Union-Separation discourse) neither section possessed the capacity to act without a majority among the three principal sectional actors. The temporal diffusion of preferences of each of the three sections on Dimension^2 was important because they forecast short- and long-term possibilities for resolving the secession crisis. As illustrated, the North ("A") and the lower South ("C") do not share

---

[34] See Barry R. Weingast, "American Democratic Stability and the Civil War: Institutions, Commitment, and Political Behavior," in Bates, Greif, Levi, Rosenthal, and Weingast, eds. *Analytic Narratives* (Princeton, NJ: Princeton University Press, 1998).

immediate preferences – although the range of longer-term preferences of the lower South extends to include support for the Union. The upper South ("B") has no immediate preference for either Union or Separation, yet its long-term range of preferences exhibits a strong tendency for Union.[35]

On Dimension[3] (the northern-southern discourse), the three sectional actors divide more clearly. The immediate and longer-term preferences of the North ("A") center around the northern pole. The immediate and longer-term preferences of the upper South ("B") and the lower South ("C") are anchored decisively around the southern pole.[36]

Given the North's representational majority on Dimension[1] and the unlikelihood of an immediate resolution of the conflict on Dimension[2], a small but committed group of southern separatists repeatedly attempted to force a final resolution of the sectional conflict on Dimension[3]. Northern leaders clearly adopted a different strategy, which President Lincoln publicly articulated in his First Inaugural Address in March 1861. In unequivocal terms, Lincoln promised he would not use coercive force to resolve the conflict *unless* "violence and bloodshed" were "forced upon the national authority."[37] In striking contrast to the rhetoric of secessionist leaders, Lincoln repeatedly defended the Constitution's system of majority rule (in other words: Dimension[1]), described "the Union of these States" as "perpetual" and secession as "the essence of anarchy" and "despotism" (Dimension[2]), and dismissed the salience of sectional distinctions (Dimension[3]). Lincoln further appealed to the South:

We are not enemies, but friends. We must not be enemies. Though passion may have strained it must not break our bonds of affection. The mystic chords of memory, stretching from every battlefield and patriot grave to every living heart and hearthstone all over this broad land, will yet swell the chorus of the Union, when again touched, as surely they will be, by the better angels of our nature.[38]

---

[35] For support of the proposition that the longer-term preferences of the upper and lower South included a return to the Union, see David M. Potter's description of the inherent weaknesses of secession sentiments in *Lincoln and his Party* (1942), pp. 210–218; 230–232.

[36] Aside from the historical fact that the American Civil War was in fact a sectionally based conflict, contemporaneous evidence before the war and the scholarly literature since confirm and clarify the reality of this third dimension. For two recent works, see Don E. Fehrenbacher's *The Slaveholding Republic* (New York: Oxford University Press, 2001) and *Sectional Crisis and Southern Constitutionalism* (Baton Rouge, LA: Louisiana State University Press, 1995).

[37] Lincoln, "First Inaugural Address," 6: 7, 11.

[38] Lincoln, "First Inaugural Address," 6: 11–12.

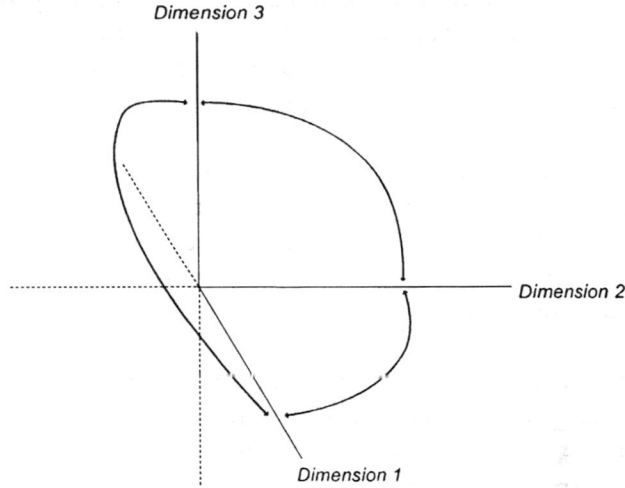

Dimension 1: U.S. Constitution
Dimension 2: Union/Separation
Dimension 3: Northern/Separation

FIGURE 9.5. A Dimensional Representation of the Secession Crisis

Lincoln's rhetoric

Neither Lincoln nor the most radical secessionists were particularly successful in determining the rhetorical dimension on which the secession crisis would be resolved. Immediately after Lincoln's Inaugural Address, no additional state seceded nor did a single upper South state fully renounce the renegade secessionist states. The simultaneous advocacy of these different rhetorical strategies was not without effect, however. As illustrated in the three-dimensional space in Figure 9.5, these appeals effectively induced a cycling amongst the various terms on which to settle the secession crisis.

Although this cycling of discourses could be expected to induce a highly unstable political environment, the persistence and predictability of the various rhetorical appeals produced a type of stability that clearly benefited the North's commitment to resolve the sectional conflict on Dimension[1]. The longer the secession crisis remained unresolved, the more the North could anticipate the states of the upper South and several of the lower South voluntarily returning to the Union rather than enduring the stalemate on Dimension[2] or the uncertain consequences of forcing a resolution of the conflict on Dimension[3].

Given the special dynamics of this constitutional stalemate, congressional Republicans not surprisingly did not become actively engaged in resolving the secession crisis before Lincoln's inauguration. As early as January 10, 1861, southern leaders like Mississippi Senator Jefferson Davis told the Republicans that "we have come to the conclusion that you mean to do nothing."[39] Lincoln also perceived benefits from a slower, more deliberate process of reconciliation.[40] In his First Inaugural Address, Lincoln advocated assembling a constitutional convention at an indefinite future date, appealing directly to his fellow "[c]ountrymen, one and all" to "think calmly and *well* upon this whole subject. Nothing valuable," he insisted, "can be lost by taking time." Lincoln additionally implored southern leaders that even if their cause was "the right side of the dispute, there still is no single good reason for precipitate action."[41]

Lincoln's admonition was not only prophetic of how the Confederate attack on Fort Sumter in April 1861 would precipitate a constitutional cascade into civil war, it also revealed his acute understanding of how easily a single act of violence could irrevocably alter the anticipated course of the sectional stalemate. For the introduction of coercive force by the North – the option Lincoln specifically renounced – likely would unify the upper South and lower South in defense against a common aggressor, thereby strengthening the South's capacity to secure secession or representational concessions from the North, especially since it was commonly believed that after a few skirmishes the North would offer concessions rather than accept the costs of a protracted civil war.[42] A similar unilateral action by the secessionist states likely would unify the northern states. For if the North did not collectively respond in kind, the authority of the Union would be diminished and the uncommitted states of the upper South could expect greatly reduced costs from issuing

---

[39] Jefferson Davis, "Remarks on the Special Messages on Affairs in South Carolina," in Jon Wakelyn, ed., *Southern Pamphlets on Secession* (Chapel Hill: University of North Carolina Press, 1996), p. 133.

[40] In Pittsburgh, Lincoln declared: "there is no crisis, such a one as may be gotten up at any time by designing politicians." "If the great American people will only keep their temper, on both sides of the line, the troubles will come to an end . . . just as other clouds have cleared away in due time, so will this." Quoted in Gabor Borritt, "Abraham Lincoln and the Question of Individual Responsibility," in *Why the Civil War Came* (New York: Oxford University Press, 1996), p. 23.

[41] Lincoln, "First Inaugural Address," 6: 11.

[42] See Barney, *The Road to Secession* (1937), p. 197; Potter, *Lincoln and His Party* ([1942], 1970), pp. 212–213; and Crofts, *Reluctant Confederates* (1989).

their own secessionist declarations – again strengthening the South's collective bargaining position against the North.[43]

The North and the South thus failed to avoid the tragedy of civil war because the Confederate Army's attack on Fort Sumter and Lincoln's subsequent call for 75,000 federal troops effectively framed the sectional conflict in terms of the one discourse within which the North and South were imagined to share no immediate or long-term preferences, the discourse that crudely but effectively divided the nation and its residents into two sectionally distinct identities.[44]

PART III: RECONSTRUCTION AND A NEW NATIONAL RULE OF APPORTIONMENT

Reconstitution of the Union after the four-year civil war that followed the Fort Sumter incident was complicated by the immense human toll of the war and the ambivalence many northern leaders had concerning the South's political restoration. Northern anxieties were heightened by disheartening accounts of continued violence against the formerly enslaved. In many southern states, moreover, former secessionists were elected or appointed to positions of political authority, and several state legislatures audaciously enacted the so called "black codes" which effectively denied full civil rights to the newly freed.[45]

[43] For a contemporary argument see "What are We Fighting For," *The Knickerbocker* (New York), July 1861, LVIII(1): 66–67: "Suppose we had yielded at first to the wishes of the seven seceded States. . . . Congress meets again. Virginia, and North Carolina, and Tennessee are represented there, with other States who sympathized with the seceders. . . . They claim to have their way, demand further concessions, and threaten . . . to join the 'Southern Confederacy'. . . . What a humiliating spectacle. . . . The right to secede granted, there would be nothing left of us."

[44] For an account of the upper South's reaction to Lincoln's call for federal troops, see Crofts, *Reluctant Rebels* (1989); J. G. Barrett, *The Civil War in North Carolina* (Chapel Hill: University of North Carolina Press, 1963); Joseph C. Sitterson, *The Secessionist Movement in North Carolina* (Chapel Hill: The University of North Carolina Press, 1939). For a theoretical discussion of decision making as a function of shifts in dimensional salience rather than preference changes, see Bryan D. Jones, "A Change of Mind or a Change of Focus? A Theory of Choice Reversals in Politics," *Journal of Public Administration Research and Theory* (1994), 2: 141–177.

[45] Among numerous works on the Reconstruction era, see Earl M. Maltz, *Civil Rights, The Constitution, and Congress, 1863–1869* (Lawrence, KS: University Press of Kansas, 1990); Eric Foner, *Reconstruction: America's Unfinished Revolution, 1863–1877* (New York: Perennial Library, 1988); Michael Les Benedict, *A Compromise of Principle* (New York: Norton, 1974); W. R. Brock, *An American Crisis: Congress and Reconstruction, 1865–1867* (New York: Harper & Row, 1963); Joseph B. James, *The Framing of the Fourteenth Amendment* (Urbana, IL: University of Illinois Press, 1956).

Republican Party members also anticipated that once the southern states were readmitted into Congress, their national representatives would form an alliance with northern Democrats. This coalition, many feared, "would be sufficient to overrule the friends of progress here, and this nation would be in the hands of secessionists at the very next congressional election and at the very next presidential election." Ratification of the Thirteenth Amendment in 1865 only compounded the threat. The constitutional delegitimization of human slavery nullified the original Constitution's three-fifths apportionment formula and thereby guaranteed southern states between ten to fifteen additional members in the House and Electoral College. According to calculations published in the *Chicago Tribune*, this southern bloc required only twenty-nine northern votes to control the House of Representatives. Pennsylvania Representative Thaddeus Stevens spoke for most Republican Party members when he admitted he had no desire "to grant [the South] this privilege at least for some years."[46]

In addition to delaying the South's restoration, Republican leaders in early 1865 rallied around the idea of a constitutional amendment guaranteeing black suffrage. By extending this right, Thaddeus Stevens later explained, Republicans hoped that a coalition between freedmen and southern Unionists would emerge "to divide the [South's] representation, and thus continue the Republican ascendancy" within the national government.[47]

By mid-1865, however, several developments dampened Republican enthusiasm for the establishment of black suffrage. Lincoln's successor President Andrew Johnson, for one, signaled he did not support the reform. Without Executive support, congressional Republicans rightfully feared their advocacy of this reform might either split their party or, worse yet, give northern Democrats a potent campaign issue for the upcoming 1866 elections. Once several northern states rejected suffrage extension within their states Republican leaders pragmatically refocused their energies toward devising a new rule for apportioning representation in the U.S. House.[48] As one Republican openly confessed, given

---

[46] *Congressional Globe*, 39th Cong., 1st sess. (Jan. 24, 1866), p. 404; James, *The Framing of the Fourteenth Amendment* (1956), pp. 22–23; George P. Smith, "Republican Reconstruction and Section Two of the Fourteenth Amendment," *WPQ* (1970), 13: 830–834; *Congressional Globe*, 39th Cong., 1st sess. (Jan. 31, 1866), p. 536.

[47] See Eric Foner, *Reconstruction* (1988), p. 178; James, *The Framing of the Fourteenth Amendment* (1956), pp. 21–23; *Congressional Globe*, 39th Cong., 1st sess. (Dec. 18, 1865), p. 74.

[48] James, *The Framing of the Fourteenth Amendment* (1956), pp. 15, 120, 16–17; Benedict, *A Compromise of Principle* (1974), pp. 113–116; and Eric Foner, *Reconstruction* (1988), pp. 222–224.

"existing prejudices and existing institutions," it was hoped that a new apportionment rule would effect "indirectly what we may not have the power to accomplish directly."[49]

When the Thirty-ninth Congress began its deliberations on the terms of a new apportionment rule in January 1866, members concentrated their attention on two basic proposals. The first called for a House apportionment based on legal voters; the second called for an apportionment according to population with a reduction if a state prohibited the right to vote based on race or color. Support for these proposals divided congressional Republicans along roughly geographical lines. Northwest Republicans supported the legal voter basis; they argued that these terms offered the surest way to guarantee either black suffrage or a reduction in the South's national representation. New England Republicans supported the population basis because, they contended, the voter basis would "cheapen suffrage everywhere" by inducing "an unseemly scramble . . . to increase by every means the number of voters."[50]

The different expectations that emerged as these political actors considered their decision-making capacities under both terms of apportionment threatened the larger reconstruction process. Midwesterners claimed their intent was only to increase the number of black voters in the South and they quickly noted that New England opposition to a voter basis grew out of the fact that it would transfer representation from the older northeastern states to the newer and faster-growing northwestern states. New Englanders observed that their region under a male voter basis would be disadvantaged because they possessed a higher ratio of women to men than the other northern states. And as one Senator bluntly stated:

We, of the old States, are not of opinion that the new States, made up as they are in the beginning, are any better able to conduct the affairs of Government than we are ourselves. We are willing to concede to them equality, not superiority. It would, therefore, as I have said, and as has been argued . . . produce an inequality and a very considerable and striking one, so far as some of the States are concerned.[51]

[49] *Congressional Globe*, 39th Cong., 1st sess. (Feb. 7, 1866), p. 705.
No less than 54 constitutional amendments on the House apportionment method were proposed between 1864 and 1868. See Herman V. Ames, *The Proposed Amendments to the Constitution*, Annual Report of the American Historical Association (1897), II: 367–384.

[50] *Congressional Globe*, 39th Cong., 1st sess. (Dec. 5, 1865), pp. 9, 10; (Jan. 8, 1866), pp. 141–42.

[51] *Congressional Globe*, 39th Congress, 1st sess. (Feb. 7, 1866), p. 705.

A special fifteen-member Joint Committee on Reconstruction considered both apportionment rule proposals, but its New England members
ensured that the committee would recommend population as the
apportionment basis. After several minor changes in the terms of the
Committee's constitutional amendment proposal, the House adopted
the amendment on January 31, 1866. This amendment proposal did
not receive the required two-thirds majority in the Senate. Northern
Democrats rejected it as a blatantly partisan plan designed to punish only
the South. Interestingly, five radical Republicans also opposed the House-
approved amendment, but they did so because it provided states with
constitutional authority to discriminate based on race or color. Massachusetts Senator Charles Sumner condemned the House amendment as
"the meanest & wickedest proposition ever brought into Congress," and
he privately predicted "People will sometime or other thank me for
having resisted it. Many will think it the best thing of my life."[52]

In April 1866, the Joint Committee on Reconstruction proposed a new
constitutional amendment. Section 2 of this five-section amendment
contained the terms of a new rule of apportionment. Although resembling
the apportionment amendment previously rejected by the Senate, the
Joint Committee proposal included several notable changes. Section 2
allowed the disenfranchisement of former rebels and noncitizens without
any reduction in a state's congressional representation. It also explicitly
recognized suffrage rights for "male citizens not less than twenty-one
years of age" – much to the consternation of the women's suffrage lobby.
Perhaps most significantly, the new standard for reduction of a state's
House representation was to be *proportional* to the "number of male
citizens." The earlier amendment had required that whenever suffrage
rights were denied or abridged, "*all persons* of such race or color" were
excluded from a state's apportionment population.[53]

[52] Benjamin B. Kendrick, ed., *The Journal of the Joint Committee of Fifteen on Reconstruction* (New York: Columbia University Press, 1914); and James, *The Framing of the
Fourteenth Amendment*, pp. 55–66; *Congressional Globe*, 39th Cong., 1st sess. (Jan.
31, 1866), p. 538; *Congressional Globe*, 39th Cong., 1st sess. (March 9, 1866), p. 1289;
"Charles Sumner to Gerrit Smith, February 12, 1866," *The Selected Letters of Charles
Sumner*, Beverly Wilson Palmer, ed. (Boston: Northeastern University Press, 1990) 2:
357; "Charles Sumner to Horatio Woodman, March 18, 1866," *Selected Letters*, 2:
357–358; "Charles Sumner to the Duchess of Argyll, April 3, 1866," *Selected Letters*,
2: 359.
[53] See *Congressional Globe*, 39th Cong., 1st sess. (April 30, 1866), p. 2286; Horace Flack,
The Adoption of the Fourteenth Amendment [Gloucester, MA: P. Smith, 1965 [1908]),
pp. 115–116.

After several minor revisions, Congress approved the Joint Committee's amendment in June 1866.[54] As amended, the final version of Section 2 of the Fourteenth Amendment provides:

Representatives shall be apportioned among the several States according to their respective numbers, counting the whole number of persons in each State, excluding Indians not taxed. But when the right to vote at any election for the choice of electors for President and Vice President of the United States, Representatives in Congress, the Executive and Judicial officers of a State, or the members of the Legislatures thereof, is denied to any of the male inhabitants of such States, being twenty-one years of age, and citizens of the United States, or in any way abridged, except for participation in rebellion, or other crime, the basis of representation therein shall be reduced in the proportion which the number of such male citizens shall bear to the whole number of male citizens twenty-one years of age in such State."[55]

Congress submitted this amendment to the states for ratification on June 16, 1866. Every southern state, except Tennessee, initially rejected the amendment. By 1868, all but four of the secessionist states had ratified the amendment and been readmitted into Congress. Many Republicans were dissatisfied with the Fourteenth Amendment, however, because it did not guarantee suffrage rights for African-American males. Pennsylvania Representative Thaddeus Stevens privately called the amendment a "shilly-shally bungling thing" and Boston abolitionist Wendell Phillips dismissed it altogether as a "fatal and total surrender."[56]

To compound this disappointment among Republicans, during the 1868 elections former secessionists demonstrated their willingness to use violence and intimidation to regain political control in the southern states. In Tennessee, for example, Ku Klux Klan terrorism dramatically reduced Republican votes over those of the previous year. In Louisiana, according to historian Michael Les Benedict, the election "was marked by widespread violence, including several outright massacres of black men." Most outrageously, in Georgia, former rebels elected to the state legislatures succeeded in expelling its African-American members with

---

[54] Specifically, the term "elective franchise" was replaced with the more positive-sounding term "right to vote." The reduction mechanism was made to include denial or abridgment of voting in *state elections* as well as federal elections. The reduction mechanism was also amended by replacing the term "citizens" with "inhabitants." James, *The Framing of the Fourteenth Amendment*, p. 148.

[55] *Congressional Globe*, 39th Cong., 1st sess. (June 8, 1866), p. 3042 (Senate); 39th Congress, 1st sess. (June 13, 1866), p. 3149 (House).

[56] As quoted in Stampp, *The Era of Reconstruction* (1965), pp. 141–142.

the implausible argument that Georgia's new constitution did not explicitly guarantee this privilege.[57]

When Congress reconvened after the 1868 elections, both the House and Senate agreed to a constitutional amendment prohibiting the states from restricting voting and officeholding rights on account of race, color, nativity, property, creed, or previous condition of servitude.[58] However, in the conference committee convened to reconcile minor differences in the two versions of the proposed amendment, the officeholding protection and several other restrictions were deleted from the final language of the amendment. In its final form, Section 1 of the proposed Fifteenth Amendment guaranteed: "The right of citizens of the United States to vote shall not be denied or abridged by the United States or by any State on account of race, color, or previous condition of servitude." By 1870, this amendment was ratified and effectively ended the formal reconstitution of the American Union.

CONCLUSION

This chapter examined a third constitutional change in the national rule of and its relationship to the larger constitutional changes signified by the American Civil War and the Union's subsequent reconstruction. In particular, this rule change resulted in the abandonment of the U.S. Constitution's double rule of apportionment and in the formalization of a new apportionment rule in the Thirteenth, Fourteenth, and Fifteenth Amendments to the U.S. Constitution. As in the two previously studied changes, the process effecting changes in the larger constitutional order followed a two-part sequential process. The first part of the process entailed a breakdown in the consensus for the existing rule of apportionment followed by a breakdown in the consensus for the larger constitutional order. This breakdown was initiated when eleven southern states voluntarily seceded from the Union. The second part of the process followed in a similar order: The formation of a consensus for a new rule of apportionment preceded the formation of constitutional consensus for

---

[57] Benedict, *A Compromise of Principle*, p. 329.

[58] *Congressional Globe*, 40th Cong., 3rd sess. (Feb. 9, 1869), p. 1040, (Senate approval); (Feb. 20, 1869), p. 1428 (House approval). The single substantive difference between the two amendments was that the Senate version prohibited discrimination based on education, whereas the House version did not.

a new constitutional order. Whereas the first part of this process was initiated through the consensual actions of the eleven southern states, the latter was effected only after a four-year civil war and the national government's coercive occupation of the southern half of the United States.

The act of voluntary secession amidst common interests, limited government, and economic plenty, and the willful act of coercion amidst constitutional traditions of consent and the rule of law have long endured as two of the most vexing puzzles of American political development. This account explains the former as motivated primarily by the fears of southern statesmen that the existing apportionment rule effectively made their sectional preferences and identity – in which so much had been invested over the years – politically irrelevant. A double irony thus becomes apparent. The apportionment rule that prompted these fears was the same rule that made the constitutional order possible in 1787. Moreover, this same rule established both a representative form of national government and the means by which various political representatives became disastrously unrepresentative of the discrete or common interests of their constituents and the nation.

The North's ultimate refusal to allay southern fears can also be accounted for by the Constitution's rule of apportionment. As this rule steadily increased the decision-making capacities of the northern states, especially after 1820, their agents within Congress became increasingly less willing to recognize and to negotiate with their southern cohorts as equals. Secession was resisted therefore, not only because it threatened to establish an undesired precedent for future attempts, but also because northern representatives perceived that the existing constitutional rule of apportionment rightfully endowed them with the constitutional authority to govern the nation.

In the aftermath of the American Civil War, a new national rule of apportionment was defined with the ratification of the Thirteenth Amendment in 1865. The amendment's delegitimization of human slavery ended the applicability of the original Constitution's three-fifths clause, thereby promising an increase in southern state representation within Congress and the Electoral College. The Fourteenth Amendment, ratified in 1868, modified this rule by defining a procedure for reducing a state's national representation in proportion to the number of eligible individuals whose right to vote was denied or abridged. Two years later, and just prior to the 1870 Census and the first expected reapportionment of national representation since the secession crisis, the Fifteenth Amendment was ratified and further reinforced the new apportionment rule by explicitly curbing federal and state authority to deny or to abridge the voting rights of eligible adult males.

Congress subsequently reapportioned the U.S. House of Representatives in accord with the full population terms required by the Thirteenth and Fourteenth Amendments.[59] Congress's refusal to adhere to the letter and spirit of the Fourteenth Amendment's Section 2 reduction provision and the inability (and often unwillingness) of other national institutions to sustain the explicit protections afforded by the Fourteenth and Fifteenth Amendments were clear signals that, although the bonds of Union had been formally reconstructed, the events of the preceding decade left an undeniable chasm between the words of the U.S. Constitution and the working constitution of the American political order.[60] Perhaps the depth of this chasm between form and practice was nowhere more apparent than the supplementary apportionment legislation enacted by Congress and approved by President Grant in 1872. In response to demands for increased state representation after the U.S. House had already been reapportioned once in accord with the 1870 Census, this legislation increased the House size by an additional 9 seats, to 292 members. Not only did the subsequent interstate apportionment of these seats again ignore the explicit reduction requirements of Section 2, but this supplementary legislation also violated the explicit constitutional requirement for a division of representation solely according to population.[61] How and why this new national rule of apportionment and the American political order subsequently were defined and developed in the wake of the American Civil War and its attendant constitutional

---

[59] 17 Stat. L. 28 (Feb. 2, 1872).

[60] See, for example, the 1870 Naturalization Act, in which Congress arbitrarily excluded individuals of Chinese ancestry (Xi Wang, *The Trial of Democracy: Black Suffrage and Northern Republicans, 1860–1910* (Athens, GA: University of Georgia Press, 1997); for the distortion of customary population requirements for the admission of new western states see Charles Stewart and Barry Weingast, "Stacking the Senate, Changing the Nation: Republican Rotten Boroughs, Statehood Politics and American Political Development," *Studies in American Political Development* (1992), 6: 223–271; see also the infamous U.S. Supreme Court decisions in *U.S. v. Reese*, 92 U.S. 214 (1876) and *U.S. v. Cruikshank*, 92 U.S. 542 (1876).

[61] 17 Stat. L. 192 (May 30, 1872). In particular, the legislation assigned an additional House seat to Florida and New Hampshire that was unwarranted by their respective populations. New York and Illinois each were denied an additional seat warranted by their populations. Margo Anderson, *The American Census: A Social History* (New Haven, CT: Yale University Press, 1988), p. 80.

distortions are inquiries that have already been diligently and eloquently engaged by others.[62]

[62] See Scott C. James, *Presidents, Parties and the State. A Party System Perspective on Democratic Regulatory Choice, 1884–1936* (Cambridge, UK: Cambridge University Press, 2001); Eric Schickler, *Disjointed Pluralism: Institutional Innovation and the Development of the U.S. Congress* (Princeton, NJ: Princeton University Press, 2001); Dan Carpenter, *Forging of Bureaucratic Autonomy: Reputations, Networks, and Policy Innovation in Executive Agencies, 1862–1928* (Princeton, NJ: Princeton University Press, 2001); Richard F. Bensel, *The Political Economy of American Industrialization, 1877–1900* (Cambridge, UK: Cambridge University Press, 2000); Sidney M. Milkis and Michael Nelson, *The American Presidency: Origins and Development, 1776–1998* (Washington, DC: Congressional Quarterly Press, 1999); Anna Harvey, *Votes Without Leverage: Women in American Electoral Politics, 1920–1970* (Cambridge, UK: Cambridge University Press, 1998); Gretchen Ritter, *Goldbugs and Greenbacks: The Antimonopoly Tradition and the Politics of Finance in America* (Cambridge, UK: Cambridge University Press, 1997); Rogers M. Smith, *Civic Ideals: Conflicting Visions of Citizenship in U.S. History* (New Haven, CT: Yale University Press, 1997); David Plotke, *Building a Democratic Political Order: Reshaping American Liberalism in the 1930s and 1940s* (Cambridge, UK: Cambridge University Press, 1996); Ballard C. Campbell, *The Growth of American Government: Governance from the Cleveland Era to the Present* (Bloomington, IN: Indiana University Press, 1995); Kenneth Finegold and Theda Skocpol, *State and Party in America's New Deal* (Madison, WI: University of Wisconsin Press, 1995); Gerald Berk, *Alternative Tracks: The Constitution of American Industrial Order, 1865–1917* (Baltimore: Johns Hopkins University Press, 1994); Theda Skocpol, *Protecting Soldiers and Mothers: The Political Origins of Social Policy in the United States* (Cambridge, MA: Harvard University Press, 1992); Karen Orren, *Belated Feudalism: Labor, the Law, and Liberal Development in the United States* (Cambridge, UK: Cambridge University Press, 1991); Richard Franklin Bensel, *Yankee Leviathan: The Origins of Central State Authority in America, 1859–1877* (Cambridge, UK: Cambridge University Press, 1990); Martin J. Sklar, *The Corporate Reconstruction of American Capitalism, 1890–1916* (Cambridge, UK: Cambridge University Press, 1988); Margaret Susan Thompson, *The "Spider Web": Congress and Lobbying in the Age of Grant* (Ithaca, NY: Cornell University Press, 1985); Richard Franklin Bensel, *Sectionalism and American Political Development, 1880–1980* (Madison, WI: University of Wisconsin Press, 1984); Stephen Skowronek, *Building the New American State: The Expansion of National Administrative Capacities, 1877–1920* (Cambridge, UK: Cambridge University Press, 1982).

10

Conclusions

THE GREAT QUESTION which in all ages has disturbed mankind, and brought on them the greatest part of those mischiefs which have ruined cities, depopulated countries, and disordered the peace of the world, has been, not whether there be power in the world, not whence it came, but who should have it. The settling of this point being of no smaller moment than the security of princes and the peace and welfare of their estates and kingdoms, a reformer of politics. . . . should lay this sure and be very clear in it; for if this remain disputable, all the rest will be to very little purpose.[1]

Lots of things depend on lots of things.[2]

The preceding chapters offer detailed descriptions, explicit causal explanations, and a unifying theory that accounts for the creation and recreation of the American political order from 1700 to 1870. A comparative historical analysis of the conditions and decisions comprising three constitutional changes in the national rule of apportionment was the means employed for confronting and understanding the violent and consensual origins of this order in 1776, its peaceful transformation in 1787, and its ultimate breakdown and reconstruction after 1861. The first apportionment rule change studied began in the wake of the Declaration of Independence and culminated in 1781 with the formalization of the equal state apportionment rule in the Articles of Confederation. The second apportionment rule change was initiated by the states' decisions to attend the 1787 Constitutional Convention and was completed with the subsequent ratification of the U.S. Constitution. The second

[1] John Locke, *The First Treatise on Government*, sec. 106.
[2] Ideal Baldoni, Democratic Party Chair, St. Joseph County, IN, 1968.

apportionment rule divided representation among the states on a pro-portional basis in the U.S. House of Representatives and an equal state basis in the U.S. Senate. The third and final rule change examined began with the voluntary secession of eleven states in 1860 and 1861 and ended after the American Civil War with the reunification of the Union and the ratification of the Thirteenth, Fourteenth, and Fifteenth Amendments.

Four research questions were identified to guide our study of each apportionment rule change. The first two questions inquired when and how do constitutional changes in apportionment rules occur. Answers to these questions required detailed descriptions of the particular contexts, actors, and decision-making sequences that constituted each specific change. The third question asked why these changes occur and required clarification of the particular and general causes of this type of consti-tutional change. The fourth research question demanded an accounting of the immediate and longer-term consequences of each apportionment rule change. An answer to this final question required construction of a theoretical framework for understanding how and in what ways appor-tionment rules are related to the creation, maintenance, and breakdown of political orders.

To answer the first research question, this study defined constitutional rule change as an alteration of the capacities and practical limits that define the formal or customary content and uses of collective authority. Constitutional changes in apportionment rules, I proposed, affect the terms or procedures that determine the intragovernmental distribution and possession of collective decision-making authority. Because of their anticipated consequences apportionment rule changes typically entail the abandonment of the existing rule of apportionment and the creation of a new rule.[3] Beyond identification of three sequential apportionment rule changes, this study answered the first research question by reconstruct-ing the long- and short-term developmental patterns for several types of social and political conditions. It focused on the development of

---

[3] Five constitutional changes in the national rule of apportionment were identified as fitting the criteria of this definition. This study completed detailed examinations of the first three changes. The fourth apportionment rule change was initiated after the 1920 Census with the abandonment of the traditional practice of a decennial reapportionment of the U.S. House. The 1929 Census Act subsequently established a new "automatic" and non-legislative apportionment process that effectively fixed the U.S. House size at 435 mem-bers. The fifth identified constitutional change in the national rule of apportionment was initiated by the U.S. Supreme Court in the early 1960s. In addition to voiding long-standing state districting practices, the Court mandated that intrastate legislative districts must consist of equal populations as nearly as is practicable.

economic and demographic conditions, and on changes in governmental structure and capacities and the concept and institutions of political representation.

Reconstruction of the developmental patterns associated with these four macrostructural conditions prior to each apportionment rule change served several critical purposes. The first purpose was the specification of the larger contextual conditions within which each change was embedded. The second purpose was the identification of the developmental dynamics latent within the status quo prior to each particular change. The "status quo" was never portrayed as a static or neutral reference point for understanding the subsequently observed process of change; rather, at the time of each change it was represented as a dynamic moment that suggestively pointed toward immediate and longer-term developmental trajectories. The third purpose was to test claims that there were direct causal relationships between one or more of these structural conditions and the three identified apportionment rule changes. As the preceding accounts reveal, this study lends no support to these claims or to related alternative hypotheses that propose these rule changes reflect or were prompted by economic, demographic, institutional, or ideological changes.[4]

The second research question asked: How do constitutional changes in the rule of apportionment occur? As described in Chapters 2 and 3 (Change I), Chapters 5 and 6 (Change II), and Chapter 9 (Change III), apportionment rule changes are initiated and aided by the entrepreneurial actions of a small number of individuals. The changes are completed, however, only after a process of negotiation among a larger set of politically relevant actors. These negotiations are directed toward and effect two distinct ends: first, the abandonment of the existing rule and second, the establishment of a new rule. With reference to the three apportionment rule changes examined in this study, Table 10.1 reveals that such negotiations do not always or necessarily end with consensual or peaceful agreements. Negotiations associated with the abandonment of the first rule and with the completion of the third apportionment rule change broke down and ultimately were resolved through coercive, not consensual, means.

---

[4] Elimination of these alternative structural hypotheses thus lends indirect support to the credibility of this study's actor-centered hypothesis and theory. See Arthur Stinchombe, *Constructing Social Theories* (New York: Harcourt, Brace & World, 1968), p. 25. For more on the importance of fair causal comparison of relevant alternative hypotheses, see Richard W. Miller, *Fact and Method: Explanation, Confirmation and Reality in the Natural and the Social Sciences* (Princeton, NJ: Princeton University Press, 1987).

TABLE 10.1. *Apportionment Rule Creation*

Rule Creation: Rule Abandonment:	Consensual means	Coercive means
Consensual means	Change II (1787–1789)	Change III (1860–1870)
Coercive means	Change I (1776–1781)	

This study provides two distinct answers to the third research question: Why do constitutional changes in the rule of apportionment occur? The first answer consists of the particular and highly detailed accounts of the historical contexts, the principal political actors, and the decision-making motives and negotiations that defined each of the three changes. To summarize these accounts here would be both tedious and a misrepresentation of the totality of discrete circumstances, personalities, interests, and choices that affected and effected each particular change.[5]

The second answer explains all three changes in terms of the generalization that apportionment rule changes are caused by changes in political expectations concerning decision-making capacities and governmental authority.[6] Apportionment rules are abandoned when these expectations are either unfulfilled by the existing constitutional framework or when there is a divergence of expectations within the set of politically relevant actors. Conversely, the creation and consensual establishment of a new apportionment rule occurs when there is a convergence of these two types of political expectations.

But what is the common microlevel (or actor-centered) motivation that grounds the causal relationship between changes in these two expectations and changes in rules of apportionment? This study concludes that those who engage in the creation, maintenance, and dissolution of collective authority are motivated by their desire to attain sufficient levels of certainty regarding the protection or promotion of their discrete and common interests. From the perspective offered within the

[5] This first answer thus heeds the insight of the nineteenth-century English poet William Blake that: "To Generalize is to be an Idiot. To Particularise is the Alone Distinction of Merit." As quoted in Patrick Riley, *The General Will Before Rousseau* (Princeton, NJ: Princeton University Press, 1986), p. xii n.6.

[6] This second answer thus responds to what Gary King, Robert O. Keohane, and Sidney Verba identified as "one of the most important achievements of all social science: *explaining as much as possible with as little as possible*." (*Designing Social Inquiry: Scientific Inference in Qualitative Research* (Princeton, NJ: Princeton University Press, 1994), p. 29.

intragovernmental constitution, stable constitutional orders are like long-term contracts in that parties are not principally motivated by the maximization of relative or absolute individual gains but by the desire to maintain a stable yet flexible relational framework that yields consistent streams of discrete and collective benefits.[7] Rules of apportionment constitute one of the most significant and elemental means of securing immediate and longer-term certainty because they define the basis for participation within the collective decision-making process. It follows that when there are changes in relative expected levels of participation or changes in the expected range of interests deemed worthy of collective recognition, protection, or promotion, politically relevant interests and their agents are motivated to consider the means by which they can retain or increase their relative decision-making positions.[8]

---

[7] Hobbes similarly proposed that individuals commonly seek the maximization of their capacities to ensure their own self-preservation. To accomplish this end, according to the Hobbesian account, individuals ultimately agree to forsake participation in the process of collective decision making. This solution parallels the classic account of Pisistratus' seizure of the power to rule ancient Athens. According to Aristotle, Pisistratus led an armed parade of the people into the Theseum, where by custom all weapons were left outside before entering. When Pisistratus' speech could not allegedly be heard by everyone, he had them reassemble at the gate of the Acropolis in order to speak to them. "When he had finished the rest of his speech, [Pisistratus] told the people" his men had seized "their arms, saying that they should not be startled or disheartened but should go and attend to their private affairs, and that he would take care of all public affairs." *The Athenian Constitution*, ch. 15.5. No doubt the Pisistratian exchange of public abstinence for private peace and well-being appeals to many individuals and it offers a microlevel foundation for monocratic (and state-centered) accounts of the creation, maintenance, and dissolution of Leviathanlike constitutional orders. Unfortunately, it is difficult to see how individual interest of this purely private sort can be used to ground accounts of more complex democratic forms of governance in which the intragovernmental constitution of an order contains a plurality of interests. This account has sought to devise a credible account of the creation, maintenance, and breakdown of "plural" forms of government. For this end, it proposes that the various interests and individuals who seek and become engaged in public affairs are motivated to achieve sufficient decision-making capacities to ensure the collective protection or promotion of their particular interests and of the common good. The desire for certainty describes the motives of both those who accept the Pisistratian exchange and those who seek to participate in the process of collective decision making.

[8] The most obvious means of altering relative decision-making capacities (and, therefore, one typically exacting the most resistance and the highest transformation costs) is the wholesale change in the rule of apportionment. Other (less costly) means to achieve a similar end are also conceivable. Relative decision-making capacities, for example, are affected by changes in the number or composition of the set of principal political interests and their agents. The distributional consequences of formalized rules of apportionment can also be altered by the addition of informal dimensions of these rules that are more amenable to incremental adaptations. Moreover, political interests or their agents

Changes in political expectations do not catalyze instantaneous attempts to abandon rules of apportionment nor does every attempt necessarily yield a new division of collective decision-making authority. Such attempts must be envisioned, organized, and assessed in terms of their likely costs and benefits. Moreover, even when initiated, the consensual abandonment and creation of old and new apportionment rules typically are the outcomes of a process of negotiation, not of spontaneous agreement. Constitutional entrepreneurs are the individuals who bear the intellectual, social, and (sometimes) personal costs of initiating these negotiations. But beyond divergent expectations and entrepreneurial agents, what insights does this study offer into the process of negotiations by which apportionment rules are abandoned and new rules are created?

Consider the two distinct dimensions of the process of negotiation illustrated in the following tables. These tables define expectations for governmental authority and decision-making capacity in terms of a simplified range consisting of relative increase, maintenance of the status quo, and relative decrease. The resulting matrix of expectations offers a template for assessing the types of interests that become engaged in historical instances of rule abandonment and rule creation. For each of the three historical cases of rule abandonment examined in this study, we can represent the expectations of the principal political actors who *initiated* this process as I_I, II_I, III_I. For each change, the other principal political actors who subsequently *responded* and engaged in negotiations can be represented as: I_R, II_R, III_R. Recall that for each instance of rule abandonment, this study assumed that the negotiation process could be modeled in terms of unitary actors. For each of the three changes, the primary expectations of the principal unitary actors are identified in Table 10.2

In addition to revealing a diffusion of expectations across the three changes, Table 10.3 also suggests a basis for explaining why particular alignments of expectations may be less likely to yield consensual settlements. Recall that Changes I and III ultimately ended in civil war whereas Change II was defined by the peaceful and consensual abandonment of the existing rule of apportionment. In both of the former changes, there were principal political actors who perceived that their short- and

who attain satisfactory levels of certainty regarding the promotion or protection of their interests at lower or higher levels of collective authority may consent to reductions in their relative decision-making positions at an intermediate level.

TABLE 10.2. *Initiators' and Respondents' Expectations*

	Initiator's Expectations (I)		Respondent's Expectations (R)	
Change				
I.	I_I.	**Great Britain:** +Governmental Authority +Decision-making Capacity	I_R.	**American Colonies:** Status Quo
II.	II_I.	**Virginia:** +Decision-making Capacity	II_{R1}.	**Massachusetts:** +Governmental Authority
			II_{R2}.	**Pennsylvania:** +Governmental Authority, +Decision-making Capacity
III.	III_I.	**Lower South:** +Governmental Authority +Decision-making Capacity	III_{R1}.	**North:** Status Quo
			III_{R2}.	**Upper South:** +Governmental Authority, +Decision-making Capacity

TABLE 10.3. *Apportionment Rule Abandonment*

Decision-making Capacity:	Governmental Authority:	Increase (+)	Status Quo	Decrease (−)
Increase (+)		I_I III_I II_{R2} III_{R2}	II_I	
Status Quo		II_{R1}	I_R III_{R1}	
Decrease (−)				

Note: Cases: I (Chapter 3), II (Chapter 6), III (Chapter 9); I = Initiators; R = Respondents.

long-term interests were favored by maintaining the status quo. These actors were thus never inclined to engage in serious negotiations. The parties most committed to bringing about some form of change therefore became increasingly open to alternative means of achieving their goals. For the principal interest who initiated Change I, these means took the form of naked coercion. For the principal interest in Change III, secession was selected as the means for disrupting the status quo. Each of the three principal political actors associated with Change II were

TABLE 10.4. *Apportionment Rule Creation*

Decision-making Capacity:	Governmental Authority:	Increase (+)	Status Quo	Decrease (−)
Increase (+)		II III		
Status Quo				
Decrease (−)				I

Note: Cases: I (Chapter 4), II (Chapter 7), III (Chapter 9).

predisposed to engage in serious negotiations concerning alternatives to the status quo.

Table 10.4 uses the same matrix of expectations to identify the general points of convergence on which consent for each new rule of apportionment emerged.

To conclude that the mere convergence of expectations solves the constitutional action problem described in the Preface overlooks both the problematics of consent and diversity, and the range of solutions exposed in the details of the preceding historical accounts. Recall, for example, that consent for the Articles of Confederation followed only after the adoption of a "minimization" solution that severely reduced each state's decision-making capacities and the new national government's collective authority. Consent for the U.S. Constitution followed the introduction of a different solution. Recall that national governmental authority was expanded over a range of discrete and common interests, and that the new double rule of apportionment for the future U.S. Congress effectively "split the difference" between several stubborn voting blocs within the 1787 Constitutional Convention. Finally, consent for the new national apportionment rule formalized in the three Civil War amendments to the U.S. Constitution depended on a third solution: the limitation of the number of political interests permitted to participate in negotiations over the terms of this new rule.

The variability of these solutions reaffirms this study's initial critique of the prospects of devising a general or permanent solution to the paradox of constitutional consent. Identification of when, how, and why these particular solutions were devised also confirms that the art and import of creating consensual constitutional orders ought not to be conceived as hidden behind a hypothetical veil or the blind hand of *fortuna*.

This study, rather, concludes that these creative acts are born out of the special dynamics opened by the willingness to engage the diversity of the human condition, the constraints of particular historical circumstances, and the liberty and limits of human imagination.

The fourth and final research question anchoring this study asked: What are the immediate and longer-term consequences of apportionment rule changes? To answer this question required extending the inquiry beyond each moment of apportionment rule change. Appraisal of the consequences of the three changes studied was facilitated by the sequential nature of the changes and by familiar and well-documented eras and events associated with each change: the American Revolution and the creation of the United States under the Articles of Confederation; the 1787 Constitutional Convention and the comparatively peaceful transformation of the political order under the U.S. Constitution; and the voluntary secession of eleven states from the United States and the coercive reconstruction of the political order by the Civil War and the Thirteenth, Fourteenth, and Fifteenth Amendments.

To appraise the consequences of these apportionment rule changes, this study further clarified the nature of the relationship between apportionment rules and the larger set of constitutional rules within which they are embedded. It demonstrated that apportionment rules, like all constitutional rules, have immediate and long-term informational consequences. In particular, apportionment rules establish a minimum level of decision-making coherence required for coordinated collective action. Apportionment rules, furthermore, convey valuable information regarding the expected intragovernmental division of collective decision-making authority. In "plural" constitutional orders – that is, those in which intragovernmental representation is open to a multiplicity of socially organized interests – apportionment rules are especially significant because they define the terms (and thus the reciprocal nature) of the relationship between governmental authority and societal interests.

To clarify the consequences of apportionment rule changes within plural constitutional orders, this study proposed a theoretical framework relating changes in political expectations for decision-making capacities and expected levels of governmental authority to the creation, maintenance, and breakdown of political order. The possibilities of order creation were closely associated with the convergence of these expectations among the set of constitution-making agents and the principal political actors they represented. Conversely, the dissolution of consensual constitutional orders became possible when these expectations diverged or were not satisfied by the existing set of constitutional rules.

But how are consensual constitutional orders with plural apportionment rules maintained between their moments of creation and dissolution? For the problematics of constitutional consent amidst diversity are constant and commonly exacerbated by the selection and establishment of a new apportionment rule over rival rules. In addition to general informational benefits, apportionment rules typically have distributional consequences that either immediately or over time became dissonant with the range of relevant political expectations for decision-making capacities or levels of governmental authority. Under these conditions, how is the voluntary participation of a diversity of interests within a common constitutional order sustained?

A full answer to this question requires a deeper grounding in the particular circumstances and individuals that constitute the development of a constitutional order over time. At a more general level, however, the decidedly nonhistorical answers offered by Hobbes and Locke (and their modern counterparts) suggest that both negative and positive incentives compel and sustain voluntary participation. The Hobbesian account suggests that political stability is positively motivated by the benefits of domestic peace and international recognition, and negatively motivated by the extreme costs and risks of evading or overthrowing the Leviathan. The Lockean account of order maintenance extends the range of positive incentives in two noteworthy ways: by restricting the boundaries of collective authority over life, liberty, and property (thus indirectly creating individual incentives to maintain the constitutional status quo) and by providing for periodic opportunities to elect the set of political agents. Contemporary theorists, aware of the insufficiencies of these incentives, have suggested additional positive incentives. Both Robert A. Dahl and Adam Przeworski, for example, posit elite pacts and electoral competition as necessary conditions for democratic stability.[9] Barry R. Weingast adds the necessity of reelection-minded elites and a vigorous civic culture (or at least its voting population) that values the procedures of democratic institutions more than the immediate promotion or protection of its material or cultural interests.[10]

Exogenous forces from without or from below have no doubt had a profound influence on political actors and political orders, especially the

---

[9] See Robert A. Dahl, *Pluralist Democracy in the United States* (Chicago: Rand McNally, 1967); *Polyarchy: Participation and Opposition* (New Haven, CT: Yale University Press, 1971); Adam Przeworski, *Democracy and the Market* (Cambridge, UK: Cambridge University Press, 1991).

[10] Barry R. Weingast, "The Political Foundations of Democracy and the Rule of Law," *American Political Science Review* (1997), 91: 245–263.

extraordinary constitutional challenges prompted by war and revolution. Whether these forces can also be used to construct rigorous *and* realistic accounts of the creation and maintenance of democratic constitutions remains to be demonstrated. Clearly, application of such an approach to explain the constitutional development of the United States can be made persuasively only from the safe distance of ad hoc theorization or incomplete knowledge of the corpus of historical evidence. This account does not discount the import of changes within the external or domestic constitutions of a particular political order. Rather, it assumes that the weight of these changes and the special problematics of consensual constitutional orders amidst diversity must ultimately be measured and explained first in terms of developments within the intragovernmental constitution of a political order.

To focus these measurements and explanations, this account suggests special attention be given to the range of negative incentives latent within established consensual constitutional orders. The incentives for maintaining the constitutional status quo include: (1) transformation costs, which increase with the complexity and diffusion of collective decision-making procedures; (2) information costs, incurred from the search for and dissemination of viable alternatives to the constitutional status quo; (3) discounting uncertainty, which increases for the long-term benefits of constitutional alternatives compared to the constitutional status quo; (4) recognition costs, which increase the more the terms of the existing rule of apportionment fail to reflect a social interest's natural identity or capacities; and (5) exit costs, or the costs and risks associated with the subversion of or secession from the constitutional status quo.

In addition to these negative incentives, attention should also be given to the range of procedures and norms that offer positive incentives for voluntary participation under democratic constitutional orders. Procedures that encourage deliberation, for example, facilitate the identification and authorization of both common goods and collective boundaries.[11] Deliberation also increases the opportunities for the formation and collective authorization of bundles of unrelated discrete goods. As a result, the net absolute expected utility associated with voluntary participation under an established constitutional order increases.

---

[11] See Amy Gutmann and Dennis Thompson, *Democracy and Disagreement* (Cambridge, MA: Belknap Press, 1996); Jack Knight and James Johnson, "Aggregation and Deliberation: On the Possibility of Democratic Legitimacy," *Political Theory* (1994), 22(2): 277–296.

Several norms also promote voluntary participation. A norm that promotes the minimization of the distributional consequences attributable to an established apportionment rule may compel the creation of mitigating secondary institutions at different levels of aggregation. Another norm might promote the minimization of unnecessary collective choices among discrete goods, thereby protecting the range of benefits offered under the existing constitutional order.

Whereas the logic of maximizing absolute gains and minimizing relative losses suggests a potentially generalizable solution to the constitutional action problem identified in the Preface, the historical development of the American constitutional order between 1776 and 1861 ends with the ironic constitutional fate experienced by other efforts to create and maintain collective authority. The voluntary secession of eleven states and the American Civil War remind us that even when net expected benefits exceed the net expected costs of consent, the rational republic is not immune from the trials and tragedies of dissolution. To enquire why this is so requires pondering much deeper mysteries concerning the nature of representational relationships, the constitution of the human mind, the possibility of more complex matrices of structure and agency, and the constancy of our venal desires to secure recognition and relative gain by dividing, deceiving, and dominating others.

Acknowledgments

Over the years, numerous institutions, individuals, accidents, and an act of nature have assisted, compelled, and unwittingly guided my steps down the long pathway traveled to complete this work. Some of the most important individuals that I have not sufficiently thanked are the benefactors and staffs of the libraries at the University of Virginia, Johns Hopkins University, The Catholic University of America, the University of Chicago, and the Library of Congress. They were the silent but active partners who made everything good in this work possible. Indeed, it is no overstatement to say that without their long-term vision, their professional care, and their personal diligence this book could have been conceived but it certainly could not have been initiated or finished.

Many others deserve public praise. Three invited lectures at critical points along the journey allowed me to present various parts of this work before inquisitive and thoughtful audiences of political scientists, historians, and economists. For these opportunities, I would like to acknowledge Jac Heckleman and the Economics Department at Wake Forest University, Beth Dougherty and Beloit College, and Norman Schofield and The Center in Political Economy at Washington University in St. Louis.

I am equally as grateful and indebted for the careful comments, suggestions, and encouragement offered by the following individuals on parts or earlier drafts of this work: Henry Abraham, Janet Adamski, John Aldrich, Richard Bensel, Vernon Burton, Michael Cain, James Ceasar, Joe Cooper, Martha Derthick, Keith Dougherty, John Echeverri-Gent, Scott Gerber, John Gerring, James Fearon, Charlie Holt, Sam Kernell, George Klosko, Margaret Levi, Carol Mershon, Sid Milkis, Douglass

North, David O'Brien, Tim O'Rourke, Adam Przeworski, Mark Rush, Frank Smith, Barry Weingast, and several anonymous reviewers. Finally, no song of public thanks could be complete without some expression of my gratitude for the magnanimous dispositions, extended comments, and repeated good counsel of Lew Bateman of Cambridge University Press, Michael Holt, Jack Knight, Peter Onuf, Jack Rakove, and David Waldner.

The contributions of each of these individuals, although noteworthy exemplars for their respective professions, pale however when compared to the support, sacrifices, insights, and inspiration offered by my family and, most especially, my wife Anne.

Index

Printed in the United States
54709LVS00004B/7-9